CYPRIAN

HIS LIFE · HIS TIMES · HIS WORK

CYPRIAN

HIS LIFE · HIS TIMES · HIS WORK

BY

EDWARD WHITE BENSON, D.D., D.C.L.,
SOMETIME ARCHBISHOP OF CANTERBURY

PUBLISHERS
Eugene, Oregon

Wipf and Stock Publishers
199 W 8th Ave, Suite 3
Eugene, OR 97401

Cyprian: His Life, His Times, His Work
By Benson, Edward W.
ISBN: 1-59244-956-5
Publication date 10/18/2004
Previously published by Macmillan and Co., 1897

PREFATORY NOTE.

A few days before my father left Addington for Ireland, in the September of last year (1896), he called me into his library, and handed me the proof of the preface of his Cyprian—the book that is here presented—asking me to criticise anything that struck me in it.

The following day I brought him a paper of minute suggestions. He went through them with the utmost patience, accepting some, and carefully justifying the rejection of others. When he had finished, he said, "You seem to find my style very obscure!" (smiling) "you are not the only person who does." I ventured to say that I thought he was too careful to avoid the obvious: "No," he said, "it's not that: I only wish to say the obvious thing without the customary periphrases:—it all comes of hours and hours spent with intense enjoyment over Thucydides, weighing the force of every adjective and every particle." I went on to ask whether the Cyprian was really finished, and reminded him of how more than fifteen years before, when he was at Truro, he had come out of his study one evening, and announced that his Cyprian was "practically finished." "Yes," he said, "it is all done: only a few corrections and verifications to make." I asked whether he was not glad it was done: "I ought to be;" —he said, and began turning over some of the proofs on the table: then he looked up with a smile: "but I am not really glad—my only amusement will be gone."

And this was literally true: my father was less capable of "amusing himself," of resting, than any one I have ever known:

his holidays were merely a change from one intense kind of work to another: if he was in a place of artistic or antiquarian interest, he worked at pictures and churches, as though it were the business of his life: he stored his mind with precise and graphic impressions. In scenes of natural beauty, he studied detail like an artist. At home, when at work, at Lambeth and Addington, he had a "Cyprian" table, where his books and papers lay often untouched for weeks together: late at night, early in the morning, when all his official work had been done with the minute precision so characteristic of him, he stole an hour from sleep for his beloved book: but I have the authority of the Bishop of Winchester, who was with him constantly at all times and places, for saying that not only did he never let his literary work interfere with his official work, or constitute a reason for avoiding a piece of business, or deferring an engagement—but that he regarded it in the strictest sense as a recreation only.

Thirty years ago, when he was Headmaster of Wellington College, he found that his professional work was so absorbing that he felt himself in danger of losing sight of study, of erudition, of antiquity, and resolved, on the suggestion of his dear friend Bishop Lightfoot, to undertake some definite work, which might provide both a contrast to and an illustration of modern tendencies and recent problems.

Year after year, at Lincoln, at Truro, at Canterbury, these patient pages have grown: sometimes weeks would be consumed in the elucidation of some minute technical point: he even undertook, a few years ago, a journey to North Africa to study his topography: of late he has often sighed for "six weeks of unbroken leisure!—I could finish my book." The first hundred and fifty pages were put into print so long ago that when he had reached the end, they required to be entirely revised and

PREFATORY NOTE.   v

rewritten. But at last it was finished, and he took the whole book with him to Ireland, most of it in proof and part of it in MS., in order to endeavour to see the end.

Two significant entries in his Diary in the last year of his life may here, I think, with advantage be quoted, to show how his hopes were bound up in the book, with how definite a purpose of self-education it had been planned and carried out, and how ardently he desired that it should serve true and high ends.

Friday, March 6, 1896.

Finishing what I really think is the end of my Cyprian:—the examination of the Lists of Bishops who attended Councils under Cyprian. The test of genuineness which they offer was one of the first things that struck me. I then wrote out at (sic) the Lists and criticized them. This can certainly not have been later (if so late) than 1865, and I have to-day sent that originally written list and notes, with fresh notes made to-day to the University Press. So that my 'copy' is at least 30 years apart in its work.

. . . .

I pray God bless this Cyprian to the good of His Church. If He bless it not, I have spent half my life in building hay and stubble, and the fire must consume it. But please God, may it last.

Sunday, March 22, 1896.

Have now practically finished a big book, unless I add a few of the Greek comments. If it ever sees the light, many will think it a very odd book. Folk are edified in such different ways. But it has edified me, which is what I began it for.

To emphasize the event, or "to adorn a tale" would be out of place here: I have merely tried to indicate the history of the book, and the significant fact that the completion of his only literary enterprise coincided so strangely and so majestically with the termination of his earthly energies.

ARTHUR CHRISTOPHER BENSON.

Jan. 1, 1897.

EDITORIAL NOTE.

AMONG the last proofs which my father corrected was found a memorandum to write an Appendix dealing with the Rev. E. W. Watson's valuable Essay on the Style and Language of S. Cyprian in the 'Studia Biblica et Ecclesiastica,' vol. IV. (Oxford, 1896). In all other respects the book had been completed.

Mr Watson has since most kindly verified some complicated references from two important codices in the Bodleian.

I must here also be allowed to record my sincerest gratitude to my father's dear and honoured friend, M. Alexis Larpent, who gave him invaluable assistance in verifying references and suggesting corrections, compiled the index, and in conjunction with my brother, Mr E. F. Benson, corrected the final proofs.

A. C. B.

Feb. 12, 1897.

DUOBUS MARTINIS

ANIMÆ PATERNÆ
SPEI MATURESCENTI

IN PACE

PREFACE.

IT is a long time since I fixed on the Life and Work of Cyprian for a special study. The reason, I think, was first this.

In times which, like ours, were both extraordinarily picturesque and extraordinarily crowded with business, a powerful and fascinating personality appeared to me to have done most to turn the Pagan to the Christian temper, to have dealt masterfully with lasting problems in the Church, to have left behind him a living 'Theory'—so living that the *ecclesia principalis* has never ceased to fret over it and retouch it. In short he appeared to be among us.

He was tempted into the noble and alas! too fruitful error of arraying the Visible Church in attributes of the Church Invisible. But he said and shewed how men might gravely dissent without one wound to peace. He spoke a watch-word of comprehension which, for lack of the charity which possessed him, we do not receive in the churches, although it must needs precede the Unity we dream of.

I hope that in this study I have not ever been unmindful of the present, and yet have not committed what I hold to be a grievous fault in a historian, the reading of the present into the past. I have tried to sketch what I saw. It is only thus that the past can be read into the present— the 'Lesson of History' learnt.

That we have some need of the Lesson of the Cyprianic times I feel sure. Sure that it might have saved us some of our losses.

Still I was not overcareful to point the morals in places where it could escape no thoughtful reader wherein they lie, or what they are. Such simpler morals are of infinite value to a student who draws them out for himself. Not of much value to one who should read them over and think that he had always thought them.

As I have dared to take the reader into confidence by placing two names, sacred to me, on a leaf of this book, I may perhaps be allowed to explain why work so long ago commenced is so late committed to the reader's indulgence. At school under Prince Lee the very name of Cyprian had attraction for me. At Trinity Lightfoot and I read the *De Unitate* together on Sunday evenings in my Freshman's term. At Wellington, at Lincoln, at Truro, at Lambeth, even at this Addington—*cara ubi tot cara*—minutes only of the day, often of the week, have been all that what I am not ashamed to call a life of labour has left me. Therefore I feel that if my love for the man has surpassed my ability to know him, I may humbly ask that some excuse may be allowed me.

If the earlier part of this Life is somewhat thin, that is because I thought it not worth while to bring up its *primitiæ* to the same level and same fulness as those days of Cyprian when the real problems of Church and World were upon him and he wrestling with them.

The Texts of the Latin Versions witnessed to in his writings are too special and too large a work to be included here.

The smaller type is for student-studies not essential to

the main course of story or comment, although they often shew the source of the text. Some nevertheless I commend to the general reader who will soon see whether or no they have interest for him.

To Prof. Lanciani I owe the map which illustrates the chapter on Xystus. The two others are compiled. They of course owe their accuracy to M. Charles Tissot and to the grand Archæological Atlas of Tunisie which is being published by the Minister of Public Instruction and Beaux-Arts.

I must express my gratitude to my friend M. Larpent for his minute and learned assistance to me while seeing the work through the Press, and to the University Press itself and the Publishers for their patience.

EDW: CANTUAR:

ADDINGTON.
September, 1896.

CONTENTS.

		Page
Chronology of the Times and Writings of Cyprian	. .	xxi—xxiii

INTRODUCTION.

Carthage and her Society . . . . xxv—xxxvii

CHAPTER I.

THE LAST OF THE LONG PEACE.

Section		
I.	Cyprian's Preparation in Heathendom	1
II.	Cyprian's Preparation under the Church	7
	'THAT IDOLS ARE NOT GODS'	10
III.	Lay-work	13
	'TO DONATUS' ['THE GRACE OF GOD'] . . .	13
IV.	Cyprian Deacon	17
V.	Presbyterate	19
VI.	Helps to Laymen's Scripture Studies	22
	'TO QUIRINUS' ['TESTIMONIES']	22
VII.	Cyprian made Pope of Carthage	25
	Cyprian's Title of 'Papa'	29
VIII.	Cyprian's view of the Authority and the Design of the Episcopate .	31
IX.	Divergence of Cyprian's from Modern Views	35
X.	A Bishop's Work uphill	41
XI.	Discipline—Clerical and Lay	44
	Of Clerics not to be 'Tutores'	47
	Of Christians not to train for the Stage . . .	51
XII.	The Eighteen Months continued. Virginal Life in Carthage .	51
XIII.	Literary Character of the Book 'OF THE DRESS OF VIRGINS' .	57

CHAPTER II.

THE DECIAN PERSECUTION.

Section		Page
I.	The Roman Theory of Persecution	60
II.	The Outbreak of the Decian Persecution—Rome	64
	Of Genuineness in Nomenclature	72
	On Etecusa and Numeria	74
III.	The Persecution at Carthage.—1. The 'Stantes'	75
	2. The 'Lapsi'	79
	On the Form and Contents of the Libelli.	82
IV.	The Retirement of Cyprian	84
V.	Interference of the Church of Rome	87
VI.	The Lapsed and the Martyrs	89
VII.	The Cyprianic Scheme for Restorative Discipline	95
	On the 'Proof' of Roman Confession which is derived from these events	98
VIII.	The adopted policy was Carthaginian, not Roman	99
	On the Thirteen Epistles of which Cyprian sent copies to the Romans	102
IX.	Diocesan Disquietudes	106
X.	Declaration of Parties—Novatus and Felicissimus	108
	Budinarius and Sarcinatrix	117
XI.	Growth of the Opposition at Rome—The Confessors and Novatian	118

CHAPTER III.

SEQUEL OF THE PERSECUTION.

I.	Cyprian's 'FIRST COUNCIL OF CARTHAGE':	
	Question 1. The Title of Cornelius	129
	Question 2. Decision on Felicissimus	131
	Question 3. Novatianism	134
	Four different Pictures from the year 250	148
	Of Cyprian before his own Presbyters	148
	Of Cyprian before the Roman Presbyters	150
	Of Felicissimus as a more faithful representative of the Church	153
	Of the Evanescence of Novatus under Ritschl's Analysis	154
	Question 4. The Decision on the Lapsed	156
II.	Advance of Novatianism—Return of the Confessors	159
III.	Continued Action against Novatianism—Roman Council of A.D. 251, Antiochene of A.D. 252	163
	Difficulties in identifying Hippolytus, through whom Dionysius wrote to the Romans, with Hippolytus of Portus	169
	Why is Dionysius' Epistle to the Romans called διακονική?	171

CONTENTS.   xv

Section   Page
  IV. Constitutional Results of the First Council 172
   V. Corollaries:—Puritanism: Saint-Merit: Flight from Suffering.
         The 'DE LAPSIS'.   174
         Mai's supposed Fragment of Cyprian   179

CHAPTER IV.

CYPRIAN 'OF THE UNITY OF THE CATHOLIC CHURCH.'

   I. Time and Substance of the Treatise   180
  II. Two Questions on Cyprianic Unity. 1. Was it a theory of Convic-
         tion or of Policy? 2. Does it involve Roman Unity?   .   186
         *Catena of Cyprianic passages on the Unity signified in the
         Charge to Peter*   197
 III. The Appeal of the modern Church of Rome to Cyprian on '*The
         Unity of the Catholic Church*'—by way of Interpolation . 200
         How to make the best of the Forgeries now .   .   .   219
         Note on the Citation from Pelagius II.   220

CHAPTER V.

THE HARVEST OF THE NEW LEGISLATION.

   I. The softening of the Penances—'THE SECOND COUNCIL'   .   . 222
  II. The Effect on Felicissimus and his Party 225
 III. The Legacy of Clerical Appeals under the Law of the Lapsed—
         'THE THIRD AND FOURTH COUNCILS.' Episcopal Cases. The
         Spanish Appeal against Rome   230

CHAPTER VI.

EXPANSION OF HUMAN FEELING AND ENERGY.

   I. The Church in relation to Physical Suffering:
        1. Within itself.—The Berber Raid   236
              Of Genuineness Geographical   239
        2. The Church in relation to Heathen Suffering.—The Plague 240
        3. The Theory.—Unconditional Altruism. 'OF WORK AND
              ALMSDEEDS' 246
  II. Resentment.—'TO DEMETRIAN' 249
         Of the Style of the Demetrian   256
 III. The Interpretation of Sorrows   256
         'ON THE MORTALITY' 260
         'TO FORTUNATUS' ['EXHORTATION TO MARTYRDOM']   .   .   . 264

Section		Page
IV.	Intelligent Devotion.—'ON THE LORD'S PRAYER'	267
	Table shewing the Verbal Debts to Tertullian in Cyprian's Treatise De Dominica Oratione	275
	On the Characteristics and Genuineness of the De Dominica Oratione	280
	Comparison elucidating the Dates	287
V.	Ritual—1. The Mixed Cup	289
	2. The Age of Baptism	295
	Objection to Council III. on account of its Antipelagianism	297

CHAPTER VII.

THE ROMAN CHAIR.

I.	The End of CORNELIUS	298
II.	The Sitting of LUCIUS	304
III.	STEPHANUS. The Church not identified with or represented by Rome	307
	1. The Spanish Appeal	311
	2. The Gaulish Appeal	314

INTERCALARY.

Presbyters as Members of Administration 323

CHAPTER VIII.

		THE BAPTISMAL QUESTION	331
I.	1.	The Tradition of Africa	335
	2.	The Tradition of Asia Minor East	339
II.	1.	Position of the Leaders—Cyprian and Stephen	342
		Dates (Council of Iconium and other)	347
	2.	Acts and Documents	349
		FIFTH COUNCIL, FIRST ON BAPTISM	349
		SIXTH COUNCIL, SECOND ON BAPTISM	351
		Did Stephen excommunicate the Bishops of the East?	354
		Dionysius the Great	354
		That there is no reason to suppose letters are missing from the Correspondence with Stephen	360
		That the Epistle to Pompey (Ep. 74) and Stephen's Epistle quoted therein are earlier than the Third Council	361
		That Ep. 72 to Stephen is rightly put down to the Second Council, not the Third	362
		That Quietus of Buruc who spoke in the Seventh Council is Quintus the Mauretanian, Recipient of Ep. 71	363

Section			Page
	Seventh Council, Third on Baptism		364
	Firmilian and his Letter		372
	On the Genuineness of the Epistle of Firmilian		377
	Quotations of Scripture in Firmilian		386
	Basil and the Letter of Firmilian		388
	The Nameless Author 'on Rebaptism'		390
III.	The Arguments		399
	Cyprian's. 1. Objective		401
	2. Subjective		405
	Baptism in the Name of Christ alone		406
	3. Historical		408
	4. Biblical		411
	Stephen's Arguments		413
	On the Force of Stephen's Nihil innovetur nisi		421
IV.	Ecclesiastical Results.		
	1. The Unbroken Unity		423
	2. The Baptismal Councils failed doctrinally—and why		424
	3. The Catholic and the Ultramontane Estimate of Cyprian		432

CHAPTER IX.

Expansion of Christian Feeling and Energy (resumed).

		Page
The Secret of Conduct		437
1. 'Of the Good of Patience'		437
2. 'Of Jealousy and Envy'		448

CHAPTER X.

The Persecution of Valerian.

			Page
I.	1.	The Edict and its occasions	456
		Macrian. The 'Uprising of Nations'	457
		On Kephron and the Lands of Kolluthion	463
	2.	Treatment of Cyprian	464
	3.	Numidian Bishop-Confessors	471
	4.	'To Fortunatus' ['Of Encouragement to Confessorship']	474
	5.	Rome. Accession of Xystus and his immunity	475
II.	1.	The Rescript	477
	2.	Rome. The Exclusion from the Cemeteries	481
	3.	Memorials of Xystus and his Martyrdom	487

CHAPTER XI.

THE BIRTHDAY

	Page
THE BIRTHDAY	493
Where was Cyprian Martyr buried?	509
Where was Cyprian tried and executed?	512
The Dress of Cyprian	513
The Soldiers and Officers named in the Trial	516
Of the Massa Candida	517
Acta Proconsularia	518

CHAPTER XII.

AFTERMATH.

APPENDICES.

A.	'PRINCIPALIS ECCLESIA,' *Note on the meaning of* Principalis (p. 192)	537
B.	*Additional note on* Libelli *and two extant specimens of them* (pp. 81—84)	541
C.	*The Intrigue about* Manutius' Text. *Visconti's Letter* (p. 212)	544
D.	*The Intrigue about the* Benedictine Text. *Additional note on* du Mabaret (p. 213)	546
E.	*Text of the* Interpolation *in* De Unitate c. IV. *with new collations*	547
F.	*On points in the* Chronology *of* Valerian's *Reign* (pp. 456 sqq.)	552
G.	*On the nameless Epistle* Ad Novatianum *and the attribution of it to* Xystus (p. 476)	557
H.	*Examination of the* Lists *of the* Bishops *attending the* Councils. (*Genuineness. Seniority*)	565
I, K.	*The* Cities *from which the* Bishops *came to* the Seventh Council on the First of September, A.D. 256	573
L.	*On* S. Cyprian's Day *in* Kalendars. *And how it came to be in England on the 26th instead of the 14th of September*	610

MAPS.

	Page
The Cemeteries on the Appian Way near Rome	481
Carthage (Environs of)	509
Proconsular Africa and Numidia to illustrate the writings of Cyprian	573

WOODCUTS.

Loculus of Fabian	66
Loculus of Cornelius	124
Loculus of Maximus	162
Coins of Cornelia Salonina	300
Ninth Century figures of Cyprian and Cornelius from the Cemetery of Callistus	302
Loculus of Lucius	306
Well of the Legend of Stephen's baptizing in Cemetery of Domitilla	332
List of Books quoted	621
Index	626

ERRATA.

p. 48. *Instead of* Cæcilius, *read* Cæcilianus.

p. 120. n. 4, *read* Privatus of Lambæse had Five adherents,...Five Bishops attended Cornelius at the reconciliation of Maximus.

p. 160. *Read*, the Bishop Evaristus, who had been probably one of Novatian's consecrators.

CHRONOLOGY

OF THE

TIMES AND WRITINGS OF CYPRIAN.

A.D. [Easter]	Consuls (see margins)	Emperors	Bishops of Rome	Events	Treatises and Letters
246 [Apr. 19]	Praesens Albinus	Philip since Feb. or March 244	Fabian since Jan. 10, 236	Cyprian converted	Ad Donatum Quod idola dii non sint
247 [Apr. 11]	Philip II. Philip			Cyprian presbyter	
248 [March 26]	Philip III. Philip II.			after June Cyprian Bishop cf. *quadriennium*, Ep. 59. 6, *in* A.D. 252 Popular persecution at Alexandria	Ad Quirinum. De habitu virginum Epp. 1, 2, 4
249 [Apr. 15]	Æmilian II. Aquilinus	Sept. or Oct. Decius		Trial of Novatus approaching Decian persecution, 7th	
250 [Apr. 7]	Decius II. Gratus	end of 250 Decius leaves Rome for Thrace and Macedonia against Goths and Priscus	Jan. 20 mart.	Jan. med. Cyprian retires Apr. The Proconsul's tour Moyses, Maximus, &c. incarcerated Felicissimus joined by 'the Five Presbyters' Nov. Persecution relaxed in Carthage Dec. 31, Moyses dies in prison at Rome Febr. March, Julius Valens proclaimed and slain	Epp. 5—40 Epp. 41—43
251 [March 23]	Decius III. Decius		March 5, Cornelius	Celerinus comes from Roman Confessors to Cyprian, Ep. 37. 1 after Easter Cyprian returns. March, Novatus to Rome April, 1st Council of Carthage under Cyprian Anti-election of Novatian 1st embassy of Novatianists Embassy from Cornelius to Carthage Reconciliation of Roman Confessors, Ep. 54 June, Roman Council de Lapsis 2nd Embassy, Novatus and Evaristus, Ep. 50	Epp. 44—53 De Unitate and De Lapsis read to Council
252 [Apr. 11]	Gallus II. Volusian	Oct. Valerian Censor Nov. Decius killed Gallus		Persecution of Gallus, 'edicta feralia,' Ep. 58, 9 'ad leones' The Berber-Raid, Ep. 62 Council at Antioch The Plague at Carthage Proscription of Cyprian. Epp. 59. 6, 66. 4	De Opere et Eleemosynis Ad Demetrianum Epp. 55—59, 62 De Mortalitate De Oratione Dominica

TIMES AND WRITINGS OF CYPRIAN.

Year	Consuls			Writings
253 [Apr. 3]	Volusian II. Maximus	tioch by Sapor before *May* 253 *May*, Æmilian	Privatus attempts to appear, *Ep.* 59, 10 Pseudo-consecration of Maximus, *Ep.* 59. 9 ", of Fortunatus, *Ep.* 59. 11 Persecution diminishing at Carthage. Outbreak at Rome. Exile of Cornelius "Peace"	*Ep.* 60
		Jun. med. Cornelius dec. *Jun.* 25, Lucius		*Epp.* 61, 63—65
254 [Apr. 23]	Valerian II. Gallienus	Valerian and Gallien *bef. Oct.* 22, 259 *C. I. L.* VIII. 2482 *March* 5, Lucius *May* 12, Stephanus	*Sept.* 3rd Council, *Ep.* 64	
255 [Apr. 8] 256 [March 30]	Valerian III. Gallienus II. Maximus II. Glabrio		*Autumn*, 4th Council. Spanish and Gaulish appeals 5th Council, 1st on Baptism *bef. Easter*, 6th Council, 2nd on Baptism	*Epp.* 3, [p. 234] 66—68 *Epp.* 69—71 (cf. 73. 1) De Bono Patientiæ De Zelo et Livore
			Sept. 1, 7th Council, 3rd on Baptism	*Epp.* 72, 73 Sententiæ Episcoporum *Epp.* 74, 75 (Firmilian) before winter
257 [Apr. 19]	Valerian IV. Gallienus III.	*Jun.* Valerian to East *Jul.* The Edict	Persecution of Valerian, 8th Exile of Dionysius *Aug.* 30, Trial of Cyprian before Paternus *Sept.* 14, to Curubis	De exhortatione martyrii *Epp.* 76—79
258 [Apr. 11]	Tuscus Bassus	*Aug.* 2, Stephanus dec. *Aug.* 31 ?, Xystus *Jun.* 29, SS. Peter and Paul moved to Catacumbas *Aug.* 6, Xystus mart.	Returns to Carthage *Sept.* 14, Cyprian martyred	*Epp.* 80, 81
259 [March 27] 260 [Apr. 15]	Æmilian Bassus Sæcularis II. Donatus II.	*Jul.* 22, Dionysius 2nd Capture of Antioch by Sapor Valerian captured *Oct.* Gallienus' Edict of 'Peace'	Persecution practically over in Rome	

INTRODUCTION.

CARTHAGE AND HER SOCIETY.

A SAILING vessel running before a fair wind from Ostia, could reach Carthage on the second day. Yet to the Roman Africa never lost the sense of distance and weirdness. His business transactions with it were enormous. It is all strewn with relics of his factories, yet his scientific notes on it were as weird as the tales of its wild men. Its lion understood what was said to him. Its python checked his legion. New species of creatures were continually produced there. His armies trod floors of salt over bottomless pits. He quarried Atlas, his precious tables were made of its wood, yet it was the mountain 'of fable,' the inexhaustible, inexplorable mountain. Even in the sixth century his description of Mt Aures is merely fantastic. He never shook off his feeling about the city which had wrestled with him for the empire of the earth, and had been so foully thrown. He still heard with awe that, where other nations called on their gods, the African breathed only the name of 'Africa' before a new enterprise.

Into this region opened two glorious gates, the valley of Egypt and this other. Through these two must pass and repass all that the Mediterranean fetched and carried to or from the infinite Soudan. Through this alone went all that they lent or borrowed from the antient and resourceful civilizations which lay between Sahara and the sea, and all the human hosts which served and violated the multitudinous interests there involved.

For its coast from the Nile to the Atlantic lay thus. First a lowland of dunes, whose sands invaded the sea in two vast Syrtes, swept by the hurricanes from the Sahara over the rocky rim, and swirling in shoals and quicksands and shifting banks, along ever-shifting currents. Then down upon these, slope after slope, fell the buttress ends of two Alpine chains which, barring breaks and rents, rolled out their snowy ridges side by side to the Atlantic: the northern chain, a vast rampart cresting along over the iron-bound coast which it made; the southern falling by plateau after plateau till it plunged its roots in Sahara, and flung its torrents into leagues of salt lakes. Between the twin giant ridges, sometimes linked together by cross fells and yokes of lower height, were high plains and hollows full of mountain basins and small streams, so that there were endless rich sheets of land and fertile slopes, and sometimes a succession of fat plains, as on the Medjerda, as well as oases of bewildering fertility out in the deserts. Horses and cattle, cereals, the heaviest wheat and largest yield then known, minerals, unique marbles, palm groves southward and olive woods northward, and mountains of cedars stocked and stored the land. The yield of oil was prodigious, and a third of all the corn consumed in Rome and Italy was grown here.

These three lines, the northern slopes, the southern terraces, and the vast central lap, were thick from immemorial time with native villages, most of which grew into towns of which scarcely one was insignificant in its possession of some source of well-being.

It was on the brow of the seaward head, between highlands and lowlands, where the ends of the two chains brought the westering shore to a sudden stop and turned it north,—it was in that gate, commanding the mouth of the Medjerda valley, that Carthage had long since sat herself down, *Italiam contra*, and looked straight north to Rome. So dangerously near it was, that Cato shewed the senators a fresh fig pulled two days before in Carthage, as a token that both could not exist.

*   *   *

The end of her power had been the beginning for her of unequalled wealth. When her warships had been towed out to sea and fired she became a neutral, free of the seas, while war kept out of commerce all the maritime peoples of the East for half a century.

But that prosperous interval stifled the spirit of a state for which Hannibal had not been ambitious enough, when he sketched an honourable peace and Africa for a safe dominion. The pursuit of gain thinned their troops and filled them up with mercenaries. The fifty years over, they had nothing but the wish for peace and a readiness to give and keep any required guarantees, to oppose to the stolid animosity of Cato and the craft of Masinissa. It would have been a sore exchange for mankind if semi-orientals scrambling into democracy through constitutional decay had prevailed. But the Roman policy, inspired by both fear and greed, its secret instigation of the barbarian, its simulation of impartiality, has been called by the calmest of historians 'diabolic.' It flared out in the atrocities of the siege and the capture. Through seventeen days the city, which lately contained 700,000 people, burnt as 'one funeral pyre.' Then the plough was foolishly dragged about her vitrified walls.

*   *   *

A quarter of a century, and her history began again through Caius Gracchus, but in a dreary fashion. She loomed too large still to be left to Phœnician boatmen and Libyan mapalia. The capital was suddenly repeopled and the lands allotted to Roman colonists, old soldiers, speculating farmers, and hosts of slave labourers. But still jealousy would permit no real development. They had to protect themselves. There was no military station. The walls were never restored, and something forbade the inhabiting of the precinct, so that 'the ruins of Carthage,' in which Marius was seen sitting, were half a mile perhaps from bazaars and basilicas.

But all was changed once more when great men and statesmen, a Julius and an Octavius, undertook the thing. Then began a real policy, selfish enough, but a policy which enriched vast classes, created a yeomanry, found a subsistence for every peasant, and fed Italy. Carthage first, and then the old towns began to receive privileges as municipia and colonies, sometimes titulary, but often with many settlers capable of Romanizing the thick and thickening population. They slid quietly from the administration of *Sufetes*, 'Judges,' to that of *Duumvirs* and *Decurions*. After Trajan's time nearly all towns had received honours and privileges, and took occasion to glorify themselves with little municipal buildings and large market-places, above all with amphitheatres. Many temples and basilicas and arches, though not perfectly pure in taste, were great and stately, as they consecrated themselves in marble to their own Severus, to his Julia, Geta and Caracalla.

Wealthy villas, surrounded themselves with dependents and with industries, had to be taken into account in the communal system like small towns, and were less easily dealt with.

The Roman farmer of Africa has left his mark. His Moorish successors, though for civil and religious purposes using the Arabic Kalendar, name the months of their agricultural operations from his Latin. He was proverbial for two points. His daughters worked as well as his sons, and his own implement was the *Oculus Domini*. He worked and made everyone work. Pliny saw him or his native tenant in Byzacium yoking an old woman with an ass, a practice not dropped until of late. He held his land usually upon a military tenure.

The brilliant Third Legion executed works of immense magnitude and of admirable utility, while from its soldier towns it fenced civilization off from the Berber hordes. A few of their clans were more or less ticketed and enrolled, but all were subjects in the eye of the law, generally rebels but subjects.

The whole civil and military organization, from the Proconsul's Staff and Office downwards, was without a break, absolutely continuous, intelligible, minute and instant. We know it from their innumerable monuments as precisely as we know that of counties, parishes and boroughs.

Yet a fearful shadow dogged all this national genius and individual vigour, the inherent vice of the Roman spirit, the scornful inhumanity with which uncivilized populations were unhelped and repelled. It was

INTRODUCTION.

this, with its ever-growing train of consequences, this and not the Vandals, which wrought the last wreck.

* * *

Of material Carthage we have less solid knowledge than of any great city. Carthage has been learnedly rebuilt in the air, its temples and streets mapped and named by departments, but all are as visionary as mirage. Archæology has spoiled Carthage for museums as Arabs did for harems, and Italian Republics for cathedrals. Until science and system explore what lies interred under cloisters we can know little of a city whose two effacements were not more wonderful than itself in its majesty. When Cyprian was there in the height of his repute, Carthage is reported by Herodian to have been in population and wealth the equal of Alexandria and second only to Rome. Its beauty matched its rank.

The first few steps in it to-day are enough to shew us that these Arab quarters were laid out by no Arab hand. Two streets of great length through its largest dimensions, intersect at right angles, and pass out of the city northward and westward as imperial roads. For the outer city and environs they form base lines each way for many other streets set out at right angles, and frequently interlaced again with convenient diagonals. In the inner city, with its winding edge and cliff, its heights and steeps, the streets still made a singular symmetry of squares and triangles, so that space was rapidly traversed and every awkward plot made serviceable. Most of this literal geometry was Roman, but in the older citadel-region and religious quarters there are traces perhaps of those streets with which, earliest of all world-cities (it was believed), Carthage was laid out in regular plan. In another feature this Inner City resembled modern sea-ports and was unlike ancient ones. The harbour was excavated in regular basins, outer and inner. The outer oblong, for vessels of commerce, the inner, called Cothon, fitted for 220 full-sized triremes. This ran round, or nearly round, a circular island, from which the Punic admiral's quarters had commanded the lake of Tunis and the sea. All was constructed at the one corner which gave a straight shore, south and north, for quays and a short end southward and sheltered for the harbour mouth. Everywhere there was a genius for adaptation visible. At the intersection of the two great streets are the extraordinary reservoirs, Roman too, but on Punic lines. The substructure of the citadel—a unique contrivance (except so far as it resembles the sub-structure of the Temple)—is a nest of chambers where water was purified and stood in vast volume. Of the triple wall of the inner city, itself containing stabling and barracks, without believing all that is in Appian, we may believe wonders.

At the heart of the isosceles triangle which, as we can perceive, the city shaped out, rose three hundred feet high, the famous Bozrah—climbed by three streets of rapid gradient—the Byrsa of the legend, and of the most 'truthful and moving' of all siege narratives save one.

On the crown of it had been in all Punic time the tutelary temple of Eschmoun, heavily pillared and yellow stuccoed, replaced perhaps in the times we are busy with, by the Corinthian or Ionic temple, of whose columns a few fragments remain. Now it is the chapel of the saint and king who died on the shore below in the arms of Joinville. Here were the Basilicas, where Cyprian pleaded, the great Library he used, the Senate House, the Prætorium facing the sea—and all the home of a State.

Close by the inner side of the harbour rises a miniature Byrsa, on which perhaps Cælestis had her shrine—Ashtaroth, the 'abomination of the Sidonians,' and the despair of Virgil, after whom Gracchus tried to re-name the town Junonia.

The fragments which thickly strew the ground are all Roman. The Punic city lies below them under a deep layer of calcined earth and wood ash. Nothing of it presses on our eyes but the enormous tufa blocks marked with fire, the bases of the ramparts. Within their northernmost reach but seemingly beyond all old dwellings is the city of the dead, little hills and dells of limestone, *Djebel Khaoui*, where lie hundreds of thousands. Their places have been sunken, burrowed, and scooped, tenanted, re-tenanted and desecrated again. Thousands of dull monuments teach us nothing but names. These date onward from the second Phœnician epoch. Their forefathers had buried in the Inner Town. The ponderous sepulchres of the oldest Phœnician lords are in the sides of Bozrah. Tertullian had shuddered at what he saw disclosed when the Odeon was excavated. Here are Christian emblems, and here are beheaded skeletons with their heads laid carefully upon their laps. And who are these?

Within the ramparts partly, but for miles outside them, stretched the woods and gardens of the Roman peers, an extent of 'Horti' unmatched at Rome, and across them from the western hills strode the colossal aqueduct.

If we did not know that the marble wealth of its structures, so conveniently stratified for a second quarrying, had tempted not only anti-Christian Tunis, but supremely Christian Pisa, we should gaze with blank eyes upon the blank spaces where such marvels have been. Of Amphitheatre and Circus no trace but immense shallow troughs in the soil. Of Theatre, Odeon, Forum itself, scarce a sign. The Christian Fathers did not prophesy in vain, when they declared that these, the most prominent, most imposing institutions of that age, were dissolving the primary institutes of society and nature—respect for Life, for Virtue, for Government, and for Justice itself. About the Amphitheatre Tertullian refuses to reason with Christians. He can consider it an open question only for men still heathen. In the Circus mere madness is king, no authority acknowledged. Cyprian tells them this Theatre is the apotheosis of sin, this Forum the living spirit of Falseness. It is a strange note of our city that all these have been not ruined but annihilated.

Faintly then we may picture to ourselves a material something not wholly unlike what Carthage was. Scarcely any city yields so many scenes. The streets gathering themselves in unique symmetry to the feet of sudden steeps and many-tinted marble heights, or opening full on the glistening quays and the breathless harbour: graceful hills about it crowned with shrines and villas, great levels spreading in chase or garden; low 'difficult hills' with 'artificial passages,' which yoked the neck of its foreland; the vast lake where navies of commerce and of pleasure rode close to the streets, severed by a thread from the open sea; mountain crests in snow watching from the distances; through all and over all the keen light and intense blue of Africa.

*   *   *

More to us than the splendours of the place is the population, its habits and temper.

One of its unlikenesses to other capitals was the way in which it was made and kept a city of Peace, luxurious but not idle Peace. The policy of its re-peopling did not suffer it to be a military centre. A third of the Third Legion was always quartered, not at Carthage, but wherever the Proconsul was, and the brilliance of his court was unsurpassed.

When Carthage called the Gordians to the Empire, ten years before Cyprian became a Christian, the military ceremonial of Rome was punctiliously represented there, but Maximin taunted the city which would make Emperors, with being kept in order by a handful of lictors, having no weapons but hunting-spears, and no drill but the dance. The population of the rich territory outside was not more martial. They poured in armed only with hatchets and country sticks. It was the more striking because their neighbour Numidia was a land of forts and camps, and, thanks to its marvellous old Masinissa, famous for its native javelin men, who rode without bit or bridle and 'steered' their barbs, the costliest in the world, with cord and switch.

Three of the finest of earth's races lived together in its circuit. The Roman, as he is best known, so is he also least patient of a rapid touch. We need say here no more than that of all the vast institutions and organizations of power, rule, pleasure, corruption which we may touch on, he was the creator. The Romans of Carthage did not see themselves, as at home, sending out, as from a source, all the legislative, administrative and executive powers, and receiving the appeals and prayers of all nations, nor yet, as in other capitals, few in number but sovereign through military peace and unswerving law. At Carthage the commerce, wealth and social influence of their preponderating numbers were shared by Punic families Latinized since the last colonizations. If the native race largely supplied them with slaves, it had also an independent population within the city naturally recruiting itself from the clans.

The Berber—by this, its northern name, we may call the earliest universal stock of the continent whom the antients knew by many names— the Berber may be studied now as well as at any of his unrecorded eras. He is unchanged. He is nearly half the population. In large districts he talks 'Libyan' still, which his masters never allowed on coin or document, and seldom indeed could speak. He is no child of Shem like the Arab he lives with. His notions are of equality among men, honour for women, village communities (in the hill-tops if possible), neighbourly federation. He is tall, strong, supple, healthful, often 'like a bronze' for form and colour, often fair and blue eyed. We do not know whether he came in by Gibraltar. Before our times he had learnt enough of Roman manners along the seaboard. How the Roman used him and what he made of him in the interior we shall tell by and bye. Of his third century relations to Christianity we know nothing at all. In his time he has learnt the Phœnician, Roman, and Christian religions, and he retains little spots of each. All that was important in them he dropped before Islam. He saw all other races in and will see them out.

The administration of law was perforce rigorous. The complicated agrarian and military conditions under which land was incessantly being acquired, leased, sub-let, and transferred by Roman farmers; antient freeholders and tenants being generally maintained in their rights, and an elaborate *corvée* system worked with an eye indeed to the benefit of Italian proprietors, yet with a tendency to keep peasant-life tolerable, and not to aggravate traditional service—all this developed highly in 'Africa, nurse of pleaders,' some branches of legal skill. Inscriptions witness to the care with which peasant farmers had their cases heard, and the awards recorded monumentally for future information and security.

The moving part of the population consisted, not, as with us, of people making their way up to the metropolis to be lost in it, but of families and masters, often veteran soldiers, halting on their way up the country, and often increasing their little capital by the ingenious use of opportunities which a seaport offered in the way of new arrivals, commodities accessible, and industries in requisition. But finally they were in quest of rich rewarding plots of soil, as near as might be to the countless little towns which were growing out of villages and Punic stations in the plateaux and slopes of Atlas. After a while they and their factors again crowded the quays with their produce, and employed a conflux of foreign sailors, porters, dock-labourers, to which the 'Rhuppapai' of the Piræus was a small orderly company.

Meantime the ultimately ruinous transfers of land were proceeding, by which the superior ownership was concentrating itself under fewer and fewer titles. Farms were therefore ranging themselves more and more round the bright towns, rich in every natural advantage of water and wood and quarry, while enormous tracts of land were being afforested.

All this implied an immense class of lawyers and agents, of architects and engineers, builders of aqueducts and road makers, with Colleges of Surveyors who had never found it convenient to drop the augural system which gave a Divine sanction to their mensuration. Their verdicts must be no more disputed than those of the magistrates, who similarly supported their excellent character for justice by conjuring tricks, by retaining priestly functions, by a grave acting of religious sentiments which few of them entertained. If there was one thing they disliked, it was having to punish opinions which at first seemed to them only eccentric. Yet the Christians turned even this into a grave necessity.

* * *

How could there be many races without many gods? Yet these Christians would have but one God, and Him a new one. How could so many races have unity or coherence without the *cultus* of the one Emperor?

Before his bust in the standard of the legion, before his image in the shrine of the domestic cloister, incense went up continually. He might be vile, but he was the Unity of Man. His *numen* was an earthly Providence—practically more useful than a heavenly one—so useful that after a temporary interruption by Christian Emperors the same cultus revived and still flourishes on the same earthly centre.

Among Celts and Africans schools of Latin were a necessity. They naturally became schools of Rhetoric. Spain, Gaul and Africa were each famous, and Augustine admits no rival to Carthage except Rome, for Professors of Oratory and of all the knowledge which oratory demands. Fronto, with his 'gravity,' glorified as '*the* Orator' and canonized by Aurelius' lavish friendship, was of Cirta. But as of old it was remarked that Africa had produced 'no astronomer,' so to the last she reared no philosopher.

Augustine, who owed so much to its schools, cannot be said to speak of Carthage with affection. Its 'riot of flagitious loves' which swept away even 'the more sedate,' its stage dancing and scenic shame, and scarcely less the falsity of its rhetorical training and the objects to be effected by that training, made Carthage a blot on his memory. He speaks with yet further horror of street scenes in which he never took part, the abominable *eversiones*, which seem to have perpetuated the tradition of those Punic riots in which, as at Alexandria, Polybius says the youths took as much part as the men.

But in general her citizens were as 'enamoured' of Carthage as Pericles wished his countrymen to be of Athens. The feeling is not ill represented by Apuleius, himself 'a half Gætulian, half Numidian' from Madaura. He speaks of her schools, her commerce and her religion as the never worn out boast of her *alumnus*. Devotion to her as the one lasting rivalry between two distinguished friends of his own.

Cyprian himself, confessing to the full the stains upon his own grave professional life, yet exclaims as to Carthage itself, 'Where better, where gladlier might I be than in the place where God willed me to believe and grow?' (*credere et crescere*).

* * *

Of the Phœnician population of Carthage there has been much to imagine, little to know. Scant record but an enduring type. More than sixteen centuries before Christ they had stepped hither, point by point along the Mediterranean coasts on their way to Spain and outward. Here an island, there a foreland or a peninsula had served their turn and made them masters or controllers of the moving currents of wealth. But this was far their noblest settlement. About the eighth century it may have been reorganized, receiving the name which appears on coin and monument, Kart Hadasat, the NEW CITY which Cato tried to pronounce in his 'Carthada.' They checked the advance of Cyrene, planting along the edge of the Lesser Syrtis, as far on as the Greater, a chain of advanced posts, whose collective name of *Emporia* stamps the spirit of their foundation and indicates their wealth. Where there were lagoons they rejoiced, and made them serviceable with quay and aqueduct and causey. These towns they lost and won again and again in conflict with native princes. They cared nothing for the peoples among whom they fared, and nothing for their broad lands. They paid tribute readily to the inland tribes, until the day came when it could be repudiated. A hard unsympathetic spirit marked their rule. They amalgamated no tribes, allied no governments, conciliated no loyalty. Their nearest neighbour, Utica, whose interests seemed identical with those of Carthage, was first to turn on her when her stress came.

They had brought a rich material dowry to their new country:—purple murex which on the seabanks of the Isle of Meninx became a source of untold wealth; olive, vine, artichoke, pomegranate, the date-palm which soon possessed the land. The first of all treatises of gardening was Mago's. They imbedded the city in gardens. That they did not introduce deer or boar is just a token of how little to them was the inland. But they almost adored the native horse, and stamped him on their coins with perfect appreciation of his points.

They also brought with them worships which had the fascinations of orgy, cruelty and secrecy, worships ever deadliest to the religion of revelation. The Romans favoured or adopted the service of the 'Dæmon' or 'Genius of the Carthaginians,' Baal or 'Heracles' or Eschmoun; as well as of Astarte, Tanit, the 'Juno' or Virgo Cælestis, of whose observances there are not wanting traces in the Moslem villages of to-day. But everywhere there is the commercial touch. Amongst the most important of our Punic inscriptions are two tariffs which tabulate for Carthage and Marseilles the fees and perquisites of sacrifices and the price of victims. Of two Punic words in Augustine, one is 'Mammon,' which he renders 'Lucre,' and he quotes one proverb, 'The Plague asks a coin: give two to be rid of him.' Commerce was their aristocratic life, seacraft and ship-building their ancestral pride. 'Thy benches of ivory; fine linen with broidered work of Egypt thy sail;...wise men thy calkers'; so Ezekiel touches in the Tyrian galley, such a ship as sailed with its annual freight of 'Firstfruits' from the daughter Carthage. A gainful people, high and low, intriguing and bribing for office, says Polybius, with a bribery which at Rome in his time would have been penal and capital; ambitious with a passion which Hannibal himself failed to gratify.

The character of the race was permanent like its physiognomy; in both they were *Chenani*, as they called themselves to the last, genuine Canaanites.

When the last Colonia settled 'within the vestiges of great Carthage,' there were some thousands of Chenani lingering there, safer than among Libyan nomads. They were not ejected. There was nothing to hinder the redevelopment of their antient tastes, but everything to promote them. The Romans who had been so scared when the jackals pulled up the boundary rods were only too glad to adore and to endow the gods in possession.

It is not hard, then, to understand how under the Empire the rich and able Chenani prospered, and how their craftsmen, labourers and sailors found more employment than ever on the quays, harbour and lake, where rode fleets of all nations. The memory of their past was written in colossal characters all round them, and would have tended to keep a less supple people separate in the pride both of achievement and of suffering, and probably in a distinct quarter of the city. But of this we hear nothing. And although some great Punic families probably withdrew gradually to their remoter estates, as the Mahomedan gentry now slip away from Algiers even against the wish of the French, yet at any rate in Carthage strong interests promoted fusion.

It is more hard to say what hold Christianity took on them. The copious Augustine, who flashes into every corner, finds it needful to call attention to only two Punic words, even incidentally. The second was *Messiah*. We must not assume from this that the language had receded in the two previous centuries, for Cyprian and Tertullian mention none. The two Sacraments were known among them by beautiful names, meaning *Salus* and *Vita*, which Augustine supposes must have come to them through some original Apostolic channel of their own. Yet in the Cyprianic documents, flowing over with sacramental language, there is but one doubtful allusion, 'Laver of Health,' and that is in the retranslation from Firmilian.

For official use Punic had been soon disallowed, and in Carthage the Phœnicians soon became bilingual, but the Romans never. In the more primitive towns alone Punic was talked by the lower orders, and was patriotically kept up by higher circles, together with a little shocking Greek, and no Latin to speak of. That was the case in Tripolis. Forty miles from Hippo it was necessary in the fourth century to place a Punic-speaking Bishop in the town of Fussala, and the saintly Valerius took Augustine for his coadjutor because it was impossible for him as a Greek to teach effectively. Phœnician then was a living tongue, and it had, we know, an eloquence of its own. Severus was 'very prompt with it.' Its old literature was read, and 'the learned found much wisdom in it.'

There was a free use by the population of an incorrect Latin, of which we have examples in the Letters of Celerinus and Lucian, and relics in many forms. The anti-Donatist 'Psalm' or Ballad, made to be sung about by the *idiotæ*, was in Latin. It was scoffingly said that if Donatism were the only genuine Christianity, as it claimed to be, only two of the Pentecostal tongues were worth anything, for it talked only Punic and Latin. There is no trace of a Phœnician Christian Literature. Of a hundred and forty or fifty names of Bishops in the Cyprianic papers, not more than a dozen may be non-Latin, but apparently not more than one may be Punic. All the facts look one way, and they scarcely could be what they are if Christianity at the time we speak of had taken hold of the Phœnician nationality in either its lower or its cultivated strata. The Latin Christian speech which there developed was due to the fact that while the Church in Rome was still a Greek Church, a Church of foreigners, the most advanced classes in Carthage, of Roman origin and Latin tongue, were the most Christian. And when the jurists and the rhetoricians were touched, they were the very men qualified to form with accuracy the new vocabulary of the new subject, and not to be deterred by the necessity for fresh combinations of words when they set out to express truth with strength. The languid literature, for such it had been, was regenerated.

* * *

Their 'Africa'—for the Roman of Carthage was as proud of that name, which had somehow come in with him and was unknown to the Greeks, as the Londoner is of 'England'—had begun to glory in having saturated itself with all the religions, all the pleasures, 'of the Greeks.' What that meant for morals moralists tell. Salvian groans that the city itself was so little purified by Christianity till the strong, pure Vandals came in. It is enough for us to say that, for the masses, the standard, much more the discipline, of morals went down before the flood, unstemmed by the pious propitiation of 'dæmons,' ever multiplying, swarming on every branch of life, while all life was pervaded by a sense of the unreality of God.

Exceptions were eminent, possibly numerous. The monuments shew that the old chaste, grave, diligent virtues were in honour. Of the many lecturers in philosophy few, perhaps, were not in some small degree effective in raising the moral tone of their best disciples. Some worked a stern, if self-satisfied, code. But when the best was done, the individual only was moved or raised, and the individual grew daily of less and less account.

The one thing desirable, the one thing unattainable by any known method, was a re-casting of Society, such that selfishness should be discounted as an evil, the source of evil, and yet the individual be made of full account. A Society faithful to the Individual, the Individual devoted to the Society.

Meantime there had been growing up for more than a century and a half in every grade of society a kind of Union, or rather a kind of 'People,' for this was what they meant to be, although not in any sense a nation. They were uniformly loyal to the Government, save only as to the one article of bearing arms in its service. But averse, even adverse, to almost every other influence, rule, tone, opinion, habit and sacred observance of every locality in which they were found.

It was understood that they were bound together in a federal network, and their leading officials generally well known, and that by the same official titles in all countries. They sought the individual whom they thought likely to join them. They cared for the stranger. If he became one of them, they made him, wherever he travelled or settled, one of a circle of pledged friends with vowed teachers. God and Life and Death were not the same things to them as to any others. There were daily, and sometimes more frequent gatherings of their local groups. In public life they were irreproachable except for their strange conventions, betraying their new associations by nothing sometimes but a deranged character. Yet the least moral of their neighbours had more than doubts of their secret licentiousness. Few knew the affiliations of their tenets or theories. Historically and 'scholastically' they were bound up with the Jews, but Judaic hostility to them was unsleeping. Admired professors of philosophy considered that, with more or less clearness, their ethical notions were unaccountably sound, but so disfigured by being adapted to fit such hopeless people, and their evidently philosophic Founder so disguised behind a wild story and a sacrilegious theory, that if the ethics had no practical effect on them this could not be wondered at.

Their unpopularity must rest on some deep contradiction to human principle, or it could not be so instructive and universal. Social harass, popular outbreak, magisterial severity, imperial thunder were perpetually breaking on them, and were less than unavailing; in fact stimulated interest in them and adherence to them. Until lately they had been a non-descript between ethnics and Jews, a *Tertium Genus* whom 'our recognized tolerance' could scarcely be expected to tolerate. Yet people began slowly to be aware that the singular persons whom they knew belonged to an invisible 'majority.' 'We are men of yesterday,' says Tertullian, yet they were 'filling cities, islands, castles, boroughs, council rooms,—even camps,—the tribes, the decuries—palace, senate, forum—

every place but the temples.' They had come in so insensibly that some of them still plied former callings inconsistent with their principles. Now and then some were seen in the *cunei* at the habitual spectacles.

Here in Africa—at the Gate which all passed through—there was no doubt such another hospice on the quay as there was at Portus. There were no doubt in the town Basilicas and 'Fabrics,' such as Fabian had, and built at the same time in Rome. The private estate of their well-known chief was large and beautiful. Then all along both ridges of Atlas, and on to where he dipped to his own ocean, there was not a town where they had not a footing and a constitution, officers and an inner circle; not a farm where they did not claim a slave, if not a son. Their officials, 'servants' 'sub-servants' and 'followers,' flitted to and fro with missives and carried monies on ships, through prison doors, among barracks and mines. When they were recognized they were gone. Their 'Overseers' convened themselves for deliberation when and where they pleased. Their public death-scenes from time to time were to their sect a kind of grave festival.

It was and is vain to try to ascertain where and by what avenues the flood had poured in. Cyprian only knew that the 'sacerdotal unity,' the one order of bishops, traced to the 'primal church' of Rome. Augustine only thought that the Punic Sacraments, called by names not borrowed or rendered from the Latin, traced to some other Apostolic source. That is all. They were there and they were one. The Christians had in fact come into possession as the Phœnicians themselves had come into possession of harbours and marts, not like the noisy Roman colonies, but without violence or observation.

It is with a few years of this People that we are now to concern ourselves.

CHAPTER I.

THE LAST OF THE LONG PEACE.

I.

Cyprian's Preparation in Heathendom.

SUCH was the city and the society in which, possibly after long practice as an advocate, Thascius Cyprianus became the most eminent master of forensic eloquence[1]; that is to say the leading member of the highest of the professions[2].

Of his birthplace or family we know nothing; both his names[3] are almost unique in the nomenclature of antiquity,

---

[1] ...in tantam gloriam venit eloquentiæ ut oratoriam quoque doceret Carthagini. Hieron. *comm. Jon.* c. 3. Cyprianus primum rhetor, deinde presbyter, ad extremum Carthaginiensis episcopus martyrio coronatur. Euseb. *Chronicon* II. Olymp. 258.
...et magnam sibi gloriam ex artis oratoriæ professione quæsierat. Lactant. *Div. Inst.* v. 1. ...tantæ vocis tuba quæ forensium mendaciorum certamina solebat acuere...suam et aliorum linguas docuerat loqui mendacium. In alia schola, &c. Aug. *Serm.* 312, c. 4 (4).

[2] On the high rank and fortunes attained by many advocates and rhetores from and after the second century, see L. Friedländer, *Darstellungen aus d. Sittengeschichte Roms*, B. iii. c. 4 § 1 (1888—90, vol. I. pp. 322—330) and note in supplement.

[3] Thascius Cyprianus he is called by the proconsul. (*Acta Proc.* 3, 4, cf. Pontii *Vit. Cypr.*), and in the singular heading of *Ep.* 66 he styles himself 'Cyprianus qui et Thascius.' After his adoption, according to Jerome (*De Viris Ill.*), of the 'cognomentum' of the presbyter who converted him, he became Thascius Cæcilius Cyprianus, and in his proscription (which he himself quotes *Ep.* 66) is called Cæcilius Cyprianus. But the adoption must be doubtful, since every MS. and ed. Man. reads 'Cæciliani' as the presbyter's name in the only place where Pontius mentions him (c. 4), and Pontius adds nothing on the subject. The pleasant fancy was likely to occur to biographers. The only recurrence of the prænomen which I find is in the African Kalendar, which commemorates a 'Tascius Martyr' on Sept. 1. Its rarity no doubt leads to the misnomer *Tatius* (*Tassius, Tarsus*) Cyprianus in the Decree of *Conc. Rom.* 1. *sub* Gelas., Labbe v. c. 388.

The name Cyprianus occurs later, among African Christians possibly called after him—*e.g.* one of the Fathers in the Carthaginian council of A.D. 416 (Aug.

and when he speaks affectionately of Carthage as the happiest place on earth to him,—'where God had willed that he should believe and grow up (in the faith),' he would scarcely have omitted to claim a native interest in the beloved home, had he possessed it[1].

All that to us is represented by the influence of the press lay in an ancient capital within the power of eloquence. Far from any shade of unreality resting on them the teachers of oratory were courted leaders in society. The publicity of life, the majesty of national audiences, the familiarity of the cultivated classes with the teaching of the schools, required the orator to be not only perfect in the graces of life, but to be versed in ethical science; to be armed with solid arguments as well as to be facile of invention; not less convincing than attractive; in short to be a wit and a student, a politician and an eclectic philosopher.

At the age of nearly thirty Cicero was still placing himself under the tuition of the Rhodian Molon[2]. Augustine's fourth

Epp. 175, 181) is so named, as is also the Deacon who carried the remarkable correspondence between Jerome and Augustine (Aug. *Epp.* 71 et sqq.); a Presbyter, to whom Jerome writes as Presbyterorum studiosissime,' *Ep.* 140 (139) (13) on Psalm 89 (90); and a Donatist Bishop (Aug. *c. litt. Petil.* iii. c. 34 (40)); in *C. Insc. Gr.* IV. 8954 from Bethlehem, 9203, 9412 Κηπρη(α)-νου; in *C. Inscrr. Latt.* VIII. i. 455, 2291 (a Bishop of Bagai), VIII. ii. 10539; and in Procopius as the name of a 'Dux fœderatorum' in the Vandal and Gothic wars. Thus Pape properly calls it a late name.

The origin of both names is unknown. The Mozarabic Vesper Hymn for his day begins 'Urbis magister Tasciæ,' *Lit. Moz.* ed. Migne II. c. 1201 (ed. Card. Ximenes, 'Tusciæ'), but this cannot be identified with the African town Thacia (*Tab. Peut.*), Θασία (*Ptol.*), or regarded as more than a guess. See also *Corp. Inscrr. Latt.* vol. XII. n. 3277 Q. TASGIVS FORTVNATVS.

From the connection of Cyprus with Carthage it might have seemed possible to derive *Cyprianus* thence if *Cyprius* had been an ascertained proper name, but scarcely otherwise. Pape connects it with 'Copper.' If derived from Cypris it would, as other derivatives of divine names, Apollonius, Herculanus, &c., be more common. Names given after this goddess come generally from Aphrodite.

[1] The birthplace is not really indicated by the passages quoted from Prudentius *Peristeph.* xiii. 3 'est proprius patriæ martyr,' and Suidas, s.v. Καρχηδών...ἐξ ἧς ὡρμᾶτο, even supposing their authority to be sufficient. Jerome's 'Cyprianus Afer' cannot be taken, as by Fechtrup, to mean necessarily a native of Africa.

[2] For the third time Cic. *Brut.* 91.

book on Christian Doctrine shews us that five centuries and a changed religion did not abate the value placed on technical perfection. No statesman's name had for generations commanded such reverence as was paid in Cyprian's times to the life and memory of Timesitheus the Rhetorician, whose daughter the young African Emperor had espoused[1], and whose honour and universal cultivation and experience had for a brief interval restored purity to the court, dignity to the senate, and discipline to the camps of Rome.

Ob. A.D. 243.

To the well-moulded strength of Roman eloquence Africa, 'nurse of pleaders[2],' had added a fervour not unlike that with which Ireland has enriched the English bar. With a powerful memory[3], and a methodic, classificatory mind, Cyprian had pursued the highest literary culture. 'What gold, what silver, what raiment he brought with him out of Egypt!' exclaims Augustine. And Jerome, treating the conquest of the literary world by Christianity as grander than any triumph over mere power or luxury, and seeking an instance of the true 'Kings of the World,'—'who are last of all to hear the word, yet 'at length, like the Ninevite, descend from their thrones to 'plebeian levels, lay aside the radiance of their eloquence, put 'away the intoxicating draught of words, and thenceforth 'content themselves with the majesty of Christian thoughts' —selects the great Carthaginian master[4].

---

[1] Jul. Capitol. *Gordiani Tres* c. 23 'causa eloquentiæ digrum parentela sua putavit.' [The incredible name *Misitheus* given him by Julius, and that of *Timesicles* by Zosimus (i. 17, 18) are both mistakes. His name was in full *C. Furius Sabinius Aquila Timesitheus*. See two interesting Inscriptions in Orell., *Inscrr. Latt.* v. 3, pp. 103, 4, n. 5530, 1. The former with facsimile and full comment in L. Renier's and J. B. Monfalcon's ed. of J. Spon (Lyon 1857) pp. 162, 3.]

[2] Juv. *Sat.* vii. 148 'nutricula causidicorum Africa.' Domitius Afer and Julius Africanus in the time of Nero were orators whom Quintilian (x. 1, 118) compares to the ancients; the latter he describes as 'concitatior sed in cura verborum nimius.'

[3] Memoriosa mens, Pont. *Vit.* 5. Cf. preface to *Testim.* 'quantum mediocris memoria suggerebat.'

[4] *Comm. in Jon.* c. 3. So Greg. Naz. *Or.* xxiv. 6 ...τὸ τῶν λόγων κράτος, τῶν τε κατὰ φιλοσοφίαν καὶ ὅσοι τῆς ἄλλης παιδεύσεως, καὶ τούτων ὃ βούλει μέρος· ὡς μᾶλλον μὲν τὸ ποικίλον ἢ τὸ ἄκρον ἐν ἑκάστῳ θαυμάζεσθαι· μᾶλλον δὲ τὸ εὐδό-

No accessions, indeed, to the Christian ranks were more important than the conversions of the great lawyers. Versed in letters and in modern thought, practised in the sifting of evidence, cold to the voice of enthusiasm, moving in that circle of refined habit of which Minucius gives so delicate a picture in his barrister's holiday at Ostia, accustomed moreover to see Christians at the worst worldly advantage, they became witnesses and disciples at once. Nor are any phenomena more significant of the hold which was being gained upon the Roman world than first the conversion, and next the superiority to contemporary ethnic writers, in genius alike and in cultivation, of a Tertullian, a Felix, a Cyprian.

The position he had attained might alone imply that at the time when he first attracts our notice Cyprian had passed middle life[1]. His wealth was affluent, his landed property large, his gardens in Carthage spacious and beautiful[2]. The home of which he speaks to Donatus as no longer fair to the purged eye is sketched apparently from his own: it is a villa of more than Pompeian richness, with frescoed walls, gilded ceilings, and marble-lined saloons[3].

κιμον ἐν ἑκάστῳ τῆς περὶ πάντα πολυμαθίας. It is evident that Gregory had read some at least of his treatises (and see also c. 7). There is no ground for supposing his other Cyprian to have written anything.

[1] Pearson rightly sets aside Baronius' inference from the *Ad Donatum* c. 3 'senio,' as to his age, and observes that Pontius gives no hint of it. This would be strange in a biographer, and although *supergressus vetustatis ætatem* Pont. *Vit.* 2 may mean 'surpassing all antiquity,' it is just possible that in his superfine style he may parallel *veteribus* by *vetustatis* and *senibus* by *ætatem*, thus implying old age. Antiquity is not part of the antithesis, and he is contrasting Cyprian with those who had heard the truth all their lives. Gregory Nazianzen, calling him (*Or.* xxiv. 6) τὸ τῆς νεότητος ἄνθος, confuses him with the Oriental Cyprian who was somewhat over 30 according to the story.

[2] Pont. *Vit.* 2, *ad Donat.*, 1, 15.

[3] *Ad Don.* 15. Compare Vitruv. vi. 5 (8) 'Forensibus autem et disertis (atria) elegantiora et spatiosiora ad conventus excipiundos.' I do not introduce to the text Gregory's ὁ πλούτῳ περιφανὴς καὶ δυναστείᾳ περίβλεπτος καὶ γένει γνώριμος...συγκλήτου βουλῆς μετουσία καὶ προεδρία because there is no knowing whether he has the right Cyprian before him. *Or.* xxiv. 6. The end of *Ad Don.* c. 3 has no relation to his own position. 'Fascibus *ille* oblectatus...*Hic* stipatus clientium cuneis' are picturesque illustrations simply.

His personal address was conciliatory yet dignified, his manner affectionate, his expression attractive by a certain grave joyousness. His dress, quiet yet appropriate to his rank, was remarked on as answering to his calm tone of mind[1]. He never thought it necessary to assume the philosopher's pall, which Tertullian had maintained to be the true dress of a Christian, for to him the bared arm and exposed chest seemed rather pretentious than plain[2]. Augustine, when acknowledging the benefits he had derived through Cyprian's intercessions, dwells especially on the never-hardened tenderness of his character. 'Gentle he was when he 'had yet to endure amid various temptations this world's 'perils[3].' Even to the last his friendship was claimed by senator and knight, by the oldest heathen houses, and the highest ranks of the province[4].

Yet wealth and elegance, cultivation and good sense, might have left him the mere ornament of his circle or perhaps of

---

[1] Gravis vultus et laetus nec severitas tristis nec comitas nimia...nec cultus dispar a vultu, temperatus et ipse de medio; non illum superbia saecularis inflaverat, nec tamen prorsus adfectata penuria sordidarat. Pont. *Vit.* 6. Gregory Nazianz. surely had read the passage which he thus beautifully condenses, τὸ περὶ τὰς ἐντεύξεις ὑψηλόν τε ὁμοῦ καὶ φιλάνθρωπον, ὡς ἴσον ἀπέχειν εὐτελείας καὶ αὐθαδείας. *Or.* xxiv. 13.

[2] *De Bono Patientia* 2 'exserti ac seminudi pectoris,' &c. That is, he condemns the mode of wearing the Pallium which Justin kept and which Tertullian recommended as ascetic and Christian. It is represented in the Cemetery of Callistus on two figures of teachers (de Rossi, *R. S.* vol. II. p. 349, Tav. xv. 7, 9). These belong to the middle of the second century, and the fashion does not reappear. If Gregory Nazianzen means that Cyprian wore the *pallium* (as he seems to do, *Or.* xxiv. 13, when he praises in him τὸ περὶ τὴν ἐσθῆτα φιλόσοφον) it is one of his countless mistakes about him.

[3] *Serm.* 312, c. 1.

[4] Pont. *Vit.* 14. And this heathen respect for him remained. Greg. Naz. says τὸ μὲν ὄνομα πολὺ παρὰ πᾶσι Κυπριανοῦ καὶ οὐ Χριστιανοῖς μόνον ἀλλὰ καὶ τὴν ἐναντίαν ἡμῖν τεταγμένοις...*Or.* xxiv. 17. Dr Peters, p. 38, solemnly works out, as if from Lactantius, that a nickname 'Coprianus' was effectually used at Carthage to laugh away Cyprian's influence. All that Lactantius says is *Divin. Instt.* v. 1 that *he had heard* an accomplished man break this sorry jest, say fifty years at least later. The point of it was that 'so elegant a wit, meant for better things, had devoted itself to old wives' fables.' Cf. inter copreas, Suet. *Tib.* 61. Scurra qui incopriatur, *Gloss. Isidor.* ap. M. Martini *Lexic. Philol.* (1698) v. II.

the church, but for his instinctive delight in concerting action with others and in gathering influential men about him, a finely developed tact in approaching the right person at the suitable moment, and a real laboriousness in keeping people of weight informed of all they could desire to know. Such habits may belong to men of small conceptions; if they are the accompaniments of genius, such a genius moves the world.

The peculiar expressions of two authorities, one of whom from local opportunities, the other from the character of his investigations, may have seen good reasons for their words, imply that, in somewhat more than the common function of an advocate, he had concerned himself with maintaining polytheism. Whether in processes touching temple endowments, or in procedures against Christians, in panegyrics, or in some more speculative way, cannot now be determined, but Jerome distinctly speaks of his having been a 'vindicator[1] of idolatry,' and Augustine dwells on 'the garniture of that 'noble eloquence whereby the crumbling doctrines of dæmons 'were once undeservedly decorated,' 'that eloquence wherein, 'as from some precious goblet, he once drank pledges to 'deadly errors[2].'

The purport of the Christian rites had nevertheless not escaped his earlier observation as a moralist. Like many a noble heathen he had known what it was to rebel against sensual habit. The power of Baptismal Grace had been mentioned in his hearing and not excited his derision. Yet the suppression of passion and surrender of indulgence was still

---

[1] *Comm. in Jon.* 3 'adsertor idololatriæ,' cf. Optat. i. c. 9 'adsertoribus ecclesiæ Catholicæ.' So Aug. *Conf.* viii. 2 says that Victorinus the rhetorician had up to an advanced age defended with fanatic eloquence (ore terricrepo) the monstrous foreign gods. In an inscription of A.D. 495 on Donatus Bishop of Tanaramusa (*C. Inscrr. Latt.* VIII. ii. n. 9286) he is styled (mu)LTIS EXILIIS (saepe) PROBATVS ET FIDEI CATHOLICAE ADSERTOR DIGNVS INVENTVS. As to Cyprian we scarcely dare quote Gregory Nazianzen for such a fact. But his δαιμόνων ἦν θεραπευτής...καὶ διώκτης πικρότατος may represent the same tradition. *Or.* xxiv. 8.

[2] *Serm.* 312, c. 2 (2).

an incredible dream to the observer of human nature[1]. At last, with closer observation, came the recognition of a Divine Presence in the world, adequate even to those effects. A presbyter of high character in the city, Cæcilian by name, was permitted to crown a long life and devoted friendship for Cyprian by imparting to him the *Nova Vita* of the world[2].

A.D. 246.
A.U.C. 999.
Coss. C.
Bruttius
Præsens,
C. Alb...
Albinus.

Cyprian became a Catechumen of the Church of Carthage, famous already for her 'faith, organization, and quietude[3].' The head of the society was Donatus[4].

II.

Cyprian's Preparation under the Church.

The period of Catechesis would naturally engage so energetic a convert in that closeness of study which Pontius indicates, and which his enormous classified copiousness of illustration evinces to have been at some time bestowed by Cyprian on Scripture. But, qualified as his mature reason may have been for reflection, the habits of the man instantly translated thought into life. His work never became speculative, scarcely ever was purely doctrinal. He read to practise[5]. His friend dwells on the vividness with which in the conversations of these and the subsequent months he analysed for himself and for the group which surrounded him lessons of 'God-pleasing' lives to which his new readings introduced the

---

[1] Cum in tenebris...jacerem...vitæ meæ nescius, veritatis...alienus...'Qui possibilis,' aiebam, 'tanta conversio?'... desperatione meliorum malis meis...et favebam. *Ad Don.* 3, 4.

[2] ...viri justi et laudabilis memoriæ Caeciliani et ætate tunc et honore presbyteri, qui eam ad agnitionem veræ divinitatis...*non jam* ut amicum animæ coæqualem sed tanquam novæ vitæ parentem. Pont. *vit.* 4. Dom Maran conjectures without any ground that he is the Cæcilius Natalis who is converted by Octavius in Minucius Felix.

[3] Novimus Carthaginiensis Ecclesiæ fidem, novimus institutionem, novimus humilitatem. *Ep.* 36. 3, from Roman clergy (Novatian). Cf. 'in operibus fratrum' *Epp.* 10. 5, 'antecessoribus' 15. 1, 16. 1.

[4] *Ep.* 59. 10.

[5] Prudentius well touches this characteristic, '*Vivere justitiam* Christi penetrare dogma nostrum.' *Per.* xiii. 32.

man of the world. He gives us the very words[1] of one vivid relic of Cyprian's talk. It is about Job, and though the wording differs throughout, the thoughts are almost identical with his later reflections on the character which appear in the book Of Patience.

How deep-dyed a stain rested on society is seen in the singularity which was attached to the fact that from the moment of his entrance into the ranks of the Catechumens, and 'before the insight of the second birth,' the new convert devoted himself to perfect chastity[2]. What he felt to be the moral obligation of his position is no doubt expressed in one of the headings of his 'Testimonies,' soon afterwards compiled —'that a Catechumen ought to sin no more.' This is however singularly deduced from a false reading of St Paul 'Let us do evil *while good is coming*—whose damnation is just[3].'

Thus early[4] also he reverted to the primitive examples of liberality, and in seeking to palliate the incurable pauperism of his time parted with his property, whole farms apparently at once[5], and distributed all the proceeds.

---

[1] Observe the direct tenses, and the introduction of *dicebat*. Pont. *Vit.* 3. Compare *De B. Pat.* 18. Observe also how a forger of either of these pieces would have copied *words* from the genuine one—while two independent forgers could never have so coincided in thought and tone. The one *word* of coincidence is the calling of GOD's commendation a 'blessing' (*benedictio —benediceret*).

[2] This alone shews how the χαμευνίαι and ἀγρυπνίαι attributed to him by Greg. Naz. are in a false key, and do not belong to *this* Cyprian. *Or.* xxiv. 13.

[3] 'Faciamus mala *dum veniunt bona*: quorum damnatio justa est,' Rom. iii. 8 ap. *Test.* iii. 98.

[4] 'Rudis fidei et cui nondum forsitan crederetur,' Pont. *Vit.* 2, *i.e.* whilst his conversion was probably distrusted, like St Paul's, Acts ix. 26.

[5] The text here is interesting. 'Distractis rebus suis ad indigentium multorum pacem sustinendam, tota prope pretia dispensans, &c.' is Hartel's reading in Pont. *Vit.* c. 2. But 'pacem' in this material sense (and not meaning 'freedom from persecution') is intolerable. The reading of Bodl. MS. 1. (MS. Bodl. Laud. Misc. fol. 192) 'indigentiam multorum pauperum' is not only good sense, but also accounts for 'pacem' through an intermediate abbreviation p͞m.

For *pretia* most editions have *pretio*, but *pro proelia preda* is the reading of Cod. T, the favourite of Hartel. The corrupt *proelia preda* indicates more than the word *pretia* only, and Fell's 'tota *prædia pretio* dispensans' is too harsh. Dr Hort once suggested to me

Two works of Carthaginian authorship had probably been, in the hands of his friend Cæcilian, instrumental to his conversion,—the *Octavius* of Minucius Felix, and the *Apologeticum* of Tertullian. Tertullian's passionate genius was the first to grapple with the amazing difficulty of making the speech of the Roman a vehicle for Theology. That his style was hard, dark, *granitic* is no wonder. Cyprian henceforth was his devoted yet discriminating disciple. He daily called for some manuscript of his in the famous phrase 'Give me The Master[1].'

His first labour probably was, with the condensation and the lucid arrangement of a pleader, retaining as far as possible the words of his originals, yet avoiding whatever was displeasingly rugged or ambiguous, to produce for those who had witnessed his activity in the opposite camp, a telling little résumé of Minucius' anti-polytheistic arguments[2], and of Tertullian's magnificent presentment of the Person of Christ.

It came out, we know not when, as a Thesis headed

'*pretia prædiorum*,' and Dr Westcott '*tota prope prædia*.'

Bodl. MS. 1. originally read 'tota *pro plurima* pretia,' but has been corrected into *propria*, by changing the tall *l* of the original abbreviation *plīa* into a tall *r* in shape like others. This MS. which was full of errors was corrected throughout by a contemporary hand, and we have here perhaps the right reading, 'tota propria pretia.' Quite a Pontian way of expressing that as in Acts v. 4 the prices 'after it was sold were his own.'

The passage is evidently a reminiscence of Acts iv. 34 which in the *Versio Latina Antiqua* ran 'Nec enim indigens aliquis erat in eis. Quotquot enim possessores *prædiorum* aut domorum erant venderǝles adferebant *pretia* venalium.' And Augustine, *Ep.* 185, ix. 36, quotes Acts iv. 32 as 'et nemo dicebat aliquid *proprium*.' See P. Sabatier, *Bibll. SS. Latt. Verss. Antt. l.c.* Cyprian *de unit.* 26 has 'fundos...in usus *indigentium pretia*.' *De op. et el.* 25 '*prædia...dispensandam... distracto*.'

[1] 'Da Magistrum.' Hieron. *de Virr. Ill.* 53.

[2] A simple juxtaposition of passages shews the *Octavius* to be the original, and Jerome in his *de Virr. Ill.* to be right in naming Minucius earlier than Cyprian. Divisions 1 and 2 of the tract are compiled from Minucius 20—27, 18, 32. The 3rd from Tertullian *Apol.* 21—23. Cyprian had also read (*Quod Id.* 9) the *De Testimonio Animæ*.

'THAT IDOLS ARE NOT GODS[1].' It is the work of a learner, not of a teacher[2].

A little later he challenges the world's *Life*: this was his review of the world's *Creeds*.

1. The popular Divinities can, he argues, be identified with historical benefactors. Their variety, the survival of local tradition about them, the inferiority of one national group to another, the occasional suppression of one group by another, sufficiently demonstrate this. The indigenous Roman group was one of the least prominent or least respectable. Who could credit Picus or Tiberinus, Pavor or Cloacina with the rise of Rome? To native deities the greatness of the Empire owed nothing. After lodging this shaft, he accepts the theory, —supported by a consensus, as he says, of the master minds of antiquity,—of the operation of wandering and impure spirits. Their presence is sufficient to account for the many phenomena of vaticination and possession upon which the superstitious fabric of worship has been raised to obstruct the rational service of God. Their office is to 'confound true with false,—deceiving and being deceived.' He then confidently challenges their votaries to be present at a Christian Exorcism. He speaks of extraordinary scenes—the confessions, the lamentations, the departure of these spirits—as familiar events[3].

---

[1] For the title 'quod Idola dii non sint,' kept in all the manuscripts, and confirmed by Jerome *Ep.* 70 (84). 5 ad Magnum, and by Cyp. *Ep. ad Fortunat.* opening with the same words, nearly all editions have substituted 'De Idolorum Vanitate,' so destroying the modest character of a simple thesis. There is no shadow of ground for Peters' treatment of this and the Letter to Donatus as together forming an Apologia proper.

[2] Pontius omits it from the list of his works. Jerome (*l.c.*) praising its learning (*historiarum omnium scientia*) did not know how simple a compilation it was. For instance, it betrays no further acquaintance than comes through Minucius (c. 21) with Euhemerus the Rationalist, whose Ἱερὰ Ἀναγραφή, translated by Ennius, was exactly to Cyprian's purpose.

[3] I am not sure that Cyprian means to say that he had been an eyewitness, although, if not, he should have written still more guardedly. He however only says 'videas' *Quod Id.* c. 7; and again *ad Demetrian.* 15 'videbis.' 'Sub

2. In contrast with all this confusion rises the majestic truth of the Unity of God. He attempts no proof of this; only illustrates it, and not felicitously, from analogy and from traces of it in the universal consciousness.

3. Now comes in the impressive history of Judaism and the exact correspondence of its greatness, and its dispersion, with predictions which had linked its destiny to obedience. Those same predictions had anticipated a universal nation in union with God incarnate. The appearance of Christ, the misinterpretation of His work and Person, the testimony to His Resurrection, are facts before the world. The illumination of the individual by Faith in Him, and the coming elevation of the Race of Man, are beginning to fulfil themselves. He concludes, for perhaps the first time in the Christian argument, by putting in evidence the

---

manu nostra,' 'a nobis' are not conclusive. They are taken from Minucius c. 27. Besides, the very strong language of Cyprian 'videas illos nostra voce et oratione majestatis occultæ flagris cædi, igne torreri, incremento poenæ propagantis extendi, ejulare, gemere, deprecari' looks like a mere amplification of Minucius' 'quoties a nobis et tormentis *verborum, orationis incendiis* de corporibus exiguntur,' who is more special also in that he speaks of Saturn, Serapis, Jupiter being thus expelled. Cyprian repeats his own words in *ad Don.* 5. In a strange passage *Ep.* 69. 15, though exorcism is not always successful, baptism 'must be held' to overpower the Devil (diabolus). Personal testimony to the phenomena is hard to find, though appeals to the knowledge of readers, even pagans, are numerous. *Ep.* i. *ad Virgines*, under the name of *S. Clement of Rome*, c. 12 [Wetstein, *Nov. T. Gr.* t. II., see Bp. Lightfoot, *Ap. Fathers*, pt. 1 (Clement), vol. I. p. 407, (1890)] recognises in the second century

both the reality of exorcism and the vain attempts at it. [Cf. *Recognit. Clement.* iv. 20.] A large collection of passages is in Dissert. I., in H. Hurter's *SS. Patr. Opuscula*, vol. I. St Ambrose, *Ep.* 22. 9, has 'cognovistis imo *vidistis*,' which he ought not to have written, as Tertullian ought not to have written *Apol.* c. 23, except they had been spectators themselves also. However Greg. Naz. *Carm.* II. ii. 7, 80—83, says of himself,

...καὶ γὰρ ἐγὼ Χριστοῦ λάχος οὔνομα σεπτὸν

πολλάκι μοῦνον ἔειπον· ὁ δ' ᾤχετο τηλόθι δαίμων

τρύζων, ἀσχαλόων τε, βοῶν σθένος Ὑψιμέδοντος.

Damascius' *Life of Isidore*, Phot. *Bibl.* 242; 551 H (ed. Bekker). Theosebius adjures a dæmon, 'setting before it the sun's rays and the God of the Hebrews.' The dæmon was driven off, exclaiming that it 'reverenced the gods, and was ashamed before him too.'

continuous sufferings of believers in attestation of their credibility[1].

The brilliant little pamphlet[2] cannot but have had an effect, none the weaker because the reasonings were not new. It was even more remarkable that language which had been half a century before the world should have been taken up, pointed, edged, polished by the famous Thascius. The destructive details of the argument had indeed long fermented. Polytheism had halted, unable either to remove them or repair them. The very attempts made to tinge the legends with Christian morality pointed the fatal contrast[3]. From before Cicero's day until now the thoughtful Roman had looked on religion with the same sad eye. Like Cicero, Cyprian must have long contemned Acca and Flora and the Bald Venus, yet underneath all had recognised a supernatural basis. Like him he had from time to time distrusted the most refined pleasures: like him had despaired of society. And even now, though the Person of Christ had risen before him as the Regenerator, he could not yet grasp the conception that the Faith would effect the reconstruction of society or the amelioration of governments. A pure society within society, and eternal salvation for its holy members, is all that he yet hopes for. He deliberately excludes providence from history. Nations rise and fall by some external indecipherable law of change, without conscience and without reward[4].

---

[1] Ac ne esset probatio minus solida... dolor qui veritatis testis est, admovetur, &c. *Quod Id.* 15. This remark and the homethrust at the inadequacy of the Roman gods originate (so far as I know) with our author.

[2] The qualities which Jerome (*l. c.*) justly notes in it are *brevitas* and *splendor*.

[3] See Möhler (ap. Peters, p. 61), *Kirchengesch.*, pp. 583 ff.

[4] *Quod Id.* 5 'regna non merito accidunt sed sorte variantur.'

III.

Lay-Work.

We may perhaps assume that Cyprian received baptism at the time most usual in Africa, the season of Easter[1]. In the autumn holidays next ensuing, and in his own gardens, he places the time and scene of a monologue—a brief Christian Tusculan—addressed to a fellow-neophyte[2] and brother rhetorician, Donatus. The subject was one in which Cicero would have gloried,—THE GRACE OF GOD[3].

A.D. 246. Easter Day, April 19.

He paints the scene with a fulness of colour which will ask further criticism, but with the tenderness of one who feels that a higher call is robbing it of its charm. From the busy thoughtless sounds of the slave-household they retire to a 'viny cloister,' and here Cyprian pours forth the freshest intensest expressions of relief from the old passionate thraldom, and of joyous restfulness in Christ. We discern what Cyprian will be; there is no spiritual analysis; there is no subtlety of doctrine; but there is the deep avowal 'whereas I was blind now I see.' There is the modest claim to have the evidence of new life examined; the confident assertion of a power above the powers of darkness.

Behind the two friends lies the awful background of a fast corrupting society, surrendering itself to unblushing evils, private and public. They pass 'Life' in review. Lowest in the scale lie the Criminal classes—whole sections defiant of law, threateningly aggressive upon society. War is incessant, aimless war. The arena is visibly deadening humanity. The

---

[1] Tert. *de Baptismo* c. 19.

[2] *Ad Don.* c. 15 'Tu tantum, quem *jam* spiritalibus castris militia cælestis signavit.'

[3] The MSS. up to the eleventh century give no title. In that century '*Epistola ad Donatum*' began to be used. Rufinus begins his letter to Ursacius, which is the prologue to his translation of Origen's Homilies on Numbers, with 'Ut verbis tibi, frater, beati martyris loquar: Bene admones, Donate carissime.' The title *De gratia Dei* is Bp. Fell's invention from Pontius' allusion 'Quis emolumentum gratiæ per fidem proficientis ostenderet?' Pont. *Vit.* 7.

theatre with its unnatural subjects and impure spectacles is the divinisation of lust.

In fixing upon the arena as a degradation in comparison of which slavery, that 'abyss of misery,' may be passed in silence, Cyprian is true to nature. The delight in blood has become a systematized passion. He marks 'the simplicity, 'the manly health and grace, of the youths trained to mutual 'murder under the eyes of their own fathers; the brother waits 'his turn in the den, above which sits the expectant sister; 'the mother pays a higher price for the ticket to witness her 'child's deathwound on a gala day, and there is not the faintest 'sense of guilt on any conscience[1].' In thus regarding the unknown individual man and the affections which ought to centre on him as a precious thing, the Christian idea restores something to the world which civilisation had taught an Antonine, an Aurelius to ignore. The appalling proportions of the crime to which every city dedicated its grandest building, may be judged from the fact that when Cyprian became bishop, within two years from this time, the Emperors Philip had just celebrated 'The New Age[2],' on the completion of Rome's first thousand years, by the combats of that thousand pair of gladiators, whom the gentle Gordian had provided to adorn his own triumph.

Meantime the horrors of private licentiousness, from which the veil is from time to time rent by some *cause célèbre* in which the very evidence is criminal, the corruption and inhuman procedures of the judicature, the degrading competition for official rank, and the trembling insecurity of military dominion, stamp the decline of public and domestic morality[3].

Were those the dreams of despondency and world-

---

[1] *Ad Don.* 7. The indignation of 'the Master' had already boiled over in the *De Spectaculis*.

[2] A.D. 248. The coins fix the 'milliarium sæculum' or 'novum sæculum' to the 3rd consulship of the elder Philip. Euseb. (*Chronic.* II.) dates it wrongly A.D. 247. Clinton, *Fast. Rom.* I. pp. 264—5, Jul. Capitol. *Gord. Tres* c. 33.

[3] *Ad Don.* 9—13.

weariness? The answer is not to be gained by collecting scandalous anecdotes. But, apart from the end to which all was tending, we might conclude Cyprian's generalisations to be just from his treatment of the courts of law. A successful experienced man here speaks in terms to provoke reply, if reply were possible, on a subject on which declamation would defeat itself, and his shades are as dark as elsewhere[1]. On other points we can compare the language of the satirists, but it is since the age of Juvenal that the tide of corruption has engulfed the judgment seat. False glitter, intrigues, assassinations which swarmed about the persons of numerous petty kings and kingly magistrates, fill the outline which is traced by the violent deaths upon the world's throne, within the last ten years, of eight Emperors, unshielded by either the highest philosophic virtue or the lowest animal ferocity[2].

Yet wider still the sketch of Cyprian ranges as with statesmanlike instinct he marks the no less fatal symptoms of political dissolution, presented by vast accumulations of locked-up capital, by the abnormal growth of grazing land[3], and the gradual elimination of the independent labouring class[4]. Lastly,—and at Carthage it was probably more complete than at Rome—there was the disruption of the client-bond and the disowning of obligation between rich and poor.

What then is the moral, or what the remedy? There is but one; one calm, one freedom. All that the individual can do is to seek deliverance from this world's 'whirlpools,' to approach the 'Gift of God,' and be 'greater than the world': to become 'a home of God'[5] and entertain the indwelling Spirit[6],—not indeed in ascetic retirement, for the hermit-life

---

[1] *Ad Don.* 10.

[2] A.D. 235, Alex. Severus. A.D. 238 Gordianus I., II., Maximinus, Maximus, Pupienus, Balbinus. A.D. 244 Gordianus III.

[3] Continuantes saltibus saltus. *Ad Don.* 12.

[4] De confinio pauperibus exclusis. *Ad Don.* 12.

[5] *Ad Don.* 15, mark the expression '*domum*...quam Dominus insedit *templi* vice.'

[6] Rettberg's ignorance of scripture language betrays his penetration into

has not yet presented itself as the sole remaining refuge,—but through inner purity, in sweet domestic life, in a round of prayer and study[1]. Such is the moral of the scene with which the holiday evening closes,—the sober banquet, the sweet chant, the memory stored with Psalms.

All this needed expansion into fuller richer life: yet it was something when the fortunate man of the world began even thus to live. The conditions of the new problem are stated, though their connection is not yet perceived. On one side the needs of modern life, on the other his own spiritual experience thus far as a pagan. 'I seconded my own be-'setting vices; I despaired of improvement; I looked on my 'faults as natural and home-born; I even favoured them. 'But so soon as the stain of my former life was wiped 'away by help of the birth-giving wave, and a calm pure light 'from above flooded my purged breast; so soon as I drank of 'the spirit from heaven and was restored to new manhood by 'a second nativity; then, marvellously, doubts began to clear; 'secrets revealed themselves; the dark grew light; seeming 'difficulties gave way; supposed impossibilities vanished; I 'was able to recognise that what was born after the flesh and 'lived under the rule of sin, was of the earth earthy, while that 'which was animated by the Holy Spirit began to belong to 'God[2].' These mighty experiences of his Baptism support rather than invalidate his biographer's account of the Charity and Purity of his devoted preparation for it. Pontius had known no parallel, he tells us, of such early fruits of Faith, but to Faith he expressly attributes them, and so to the Grace of God, 'although the second birth had not yet illuminated the novice with the *whole* splendour of the light divine[3].'

perceiving this 'tone of mystical union with God' to '*be grounded on a pantheistic view*,' and to be found only 'in these excited early writings.'

[1] Sit tibi vel oratio assidua vel lectio. *Ad Donat.* 15.

[2] *Ad Don.* 4.

[3] 'Pro *fidei* festinatione,' 'nondum secunda nativitas novum hominem splendore *toto* divinæ lucis oculaverat,' Pont. *Vit.* 2. There is no need therefore to attribute to Pontius a semipelagianism;

When Cyprian speaks of his unbaptized life as one of 'darkness, ignorance of self, estrangement,' he is not dwelling on the short interval between conversion and baptism but on his life as a whole. As yet the subtleties were not which would assign the stage of attraction and approach rather to the heathen than to the Christian side of life. Very feeble do they shew beneath the dawn on which Cyprian's gaze was fixed. Divine Grace has fallen as a psychological fact within his personal experience while he contemplates society as barren and corrupting through lack of an inspiration. He will not be long in claiming the regeneration of society from the same source which he already recognises as the renewal of the man.

We need not look to him for Theology proper, for doctrinal refinement, for the metaphysic of Christian definition. We shall find him busy with moral conditions, the work of grace, the bonds of union: the sanctification of life through the sacraments, the remodelling of life through discipline; the constitution of the church in permanence, the transforming social influences which are to control the application of power and wealth, to charge science again with the love of truth, art with the love of beauty, and to create a new benevolence. The 'Charismata of Administrations,' 'helps, governments[1],'— these are his field.

IV.

Cyprian Deacon.

The indigence of the Carthaginian poor was, owing to the causes which Cyprian himself had indicated, a constantly deepening gulf. Fifty years later treasures were still thrown

none to find (with Tillemont Tom. IV. note 4 on S. Cypr.) a contradiction between him and Cyprian, as to whether the two 'vows' were before or after Baptism. Pontius clearly speaks of resolutions formed and kept before it:

Cyprian of the struggle and the fears of self which preceded it, and of the intense relief and peace which followed it.

[1] $\delta\iota\alpha\kappa o\nu\iota\alpha\iota,\ \dot{\alpha}\nu\tau\iota\lambda\dot{\eta}\psi\epsilon\iota\varsigma,\ \kappa\nu\beta\epsilon\rho\nu\dot{\eta}\sigma\epsilon\iota\varsigma.$ 1 Cor. xii. 5, 28.

into it in vain. The first outbreak of the anger of the separatist Donatus against the Catholics, his famous exclamation 'What hath Emperor to do with Church?,' was occasioned by the mission of Paul and Macarius to Carthage from Constans 'with relief for the poor'; 'that poverty might be able to breathe, be clothed fed and comforted.' They came 'bringing what we may almost call *Treasuries* to expend 'upon the poor[1].'

To the sacrifice of his farms in their cause Cyprian did not hesitate to add that of his delightful Gardens. Friends bought them in[2], and insisted on his residing there. Later on he was only too anxious to sell them again. Everything shews him to have been free from family ties[3]. A reasonable interpretation suggests that he entered the order of Deacons. And as we shall have more than one occasion to remark the intimate relations subsisting between a Deacon and some Presbyter to whose labours he was specially attached, so we find him, possibly in this capacity, taking up his quarters in the house of his aged father in the faith, the Presbyter Cæcilian[4], and by his attention soothing his last

---

[1] Optat. iii. 3.

[2] Pont. *Vit.* 15. Perhaps Pontius was concerned in this transaction, for he says they were 'de Dei indulgentia restituti.'

O. Ritschl, pp. 6, 7, conceives that the Horti must have been confiscated later and that Pontius mistakes this for charitable sale now. Pontius' personal knowledge seems to present to him no difficulty, nor yet the question how the confiscation was taken off.

[3] There is no token of his ever having married. Pontius as a fine writer is obscure. Yet it is inexcusable for Baronius (*Ann. Eccles.* A.D. 250, x.) to have misunderstood what he says of Cæcilian's wife and children to mean Cyprian's family renounced in favour of celibacy. Bp. Fell is worse in misreading what Pontius says of *Job's* wife so as to prove Cyprian's marriage. Pont. *Vit.* c. 3 'Illum (Job) non *uxoris suadela* deflexit.' Fell ad loc. 'conjugatus ergo erat Cyprianus.' Let us hope that prepossession is less blinding in our own day. In all his letters from his retirement there is no reference to a home of his own.

[4] I can give no meaning to the words of Pontius the Deacon 'Erat sane illi etiam de nobis contubernium...Cæciliani,' except that assigned to them by Pearson (*An. Cypr.* A.D. 247), 'while still of *our* body (the diaconate) he had quarters with Cæcilian.' Pont. *Vit.* 4. Pontius himself resided with Cyprian from before his first retirement till his

days[1]. For Cæcilian shortly afterwards died, commending his wife and children to the grateful affection of his convert[2].

V.

Presbyterate.

What we now naturally enquire is the exact character up to this time impressed, in the eyes of the Carthaginian church, upon a layman by his becoming a cleric. Was it official and administrative, or mystical, or didactic, or benevolent? From Tertullian we may collect answers to these questions with unusual clearness—answers consistent with each other though not always rendered from the same points of view.

The position of the clergy had been expressed in terms borrowed from the civil constitution—terms which there is no reason to think were disputed at Carthage as either arrogant or inadequate. The laity were the Commons or *Plebes*[3], the Clergy were the *Ordo*, that is they were the Senatorial Order in the Church; Ordo being the regular name of the Senate, the Decurions, in the provincial and Italian towns. Cyprian when a layman is called a 'Plebeian' by Pontius, and he himself addresses letters 'to those who stand fast in the Commons,' and 'to the Commons of Leon and Astorga.' As the senators in court and in basilica had the common-bench (consessus), so had the clergy in the congregation. 'The 'difference between the Order and the Plebes is constituted 'by the authority of the Church, and by the consecration

---

death. See also the relation of Felicissimus to Novatus pp. 102 sqq. Cyprian's diaconate seems also implied in Pont. *Vit*. 3, 'Quis enim non omnes honoris gradus crederet tali mente credenti?'

[1] Demulsus obsequiis. Pont. *Vit*. 4.

[2] Pontius, *Vit*. 4, says he made Cyprian 'pietatis heredem,' not that he appointed him curator or tutor to the family. This would have been contrary both to the Christian rules which withheld ordained persons from taking those offices, and to the Roman usage of appointing the nearest relations. See below pp. 44 sqq. Fechtrup p. 10, n. 2 needlessly hence infers that he was a layman still.

[3] '*Plebs* hominum dicas sed *Plebes* ecclesiarum. Ebrard in Græcismo.' Ducange.

'of the Office indicated by the sitting together of the
'Order[1].' Tertullian does not attribute to the clergy spiritual
descent from the Apostles, nor regard them as having been
typified by the Levitical Priesthood, or as occupying their
relative position towards the people. But he regards the
Office as none the less 'sacerdotal' although in origin
ecclesiastical, and not immediately divine. 'A woman is
'not permitted to speak in the church, nor yet to teach, nor
'baptize, nor offer, nor claim to herself the rights of any
'masculine function, much less of the sacerdotal office[2].' The
right of giving baptism belongs to the chief priest, 'that is
the bishop,' and heretics offend in the moveable character of
their orders and in that they 'enjoin sacerdotal offices to
laymen[3].' Nevertheless the functions of the Order were not
significant of any alienation or absorption of the priesthood
of believers; they involved during their exercise only its
suspension or dormancy. Where there is a destitution of
clergy the sacerdotal powers of the laity revive, to the extent
of performing sacramental acts. 'Where there is no Bench
'of the ecclesiastical order you (a layman) offer (the sacrifice)
'and you baptize and are your own sole priest[4].'

The priesthood had been actually imparted by Christ to
all Christians, for 'Jesus the High Priest and Lamb[5] of the

---

[1] Differentiam inter Ordinem et Plebem constituit Ecclesiæ auctoritas, et Honor per Ordinis consessum sanctificatus. *De Exhort. Cast.* 7. Honor is like Ordo a constitutional word, signifying the Office of any magistrate or dignity. Bp. Lightfoot in his *Dissertation on the Christian Ministry* [*Ep. to Philippians* p. 254 (1868)] translates thus '...the consecration of their rank by the assignment of special benches to the clergy.' The Bishop well observes that these passages coming from a Montanist bear witness to the fact that the doctrine of an universal priesthood was common ground to himself and his opponents. And this of course is equally true as to the doctrine of the exercise of the functions of the priesthood by the Order only. *Ep.* 59. 18, note the form '*congestus*.'

[2] *De Veland. Virgin.* 9.

[3] *De Præscript. hæretic.* 41.

[4] *De Exh. Cast.* 7. Adeo ubi ecclesiastici ordinis non est consessus et offers et tinguis et sacerdos es tibi solus.

[5] Adopting Scaliger's emendation 'Nos Iesus summus sacerdos et *Agnus* Patris de suo vestiens,' *De Monogam.* 7, for the common reading *magnus*; compare Cypr. *Ad Fortunat. præf.* 3, of which this passage was perhaps the

'Father clothing us from His own [clothing], because they
'that are baptized in Christ have put on Christ, hath made us
'priests to His Father, according to John.' So complete is
the sacerdotal character of the Christian layman that he is
subject to rules laid down for the Jewish Priesthood: thus,
the young man who was not suffered to bury his Jewish
father was prohibited because, being a Christian, he was a
Priest and could not (according to the law of the Priest)
attend the funeral, although Christians may bury Christians
because these live still in Christ. Again, 'Assuredly we are
'Priests called by Christ, and therefore bound to single
'marriages only, according to God's ancient law which then
'in its own priests prophesied of us[1].'

The fancifulness of the conclusions does not affect the
theory from which he derives them. He argues from what
was generally accepted to what he himself advanced. In his
time the substantive priesthood of the laity was an understood
reality. This it was which was perceived to be fore-shewn in
the Levitic priesthood, not that official priesthood of the clergy
which was rightly constituted by the authority of the Church.

Then there were the beliefs and associations which invested
the order of the Presbyterate at the time when Cyprian was
received by Donatus to their own bench[2]. We shall see how
they were presently varied.

We shall see too how grave was the business which came
before the 'consessus,' and how necessary that men of affairs
should have seats on it.

All that his Biographer records of Cyprian as a member
of the Bench of Presbyters is that he was no less active in
that office than he had been as a Plebeian, no less eager to
translate the ancient saints into modern life[3].

A.D. 247.
A.U.C. 1000.
Coss. Imp. Cæs.
M. Jul. Philippus
Pius Fel.
Aug.
Parth.
max. II.
Imp. Cæs.
M. Jul. Severus
Philippus
Aug. f. Pi.
Fel. Aug.

seed—'...de *Agno*. .lanam ipsam et pur-
puram misi, quam cum acceperis tuni-
cam tibi pro voluntate conficies et plus
ut in domestica tua adque in propria
veste lætaberis,' &c.

[1] *De Monogam.* 7, cf. *De Exh. Cast.* 7.
[2] Non post multum temporis allectus
in presbyterium. Hier. *de Viris Ill.* 67.
[3] Pont. *Vit.* 3 "multa sunt quæ adhuc plebeius, multa quæ jam presbyter

VI.

Helps to Laymen's Scripture Studies.

Of that activity in one of its applications we have still a noble instance in at least two of the books of classified texts skilfully grouped under pithy headings, entitled To QUIRINUS, —the 'dear son,' or layman, at whose request they were compiled.

Since in Augustine's mention of the books the name of TESTIMONIES is used, and Pelagius compiled his 'Testimonies to the Romans' in imitation and indeed in completion of it,— as he himself stated,—and since this name appears in the earliest manuscript, if not in slightly later ones[1], it is probable enough that a title, which so neatly describes the work, was of Cyprian's own giving.

It was also vulgarly called 'Against the Jews'; but was perhaps not so much intended for as found to be a serviceable manual in the contemporary controversies[2].

---

fecerit, multa quæ ad veterum exempla justorum imitatione consimili prosecutus...'*hæc debent facere*,' dicebat, 'qui Deo placere desiderant.' et sic (per) bonorum omnium exempla decurrens, dum meliores semper imitatur, etiam ipse se fecit imitandum." Cf. Euseb. *Chronicon*, Ol. 258, 2.

[1] Hartel, p. 35, entitles it thus: 'Ad Quirinum (Testimoniorum Libri Tres),' which can represent nothing ancient, and his own note is as follows: "*Aug. c. ii. epp. Pelag.* l. iv. c. 21 (p. 480 d) Cyprianum etiam ipse hæresiarches istorum Pelagius cum debito honore commemorat, ubi *testimoniorum* librum scribens, eum se asserit imitari, 'hoc se' dicens 'facere *ad Romanos* quod ille fecerit *ad Quirinum*.' *et ejusdem libri c.* 27 merito et *ad Quirinum* de hac re absolutissimam sententiam proponit cui *testimonia* divina subjungeret. Hieron.

Dial. c. Pelag. c. 32 quumque se imitatorem imo expletorem operis beati Cypriani scribentis *ad Quirinum* esse fateatur." The Sessorian MS. (sæc. VII. Mai, or VIII.-IX. Reifferscheid) has 'Testimoniorum incipit ad Quirinum'; the word 'explicit' before 'Testimoniorum' refers of course to the preceding treatise. Surely from these facts one would *not* 'conjecture that the genuine title was 'Ad Quirinum' merely. Does the note at the end of Bk. III. in MS. L imply that it was sometimes called NUMERI—'Ad Quirinum numēr. līb. III. ex.'? Hartel p. 184. Cf. Caecili Cipriani ad Quirinum liber II. exp̄ incip̄ ad eundem excerpta capitulorum numero LXX. (Cod. M), Hartel p. 101. Here LXX. is in error for CXX.

[2] See on Novatian's controversial books p. 123 and notes. Since out of nearly a hundred passages collected in

The first book assembles the chief scriptures which foretold disobedience and forfeiture of grace on the part of the Jews, and the inheritance of all the Church's privileges by the Gentiles: the substitution of a new Circumcision, Law and Testament for the ancient ones, of a new Baptism, a new 'Yoke': how the old Pastors, the old House of God, the Temple, and the Sacrifice were to come back in nobler form; how the cessation of the Priesthood and the succession of Christ as true High Priest[1] were predicted and accomplished; how to the Jewish nation there remained now nothing but to purge by baptism the blood of their slain Messiah and to come over to His Church.

In the second book Cyprian treats of the Mystery or 'Sacrament of Christ[2]'—the adequate fulfilment of prophecy in Him, and the grandest notes of His Person. The clearness and force of these most brief summaries or articles of Christology are very impressive, nor less so the spirit of personal devotion which they breathe.

The third book[3], separately issued, resembles the others only in arrangement. It is a commonplace-book, meant for rapid and frequent reading, of texts for Quirinus' use on the Christian life, duty and doctrine[4]: the tone very pure and spiritual.

the first book, only twenty come from the New Testament, and these almost all bearing on the fulfilment of the Old, and as each heading notes a contrast of Old with New, it is somewhat less clear to me than it was to Rettberg pp. 231 sqq. that Cyprian had no eye to the Jewish sects in this compilation. Again, the last heading, *Test.* i. 24, gives the point of the whole.

[1] *Test.* i. 17.
[2] See *Test. Proem.* (Hartel p. 36, l. 13) and notes in MSS. A and B at end of *Test.* Bk II. (Hartel p. 101).
[3] *Test.* iii. ti. 4 is thrice quoted by Augustine *Retr.* ii. 1 ; *de Prædest. sanctt.*

iii. (7); *c. II. epp. Pelagg.* iv. 9 (25).

[4] Salubre et grande compendium...in breviarium pauca digesta et velociter perleguntur et frequenter iterantur, *Test.* iii. *Proem.* No. 6 is perhaps the first explanation in Latin of misfortunes as a divine probation and is the keynote of his treatise on *The Mortality.* No. 28 marks the slight tendency which Cyprian had to Novatianism before Novatian. No. 46 on silence of women seems oddly placed. Rettberg argues that this book belongs to the early years of his Christianity from the 'texts against heretics' being other than those which he used afterwards. Unless he refers

His touches upon Faith are well worth reflexion—That the very difficulty of the subjects demands that dogma should be simple; that belief is not independent of will; that cause and effect are proportionate, as elsewhere so in faith; that faith requires patience as an essential character of itself[1].

Cyprian's copious memory, to which Pontius bore witness, receives remarkable illustration from these books. That such a work could be compiled out of Scripture at all by a memory unassisted by concordance or index is surprising. Add to this that the selection is so well made, and that the memory had been so recently introduced to the Bible. He mentions that he had avoided diffuse selection, and confined himself to what a 'moderately good memory' had suggested[2]. But all this would be truly unimaginable if he had been debarred from the study of Scripture until he entered on the duties of a presbyter, and had been taught only orally whilst he was a layman[3]. Quirinus himself must have been such a layman, for Cyprian seeks to provide him only with profitable 'reading towards forming the first lineaments of his faith.' Yet he assumes that Quirinus will presently 'be searching into the 'Scriptures old and new more fully, and reading through the

(which I doubt) to what is here said as to Novatianism, I do not know what texts he means. But the fact does appear, I think, from the 28th heading just mentioned standing without the qualification which he would have added later.

[1] No. 52, Credendi vel non credendi libertatem in arbitrio positam. (Compare Coleridge *Aids to Reflection*.) No. 53, Dei arcana perspici non posse, et idcirco fidem nostram simplicem esse debere. No. 42, Fidem totum prodesse, et tantum nos posse quantum credimus. No. 45, Spem futurorum esse, et ideo fidem circa ea quæ promissa sunt patientem esse debere.

[2] *Test. Proem.* compare Pont. *Vit.* c. 5 'tam memoriosa mens.'

[3] This ultramontane thesis is delivered, and Cyprian's study of Scripture limited to 'about the inside of a year,' by Peters, p. 80, in the face of Pontius' account (*Vit.* 2, 3) how Cyprian as a layman was teaching others how to use Scripture, and of these very prefaces to Quirinus. So Novatian to the Plebes at Rome, 'Nam qui sincerum Evangelium...non tantum tenetis verum etiam animose docetis,' *De Cib. Jud.* c. 1. Peters alleges the bare fact that the 'Quod Idola' and the 'ad Donatum' contain no quotations; to which (so far as it is true) the aim of those pamphlets is an answer in full.

'whole of the volumes of the spiritual books' and 'equally 'with ourselves be drinking of the same springs of divine 'fulness.'

To our knowledge of the wording of the actual versions which the African Christian thus studied these books are necessarily a very important contribution. In this light we hope to return to them again.

VII.

Cyprian made Pope of Carthage.

So rapid had been the progress of Cyprian through the Diaconate and in the offices of the Presbyterate[1] that he was still a Novice[2], according to usual account, when the public opinion of the laity[3], immediately upon the voidance of the see of Carthage by the demise of Donatus[4], unanimously called him to that post. The apostolic warning against the elation of a neophyte was afterwards quoted against him. Some defended the step by the instance of the Vizir of Meroe, baptized by an evangelist after an hour's instruction. But others rested on the exceptional character of the man, his mature and gentle wisdom, his vast knowledge, sagacity and diligence, and that rapid energy, so needed by the stagnant church, which swiftly carried him through the circle of investigation and acquirement, and then unrestingly through administrations, reforms, and new creations.

A.D. 248.
A.U.C. 1001.
Coss. Imp. Cæs. M. Jul. Philippus P. F. Aug. Parth. max. Ger. max. Carp. max. III. Imp. Cæs. M. Jul. Philippus P. F. Aug. Germ. max. Carp. max. II.

Cyprian declined the office. His own desire was to see it exercised by one of his elders in years and in the faith[5]. A small portion of the church, but among them five of the

---

[1] Pont. *Vit.* 2 ...et præpropera velocitate pietatis pæne ante cœpit perfectus esse quam disceret. 3...quis enim non omnes honoris gradus crederet tali mente credenti?

[2] Adhuc neophytus...novellus. Pont.

Vit. 5.

[3] Suffragium vestrum.—vestra suffragia, *Ep.* 43. 1, 5.

[4] *Ep.* 59. 6, 10.—On the date see p. 41, note 2.

[5] Antiquioribus cedens. Pont. *Vit.* 5.

most influential[1] members of the bench, held the same view. Some of the firmest friends of his after-life had belonged at first to that minority, but the five presbyters maintained for many years an organized opposition. The mass would now brook neither opposition nor refusal. They surrounded his house and filled the avenues by which it was approached. He concealed himself; he would fain have escaped by a lattice[2]; but the tumultuous demonstration (a sufficient indication of the present security of the Christian population) lasted until he reappeared and signified his consent, when it was succeeded by rapturous joy.

Whether as in some untrustworthy statements concerning Alypius and Ambrose he was carried away and consecrated on the spot, or what further steps were allowed to be necessary before his consecration, we do not know. It must remain matter of doubt whether the bishops of his province were summoned to elect him. He himself enumerates more than once the requisites of a regular episcopate as three, and says that they were regarded in Africa as essentials; first, the choice of the neighbouring bishops of the province assembled at the see[3]; secondly, the 'suffrage,' that is, the presence and support of the Plebes at that choice; thirdly, the judgment of God. To these he adds, in vindicating the perfectness of the election of Cornelius at Rome, the testimony of a large

---

[1] *Ep.* 43. 4 ...ætas...auctoritas.—On their identification see below, p. 110, n. 4.

[2] Pont. *Vit.* 5. I hope this is what Pontius means by 'potuisset fortasse tunc illi apostolicum illud evenire, quod voluit, ut per fenestram deponeretur, si jam tum apostolo etiam ordinationis honore similaretur.' Freppel 'il y songea un moment, mais son humilité redouta ce trait de ressemblance avec Paul.' Rather 'if he was being made like him in one way, by ordination, he might (if he had had his own will) have been made like him in another, by escaping through the lattice.' Whether S. Paul could be considered an ordained apostle when at Damascus (Acts ix. 25) is another matter.

[3] *Ep.* 67. 5 '...apud nos quoque et fere per provincias universas tenetur, ut ad ordinationes rite celebrandas ad eam plebem cui præpositus ordinatur episcopi ejusdem provinciæ proximi quique conveniant, et episcopus deligatur plebe præsente...' He also distinguishes the 'episcopatus deferretur' from 'manus ei...imponeretur.'

In *Ep.* 59 it may be observed that he says of himself (6) '...populi universi suffragio...*deligitur*,' and (5) 'post coepiscoporum *consensum*.'

majority of the clergy. But since we observe that, although he has more than once to maintain his own title[1], he omits, as his biographer does, the mention of any such choice by his provincial bishops, claiming nevertheless to have had 'the consensus of his fellow-bishops[2],' it is probable that such a call by acclamation superseded further election[3], and that their 'consensus' was simply their imposition of hands.

The picture drawn in earlier canons and constitutions shews us the people electing their bishop, and declaring their choice on the Lord's day in the presence of the presbytery and neighbouring bishops, in answer to the thrice-repeated questions of the principal bishop, 'Is this the man whom ye desire for a Ruler? is he blameless, and is he worthy[4]?' Nothing is more likely than that Cyprian was himself ordained thus in a way more primitive than that which he afterwards describes as customary[5]. The ordaining bishops were those of his own Province of Africa, according to its dignity, not

---

[1] *Ep.* 43. *Ep.* 65.

[2] *Ep.* 59. 5... The very expression 'all the bishops consenting' to the choice of the people occurs in the primitive Coptic Canon 31 (Bunsen, *Hippolytus and his age*, vol. II. p. 308, vol. III. p. 42, 1852).

[3] Tillemont compares the election of Alexander of Comana at the same period. There it would seem that Gregory Thaumat., having satisfied himself of the fitness of the person, proposed him to the people, and on their consenting, consecrated him. Tillem. vol. IV. Art. viii. on S. Greg. Thaum. p. 331, quoting Greg. Nyss. *Life of S. Greg. Thaum.*

[4] The 65th canon of the Coptic collection, 'literally agreeing with the *Apostolical Constitutions*, B. viii. c. 4.' Bunsen, *op. cit.* vol. II. p. 336, vol. III. pp. 49, 50 (1852).

[5] The primitive 'Apostolic Canons' shew us the bishop elected by his flock and accepted by the neighbouring bishops; Cyprian's rule as elected by the neighbouring bishops, accepted by the flock. The process of change may have gone on through the other custom prescribed by those canons in appointing a bishop to any congregation, not having before had or elected a bishop of its own, in which twelve men at least were ready to guarantee a sustentation fund. In such case the neighbouring churches proposed a bishop to the new congregation who by three deputies examined and (if satisfied with their report) accepted him. The proposers must in practice or officially have been the bishops; subsequent elections in such sees would easily follow the precedent of the first election, and as sees multiplied this would become the usual mode. Coptic collection, canon 16. Bunsen, *op. cit.* vol. II. p. 305, vol. III. pp. 35—36.

the primates of the neighbouring provinces of Numidia and Mauritania[1].

The 'suffrage' of the laity was adequately signified by their presence and their testimony to good life and conversation. There is no indication that the 'suffrage' implied any recording of votes; under the tutelary empire the word had long ceased to bear any such meaning[2] in political affairs, and there is no ground for fancying that this sense was revived by the Church of Carthage.

In what way distinct from these the third requisite—'the Judgment of God'—was looked for is somewhat more difficult to perceive. Some have supposed, as in the choice of Matthias, a casting of lots with prayer. Evidence of this there is none[3]. But by those who relied upon the special providence and guidance of the Father, His Judgment was recognised in the fact of the election and ordination proceeding in due order without interruption[4]. Cyprian claims to enjoy 'the Judgment of God and Christ' as a token of the genuineness of his apostleship upon the ground that he is *de facto* bishop; that 'the 'God who made him to be this is the God without whose will 'the sparrow falls not[5].'

---

[1] Münter, *Primordia Eccl. Afr.* p. 45.

[2] In *Ep.* 57. 5 the ordination made in the *presence* of a plebes fully conversant with the life and conversation of the bishop elect is said to be 'de universæ fraternitatis *suffragio*.' '*Suffragium* sceleris' is the *support* which the stern crime of Brutus gave to his own authority. *Quod Idol.* 5. 'Suffragia sæpe repetita' are the cries with which the mob demanded Cyprian for the lions, Pont. *Vit.* 7. Christ is our *Suffragator* in a gloss on *Advocatum* which in the common text of *Ep.* 55. 18 displaced *justum* in 1 Joh. ii. 1—a word which seems to imply the utter disappearance of any idea of united opinions. The '*Votes*' in Copt. Can. 65 seem to mean the previously expressed assent. Bunsen, *op. cit.* vol. III. p. 50.

[3] H. Dodwell, *Diss. Cyp.* 1, considers the word κλῆρος to be evidence.

[4] The Coptic Canon 65 seems to describe a distinct appeal to Heaven as following upon the enquiry whether the elected person is of pure character— 'And if they all together have witnessed that he is such an one according to the truth, God the Father and His only-begotten Son Jesus Christ our Lord and the Holy Ghost *being judge* that these things are so...'

[5] *Ep.* 66. 1, 9, to Pupienus; to whom he would take the strongest ground he could. So also to Cornelius 59. 6. Somewhat similarly an opportunity of

Cyprian's title of 'Papa.'

The Roman clergy in addressing Cyprian and in writing about him style him 'Papa,' 'Papas,' or Pope of Carthage, as do also the Confessors of his own city[1]. This title has been attempted to be explained by the statement that it was a common synonym for 'Bishop,' or that the Romans at least felt no difficulty in extending the title used by their own bishop.

Pearson[2], Bingham[3], Routh[4] have added their weight to the belief that all bishops were so called. This however was apparently not the case in the time of Cyprian. By the end of the 5th century no doubt Papa was a common title in distinguished sees. Sidonius Apollinaris (Bp. 472) speaks of the Popes of Rheims, Lyons, Arles, Vienne, Marseilles and others, usually. Even in the 4th century the name was not uncommon. Augustine is frequently addressed as Pope by his correspondents[5], especially by Jerome, and Jerome himself so calls Epiphanius, John of Jerusalem, Athanasius, Chromatius of Aquileia, as well as Anastasius and Damasus Bishops of Rome, and Theophilus of Alexandria[6].

The Bishops of Alexandria however had the appellation earlier than the rest. Both Athanasius and Arius call Alexander (*d.* A.D. 326) the 'Pope' of that see, and the first distinct use of the title there is in the instance of Heraclas who probably died in A.D. 246 and is so styled formally by his successor Dionysius the Great[7].

It now will seem remarkable that within two or three years of the death of Heraclas Cyprian is called Papa frequently by the Roman clergy and confessors, as well as by the native confessors—especially

---

martyrdom, even when it is rightly (as coming in the order of providence) avoided by flight, is called an occasion when...'corona *de dignatione Dei* descendat, nec possit accipi...,' *De Laps.* 10.

[1] *Ep.* 30. Cypriano Papæ Presbyteri et Diaconi Romæ consistentes s.—optamus te, beatissime ac gloriosissime papa, semper in Domino bene valere...(*in fine*).

Ep. 31. Cypriano Papæ Moyses et Maximus Presbyteri et Nicostratus et Rufinus et ceteri qui cum eis confessores s.

Ep. 36. Cypriano Papati Presbyteri et Diacones Romæ consistentes s.

Ep. 23. Universi Confessores Cypriano Papati s.

Ep. 8. 1. Didicimus secessisse benedictum Papatem Cyprianum. (Cleri Rom.)

[2] *Vind. Epistt. S. Ignat.* p. I. c. xi. 2.

[3] J. Bingham, I. pp. 65 sqq. (1855).

[4] Routh, *R. S.* III. pp. 235, 268.

[5] Aug. *Ep.* 68, 81, 119, 216.

[6] Hieron. *Epp.* 81 (66), 86 (70), 88 (71), also *Contra Johann. Hierosolymit.* 4.

[7] Euseb. *Hist. Eccles.* vii. 7. Gregory of Neocæsarea (Thaumat.) addresses his *Canonical Letter* to (ἱερώτατε) Πάπα in A.D. 258 (?), but it is difficult to say whether this is a circular letter to bishops, or to priests, as Greek priests and hieromonachi are so called, or to a particular bishop.

remarkable when we further observe that the Bishops of Rome with whom so many letters pass to and fro are never once so designated. This corresponds however with the evidence of inscriptions. We have from the Roman Catacombs a series of the monumental slabs first laid over the Bishops of Rome in the 3rd century. We have Urban's, who was bishop from A.D. 222 to 230; we have the monument of Anteros who sat in 235 and 236, Fabian's from 236 to 250, Eutychian's from 275 to 283. Again we have that which Damasus placed over Eusebius who died in 309, and that which Damasus made for himself. Yet the first appearances of the title Papa at Rome are in inscriptions to the honour of Marcellinus A.D. 296—304 and Damasus 366—384.

De Rossi attempts to account for the fact that the third century monuments call the Roman bishop in each case Episcopus and not Papa, by the theory that this name still bore only the sense of affectionate reverence in which it arose, was not yet a recognised title, and therefore not appropriate to a monument. He observes that the earliest inscriptional use of the word is with the adjectives *meus, suus, noster*, and accordingly in the two earliest instances of the Roman bishops, the admirer who erects the inscription calls him '*his* papa' in each instance. 'By order of his papa Marcellinus this Severus, deacon, made a double chamber[1]...' 'Furius Dionisius Filocalus inscribed this, adorer and lover of Damasus his papa[2].' And of this usage in application even to priests various early examples are given.

But the point to be observed is that so very long before any bishop of Rome appears with the title in *any* sense it is used as a *formal* mode of address to Cyprian by the clergy of Rome.

We have then this curious result that when Gregory the Seventh, in 1073, published the edict that the world should have but one Pope[3], he appropriated a title not original to his see, which had belonged to the great African sees far earlier, and in the meantime had been very widely adopted.

I believe however that the earliest instance of the use of the name is in connection with the see of Carthage. It seems so improbable that Tertullian should attack a Roman regulation that I must think his *De Pudicitia* was addressed to the then bishop of Carthage (A.D. 211—220).

---

[1] Cubiculum duplex cum arcisoliis et luminare
Jussu p(a)p(æ) sui Marcellini Diaconus iste
Severus fecit...
G. B. de Rossi, *Inscrr. Chr. Urb. Romæ*, I. p. cxv., II. p. 55.

[2] Furius Dionisius Filocalus scribsit Damasi s pappæ cultor atque amatot (amator). De Rossi, *Roma Sott*. I. p. 121, II. 200, 201.

[3] [Ennodius xliii., lxxx. refutes Simond's assertion (*ad Enn. Epp*. iv. 1) that his use of the word is limited to the Roman see.]

It is the much condemned assumption of the authority of Episcopus Episcoporum by a predecessor which makes Cyprian in council so anxious to disclaim the appearance of it, as well as the African canons so distinct in repudiating it. Now in chapter 13 Tertullian, with ironical emphasis, calls the bishop in question Bonus pastor et benedictus papa, and Benedictus Papa is the very word used of Cyprian in *Ep.* 8. 1. Because Callistus issued an edict[1] like the one which Tertullian condemns, it would not follow that he was the only bishop who did so, rather perhaps the reverse. If Papa was originally then of Carthaginian usage, this is but one of many instances in which the African Church led the Latin forms.

Lastly, we may observe that if the Roman letters to Cyprian were not genuine, but belonged to the fifth century, or even the fourth, and were written in the interests of the papal see, we should not have had the name Papa carefully attributed by the Romans to Cyprian and entirely withheld by them and by all the letter-writers from the bishop of Rome.

VIII.

Cyprian's View of the Authority and the Design of the Episcopate.

And what then was, in Cyprian's thought, the Office to which he had been called?

It is evident that we must ascertain this before we can enter into the spirit of his administration. For that office was undertaken by him with clear ideas upon its import, and was not gradually invested with them by mere administrative convenience.

There are two main outlines possible. Which of the two was before him?

Did he find himself called to be chief arbiter and judge of the Christian congregations, the president of their committees, the guardian of their doctrine and customs, of the Scriptures and their interpretation, the principal of those functionaries who for the sake of order, regularly and alone, within a certain district exercised that priesthood which in theory

---

[1] Hippol. *Refut. omn. hæres.* ix. 12 (ed. L. Dunker and F. G. Schneidewin); cf. Tert. *de Pudicit.* 13.

belonged equally to all believers? Had his office thus risen naturally out of the presbyterate, as the presbyterate had grown out of the whole community? or, if this enquiry surpassed the curiosity of the age, did he regard himself as delegated to be their head-priest by a nation of priests?

Or did he regard his office as something different in kind from all such conceptions of it? as a line traced in the Divine Plan? indicated and assumed, if not defined, in the New Testament? deducible from it by reasoning, such as evolves from the same writings the doctrine of the Holy Trinity? as a power not there reduced to terms, but constant in exercise; endowed with a grace specific, exclusive, efficient?

These questions receive a full answer in Cyprian's writings. As matter of order, the eminence of the rank of the bishop was visible to the Roman world. He was the Chief of the Christian Society; the confiscation of his property was the first, for a time the only, edict of persecuting magistrates. In the assembly from the midst of the separate semicircle of the presbyters[1] rose his chair or Throne, already the universal name and symbol of his authority. He was specially the Preacher[2] in his church, the chief instructor. Again he was the principal arbitrator in disputes. As to morals and discipline, whether clerical or lay, he was 'Judge in Christ's stead' of disqualifications[3] from communion, propriety of restoration, suitableness for any office. But in this capacity Cyprian felt at all times bound to act on the principle which in one of his earliest letters he lays down—'to do nothing 'without the information and advice of presbyters, deacons, 'and laymen[4].'

---

[1] *Epp.* 39. 4. 40, &c.

[2] *Ep.* 55. 14...legeram et episcopo *tractante* cognoveram. And of false bishops...quorum *tractatus*...mortale virus infundit. *De Unit.* 10. One of the sadnesses of the exile is...quod...nec *tractantes* episcopos audiat. *Ep.* 58. 4.

[3] ...nec episcopo honorem sacerdotii sui et cathedræ reservantes, *Ep.* 17. 2.

[4] ...præsentibus et judicantibus vobis (*i.e.* plebe). *Ep.* 17. 1, cf. 3.—Cf. *Ep.* 14. 4; 19. 2. Cf. as regards ordination *Ep.* 38. 1...solemus vos ante consulere et mores ac merita singulorum communi

That which has been for centuries the supreme title of episcopal greatness, the title of Pontiff, he would have rejected with disdain and horror. On Tertullian's lips it had been a gibe[1]. In Cyprian's language it was reserved for Caiaphas after the priesthood had passed from him by his condemnation of his own High Priest[2]: but that the Bishop was simply the delegate or representative of the people in their sacerdotal aspect is a thought which never took shape from his pen. For him the Bishop is the sacrificing priest[3]. Christ was Himself the Ordainer of the Jewish Priesthood[4]. The Priests of that line were 'our predecessors[5].' The Jewish Priesthood at last became 'a name and a shade,' on the day when it crucified Christ[6]. Its reality passed on to the Christian bishop; each congregation (diocese) is 'the congregation of Israel'; the election of the bishop in their presence is made in accordance with the Law of Moses[7]: the lapsed or sinful

consilio ponderare. Cf. *Ep.* 43. 7, *Ep.* 30. 5 (at Rome).

[1] Tert. *De Pudicit.* 1. See below, p. 197.

[2] *Ep.* 3. 2; *Ep.* 59. 4. So fast did the feeling change that Pontius *Vit.* c. 9 calls Cyprian 'Christi et Dei pontifex' in contrast with the 'pontifices hujus mundi' and e. 11 'Dei pontifex' simply.

[3] Throughout the letters of Cyprian the bishop is more frequently called *sacerdos* than *episcopus*. The word 'sacerdos' is never, I believe, distinctly applied to a presbyter, though once or twice the whole clerical body is spoken of as *sacerdotes et ministri*. In *Ep.* 63 (14, 18, 19) at first sight it might seem that the arguments there addressed to 'Sacerdotes' as to the mixture of wine with the water in the Eucharist were addressed to or at least included presbyters, but the opening of the letter shews that he confines his remarks to the bishops (episcopi), of whom the majority, he says, are correct in practice, but others not so. Again, his own presbyters were not in fault, and it would be contrary to his principles to address the presbyters of another. Even in this epistle therefore 'sacerdos' means bishop. In *Ep.* 40 he says Numidicus had been rescued from death at his martyrdom by God, 'ut ...et desolatam per lapsum quorundam presbyterorum nostrorum copiam gloriosis sacerdotibus ornaret.' This is the *general* use of the term, as in 'sacerdotes et ministri,' and he indeed adds 'et promovebitur quidem...ad ampliorem locum,' *sc.* episcopatum, so that 'sacerdos' does not lose here its proper reference. In *De Zel. et Liv.* 6 it might equally be maintained that the words were distinguished or that they were rhetorically paralleled, 'dum obtrectatur sacerdotibus, dum episcopis invidetur.'

[4] *Ep.* 69. 8. [5] *Ep.* 8. 1.
[6] *Ep.* 66. 3; 59. 4.
[7] *Ep.* 67. 4.

bishop is prohibited from sacrificing by the Mosaic statute against uncleanness; his communicants are tainted by his sin[1]. The presbyterate is the Levitic tribe[2], exempt from worldly office, debarred from worldly callings, living on the offerings of the people, as their predecessors on the tithes, devoted day and night to sacrifice and prayer. So precise is the application, that the people are to rise at their coming in pursuance of the Levitic direction[3].

Again there is another aspect of the same office. The Apostles were bishops. Matthias was ordained a 'bishop.' And still the bishop is the Apostle of his flock[4]. From the Twelve through successive ordinations he derives that character[5]. His order is of divine creation. The diaconate is the institution of his predecessors.

He is not only a Judge. He is Judge in Christ's stead[6]. Contempt of his government[7] is the parent of heresy; it is expressly condemned in the Law, in the books of Samuel, by the example of St Paul and of our Lord. To maintain the same faith and worship and yet invade the office of the rightful bishop is identically the sin of Korah[8]. For the Laws about the High Priest are not merely applicable to the Bishops; they were ultimately intended for them, and now they apply to them alone.

---

[1] *Ep.* 65. 2; 67. 1, 9.

[2] *Ep.* 1. 1.

[3] Levit. xix. 32, so interpreted *Testim.* iii. 85.

[4] ...apostolos id est episcopos et præpositos, *Ep.* 3. 3. Cf. *Ep.* 45. 3. The reading 'de ordinando in locum Iudæ *episcopo*,' *Ep.* 67. 4 (Hart. p. 738), is not only supported apparently by all MSS., against edd., but is required by the 'episcoporum et sacerdotum' which follows.

[5] ...apostolis vicaria ordinatione succedunt, *Ep.* 66. 4.

[6] *Ep.* 59. 5 'vice Christi.' Cyprian's use of *Iudex* not *Arbiter* is important on account of his legal exactness.

[7] *Ep.* 66, *Ep.* 3, *Ep.* 59, *Ep.* 43. The Scriptures quoted are Deut. xvii. 12, which is cited five times, 1 Sam. viii. 7. Sir. vii. 29, 31. Acts xxiii. 4, 5. Matth. viii. 4. Jo. xviii. 22, 23. Luc. x. 16.

[8] *Ep.* 69. 8.

IX.

Divergence of Cyprian's from Modern views.

In these opinions of Cyprian the first point which invites attention is their dissimilarity to any scheme of the Christian ministry now held. A parallel between that ministry and the three Levitic orders is indeed familiar to us, but not the same parallel which Cyprian draws. Although disobedience to the Bishop is the sin of disobedience to the High Priest, yet his Bishop is not pourtrayed as surrounded first by the Priests, and secondly by the Deacon-Levites. The Order of Bishops with him answers to the 'Priests of God,' the Presbyters are the Tribe of Levi. The New High Priest is Christ eternally[1].

Secondly, neither would any school now interpret the Mosaic precepts with anything like the literalness which he always uses. For instance, the territorially endowed ministry of all Christendom gives up what was in his eyes an essential resemblance to the house of Levi, their right to maintenance by offerings without land.

Third, the method of election to bishoprics is extinct through the whole world. Nowhere do neighbouring bishops meet and, requiring the testimony of the laity over whom he will preside, elect or nominate for them a bishop[2]. Various as have been the phases through which that election has passed, none can be more alien from the spirit of Cyprian's prescriptions than the two which divide the Western Church between them. In one the lay, in the other the ecclesiastical element has reduced its copartner to a shadow: in each the surviving element has merged in a single individual, a single nominator to all sees within his supremacy. Here it is the monarch, there the one bishop of Rome[3]. Measured by ancient standards neither section could criticise the other, yet to the purposes

---

[1] *Ep.* I. 1, *Testim.* i. 17. *Ep.* 63. 14.
[2] *Ep.* 67. 4, 5
[3] Where concordats exist the laity nominate in the person of the sovereign. The bishop of Rome in the præconisation of bishops or in appointments by brief elects and constitutes.

of each no machinery could be better adapted than the present, and ancient standards were not uniform. No mean analogy is that of England, where a minister of the Crown, selected from popular representatives, nominates, the chapters as representatives of the diocesan presbyterate accept or reject, and the comprovincial bishops consecrate[1].

Fourth, the presbyters had no voice or vote in the election of the bishop distinct from that of the laity: their influence was great, but in government they scarcely appear as an order[2]. The very name of priesthood (as represented by *sacerdotes, sacerdotium*) did not descend from the episcopate upon them until after Cyprian wrote. Their then designation, as the Levitic body of the church, similarly descended upon the deacons[3].

Fifth, while the virtue of Aaron's Priesthood and the grace of Apostleship still flowed, as it were, from a divine source through the world, those who received it were not a college with power to invite or coopt or to increase their numbers at their pleasure. It was the Christian *plebes* which to every individual bishop was the fountain of his honour[4]. It was they who by the '*aspiration* of God' addressed to him the call

---

[1] See Dr Pusey, *The Councils of the Church*, p. 10 ff.

[2] Presbyters in *Conc. v. de Bap.* 1, are said 'adesse'—'plurimi Coepiscopi cum Conpresbyteris qui aderant,' *Ep.* 71. 1.

[3] Perhaps the first use of *Levitæ* for *Deacons* is nearly contemporary with Cyprian's application of *Levitica tribus* (*Ep.* 1. 1) to presbyters (A.D. circ. 245) Origen, *Hom.* xii. 3, in Jerem. (Delarue v. iii. 196 [1740]), and it is in a way which shews his use of both words to be unfamiliar. Εἴ τις οὖν καὶ τούτοις τοῖς ἱερεῦσι (δείκνυμι δὲ τοὺς πρεσβυτέρους ἡμᾶς) ἢ ἐν τούτοις τοῖς περιεστηκόσι λαὸν λευΐταις (λέγω δὲ τοὺς διακόνους) ἁμαρτάνει... The first formal use of them I trace is in *II. Conc. Carth. sub Genethlio*, A.D. 390, Can. 11. (Labbe, II. c. 1244), where to a question put with the words 'episcopus, presbyter et diaconus' Genethlius himself replies, using 'sacrosanctos antistites, et Dei sacerdotes, nec non et Levitas.' In this form Aurelius repeats it *Cod. Can. Ecc. Afric.* Can. III.(Labbe, II. c. 1261). In Can. X. of *II. Conc. Carth.* and in Can. IV. of *III. Conc. Carth.* A.D. 397 (al. 398) the form appears in titles only, not in Canons. And so it spreads.

[4] A bishop could ordain a lector, a subdeacon, a deacon, even a presbyter, without more than a nominal reference to the *plebes*. But the whole *collegium sacerdotale* could not elect a bishop.

to enter on the inheritance of that priesthood and the dispensation of that grace. On them rested also the responsibility and duty of withdrawing from him and his administrations if he were a sinner. 'A people obedient to the precepts of the 'Lord and fearing God is bound to separate itself from a 'sinful prelate, and not to associate itself with the sacrifices 'of a sacrilegious Priest; forasmuch as they have mainly the 'power either of electing worthy Priests (*i.e.* Bishops) or of 'refusing the unworthy[1].'

Sixth, hence when a bishop had been appointed to a see, he was, so long as he remained in faith and charity, the visible pillar, foundation, and indeed the embodiment of his church. 'The bishop is in the church, and the church in the 'bishop, and if anyone is not with the bishop he is not in 'the church[2].'

Seventh, in the councils there was no elective, no mutable representation. Each diocese elected its bishop once for all to be, among other functions, the representative of his church and constituency; a life member of the conciliar body. They needed no other.

Eighth, the temptations incident to this copious authority were not without an antidote in the popular character of the commission and the popular duties it involved. To the bitter attack of Pupien Cyprian replies 'all the brethren and the 'heathen also well know and love my humble character: you 'knew it and you loved it when you were in the church and in 'communion with me...I am daily the servant of the brethren. 'I receive those who come to the church, one after another, 'with goodwill, with prayers, and with joyfulness[3].'

Lastly, it has been accurately shewn that there is no clear development of these opinions on Priesthood in the writings of the Apostolic Fathers, in Justin, or in Clement of Alexandria[4].

---

[1] *Ep.* 67. 3. On the refusal of the Spanish churches to communicate with their bishops Basilides and Martial.

[2] *Ep.* 66. 8.   [3] *Ep.* 66. 3.

[4] *Dissertation on the Christian Ministry* in Bp. Lightfoot's edition of the

I am not so sure that there is no trace of them in Irenæus[1]. We have seen that in Tertullian they exist side by side with clear enunciations of the doctrine of an essential priesthood inherent in all Christians, but exercised in fully developed churches by the organic ministry alone.

This universal Lay-priesthood is not dwelt upon in Cyprian, but there is no sufficient reason to question his belief in it. Nor is it a specially Christian doctrine; it is coæval with the religious instinct of mankind. It had no doubt been obscured in pagan Greece, and even in Rome many shrines had special endowments and ministers, and to the last both retained traces of functions appropriate to priest-kings. But the principal sacrificing priests of the Roman state, the pontiffs and the augurs, were 'lay men,' not separated from the rest of the people. The celebrants in the sacrifices were generals, senators, and magistrates[2]. The Jewish nation had been founded as a priesthood, in which the functions proper to the whole manhood of the race were deputed first in theory to the eldest sons and then to the single tribe, yet frequently resumed for sufficient cause by kings and prophets. This royal priesthood became, when

---

Epistle to the Philippians, 1868, pp. 247 sqq.

[1] Irenæus handles the episcopate more 'as the depository of apostolic tradition' than as 'the centre of unity' (Bp. Lightfoot, *op. cit.* pp. 237, 8), because his whole object is doctrinal, not governmental. The whole Church is to him a 'depositorium dives,' into which the apostles stored 'omnia quæ sint veritatis,' *c. Hæres.* iii. 4. The notes however of a church (possessing *charismata* and so) capable of witnessing to apostolic truth he makes to be three, viz. 'apud quos est (1) ea quæ est ab apostolis ecclesiæ successio, (2) et id quod est sanum et irreprobabile conversationis, (3) et inadulteratum et incorruptibile sermonis constat.' These three he parallels with the 'apostles, prophets, doctors' of 1 Cor. xii. 28, *c. Hæres.* iv. 26. See also the commencement of the same section and compare iv. 26, iii. 3, v. 20 '...episcopi quibus apostoli tradiderunt ecclesias.'

In Justin it is true, *Dial. c. Tryph.* 116, that the whole Christian people are the high-priestly family, but we must mark also the church-function of the προεστώς alone, *Apolog.* i. 65—ὁ προεστώς...λαβὼν...εὐχαριστίαν...ἐπὶ πολὺ ποιεῖται. Οὗ συντελέσαντος τὰς εὐχὰς καὶ τὴν εὐχαριστίαν...

[2] ...flaminicæ et ædiles sacrificant, Tert. *de Idolatr.* 10.

Judaism broadened into Christianity, the inheritance of believing humanity[1]. The right to approach the Father with prayers and intercessions, the duty of purity, the unworldliness, which all exercise of the right implied, were sacerdotal characters which none failed to recognise. We have seen, however, that strongly as Tertullian represents this view, he no less strongly recognises the 'priestly discipline[2]' and the separateness of the *office*. And 'it seems plain from his mode 'of speaking that such language was not peculiar to himself, 'but passed current in the churches among which he moved[3].' What is distinctive therefore in Cyprian's theory simply regards the *origin* of that office. According to him, it is (1) an inheritance from the apostles, (2) and a succession to the Levitic Priesthood, only more glorious in being the fulfilment of that priesthood as of a type.

And now, we must observe that from whatever source the theory sprang it was not an emanation from the *policy* of Cyprian. And although it would be equally inaccurate to say that the policy sprang from the theory, yet the influence of the view in moulding both then and ever since all vigorous church-life which has had any continuity, all Christian organization which has enjoyed any extension, can scarcely be over-estimated. From the very first Cyprian believed that he read that doctrine in Scripture, and in Scripture as a whole. Whencesoever derived, it came to him in his 'novitiate.' We find it in strongest and completest terms in his first epistle and in his first application of texts in the Testimonies. The whole period of his episcopate added nothing to the distinctness with which he realised it, although his discussions and his 'visions' reflected and impressed it[4]. There is no room for the hypothesis that the exigencies of his position towards the Novatianists, towards his own presbyters, or towards

---

[1] Tert. *de Monog.* 7.
[2] *Ibid.* 12.
[3] Bp. Lightfoot, *op. cit.* pp. 253, 254.
[4] *Ep.* 66. 10.

the see of Rome, determined or in the least developed his belief[1].

And whence then did this form of Christian thought originate? I see no proof, and to me it is incredible, that he or other Africans should have derived any such scheme, consciously or unconsciously, from *Pagan* constitutions, which appeared to them all in the light of a purely demoniacal and satanic system. Nor yet is it possible that they inherited them from any *Judaizing* forms of Christianity. For not only is sacerdotalism not one of the characteristics for which Judaizers are ever reprehended[2], but in fact the very essence of Judaism lay in looking back to the literal circumcision, the literal passover, the literal centralising of the church upon Jerusalem. Towards Gentile Priests, towards Levites from the uncircumcision, they had no propension. Neither to heathenism nor to legalistic sects can we trace back the fruitful powerful theory now accepted in Africa.

Was it then but an unconscious straining first of language, then of feeling, lastly of thought, which gradually warped with a hieratic distortion offices originally politic and didactic? Did the contemplative study of numerously fulfilled types draw men by a seemingly irresistible attraction to imagine an actual continuity, totally unreal, between a sacrificial priesthood and what was designed only for a hortatory college?

Or, was the belief a legitimate development of the principles of the apostolic church, parallel with and analogous to the growing light on cardinal doctrines which similarly nothing but use could illustrate? And are all the forms in

---

[1] O. Ritschl (pp. 50, 222, 223) rightly states that the theory was not developed without the events. No practical theory of a polity could be. But when he says that it broke out as a new perception in *Ep.* 43, he not only overlooks the early *Ep.* 33, but fails to discern what is more important, that the conception of the Church which Cyprian applies to life in his first writings requires for its potential nucleus that theory which the formula so soon consolidates.—[The text was written some years before Ritschl appeared.]

[2] Bp. Lightfoot, *op. cit.* pp. 257 sqq.

which it may be said to live among us broken lights of the same truth?

The alternative is an important one. It will be answered by thinkers according to their schools, and cannot be determined by history alone. We shall find further illustrations of it in the progress of the history, but it becomes at this point a debate of metaphysical theology.

X.

A Bishop's work uphill.

A few months only were left to the unsuspecting Christians of a 'Thirty-eight years Peace[1]' which had assisted the extension of the church without promoting either its devotion or its organization, when, some time between the July of A.D. 248 and the following April[2], the figure of the well-known advocate, now for some time missed from court and forum, and grown familiar to Christians in the semicircle of presbyters, took the white linen-covered chair of the illicit assembly in some merchant prince's basilica[3], and the voice

A.D. 249.
A.U.C. 1002. Coss.
...Fulvius Æmilianus II.
L. Nævius Aquilinus.

---

[1] Sulpicius Severus *Chronicor.* ii. 32 'interjectis deinde annis VIII et XXX Pax Christianis fuit,' *i.e.* from the end of Sept. Severus (*d.* 4 Feb. 211), about which time the ferocities of the proconsul Scapula elicited Tertullian's fierce 'Ad Scapulam.' Freppel, p. 168, quotes Origen, *c. Cels.* vii. 26, speaking of the rapid multiplication of the Christians.

[2] The 59th epistle was written after the 15th of May, the Ides, A.D. 252 (*Ep.* 59. 10). Cyprian had then been bishop for a 'quadriennium' (*ib.* 6), *i.e.* at least for two or three months beyond three years, at most for four years. This makes the earliest date possible for his accession to be June A.D. 248, the latest possible April A.D. 249. He was certainly bishop on Easter Day, April 15, A.D. 249; for in *Ep.* 29, after Easter A.D. 250, he mentions that he had made Saturus read a Lesson, with the consent of the clergy, on the two last Easter Days.

The Decian persecution began in the end of A.D. 249, or the very beginning of A.D. 250. For all that happened Tillemont allows two years (vol. IV. S. Cypr. Art. VI.). Eighteen months is the utmost possible, and probably the episcopate began not long after June A.D. 248. More than four years would be called a quinquennium; in *Ep.* 56. 1 a 'triennium' is two years and three months; in *Ep.* 43. 4 little more than a twelvemonth is a 'biennium.'

[3] The Basilicæ common in great houses, and not those of the law-courts, were probably the models of the first

that had defended the state-religion rose before an altar which, still standing in its old place sixty years later[1], seemed to reproach the departing schismatic with the shadows of Cyprian and of Unity.

Of his sermons, unless the tract on Patience is a sermon remodelled, not a record has reached us: a singular contrast to the vast monuments of Augustine's preaching. We should have gladly learnt the tenor of that first exhortation which, after the usage of the African bishops, he opened and closed with the double[2] salutation 'In the Name of the Lord,' and have caught the first note of those thirteen years of ineffaceable teaching. But there is in the whole man such oneness that we can scarcely question that, as in his letters and pamphlets, so from his bema Christian life was taught as a social science. 'In the quiet time he had served *discipline*[3]' is his own epigrammatic tale of his first few months. There was nothing wavering in him, or tentative; there was no feeling for a clue. He entered on restoration and organization with a theory clearly ascertained, and a practical devotion to its consequences. 'The church is one. She holds and owns 'all the power of her Spouse and Lord. And in her we pre-'side. For her honour and her unity we do battle. Her grace 'and her glory we alike maintain with faithful self-devotion. 'We have God's leave to water God's thirsting people. We 'keep the bounds of the springs of life[4].' Such was his estimate of his duty and his responsibility. To revive in a worldly laity, with a staff of caballing clergy, the reality of their professions and of their offices, to reanimate church life with half-forgotten forces, was his first task, and in that primitive age no light one. Not only had he from the

---

churches. See R. Burn's *Rome and the Campagna*, Introd. p. l. That used by Cyprian's congregation was maintained afterwards as a church.

[1] Optat. i. 19 'erat altare loco suo,' &c.

[2] ...salutatione scilicet geminata. Optat. vii. 6, note p. 162, ed. Albaspinaei. Paris, 1631.

[3] *Ep.* 59. 6.

[4] *Ep.* 73. 11.

first to bear 'contumely toward his office[1]'; not only did opponents, the five presbyters and others, 'turbulent men whom he could scarcely rule[2],' render his administration difficult; the glaring abuses of the episcopal office were yet harder to cope with. Socially known as leading men, but unprovided with material independence, or with position equal to that of a provincial magistracy, some bishops were engrossed in agriculture, some absent in commerce, some even engaged in usury[3]. There was the free-living bishop actually enriched by the opportunities of his post, ready to abjure the faith on the prospect of danger, ready to resume his office when peril was past[4]. There was the immoral bishop on the verge of excommunication[5]. Some were secure in their position though notorious for their frauds in the bazaar, or their complicity in the slave-trade of the Sahara[6]. Some again were too ignorant to prepare their catechumens for baptism, or to avoid heretical phrases in their public prayers, too indifferent even to abstain from using in their liturgies[7] the compositions of well-known heretics. Cold and dark are the shades which are flung athwart the bright tracts and around the glowing lights of the scenes of this early church life. If it was possible for such men to be bishops we can understand how among their presbyters they tolerated the makers of idols and the compounders of incense, or among their laity astrologers[8] and theatrical trainers[9].

In that fierce surge of mingling races, tyrannous classes, inhuman superstitions, the struggle of life and the shock of interests was, upon a comparatively narrow space, tenfold more violent and more unscrupulous than in the most intense

---

[1] *Ep.* 16. 1, 2.
[2] *Ep.* 27. 3: see above I. VII.
[3] *De Laps.* 5, 6.
[4] *Ep.* 65. 3.
[5] Auct. *de Rebaptism.* 10.
[6] Aug. *de Bapt. c. Donatt.* vii. 45 (89) 'Cum collegis fæneratoribus, insidiosis, fraudatoribus, raptoribus non privatam mensam sed Dei altare habebat commune Cyprianus.' *Ibid.* iv. 9 (12); c. *Ep. Parmen.* iii. 2 (8). Cf. Can. 18, 19, 20 *Conc. Elib.* (305—306?), Can. 13 *I. Conc. Carth.* (348).
[7] Aug. *de Bapt. c. Donatt.* vi. 25 (47).
[8] Tert. *de Idolatr.* cc. 7, 9.
[9] *Ep.* 2.

centres of our energies. The new sect had been for the third part of a century not only unharmed but prosperous: that hollowness and insincerity should have grown up in it was inevitable. We can but recognise as they did themselves that the persecution of the church was mercy to the world. We shall find reason to believe that its end was answered. And for the present, we shall see that the troublous years which followed were more favourable by far than profoundest peace could have been to the grand combinations of one master spirit.

XI.

Discipline—Clerical and Lay.

We must now pass in review the measures of Cyprian's eighteen months[1] of peace, remembering that, illustrative as they are, they are but a prelude.

One passing glimpse of what seem active methods shews him to us with a band of the 'Teaching Presbyters,' examining into the qualifications of Readers, testing all who were preparing for the clerical office, and placing the approved in a kind of rank as 'Next the Clergy.' On one such occasion these agree to appoint Optatus one of the Readers to be 'Teacher of Catechumens,'—to do for many what Cæcilian had done for Cyprian, but still as a Reader[2]. Again on two

Easter,
A.D. 249,
A.D. 250.

---

[1] Counting from June 248 A.D.— See p. 41, note 2.

[2] *Ep.* 29 '...quos jam pridem communi consilio clero proximos feceramus, quando aut Saturo die Paschæ semel atque iterum lectionem dedimus, aut modo cum presbyteris doctoribus lectores diligenter probaremus, Optatum inter lectores doctorem audientium constituimus, examinantes, &c.' In this interesting passage there must be some fault, for *presbyteris* cannot be dative: Dr Hort conjectures that *coram* may have disappeared after *cum*. Hartel reads *doctorum*, which is not a Cyprianic construction. 'Presbyteri doctores' are like Aspasius in *Passio SS. Perpetuæ et Felicit.* xiii.; the Doctores no longer a distinct Order as in *Teaching of the XII. Apostles* xi. xv., or *Shepherd of Hermas*, Vis. III. 5. See Dodwell, *Diss. Cyp.* vi. I cannot think 'die Paschæ semel atque iterum lectionem dedimus' means 'we gave him two passages to read aloud in examination.' Compare *Ep.* 38. 2 '...dominico legit.' In *Ep.* 38. 1 he speaks of his 'practice' of consulting presbyters, deacons and laity on the fitness of candidates.

consecutive Easter Days they assign to Saturus, though not yet a Reader, the Reading of the Lesson. It is not quite possible to say whether all this was new, or old with a new life in it. But this gathering of the best-read presbyters about their bishop in the training of the young clergy was a sure sign of progressive improvement.

The monuments of this time are one Treatise and three Letters which the sagacity of Pearson restored to their place as the earliest in the collection. About another, however (the third), he was mistaken[1].

His first epistle deals with the case of one who had, contrary to an existing rule, left a clergyman 'Tutor' by will to his property. It forbids the sacrifices[2] to be offered for his repose.

Geminius Victor of Furni[3] near Carthage had in his will nominated as 'Tutor' Geminius Faustinus a presbyter. A statute[4] of a former council had ruled thus: 'No one is to 'appoint by his will a cleric and minister of God to be a *tutor* 'or *curator*, since every one who is honoured with the divine 'priesthood and appointed to the clerical ministry ought only 'to serve the altar and sacrifices and be free for devotions and 'prayers...' 'if any shall have so done, no offering shall be 'made for him nor sacrifice celebrated[5] for his repose.' Cyprian accordingly enjoins that at Furni there shall be no 'oblation' for Geminius Victor, or any 'deprecation frequented' in the church in his name.

The next transaction in which we mark the strong, considerate ruler, is the answer to Eucratius, the bishop probably of the distant seacoast colony of Thenæ or Tain[6]. It furnishes

---

[1] On *Ep.* 3 Rogatiano see pp. 234, 235 and note.

[2] Compare Tert. *Monog.* 10.

[3] About 28 miles west of Carthage which latter had a Porta Furnitana; see *Appendix on Cities*.

[4] I avoid the word canon in speaking of Councils which had not yet employed t. '...statutum sit' 'formam nuper in concilio a sacerdotibus datam,' *Ep.* I. 1, 2. Bunsen, *Hippolytus and his age*, vol. II. (1852) p. 223.

[5] *celebraretur*, i.e. no gathering of a congregation of friends for the purpose, as *frequentetur* also implies. *Ep.* I. 2.

[6] *Ep.* 2. Eucratius spoke in the council of ten years later in support of the second baptism of heretics. (*Sentt.*

an instance of that careful weighing of individual cases which lays the basis of permanent enactments. An Actor, who had left the profligate and corrupting stage[1] as a matter of course in obedience to Christian principles, felt no scruple in imparting his skill of voice and gesture to heathen youths or slaves. He had no power to enfranchise, or withdraw them from their profession, why hesitate to improve and elevate, perhaps chasten their performance? Similar casuistries every day impede practical morality, and the Africa of the third century was rife with them. With the touch of truth Cyprian exposes the man who was ready to form others to take the place from which he had escaped conscience-stricken; suggests his maintenance, if he really has no other means of living, by the church; and offers him, if Thenæ is too poor, food and clothing at Carthage.

The difficulty Eucratius had felt in dealing with the case lay in the absence of any rule excluding from the church elocutionists or others who only trained actors. A genuine fragment belonging to the second half of the third century[2] supplied the omission. 'If one has the mania of theatrical 'shows, or if he has been a declaimer in the theatres, let 'him cease or let him be cast out. If he teach the young '(in theatrical shows) it is good that he should cease. If 'he does not make a trade of it, let him be forgiven[3].' In A.D. 305 or 306 the Synod of Elvira enacts the rule requiring a converted performer[4] to renounce his profession before

Epp. 29.) His successors appear in Councils up to A.D. 641. See *Appendix on Cities.*

[1] Cf. Bingham (1855), vol. IV. p. 85.

[2] Bunsen, *Hippolytus* (1852), vol. II. p. 314; it is later than Cyprian's letter, if not based upon it.

[3] From the Alexandrian form of the Apostolic Constitutions which is still extant in the Abyssinian text and Arabic translation therefrom, as well as in the Coptic and Syriac; and which forms the groundwork of that separate collection which now appears as the *Eighth* Book of our Greek text. Bunsen (*op. cit.*). *Apost. Constt.* viii. c. 32 τῶν ἐπὶ σκηνῆς ἐάν τις προσίῃ ἀνὴρ ἢ γυνή... ἢ παυσάσθωσαν ἢ ἀποβαλλέσθωσαν.

[4] *Conc. Eliberitan.* can. 62. *Pantomimus* synonymous under the Emperors with *histrio.* L. C. Purser ap. Smith, *Dict. of Greek and Rom. Antiquities, s.v.* (ed. 1891).

reception into the church, and to be excluded upon any attempt to resume it.

In the 'fourth' letter he appears with Cæcilius, the senior bishop of the province, and other bishops and presbyters, taking strong measures for the suppression of a shocking fanaticism which allowed a supposed purely spiritual union between certain junior clerics and professed virgins[1]. In immediate connection with this subject appeared his treatise 'OF THE DRESS OF VIRGINS.'

In these letters the authority of the Bishop of Carthage is invoked or exercised beyond his own diocese, and wears already something of a metropolitic aspect.

One more exemplification of the system and appliances of discipline may be mentioned as belonging to this interval, in the investigation before the bishop and assessors of certain charges of cruelty to a father and a wife[2] which impended over an eminent presbyter, Novatus, the future schismatarch. To this we shall return hereafter.

When the persecution was past, Cyprian's calm judgment of his previous experiences was that 'long Peace had cor-'rupted a divinely delivered discipline; that Faith had been 'taking her ease and half asleep[3].'

Of Clerics not to be Tutores.

We are bound to take some of these subjects in detail, not only because of their intrinsic interest and importance, but because they afford us the first opportunity of weighing the objections which have been advanced by a clever writer against the genuineness of the Cyprianic letters[4]. Mr Shepherd repudiates the authenticity of the First Letter and of the canon on which it is based.

Against these documents Mr Shepherd argues, that since the Carthaginian councils of A.D. 348 and A.D. 419, in forbidding the exercise of secular offices by the clergy, did not reënact this canon it must have been unknown to them[5]. He states also that 'the office

---

[1] The συνείσακτοι, v. p. 54. *Ep.* 4.
[2] *Ep.* 52. 2.
[3] *De Laps.* 5.
[4] 'Letters on the genuineness of the writings ascribed to Cyprian,' by the Rev. E. J. Shepherd.
[5] Second letter, p. 25.

'of *Tutor* was one which a clerk, if he had no legal exemption, was 'compelled to serve.' That again the ministers of Cyprian's and still later times did engage in business (a practice allowed by the fourth council of A.D. 398), and 'were therefore very far from being 'always engaged in serving the altar and sacrifices, and employed in 'prayers and supplications.' That, although the evils which flowed from clerics taking the office of 'Tutor' were so many that Justinian prohibited it, yet they were 'at first' (in Mr S.'s opinion) proper persons to undertake such a charge, and actually did so (since the 17th canon of the 4th council of Carthage orders that, not the bishop himself but, his archpresbyter or archdeacon should take charge of widows and orphans). It is besides 'exceedingly pre-posterous' to imagine that the bishops of Cyprian's age, whom he censures for secularity, should have passed 'any law against secular pursuits,' when meantime even Cyprian himself was 'the victim of such an appointment from his own spiritual father Cæcilius,' 'to say 'nothing,' he adds in a note, 'of the wife who was also entrusted 'to him; and I suspect that a young African widow, probably not 'much out of her teens, would have been quite as serious a charge 'as the children.'

It is necessary to quote this passage, not because it is flippant, but because it evinces that the critic has not possessed himself of the most accessible information[1]. In the whole argument I do not detect one correct statement. It is well known that the power of a Tutor or Curator had 'respect to the property and pecuniary interests, not the *persons* of the pupilli' or wards. He was a trustee. His business was 'the preservation of *property*[2] during minority'; to guard against the minor's being defrauded: debts could not be recovered, nor were engagements valid, if incurred by a minor without his sanction. He was also bound to improve the property. The office of *Tutor* subsisted up to the ward's fourteenth year; that of *Curator* between the fourteenth and the twenty-fifth, at which he came of age.

There is no reason to suppose that Cyprian was Tutor or Curator of the property of his friend's family. Pontius describes a deathbed scene (accersitione jam proxima) in which Cæcilius commended them (commendavit) personally to his convert's affection (pietatis). It was improbable that Cyprian should have been named *Tutor* in the will, for by blood he was not related to Cæcilius, and the usage was so invariable by which the nearest relations and next heirs were appointed Tutors, that it was a special slur if any of

---

[1] *E.g.* Mr G. Long's article *Dict. Gk. and Rom. Ant.*

[2] The res and the pecunia. He was called upon 'negotia gerere' and 'auctoritatem interponere.'

them were passed over[1]. Incidentally, we observe that in this very letter *Geminius* Victor nominates a relative *Geminius* Faustinus.

Thus much for the legal criticism. Into the possibility of secular-minded men passing an anti-secular statute I need not enter; because the letter speaks of the rule having been made *before* the age of Cyprian, and being now enforced by him against a secularity which had grown up, as he says elsewhere[2], during the long security.

We must now look into the argument from the canons. Granted that at this time the clergy could not live on their allowances, and long afterwards eked their living out by handicraft, by farming, or by literary occupation[3]. But the point of canon after canon is this:— That they were not to administer the property of *other* people. The distinction escaped Mr Shepherd. They are not to be agents or stewards[4], nor farm-bailiffs, nor accountants[5], nor contractors, factors, or managers[6], in short, not '*implicati obnoxii alienis negotiis*' at all. The reason is not only obvious, but indicated. The opening for peculation, or at least for suspicion, caused the church to be ill spoken of, if they accepted such offices. The grounds for the prohibition of these agencies applied tenfold more to Tutorship of minors with property. The Tutor in Persius[7] sighs for the decease of the ward. And while the church as a corporation undertook from the first not only the *tutela*, but the maintenance of destitute orphans and widows, and appointed her proper officers, Deacons (and after a time Archdeacons), to care for them, it became only the more important that her clergy should not enter into private relations of the kind.

Now the Council of A.D. 348, which Mr Shepherd alleges as the earliest forbidding secular employment to the clergy, supplies evidence worth attention that there did exist an earlier rule forbidding clergy to exercise *tutela pupillorum*. In that Council (c. 6) the bishops settle that the clergy are not to become *agents* or *factors*. They do not exclude them from the office of tutors. One bishop then enquires whether persons already engaged as agents, factors, or tutors, ought to be admitted to orders. The Council allows it (c. 8) 'if they have first wound up and exhibited their accounts, and had them approved.' These two canons are only intelligible

---

[1] Te sororis filius...notavit, quum in magno numero tutorem liberis non instituit. Cic. *pro Sest.* 52.

[2] *De laps.* 5 '...disciplinam pax longa corruperat.'

[3] *IV. Conc. Carth.* A.D. 398, cann. 51, 52, 53 'artificium, artificiolum, agricultura, literæ.'

[4] *I. Conc. Carth.* A.D. 348, can. 8.

[5] *Ibid.* can. 9.

[6] *III. Conc. Carth.* A.D. 397? can. 15.

[7] Pers. *Sat.* ii. 12 '...pupillumve utinam quem proximus hæres Impello expungam': the next of kin being tutor by the XII. Tables, unless the will had nominated someone else.

if we assume the reality of that earlier canon mentioned by Cyprian. Unless it existed previously, the Council would have left matters in this incomplete position, that tutors could only become clerics by resigning office, but that clerics might freely become tutors. Assume however that clerics were already forbidden to become tutors, and we see why they are not forbidden in canon 6. Again, clerics being already incapable of becoming tutors, and others being now also excluded, the question naturally arises, which is settled in canon 8, 'Is it impossible for a tutor, and persons holding such posts, to become clerics?' The omission in the Sixth and the inclusion in the Eighth canon are both simply explained.

Lastly, there is a mistake even in the assertion that a Tutor was obliged to serve unless he had a legal exemption. Those tutors (called *legitimi*) who were appointed by magistrates when people died intestate *were* so compelled. But a tutor appointed by a will could 'abdicate,' or renounce. Certain offices were however considered by the law as exemptions, and the African bishops of the third century desired to make the clerical office such an exemption by internal regulations, since the government could not sanction it, until in the reign of Justinian, the canon was adopted into the imperial legislation. The sole penalty then lay at this time against the testator, and none was possible except the omission of his name from the intercessions for the departed. No steps could be taken against the cleric tutor, who might know nothing of his appointment until the will was read, and who certainly could not assign to his heathen neighbours, as a ground for renunciation, that he was a Christian presbyter.

Perhaps none of Mr Shepherd's 'criticisms' had more force in shaking confidence in Cyprian's letters than his attack on this one. Yet the objections are merely legal and historical misconceptions. The circumstances of the letter are, as we have shewn, perfectly consistent with the rather intricate conditions of the time; the early existence of the disputed canon is demonstrated by the wording of the later ones, and the authenticity of the story illustrated by the very names.

And here, lastly, we must add the consistency with which we find a member of the same family of Geminii speaking as bishop of the same town of Furni (*Sentt. Epp.* 59) several years later in the Council of A.D. 256. It is not impossible that it may have been Geminius Faustinus himself, and that he too may be the Bishop Geminius (*Ep.* 67) who signed the synodic letter in A.D. 254.

Of Christians not to train for the stage.

Such passages as are already quoted preclude any doubt as to the legality of quitting the theatrical profession in the third century, and shew that a law of Valentinian in A.D. 371 (*Cod. Theodos.* XV. tit. VII. 1), which (although it could not place it at the option of any clergyman to emancipate any master's slaves by communicating them) made the reception of the last sacraments necessitate an actor's manumission in case of recovery, was not (as asserted) the first step which was taken towards emancipation of actors.

A more sweeping measure submitted to Arcadius and Honorius by the African episcopate in A.D. 401[1], namely that the adoption of Christianity should at once release actors who wished to relinquish the calling, operated towards the reformation of the stage as well as to the redemption of individuals from its corruption.

In Cyprian's time then it was possible for an actor to retire from the stage, and yet, though a Christian, to set up as a trainer of actors—a profession forbidden immediately after; so that the Second Epistle is definitely fixed to Cyprian's time.

Yet Mr Shepherd, ignoring the Alexandrine fragment and the Elvira canon, and supposing the law of Valentinian and the Synod of 401 to prove that no actor could ever leave the stage[2]—an absurd position, as if all actors were slaves—and then assuming it to be 'a moral impossibility' that *any* Christian could wish to exercise that profession[3], or *any* bishop doubt how to proceed in such a case, has in this superficial mode made his telling attack upon a letter which is as demonstrably authentic as any of Cicero's.

XII.

The Eighteen Months continued. Virginal Life in Carthage.

The Virginal Life as it appeared in Carthage was one of brilliant light and darkest shade. While Cyprian recognises its evils both by sorrowful confession[4] and by actual legislation[5], he speaks of its devotees as the Flower of the Church.

---

[1] *Cod. Cann. Eccles. Afric.* can. 63.

[2] This was the extremest kind (maxima) of *minutio capitis* to which actors could be subject: to some this disability was merely technical.

[3] How idle this line of presumptive argument is we may think when among occupations exercised by Christians just before, we find incense-making, idol-carving (by clerics), idol-painting, temple-building. Tert. *de Idolatr.* 7, 8.

[4] *De Habit. Virgin.* 19, 20.

[5] *Ep.* 4.

He treats it as a practical and precious institution, without breaking like Tertullian into wild reproaches against mere corrigible vanities which occurred, nor yet glorifying the order with the title of Brides of Christ. Self-dedication to the unmarried state was considered a Christian 'Work' in the same sense in which Almsgiving was 'Work[1].' But there were at present no associations for common life, no common head, no peculiar dress[2], no special regulation for either charity or liturgy. The right conception of the 'work' was, says Tertullian, (and that it usually prevailed, he implies,) that it should be as secret as almsdeeds and prayer. Obviously we are in the rudiments of organization when Cyprian suggests to the elder women to assume some position, and to the younger to pay them some deference[3]. No specific allegiance seems to be expected from the order even to the bishop, for while his assurance that he addresses them 'affectionately rather than officially' indicates that his official position was recognised, he adds that he is too conscious of his own inferiority to claim the right to criticize[4]. The active duties of all Christian women were theirs, only so much more widely as the fuller leisure allowed—to visit the sick, to frequent the offering of the sacrifice and the preaching of the word[5]. The visiting of orphans and widows, whether poor or rich; the visiting of dæmoniacs, with continuous prayer and fasting to be enabled to use on their behalf the gift of healing, if they had reason to believe that they had received it; intercession for the church, for the holiness of its clergy and for its deliverance from false clergy, are employments suggested in the early letters which pass under the name of Clement[6]. To speak in church, teach, baptize or do any clerical act was

---

[1] Tert. *de Vel. Virg.* 13; cf. *de Orat.* 1. 17.
[2] *Ibid.* 9. Cf. 3 'Arbitrio permissa res erat.'
[3] *Hab. Virg.* 24 'Provectæ annis junioribus facite magisterium.'
[4] '...nec quo...aliquid ad censuram licentiæ vindicemus,' *Hab. Virg.* 3.
[5] Tert. *de Cult. Fem.* 2. 11.
[6] See below, note 3, p. 56.

forbidden as of course[1]. They entered on the life by private resolution[2], not by public vow; marriage might be looked on as a departure from holy purpose, but not as violating rule, and in some cases it was right[3].

The order[4] of sexagenarian 'Widows,' (who must have married but once and brought up children,) had a seat of honour in the Church[5], but in Tertullian's time was first seen by permission of the then bishop 'the monstrous marvel' of a maiden seated among them[6], and unlike them sitting unveiled. The meaning of this was that, as girls under the betrothal age of twelve years wore no veils[7], a claim had been made by certain dedicated virgins to continue the symbolic freedom of the age of innocence, and at least in church[8] to lay aside the covering which elsewhere public opinion enforced. They argued too that St Paul had enjoined veils for 'women' or 'wives[9]' not for the whole sex. They now treated as injurious to themselves the assumption of a veil by any of their sisters, and finally obtained a general rule in their own sense, to the distress of the more retired[10]. The avowed object was to confer a distinction which should make the order more attractive[11].

The 'work' was 'secret' no more. However by general and Scriptural arguments, appeals to the use of other churches, and unhappily to wrecks which had increasingly marked the history of the order, Tertullian seems to have effected the

---

[1] Tert. *de V. V.* 9.
[2] Decreverint, *Ep.* 4. 1.
[3] *Ep.* 4. 2.
[4] The Viduatus Tert. *de V. V.* 9.
[5] ...ad quam sedem praeter annos sexaginta non tantum univirae, id est nuptae, aliquando eliguntur, sed et matres, et quidem educatrices filiorum, Tert. *de V. V.* 9. Their functions (*IV. Conc. Carth.* c. 12) were to baptize and catechize women.
[6] Tert. *de V. V.* 9.
[7] *Ibid.* 11. 16.

[8] Tert. *de Orat.* 21, 22.
[9] πᾶσα δὲ γυνή, κ.τ.λ. 1 *Cor.* xi. 5. Tertull. disposes of this in *De Orat.* c. 22. Jerome dwells in an unadvised sense on the distinction between 'mulier' and 'virgo,' *De perpetua Virginit. B. Mariæ*, 20.
[10] It will be observed that 'to take the veil' meant originally to adopt the usual dress of young women of their own age.
[11] Tert. *de V. V.* 14.

restoration of the usual dress[1]. Cyprian has no complaint against departures from the rule. And if this be so we may remark here one of the instances in which Tertullian's Montanism was no bar to his catholic influence.

Christian women had now refrained as a rule for half a century from public festivals and arena spectacles as well as from temples. But an incipient tendency to reform society appears when the Virgins are desired to stay away from weddings on account of the coarseness of the customs, and from the baths in which both sexes appeared in undress[2].

The popularity and sentimental admiration which now attended the order led to vast evils. Even Cyprian with all his moderation ranks the Virgin next to the Martyr. Vanity, exaltation, sense of security, led many, the solitary converts of heathen hearths, or of circles in which Christian doctrines had not yet dissipated heathen indifferentism on such subjects, or which shared their blind confidence in the magic of a vow, to seek homes in the houses, and even share the chambers of Christian men and clerics who had bound themselves under the same obligation[3]. The power of ecstatic feeling may confessedly sometimes overpower even continuous temptation, and Cyprian wishes in dealing with this dreadful scandal not to assume that every such case was one of actual guilt[4].

---

[1] It is, as Bingham, vol. II. p. 404 (ed. 1855), writes, true that Tertullian's object was to induce all virgins to use the grave habit of matrons; but he has also in view a body of virgins, who though they did not live in a society were distinctly dedicated. *De V. V.* 16 'Nupsisti enim Christo.' Cf. 14.

[2] Bunsen must have forgotten this passage, *De Hab. Virg.* 19, when in *Hippolytus and his age*, vol. II. p. 273 (ed. 1852), he refers an apostolic canon to the East on account of this promiscuous bathing. Rettberg's anti-monasticism leads him into the ridiculous belief that only Christian maidens then took the bath.

[3] *Ep.* 4.

[4] ...dum adhuc separari innocentes possint, *Ep.* 4. 2. Chrysostom (*Contra eos qui ap. se habent virg. subintrod.*) does assume it, and scouts every plea of 'Perfection,' 'Philosophy,' 'Piety,' or 'Brotherhood.' Gregory of Nyssa *de Virginitate*, 23, and Jerome, *Ep.* 22, *ad Eustochium*, and Epiphanius, *Hæres.* 78, 11, agree with him. Basil, setting aside any such question, treats the mere fact as a scandal, deserving excommunication, *Ep.* 55 (198). See

He however adds to the instant separation a dreadful ordeal[1].

The repetition of similar griefs for a century and a half in the councils of Carthage, their prevalence in Spain and reappearance in Constantinople[2], establish the inevitable dangers of a position which the cœnobitic or conventual system arose to fortify. The earliest formation of such societies was intended perhaps to meet the case of homeless virgins[3]. But at present lacking the finality of a recognised vow, lacking fixity of discipline or prescribed occupation, the Virginal Life was little more than the expression of a fresh intense sentiment[4], a revolt against the universal degradation which enveloped city life. Its own corruption is a warning as to the danger of revivals attempted under incomplete conditions.

In his treatise upon 'THE DRESS OF THE VIRGINS' Cyprian is concerned with what seems less important yet in reality lay nearer to the fountain of the mischief. He applies himself not only to the correction of vanity, but to purify and exalt the influence of women on the community. The privacy and subjection of the married limited their influence. That of an order professed yet free to come and go might be almost boundless. Many of the Virgins, as is natural, belonged to the wealthiest class, and, without re-

---

Suicer s. v. Συνείτακτος. In *I. Conc. Carth.* cc. 3, 4 A.D. 348 excommunication is pronounced against laics guilty of the practice. It was forbidden by *Conc. Nicæn.* 3, by civil law under Honorius, and again and again by canon for several centuries. See Canon E. Venables in *Dict. Chr. Antiq. s. v.* subintroductæ.

[1] *Ep.* 4. 4. A treatment which Ambrose, *Ep.* 5 (*Syagrio*), condemns in the strongest manner.

[2] When Chrysostom speaks of them as 'fresh, paradoxical and inexplicable.' *Op. cit.* 1.

[3] *III. Conc. Carth.* can. 33.

[4] Freppel, p. 159, incorrectly represents the advice of Cyprian as 'a series of rules' preparatory to an expansion of the 'religious' life in better times, and supports the illusion by construing the interference with the scandals into a prohibition 'to live under the same roof as men' and a recommendation 'to *distinguish themselves from the rest of their sex*' by more modest dresses. All that he does require is that they should dress like other staid Roman ladies of their own age and live in proper homes. So Augustine, *Ep.* 111 (al. 122), speaks of a Sanctimonialis taken captive by barbarians and restored to *her parents*.

signing rank or home (which indeed no existing organization enabled them to do), sought in their resolution protection against social corruption with independence and respect among the Christians. To them no occasion presented itself obviously requiring a change in their dress or ornaments. In fashions half Roman, half Tyrian they still 'buried the neck[1]' in masses of gold chain and pearl, still piled the hair in grape-like clusters, loaded arms and feet with bracelets, outlined the almond-like eye with antimony, dyed the cheeks 'with crimson falsehood,' tipped toes and fingers with henna. A strange sketch of a sister! Modes against which Cyprian alleges Scripture, sense and feeling. Yet this can have been but a small portion of the picture. We may be sure there was much to reverence and much to love in that which excited in the great organizer, in the world-worn lawyer, such intense enthusiasm.

Grave matter for reflection in this essay are the 'reverence and fear' with which he scarce reproves, the self-abasement with which he asks their prayers[2]. The motives are at once too low and too lofty upon which he lauds their choice of a virgin-life,—the escapes namely from marriage-trouble, their union with Christ, their anticipated superiority in the resurrection-life. There is latent in these motives a subtle selfishness and pride, such as it seems true foresight might have shunned without waiting for experience. But woman's unapproached power in alleviating human wretchedness, and in the revival of aspirations after purity; the influence of great examples of self-sacrifice upon a sordid and luxurious age; the effective operation of frequent intercession, are more substantial and less obtruded motives. They were real then, and they are real for ever; still destined to be at last as effective as they are sound in shaping the nobler monasticisms of the future[3].

---

[1] *De Hab. Virg.* 14, 15, 21.
[2] *De Hab. Virg.* 3, cf. 24.

[3] The two Epistles to Virgins, extant in Syriac, ascribed to Clement of Rome,

XIII.

Literary character of the Book 'Of the Dress of Virgins.'

This book is less analogous to Tertullian's very Montanistic tract 'Of the Veiling of the Virgins' than to that author's two books on the 'Apparelling of Women.' Those obligations to eschew frivolity and purify their own society, which Tertullian had drawn out for the sex, are here specialised for a single class.

We have found already that the amplest plagiarism was permissible; and, this assumed, there is much literary interest in observing how a master of style like Cyprian deals with the rocky genius of his own 'Master.'

A more delicate taste abjures the coarser appeals and modifies, though unable to abandon, the materialism. Thus still, equality with angels is literally begun for those who 'are not given in marriage[1]'; wool-dyeing is unnatural because there are no purple or scarlet sheep; hair-dye unlawful because 'we cannot make one hair white or black.' His own sufficiently bold phrase that cosmetic arts are 'the siege and storming of the Truth of the face' is worked up with Tertullian's passionate 'they lay hands upon God.' Like his

---

were first printed in J. J. Wetstein's *N. T.* vol. II. The first is both from its readings of Scripture (Bp. Westcott, *Canon of Scripture*, p. 186 n. (ed. 1881)), and also from its topics and omissions (see Wetst. *Proleg.* pp. iv—vii), a work of the second century, and probably of the first half of it. The pretences to purity under similar though less outrageous conditions (*Ep.* i. 10) are not accepted, and are so coupled with warnings against idleness, roaming, pretexts of visiting, Scripture reading and exorcizing as to shew what the dangers of the profession of Virginity unprotected were before the time of Cyprian. The second epistle is not to Virgins, but prescribing caution and decorum to travelling clerics (somewhat too minutely) exhibits the same dangers from another point of view. Freppel (*Pères Apostol.*, pp. 214 sqq.) holds these to be genuine, as do other Roman divines. See Bp. Lightfoot, *Apostolic Fathers*, I., *Clement*, vol. I. pp. 407 sqq. (1890).

[1] *De Hab. Virg.* 22. Cf. 14, 15, 17.

predecessor he ascribes the invention of the toilet, 'woman's world,' to apostate angels who lived before the flood; but he spares us Tertullian's Byronic picture of spirits sighing for a lost heaven yet scheming an eternal hell for their beloved. He cannot part with 'the evil presage' of the then fashionable 'flame-colour' of hair, but avoids suggesting the horror of wearing 'the despoilment of the strange woman, of the head devoted to gehenna.'

The warning to the innocent though over-drest girl 'thy 'beholder hath in heart gratified his lust; thou art become a 'sword to him¹' is softened into 'though thou fall not thyself 'thou destroyest others, and makest thyself as it were a 'sword and a poison draught to the beholders².' 'Modesty is sacristan and priestess of the shrine' becomes 'in those shrines the worshippers and priests are we³.'

So he preserves the fine turn 'Plainly the Christian will 'glory even in the flesh,—but only when it has endured,—torn 'for Christ's sake; that the spirit may be crowned in it, not 'that it may draw the eyes and sighs of youth after it,'—but preserves it more gracefully, 'If we are to glory in the flesh it 'must plainly be then, when it is tormented in the confession 'of the Name, when woman proves stronger than torturing 'man, when she suffers fires or crosses or sword or wild beasts 'that she may be crowned⁴.'

The gain and loss of the Master in the disciple's hand are evident; the chief gain was that he became more readable: but Cyprian's merit was not limited to the turn of a phrase or the smoothing of a 'Postremissimus' into an 'Extremi et minimi⁵,' or the inweaving of expressions as beautiful as his 'Law of Innocence⁶.' To Augustine, who in him and Ambrose finds the leaders of Christian eloquence, though he criticizes severely the richness of his earlier writing, this

---

[1] Tert. *de Cult. Fem.* 2. 2.
[2] *De Hab. Virg.* 9.
[3] Tert. *C. F.* 2. 1; — *H. V.* 2.
[4] Tert. *C. F.* 2. 3; — *H. V.* 6.
[5] Tert. *C. F.* 2. 1; — *H. V.* 3.
[6] *De Hab. Virg.* 2.

treatise must have appeared very perfect in style. It furnishes him with illustrations both of the 'grand' or 'moving¹' style, and of the 'temperate².'

---

¹ Viz. *de Hab. Virg.* 15 Si quis pingendi artifex, *to* 16 auspicaris.

² Viz. *de Hab. Virg.* 3 Nunc *to* augescit, and 2 Quomodo *to end.* Aug. *de Doctr. Christiana* iv. 21 (47, 48, 49), 'Quos duos ex omnibus proponere volui.' The classification (iv. 17 (34)), adopted perhaps from Cic. *de Orat.* II. xxix. 128, 129, is (1) ut doceat, poterit parva submisse; (2) ut delectet, modica temperate; (3) ut flectat, magna granditer dicere. In ecclesiastical eloquence all the topics are 'magna,' but the 'submiss' style is for instruction, the 'temperate' for praise or blame, the 'grand' for arousing energy.

CHAPTER II.

THE DECIAN PERSECUTION.

I.

The Roman Theory of Persecution.

THE disorder and worldliness which have been described were such as in Cyprian's convictions were past correction from within. Possessed with this idea he was visited by intimations of coming trial which wore a supernatural character[1]. And it came. The Decian persecution was co-extensive with the Empire, and aimed at the suppression of Christianity by the removal of its leaders. It was not perceived that it had passed the stage in which it depended on individuals.

But before we enter on this scene of our history, it may be well to lay down the principles upon which harmless people were so cruelly handled on account of their opinions by the law-loving and tolerant state of Rome. The question admits of a less simple answer from the fact that the Christian legists of the Theodosian and Justinian codes have expunged the obsolete statutes. If the chapter of Ulpian 'Of the proconsul's office,' which recited[2] the provisions applicable to Christians in the middle of the 3rd century, were extant we should have the answer to our hand. We can however frame one correctly though circuitously.

(1). In the first place the Julian Law of Treason included among state offences and in very general terms the holding

---

[1] On the visions of Cyprian and others see infra.

[2] Lactant. *Div. Instit.* v. 11.

of any assembly with evil intent[1]; then too it promoted by every means the laying of informations under this head, admitting evidence inadmissible in other cases, that of infamous persons, soldiers, women[2], and of a man's own slaves[3]. These enactments seem prior to the time of Alexander Severus, or even contemporary with the Antonines, while from Marcus Aurelius dates the *post mortem* trial for treason and the confiscation of the estate of heirs.

Now provincials could secure the freedom of their religious meetings by registration of their cultus as a *religio licita*. But there was no province for which Christianity could be registered. It was a *tertium genus*, not ethnic, nor Judaic[4]; and any other associations for religious rites, save only unions for securing funeral celebrations for their members, were illicit. It is strange to think that the Church must have subsisted for some time at Rome under the external aspect of a Burial Society; occupied its catacombs, had its staff of fossors, and entombed its martyrs in this light. No clubs except those of very poor persons were allowed to have common funds; they might not assemble oftener than once a month; and no permanent 'Master of sacred rites[5]' was allowed. The State[6] was the one society which should engross every religious and social interest beyond those of the family. Monotheism even when licensed was looked on as anti-national and anti-imperial. A monotheistic society then, understood to have adherents from all classes of society, branches everywhere, daily meetings, permanent religious chiefs, was on all sides

---

[1] Quo (*crimine majestatis*) tenetur is, cujus opera dolo malo consilium initum erit...quove coetus conventusve fiat... Ulp. ap. *Dig.* xlviii. 4 (1).

[2] *Dig.* xlviii. 4 (7, 8).

[3] *Cod.* ix. 8 (4, 6, 7).

[4] Tertull. *ad Nationes* i. 8. 20. *Scorpiace* 10.

[5] Magister sacrorum, cf. Tert. *ad Nat.* i. 7.

[6] See E. Renan's excellent account of the restrictions on collegia, *Les Apôtres*, c xviii. The following are the most important of his citations: *Digesta* i. 12, De officio Præfecti urbi; iii. 4, Quod cujusc. universitatis...; xlvii. 22, De collegiis et corporibus. See also Mommsen, *De Collegiis et Sodalitatibus Romanorum* (1843).

amenable to laws of Treason. Delation was easy and enriched.

(2). The application of tests was familiar to the Roman magistracy. While a slave or provincial could be tortured, a freeman, suspect of religious engagements hostile to the State, could be summoned to take part in a sacrificial feast, or at least to offer incense before an imperial statue, to which the least mark of disrespect was treason. Whatever other scruples were allowed for, none might doubt the present divinity of the emperor; no beliefs could interfere with a mechanical act of obedient veneration.

Imperial edicts possessed by the Lex Regia[1] the force of Law. Such were issued from time to time to require the general application of this test. It was further competent for any magistrate who feared the growth of a dangerous class in his district, or was pressed by popular feeling, to summon a neighbourhood or any residents in it to take the test under former edicts. This mode of action is exhibited in far the larger number of arrests which led to confessorship and martyrdom. 'Persecution' of this kind, as the Christians very naturally called it, was incessantly simmering in some province or other, intensified by the policy of one emperor, moderated by the broader policy of another, at times ceasing for years in particular districts.

(3). The difficulties of soldiers. To quit the army prematurely without approved cause was treason. For a Christian to remain unsuspected or if suspected to avoid disobedience was scarcely possible. The sacrifices to the standards, the military oaths, the religious decorations, the festivities, the wreaths distributed not simply in honour of the emperor but in honour of his divinity, were endless snares. Thus the martyrologies name many soldiers. And if the victims of

---

[1] Quod principi placuit legis habet vigorem utpote cum Lege Regia.. populus ei et in eum omne suum imperium et potestatem conferat. Ulp. ap. *Dig.* i. 4 (1); Gaume, *Révolution*, tom. VI. c. 1. Justinian, *Instt.* I. tit. 2. On which see J. B. Moyle's note (ed. 1883), vol. I. p. 95.

a town persecution were easily multiplied by report, the deaths of disloyal privates in a regiment would seldom transpire.

(4). The application to Christians of repeated torture was represented from such different points of view and involved so singular a dilemma that we must pause to consider the theory of it. It was no new thing. It was constantly applied to slaves and provincials to induce them to *confess suspected crime*. It was applied to Christians because to be a Christian was equivalent to having gross crimes to confess. A secret society which could not ask for a license, which at Rome pretended to be a burial society, and was evidently much more, lay under charges of hideous unnatural orgies.

Then again the usage did not allow confessions wrung out by the first torture to be acted on: it must be repeated lest perhaps the first avowal should have been only obtained by pain[1].

The confessor confessed his religion at once and consistently. Then he was tortured to make him deny it, for denial in this case amounted to a promise to be guilty no more, since it was well understood that denial would involve exclusion from his sect.

Thus then to the magistrate torture appeared a lenient discipline for such criminals. He could not understand their declining to be let off so cheaply. He did not consider it a punishment at all, but a condonation of the past while it sufficiently secured the State from a repetition of the offences. The secret crimes whatever they might be were allowed to pass in the account. The magistrate's sense of his own benevolence is quite characteristic of genuine Acts of martyrdom.

But to the Christian who knew there were no crimes to be

---

[1] Interrogavi ipsos, an essent Christiani: confitentes *iterum ac tertio* interrogavi, supplicium minatus: *perseverantes* duci jussi. Plin. *ad Traj.* 96.

divulged the tortures seemed iniquitous indeed. Tertullian[1] and Cyprian[2] justly exclaimed against a ferocity which actually reversed the law, by applying to those who without hesitation confessed the crime of Christianity tortures which in all other cases were reserved for such as denied the legal charge.

Finally, as their numbers grew the fruitless attempt at repression was aggravated almost to desperation lest the whole system of public worship and of that domestic religion, on which rulers relied for sobriety of morals among a large class of the population, should go down before the undisguised contempt of men who acknowledged none of the authorised sanctions and were believed to live in private shamelessness.

II.

The Outbreak of the Decian Persecution.—Rome.

Philip had been so tolerant of these Christians that he appeared in their approved legends as a penitent on Easter Eve[3]. Decius was as antichristian as he was virtuous[4]. He was, we are told, 'in life and in death worthy to be ranked with the Romans of old time[5].' The luxury of his predecessors, the mustering of the Goths, the prevalence of Christianity, were all alike to him hateful forms of dissolution in society, government and religion. He was to correct, to arrest, to repress them all. His 'knowledge and universal forethought[6]' failed him in the one great sign of the times. But he knew how to strike. It is amazing that one man, even a Roman emperor, should after thirty-eight years of religious liberty have been able in a moment to deal blows

---

[1] Tert. *Apol.* ii. 'hoc imperium, cujus magistri estis, civilis non tyrannica dominatio est.' Cf. *Ep.* 31. 5 (*conff. ad Cyp.*) 'nefarias contra veritatem leges.'

[2] *Ad Demetr.* 12.

[3] Euseb. *H. E.* vi. 34. His βασιλεία εὐμενέστερα ἡμῖν rests on the sound authority of Dionysius ap. Eus. vi. 41.

[4] Zosimus i. 21 ...γένει προέχων καὶ ἀξιώματι προσέτι δὲ καὶ πάσαις διαπρέπων ταῖς ἀρεταῖς.

[5] Fl. Vopiscus *Aurelianus* c. 42.

[6] Zosimus i. 22 ...τῇ Δεκίου πεποιθότες ἐπιστήμῃ καὶ περὶ πάντα προνοίᾳ.

so rapid and accurate. In October A.D. 249 he reluctantly but successfully headed his confiding master's legions against him, and by the following January his edict[1] was doing deadly execution. This edict seems to have fixed capital penalties in the first instance on the bishops only[2]. The great Origen indeed was held no less important, and was subjected to extreme tortures with care to avoid releasing him by death. The new bishop of Alexandria, Dionysius, after awaiting the soldiers four days in his house, as they roamed the neighbourhood in search of him, fled at last upon some divine intimation. Gregory Thaumaturgus took many of his flock into the wilderness. The two patriarchs of Antioch and Jerusalem died speedily in prison, namely Babylas and 'the bright age and hoary head of Alexander[3].' At Rome Fabian, who fourteen years before had been chosen upon the descent of a Dove on his head in the elective assembly[4], was executed on the 20th January A.D. 250[5].

A.D. 250. A.U.C. 1003. Coss. Imp. Cæs. C. Messius Qu. Traj. Decius P. F. Aug II. ...Vettius Gratus.

The dismay caused by this blow was very great. His people elected no successor to Fabian when they laid him behind the stone which, still bearing the contemporary record, preserves a slight but certain memorial both of their dejection and of the order-loving spirit of that Church. The name 'Fabian Bishop' is cut deep with rude firm strokes. Not much later, but after the stone had been placed against the

---

[1] πρόσταγμα Dionys. ap. Eus. vi. 41 et passim. Greg. Nyss. *Vit. Greg. Thaum.* gives an exaggerated summary of it. (See Fechtrup, p. 44.) On the forged edict see Tillemont, note ii., *Sur la Persécution de Dèce*, vol. III. p. 699.

[2] Rettberg, p. 54. In *Ep.* 66. 7 the bishops are spoken of in connection with this persecution as suffering proscription, imprisonment, banishment and death.

[3] Eus. *H. E.* vi. 39.

[4] Eus. *H. E.* vi. 29.

[5] *Cat. Liberian.:* Fabius ann. XIIII m. I d. X... Passus XII kl. Feb... *Cat. Felician.:* Fabianus...Sedit annus XIIII mense I dies XI...et passus est XIIII KL feb...qui sepultus est in cimiterio calesti uia appia XIII KL febr. The XIIII and the XII kl. feb. are both mistakes for XIII, and the real length of the see-tenancy 14 years and 10 days. See R. A. Lipsius, *Chronolog. der Römisch. Bischöfe* (1869), pp. 199, 263, 266, 267, 275.

hollow cell, the addition of 'Martyr' has been deeply scratched[1]. Without proper authentication[2] or in the vacancy of the see

the appellation could not be attached even to so sacred a grave in the catacomb chapel. The age in which martyrs were lightly multiplied was not come.

Neither was the fanatic zeal for martyrdom at flood. The Roman Church would not now select one of her leading men for immediate death, and for sixteen months elected no bishop[3]. The clergy of the metropolis was a regularly organized body, well able to act in concert, and requiring more than a passing notice to enable us to understand their remarkable relations with Carthage and her bishop.

The wisdom of the Church was everywhere not to traverse or break up, but to adopt administrative lines and civil areas

---

[1] The letter-cutter of Fabian's inscription was not a good one like his predecessor's. The letters are unequal, the apices not elegant or exact, the punctuation ugly. The inscription is not a later honorary one, like Anteros's. The abbreviation is unusual, (in an honorary inscription it would have been full MAPTYP,) and is weakly cut or rather scratched after the slab was in its place.

[2] I believe this explanation of de Rossi (*R. S.* vol. II. pp. 58 sqq.) to be real. Compare Optat. i. 16 '...et si martyris, sed *necdum vindicati*,' and Cyp. *Ep.* 12. 2.

[3] The ultramontane statement of this fact is that 'it appeared to the pagans that the most terrible blow they could inflict on the Church was to hinder the election of a successor to Saint Peter.' Freppel, *S. Cyprien*, p. 173. It is needless to say that there is no evidence for any of the three assertions involved.

THE CONFESSORS AT ROME.

which had already impressed characters and unities on groups of population. The 'City of God' thus grew so firmly with its organization in accord with the ideas of the people, that in after-time the ecclesiastical division was often thought to be original. In fact it remained as a sort of original while fresh delimitations succeeded one another on its surface. One of the earliest examples seems to belong to this time.

Augustus had divided the City into fourteen Regions, each with its Curator, and for some purposes grouped in pairs[1]. Alexander Severus (A.D. 232—235) amplified the powers and rank of these curators and attached them as a bench for certain causes to the Prefect of the City.

Very soon after their reconstitution by Alexander, Fabian (236—250) 'divided the Regions to the Deacons[2].' That is, apparently, he assigned two Regions to each of the Seven Deacons. But he is also said to have created the seven subdeacons. He thus took the municipal divisions, to which attention had recently been drawn, either singly or in pairs, into the church organization, and also retained the apostolic number of deacons.

The Presbyters a few months later[3] were forty-six in

---

[1] *Dict. Gk. and Roman Antt.* II. p. 541 *b*.

[2] 'Hic regiones divisit diaconibus.' *Liberian Catal.* ed. Mommsen, *op. cit.* p. 635. *Lib. Pontif.* adds 'et fecit septem subdiaconos.' Augustus' curators had certain religious functions, and were chosen annually by lot (see Sueton. *Augustus* 30; Dio Cass. lv. 8). Alexander required them to be *consulares* (Lamprid. *Alex. Sev.* 33). Before the appointment of various kinds of governors he put their names up for objections to be made, 'as Christians and Jews did,' he said, '*in prædicandis sacerdotibus.' Ibid.* 45. His organization soon passed away, but not so the Christian, which apparently adopted it. See Harnack, *On the Origin of the Readership, &c.*, and Essay by J. Owen, with supplementary note. London, 1895.

When the Felician Catalogue (*cod. Bern.* Lipsius *op. cit.* p. 275) has 'Hic (*Fabianus*) regiones dividit diaconibus et fecit septem subdiaconibus. VIIq notariis inminirent ut gesta martyrum fideliter collegerent...' may we not remove the stop after 'subdiaconibus' and render 'and caused them (the deacons) to superintend seven subdeacons and seven notaries in order to collect the Acts of the martyrs'?

[3] Letter of Cornelius, Eus. *H. E.* vi. 43.

number; and since in the persecution of Diocletian (half a century later) there were 'upwards of forty basilicas[1]' it has been concluded too hastily[2] that each presbyter had charge of one basilica. This is contrary to all we know of early organization. Only in the smallest country places were churches anything but collegiate. To each of the deacons there was a subdeacon and six acolytes. Exorcists, readers and doorwatchers amounted to fifty-two.

Such was the administrative body required for the fifty thousand[3] Christians of Rome in the middle of the third century, and such as remained at liberty of the seven[4] great Treasurers or Visitors, called Deacons, together with the forty or more Presbyters, now took in commission the Episcopal conduct of internal affairs and of the relations with other

---

[1] Optatus, ii. 4. Neander thinks this number must be exaggerated; but these basilicas were not public buildings, but those which were frequently attached to great houses.—R. Burn, *Rome and the Campagna*, p. 1. The need for dispersion and small congregations entirely explains the number. Many of these would be like private chapels, while in the regularly used ones there would be always a consessus.

[2] By Routh, *Rel. S.* vol. III. p. 60.

[3] This estimate formed by Bishop Burnet (*Travels in Switzerland, Italy...* (1685-86), ed. 1724, pp. 217-220), approved by W. Moyle (*Works*, II. p. 152) and accepted by Gibbon c. xv. to illustrate the insignificance of the Christians, who thus amounted to less than one twentieth of the population, seems to me too large rather than too small. Burnet estimates from the 1500 widows, virgins and 'thlibomeni' or afflicted people who received relief. (Cornel. ap. Eus. *H. E.* vi. 43.) His reckoning is roughly verified by the ascertained proportion, three per cent. at Antioch, of the widows and virgins receiving alms (3000) to the whole number of Christians (100,000). Chrysostom, ed. Bened. VII. pp. 658, 810. The population of Antioch was 200,000, *id.* II. p. 597. But we must consider that the incessant wars would tend to make the proportion of widows and dependent children larger in the capital. From the monuments also Bp. Lightfoot thinks we might conclude the Christians to be fewer in proportion at this time. *Address on Missions*, S.P.G. (Macmillan, 1873.)

[4] A later opportunity will occur for illustrating the importance of these high officers (p. 114). At present we may notice that seven remained at Rome the fixed number of deacons. The college of cardinals retains the form of seven deacons still. Until the 9th century the Elect to the See of Rome was always a priest or deacon, the latter by preference. See Duchesne, *Orig. du Culte Chrétien*, p. 349 *n*. On the other hand Constantinople in Justinian's time had a hundred deacons. Routh, vol. III. p. 61.

Churches, particularly that of Carthage. Their tone was at first chiefly influenced by the powerful character of one whose stern uncharity severed him at last from a Church which he seemed born to govern, and by others whose rigid counsels sounded more impressively from their dungeon depth, and who were saved to the cause of unity only through the affectionate wisdom of Cyprian. Of the first great Puritan, Novatian, we shall have occasion to speak more fully. Two of the Presbyters, the aged Moyses, probably of Jewish birth, and Maximus, whose gravestone possibly still confronts us in the Vatican[1]; two of the Deacons, Rufinus and Nicostratus, the latter afterwards an active propagator of Novatianism in Cyprian's own diocese, were thrown into prison at the time[2] of Fabian's execution, along with the laymen[3] Urbanus, Sidonius, Macarius[4], and with one Celerinus, who deserves more than passing mention. This man's story not only is a remarkable illustration of the time, but tessellated together, as it requires to be, out of many distant allusions in scattered letters, it is one of the most interesting proofs of the genuineness of the whole correspondence. It is morally impossible that such a complete tale could be recomposed out of such slight touches, were those touches not truthful; morally impossible for the most ingenious forger to have constructed a character and then to have dotted it about so fragmentarily as not to support his aim by one cross-reference. It is only by writing out every passage in which his name occurs, comparing these with the African commemorations of confessors, and with a passage of Eusebius[5], that we extract the following narrative.

Celerinus was a native of Carthage, established in Rome. His grandmother Celerina had died by martyrdom in some

---

[1] The loculus ΜΑΞΕΙΜΟΥ ΠΡ(εσβυτέρου), de Rossi, *R. S.* vol. I. tav. xix. 5. See below p. 162, note 4.

[2] *Ep.* 28. 1 '...primores et duces...surgentis belli impetus primos...fregistis.'

[3] Note in *Ep.* 49. 2 '...Maximum presbyterum...ceteris...'

[4] Probably a Carthaginian. *Ep.* 21. 4; 51. 1. Tillemont, vol. III. p. 441, confuses him with Celerinus.

[5] *H. E.* vi. 43.

70   THE DECIAN PERSECUTION.

earlier persecution: so had her son and son-in-law, Laurentinus and Egnatius, both of them soldiers in the Roman army. They were commemorated in the African Church as Cyprian records[1], and the African kalendar yet retains their names on the 3rd of February. Augustine preached[2] in a church dedicated to Celerina, and it was given up to the Arians under Genseric[3].

At the time when the Bishop of Rome was executed, Celerinus was tortured in the presence it would seem of Decius himself. A Carthaginian friend of his, Lucian, a man of humble birth and small reading[4], congratulates him in a misspelt, ungrammatical letter[5] upon having prevailed against 'the chief Snake, the Quarter-master of Antichrist[6].' Cornelius, bishop of Rome, mentions this same Celerinus in a Greek letter to Fabius[7] of Antioch as having 'borne every sort of torture and mightily overcome the adversary,' and he mentions him in company with Sidonius (a Punic name) and others with whom the former allusion[8] in Cyprian also connects him. What these tortures were we learn from a quite different source[9]. He was liberated from prison in the course of the year A.D. 250, and about December conveyed letters from Moyses to Cyprian[10], who by this time, as we shall see, was in retirement. Cyprian mentions having seen the terrible scars of his torture, and witnessed the broken health which had resulted from nineteen days in the stocks under irons almost without food or water. He speaks of him as the earliest of the Roman sufferers in this persecution, 'the first at the conflict of our time,' 'the standard-bearer in front of Christ's soldiers.' His history and that of his family, as well as his personal character, which

A.D. 250, December.

---

[1] *Ep.* 39. 3.
[2] Aug. *Serm.* 48.
[3] Morcelli, vol. II. p. 65. Victor Vit. I. 9 (3).
[4] *Ep.* 27. 1.
[5] It should be read in Hartel's edition with the remarks in his preface p. xlviii., on the vulgar tongue.
[6] *Ep.* 22. 1 'Metatorem.'
[7] Eus. *l.c.*
[8] *Ep.* 49. 1, 2.
[9] *Ep.* 39. 2.
[10] *Ep.* 37. 1.

Cyprian describes as that of 'an honest and sturdy confessor, 'self-restrained, guarded and shamefast, with all the lowliness 'and awe that befit our religion,' made the Bishop desirous to enrol him among the clergy of his native place, and he proposed to make him a Reader[1]. But as he had been in a manner naturalised at Rome, Cyprian explains the step somewhat laboriously to the clergy there. The 'glorious looks and 'modest bearing of one who now lived only through a kind 'of resurrection' would, at his daily reading of the Gospel[2], stir the brethren to some imitation of his faith. A vision which the young man had overcame some scruples of his, and he was ordained along with the young Aurelius, who had himself been a 'Victor' before both the native magistracy and the proconsul[3]. To each were assigned at once the daily commons and monthly dividends of a presbyter, and they were designate for seats on Cyprian's Bench, when they should be of age to take that rank.

The martyr spirit however had not nerved every member of the family. His sister Candida had offered sacrifice. His sister Etecusa or Numeria, while actually on the ascent of the Capitol, found at the Chapel of The Three Fates some officer to whom she paid[4] a sum of money to be excused. Both were cut off from communion, and then full of remorse

---

[1] *Ep.* 39, and compare 38.

[2] ...cottidie...evangelica lectio... *Ep.* 39. 4.

[3] *Ep.* 38. 1.

[4] 'Numeria...this is what I have ever called Etecusa, because she counted out (numeravit) bribes for herself to avoid sacrificing.' I fear Celerinus cannot be acquitted of this bitter jest. *Ep.* 21. 3. This passage does not seem to have been taken into account in illustrating the topography of the slope of the Capitol. See Burn's *Rome and the Campagna*, p. 131. The temple of the Tria Fata was not, as Goldhorn (p. 46 n.) says, close to the Temple of Janus, but higher up, for the Papal procession on Easter Monday in the middle ages 'intrat sub arcu triumphali [sc. Sept. Severi] *inter templum Fatale et templum Concordiæ*,' *Ordo Rom.* xi. *Auct. Benedict.* ap. Mabillon and Germain *Mus. Ital.* II. p. 143; and with this agrees Procopius *de Bello Gotth.* i. 25, who says the temple of Janus is ἐν τῇ ἀγορᾷ πρὸ τοῦ βουλευτηρίου (*i.e.* Concord) ὀλίγον ὑπερβάντι τὰ τρία φᾶτα. When Anastasius in the passages alluded to by Pearson (*Ann. Cypr.* A.D. 250, s. xiv, which will be found in *Vit.*

devoted themselves to the sufferers whom now they envied, and especially to the relief of their compatriots, the refugees, who, driven from Carthage by the edict, found like other foreigners their obscurest hiding-place among the crowds of Rome. These they met upon their landing at Portus[1] and had no less than sixty-five of them under their care at one time. Celerinus pleaded for their restoration; and their case was heard by the Roman presbytery[2]. But their readmission was postponed until the election of a new bishop. The temporary adhesion of Celerinus and his friends to Novatian at that election will be noticed in its place.

Ap. 7, A.D. 250.

It was close on Easter A.D. 250 when his sisters yielded, so that the 'Day of Joy' and its whole season were spent by him in sackcloth and ashes and tears. At last in utter agony for Candida's 'Death to Christ,' he wrote an affecting but ill-judged appeal to Lucian at Carthage[3]. He prevailed on the suffering confessors there to interpose their unmeasured popularity in subversion of the judgment of the constituted authorities of the Church.

A fatal system thus simply originated, which presently began to threaten the whole organization of the Church.

Of Genuineness in Nomenclature.

We must pause upon certain exceptions to the genuineness of the correspondence in which the above account is extant. We may first, however, ask whether it is possible that a tale such as this could be sown in such minute fragments over such a number of epistles as a glance at the footnotes exhibits unless that tale were

---

Honor. i. Labbe, vol. VI. c. 1419 and *Vit. Hadriani* i. Labbe, vol. VIII. cc. 505 and 512), speaks of S. Adrian and of SS. Cosmas and Damian as being 'in Tribus Fatis,' this can only mean, as Bunsen saw, that the lower end (or ? north side) of the Forum came to be so called.

[1] See Rossi, *Bollettino di Archeol. Crist.*, anno iv. p. 50, for interesting illustrations of the necessity for such provision at Portus: particularly the erection by the senator Pammachius, S. Jerome's friend, of a hostelry there for Peregrini.

[2] Præpositi, *Ep.* 21. 3.

[3] *Ep.* 21. 2.

true; and then again that Eusebius should have preserved such a corroboration of it, and that even a title of a sermon of Augustine should incidentally illustrate it? or what object could possibly have been served by inventing such a character and then taking such extraordinary pains to avoid presenting it as a whole?

The critic[1] ingeniously argues against the genuineness of the letter of Celerinus from Rome and the reply of Lucian from Carthage[2], on the ground that they would evince an incredibly 'close and intimate connexion' between the two Churches. 'The *Roman* 'confessor,' he says, 'supports his prayer (to the African Confessor) by 'stating that Statius and Severianus, and the Sixty-five African Con- 'fessors who had been cared for by his lapsed sisters, joined in it.' He then quotes the greetings sent from Rome by 'Macarius and his 'sisters Cornelia and Emerita, by Saturninus [a confessor], your 'brethren Calpurnius and Maria,' &c., and Lucian's counter-greetings to the same persons, and to 'Collecta, Sabina, Spesina, Januaria, 'Dativa, Donata, Saturus with his...[3], Bassianus and all the clergy, 'Uranius, Alexius, Quintianus, Colonica, &c., Alexius, Getulicus' and from his own 'sisters Januaria and Sophia.' From these extracts he argues that, if they ever formed portions of real letters, *the Churches must have been neither more nor less than one family:* that these common names without further description would have conveyed no distinctive information between Rome and Carthage: that, as it was impossible that there could be such intimacy between such places, the letters cannot be authentic.

The ingenious critic conceives a letter in some persecution in England to a Christian in New York and writes out a parallel list of vulgar names and surnames.

This was no doubt more diverting than to trace laboriously the history of Celerinus, and to arrive at the fact that he was *not* 'a Roman Confessor' writing to a Carthaginian, but a Carthaginian resident in Rome, whose family were eminent sufferers among the Christians of Carthage and who must have been well and widely known among them. All the names mentioned on both sides are but twenty-two, and of these several are brothers and sisters, surely not a very large circle. Then, it must be observed as natural, that the more numerous remembrances are those sent from Carthage; which the refugees had been quitting for Rome, and they are sent through the persons who were receiving and caring for them. One of those saluted is *Bassianus a cleric.* Now mark that in *Ep.* 8. 3 the Roman clergy advise the clergy of Carthage of the arrival at Rome

---

[1] Mr Shepherd's First Letter, p. 12, &c.

[2] *Epp.* 21 and 22.

[3] *Ep.* 22. 3. *Cum suis* 'with their friends' is sufficiently familiar.

of Bassianus seemingly as bringing letters and, according to usage[1], a Cleric.

Mr S. thinks it suspicious that the 'most common names in Carthage' are used. The argument tells the other way. They *are Carthaginian* names, much more common in Carthage (as inscriptions testify) than elsewhere. This is true of those he quotes—Victor, Donatus, Donata, Januaria. He should have added Dativa. Names expressive of 'God's Gift' are as Phœnician as they are Hebrew. But also Getulicus, Saturninus, Uranius point to the country and to the Punic worship which they represent. How should 'a Gaulish Bishop in the 5th century, a stranger to Africa, in the days of Cæsarian, Bishop of Arles,' forge with such nicety as to evolve so appropriate a list of names? But again the names are not all common. Is *Spesina* a familiar name to Mr S.? He will not find it in all the thousands of inscriptions in Muratori and Gruter. Yet it does occur just where it should if these letters are genuine. It is the name of a martyr in the *African* Kalendar[2]. [And since this was written it has appeared in several African inscriptions[3].]

On Etecusa and Numeria.

Etecusa the Carthaginian obtained exemption from sacrificing at Rome by payment. Her brother Celerinus entreats that the first martyrs selected for death among the prisoners at Carthage may 'istis sororibus nostris *Numeriæ* et Candidæ tale peccatum remit-'tant. Nam hanc ipsam *Etecusam* semper appellavi...*quia pro se* 'dona *numeravit* ne sacrificaret' (*Ep.* 21. 3). As translated by Dr Wallis 'our sisters Numeria and Candida, for this latter I have always called Etecusa...because she gave gifts,' the passage is, as he observes, 'altogether unintelligible.' Hence the conjectures *et aëcusam* (ἀκούσαν), ἀτυχοῦσαν (Dodwell, *Diss. ad Ep.* 21), and Hartel's *excusatam*. No various reading except *Ettecusam* and *et recusam*.

Let us observe however that *Numeria* is not a real prænomen (Varro, *Ling. Lat.* ix. 55); that the whole letter fails in taste and in grammar; that *hanc ipsam* may perfectly well be predicative; and that *hanc* need not refer to the last named, who in this Latin would more commonly be *istam*. Hence we may understand that *Numeria* is the sobriquet which Celerinus says he has affixed to

---

[1] See *Epp.* 7, 8, 9, 35, 36, 44, 45, &c.

[2] ap. Morcelli, vol. II. p. 369 'M. Jun. vii. Id....Spisinæ.'

[3] *C.I.L.* VIII. 1. *Spesina* 2152. 4442. 4687. 4935. 5804. *Spessinia* 5190. *Ispesina* 150, all Numidian.

his sister because she paid (*numeravit*) for immunity. 'Ask re-'mission for these sisters of mine *Numeria* and Candida, for so 'indeed (*hanc ipsam*—by this particular name *Numeria*) have I 'always called Etecusa, because she *paid down* bribes to be excused 'from sacrificing.'

We find Tecusa in de Rossi, *R. S.* vol. II. tav. lvii. (6), in conjunction with Laurentius, which (or Laurentinus) was the name of a martyred uncle of Celerinus in the same persecution, *Ep.* 39. 3 (Laurentius, *omn. edd. exc. H* 'Laurentinus').

[In the indexed volumes of *C. Inscrr. Latt.* TECUSA (Taecusa once) occurs in 6 inscriptions, of which 3 are African, vol. VIII. i. 3306 at Lambæse, 8261 Azíz ben Tellis, VIII. ii. 10505 Hadrumetum ; 2 Sardinian (vol. X. ii.) 7590, 7943; and 1 at Ostia (vol. XIV.) 1657. There is a martyr Tecusa at Ancyra (? under Diocletian), 18 May, Basil *Menolog.*, Migne, *Patr. Gr.* V. 117, c. 464. *Acta Sanctt. Bolland.* (*s. die*).]

There is no instance of *Etecusa* and to read *Et Tecusam* from Τῷ may be best. The v.l. *et recusam* strongly supports it. And it suits Celerinus' emphatic style.

We should then have an interesting trace of the family at Rome and of Tecusa's restoration.

III.

The Persecution at Carthage.—1. *The* 'STANTES.'

The episode of Celerinus links together the sufferers of the two cities. Great had been the dismay caused by the arrival of the edict at Carthage. It required from everyone some simple test of unchristianity before a specified day[1]. The 'Bishop of the Christians' was expressly named, and probably he alone. But anyone who failed to 'profess' might be legally summoned and interrogated. Some were dragged before the magistrates and some maltreated by the populace. The numbers who suffered were possibly not great, but their sufferings were intense. The edict prescribed confiscation, banishment, mine-labour, imprisonment with starvation as penalties, and torture as the means of inquisition. In each

---

[1] *De Lapsis* 3 '...quisque (=quisquis) professus intra diem non est Christianum se esse confessus est.'

THE DECIAN PERSECUTION.

April,
A.D. 250.

town five commissioners[1] were associated with the magistrates. The tortures were not used until the arrival of the Proconsul in April[2]. He found the severities so much abated that some of the exiles had returned, but after presiding over this tribunal in the capital[3], he made a tour of the province, with his twelve dreaded fasces[4], exercising such rigour that some conspicuous confessors yielded, while others died under his engines[5].

While the persecution of Diocletian was based on the determination that, cost what it might, Christianity should be extirpated, that of Decius at first assumed that it might be dissipated by a mingling of ferocity with forbearance,

[1] Primores, *Ep*. 43. 3. 'Persecutio est hæc alia, et alia est temptatio, et quinque isti presbyteri nihil aliud sunt quam quinque primores illi qui edicto nuper magistratibus fuerant copulati, ut fidem nostram subruerent, ut gracilia fratrum corda ad letales laqueos prævaricatione veritatis averterent. eadem nunc ratio, eadem rursus eversio per quinque presbyteros Felicissimo copulatos ad ruinam salutis inducitur, &c.' That is, 'The five presbyters are as ruinous to the Church as ever the five magnates were.' To interpret it of visions, or of the presbyters actually torturing martyrs, is absurd indeed. It is only just as obscure as a Cyprian, wanting to say so strong a thing, would feel bound to make it.

We may compare *Ep*. 52. 2 where he says of Novatus '*qui* in ipsa persecutione...alia quædam persecutio nostri fuit.'

[2] See note on xiii Epistles, *Ep*. 11 infr. pp. 102 sqq. Morcelli, vol. II. p. 12 and p. 102, calls him FORTUNATIANUS. The Greek Menæa (April. Venet. 1614) Ap. 10 describe an African martyr Terentius as suffering under Fortunatianus as ἡγεμών, *i.e.* 'Præses'; rightly so rendered in *Boll. Acta SS.* p. 860.

P. F. Zinus' Latin version of Greek MS. at Venice calls him 'præfectus'; Galesinius (*Acta SS.* p. 861) 'præfectus seu præses'; Martyrol. Rom. Baronii 'præfectus.' Sirlet (ap. Canisius, *Thes. Monumm.* vol. III. pp. 422 and 482) has 'præses' Ap. 10 and Oct. 28. The Menologium of Emp. Basil has ἡγεμών (Migne, *Patr. Gr.* v. 117, c. 396). The extant Latin Acta comes from Greek versions of the original Latin, Terentius' relics having been preserved at Constantinople.

These references to the sources of Morcelli's knowledge I owe to the research and kindness of the Rev. Chas. Hole.

But I must conclude from them that Terentius belonged to Numidia or the Mauretanias under the jurisdiction of a *præses* or *præfectus* (ἡγεμών): and not to Africa Proper under its Proconsul or ἀνθύπατος; and that hence the grounds are not sufficient for placing Fortunatianus on the Roll of the Proconsuls.

[3] *Ep*. 10. 4.

[4] *Ep*. 37. 2. The proconsuls of Africa and Asia bore these insignia: others but six.

[5] *Ep*. 37. 1; *Ep*. 56. 1.

visiting the leaders with uncompromising sternness, while allowing implicit understandings with many of the inoffensive followers.

There were, however, many who instantly sacrificed property and citizenship by voluntary exile: many who sought hiding in the crowds of Rome. The first inmates of the prison at Carthage were a presbyter Rogatian, 'a glorious old man' who had been left by Cyprian, during his absence, trustee of his charities, and a 'quiet soberminded man' by name Felicissimus[1]. These were dragged thither by the multitude. Regular committals soon swelled the number. Women and even lads were imprisoned[2], who had met with equal defiance the threats and the kindly persuasions of the magistrates[3]. They declined to taste the sacrificial victim, or sprinkle the incense, or to put on the liturgic veil. Two terrible cells were assigned to them where hunger, thirst and intense heat soon did their work[4]. After a short time fifteen persons had perished there, of whom four were women, besides one in the quarry, and two under torture. Mappalicus[5] was one of the latter. His limbs and sides streaming from repeated blows of the torture-claw, he said to the proconsul as he was remanded to the cell, 'To-morrow you shall see a contest indeed.' Next day he was tortured again and died.

April 17, A.D. 250.

Some scenes were yet more dreadful. Maidens were not spared the Lupanaria[6]. Subordinates were allowed to invent new tortures[7]. Numidicus[8], a presbyter of the neighbourhood, prepared many for death, and then with his wife was tortured

---

[1] *Ep.* 6. 4; *Epp.* 7, 41, 42, 43. See Pearson *Ann. Cypr.* A.D. 250 s. vi. as to the Roman Martyrologies and Baronius following Bede's error in making Rogatian and Felicissimus Martyrs and assigning a day for their martyrdom, whereas their living example is the point of Cyprian's address.

[2] *Ep.* 6. 3.

[3] Blanditiæ.. voce libera. *Ep.* 10. 1, 2.

[4] *Ep.* 22. 2.

[5] *Ep.* 10. 2. xv Kal. Mai commemorates Mappalicus in Martyrol. African. Morcelli, *op. cit.* II. p. 365, and the date suits this letter.

[6] *De Mortalitate* 15.

[7] *Ad Demetrian.* 12.

[8] *Ep.* 40.

by fire. The wife was actually burnt alive, and he was left for dead, a shower of stones having been hurled upon him at the stake. His daughter found him breathing still; he was revived, and afterwards enrolled in the presbyterate of the capital.

Many were after double torture dismissed, some into banishment[1], some to bear the brand for life, as a second 'seal in their foreheads[2],' some to resume former occupations, beggared of all they possessed. Some quailed and fell, who on second thoughts returned to avow their faith, forfeit their all, and undergo their torture[3]. Bona[4] was dragged by her husband to the altar, there to justify her reappearance from abroad; but exclaiming 'The act is not mine but yours' as the incense fell from her hand, she was exiled again. No martyrs were more honoured than Castus and Æmilius, who for such recantation were burnt to death[5].

May 22, A.D. 250.

The devouring passion for martyrdom was still in the future, yet already survivors envied 'The Crowned.' The fervid temperament of Africa was aflame. Rhetoric apostrophised 'The Happy Prison! Gloom more brilliant than the Sun himself[6]!' yet even such rhetoric seems colder to us than the everyday terms of their common speech which called every such death a 'Confession in blossom,' a 'Purple Confession[7].'

Still at the very summit of their enthusiasm their leader never suffered them to forget that enthusiasm was not the solid height itself but only a glory which bathed it. 'He that 'speaketh the things that make for peace and are good and

---

[1] *Epp.* 14. 21.
[2] Pont. *Vit.* 7 '...tot confessores frontium notatarum secunda inscriptione signatos et ad exemplum martyrii superstites reservatos...'
[3] *Ep.* 24.
[4] *Ep.* 24.
[5] *De Lapsis* 13, see Augustine's sermon cclxxxv. on their day. This was May 22, Morcelli, vol. II. p. 368.
[6] *Ep.* 6. 1.
[7] ...in tam florida confessione *Ep.* 21. 1; floridiores (*i.e.* martyres)...floridiorum ministerium, 21. 3. Rutilorum, *Ep.* 42.

'just, according to the bidding of Christ, he it is who is the 'daily Confessor of Christ¹.'

But how great a step had been gained in human thought and feeling when numbers of delicate and educated persons surrendered all that made life beautiful or even tolerable and accepted all that was hideous and unendurable, simply because immortality had become a certainty, and the revelation of God's character and Christ's presence a reality amid a world of scepticism and vice.

The Persecution at Carthage.—2. *The* 'LAPSI.'

Nevertheless, where these sober truths rose into passionate sentiment there also the sensibilities to suffering and to ridicule were equally high-strung. Nor had the recent life of the Church been so rigorous or disciplined as to make constancy under trial characteristic of its masses. Yet Cyprian, in spite of long forebodings of what under such circumstances would be the result of the worldly habits of the bishops and the gentile associations and extravagance of the laity, was not prepared for the first spectacle upon the arrival of the edict. Even he was appalled at the rush of faithless Christians to the Capitol² or to the Forum to sacrifice amid the jeers of the populace; their unwillingness to be deferred till morning, when darkness closed upon their throng, their piteous production of children and newly-baptized infants to drop incense from their small fingers. Most of the clergy

---

¹ *Ep.* 13. 5.
² *De Laps.* 8, cf. *Ep.* 59. 13. The Byrsa or Bozrah. So elsewhere in municipia the 'Idolum Capitolii' is a recognised term. See Council of Elvira, canon 59, and Hefele (*H. d. Concil.* ed. De_arc, vol. I. pp. 159, 160) upon it. At Cologne the old Capitol is still so called.

Compare with the scenes just touched by Cyprian the painfully graphic narrative of Alexandrian events by Dionysius. Eus. *H. E.* vi. 41.

fled[1], some lapsed[2]; there remained in the city scarce enough to carry on the daily duty[3]. Many provincial bishops fled to Rome[4]. One at least, Repostus of Tuburnuc, carried the main part of his flock back to paganism[5].

Even in Rome there were fears at one moment lest 'the 'brotherhood should be completely rooted out by this head-'long return to idolatry[6].' Although it may or may not be a literal statement that the lapsed at Carthage were 'the majority of the flock[7],' yet their Bishop may well have felt 'like one sitting amid the ruins of his house.'

Thus were being formed the vast classes of 'the Incensers' and 'the Sacrificers[8],' whose self-excision from the body of Christ was palpable. The act of the latter class was held the more odious whether from the fuller ceremonial, or from the material pollution ascribed to the victim's flesh. Yet greater perplexity resulted from the conduct of others who, although not stronger to confess their faith, were less bold to abjure it. The constitution of the courts which had to enforce uniformity, and the number of inferior officials employed in a service which attempted to deal with individual beliefs, opened a door to any evasions which friendship, favour, or cupidity could devise. As in the days of Trajan, the approved form of profession was still to take part in sacrifice, but it was possible also to tender allegiance in writing[9]. The name of one who 'professed' in this

---

[1] *Ep.* 34. 4.
[2] *Ep.* 40.
[3] *Ep.* 29.
[4] *Ep.* 30. 8.
[5] *Ep.* 59. 10. Tuburnuc was a small municipium and Hot-Wells, about 12 miles south of the Gulf of Tunis, or 22 from Carthage. Tissot II. 780 (by inadvertence?) makes this see one of 'emplacement inconnu,' but in pl. viii. marks the place, which is no doubt the see. In Numidia was a Θουβούρνικα κολωνία (Ptol.), an *oppidum civium Romanorum* (Plin.), (*Corp. Inscrr. Latt.* VIII. 1, p. 121). G. Wilmanns assigns the bishops 'Tuburnicenses' of A.D. 411 and 646 to the latter. Morcelli, vol. I. p. 333, gives them to the former. One would naturally place Cyprian's Repostus nearer to him. No trace remains of any place answering to Hartel's Sutunurcensis, or the readings Suturnucensis, Quoturnicensis, Sutun-urcensis, Utunurcensis.
[6] *Ep.* 8. 2.
[7] *Epp.* 11. 1; 14. 1.
[8] Thurificati, Sacrificati.
[9] See below the note on the LIBELLI.

form was subscribed either to a renunciation of Christianity, or to a denial of that crime, or else to a statement of having recently or habitually attended sacrifice, and sometimes (unless Augustine[1] has fallen into an unlikely error) to a mere declaration of readiness to comply. This document was delivered to a magistrate, entered on the Acta, and finally published in the Forum.

In the persecution of Diocletian timid Christians were sometimes represented at the altar by a slave[2] or by a heathen friend; sometimes attendants connived at their slipping past the altars without actually making the oblation[3]. It would seem that in the Decian persecution too a proxy[4] sometimes performed the act which the accused afterwards claimed as his own; while in heartrending cases, which came later to light, the heads of families often dechristianized themselves to deliver wife, children and dependants from beggary and torture[5].

Venal or kindly fraud provided further a different security from molestation. Certificates at high rates of payment were offered and almost thrust on persons who believed themselves, after a private avowal of their faith, to be simply purchasing exemption from the obligation to conform. This is a species of confiscation and has seldom given offence[6]; but it is evident, from the endeavours of Cyprian to awaken penitence on account of them, that the contents of these certificates or 'libels' were not unobjectionable. Indeed it is impossible that they can have sanctioned exemption without some grounds being alleged. Nor can those grounds have been any other than that the certifying

---

[1] Aug. de Bapt. c. Donatt. iv. 4 (6).
[2] Petr. Alex. c. 6, 7. The slave, if a Christian, received in such a case one year's penance and his master three. Routh, Rel. S. vol. iv. pp. 29, 30.
[3] Petr. Alex. Can. 5. For this offence the penance was of six months, Routh, op. cit. p. 28.
[4] See note on Libelli, p. 82.
[5] Ep. 55. 13. Tert. de fug. 5, 12, 13.
[6] On the Montanist view, however, see Tillemont, Notes sur la Persécut. de Dèce, n. iii., vol. III. p. 702.

magistrate had satisfied himself of the sound paganism of the recipient.

The unworthiness of these transactions must not mislead us into conceiving that Christian truth had little hold upon those who were concerned in them[1]. 'Parliamentary certificates' of conformity were in our strictest age given and received by the strictest Puritans and churchmen without any pretext of fact. Intense devotion to formal truth has to the southern and eastern temperament seemed often not inconsistent with insensibility to fine veracity. To detect that lurking source of so much false doctrine and false practice was a part of Cyprian's moral office, and he speaks of the tears of sorrow and surprise with which many first recognised the gravity of the fault. Even Peter of Alexandria, in the midst of similar displeasure with the Lapsed under Diocletian, cannot forbear, before he passes on to place the sin in its true light, to glance at its aspect as a mockery of heathen power; calling his flock 'clever, designing children befooling dull ones.' When we are treating of Africans or Romans in the third century we cannot infer that there was no truth of conviction because we find that conviction was dissembled. To them the system came so naturally, that when enquiries began it was found that the numbers of these 'Libellatics' or certificated persons with whom Cyprian himself had to deal amounted to some thousands[2].

On the Form and Contents of the Libelli.

I have in the text presented a correct account, I believe, of the various ways in which the vast class of Libellatici arose. The difficulties raised by various authors have arisen from their assuming that the Libelli were all of one kind, or that there could be any systematic and regular procedure for the evasion of procedure[3].

---

[1] *De Laps.* 27.
[2] *Ep.* 20. 2.
[3] Tillemont (vol. III. p. 702) alone perceived there might be *two* ways. 'Peut-estre que l'on faisait et l'un et l'autre.' Dom Maran thought the distinction was only whether persons had been present or not at the registering of their names. *Vit. Cypr.* vi. Rigalt (ap. Fell, *Ep.* 30) that the libelli were declara-

On the contrary, every conceivable means would of course be adopted. Accounts are not irreconcilable; they only describe different things. Cyprian's language is accurate to technicality in the use of professional terms.

I. (1) The libellus which the suspected men tendered is clearly characterized in *De Laps.* 27, 'et illa *professio* est denegantis, *contestatio* est christiani quod fuerat[1] abnuentis.' In *Ep.* 30. 3 '*Professio libellorum*' is again the *exhibition* or *putting in* of such statements. *Profiteri* is elsewhere the technical term, 'Christi negationem *scriptam profiteri*' Act. SS. *Agapes, Chionae, Irenes*, &c., Ruinart, *Acta Mart.*, Ratisb. 1859, pp. 424—5[2]. Again, *contestatio* means the plea or statement of his own case made by either party to a suit; it answers to the διωμοσία of the Athenian Courts; the Roman clergy correctly argue in *Ep.* 30. 3, that although a man may not have approached the altar, he must take the consequences (*tenetur*) if he has put in a *legal affirmation* (*contestatus sit*) *that he had done so*.

In the above passages a Libellus is plainly a document emanating from the recanting Christian. Such persons are in *Peter of Alexandria* (Can. v.) described as giving a libellus, χειρογραφήσαντες. The nature of the contents of it is indicated in the passage of the *De Lapsis* 27, 'He has declared himself to have done whatever evil another actually did' (*faciendo commisit*), which implies a representative in the sacrificial act.

The offence of the Bishop Martial (*Ep.* 67. 6) who was 'stained with the libellus of idolatry,' is explained by the use of the word *contestatus*. In the public proceedings before the Ducenary Procurator (actis publice habitis apud D. P.) he had appeared, and put in a declaration that he had denied Christ and adopted a heathen cultus. He is not accused of having ever actually sacrificed, and the libelli of others, as Augustine says, contained only a declaration of readiness to do so.

(2) A second class (*sed etiam*) are spoken of by Novatian and the Roman clergy in *Ep.* 30. 3 as having virtually 'given acknowledgments, quittances or discharges[3]' (accepta fecissent), though not

---

tions either of heathenism or of Christianity, but tendered (the latter with bribes) only by the people, and not given by magistrates: Fechtrup that they were magisterial certificates only. Fechtrup's special pleading is matched by his inscience of every technical law term, pp. 66—76.

[1] This peculiar phrase occurs again *ad Demetr.* 13, 'id quod prius fueram.'

[2] So Aug. *de Bapt. c. Donatt.* iv.

4 (6) '...se thurificaturos *professi erant.*'

[3] *Accepta fecissent* is apparently the best authenticated reading. *Accepta facere* is a common term (Dirksen, *Manuale, s.v.* accepto acceptum). But the other reading, *acta facere*, which Neander adopts, is equally possible here in meaning. It is 'to put in a plea in a legal process.' 'Inter quem et creditorem acta facta sunt.' Scævola ap. Forcellini.

present in person (cum fierent). They had put in a *legal* appearance (...*præsentiam suam...fecissent*) by commissioning a proxy to register their names on the magistrates' list of conformity (*ut sic scriberentur mandando*). Novatian argues that as one who orders a crime is responsible for it, so one who sanctions (consensu) the reading in public (publice legitur) of an untrue statement about himself is liable to be proceeded against as if it were true.

II. The other kind of *libellus* which emanated not from the renegade but from the magistrate is described with equal precision.

In the letter to Antonian (*Ep.* 55. 14) Cyprian says some of the Libellatici had received (*acceptus*) such a libellus. An opportunity for obtaining one had presented itself unsought (*occasio libelli oblata...ostensa*), and they had in person or by deputy (*mandavi*) gone to a magistrate, informed him that they were Christians and paid a sum to be exempted from sacrificing. But as no magistrate could issue an order simply staying the execution of an edict, his certificate must have contained a statement of the satisfactory paganism of the holder. This is why Cyprian tries to awaken their consciences, while they themselves were disposed to plead that they had avowed their religion and that the form of the document was the magistrate's affair.

Again, in the *Ad Fortunatum* c. 11 Christians are urged if a libellus is offered them (*libelli...oblata sibi occasione*) not to embrace the gift (*decipientium malum munus*), by the example of Eleazar who refused the facilities offered him by the officers (*a ministris regis facultas offerretur*) for eating lawful flesh as a make-believe for swine's flesh. The official connivance in each case would have enabled them to seem to do what they did not. The *libellus* is here something offered and is a *munus*.

Nothing is more clear than that the *libel* included two kinds of documents. Whether any document was issued in cases of registration is not clear, but all three sorts of persons are included in the name Libellatici. [See *Appendix*, p. 541.]

IV.

The Retirement of Cyprian.

While these scenes were passing Cyprian was away from the city. He had left it before the end of the month of January[1]; so suddenly that Caldonius writes to him as if unaware of his departure[2]. The place of his retreat is un-

---

[1] Lipsius, *op. cit.* p. 200. [2] *Ep.* 24.

known¹. He made over part of his still large property to one of the presbyters Rogatian, for the use of the sufferers, forwarding further instalments to him as need arose². The populace sought for him with cries of 'Cyprian to the Lions,' and the government published a Proscription of him and of his trustees³.

Dec. A.D. 249, Jan. A.D. 250.

Nothing in his career is more remarkable than the calm decision with which he took a step which to many would seem questionable, and which his 'Master' had beforehand branded⁴ with disapproval. His own rational view that a course sanctioned by Christ was legitimate,—was for some men a duty, the neglect of which aggravated the guilt of any subsequent wavering⁵,—was not the only consideration which determined his action. Clerics engaged daily in ministrations, spiritual and corporeal, were not free to depart, such absentees had forsaken their special calling. The absent bishop reserved their restoration, upon their returning, for the decision of the whole plebes, and suspended during the interval their 'monthly dividend⁶.' So wide was the line which, like a true statesman, he inevitably and unshrinkingly drew between their functions and his own. The presence of the bishop on any one spot was infinitely less important than uninterrupted government. It was not the martyrdom of a saint which was in question but the maintenance of rule. Some years later, when his death seemed to him likely to be at last more

---

¹ Pearson and Tillemont in giving him Victor the Deacon for a companion must rely on the spurious close of *Ep.* 13, which is given only in Rigalt's 'codex remensis,' yet taken into the text by Baluze, and on *Ep.* 5, where the name is spurious, omitted by Hartel.

The scientific construction of history without evidence is illustrated by O. Ritschl's statement that the place must have been known to the magistrates, or easily discoverable because his correspondence was large.

² *Ep.* 7.
³ *Epp.* 66. 4; 59. 6; Pont. *Vit.* 7.
⁴ Tertull. *de Fuga in Persecutione.*
⁵ *De Laps.* 10. The words 'Dominus in persecutione secedere et fugere mandavit' referring to Matth. x. 23 shew that it is not necessary to interpret *Ep.* 16. 4 '...Dominus, qui ut secederem jussit' of 'visions, &c.' rather than of Scripture.
⁶ *Ep.* 34. 4.

useful than his energies, he remained, against all solicitations, to die among his people. And gladly now would he have braved danger in the activity of the presbyterate 'if the conditions of his place and degree had permitted[1].' But his presence in Carthage would have attracted danger upon others[2]; would have provoked riots in the aroused state of heathen feeling[3]. Tertullus[4], the devotee of prisoners and martyrs, was himself the prime mover[5] and most strenuous advocate of the concealment of Cyprian. Yet such a charm invests even the most rash exposure of life, that there possibly will never be wanting suggestions that the first duty of Cyprian's life was to throw it away. Leaving fanaticism however to its doubts, and scepticism to its sneers on this particular, we pass to the use he made of that life. His pre-eminent work sprang into light before him. Instantly we find him blending a life of devotion and eucharist[6] with intensest and widest activity. We find him not only swaying and sustaining the Church of Carthage; he forms and guides the policy of the West. Repelling a singular aggression of the Roman clergy, he suggests to Rome the measures of the Church. The faith and polity of the Church are menaced simultaneously by the two worst dangers: by Indifferentism bidding for popular support with newly invented indulgences and saintly merits, and by Puritanism armed with specious ideals. To the victorious[7] firmness and sweet persuasiveness of Cyprian it was due that in his age Christianity did not melt into an ethnic religion or freeze into a sect.

[1] *Ep.* 12. 1; cf. *Epp.* 5. 1; 6. 1.
[2] *Epp.* 7; 14. 1.
[3] *Ep.* 43. 4.
[4] *Ep.* 12. 2.
[5] *Ep.* 14. 1.
[6] *Ep.* 12. 2 '...et celebrentur hic a nobis oblationes et sacrificia ob commemorationes eorum.' A painful incident of one of his communions is related *De Laps.* 25, see p. 108 infr.
[7] 'Victoriosissimus Cyprianus,' Aug.

V.

Interference of the Church of Rome.

We must pursue these lines in detail. Immediately upon his retirement the Roman presbyters and deacons, then holding the administration of their see[1] in commission during its vacancy, despatched two letters to Carthage, one detailing to Cyprian himself very fully the glorious martyrdom of their own bishop, and evidently pointing hints from his example[2]; the other exhorting Cyprian's clergy to supply by their devotion the void created by the fugitive[3]. 'The unfaithful 'shepherds of Ezekiel and the hireling shepherd of the Gospel, 'the Good Shepherd Himself and the faithful pastorate of 'Peter must be their warning and their pattern. They them-'selves at Rome have reaped the reward of not deserting the 'brotherhood, in the general fidelity of their Church in spite 'of the lapse of some eminent and timorous persons.' This, after the remark that Cyprian's clergy justified his absence as being an 'eminent person,' persecution impending[4]. Such a sarcasm might perhaps have seemed intelligible had it followed the return of their own envoy, sent with the news of Fabian's martyrdom to Cyprian, and bringing back the startling news of his disappearance. Ultramontane ingenuity has indeed so narrated the facts[5]. But it was Carthage which had communicated both fact and justification, and unfortunately the two Roman letters were sent together by the same hand, nor can the former, which has not survived,

Jan. 20, A.D. 250.

---

[1] Cf. *Ep.* 14. 2 '...gerenda ea quæ administratio religiosa deposcit.'

[2] *Ep.* 9. 1.

[3] This is *Ep.* 8. That on Fabian is lost.

[4] N. Marshall (London, 1717) correctly 'hath retired for a certain reason, wherein you seem to think he hath acted well and rightly, as being a distinguished person, and standing as such the more exposed.' *Ep.* 8. 1. Hartel spoils the sense by his comma before 'certa ex causa.'

[5] Freppel, p. 174. Full of admiration of his Church's 'traditions of vigilance and universal solicitude' he magnanimously sympathises with Cyprian's sensitiveness to what might have seemed 'an indirect censure.'

have been less wounding than the latter. Cyprian responds however with fervour to the eulogy on Fabian, but returns to them their other letter with a dignified hope that it may prove to be a forgery, since it lacks both authentication and address, and surprises him equally by its matter, its style and even the paper it was written on[1]. It is indeed a singular document. We might have wished to share Cyprian's suspicion, did not a later letter of his shew that his delicate doubt was but a criticism of the missive[2]. It is, when printed according to the genuine text, a remarkable illustration of what has been often pointed out, the deficiency of the Church of Rome at that period in literary cultivation. The inelegance of its style and the incorrectness of its constructions and forms of words place it by the side of the four other epistles[3] which emanate from less cultivated persons, and distinguish these from all the rest of the correspondence. No further caustic criticism was provoked. He had awakened them to the sense of his position and their own. Their answer gave him full assurance of support, and with a vigorous letter from the Roman to the Carthaginian Confessors[4], came opportunely and helpfully. Their third Epistle was from the strong, clear, pedantically clear, pen of Novatian[5] and was sent after a consultation with 'Bishops Present' as they were called—neighbouring bishops and bishops then in Rome on

---

[1] *Ep.* 9. 2.

[2] In *Ep.* 20. 3 he calls it plainly 'vestra scripta' and quotes a passage from it with a slight improvement in the wording. Fechtrup (p. 47) ponderously thinks he had made and now detected the mistake.

[3] *Epp.* 21—24. The errors are not due to the inaccuracy but to the correctness of the text, which elsewhere exhibits no such phenomena. See Hartel's Preface, p. xlviii. Does *chartæ ipsæ* in *Ep.* 9. 2 further indicate the poverty of the scribe? One would gladly learn what honour was covertly intended for the Church of Rome by this composition, upon the theory that the whole Cyprianic correspondence was forged in her interest.

[4] These two crossed his *Ep.* 20, see *Ep.* 27. 4, and are lost like that on Fabian. The principal contents of the former are given in *Ep.* 30. 3, and it was widely circulated with two of Cyprian's. Their letter to Sicily (*Ep.* 30. 5) is also lost (see p. 95).

[5] *Ep.* 30; compare *Ep.* 55. 5. On Novatian's style see p. 122 and note.

account of the persecution or other causes, for before it was written they had learnt how much they and the Church owed to Cyprian's preservation. It is possible too that the need for seclusion which Novatian[1] felt in his own case, as we shall see, had something to do with the change or at least the suppression of opinion from Rome on this subject, so soon as Novatian became their scribe.

Their last letter also penned by Novatian is in thorough accord with the vigorous steps which, as we shall see, Cyprian took and proposed to take as difficulties developed[2].

VI.

The Lapsed and the Martyrs.

For in the meantime mightier issues had blazed out. The merit of confessorship and the remorse of the lapsed had come face to face, and the conception had been entertained that the faithful might mediate for the fallen. Even in Tertullian's time certain penitents had by their intercession procured restoration to communion for others. He intimates a doubt of the validity[3] of this system in his earliest work, while apparently implying that it was of no long standing; but as a Montanist, however exaggerated his language, he shews that it had become more common under the patronage of the contemporary bishop whom he attacks[4].

Now, however, the question was no longer one of the dispensation of private sin. No contrast could be stronger than that between the Confessors and the Lapsed, and it was exhibited on a great scale. The sufferers were not only

---

[1] See pp. 121, 122.
[2] *Ep.* 36; see p. 122, n. 3.
[3] *Ad Mart.* 1. Note the words *quidam* and *si forte*.
[4] Jam et in martyras *tuos effundis* hanc potestatem. *De Pudic.* c. 22.

faithful to the Church, they were saving its existence[1], and at the same time demonstrating that the attractions and the terrors of heathenism were not powerful enough to hold the world. Gratitude to them knew no bounds. Ministers to their wants flocked to the prisons[2]. Men prayed all night upon the earth that they might themselves be captured so as to attend on those[3] who had been tortured. 'The Offering' was made regularly in their cells. From his retirement Cyprian has to recommend less demonstrative sympathy[4], and to enjoin that only one presbyter with one deacon should perform that service, and that these should so succeed one another as not to cause the constant attendance of any to be remarked. Every death among them was communicated to him that he might 'celebrate the oblations and sacrifices' of commemoration, and was calendared for future observance[5].

At Rome the martyred Fabian himself had made the compilation of such registers a duty of the subdeacons with their clerks[6]. A few years later began under Gregory Thaumaturgus the substitution for pagan feasts of wakes over the martyred remains which he conveyed to various localities[7].

Thus everywhere the veneration for the martyrs rose in proportion to the magnitude of the interests at stake. Cyprian

---

[1] *Ep.* 37. 4 '...nutantem multorum fidem martyrii vestri veritate solidastis.'

[2] *Ep.* 5. 2.

[3] The only intelligible sense I can give to *Ep.* 21. 3.

[4] Hefele suggests that some of the calumnies against Cæcilian arose from his requiring similar prudence. *H. des Conciles* (ed. Delarc) vol. I. p. 172.

[5] *Ep.* 12. 2. From the recitation of their names in the list or canon arose the term 'canonize.' Cæcilian, A.D. 312, rebukes Lucilla's veneration for a relic of a martyr, '...et si martyris, sed necdum *vindicati*,' *not yet acknowledged*. Opt. i. 16. The delay necessary for such enrolment is a probable explanation (as has been already observed) of the title *Martyr* being added, though not much later, to the epigraph of Fabian, about whose martyrdom there can be no question; see pp. 65, 66 and notes.

[6] 'Notarii,' *Felician Catalogue* (Lipsius, *op. cit.* p. 275). Cf. Pearson, *Minor Theolog. Works*, vol. II. pp. 314, 315.

[7] Greg. Nyss. *Opp.* t. III. p. 574, ed. Morell.

himself, who was not without some apprehension of the coming mischief; who had written so wisely, 'He who 'speaketh things peaceful and kind and righteous after the 'precept of Christ, is every day a Confessor of Christ'; who elsewhere so invariably softens Tertullian's rhetoric, himself now exaggerates it even to bad taste[1] in addressing the confessors.

A significant change had taken place even in the common use of terms. Only seventy years before this the sufferers of Lyons and Vienne had, in their last prison, after their last contests with the wild beasts, sharply reproved the application to themselves of the name of Martyr, ascribing it to those alone who had followed to the death 'the Faithful and True Martyr' of the Apocalypse[2]. At the end of the second century we have indeed a fragment from one who styles himself 'Aurelius Cyrenius Martyr[3]'; whom, if we rightly understand him, the men of Lyons would have disowned. But Tertullian early addressed imprisoned Christians only as 'martyrs designate[4]' and seems much later to repudiate and ridicule the growing fashion by his question, 'What martyr is 'a dweller in this world, a petitioner for pence, a victim to 'doctor and money-lender[5]?' But now Cyprian uses it freely of all who are in prisons or in mines[6], while 'Confessor,' once reserved for those awaiting death, is applied to any sufferer, and even flight is honoured as a 'private confession[7].'

The captives were in Cyprian's eyes 'the friends of the Lord, who would sit with Him in judgment,' whose intercessions already avail[8] in the unseen world. But the faction

---

[1] Although allowance must be made for the then freshness of metaphors now trite, I cannot share Freppel's transport at *Ep.* 10, '...ce langage tout frémissant de poésie lyrique.'
[2] Euseb. *H. E.* v. 2.
[3] Routh, *Rell. Sac.* I. p. 451.
[4] *Ad Martt.* 1.
[5] *De Pudicit.* 22. I am unable to adopt the common explanation of this savage passage.
[6] *Epp.* 15. 1; 76. 6.
[7] *De Laps.* 3.
[8] ...prærogativa eorum adjuvari *apud Deum* possunt (*Ep.* 18. 1); ...adjuvari *apud Dominum* in delictis suis possunt (*Ep.* 19. 2). Rettberg, who belongs to that class of historians which thinks in-

which had at all times been unfriendly to him attributed to them such spiritual supremacy on earth as threatened to disorganize the whole fabric of the Church.

Among the Lapsed there had at once set in a violent revulsion, a passionate desire to recover or to reassert their place in the forsaken Church. Some reappeared at the tribunals, and received sentence of exile[1]; some, like Castus and Æmilius, of torture and death; some, like the sisters of Celerinus, dedicated themselves to the service of the confessors[2]; others entered unmurmuringly on penance of indefinite duration[3]. Unhappily most preferred to rely on a vicarious and imputed merit. At first a letter from a 'martyr' to a bishop prayed only that the case of a fallen friend might after the restoration of peace be examined into; a due period of penitence and the imposition of hands being understood to be at least as necessary as after other open falls. Some, like the torn and tortured Saturninus, forebore even this petition. Mappalicus in dying requested it only for his sister and mother[4].

But the factious presbyters, who in the simplicity and devotion of these men saw so promising a weapon against the absent bishop, ventured now to anticipate not such enquiry only, but even the death of the martyr which alone could have given validity to his appeal[5]. Upon the strength of papers signed by still living confessors they 'offered the names[6]' of lapsed persons at the Eucharist as of duly restored penitents and gave them communion[7]. Then these Libels began to be carelessly drawn: they sometimes specified only

---

sight consists in the ascription of low motives to great minds, sees in this language the bidding for support against the factious clergy.

[1] *Ep.* 24.
[2] *Ep.* 21. 3, 4.
[3] *Ep.* 56. 2.
[4] *Ep.* 27. 1.

[5] *Ep.* 16. 3.
[6] On *Nomen offerre* see the correct though not very lucid remarks of L'Aubespine, *Observatt. Eccles.* L. I. § vii. (1623), reprinted in his edition of Optatus, 1679. (Prieur's Optatus, 1676, p. 21.)
[7] *Ep.* 34. 1. Cf. *Ep.* 15. 1.

one of a group to whom they were granted, 'Allow such an one *and his family* to communicate[1].' They were issued in the name of a dead confessor, of a confessor too illiterate to write[2]; issued so copiously[3], that some thousands were believed to be circulating in Africa, and the very sale of them was not beyond suspicion[4]. The chief author of this issue was Lucian, the old friend of Celerinus, but very unlike him, says Cyprian, in delicacy of feeling though an honest man, and 'scantily versed in the literature of the Lord[5].' Lucian had been charged, as he announced[6], by a revered confessor Paul before his death in prison to bestow 'Peace' in his name on whoever asked it, and he did so with only the proviso, that the recipient should, when the persecution ended, present himself to his bishop and confess his lapse. He used similarly the name of Aurelius. When remonstrated with by Cyprian, he seems to have replied almost at once by promulgating in the name of 'All Confessors[7]' an indulgence to 'All Lapsed,' and desiring Cyprian himself to communicate this to the provincial bishops. A condition was annexed, seemingly meant for a concession, that they should satisfy their bishop as to their conduct since their fall. This extraordinary document is extant[8].

Cyprian regarded it as an outrage on discipline[9]. The Roman presbyters exposed its inconsistencies, but partly excused it as shewing a desire to escape from their false

---

[1] 'Communicet ille cum suis,' *Ep.* 15. 4.

[2] *Ep.* 27. 1. On this ground Lucian justified his use of the name of Aurelius, 'quod literas non *nosset*'; yet it can scarcely have been true in his case, since Aurelius was immediately after ordained Lector by Cyprian. *Ep.* 38. 1.

[3] ...gregatim...passim... *Ep.* 27. 1.

[4] *Ep.* 20. 2. *Ep.* 15. 3.

[5] *Ep.* 27. 3 '...circa intellegentiam dominicæ lectionis.'

[6] *Ep.* 22. 2.

[7] Compare ἀσπάζεται ὑμᾶς χορὸς ἅπας ὁμοῦ μαρτύρων at end of cent. iii. Lucian, ap. Routh, *R. S.* vol. IV. p. 5.

[8] *Ep.* 23.

[9] ...quasi moderatius aliquid et temperantius fieret...epistolam scripsit qua pæne omne vinculum fidei...et evangelii sanctitas et firmitas solveretur. *Ep.* 27. 2.

position by throwing the final responsibility on their bishop—which is not an unfair view[1].

It may for a moment be worth our while to glance at the modern ultramontane explanation of this step. 'Their 'imprudent charity' says Freppel 'had *forgotten* that *In-* '*dulgences have for their object to supplement the insufficiency* '*of works of satisfaction,* but not to replace them.' How was it then that not only Cyprian, but his supposed directors, the Roman presbyters, left after all the definition of an Indulgence so incomplete?—No stronger refutation of ultramontanism exists than its attempts to write history.

The Lapsed and the Presbyters who encouraged them soon despised the condition that they should satisfy the bishops[2]; but beyond the direct evils of the confessors' action lay the unpopularity[3] which it ensured for the bishops, if they did their duty. They must presently be seen rejecting wholesale both penitents and martyrs. Discipline was violated, but harmony too and reverence and affection would have no place under the random domination of merits. It is not surprising that in some of the provincial towns there was something like actual riot[4], and that the Lapsed extorted communion from the weaker presbyters by force.

From the Cyprianic correspondence it would seem that these disorders did not exist at Rome. This was no doubt due at least in part to the powerful influence of Novatian in the exactly contrary direction over the confessors whom he commends for maintaining 'Evangelical discipline[5]' and

---

[1] ...quia a multis urguebantur, dum ad episcopum illos remittunt, &c. *Ep.* 36. 2. Fechtrup and Ritschl take 'optamus te cum sanctis martyribus pacem habere,' *Ep.* 23, as a threatening. The confessors were too literal so to write. So also it is impossible to credit them with parodying the usual forms in the attestation clause 'præsente de clero et exorcista et lectore.'

[2] *Ep.* 35.

[3] Invidia, *Epp.* 15. 4; 27. 2.

[4] ...impetus per multitudinem, *Ep.* 27. 3.

[5] *Ep.* 30. 4.

who at first adhered to him rather than to the milder Cornelius. These clergy sympathize with Africa and evidently with Sicily[1], and deplore the revolt not only there but in 'nearly all the world,' but of themselves they state 'we seem so far to have escaped the disorders of the times[2].' The vacancy of their See was an adequate reason both for postponement and for patience. It was prudently employed, and, as a rule, sensibly accepted. Celerinus was the exception[3]. Cyprian's correspondents among the Roman confessors take Cyprian's view, urge humility on the Carthaginian martyrs, and at last go beyond him in strictness[4].

VII.

The Cyprianic Scheme for Restorative Discipline.

For Cyprian had lost no time. A distinct policy had become essential. The temper of the Lapsed, the increasing dangers which it threatened, the fitness of conciliating the martyrs[5], and the approach of the feverous malarious autumn of the old world city or the stagnant offensive water of the Lake of Tunis[6], would brook no delay on the part of the

---

[1] This seems to be the first mention of a Christian Church in that island. *Ep.* 30. 5.

[2] *Ep.* 30. 5, 6. Under Diocletian's persecution the Roman church was not exempt. A page of unwritten history is indicated in the epitaphs of Damasus upon the popes Marcellus and Eusebius. He borrows the sentiments and words of Cyprian to express the similar rebellion. Dam. *Carm. xi. De S. Marcello Martyre*, 'Veridicus Rector *lapsos quia crimina flere Prædixit* miseris fuit omnibus hostis amarus Hinc furor, hinc odium...' *Carm. xii. De S. Eusebio Papa*, 'Heraclius *vetuit lapsos peccata dolere:* Eusebius *miseros* docuit *sua crimina flere*. Scinditur in partes vulgus...' Even blood was shed, he proceeds.

See de Rossi, *Inscrr. Christ.* II. p. 66, 102—3, 138; also *R. S.* II. p. 201. Migne, *Patr. Lat.* XIII. cc. 384, 385. Peter Alex. Can. 5, speaks of confessors giving remission to the Lapsed under the persecution of Diocletian, but in a mild form, and he appoints them a penance notwithstanding.

[3] *Ep.* 21. 3.

[4] *Epp.* 27, 31, 32.

[5] Notes 3 and 4 on p. 94.

[6] *Ep.* 18. 1 'jam æstatem cœpisse, tempus infirmitatibus assiduis et gravibus infestatum...' Κυνὸς δ' ἦν ἐπιτολὴ ...ἐπὶ λίμνῃ σταθεροῦ καὶ βαρέος ὕδατος, Appian, *de Rebus Punic.* viii. 99.

church in dealing with the anxious multitudes who besieged her gates. So soon as the Libels appeared he wrote despatches to the confessors at Carthage, to his clergy, and with peculiar warmth and confidence to his laity[1], to Bishops in all directions[2], to a remarkable group of Roman confessors, and to the Roman clergy[3] who were still under the leadership of the able, high-minded and austere Novatian. This man, had he lived in some brief halcyon day when orthodox speculation and asceticism were in the ascendant, might have been a scholastic saint. That, in times of conflict and in the most practical of all cities, some tinge of ambition shot across his higher qualities, made his position false and his memory unenviable. At present however nothing had appeared in him but the clear and somewhat hard decisiveness which, giving point to his nobler characteristics, made him regarded as the possible head of the Roman church, when Fabian's successor should be elected. Moyses, Maximus and their fellow prisoners were as yet earnestly attached to him.

To all whom he now addressed Cyprian proposed one simple method: To reserve the cases of the Lapsed intact, whether the martyrs had given them Letters of Peace or not[4], until councils of bishops, assembling both at Carthage and at Rome[5] on the abatement of persecution, should lay down some general principles of restoration for those who deserved compassion: Then the cases to be heard individually by the bishops with the assistance of their presbyterate, diaconate and 'commons[6]': Full confession without reserve

---

[1] *Epp.* 15, 16, and 17.
[2] *Ep.* 26.
[3] *Epp.* 27 and 28.
[4] *Ep.* 20. 3.
[5] *Epp.* 20. 3; 55. 4.
[6] *Ep.* 17. 4 *Fratribus in plebe consistentibus.* *Ep.* 31. 6 puts in the strongest light the opinions both of Cyprian and of the Roman Confessors as to the part which the Plebes were to have on account of the magnitude of the affair, '*consultis* omnibus Episcopis, Presbyteris, Diaconibus, confessoribus, sed *et ipsis* stantibus *Laicis*, ut in tuis literis et ipse testaris.' *Ep.* 17. 1 '...examinabuntur singula præsentibus et *judicantibus* vobis.' Cf. *Ep.* 30. 5.

to be required in the presence of those most conversant with the circumstances: Readmission to Communion to be given by the imposed hands of the bishop and clerus: Meantime to concede to mercy and to the martyrs thus much—that any lapsed person in danger of death or in serious trouble, *who had been provided with a Libel*, might be readmitted to communion with imposition of hands by any presbyter, or in desperate cases, even by a deacon[1]: until general resolutions shall have been come to, all others, who had not obtained Confessors' Letters, must even in the hour of death be commended to the forgiveness of God without earthly communion and be assisted in their repentance. It was not for the ordinary officers to restore them to communion without directions from the bishop, or recommendation from martyrs. To all it was still open publicly to recant their denial of Christ, and to abide the issue from the heathen authorities. Thus they would be not merely restored but crowned.

The grounds of the course he advised were these:

1. That so general a question should be dealt with upon some general principle not by individual discretion[2].

2. That the Lapsed if restored at once would have fared better than the Constant who had borne the loss of all things.

3. That some regard should be had to the 'prerogative' of confessorship.

These principles he insists upon in his letters and in his pamphlet OF THE LAPSED[3]. The concession to confessors is

---

[1] *Epp.* 18. 1 and 19. 2.

[2] ...non paucorum nec ecclesiæ unius nec unius provinciæ sed totius orbis hæc causa est, *Ep.* 19. 2, cf. *Ep.* 30. 5.

[3] Freppel calls the *De Lapsis* a résumé of the letters:—fairly, but it is of their latest views, for these views gradually alter, as we shall see.

not unnatural[1]. His assurance of the divine acceptance of the unaneled penitent is nobly expressed[2]. 'They that in 'gentleness and lowliness and very penitence shall have per-'severed in good works will not be left destitute of the help 'and aid of the Lord. They too will be cared for by a divine 'healing.'

On the 'Proof' of Roman Confession which is derived from these events.

Some theory of 'development' applied to the principles both of discipline and doctrine is no less essential to the progress (and even to the construction) of ecclesiastical than of civil estates. The misfortune of Rome is not only that her constructiveness has been inconsequent and has incorporated usages subversive of the original theory, but that she does practically repudiate schemes of 'development' erected in her behalf. Her scholars are required to prove her most modern inventions to be primitive. For instance—The word Confession (*exomologesis*) is still so far from bearing a technical sense in Cyprian, that it is applied in the same page (1) to the Song of the Three Children, (2) to the Monody of Daniel, and (3) to the public acknowledgment of apostasy (*de Laps.* 28, 31), as well as (4) in *Testim.* iii. 114 to Confession of sin to God. The word 'Sacerdos' in Cyprian invariably signifies a Bishop. But a judicious limitation of these two terms to the sense of 'sacramental confession' and 'presbyter or priest' yields to the ultramontane mind the product of auricular confession as now used in the church of Rome. Is it not Exomologesis before a Sacerdos?

A similar concatenation is made of (1) Cyprian's argument that 'since even ordinary penitents could be restored only through the imposition of hands by bishop and clergy, after less offences than apostasy, the Lapsed cannot be admitted *more* easily' with (2) his requirement of *exomologesis* from the latter class, and (3) with examples drawn from some tender consciences which had revealed a merely contemplated desertion. From these passages is drawn the inference that Cyprian '*demanded sacramental* confession of *all* the less serious faults' as '*obligatory*' and 'as extending even *to bad thoughts.*'

---

[1] ...cum videretur et honor martyribus habendus, *Ep.* 20. 3. Cf. *Ep.* 18. 1.   [2] *Ep.* 18. 2.

Again, in extreme cases a presbyter 'without waiting for our presence' or 'even a deacon' might on approach of death lay his hand on a penitent who has confessed his lapse, and give him that 'Peace' which the martyrs had requested for him. This simple natural permission is by the ultramontane expanded into the following difficulties: (1) that confession *to* a deacon who was 'not the minister of the sacrament of penance' was 'an act of humility which could not fail to be very meritorious'; (2) that 'as indulgences are conferred apart from the sacrament' so 'at that date apparently deacons had the power to *apply* to the sick such spiritual favour'; (3) this particular 'spiritual favour' is defined to be 'a remission to the moribund of *all the temporal pains* due to their sins,' 'it was what we call *a plenary indulgence accorded in the hour of death*.'

This then is the way to demonstrate the primitive character of confession private, sacramental, obligatory, extending to the thoughts, and favoured with plenary indulgence. This almost incredible juggling is from Freppel's tenth Lecture on S. Cyprian at the Sorbonne, 1863, 4.

Fechtrup notes, p. 83, that *Exomologesis* in Tertullian signifies the whole course and process of public penance; which is no nearer to the Roman Use (see *de Pœnitentia*, c. 9).

VIII.

The adopted policy was Carthaginian not Roman.

The modern Ultramontane ascribes this policy to 'the 'distinguishing wisdom of that church, mother and mistress 'of all others, which indicates to Carthage the only course[1],' and assigns to Cyprian the merit of 'fully adopting this line of conduct.'

The honest Tillemont truthfully wrote 'Cyprian regulates 'in a council the business of the Lapsed, and is followed in it 'by Rome and by the whole church[2].' There is no possibility of doubt as to the origination of the whole policy.

---

[1] Freppel's *S. Cyprien*, pp. 195—215; pp. 235—241.   [2] Vol. IV. *S. Cyprien*, Art. 23.

All that the Roman clergymen have to recommend in their first coarse letter[1] is mere restoration of the Lapsed if sick and penitent: to the rest they offer no prospect but that of exhortation. Conception of the world-wide importance of the crisis, conception of *policy* they have none. There is no suggestion of investigation by the Bishops, of councils or committees, of the assistance of the laity, of modification of discipline in accordance with circumstances, of reservation until quieter times. Yet these are the important lines. Without them the plan is featureless.

And it is Cyprian who step by step develops them all in the three letters seventeenth, eighteenth and nineteenth to the Clergy and People of Carthage. In his twentieth he communicates his views and the action he had already taken, to the Roman clergy. He observes that he has seen their letter[2], 'recommending the restoration of sick penitents,' and agreed with it, 'considering united action very important.' This is the commonplace with which he proceeds to develop his own far greater scheme. Less he could not say in introducing it[3]. As the plainest exposition of it he encloses to them a budget of Thirteen Letters[4] which he had from his retirement despatched to Carthage, containing his successive comments and instructions upon the progress of affairs, and he adds a connected outline of their purport. He repeats his own three observations which had led him to direct that, while others should be deferred till the councils could be held, those who possessed martyrs' Libels should,

---

[1] *Ep.* 8. 3, see above, sect. v.

[2] *Ep.* 20. 3. Meaning *Ep.* 8, identified by the mention of Crementius, &c. The lost one, named in *Ep.* 27. 4, had not yet reached him.

[3] Observe in the same complimentary sentence how he mentions the qualifications, introduced by himself, which made all the difference: *Ep.* 20. 3 '...standum putavi et cum vestra sententia, ne actus noster, qui adunatus esse et consentire circa omnia debet, in aliquo discreparet. *plane cæterorum causas, quamvis libello a martyribus accepto differri mandavi, et in nostram præsentiam reservari, ut cum, pace a Domino nobis data, plures convenire in unum cœperimus,*' &c.

[4] *Ep.* 20. 2. On the Thirteen Letters see note at close of this section.

if in peril of death, be restored by the imposition of hands[1]. He promises the Romans a full share in the future regulation of details[2]. They in their answer, composed by Novatian and read aloud to the rest for their signatures, acknowledge the whole scheme to be entirely Cyprian's, and adopt it with a patronising deference. 'He allows them, say 'they, by virtue of their approval to share his credit, to be 'thought of as "coheirs" in his counsels because they reaffirm 'them[3].' 'Too hasty remedies,' such as they had themselves at first advised, are deprecated; point by point the Carthaginian scheme is restated and adopted. They are only solicitous to point out that in their former letter they had themselves 'lucidly' differenced three classes among the Lapsed. The more plain-spoken Confessors of Rome acknowledged the debt more candidly and less obsequiously[4].

Lastly, in a note to them which relates a new presumption of the 'martyrs' Cyprian adds that, if 'neither his own nor their letters' bring them to their senses, 'we shall act as, according to the gospel, the Lord charged us to act[5].' The Roman clergy in their last letter, also by Novatian's hand, admiringly acknowledge his 'vigour' and enforce with arguments, as he wishes, the action that has so far been taken[6].

---

[1] *Epp.* 17—19.
[2] Ut...communicato etiam vobiscum consilio disponere singula et reformare possimus, *Ep.* 2c. 3.
[3] *Ep.* 30. 1; see *Ep.* 55. 5.
[4] *Ep.* 31. 1, 6, and cf. *Ep.* 27. 4.
[5] *Ep.* 35.
[6] *Ep.* 36, see p. 122. It touches also topics of Cyprian's in *Ep.* 20.

On the Thirteen Epistles of which Cyprian sent copies to the Romans.

In Epistle 20. 2 Cyprian gives *précis* of the contents of these his Thirteen Letters, with some chronological notes, in somewhat of the same way in which Pontius (*Vit.* c. 7) gives in a few sentences a consecutive outline of Cyprian's Treatises. By writing out this sketch in clauses and lines, and placing opposite to these our own abstract of certain epistles, we shall form an opinion (1) as to whether any of the thirteen are lost, (2) as to the order in which Cyprian himself had them arranged, and wished them to be read. Thus—

CYP. *Ep.* 20. 2. Et quid egerim locuntur vobis Epistulæ pro temporibus emissæ numero Tredecim :

in quibus nec 'clero' consilium,

nec 'confessoribus' exhortatio,

nec 'extorribus' quando oportuit objurgatio,

nec universæ fraternitati ad deprecandam Dei misericordiam, allocutio et persuasio nostra defuit.
Posteaquam vero et 'tormenta venerunt,'

sive jam tortis fratribus nostris,
sive adhuc ut torquerentur 'inclusis,'
ad corroborandos eos et confortandos noster sermo penetravit.

Epp. 5, 7, 14. THREE letters to PRESBYTERS and DEACONS, on their duty: use his funds: keep the prisons quiet: *Ep.* 7 regrets own absence, which is for general good: care of widows, sick, poor, foreigners: additional supplies: *Ep.* 5. 2 speaks of the present as the *initia* of persecution as in *Ep.* 6. 4 and *Ep.* 13. 2: *Ep.* 14 is the fullest and strongest about 'pauperes' (*and so precedes Ep.* 12 q. v. inf.; its order otherwise unfixed): quotes *Ep.* 5.

Ep. 6. To CONFESSORS. '...gratulor pariter et exhortor....' Exuberant joy in their confession: they the first prisoners: note too *ingressi, initiis,* and expressions coincident with those of *Ep.* 5.

Ep. 13. To CONFESSORS. Speaks of his former 'exsultantia verba' (*i.e. Ep.* 6). Exhorts to perseverance. Severe objurgation of faulty confessors, returned *extorres* and others. Theirs is a *prima congressio* (2).

Ep. 11. To PRESBYTERS and DEACONS, with directions (7) that it be read to the BRETHREN. One continuous Exhortation to Prayer. He uses the phrase 'tormenta venerunt[1]' and describes these as devised not to be fatal but to convert. (Fechtrup pp. 39, 40 well argues that this Epistle precedes the severest stage under the proconsul, but is an advance from the imprisonment and confiscation stage.) From the allusion in *Ep.* 13. 6 to the vision described in *Ep.* 11. 6, *Ep.* 13 probably followed *Ep.* 11 in time though not in Cyprian's logical order.

Ep. 12. To PRESBYTERS and DEACONS. Some have died in prison, not from tortures; are no less martyrs (Tortures therefore have not been extreme, but might have been—which exactly corresponds with the rest. It belongs to same moment as *Ep.* 11): refers verbally to *Ep.* 5. This speaks of having '*often* written' about the Poor, '...ut sæpe jam scripsi,' which leads to placing not *Ep.* 5 and *Ep.* 7 only, but also *Ep* 14, somewhere in the group above *Ep.* 12.

Ep. 10. To MARTYRS and CONFESSORS. This and remaining Epistles all dwell on Torture as in full use; only imprisonment or exile having been used hitherto. These then belong to the Visitation of the Proconsul. This is later than *April* 17, from its mention of Mappalicus' death under torture, whose commemoration is that day in the African Kalendar. This Epistle could not be summarised more exactly than by Cyprian opposite. Various expressions coincide also.

---

[1] *Ep.* 11. 1. Compare *De Laps.* 13 'Sed tormenta postmodum venerant.'

(OF DOCUMENTS.)

Item cum comperissem &c. *the distribution of libelli,*
   litteras feci quibus martyres et confessores ad dominica 'præcepta' revocarem ;

Item presbyteris et diaconibus non defuit sacerdotii vigor ut 'quidam' disciplinæ minus 'memores,' *receiving Lapsed to Communion without authority,* comprimerentur.

Plebi quoque ipsi...animum composuimus et ut ecclesiastica disciplina servaretur instruximus.

Postmodum vero (*the Lapsed having violently extorted communion*)...de hoc etiam BIS ad Clerum litteras feci...si qui 'libello a martyribus accepto' de sæculo excederent 'exomologesi facta' et 'manu eis in pænitentia imposita cum pace' sibi 'a martyribus' promissa 'ad Dominum' remitterentur.

Sed cum videretur 1. *necessary to respect Confessors,* 2. *quiet the Lapsed,* 3. *reconcile sick penitents,   he had ordered the libelli to be complied with in this last case, as effecting the three points: all other cases to be reserved for a Council when Peace returns.*

Ep. 15. To MARTYRS and CONFESSORS. Observe Christ's 'precepts,' *i.e.* discipline as well as faith, even though presbyters and deacons be rash. This (4) mentions *Ep.* 16 to the clergy, and *Ep.* 17 to the laity, as sent same time on same subject. (? June; severities abating.)

Ep. 16. To PRESBYTERS and DEACONS. Accompanies *Ep.* 15: is precisely described opposite.

Ep. 17. To LAITY. Accompanies *Ep.* 15. A precise account of it opposite.

Ep. 18. To PRESBYTERS and DEACONS. Dated to late July or August by the '*jam æstatem* cœpisse' (1) and malaria. *Postmodum*, opposite, places the above earlier; also accurately excerpted, and expressions correspond.

Ep. 19. To PRESBYTERS and DEACONS. Accurate précis in *Ep.* 20, as opposite.

It is clear from the above comparison that no letter described by Cyprian is missing from the budget. He wished the Romans to read *Ep.* 14 with *Ep.* 5 and *Ep.* 7, and *Ep.* 13 before *Ep.* 11, out of their chronology, on account of their subjects.

The chronological order stands thus, so far as it determines itself, *Epp.* 5, 6, 7, 11, 13, 14, 12, 10, 15, 16, 17, 18, 19.

Tillemont IV. pp. 66—69, 604, 605 and Dom Maran *Vit. S. Cypr.* IX. have doubts, but Pearson saw that we had all. Fechtrup (pp. 40, 41) agrees with Pearson, and verifies with care and clearness.

IX.

Diocesan Disquietudes.

Throughout the earlier part of Cyprian's correspondence is perceptible a reliance upon his laity, a dissatisfaction with his clergy. These omit to answer his letters[1]. Some act independently of his aims. Some compromise themselves by entire deference to the injunctions of the Confessors[2] or adopt them as the strongest barrier against superior authority. In one letter[3] he throws himself on the Plebes with an almost impassioned appeal. 'My presbyters and deacons should 'have warned them. I know the quietude, the shrinking-'ness of my people. How watchful would they have been 'had not certain presbyters in quest of popularity deceived 'them! Do you then yourselves take the guidance of them, 'one by one. By your own counsel and moderation refrain 'the spirits of the lapsed.'

When he has at length obtained the entire concurrence of the Roman clergy, Novatian included[4], of their confessors[5], and of the whole episcopate African and Italian[6], he assumes a stronger tone with his own clergy[7], and requires them to circulate the whole correspondence of which he forwards them copies. This was done[8]. The affair seemed settled for the present. All the Lapsed except death-stricken persons, however armed with Martyrs' papers, even Clergy penitently ready to return to their charge[9], were reserved for the decision of the organic authority—the united Episcopate.

Lastly, in accordance with the severer tone already assumed

---

[1] *Ep.* 18. 1.
[2] *Ep.* 27. 1.
[3] *Ep.* 17. 2, 3.
[4] *Ep.* 30.
[5] *Ep.* 31.
[6] *Epp.* 25; 26; 43. 3; 55. 5; 30. 8.
[7] *Ep.* 32.
[8] *Ep.* 55. 5.
[9] *Ep.* 34. 4. They were to cease to draw their monthly dividends, though 'without prejudice,' until they could be heard.

II. IX.   DIOCESAN DISQUIETUDES.   107

by certain clergy acting in concert with some bishops who had been visiting Carthage and were in Cyprian's confidence[1], notice was duly given of excommunication to be enforced against any who, until that authority should have spoken, should give communion to any of the lapsed except in the cases already provided for[2].

By the November of the year 250 the persecution was relaxing at Carthage. The Goths had crossed the Don. Decius was leaving Rome for his last campaign. It was however still unsafe for Cyprian to return. He therefore commissioned five representatives[3] for certain important functions, which he sketched out and for which he supplied the means, in Carthage and the neighbouring districts. These were three bishops, Caldonius, Herculanus and Victor, with two presbyters, Numidicus whom, after his already mentioned resuscitation from a horrible martyrdom, Cyprian placed among the clergy of the capital, and lastly Rogatian, the aged confessor, long since charged with the dispersion of Cyprian's fortune. The letter of Caldonius, who acted with firmness, indicates by its incorrectness a scanty and provincial education[4]. This commission had enough to do, under social conditions which seemed to allow penury no upward road, in distributing alms, in helpfully subsidising confessors whose capital had been confiscated so as to enable them to resume their trades, in selecting persons capable of being employed in functions of the church[5], in maintaining communications with

Nov., A.D. 250.

? Jan., A.D. 251.

---

[1] *e.g.* as to the excommunication of Gaius of Dida. *Ep.* 34. 1.

[2] *Ep.* 34. 3.

[3] *Epp.* 25; 26, where they are his medium of communication with other bishops, 'ad collegas nostros' (*Ep.* 25). —*Ep.* 41. 1 '...vos pro me vicarios.' This epistle is written to them when away from Carthage, either visiting the neighbouring bishops or at some gathering of them: 'has litteras meas fratribus nostris legite et Carthaginem ad clerum transmittite....' *Ep.* 41. 2. There is no sign of their removal being due to the influence of Felicissimus. The resources were still Cyprian's own, *sumptibus istis. Ep.* 41. 1.

[4] ...abluisse prior*em* delictum, and the Punic Latin *extorrentes* twice for *extorres*, &c. with great clumsiness of expression. *Ep.* 24. See Hartel's Preface, p. xlviii. He should in consistency have kept those readings of T and T$_1$.

[5] *Ep.* 41. 1.

the provincial bishops, and above all in endeavouring to persuade to patience the restless masses of the Lapsed[1].

Superstition was in some quarters beginning to add terror to the anxiety for restoration. Stricken consciences had in many instances induced physical and mental prostration—even death[2]. One person had become dumb in the moment of denial and so remained. Another had died in the public baths, gnawing the tongue which had tasted the idol sacrifice.

On the other hand still more terrible signs indicated the profanity of presumptuous return. An infant girl had rejected the chalice with wailing and convulsions. This occurred in Cyprian's own presence, while celebrating during his retirement. It was found that the nurse had taken the child before the magistrates and made it taste the idolatrous wine. A woman who clandestinely presented herself at the liturgy, died in the act of communicating. One who had as usual reserved the sacred Bread at home, was, on opening its receptacle after her lapse, scared by an outburst of flame. A man found it changed to ashes in his very hands.

X.

Declaration of Parties. Novatus and Felicissimus.

The latter class of stories indicates, what was the fact, that the opinion destined to create and to perpetuate real division was already active. Evidently the question which to some was presenting itself was not when, or upon what terms, the Lapsed should be readmitted, but whether it was possible for the church to remit such guilt. Although Cyprian employs these incidents in favour of delay, they are plainly no emanation from the party of moderation. Yet he probably apprehended at this moment little peril from the sentiment

---

[1] *Ep.* 26.   [2] *De Lapsis*, 24, 25, 26.

of Puritanism It was the party of Laxity which at present appeared to be absorbing into itself every dangerous element.

It threatened him indeed from many sides. There were the crowds of Libellatics eager for return. There were meritorious confessors, wounded because their fortitude was not allowed to cover a brother's weakness.

But the conscientiously troublesome in both ranks were outvoiced by the worldly and unscrupulous who foamed at restraint. For them the Universal Indulgence franked with the name of the Confessor Paul was title enough to cancel mere episcopal restrictions[1]. Some 'refugees' who had never left the port, and others who had quickly broken their sentence and come back, skulked awhile as outlaws in low hiding-places[2]; and emerged, as the severities abated, to claim a voice in church-affairs. Some of the confessors, their heads turned by vanity, courted by female devotees, had sunk into scandalous immorality[3]. Of the lapsed many had not spent one day in penance, but had braved their shame amid the habits of fashionable and dissipated life[4]; while (as we have seen) influential persons in the provinces had extorted communion by actual tumult from unwilling clergy. Many of the clergy however were not unwilling[5], and they found ready chiefs, although perhaps not at first avowed ones[6], in the Five Presbyters who had been all along hostile to Cyprian's election and authority. Under their headship the party grew numerous and bold enough to designate itself, in a manifesto addressed to the bishop himself, as 'THE CHURCH.' To this he answered characteristically that since the day of the Charge to Peter the Church had been found

---

[1] *Ep*. 35, compare *Ep*. 22. 2.

[2] Such must be, I think, the meaning of '...aliquis temulentus et lasciviens demoratur, alius in eam patriam unde extorris factus est regreditur, ut deprehensus non jam quasi Christianus sed quasi nocens pereat.' *Ep*. 13. 4. *Extorris* is certainly used both of those who fled and those who were legally banished.

[3] *De Unitate* 20.

[4] *De Laps*. 30.

[5] *Ep*. 17. 2, 3.

[6] *Ep*. 43. 1, 2 'Nunc apparuit Felicissimi factio unde venisset....' See above, pp. 25, 43.

in unity with the Bishop; and still more characteristically that their 'roll of the Lapsed could scarcely be "The Church," since GOD was not the GOD of the dead but of the living.'

More welcome letters[1] reached him at the same moment. There were many of the Lapsed who had ever since given themselves devotedly to good works in silence. These now assured him that they would never plead their Libels; that they were living in thankful penance; biding their time for restoration to Peace on his return. They added with that gentle fervour which marked true African Christianity that 'Peace would be more sweet to them if restored in his own 'presence.' 'How I hail them,' says Cyprian, 'the Lord is 'my witness; He has vouchsafed to show what servants like 'these deserve from His goodness.'

Then in that methodic way which gave point to all his enthusiasm he requests from each side a list of their signatures, sends to the clergy of Carthage explicit instructions, and to the clergy of Rome, by a subdeacon Fortunatus[2], copies of all the papers[3].

Foremost of the presbyters stood the famous and restless[4]

---

[1] Both letters are described in *Ep.* 33. 1, 2.

[2] *Ep.* 36. 1.

[3] *Epp.* 33, 34, 35. The Roman clergy acknowledging these *Ep.* 36. 3, say there must be some 'qui illos *arment*...et in perversum *instruentes*... exitiosa deposcant illis properatæ communicationis venena,' and that not 'sine instinctu *quorundam*' would all have dared 'tam petulanter sibi jam *pacem* vindicare.' It should be unnecessary to remark that *arment* with *instruentes* means *provide and furnish*, and has no relation to *pacem* which is simply *communion*, and contains no indication of 'weitere aufständische Bewegungen.' *Quorundam* refers to the persons of whom Cyprian had told them, not to his clergy at large. Again '*deposcant illis*' means 'demand for them.' To conceive that *sibi* has dropped out before *illis* is monstrous in Latinity, and to translate it 'claim *for themselves* liberty to *give them* communion prematurely,' equally so. So, however, O. Ritschl's laboured pages, 52, 53.

[4] See p. 47. 'Rerum novarum semper cupidus,' *Ep.* 52. 2. That the leader Novatus was one of the Five appears from the whole tenor of the history of the faction more than from particular passages. Compare however *Ep.* 14. 4; *Ep.* 59. 9, and what is said of the Five presbyters acting with Felicissimus, *Ep.* 43. 3, and of Novatus acting with him, *Ep.* 52. 2. That the Five are the original opponents of Cyprian is shewn by the expression 'olim secundum vestra suffragia' in *Ep.* 43. 5, and these passages

Novatus. To these opponents Cyprian allows on the whole both age and weight of character, yet Novatus had been in poor repute[1], and had escaped an investigation[2] into his conduct only through the breaking out of the persecution. He had been charged with inhuman cruelty towards his own wife and father[3]. It is true that the assumption of Novatus' guilt, and the attributing his withdrawal to a stricken conscience, as well as general accusations of depravity and unworthy motive, may or may not be due to factious representations. But that an enquiry before Cyprian and assessors was impending over Novatus just before the persecution broke out is surely undeniable. It is a question of fact upon which, if Cyprian's direct statement be not trustworthy, what evidence is credible[4]?

---

viewed together leave no doubt as to the application of the words 'idem est Novatus qui apud nos primum discordiæ incendium seminavit, &c.' *Ep.* 52. 2. Among the rest Pearson (*An. Cyp.* CCLI. ii.) counts Jovinus and Maximus; but these had lapsed (*Ep.* 59. 10), which we have no ground for imputing to any of the Five. Pamèle includes Repostus and Felix; but of these one was a lapsed bishop and the second a bishop of some schismatic body. Dom Maran (xvii.) and Rettberg (pp. 97—112) fix upon Donatus, Fortunatus and Gordius, and rightly (*Ep.* 14. 4) I think. As to Fortunatus (afterwards the pseudo-bishop of the party) there is no doubt (*Ep.* 59. 9). But that the fifth was either Gaius of Dida (*Ep.* 34. 1) or Augendus (*Ep.* 42) is a mere guess, and the latter was a deacon (*Ep.* 44. 1). Fell, without any colour, fancies that only three presbyters, those named in *Ep.* 43. 1, remained faithful. Fechtrup conjectures with reason that the petition of Donatus, Fortunatus, Novatus and Gordius was for an immediate restoration of some Lapsed; for Cyprian answers as he always answers that request. But that it already covered a 'feine List' (p. 80) for uniting the strict confessors with the lax party against Cyprian, through his expected refusal, is a little too subtle. The phrases as to the authors of dissension in the *De Zelo et Livore* (6) do not seem to me to apply to this party, and they were written six years later. See on that treatise below.

[1] Semper istic episcopis male cognitus. *Ep.* 52. 2.

[2] Imminebat cognitionis dies. *Ep.* 52. 3. *cognitio*, the technical term of the law.

[3] *Ep.* 52. 2.

[4] On Neander's opinion, *Hist. of the Christ. Religion and Church*, vol. I. p. 312 (Bohn), see p. 130, note 2, infra. If Cyprian had *not* spoken out as to the unsatisfactory character of Novatus it could never have eluded such ingenuity as Mosheim, Neander, and Rettberg have devoted to clearing him.

This man, as a Presbyter, had some charge in an important region or ward in the city, called Mons, or the Hill. The Bozra or Byrsa itself rising some two hundred feet above the rest of the town, with the main streets leading up it, and the principal buildings on its plateau, may well have caused distinctions, local and social, like the still remembered 'Above Hill' and 'Below Hill' of such cities as Lincoln; and at least no other district can well have occupied that distinctive name[1]. In managing its church affairs he associated with himself as Deacon an energetic and determined person named

---

[1] This I venture to think must be the simple meaning of '*In Monte*,' *Ep.* 41. 1 and 2. In each place Hartel reads *in morte* and so Ritschl, &c. But in the latter clause there is no doubt as to the reading, *T* having *monte* and *Z montem*; in the former *morte T*, φ, *w*, *mortem Z* are natural corrections of what seemed obscure; but not so *monte* for *morte*, the sense of which would be obvious; whilst *im*mo ut te*cum*, *r*, *im*mo vitæ, μ, indicate both the puzzle of the scribes and that they had *monte* before them. See also p. 113, note 4. Reference to *Monte* in Numidia is absurd. Mosheim and others thought that this 'in Monte' travelled with Novatus to Rome, and gave the Novatianists the name Montenses there. Hefele (*Novatianisches Schisma* in *Wetzer u. Welte's Kirchenlexikon*, and *H. d. Conciles*, ed. Delarc, L. VIII. § 105) says that they were so called (and also *Montanistæ*, which is an invention) from confusion with the Montanists. But all this arises from a misinterpretation of Epiphanius. His words are (after he has already enumerated the Montanists in his list) (*Ancoratus* 13) Καθαροί, οἱ καὶ Ναυατᾶιοι, οἱ καὶ Μοντήσιοι, ὡς ἐν Ῥώμῃ καλοῦνται. These 'Puritans' might be of course either Novatianist or Donatist (differenced by origin only, not doctrine), and at Rome the *Donatists were* called Montenses. See Optatus, B. II. c. iv., and the passages there quoted by E. Dupin (Paris, 1702, p. 35). Jerome, *Chron.* 356; *adv. Lucif.* ad fin.; Aug. *Ep.* (165) 53, *De Unit. Eccl.* 3, *De Hæresibus* 69. Cod. Theod. L. 16, Tit. 5, xliii. (A.D. 408). There is no trace of any sect but the Donatists being so called, and they from a Mons at Rome, in a grotto of which they had their first church. In the 8th canon of the council held at Rome A.D. 386 the two sects are thus conjoined and distinguished: 'Ut venientes a Novatianis vel Montensibus per manus impositionem suscipiantur *ex eo quod* rebaptizant' (*Ep.* 4 Siricii papæ, Labbe, t. II. c. 1225).

Perhaps I may attempt here to emend this canon, since the italicised words mean (as has been seen) the opposite of the fact. They are thus paraphrased by Innocent I. in his letter to Victricius of Rouen (Innoc. 1, *Ep.* 2. 8, Labbe v. III. c. 9), '*præter eos, si qui* forte a nobis ad illos transeuntes *rebaptizati sunt*.' I propose to read in the Roman canon '*excepto quos* rebaptizant.' For the construction cf. '...excepto divina natura ut humanitas integra fiat,' S. Isidor., 'Excepto comitibus, &c.' ap. Ducange.

Felicissimus[1]. Cyprian was naturally not consulted as to this appointment, which gave to the party the control of considerable funds; his missives were systematically disregarded by them; the Lapsed freely admitted and invited to communion[2]; the agreement of the bishops in the arrangement between Rome and Carthage unheeded, and when Cyprian sent out his commission of relief and enquiry[3], Felicissimus treated it as a deliberate invasion of his diaconal office. He announced publicly that whoever had accepted its benefits, or answered its queries, should be[4] excluded from participation in the communions and all other benefits of the Hill district. This declaration appeared in his own name, and his leadership was so energetic that the Five are designated as 'his partners,' 'his satellites,' even 'his presbyterate[5].' 'His Five Presbyters were as ruinous to the Church,' says Cyprian, with their offers of Communion, 'as the Five Magnates on the Committees of Persecution[6].'

In vigorous reply to his own vigour Felicissimus with another deacon Augendus was for the time being[7] excommunicated by Caldonius and the Commission. Cyprian speaks of the moral charges against Felicissimus as now advanced upon evidence so grave as alone to constitute grounds for 'suspension' of communion with him. This enquiry is postponed until a proper court can be assembled. Cyprian's instructions to this effect are contained in the same despatch which directed their benevolent labours, and he desires that in forwarding it for the information of the clergy in Carthage Caldonius will append to it the names of the

? October.

---

[1] *Ep.* 52. 2; cf. *Ep.* 59. 1, 16. Compare 'Gaio Didensi presbytero et diacono ejus,' *Ep.* 3—. 1.

[2] *Ep.* 43. 2.

[3] See p. 107.

[4] *Ep.* 41. 2 '...*non communicaturos in Monte secum*,' to which the rejoinder runs 'sciat se in ecclesia nobiscum communicaturum non esse, qui se sponte maluit ab ecclesia separare,' *Ep.* 41. 2. Note how *in ecclesia* answers to *in monte*; it could not answer to *in morte*.

[5] *Ep.* 43. 3, 5, 7.

[6] See p. 76, note 1. *Ep.* 43. 3, 7.

[7] *Ep.* 41. 2 'interim.'

fautors of the conspiracy. This letter accordingly comes down to us followed by Caldonius' list. It gives a glimpse of the lower social classes which entered with living interest into Christianity and its debates,—classes without which the Church's work is not half done. With the two Deacons are named a small manufacturer, a seamstress, a woman who had been tortured, and two refugees. The Five Presbyters are not mentioned[1].

The prominence of a Deacon at this period need cause no surprise. Although the time had not yet come when at Rome those officers so far surpassed the presbyters in emolument and dignity, that they looked upon promotion as an injury, or when at Carthage they were described as in 'the third Priesthood[2],' and needed new canons to remind them of their subordination to the presbyterate as well as to the episcopate, and even of their duty of rendering assistance in the Eucharist[3], yet already their control of funds, their knowledge

---

[1] *Ep.* 42. In *Ep.* 41. 2 Cyprian writes 'has litteras meas...Carthaginem ad clerum transmittite *additis nominibus eorum* quicunque se Felicissimo junxerint.' Accordingly *Ep.* 42 is simply as follows. 'Caldonius cum Herculano et Victore Collegis item Rogatiano cum Numidico Presbyteris. Abstinuimus a communicatione Felicissimum et Augendum, item Repostum de extorribus et Irenem Rutilorum et Paulam sarcinatricem quod ex adnotatione mea scire debuisti. item abstinuimus Sophronium et ipsum de extorribus Soliassum budinarium.' In this strange little note it should seem superfluous to say that *adnotatio* cannot mean the kind of list by which a magistrate published the names of *absentees* summoned to appear for trial (see Dirksen, *Manuale, s.v.*). This is itself a sentence on notorious offenders and is itself the *adnotatio*, as appended to Cyprian's despatch in conformity with his instructions. *Scire debuisti* is epistolary and does not imply a former communication; compare *Ep.* 53 '...*hoc factum* his *litteris* nostris certissime *scire debuisti.*' Translate 'I am bound to inform you by a note appended by myself.' This *Ep.* 42 is not addressed to Cyprian himself therefore, as usually understood, but is a transcript of the document issued. It naturally bears no address; the vulgate heading *Cypriano S.* is not original.

On the obscure occupations named see note at end of this section, p. 117. On *extorres* cf. Baluze ad Cypr. *Epp.* 14 and 18, quoting C. Guyet, l. 2, p. 173, Baron. *Ad Ann.* 25, and his *Notes on the Roman Martyrology*, Jan. 2; see note 2, p. 109 above.

[2] Optat. i. 13 (vid. Casaub. in loc.). Hieron. in Ezech. c. 18.

[3] *IV. Concil. Carth.* A.D. 398, cc. 37—41.

DECLARATION OF PARTIES.

of business, their intimacy with the secular cares of the laity, the very fact that a district which had many presbyters had but one deacon, gave them the command of many threads of influence. Hence from Spain it is the Deacon of the church of Merida who writes in the name of the church to the bishops of Africa in protest against the return of its lapsed bishop[1] and receives their conciliar reply. Cyprian calls the office at Rome (apparently in Cornelius' words) 'the Diaconate of the Holy Administration,' and refers to it as 'the charge of guiding and piloting the Church[2].' The Deacon indeed not only had charge of the corporate funds but also acted as the official trustee of Christian widows and orphans[3]. Hence his opportunity of enriching with both adherents and property any section which he pronounced to be the true church. And it is from such transferences probably that the accusations of 'fraud and rapine' arise which are so freely showered upon unorthodox Deacons, when darker stains on character rest evidently on hearsay[4].

There is no ground for assuming that Novatus exaggerated his irregularities by actually conferring orders upon Felicissimus[5]. There is no previous or contemporary instance of such a fact, nor the slightest symptom of any presbyterian or anti-episcopalian theory (as members of unepiscopal churches have freely averred[6]) in the principles or conduct of Novatus and his following. They were in episcopal communion, they took part in the episcopal election at Carthage and opposed the nomination of Cyprian, they presently elected a new

---

[1] *Ep.* 67 'Cyprianus...item Ælio Diacono et plebi Emeritæ consistentibus.'
[2] *Ep.* 52. 1. See further p. 311 below, ch. VII. iii. 1.
[3] Ecclesiasticæ pecuniæ...viduarum ac pupillorum deposita, *Ep.* 52. 1. Ecclesiæ deposita, *Ep.* 50. See p. 68, n. 4.
[4] *Ep.* 41. 1.
[5] G. A. Poole's suggestion (*Life and Times of S. Cypr.* p. 134) that some heretical bishop was called in lacks all foundation.
[6] E. de Pressensé, *H. des Trois Premiers Siècles de l'Église Chrét.* 2me Sér. I. pp. 484 sqq. Neander, *op. cit.* vol. I. p. 313, besides Rettberg, D'Aubigné, Keyser. Fechtrup however rightly says 'nicht eine Spur, nicht ein Wort,' p. 81, n. 1.

bishop for themselves and procured his consecration. When Novatus visited Rome, he threw himself into the Episcopal election then proceeding, opposed the candidate who was chosen, and then procured an episcopal consecration for his own nominee[1]. If in any century of the Church's history the presbyteral parentage of episcopacy was forgotten or undiscovered, and any revival of latent presbyteral claim to assume an episcopal function impossible, it was in the third[2].

But, again, it is evident from the nature of the frauds attributed to Felicissimus that he was already a Deacon when he joined Novatus, and it was by complicity with him that Novatus became liable to the same accusation[3] of wronging the fatherless and widows[4].

Thus at last we have before us a complete picture of the formation of an Opposition in the third century. The original clerical element of dissatisfaction with the popular choice of the bishop had allied itself with discontent at the bishop's delegating even administrative functions to others, and with a wide-spread conviction that meritorious suffering in the Church's cause established some claim to a voice in her discipline. Lenity to the Lapsed, open admission to Communion was the rallying cry, and the rank and file of the party consisted of the multitudinous claimants for restoration with their families.

---

[1] ...illic episcopum fecit, *Ep.* 52. 2.

[2] See Bp. Lightfoot's *Dissertation on the Christian Ministry*.

[3] *Epp.* 41. 1; 52. 2.

[4] In *Epp.* 52. 2 this action of Novatus is paralleled with his creation of a Bishop, which was certainly not without the intervention of legitimate bishops. His offence lay in making Felicissimus *his* deacon, 'nec permittente me nec sciente,' *i.e.* inconsulto Cypriano. Compare *Ep.* 34. 1 'Gaio Didensi *presbytero* et diacono *ejus*.' 'Felicissimum satellitem suum diaconum...constituit' is the reading of Hartel, but the MSS. *F*, 'Felicissimum satellitem *suum suum* diaconem constituit,' and *Q*, 'Felicissimum satellitem *suum suum* diaconum constituit' are right, and supported by the further repetition in *M*, 'Felicissimum satellitem *suum suum* diaconum *suum* constituit.'

Fechtrup, pp. 110, 111, and n. 4, p. 110, says rightly that Novatus could not have ventured upon, nor Cyprian have failed explicitly to censure, so discrediting a novelty as Orders given by a presbyter.

From the counter extreme we have faintly caught in dark legendary form sterner voices demanding even in easy-going Carthage their perpetual exclusion. In the haughtier Capital this tendency alone had a chance of development. We shall see how singularly this movement was in the very person of Novatus linked to the opposite Carthaginian movement. Our next interest will be to trace the gentle yet commanding policy of Cyprian in subduing the violence of both the separations.

Budinarius and *Sarcinatrix.* (*Ep.* 42.) [Additional Note on p. 114.]

For the reason given in the text the obscure occupations of two of those partisans of Felicissimus are worth considering.

1. Soliassus (itself a name which I have not found in inscriptions) is called *Budinarius* (*budianarius* T.), to which we have no clue. Fell conjectures *burdonarius* 'mule-keeper,' but Baluze finds no trace of this word. However Sophocles *Greek Lexicon of Roman and Byzantine Periods* has 'Βουρδωνάριος *Schol. Arist. Th.* 491. Written also βουρδουνάριος *Cyrill. Scyth.* V. S. 230 A, *Leont. Cypr.* 1797 C. Also βορδωνάριος *Ioann. Mosch.* 2988 B.' These forms, *considering the Latin termination of the word,* seem to make its existence probable.

Saumaise (*Script. Hist. Aug.* p. 408) (II p. 578, Lugd. 1671) conjectures *butinarium* from *butina* which Du Cange indicates, though without examples, as a diminutive of *butta,* 'a small wine-butt' or 'bottle,' which has many relatives βουττίον, βοῦττις κ.τ.λ. (v. Soph. *Lex.* s.v.), *buttis, butica, buticula* (v. Du Cange). And he suggests that it means 'a maker of small vessels or measures' (*e.g. acetabula*). Hesychius has βυτίνη as a Tarentine word for λάγυνος ἢ ἀμίς.

2. Paula was a *Sarcinatrix.* The employment is often mentioned in inscriptions and was one of the offices of the Domus Augusta. See Orelli, *Inscrr.* 645, (5372), 7275; a fine monument ap. Gruter, p. MCXVII. 9 'Fausta Saturnia Sarcinatrix Proculeio Vernæ suo puero ingeniosissimo...' and five inscriptions on p. DLXXX, where two have Greek names and three are libertæ; one is of 'Iulia Iucunda Aug. l. sarcinatr(ix) a mundo mulie(bri),' &c. Abp. Lavigerie communicated to de Rossi one from Cæsarea in Mauretania 'Rogata Sarcinatr. Saturno, v. l. a. s.' (*Corp. Inscrr. L.* VIII. ii. no. 10938).

What the office was seems scarcely doubtful if the quotations in Forcellini are compared. Fronto, *de Differ.,* p. 2192 (Putsch) 'Sartrix quæ sarcit, sarcinatrix quæ sarcinas servat'; Nonius, c. i. 276 'Sarcinatrices non ut quidam volunt sarcitrices quasi a sarciendo, sed magis a sarcinis *quod plurimum vestium sumant.*' But as Paulus, *Dig.* l. 47, tit. 2, 83 (82), says 'Fullo et sarcinator, qui polienda aut sarcienda vestimenta accipit,' the grammarians' account (though they are anxious as to the formation of the word) is consistent with the employment being that of a 'seamstress,' or 'mender,' the 'sarcinæ' being packs of clothes. So from an old Latin-Greek Glossary in the Library of S. Germain des Prés, Du Cange *s.v.*, cf. vol. VII. p. 442 *a* l. 9, quotes sarcinatrix ἠπητρία, ἀκεστρία (*sic lege*), ἡ καλλωπιστρία. It is coupled in *Dig.* l. 15, tit. 1, 27 (Gaius) with the employment of a 'textrix' as an 'artificium vulgare.' So in Plaut. *Aulul.* III. 5, 41 the 'sarcinatores' are named with the 'fullones,' as also in Gaius *Comment.* l. iii. 143, 162, 205. In Lucil. *ap. Non.* ii. 818 the 'sarcinator' makes a patchwork quilt 'suere centonem.' What the 'machinæ' are in Varro, *ap. Non.* i. 276, 'Homines rusticos in vindemia incondita cantare, sarcinatrices in machinis' is not so clear.

Anyhow the exhibition of the social class is most interesting.

XI.

Growth of the Opposition at Rome. The Confessors and Novatian.

We have already had occasion to mention a noble group of Confessors who had been committed to the Roman prisons at the time of the execution of Fabian[1]. Their sufferings and the sight of each other's tortures were harrowing. Cyprian sent them constant encouragement, and pecuniary help from his own resources[2]. Among them were two of the seven Deacons of the city, Rufinus, of whom we have no further personal detail, and Nicostratus, who soon passed, never to return, into the ranks of schism. Of the laymen confined with them, Urbanus twice underwent the torture; the three Punic friends Sidonius, Macarius and the indomitable Celerinus[3] are familiar names already. The Presbyter Maximus[4] was in after years thought worthy to be laid among the bishops in the subterranean chapel of Cornelius; we

[1] *Ep.* 28.
[2] *Ep.* 31. 1, 5, 6.
[3] Euseb. vi. 43, et sup. p. 69.
[4] pp. 69, 162.

shall find him inspiring his fellow sufferers to an act of courage morally higher than their confessorship. But the ruling spirit among them during the year 250 was a Presbyter, who doubtless belonged to the Jewish section of the church of Rome, Moyses. His signature had been attached to the letter in which Novatian and the clergy signified their adhesion to the proposals of Cyprian, and we may not unreasonably conjecture him to be the author of the manly thirty-first epistle[1]. Had some philosophic magistrate surprised in its passage such a document, rating his severities, even while in process, as substantial happiness to the sufferer, and from a dungeon claiming the right to legislate for evidently numerous classes of mankind, he must have questioned with himself not only as to where the chief Good, but where the reality of power resided.

Moyses and his fellow-sufferers from the first gave no countenance to the theory that the merits of martyrs or confessors should cross the path of discipline; and they earned the gratitude of Cyprian by their remonstrance with those whom they were connected with at Carthage, against the line there pursued[2]. A year of confinement was nearly past when Cyprian writing them a letter of confidence and comfort, in answer to theirs, by the now liberated and welcome hand of Celerinus, traced out the progress of the four seasons of their spiritual experience, with no small remnants of his older rhetoric[3]. It must not be forgotten that such flowers of eloquence were in their freshness then, and that the brightness of a prison-house was a new theme. Some unknown members of the group had already died[4], when Moyses after eleven months and eleven days of bondage (such is the accurate record of the Liberian Chronicle, and one which

Dec. (?) 31, A.D. 250.

---

[1] That one wrote for the rest appears in the phrase 'non dicam,' *Ep.* 31. 2.

[2] *Ep.* 28. 2.

[3] *Ep.* 37. 1 'per tales talia.'

[4] *Ep.* 37. 3 'ad osculum Domini venerunt.'

even here marks the importance attached to his position) followed them[1] to a confessor's grave.

With an insight lacking to the rest Moyses had marked Novatian's progress toward an exclusive rigorism, not undiscoverable even in his first epistle, and hardening just as Cyprian softened, after that meeting-point[2]. So unchristian-like had seemed to him the 'insane arrogance[3]' of Novatian's tone that at last he had refused to act with him, or possibly to communicate with him and his uncharitable disciples (at this time five presbyters), in the visits which, like other clergy, they paid to the prisoners[4]. Moyses may well have

---

[1] Post passionem ejus (Fabii) Moyses et Maximus presbyteri et Nicostratus diaconus comprehensi sunt et in carcerem sunt missi. Eo tempore supervenit Novatus ex Africa et separavit de ecclesia Novatianum et quosdam confessores, postquam Moyses in carcere defunctus est, qui fuit ibi m. xi. d. xi. (*Liberian Catalogue*, ap. Lipsius, *op. cit.* p. 267). Considering that Fabian was martyred on 20 Jan. this looks as if it meant that Moyses died on the last day of the year; the precision of the record is due to the necessity felt for saving the memory of Moyses from the imputation of Novatianism.

[2] pp. 108 sqq.

[3] κατιδὼν αὐτοῦ τὴν θρασύτητα καὶ τὴν ἀπόνοιαν. Eus. *H. E.* vi. 43.

[4] ἀκοινώνητον ἐποίησεν Cornelius, *Ep.* ap. Eus. *H. E.*, *l.c.*, where see Valois. Although the word is classical in the sense of 'having no dealings with,' yet the bond and usages of communion can hardly fail to have affected already a term which soon was becoming the fixed word for 'excommunicated,' especially since the sentence proceeds σὺν τοῖς πέντε πρεσβυτέροις τοῖς ἅμα αὐτῷ ἀποσχίσασιν ἑαυτοὺς τῆς ἐκκλησίας.

In this same clause Lipsius (*op. cit.* p. 202) untowardly conceived that this αὐτῷ must refer to Novatus, and not Novatian, because 'The five presbyters' *must be The Five Carthaginian* Presbyters. It is to be observed that through the whole Epistle Novatian is called, possibly through Eusebius' editing, 'Novatus.' Having however not only a numerical but a presbyterian bias, Lipsius makes Moyses 'excommunicate' Novatus and his five. In that case we should have a Roman presbyter excommunicating Five Presbyters who never stirred from Carthage, and of whom it is difficult to conceive that he had heard. Ritschl, p. 68, observes also that this would make Six Opposition Presbyters there, whereas we only hear of Five. But then further, if this is so, Moyses is not said to have renounced Novatian himself at all (but only Novatus and his Carthaginians), whereas his disowning of Novatian is the very point which Cornelius wished to impress on Fabius.

The number *Five* reappears singularly in the History. Cyprian's first recusants are Five Presbyters, *Ep.* 43. 1, 3. The heretic Privatus of Lambæse had Five presbyter adherents, *Ep.* 59. 10. Five presbyters attended Cornelius at the reconciliation of Maximus, *Ep.* 49. 2. Five bishops consecrated the

been one of the presbyters whose advice Fabian had overruled when he ordained the Stoic philosopher, the epileptic, who had been exorcised as a dæmoniac, and baptized in the apparently fatal malady which ensued, yet who after his recovery had not cared to complete the right by obtaining the imposition of hands. These were harsh traits in Novatian's history, and although the language of Cornelius is cruelly bitter[1], they were traits likely to be remembered against him by the gentlest, when the man slowly moved into prominence as the withholder of forgiveness and rejecter of the penitent. Harsher yet was the story that the Deacons could not persuade him to emerge, in order to visit suffering confessors, from some small cell[2] to which he had retired during the persecution, 'because he had resolved to be no longer presbyter and belonged now to another philosophy.' The first half of the speech thus imputed to him we may unhesitatingly reject as a mistaken comment on the rest. His meaning doubtless was that he embraced the contem-

pseudo-bishop Fortunatus, *Ep.* 59. 11. Any of these Fives might as reasonably be identified with the Five Novatianist Presbyters, as the Five Presbyters of Carthage. We remember too that Cyprian sarcastically identified his own Five with the 'Five Magnates.'

[1] He talks of his 'wolf-like friendliness,' ascribes his conversion to the act of Satan, and treats the natural rule, that a person baptized under fear of death should not be admitted to Orders, as if it admitted of no equally natural exceptions. He was a narrow-minded man. Cyprian, with his larger heart, and humour rallies the prejudice (which at Neocæsarea A.D. 314 became a Canon) against Clinical Baptism by hinting that other baptism might just as well be called Peripatetic, *Ep.* 69. 16. It is true that we have no distinct information that Novatian was a Stoic, but he is constantly spoken of as proud of being a philosopher, and if his school had been any but the Stoic, Cyprian could scarcely have written *Ep.* 55. 6, 'alia est philosophorum et Stoicorum ratio, &c.' The sternness of his tone is well seen in the strange epithets with which he loads his idea of manliness— asperi et hispidi et hirti et firmi et graves mores hominum probantur, *De Cib. Jud.* c. 3. No credit can be attached to the statement of Philostorgius, *H. E.* viii. 15, that he was a Phrygian Socrates, who wrote (*H. E.* iv. 28) with a strong regard for the Novatianist discipline and had investigated the history of the sect in Phrygia, attributes its spread there to the austere character of the people and not at all to any personal influences. Cf. Sozom. *H. E.* ii. 32.

[2] οἰκίσκος, Euseb. *loc. cit.*

plative life in preference to the active, and for this his health and habits furnished an excuse which would not have been disallowed from others. To forsake the presbyterate would have been a step alien to his rigidly ecclesiastical spirit, while at the same time there is no reason to question either the fact or the sincerity of his abjuration of episcopal ambition[1]. The unsparing author of the contemporary pamphlet 'To Novatian' bears witness to his faithfulness as a presbyter, 'how he had wept for the faults of others as his own, how he 'had borne their burdens,' and dwells on 'the strength of his heavenly addresses' to the faint-hearted[2].

We may judge for ourselves that his eloquence was of no vulgar order. At a time when the Roman church possessed no Latin writer of ability, his style is pure, clear, incisive, not disdainful of verbal repetitions for distinctness' sake, or in his syllogisms afraid of prolonged pronominal clauses[3]. When he passes from explanations to reflections he has a peculiar tone of melancholy sarcasm and latent censure which seems to dwell even in the sound of his sentences.

He had been engaged in controversy with the Jews, and

---

[1] We need not believe with Cornelius (Euseb. *loc. cit.*) that his oaths on this subject were φοβεροί (...καὶ δι' ὅρκων φοβερῶν τινων...), but Neander's questioning (*op. cit.* vol. I. pp. 335, 6) that Novatian protested against the imputation is not creditable to his criticism. Novatian was a student, and a pietist and a severe man, and in delicate health. He did not wish to be dragged from retirement until the development of his views forced it on him.

[2] *Ad Novatianum*, ch. 13, in the appendices to Cyprian. On the Authorship of this Treatise see *Appendix*, p. 557.

[3] From this tone (see especially the insinuation of 36. 3) and from the pronominal peculiarities I cannot hesitate to ascribe to him *Ep.* 36 as certainly as *Ep.* 30. Compare *Ep.* 36. 2 '*hoc ipsum quod pro se ipsis* facere putaverunt animadvertimus contra *se ipsos* protulisse,' and *Ep.* 36. 3 'quando meliores *ipsorum*...impetretur' with *Ep.* 30. 4 'Nam *qui id quod* habet non custodit in *eo* ex *quo illud* possidet, dum *id* ex *quo* possidet violat, amittit *illud quod* possidebat,' and with Novatian's *de Trin.* c. 13 '...Verbum autem *hoc illud* est *quod*...Et nihilominus dum mundus *ipse post illum*,' &c. Compare again the string of short clauses commenced with *Quod si* in the above passage of *De Trin.* with *Ep.* 36. 1, 2 'qui si habent,' &c., and cf. p. 147, n. 1 inf. [A more elaborate proof of the authorship is worked out by Dr A. Harnack in *op. cit.*, inf. p. 150.]

perhaps with the Judaizing Christians, who formed so strong a party in Rome. Nothing indeed could be more important than that the vast Jewish population should be directly confronted by Christianity, and that inquirers should learn the difference between shadow and substance. His two epistles 'Of Circumcision' and 'Of the Sabbath' were thus aimed[1]. Whether that 'On the Priest' bore on the same controversy or on his own conflict with Cornelius is more than I can decide. But his extant epistle 'Of the Jewish Meats' was composed probably in this very year, and possibly during the retirement[2] which by some was so violently reprehended, as a manual repeatedly asked for by a laity who 'not only held but vehemently taught a sincere Gospel.' It is a singular and partly beautiful essay:—'The Jews are strange to the under-'standing of their law...No animals, created and blessed of 'God, are really unclean. Some have in their habits, character 'or form a figurative repulsiveness, and this was taken ad-'vantage of as a means of instruction in morals.' Here the illustrations are fanciful, as might be imagined, the pride of the swan's neck being one of them. So it was 'in some olden days when such like shadows or emblems had to be used.' But Christ had opened out 'all things which antiquity had 'shrouded in mists of symbol[3],' had 'restored them all to 'their own primal benedictions by closing the law.'

'The true meat, holy and clean, is a right faith, an un-'spotted conscience, and an innocent soul. Whoso thus feeds 'sups with Christ. Such a banqueter is God's guest. These

---

[1] So he says himself. See *De Cibis Jud.* c. 1. His *de Attalo* may have been a paper on the Abuse of Wealth. The *De Instantia* sounds like a characteristic title of a pendant to Tertullian's *De Patientia*, or a corrective to Cyprian's *De Bono Patientiæ*.

[2] Commonly headed 'Plebi in Evangelio perstanti.' He speaks of writing it during an absence which he trusts will not prove injurious to them. If this were during persecution it accounts for that change of tone as to Cyprian's retirement which we saw that Novatian imported into the Roman judgment.

[3] ...sacramentorum nebulis, *De Cib. Jud.* c. 5.

'be the banquets which sustain angels; these be the tables 'which make martyrs.'

'Christian temperance condemns both avarice and luxury[1].' These vices are severely chastised, and lastly, in language much sterner than S. Paul's[2], the partaking of things offered to idols is condemned as still in use, and apparently as being the one way now possible in which defiled meats could be eaten.

Thus then Novatian had well deserved the reputation, at which the practical Cornelius levels an unthinking sneer, of 'a master in doctrine and a maintainer of ecclesiastical science[3].' Cornelius was indeed cast in another mould. He was a Roman of the Romans. Apart even from the other popes

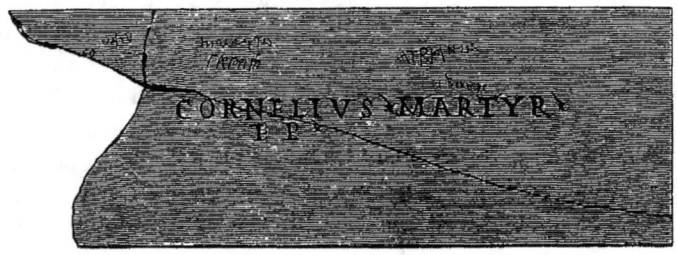

with their Greek epigraphs, he was buried under a Latin inscription among the noble Cornelii[4]. He had risen quiet and

---

[1] c. 6. On one singular revelation here made see p. 290, n. 4.

[2] ...sumentem dæmonio nutrit non Deo... c. 7.

[3] ...ὁ δογματιστής, ὁ τῆς ἐκκλησιαστικῆς ἐπιστήμης ὑπερασπιστής, ap. Eus. *l.c.* Novatian's admirable work *Of the Trinity*, must, from its mention of 'the Sabellian Heresy' (c. 12 sqq.), be some years later in date. Jerome (*de Virr. Ill.* 70) calls it a 'quasi-epitome' from Tertullian, usually ascribed to Cyprian. Under Cyprian's name it was in after times sold at Constantinople at a low price, with the object of helping on the Macedonian views of the Holy Spirit. However it is orthodox, and inexact only as prior to definition.

[4] See inf. Ch. VII. 1. The *Felician Catalogue* (Lipsius, *op. cit.* p. 275) does not mention his father's name, and the surname Castinus given in the *Liber*

respected through every order and office in the church[1]. Personally he was not other than a humble-minded man, yet somewhat irritable, and with a high sense of official dignity. Cyprian at once honoured and humoured him, and was as far superior to him in the instincts of a ruler, as Novatian was in doctrinal acuteness. He had received to Communion some who, he satisfied himself by enquiry, had been unjustly accused of lapse by the severer faction, and was retaliated upon by charges of communicating with lapsed bishops and others, or even of being himself a Libellatic[2].

The disqualifications of Novatian however for the episcopate were patent; his irregular ordination, his unpopular retirement, the judgment of Moyses on his opinions. For he had now advanced to the position of the Puritan. He held it impossible that the Church on earth should reconcile apostates. He did not indeed exclude them from hope of salvation. He maintained it to be one of the most solemn ministries to bring them to repentance; but to communion never. To communicate in their communion was to become excommunicate.

No Christian thinker as yet had struck on the now so familiar distinction between the Invisible Church and the Visible, as the reconcilement of her essential attributes with their practicable evincement. But a true sense had guided both Cornelius and Cyprian himself, (who in later years was so egregiously to fail for lack of the same simple formula,) to a standpoint of more leniency than the late resolutions had occupied. With them moved almost the whole Church. But singular to say, the immediate comrades of Moyses had, possibly in some reaction against his influence, but also

---

Pontificalis of the Pseudo-Damasus, Labbe, I. p. 683, is less likely to be traditional than invented. See Rossi, *R. S.* I. Tav. iv. 2.

[1] *Ep.* 55. 8.
[2] *Ep.* 55. 10, 11, 12. With singular unfairness Ritschl says we have no means of knowing whether Cornelius was a Libellatic. The whole tenor of his history and the debate about his title must have been quite different if he had been.

urged by a new and strange partisan, placed themselves on the side of Novatian[1].

Early in the year 251 they were liberated from prison and the election of a bishop was contemplated.

For the security of Decius was threatened. Before the commencement of the new year Priscus* had assumed in Macedonia the title of Augustus, and allied his legions with Cniva and his Goths. Decius left Rome for the scene of action. Scarcely was he gone when Julius Valens was proclaimed Emperor† behind him, and followed him as far as Illyria[2]. There was a sudden absence from the city of all the principal military officers. Valens soon fell. But the war of commanders was the Rest of the Church. And though threats abounded, and expectations of resumed persecution prevailed[3], the interval was seized[4] for an election. Cornelius, compelled to accept the result[5], was by no less than sixteen bishops[6] ordained to the See of Rome.

In that Imperial world horror followed horror and 'blood touched blood' so fast that the sense of awe only stirred uneasily from time to time and was still again. But a great people was silently rising over its vast area, for whom Providence and the Innocent Blood were realities, and whose sense of God's Love was deepened by suffering for Him. The tidings were yet some months distant of a treason against

Side notes:
A.D. 251, A.U.C. 1004.
Coss. Imp. Cæs. C. Messius Q. Traianus Decius P. F. Aug. III Q. Herenn. Etrusc. Messius Decius Cæs. [*anno verg.* Aug.].
* ? Nov. or Dec., A.D. 250.
† Feb. or March, A.D. 251.

---

[1] Eus. *H. E.* vi. 46 ...ἔτι τῇ Νοουάτου συμφερομένοις γνώμῃ.

[2] Aur. Victor, *de Cæsaribus,* 29. The rise of Valens took place in Febr. or March 251, Lipsius, *op. cit.* p. 206; that of Priscus in end of 250; see Tillemont, vol. III. pp. 324, 5.

[3] ...qui [Cornelius] tantum temporis sedit exspectans corporis sui carnifices. *Ep.* 55. 9.

[4] The events are connected by the phrase in *Ep.* 55. 9 '...*cum* multo patientius et tolerabilius *audiret levari adversus se æmulum principem* quam constitui Romæ Dei *sacerdotem.*' (1) Decius *heard* of this infringement of the edict against bishops, not being himself at Rome. (2) The *æmulus princeps* was none but Valens. (3) The events were nearly contemporaneous. If Valens had risen in March and Cornelius (according to the usual chronology) in June, Cyprian could not have thus connected them.

[5] ...vim passus est ut episcopatum coactus exciperet. *Ep.* 55. 8.

[6] *Ep.* 55. 24.

Decius like his own, of the plunging squadrons at dead of night in the all-devouring morass, of the strenuous emperor's disappearance with his loved son. When the news came at last, and the engulfed princes had been added to the gods of Rome[1], it would have been too strange if there had not survived enough of human nature to make the Christians trace an Avenger in such tragedies; but what was new was the acceptance by the mass of them undoubtingly of their own persecution as a Divine and wholesome chastisement. And, says Cyprian, their enemy had not, 'in the darkest hour of the lovers of God,' succeeded for an instant in any place in silencing their constant 'boast of His praise' until once more 'the world shone out in light[2].'

Till then security was not assured, but from the day when Decius marched out of the gates the persecution virtually dropped, and 'Peace,' which but a few months before had seemed an impossible blessing, settled tranquilly down upon the Church.

We shall not be far wrong if we fix the ordination of Cornelius to about the 5th of March[3]. Easter Day in the

March 5, A.D. 251.

[1] ...uterque in barbarico interfecti sunt, inter Divos relati. Eutrop. ix. 4.

[2] 'Mundus eluxit,' *De Lapsis*, 1. 'Ultione divina' can only refer to the death of Decius in November. This little preface must belong to a later edition, for the treatise was out by the end of March, as we shall see. See below, pp. 156, 175.

[3] *Ep.* 55. 8. The date of the election of Cornelius is thus arrived at by Lipsius, *op. cit.* p. 18, pp. 206, 207. His successor Lucius died on the 5th March after having sat eight months and ten days (*Liberian Catalogue*) in which the three added years are an interpolation. This brings his ordination to June 25, and (if we allow an average time for the vacancy) places the death of Cornelius in June, and his ordination, two years three months and ten days previously (*Liberian Catal.*), in March.

The date of the 5th of March for the *death* of *Lucius* is prettily supported by a depraved text of *Liber Pontificalis*, which says that '*Cornelius* suffered on 5th March, and committed the church treasure to the archdeacon Stephanus.' The introduction of Stephanus shews that *Cornelius* is here an error for Lucius from whose life in the same Pseudo-Damasus comes the story (Labbe I. c. 739).

The common date, 4th June, assigned to the election of Cornelius, has disturbed the chronology of the reign of Decius by making it appear that Priscus could not have revolted before April, and has led even Pearson to construct hypotheses of long recesses in the ses-

year 251 was on the 23rd of March, and Cyprian, though unable to keep the Paschal solemnity in his own church, as was the wont of the African bishops[1], returned very shortly afterwards to Carthage, after fourteen months of absence[2]. It was some expected move[3] on the part of 'the faction' which postponed his return, or the fear of a demonstration which might rekindle persecution. Nothing unusual seems to have occurred. It was recognised that the execution of the edict was suspended[4], work was instantly resumed with utmost vigour, and the bishops of the province, about the first week of April, began joyfully to muster in the metropolis.

April, A.D. 251.

sion of the First Council, and of several journeys for Novatus to and from Rome. That date rests however on the mere application of the duration of Cornelius' episcopate (two years three months and ten days) to the 14th of September, which Jerome gives as the historical date of his execution at Rome. Cornelius was however not put to death, and that day is the real anniversary of the martyrdom of Cyprian, together with whose festival the memorial of Cornelius was celebrated at Rome on account of their friendship and union.

It seems to me possible also that the coincidence of Cornelius' election and Lucius' death on 5th March may have been a cause of error in early calendars.

Eusebius, in assigning three years to the pontificate of Cornelius, blunders wretchedly by copying out the odd number of months as if they were the years. Thus, from the statements that Cornelius sate 'a. II. m. III. d. X., Stephanus a. III. m. II. d. XXI., Xystus a. II. m. XI. d. VI.' he derives his statements that they sate respectively three years, two years, and eleven years. He has Lucius more correct.

[1] *Ep.* 56. 3.
[2] *Biennium* in the loose, overwrapping time-reckoning of a Roman: *Ep.* 43. 4. See note 2, p. 41.
[3] 'Malignitas et perfidia.' He distinctly planned his return for *after* Easter, *Ep.* 43. 1.
[4] Persecutione sopita, cum data esset facultas in unum conveniendi, copiosus episcoporum numerus, *Ep.* 55. 6.

CHAPTER III.

SEQUEL OF THE PERSECUTION.

I.

Cyprian's First Council of Carthage.

Question 1. The Title of Cornelius.

EVENTS had so concurred that the first subject which would demand the attention of this, the first Council of Carthage which had met for perhaps half a century[1], was quite other than had been contemplated in the agenda.

Cyprian had at the last moment[2] received the despatch from Cornelius announcing his own election. But with it had been delivered a letter of another tenor;—a protest against the choice that had been made[3]. It was from Novatian.

The president felt himself called upon to decide whether he should lay both documents before the Council, or if not, which of the two. He was guided, he says, simply by the tone of the communications. One 'had the tone of religious sim-'plicity; the other rang with the noisy baying of execrations

---

[1] Concil. Agrippinense.

[2] *Ep.* 45. 2 '...jam tunc, fratribus et plebi,' &c.

[3] *Ep.* 45. 2. Dom Maran (*Vita S. Cypr.* XIX.) takes this letter not to have been a protest but one from Cornelius: mistakenly and against the sense of Baluze (n. p. 432) whom he edits, 'cum ad me talia adversum te (Cornelium) et compresbyteri tecum considentis (Novatiani) scripta venissent, clero et plebi legi præcepi quæ religiosam simplicitatem sonabant...'

'and invectives.' He resolved not to communicate the mass of bitter and offensive charges in writing[1] against Cornelius to an audience of partially informed, provincially-educated persons, far from the scene of action, now gathered for deliberation in files about the Altar[2], and surrounded by the excitable laity of the city. Whether even on these forcible motives he should have withheld them is a question; considering that these councils were the very types of returning freedom, both individually and corporately. We recognise in his act the benevolent despot singularly combined with the scrupulous debater. He took however the politic step of

---

[1] ...ea quæ ex diverso in librum missum congesta fuerant, *Ep.* 45. 2, nothing wonderful. Not as Rettberg (p. 125), 'ein ganzes Buch angefüllt.'

[2] Fratribus (*i.e.* sacerdotibus) et plebi, *Ep.* 45. 2 ...longe positos et trans mare constitutos, 45. 2. Hartel confuses this interesting passage by a full stop after 'intimavimus.' Cyprian says respect for the assembly forbade him to produce the railing accusation 'considerantes pariter et ponderantes quod in tanto fratrum religiosoque conventu considentibus Dei sacerdotibus et altari posito nec legi debeat nec audiri.' That is, 'he well weighed what was not fit to be read or listened to in such a place.' Further on he says, 'porro hæc fieri debere ostendimus, si quando talia quorundam calumniosa temeritate conscripta sunt legi apud nos non patimur'; that is, 'We recognise this duty if, when people have given vent to such libellous spite, we suffer it not to be read before us.' (Cf. Ephes. 4. 29.) In each passage Hartel has expunged the negatives, reading '*et* legi debeat *et* audiri' and 'apud nos patimur.' Fechtrup thinks the changes destroy the meaning; but they really only present the converse (not the reverse) if *fieri debere ostendimus* is interpreted 'we sanction these doings.' Fechtrup (p. 136 and n.) may have found difficulties in *quod* and in *si quando*. However Hartel's first reading has scarcely any support, his second none.

O. Ritschl (p. 75) makes Cyprian impart Cornelius' letter '...nur an die Bischöfe und zwar in der geheimsten Weise (*singulorum auribus intimavimus*).' But this phrase merely means that he took care that no one should be ignorant of it: *intimare* has no tint of secrecy about it (*e.g. intimaverunt* is used of the declaration of the Jews that they had no king but Cæsar, *Adv. Jud.* Hartel, App. p. 139, 15). The thought of secrecy not only takes away the contrast with Cyprian's treatment of Novatian's letter, but he says expressly *clero et plebi legi præcepi*, *Ep.* 45. 2. Ritschl has fallen into another strange mistake on '...ea quæ ex diverso in librum missum congesta fuerant acerbationibus criminosis respuimus' (45. 2), 'den Brief der Gegenpartei will er mit Erbitterung von sich gewiesen haben.' *Acerbationibus* depends on *congesta*. Yet Ritschl's whole allegation against Cyprian of unfairness in the treatment of Novatian's despatch and of untruth rests on these two errors and on the meaningless reading *retenta* in *Ep.* 48. 3.

III. I. QUESTION I. THE TITLE OF CORNELIUS.

proposing to despatch two of their own number to Rome as a delegacy to investigate and report. His old friends Caldonius and Fortunatus were selected and took their departure[1]. Their instructions were to communicate in the first instance with the bishops who had attended the ordination of Cornelius[2] and, if satisfied, to procure from them written attestations of its regularity.

This unprecedented request for credentials, although complied with, exposed Cyprian at Rome to reflections upon his innovating turn. He reasonably replied that the circumstances were novel, and his procedure a security to the title[3]. The commissioners were further charged to use their best endeavours to recompose the broken harmony of Rome[4].

One more step was taken to complete the fairness of the neutrality. Communications with Cornelius as bishop were suspended; letters of church business to the city were ordered to be addressed for the present to its presbyters and deacons[5]. All Christian travellers Rome-ward bound were cautioned to be circumspect in recognising claims for adherence[6].

Question 2. Decision on Felicissimus.

Pending intelligence from Italy the Council approached their original work. There was this further necessity for the delegacy to Rome—that if Cornelius really favoured, as was reported, the party of laxity at Rome, the position of Felicissimus might be strengthened indefinitely[7]. Before conditions

---

[1] *Ep.* 48. 2; *Ep.* 44. 1.
[2] ...qui ordinationi tuæ affuerant, *Ep.* 44. 1.
[3] *Ep.* 45. 3.
[4] *Ep.* 45. 1.
[5] This does not seem to have had any practical effect except (as we shall see) at Hadrumetum. I do not see how Lipsius infers (*op. cit.* p. 204) from *Ep.* 45 that letters to Cornelius had been already written which were now re-addressed to his Clergy.
[6] *Ep.* 48. 1, 2.
[7] Ritschl, pp. 77, 78.

of communion could be determined for the Lapsed, the affair of Felicissimus stood as a preliminary question. For, should it be decided that his reception of repentant renegades without terms of penance had been warranted by circumstances, no further discussion on the Lapsed would be required. But if the broad issue should be first decided in the opposite sense to his, it might then be too late to introduce his conduct as a disciplinary question. Condemnation would wear the appearance of being based on *ex post facto* regulation. Whereas his schism really consisted not in the views he had maintained about the Lapsed, (for the question was yet open,) but in the fact that he had re-admitted offenders when the bishops had given notice that their cases were to be reserved to a council.

There is large indication that Cyprian was not present at this debate and its decision. An honourable and experienced lawyer would naturally avoid the position of a judge in a case in which he was virtually plaintiff and Felicissimus defendant. In writing of it subsequently to Cornelius he does not employ the first person, which is I think his unvarying practice when he records decisions at which he had presided. 'To acquaint you' (he says) 'with what has passed here in 'relation to the cause of certain presbyters and Felicissimus, 'our colleagues have sent you a letter subscribed with their 'hand, and by their letter you will learn the opinion and 'decision they arrived at after giving audience to the parties[1].'

Lastly, there is intimation of the absence of Cyprian from Carthage at the very conjuncture when, as I conclude, the case of Felicissimus was before them.

In company with Liberalis, one of the senior bishops of the province, he visited Hadrumetum[2], about eighty miles from Carthage, on I know not what errand. They found the clergy there in official correspondence with Cornelius, and in accordance with the resolution of the Council (which their absent bishop Polycarp had not yet transmitted to them),

---

[1] *Ep.* 45. 4.   [2] See *Appendix on Cities*.

III. I.   QUESTION 2.   DECISION ON FELICISSIMUS.   133

desired them to communicate with the Roman Church, not at present through Cornelius, but through its presbyters and deacons. Cornelius took umbrage at this course[1]; and certainly the sole moment at which Cyprian could properly have adopted it was precisely this interval elapsing after the departure of Caldonius, before the Council had satisfied themselves of the validity of Cornelius' position. This they did (as we shall see) sometime before the return of Caldonius, that is to say, just when they were debating the case of Felicissimus. Caldonius and Fortunatus had been also provided with a transcript of the previous letters addressed upon this subject of Felicissimus by Cyprian to his laity and his commissioners. They were read to the laity of Rome, who thus, without direct appeal to them, were put in possession of the case and on their guard against clandestine negotiation[2].

That the faction and Felicissimus were immediately condemned it is almost unnecessary to relate. Cyprian himself does not record it except by implication.

But though these, their would-be patrons, were silenced, it was not yet possible to decide upon the future of the tragically situated Deniers of Christ.

---

[1] *Ep.* 48. 1. The above hypothesis of the *absence* of Cyprian from the Council during the trial of his opponent Felicissimus solves difficulties to my mind absolutely insoluble in any other way. The text exhibits grounds sufficient to recommend it. Pearson and Tillemont hold that the Council was prolonged by various adjournments. But their hypothesis was framed (1) to dispose of the long period which the false date of Cornelius' election involved, (2) to allow for this Hadrumetum visit. 'Consilio frequenter acto' (*Ep.* 59. 13), which Pearson understands 'assembled again and again,' means 'largely attended.'

Lipsius, though he has corrected the election-date, proposes to meet the second difficulty (*op. cit.* pp. 203—206) by supposing the Council, before dispersing, to have empowered Cyprian, if satisfied, to recognise Cornelius in their name. But we shall see that Pompeius and Stephanus, before Caldonius returned, abundantly satisfied the Council of the validity of the election, and that on their evidence Cornelius was acknowledged (literas nostras ad te direximus, *Ep.* 45. 1), and publication of the fact ordered. Hence it is incredible that after the *end* of the Council, Cyprian should have suspended the Hadrumetines' correspondence with Cornelius.

[2] *Ep.* 45. 4. (*Epp.* 41, 43.)

Question 3. *Novatianism.*

For the Council at once became almost a council of war on the more imperial question. Messengers came and went from the field. Seldom has a council sat amid the outbreak and clash of the questions they had to decide. Seldom has a council been more wisely guided: seldom indeed swayed by so tranquil and large-hearted a chief: seldom recalled to consider the whole range of first principles rather than to pursue or recoil from the passion of the hour.

What we now study as one of the most famous of treatises was in its first form an Essay or Oration ON THE UNITY OF THE CATHOLIC CHURCH[1] delivered at this conjuncture[2]. It must have been rapidly composed, for the occasion of it had not arisen when the prelates first assembled. For them it was in itself an education. In masterly lines and with a colouring sometimes not inferior to Tertullian's he sketched that view of the constitution of the Church which has permanently shaped its history. The great theory and its illustrations must be reserved for fuller consideration presently. Here must be indicated simply the two or three leading principles by which the crisis was skilfully faced, and an intense feeling of personal responsibility for the integrity of the Church evoked in her bishops.

Only by distinctness (it is represented) as to the Scripture ideal of Unity may be formed a compact resistance to the insinuating errors of an age whose temptation is the presentment of novel error under Christian forms. The sole practical bond of union is to be found in a united episcopate. To every member of that order is committed, not only the

---

[1] So the best MSS. call it, and apparently Cyprian himself, *Ep.* 54. 4. In the time of Fulgentius it had received already the alternative title DE SIMPLICITATE PRÆLATORUM.

[2] The date will be discussed in the section on the *De Unitate.*

regulation of his own portion of the church but a joint interest in and responsibility for the totality and oneness of all its parts. Separatism abnegates in the individual the essence and first broad principle of the religion which is a Love expanding into, or rather necessarily expressing itself in Unity. Such were the principles of which the eloquent expression was elicited from Cyprian by the arrival of intelligence which we shall now relate.

Although Caldonius and his colleague had not returned (remaining in accordance with their instructions in hope of producing some effect[1]), two other African bishops, Stephen and Pompey by name, had appeared in the midst of the session fresh from the scene at Rome. They had been present at the consecration of Cornelius[2]. Aware of the importance of the chiefly clerical agitation against it, and assured of its regularity, they had armed themselves with documents drawn up by the consecrating bishops, testimonies from the laity to the life, character and 'discipline[3]' of the new bishop, and attestations to the depositions they were prepared to make at Carthage. In their places they gave their evidence amid universal satisfaction. All the characters of a true election in the third century (as we have already specified them) had concurred; the majority of the clerics, the suffrage of the laity, the consent of the neighbouring bishops[4]. Practically nothing could now be gained by the formality of awaiting the return of the Commission. Letters of recognition were addressed to Cornelius[5]. The tidings were disseminated through all the sees of Africa with the request that they too would acknowledge the new bishop.

Scarcely can the ink have dried when four new delegates

---

[1] *Ep.* 45. 1, 4.

[2] *Epp.* 44. 1; 45. 1; cf. *Ep.* 55. 8. Impossible that they could, as Ritschl, p. 82, imagines, have voted on his election.

[3] *Disciplina* is the moral correlative to *doctrina*. His pure celibacy comes under this head.

[4] *Ep.* 55. 8.

[5] ...litteras nostras ad te direximus, *Ep.* 45. 1.

from Rome requested audience, a certain Machaeus and Longinus, Augendus a deacon of Novatian's, probably the excommunicated follower of Felicissimus, (not the only member of that party who had taken a new colour at Rome,) and, as their senior, Maximus a Presbyter, not the confessor, but one who soon after pretended to the chair of Cyprian. Their mission was personally to press the charges against Cornelius, and solemnly to announce that Novatian had been consecrated Bishop of Rome.

We must narrate the circumstances of this startling event, which had occurred after the departure from Rome of Stephen and Pompey[1], and now surprised the Council in the midst of their satisfaction.

It seems then that the party of severity, disappointed and perplexed by the election, had been stimulated to action partly by Evaristus, a bishop whom Cornelius regarded as a prime mover in the enterprise[2]. But a more important actor had appeared at Rome in the person of Novatus. He had

Circ.
March 5,
A.D. 250.

---

[1] It becomes certain that this was the order of events from the following observations. Stephanus and Pompeius are not said to have brought any news except that of Cornelius' consecration. And the sensation in the Council at the announcement by the Novatianist embassy shews that it brought the *first* news of that of Novatian. Then the Council (it is stated *Ep.* 44. 2) were able to refute and repel its charges, although they had not received (*exspectavimus Ep.* 44. 1) the report of their own commission (Dom Maran, *Vita S. Cypr.* XXI. erroneously states the contrary), because Stephanus and Pompeius had produced evidence of the propriety and regularity of the consecration.

Supervenerunt, Ep. 44. 1, it may be observed means 'came on the top of our expectancy,' *not* 'came after Novatian's embassy.' For the Council could not have at once suspended the embassy from communion as they did, if up till then they had received only Cornelius' own letters for which they had sought ratification.

[2] *Ep.* 50. The common reading *Evaristum auctorem schismatis* would not give him, as Ritschl, p. 71, supposes it would, a position ascribable to Novatian alone. *Auctor* is properly a promoter, not an originator. So the confessors accuse themselves of being *hæresis auctores, Ep.* 49. 1, for allowing (*ut paterentur*) the consecration of Novatian. Jerome calls Novatus 'Auctor' of Novatian (*de Viris Ill.* 70). Nevertheless *cum auctore* is probably the right reading, for the reading of the two better MSS. *cum auctorem* is nothing but an African construction.

troubles of his own in Carthage; an enquiry which had long hung over him was now near, and he wished to avoid it, but he crossed the Mediterranean[1] with at least some vague purpose of baffling that spirit of the rising time which by means of the episcopal order was introducing organization amid confusion, and constituting its free representative assemblies (the only free assemblies be it remembered in the Empire) into a legislative and judicatory power.

To prosecute this aim he would have to ally himself at Rome with a body which took the diametrically opposite view upon the readmission of the Lapsed to that which he had supported in Carthage. Policy no doubt shaped his ends as well as his means, yet his joining the exclusive confessors at Rome when fresh from the comprehension-party of Carthage does not perhaps after all stamp him as a mere adventurer. Rather it reveals the true character of his view. The restoration or non-restoration of the Lapsed was probably to him indifferent. The question with him was, What should be the working power? In whose hands should the settlement of the terms of church communion be vested? The real object of his activity was to resist what he considered the encroachments of episcopal influence, and to retain the regulation of such cases where it had been during the loose chaotic time before Cyprian, namely in the hands of individual clerics. He had no doctrinal view to maintain[2].

---

[1] Accompanied perhaps by some of the excommunicated Felicissimites, since Augendus, one of them (*Ep.* 42), reappears *from Rome* with the first embassy, *Ep.* 44. 1.

[2] I have omitted the statement that, according to Cyp. *Ep.* 52. 2, he had that security of the adventurer—no character to lose; because at any rate this had not come before the Roman confessors. Neander, indeed *op. cit.*, vol. I., pp. 312 sqq., with characteristic anxiety to place thinkers unprejudiced before readers, assumes that these statements are the growth of polemic rancour, and goes so far as to say that Cyprian would himself have been to blame for allowing (previous to trial it would seem) such a character among his clergy. This is uncritical. It is true that the assumption of Novatus's guilt, the attributing of his withdrawal from Carthage to a bad conscience, and the general accusations of depravity, may be classed with the usual violent moral prejudices against religious opponents, but that an

Hence though a single passage implies that his virtual enquiry into his conduct was impending just before the persecution, is as certain as a fact can be, see p. 111 sup.

Date of Novatus' journey to Rome. Nothing but some singular coincidence could have given us this date minutely. But the determination of the true date of the ordination of Cornelius removes a difficulty which beset Pearson and all earlier chronologers in attempting to fix it. In other points they have misled themselves. (1) Cornelius was supposed to have been consecrated in June 251. (2) It was inferred from the words of the Liberian Catalogue that Novatus had practised with the Roman Confessors as early as January 251. (3) It was inferred from *Ep.* 52. 2, 3 that he had fled to Rome to avoid the *cognitio* as to his conduct, which was to come off before the persecution began, *i.e.* at the latest, in the end of A.D. 249. (4) He was organizing the opposition at Carthage with Felicissimus towards the end of the persecution—towards March 23, Easter A.D. 250, *Ep.* 43. 2. (5) He was at Rome after Cornelius' consecration. To reconcile these dates it was necessary to suppose that he had made several voyages to Rome while organizing his party. But surely among his other exertions in the cause of error this would have received some notice, while the inconsistency of his shifting policy at the two centres of his activity would have attracted more observation. However, I hope to be excused for a longer examination of the story, if it were only because Lipsius himself, who detected the date of Cornelius, still imagines from (2) and (3) one voyage immediately on the death of Moyses, one or more earlier, and one after the Council. Lipsius, *op. cit.*, pp. 202, 3, takes Cyprian in 52. 3 to speak of such a voyage, although he sets down the motive assigned for it—dread of the trial—to party spite. Pacian is the fountain of this mistake [*Ad Sympronian. Ep.* 3, 6; Galland. *Bibl. SS. Patr.* vol. VII. p. 263 (1765)]. He quotes part of Cyprian's words, but paraphrases his 'ut judicium sacerdotum voluntaria discessione præcederet' by 'Romam venit...et hic latitavit.' But what Cyprian really says is that Novatus avoided excommunication for personal misdemeanours by *discession from the church during the persecution*, that is to say by getting up, or joining, the party of Felicissimus; from *Ep.* 41. 2 we see that Felicissimus took the *initiative* and excommunicated the Cyprianic side (sententiam quam *prior* dixit). In *Ep.* 52. 2 Cyprian mentions the voyage in connection with the commencement of the party of Felicissimus, but this is only a rhetorical juxtaposition because he wishes to parallel Novatus's appointment of a Bishop in Rome with his former appointment of a Deacon in Carthage. (2) Again as to the Liberian Catalogue. The words are, under FABIUS, '...Post passionem ejus Moyses et Maximus presbyteri et Nicostratus diaconus comprehensi sunt et in carcerem sunt missi. Eo tempore supervenit Novatus ex Africa et separavit de ecclesia Novatianum et quosdam confessores, postquam Moyses in carcere defunctus est qui fuit ibi m. xi d. xi'; and under CORNELIUS, '...Sub Episcopatu ejus Novatus extra ecclesiam ordinavit Novatianum in urbe Roma et Nicostratum in Africa. Hoc facto confessores qui se separaverunt a Cornelio cum Maximo presbytero, qui cum Moyse fuit, ad ecclesiam sunt reversi...,' ap. Lipsius, *op. cit.*, p. 267. Now the object of these entries, which occupy the main part of the short memoirs, is to record the action of Moyses and Maximus who were commemorated at Rome

QUESTION 3. NOVATIANISM.

change of party was not unnoticed at Carthage[1], yet it is not, as might have been expected, urged against him as a palpable refutation.

If this election of Cornelius could be overruled at once before being generally accepted or even announced; if he could establish himself at the right hand of another bishop,—one to whom the eyes of many men of highest character had been directed; if he could then secure for him recognition at Carthage; he would not only have nothing more to fear on his own account, he would be in the very best position for moderating between the episcopal power, and all who whether upon lax or upon puritan principles desired almost all individual discipline to be in the hands of the second order.

It was thus that Novatus and Felicissimus tried to restrict

as Confessors. It was important they should not be claimed as Novatianists, and Cornelius in his letter in Eusebius is anxious to vindicate them. It was needful to distinguish them from Nicostratus their companion, who though not made a bishop (as here represented) did remain a Novatianist. It is impossible to press the first entry into a chronological statement that Novatus made a voyage to Rome immediately after the death of Moyses. Its object is to record that Moyses died as a confessor before Novatianism began.

We therefore conclude that we have no statements whatever implying that Novatus made more than one journey to Rome at this period. If he did not reach Rome till *after* the election of Cornelius on March 5, where he would find growing disunion (...gliscente et in pejus recrudescente discordia... *Ep.* 45. 1) already, he would still have abundance of time to organize measures before Caldonius arrived in the 2nd or 3rd week of April only to find Novatian on the point of being consecrated. And lastly we must remark that until after the election of Cornelius had taken place no act of Novatus could be described as 'separating the confessors from the church,' for at the worst he could only have been endeavouring to procure the election of another. I conclude therefore that Novatus came to Rome immediately after the ordination of Cornelius on March 5, A.D. 251

It is annoying to find Fechtrup, who has ideas of accuracy, suggesting by the way that Cornelius' consecration may be put 'etwa vierzehn Tage später' in order to allow Novatus a fortnight more for mischief at Rome. If Lipsius' calculation, precise in itself, and solving all difficulties, is to be put a fortnight out on such subjective 'Gründe,' chronology is indeed vain (Fechtrup p. 107 and note).

[1] *Ep.* 52. 2 '...damnare nunc audet sacrificantium manus, compare the earlier '...nunc se et ad lapsorum perniciem venenata sua deceptione verterant,' *i.e.* by indulgence, *Ep.* 42. 2.

the terms of communion in their own district, and the view though unscriptural and unconstitutional is intelligible.

The spirit of Novatus illustrates itself in those presbyters of our own who, if they could, would repel from communion, celebrate or withhold marriage or funeral rites, or fix the age of confirmation, on their own judgment; who revolutionise ritual without respect to either Bishop or 'Plebes'; who admit to vows, direct the persons who take them, and pretend to dispense from them.

Maximus and the other newly liberated confessors[1], already biassed against Cornelius by the austerity of their own views, now worked upon to believe that he was ready to sacrifice the Church's purity for a spurious charity, and stimulated by the temper of Novatus, determined to elect Novatian[2]. Their high character rendered it not impossible to procure three country bishops to lay their hands, in the supposed capacity of saviours of the Church, upon his head[3], and to invest the first Puritan[4] with the attributes of the first

---

[1] *Ep.* 54. 2.

[2] '...separavit de ecclesia...' *Liberian Catalogue.* See p. 138 n.

[3] Corn. ap. Eus. vi. 43. We may dismiss the irate and simple-hearted prelate's belief that the rite was performed by them in a state of inebriety, though the assertion illustrates the possibilities of the time. Eulogius, Bp. of Alexandria, A.D. 579, had (Phot. *Bibl.* cod. 182) a preposterous story about Novatian being made pope by 'τοὺς περὶ Ἀλεξανδρείαν ἐπισκόπους'; where we should, I think, read τοὺς περὶ Ἀλέξανδρον, one of the bishops just named, though even that will not make sense of the story. 'Novatian was,' he relates, 'the Archdeacon of Rome' (no such office existed before the end of the 4th century, see Lipsius, *op. cit.*, p. 120 and note). 'The Archdeacon had an established right (ὁ τηνικάδε τύπος κρατῶν...ἐνενόμιστο) to succeed to the episcopate, but Cornelius on discovering that he was plotting his death put an end to his ambitious designs by ordaining him a presbyter.' We must receive with qualification the statement of Pacian that he became bishop without consecration (*Ep.* 2. 3). The contemporary language of the confessors and of Cornelius (*Ep.* 49 and Eus. *l. c.*) is incontrovertible. Still if we put Pacian's circumstantial expressions 'absentem...consecrante nullo...per epistolam (confessorum)' side by side with Cyp. *de unitate ecclesiæ* 10, '...nemine Episcopatum dante,...' we may suppose that some little interval occurred between his election and consecration, in which he would be called Episcopus Romanus, whereas ordinarily the consecration immediately followed.

[4] ...ὁ Ναυάτος τῆς τῶν λεγομένων

Anti-pope. He then, in strange anticipation of the policy of his rival's successors, connected the Eucharistic feast with a pledge of personal fealty to himself. 'Swear to me,' he said (for Cornelius believed he had obtained the very syllables of the form), 'swear to me'—taking both hands of each communicant between his own—'never to abandon me and return to Cornelius.' The response 'I will no more go back to Cornelius' took the place of the Eucharistic Amen[1].

Thus was commenced the Novatianist or Purist schism, which deepened its unforgivingness at last to heresy; which planted bishops in all the leading sees from Spain to Pontus, and made the mountaineers of Phrygia almost its own; which, first allowed and then proscribed by Constantine, supported by Julian, supported by Theodosius, and forbidden by his two sons, lasted on at least until the end of the sixth century[2].

This then was announced in regular form at Carthage as the election of a true bishop for Rome, one who would 'assert the gospel[3]' and preserve church-purity. Confirmatory Epistles (partly forged, as they afterwards declared[4]) were issued in the name of Maximus and the Confessors, together with despatches from Novatian himself to the other principal sees[5].

In these Novatian dwelt on the unwillingness with which he had accepted a position literally forced upon him[6]. And in a reply which the large-hearted Dionysius of Alexandria, wiser perhaps than severer censors, addressed to him, we trace a real belief that he may have followed rather than led his supporters, and that he might yet disentangle himself. If

---

Καθαρῶν αἱρέσεως ἦρξε...σχισματικὸς ὢν κυρίως ἀλλ' οὐχ αἱρετικός. οὐ γὰρ πρὸς δόγμα τι τοῖς ὀρθόφροσι διεφέρετο..., Zonar. *in Can. I. Conc. Carthag.*, ap. Migne, *Patr. Gr.* vol. 137, c. 1097.

[1] Euseb. *H. E.* vi. 43.
[2] See Tillemont, vol. III. *Les Novatiens*, pp. 471—493 and pp. 746—753.

Hefele in Wetzer u. Welte's *Kirchenlexikon* (*Novat. Schism.*).

[3] *Ep.* 44. 1, 3. See note on *Evangelium*, infr. p. 147.
[4] *Ep.* 49. 1.
[5] *Epp.* 49. 1; 55. 2.
[6] ἐκβεβιασμένος, Eus. *H. E.* vi. 45. Hieron. *de Viris Ill.* 69.

again the inference from words be as just as it is obvious, he was in fact prepared to acquiesce in a secondary place at Rome, if only accepted as bishop of a church within a church[1].

It was thus that Dionysius argued. 'If it was against 'thy will, as thou sayest, that thou wast promoted, thou wilt 'prove this by retiring. It were good to suffer anything and 'everything so to escape dividing the Church of God. And 'martyrdom to avoid schism is no less glorious than martyr-'dom to avoid idolatry[2]. Nay, it is to my mind greater. In 'one case a man is a martyr for his own single soul's sake. 'But this is for the whole Church. Even now wert thou to 'persuade or constrain the brethren to come to one mind, 'thy true deed were greater than thy fall. This will not be 'reckoned to thee, the other will be lauded. And if thou 'shouldest be powerless to sway disobedient spirits, save, save 'thine own soul. I pray for thy health and thy stedfast 'cleaving to peace in the Lord.'

Now Dionysius' actual view of the mischief which Novatian was doing was conveyed in these terms to his own namesake, then a presbyter, afterwards Bishop, at Rome: 'wheeling on to the stage most unholy teaching about God; 'falsely accusing our kindest Lord Jesus Christ as void of 'pity; setting at nought the holy Laver; overturning the 'Faith and Confession that go before it; and while there was 'some hope of their continuance or return, chasing the Holy 'Spirit away from them[3].'

Read side by side with this opinion of the man's work, Dionysius' letter to the man himself is surely a pattern of controversial sweetness.

---

[1] *Ep.* 55. 8 in fine.

[2] Καὶ ἦν οὐκ ἀδοξοτέρα τῆς ἕνεκεν τοῦ μὴ εἰδωλολατρῆσαι γινομένης ἡ ἕνεκεν τοῦ μὴ σχίσαι μαρτυρία, Eus. *H. E.* vi. 45. The text in Pearson, *Ann. Cypr.* 251, x., defective. Rufinus 'et erat non inferior gloria sustinere martyrium ne scindatur ecclesia (quam est illa ne idolis immoletur).'

[3] Euseb. *H. E.* vii. 8. The fourth Baptismal letter to Dionys. Rom.

III. I. QUESTION 3. NOVATIANISM. 143

That Cyprian was deeply convinced that ambition had a real hold on the spirit of Novatian and contributed to his action appears in a grave incidental condemnation of him penned six years later. At that distance of time, and after his unanimous councils, the allusion could not be to the opponents of his own election, nor does it in fact characterize that form of opposition. It must be of Novatian that he thinks when he writes of 'one who complained of being passed over, 'and would not brook another's preferment, and rebelled out 'of enmity not to the man but to his office,' and again of 'one 'in sheep's clothing who through the coming in of jealousy 'could neither be a peacemaker nor be in charity[1].'

When Maximus and the other delegates of Novatian presented themselves to the Council at Carthage it would have been in any case irregular to admit them to hearing prior to the report of their own commissioners. But by this time as we have seen they had received very full evidence, and were able at once to rebut many of their strenuous assertions. Until the return of the deputies they refused to hear more or to admit them to communicate[2].

We must confess however that the delegates and Novatian himself were not wholly without justification if they had anticipated that personally Cyprian might take a different view. It is far from improbable that Novatian may have had before him Cyprian's new book of Testimonies, and seen the heading 'that it is impossible for him whose offence is against GOD to be absolved in the Church[3].' At any rate when last they corresponded they had agreed upon

---

[1] *De Zelo et Liv.* 6. 12.

[2] *Ep.* 44. 1 '.. a communicatione eos nostra statim *cohibendos* esse censuimus et refutatis *interim, &c.*' *Cohibere* seems to be never used, as Ritschl (pp. 80, 81), for the purpose of making Cyprian contradict himself in consecutive sentences, here understands it 'sofort excommunicirt.' It implies a kind of 'suspension' only. *Abstinere*, sometimes with *rejicere*, is the invariable term for excommunication—see *de Dom. Or.* 18, *Epp.* 3. 3; 41. 2; 59. 1, 9, 10; 68. 2; 74. 8.

[3] *Testim.* iii. 28 'non posse in ecclesia remitti ei qui in Deum deliquerit.'

two important points. Both had held that the exclusion of the Lapsed should be for a protracted period, to be measured apparently by years. Both had agreed that the Martyrs should have a voice as to the course to be pursued. Novatian had now advanced to the conclusion that mere time could not restore their status as churchmen; he was prepared to act upon the letter of the theory which regarded[1] the separation as more properly life-long. Again, if the Martyrs' opinion was to be respected it was no less valuable when it favoured exclusion than if it recommended comprehension. If he was not aware that his own change of views was an abandonment of catholicity, how could he have expected to find Cyprian now inclining to shorten indefinitely the term of exclusion, or foreseen that the influence of the Carthaginian Martyrs would be exerted in precisely the opposite direction to that of the Roman? His ambassadors accordingly, after being removed[2] from the assembly, appealed with much vehemence to the primate in his church upon the next Station-Day[3] as well as to the laity. Either then, or on their previous removal from the Council, it was replied that Novatian had placed himself in a position external to the church, and could not return except as a penitent[4]. They were however bitterly in earnest. One or two of them conferred privately with many leading members of the church in the capital, others made the tour of some provincial towns to push the cause[5]. It was essential to the principles of such a sect that, however few and far between, all the 'Pure' believers should be united in one body.

---

[1] Ritschl holds that though there had gone on in North Africa as well as in Italy a softening of the system of exclusion, yet exclusion for life was still the theory in the instance of Lapse until the Decian persecution, pp. 15, 16.

[2] Expulsi, *Ep.* 50.

[3] *Ep.* 44. 2. Unless *statione* could describe a session of the Council on account of the presence of an altar (*Ep.* 45. 2) and of the consessus. It is used similarly, if Hartel's reading *de statione* for *destinantem* is correct, *Ep.* 49. 3.

[4] *Ep.* 68. 2.

[5] *Ep.* 44. 3.

III. I.   QUESTION 3. NOVATIANISM.   145

It is now worth while, even if somewhat tiresome[1], to follow out one intricate example of the minute finish of Cyprian's diplomacy, of his laborious care in conciliation, in the avoidance or removal of misunderstandings.

A Presbyter—Primitivus—was first despatched as the bearer of a private communication to Cornelius, briefly giving the heads of the transactions, with instructions to afford personally the fullest explanations[2]. Such explanations he was actually sent back to obtain, where his information failed, with regard to the suspension at Hadrumetum of the recognition of Cornelius' title. Cyprian's reply on this, a model of considerateness towards unduly aggrieved feelings, points to the complete success of the method adopted[3] and to the final corroboration secured through Caldonius and Fortunatus. However meantime the provisional sending off of Primitivus, which proved to be thus politic, had been at once followed up by the sending of the Subdeacon Mettius with the acolyte Nicephorus in charge of a fuller explanatory despatch[4] to meet each point of possible misconstruction; to enclose fresh copies of Cyprian's earlier letters with a request that these might be laid before the brethren; further, to announce that

---

[1] The reader may consider as he proceeds the hypothesis that these diplomatic steps,—so far from obvious in the perusal of the letters, so consistent when patiently traced, so dotted up and down, a word or two at a time,—are an incident in a large forgery, an elaborate story worked out only to be sprinkled in ineffective, indiscernible fragments.

[2] *Ep.* 44. 2. Lipsius (p. 204 n.) says that part of the correspondence here is lost. Cyprian expressly says, however, that 'et quia quibus refutatis et conpressi sunt...in epistula congerere longum fuit' will be 'plenissime singula' detailed by Primitivus, and there is no allusion to any point as having been mentioned *in letters* which we do not trace in our collection except the synodical letter about Felicissimus.

[3] *Ep.* 48. 2.

[4] *Ep.* 45. In c. 4 the MS. reading *quæ de eodem Felicissimo et de presbyteris ejusdem ad clerum istic* (*i.e.* here in Carthage) *non et ad plebem scripseram* is the opposite of the fact, for *Ep.* 43 is his weighty appeal to the laity on this exact subject. Hartel perversely ignores the printed reading of *nec* before *non*, which is essential to the sense, but dropped by the commonest kind of slip after the *-ic*. In the same line he chooses the meaningless *isdem* in preference to the equally well supported *ejusdem*.

the whole Province of Proconsular Africa had by this time been informed of the conciliar reaffirmation of the Title of Cornelius; to communicate the conciliar Resolutions on Felicissimus and his adherents; and to enclose for the Confessors, under cover to their true Bishop, a 'Brief Letter[1].' Finally when the explanation asked for through Primitivus was sent, Cyprian was able to add that the Recognition of Cornelius had been forwarded on from the Province throughout Numidia and Mauretania[2].

And now to take up the 'Brief Letter.' The concentration of energy, pathos and doctrine in so few lines is surely marvellous[3]. He touches on the depression with which the news of the Confessors' desertion had crushed him :—' Against 'God's ordinance, against the Gospel-law, against the unity 'of the Catholic foundation, to have consented to the creation 'of another bishop! that is, to a thing divinely and humanly 'impossible, the founding of a second church, the severing of

---

[1] *Epp.* 46 and 47.

[2] *Ep.* 45. 1 'Sed et per *Provinciam nostram,*' &c. Then later, *Ep.* 48. 3, 'Sed quoniam latius fusa est nostra *Provincia*, habet *etiam Numidiam et Mauritaniam* sibi cohærentes, ne in Urbe,' &c. 'Inasmuch as our Province is very widespread, and has also Numidia and Mauritania in close connection with it, therefore, &c.' (Peters, to support a scheme of 'Metropolit, Ober-metropolit, Kirchenprovinze' &c. wishes to make *habet* mean 'includes' and *sibi* 'united to each other.') The text proceeds 'placuit ut per episcopos, *retenta* a nobis rei veritate, et ad comprobandam ordinationem tuam facta auctoritate majore, tunc demum scrupulo omni de singulorum pectoribus excusso, per omnes omnino istic positos litteræ fierent.' I cannot translate *retenta* (Hartel from MSS. except μ *recente*). 'Kept secret' (as O. Ritschl, see p. 130, n. 2) cannot be the meaning, for the despatch was read to the assembly, and to conceal it would not have increased the authority. Cyprian's object was to place beyond doubt the facts of the election whatever they were. So *Ep.* 44. 1 'ut eis adventantibus et *rei gestæ veritatem reportantibus, majore auctoritate*...partis adversæ inprobitas frangeretur,' which is exactly parallel; *Ep.* 48. 2 'rebus illic...*pro veritate conpertis*'; 48. 4 '...nunc episcopatus tui et *veritas* pariter et dignitas *apertissima luce...fundata* est.' I therefore venture to propose *retecta* 'discovered, ascertained,' instead of *retenta*. The sense would thus be 'we resolved that the bishops should cause letters to be circulated among all in all directions here, now that we had *learnt* the real facts, and were in a better position to confirm your ordination, not a scruple at last remaining in any bosom.'

[3] *Ep.* 46.

III. I. QUESTION 3. NOVATIANISM. 147

'Christ's members, the rending of soul and body in the Lord's 'flock by the sundered rivalries—this is not the way to "assert 'the Gospel" of Christ¹. And we,' he exclaims, 'we cannot 'quit the Church to come out to you!—Return to your mother '—to your brotherhood.'

Dionysius the Great also wrote to them from Alexandria in their alienation². The Catholic Church could realise then what was meant by this—'If one member suffer all the members suffer with it.'

---

[1] It is remarkable that the character which seems at this time especially to attach to the word *evangelium* is that of *strictness* or *precision*. Thus in *Ep.* 55. 3 and again in *De Laps.* 15 Cyprian calls the stricter discipline 'Evangelicus vigor,' 'Evangelii vigor,' *Ep.* 55. 6 'Evangelica censura.' So *Epp.* 67. 8; 30. 4; 27. 4. This must be borne in mind in rendering such passages as '*evangelicis* traditionibus roboratos,' *De Laps.* 2. The catholic rule to have but one bishop in a city is (still with the same idea of strictness) 'evangelica lex' *Ep.* 46—'nec ecclesiæ jungitur qui ab evangelio separatur,' *De Laps.* 16. Hence it is not without a characteristic force that in *Ep.* 30 Novatian uses the terms 'Evangelica disciplina (three times), evangelicus vigor, evangelicum certamen (confessorship),' and the substantive and adjective twelve times in the first two chapters of *Ep.* 36, and addresses the book *De Cibis Judaicis*, to *you who* 'sine cessatione in Evangelio vos perstare monstratis.' After his secession 'evangelium Christi asserere' (*Ep.* 46. 2), 'assertores evangelii' (*Ep.* 44. 3) seems to have been the watchword of his sect. So even in his Greek letter to Fabius, Eus. *H. E.* vi. 43, Cornelius sarcastically calls Novatian ὁ ἐκδικητὴς τοῦ Εὐαγγελίου. The still extant type was next succeeded to and exaggerated by the Donatists. They were in the habit of accosting Catholics with ' Estote Christiani,' or 'Cai Sei, Caia Seia, adhuc paganus es, aut pagana' (Opt. iii. 11), or ' Bonus homo esses, si non esses traditor! consule animæ tuæ: esto Christianus.' Aug. *de Bapt. c. Donatt.* ii. 7 (10).

[2] Euseb. *H. E.* vi. 46 ...ἔτι τῇ τοῦ Νουάτου συμφερομένοις γνώμῃ.

FOUR OTHER PICTURES FROM A.D. 250.

It is only fair to the Reader that I should now at this point remind him that eminent critics have drawn very different sketches from those above of chief actors in the church affairs of A.D. 250.

I present outlines from two portraits of Cyprian by Otto Ritschl and by Adolf Harnack, and, by the former, one of Felicissimus in the character of the True Churchman, and one of a vanishing Novatus. I ought to say that mine were earlier in print, but a short contemplation of these may further clear some points.

It is natural that divines in Non-episcopal Confessions should not only search (as we see) for a non-episcopal ordination, but should trace the early wisdom and success of episcopal administration itself either to ignored action on the part of the presbyterate or to masterful ambitions of great prelates on behalf of their order; or again that they should if possible exhibit instances in which, as one of them naïvely expresses it, 'things really do *go* without a Bishop, and go well, if only the Clergy step full in.'

If my own judgement of what took place in those times be warped (as I think theirs is) by prepossessions unperceived by myself, it is my sincere desire to have them corrected by fact and document. To these tests I commit the difference without reserve.

The first portrait shall be that of Cyprian before his own Presbyters in the time before the Council, by O. Ritschl[1]. My abstract will be as just as I can make it.

1. *Cyprian before his own Presbyters.*

'The Roman clergy left responsible in the vacancy of their own 'see, regarded the Carthaginian see as practically vacant through 'Cyprian's retirement, its clergy as responsible like themselves, and 'themselves as responsible for suggesting to them a course like their 'own. They wrote them therefore the Eighth Epistle.'—So far well.

'Next, the Carthaginian clergy out of their perfect loyalty to

---

[1] Otto Ritschl, *Cyprian v. Karthago und die Verfassung der Kirche.* Erster Theil, Cap. i. (Göttingen 1885).

'Cyprian communicated the Epistle to him. No faction (whatever
'Cyprian may say) existed among them.
   'The Roman Letter and its probable effect were greatly dreaded
'by Cyprian. Even the loyal conduct of his clergy about it placed
'them in a position to make dangerous capital of their magnanimity.
'But its actual effect was also very great.
   'It moved at least the Four Presbyters (*Ep.* 14) to mild views of
'the course to be taken with the Lapsed, and the final result of
'their action was to make Cyprian adopt the milder view. But
'it is probable that the whole body of the Presbyters took this view
'from the first and that they selected Four of themselves to bear
'the brunt of Cyprian's anger. Cyprian was hard on the clergy,
'excusing all others and laying all blame on them. The "radical"
'presbyters who early communicated the Lapsed simply anticipated
'the necessary policy which Cyprian after a time adopted.
   'The "Visions of the Martyrs" or Confessors contributed to
'soften his procedure. The offence he took at the Confessors was no
'matter of principle, but only a personal sense of their disrespect.
   'Cyprian's attitude however was that of a strong man. He might
'have been expected to employ his money to conciliate those who
'differed from him. But he did not. He treated the Four Presbyters,
'and indeed all, with growing decision. For example; whilst in
'*Ep.* 5 he uses the language of request "*peto*," &c., afterwards, when
'the great Eighth Epistle might have wrecked their allegiance, he
'boldly in *Ep.* 14 uses the imperative mood and strain throughout.'

   To examine the above scheme—and to begin with the last
suggestion. This is not literally true. For, if in *Ep.* 5, 2 he only
uses *peto*, in *Ep.* 14. 3 he uses *oro vos*, and in *Ep.* 5. 2 occur the only
real imperatives which appear in either—*consulite et providete*. But
in tone there is no tangible difference. It is absurd to treat *hortor et
mando* in *Ep.* 14. 2 as imperious when the object of them is 'act as
plenipotentiaries for me,' *vice mea fungamini*.

   But the whole scheme may be characterized as a string of assumed
probabilities which have been already negatived by ascertainable
facts.

   The importance assigned to the illiterate Epistle Eight is necessary
to the theory but is wholly unwarrantable. A defect of humour
has kept the Critic from seeing the sarcastic force of Cyprian's treatment of it in *Ep.* 9. 2 (see pp. 87, 88 above). But in fact there is no
reason to suppose that the Eighth Epistle ever came to the hands
of the Carthaginian clergy at all. They never replied to it. They
never allude to it. For good reason. It bore no address. It was
delivered to Cyprian at the same time by the same hand—Crementius's
—which brought him the letter of the same Roman Presbyters about

Fabian's martyrdom, and it was at once returned by him to its authors for reconsideration. It proposed, as we have seen, no substantial plan. Its promoters felt ashamed of it and changed their note. Yet this is the formidable document to the guidance and terror of which we are asked to trace all the leniency of the clergy and nearly the whole policy of Cyprian.

As to the effect upon him of the 'Martyrs' Visions' it is enough to observe that the Visions are not said to have been seen by the Martyrs but by other persons, and that the one moral of all the Visions is severely disciplinary and not relaxatory.

Again the 'Radical' clergy can in no sense be said to have *anticipated* the action of Cyprian. They did indeed readmit to communion. But Cyprian's point was not that the Lapsed should be either admitted or repelled, but that they should not be admitted (1) without open repentance, (2) without the formal assent of the Church. These conditions, in which lies the gist of his whole policy, they violated. Ritschl (p. 17) quotes from *Ep.* 15. 1 *ante actam pœnitentiam, ante exomologesin...factam, ante manum...impositam* to prove that Cyprian was not angry at their action but only at their precipitancy. But he omits Cyprian's *contra evangelii legem* from the same clause, and words cannot express greater indignation than Cyprian's at the absence of enquiry and authority from their procedure.

The impossibility of other combinations and conclusions of this scheme—these are the main ones—will I hope be detected from the text and references above.

2. *Cyprian before the Roman Presbyters.*

This is our second Portrait-Sketch.

We have acknowledged that it is tempting to certain scholars to explore instances in which 'things really do *go* without a Bishop, and *go* well, if only the Clergy step full in[1].'

It is tempting even though the vacancy be one of a few months only, and even if the Clergy themselves so little acquiesce in the idea that 'things go well,' that all the time they are lamenting their limitations and longing to get the see filled.

Yet we should scarcely have expected that the vacancy of the Roman See, in which its Presbyters so changed their bearing towards Cyprian, and adopted his Policy entire; a vacancy in which his κυβέρνησις, his wisdom, gentleness and dignity as a bishop come so strongly out, would

---

[1] A. Harnack, *op. cit. infr.* p. 25. 'Dass es wirklich auch ohne Bischof geht und gut geht, wenn nur der Klerus voll eintritt, kann das Beispiel,' &c.

be selected as an *example* of the adequacy of headless, unepiscopal management.

In an ingenious and learned essay (which appeared many years after the above text was in print) Dr A. Harnack, along with much that is of linguistic importance, and a minute verification of the authorship of *Ep.* 36, has maintained an interesting thesis to that effect[1].

To him 'Epistle viii. is the masterly work of at once a Pastor and a 'Statesman (p. 25)—though not a well-educated one. Immediately on 'hearing that Carthage had by his own act lost her Bishop, the Roman 'clergy undertook the duty and adopted the style of a Bishop, and issued 'orders to the Clergy of that city. It is quite an "Archiepiscopal In-'struction" (p. 26). They pursued indeed with great political sagacity a 'double policy. To Cyprian they wrote respectfully as Bishop, to the 'Clergy they wrote with the view of getting them to ignore him as 'Bishop and take the reins of government in hand themselves.' (p. 24.)

Here we must really pause. There is in *Ep.* 8 nothing to justify the imputation of machination so mean and cruel, however prudent it may seem to some. The Roman Clergy began mistakenly. But they were in a most difficult position. Without a head themselves and not daring to elect one, they now heard that the Second City of the Empire was headless too, and that by the Bishop's own act. Persecution was afoot and he was gone. It was very natural that they should write to the authorities there without a thought that they were composing 'a pendant (*Seitenstück*) to the Epistle of Clement to the Corinthians'(p. 15). Cyprian nowhere complains of their doing so—only, in his dignified way, of their tone, *Ep.* 9; and in *Ep.* 20 says he writes to them not as bound to do so, but because they are under a mistake and misinformed. They could not know that the counsel they sent had been anticipated by Cyprian in much more minuteness; that for the liberality they recommended towards sufferers and poor, Cyprian had provided the means; that a scheme was begun by Cyprian for dealing with the Lapsed, the 'Martyrs,' and the Premature Restorers, of which they would be glad to borrow all that their own case required; that from his retirement Cyprian was governing all. When they knew, they changed their note; but from the first there was no duplicity in their conduct, rather too rough a straightforwardness.

The Clergy to whom they wrote had had solemnly committed to them beforehand by Cyprian himself all the powers which the Romans wished them to take. 'Discharge upon the spot both your own parts and mine' (*Ep.* 5. 1). 'I exhort and charge you, who can be upon the spot without 'invidiousness and with less peril, to discharge in my stead whatever 'duties the religious administration demands' (*Ep.* 14. 2).

---

[1] Adolf Harnack, *Die Briefe des römischen Klerus aus der Zeit der Sedisvacanz im Jahre* 250, ap. *Theologische Abhandlungen* (published in honour of Carl von Weizsäcker's 70th birthday). Freiburg I. B. 1892.

The Clergy who wrote were performing those very duties, just as the Romans were in the vacancy, but they were only too painfully aware that there were episcopal functions which they themselves were incapable of discharging. They took the best and widest counsel they could, calling in their neighbour bishops and such exiled bishops as were then at Rome, but 'We have thought,' say they, 'that before the appointment of a 'bishop we must take no new step, but take a middle line in attending 'to the lapsed, so that in the meantime, while we are waiting for a 'bishop to be given us by God,'—the different classes should be treated thus and thus (*Ep.* 30. 8). Again, 'We are the more obliged to postpone 'this affair, because since the decease of Fabian of noblest memory we 'have had, owing to the difficulties of circumstances and times, no bishop 'yet appointed to direct all these affairs, and to examine into the cases 'of the lapsed with authority and wisdom.' (*Ep.* 30. 5.)

This is surely not 'oberbischöfliche Unterweisung.' (p. 26.) This is not the tone of those who felt that even they themselves possessed the authority which they urge (as we are assured) their brethren to assume.

Nevertheless Dr Harnack finds that the great writer of *Ep.* 8 at once 'identifies the clergy in whose name he writes with the Bishop,' for they speak of 'Our Predecessors,' meaning the Bishops of Rome—'antecessores nostri[1].'

The passage referred to is, 'If we are found neglectful, it will be said 'to us as it was also said to our predecessors, who were such neglectful 'prelates (*præpositi*), That we have not sought that which was lost, and 'have not set right the wandering, and not bound up the lame, and were 'eating the milk of them, and clothing ourselves with the wool of them.' (*Ep.* 8. 1.) This would have been strange language to address to primitive bishops of Rome, but of course it was not. It was really addressed by Ezekiel to the Shepherds of Israel, the predecessors of all shepherds[2]. Dr Harnack admits or admires the 'sarcastic' or 'cutting' (*anzüglich*) use made of Scripture texts by the author (p. 25). This text may perhaps serve him to illustrate that criticism, but not to shew that Presbyters of Rome regarded themselves as Successors of the Popes.

The representation of the rest of the correspondence takes its colouring from these *Principia*[3]. While the letters of Novatian 30 and 36 speak an episcopal language, those of Cyprian exhibit his humiliation.

---

[1] Das Collegium spricht in ihm so, als wäre es selber der Bischof, ja es redet von 'nostri antecessores.' (p. 22.)

[2] Ezek. c. xxxiv. *vv.* 3, 4. Hartel has perhaps here deceived Harnack by omitting the reference from both text and margin, *ad Novat.* 14; Hartel, Append. p. 65. Elsewhere he has it.

[3] Yes, even to the distortion of minor facts like these. It is said that they learnt Cyprian's flight through their own delegate Bassianus—solicitously sent to enquire. Yet all that is said of Bassianus here is that he 'has arrived,' *Ep.* 8. 3, while it is distinctly said that the (Carthaginian) sub-deacon Clemen-

'Months afterwards Cyprian writes one letter, 20, to secure allies, 'humbled even to speaking of himself as "mea mediocritas"! (*cc.* 1, 2): 'writes a second 27, without waiting for an answer to the first: is silently 'ignored in two Roman letters (see *Ep.* 27. 4), but takes on him to answer 'both, with much flattery of the Confessors. At last "the ice is broken" '(p. 30), and Novatian condescends to write no more to the clergy but to 'himself. Even then a painful impression is produced by the solicitude 'with which he circulates the Roman missives.' 'What a triumph for the 'Roman Clergy' (p. 29).

In the last paragraph I have thought it only right to place before readers such a web of ingenuity spun by so distinguished a scholar. It is the meeting-point of the extremes, Presbyterian Teutonism and Ultramontanism. For I need not add that the supposed position is laid down as a truly historical and logical step from episcopacy toward the supremacy of Rome.

The only answer which can be of value is an ingenuous statement of the whole contents of the Letters. To this, as I have tried to give it above, and to the Letters themselves I confidently refer for that answer.

3. *Of Felicissimus as a more faithful representative of the Church.*

O. Ritschl's Thesis is that the consolidation of the Episcopate was a mere policy framed by an unscrupulous energetic man from moment to moment to meet the exigencies of his position, and his Doctrine of Unity a theory evolved to justify his practice. In developing this thesis he reconstructs the history of the Faction of Felicissimus. It is impossible to give more than an outline of his tedious labour, but the facts must, he maintains, have been these[1].

'Cyprian's Commission and Relief Fund, *i.e. his own* means, were 'devoted to the creation of a party by bribery and place-giving and to 'the overthrow of the Presbyters' influence at Carthage. Felicissimus 'was probably put forward by the Presbyters to defeat the plan. 'Being only a Deacon his supposed threats cannot have been really 'formidable, and therefore the adherence to him, which was very ex-'tensive, betokens only the amount of suspicion felt about Cyprian. 'His success *actually drove the Commission away* from Carthage, and 'therefore Cyprian's statement that the *plurimi* were on his side is '*untrue*.

'*Ep.* 41 exhibits Cyprian's embarrassment. He would fain ex-'communicate Felicissimus for his treatment of the Commission, but

tius brought the information. *Ep.* 8. 1. Bassianus appears from the company he is mentioned in, *Ep.* 22. 3, to be a Carthaginian cleric and refugee.

[1] pp. 57—65.

'that is hopeless; he falls back on previous offences, and after all
'reserves the decision for his coming council. The true reason for
'Felicissimus' excommunication is his simple resistance to Cyprian.
'If Augendus adheres to him *he is to be* excommunicated for this
'alone. Between the others excommunicated the only tie is their
'opposition to Cyprian. The Commission *had first applied to the
'Clergy of Carthage* to issue an excommunication. As *they declined
'to do this*, they issued it themselves. In their own opinion therefore
'they must have been always competent to do it, and having three
'bishops on their board—the number competent to ordain—competent
'they were. They returned to Carthage, and there added to the
'proscribed two names more (*Ep.* 42).

'The five hostile presbyters acquired their influence *after the ex-
'communication by the clergy of Gaius of Dida*. It is seen in the
'*refusal* of the same clergy to excommunicate Felicissimus. It comes
'out strongly when the Commission did it in spite of the clergy;
'they then had with them the majority of the Christians. The five
'were the *élite* of the clergy, and enjoyed that popular confidence
'which Cyprian forfeited by his absence.

'To them Cyprian now attributes the original opposition to his
'episcopate. He kindles good Christians against the Lapsed (such
'is the view of *Ep.* 43); sees that he can never win back the followers
'of Felicissimus, and must rid the Church—and himself—of them.

'Accordingly the Episcopal Council of A.D. 251 excommunicates
'Felicissimus and his followers.

'Thus the Episcopal power is organized in order to fight Cyprian's
'battles, and, in order to afford it a basis, the doctrine of the Unity
'of the Church is developed out of his consciousness.'

Of course no practical theory of polity is developed without events, but having already drawn out the real events as accurately as I can (and the evidence is abundant), I can only suggest further that Ritschl's heavy pages be read with the original letters side by side, and with an honest intent to reconcile some and to recognise other of the incidents—if it be possible.

4. *Of the Evanescence of Novatus under Ritschl's Analysis.*

I desire fairly to give the gist of several laborious pages[1]:—

'All our information about Novatus rests upon the statements of
'Cyprian. If we reflect on what is credible or historically imaginable
'we cannot admit that Novatus was in Rome supporting Novatian's

[1] pp. 68—75.

'election. The belief is due to the fact that Cornelius having men-
'tioned him in general terms, Cyprian, delighted with a weak parallel
'which suggested itself to him, stated that Novatus advanced in
'arithmetical progression from ordaining a Deacon at Carthage to
'consecrating a Bishop at Rome. It is unlikely too that Novatus
'should have left Carthage for fear of proceedings, since he would
'have known that he should be condemned in his absence. Unlikely
'that Cyprian should have warned Cornelius against him, just as he
'was about leaving Rome. Novatus' connection with past turmoil
'in Carthage rests on no proof: it is built up out of the combinations
'of Cyprian's fancy. It is later on when Novatus is named in con-
'nection with them.'

And I will categorically touch on these '*criticisms*' as they deserve:—

The fact is that Cyprian makes no statements about Novatus in Rome. He comments and moralises freely on what Cornelius tells him. An inventor of statements would never have cast them in a mere allusive form. We do not look for proof in such a case; the proof is notoriety. The rule of three on Novatus' progress from Carthage to Rome and so from Deacon-making to Bishop-making is a mere play of rhetoric on something told to him. The critic escapes the snares of humour.

The fear of judgment going by default is not a common deterrent from absconding. Why should it deter Novatus? As to his earlier influence against Cyprian, 'agitators' and 'certain persons' are alluded to from the very first. It is the manner of Cyprian and of many early Christian writers not to *name* adversaries so long as reticence is possible[1]. And why should Cyprian describe the career of Novatus to Cornelius until he heard that Novatus was busy near to him?

Again, Ritschl finds it of course necessary to expunge[2] *ac Novati* from all manuscripts and editions of *Ep.* 47. And so Novatus vanishes.

But yet again Ritschl himself describes Cyprian as penning *Ep.* 52. 2 in a state of 'passionate excitement' at the thought of Novatus' return from Rome to Carthage. If that were so, Why had Novatus been to Rome? What had he there been doing? And what was he expected to do in Carthage? Nothing?

---

[1] See note 4, p. 160.

[2] May I point out to students that '*et* Novatiani *ac* Novati' is Cyprian's own use when both conjunctions are to mean *and* (not *both...and*)? Compare *Ep.* 46 '*et* actui *ac* laudibus.'

Question 4. The Decision on the Lapsed.

The primary question before the Council had been what should be the position of the Lapsed? Its determination had been postponed first to the examination of the case of Felicissimus, and secondly to the unexpected outbreak of division in the election to the Roman bishopric. Both of these nevertheless depended on the solution of the original issue. Though the latter involved questions so much wider, yet its origin was in the identical question before the Council; and its present aspect illustrated the policy of free and early conciliar action such as had been concerted in Africa. The decision on Felicissimus was as we have seen a necessary preliminary to that action. These two decisions indeed had cleared off the extreme views on either side. Neither the lax nor the purist view of Discipline could now be reopened. Cyprian lets us know that the discussion was nevertheless a prolonged and earnest one[1], that the basis assumed alike by the advocates of lenity and of severity was an examination of Scripture, and that they conceived as a distinct ideal for their guidance the mercifulness of the character of God[2].

Cyprian had bestowed deepest attention on the subject. He had developed his conclusions in his elaborate paper ON THE LAPSED which he read to an audience who cannot have been less moved by the simple pathos with which it fixed the tragedies passing before their eyes, than they were strengthened by its wisdom and charity[3]. Nevertheless their leaning was to a course still milder than he suggested, and

---

[1] *Ep.* 55. 6 'Scripturis [diu] ex utraque parte prolatis,' *Ep.* 54. 3 'diu multumque tractatu inter nos habito.'

[2] The verbal resemblance of 54. 3 and 55. 11, 25 shews that the date of the letter to Antonian was very soon after the events, and therefore brings the Roman Council mentioned *Ep.* 55. 6 to June or July.

[3] *Ep.* 54. 4, *Ep.* 55. 5, 6. The libelli read to the Council were the *De Lapsis* and *De Unitate.* See pp. 174, sqq. on the former.

they were much less disposed than he to give the martyrs a voice in their decisions. The primate was loyal to the deliberative power he had evoked.

The encyclical which contained the resolutions is lost[1]. But its gist, and even its minutiæ, are extricable from an admirable letter of Cyprian. The Epistle to Antonian is in fact a pamphlet in length not far short of that On the Lapsed. Antonian was an African bishop who, while forwarding letters of adherence to Cornelius, privately acquainted Cyprian with certain difficulties which he had felt in doing so, and received from him, after the Council closed, a restatement of the whole case.

It would seem then that Cyprian in council abandoned more than one of his own suggestions. He admitted that the postponement until death of the reconciliation of the Libellatics was a severity only applicable to the very hour of persecution, when retrieval through a new confession was yet an open though terrible way. Certainly if penance was ever so worked in times of 'Peace' this could only be because Lapse was infrequent and Return more infrequent still.

After peace had been once restored to a Church which had suffered from Lapse upon a great scale, the sentence of life-long exclusion was felt to be a cruel and an impolitic[2] measure. For the utilitarian aspect of the question was a really noble one. In the later struggle with the Donatists Optatus[3] warns them that the 'Passion for Innocence' in the Church while practically unattainable could not, even if attained, be higher than the 'Utility of Unity.' Upon the natural tendency towards strictness felt by the unfallen he

---

[1] Such a document is indicated in *Ep. ad Anton.* 55. 6. For 'singula placitorum capita' has no relation to the form, nor 'ut examinarentur' to the contents of *De Lapsis*. This letter to Antonian is prior to the Second Council, A.D. 252, since it treats of the restoration of the Libellatici only, not of the Lapsed.

[2] *Necessitati temporum succubuisse* et multorum saluti providendum putasse, *Ep.* 55 7.

[3] Opt. vii. 3.

adds, 'The keys of Heaven were committed to the Apostle 'who fell, not to so many who stood firm; it was ordained 'that a Sinner should open the gate to Innocence, for an 'Innocent one might have closed it against Sinners.'

Considering therefore that penance without hope of mitigation could have no practical value, but that a return to pagan life or at best an adherence to some more tolerant schism would be its natural result, while on the other hand every spiritual help was requisite for persons who might shortly be exposed again to persecution[1], it was by this Council ruled:—

I. That an individual examination should be held not only of the facts, but further into the motives or inducements which had been presented to the weakness of the Libellatici.

II. That the Lapsed who had not sacrificed should be restored after a considerable term of penance, and after public application to their bishop for restoration[2].

III. That those who had sacrificed should be restored at the hour of death[3] if they had continued penitent.

IV. That such as had refused penance and public confession until they were in fear of death should not then be received[4].

The Council did not rule, but Cyprian assumes, that one reconciled as a dying man would not be again excluded if he

---

[1] *Ep.* 55. 6, 7, 14, 15.
[2] Traheretur diu pænitentia et rogaretur dolenter paterna clementia, *Ep.* 55. 6.
[3] 55. 17. Fechtrup, p. 129, alleges *Ep.* 55. 6 to establish against Dupin and Hefele that Rule I, when applied to 'sacrificati,' implies that some of these might be restored earlier. But although Cyprian says that their fault was of various shades, he draws the widest distinction between them and the Libellatici. 'Nec tu existimes, *Ep.* 55. 13, carissime frater, sicut quibusdam videtur, libellaticos cum sacrificatis æquari oportere.' The statement in the text is, I think, accurate.
[4] *Ep.* 55. 23.

The teaching of Dionysius is exactly the same in the beautiful fragment of his epistle to Conon printed in Pitra's *Spicilegium Solesmn.* I. p. 15 from the Bodleian *cod. Baroccian.* CXCVI. fo. 75, an excerpt of which afterwards passed for a *Canon* by a confusion at first with *Conon*. Pitra, *op. cit.*, I. p. xiv. art. v.

recovered. With a humour which he sometimes exercises upon over-rigidity he observes that the man cannot be required to die, or his spiritual guide to insist on his decease, in order to complete the conditions of his restoration. In his own strain he adds that, if GOD Himself respites him this is one more mark of the Divine pity and fatherliness. Added life takes up the pledge of holy life[1].

The Resolutions were communicated to Cornelius, to Fabius[2] patriarch of Antioch, and doubtless to the other great sees, and the Council then broke up. It was the June[3] of A.D. 251.

II.

Advance of Novatianism—Return of The Confessors.

Meantime intimation had been sent to Africa by Cornelius that his rivals shewed no disposition to sit tamely down under the rejection of their embassy. A confessor Augendus who conveyed this news was speedily followed by Nicephorus, the acolyte, bearing a private note with fuller particulars of the energetic movement with which Cyprian was to be pressed home[4].

A second Novatianist delegacy had already started, and in it the principal 'authors' of the movement. Primus and Dionysius we know but by name; Nicostratus was a freedman, probably rich; he had been one of the powerful Seven Deacons of Rome; after sharing the prison of Moyses and Maximus he was now permanently alienated from the

---

[1] Compare Cyprian's handling above. Fechtrup, p. 127, mistakenly attributes the provision to the Council; and points out that other Councils were more severe; *e.g.* Nicæn. can. 13. Arausic. I. can. 3. Epaon. can. 36. Perhaps frauds compelled them to be so.

[2] Eus. vi. 43. Cyp. *Epp.* 55. 6, 45. 4.

[3] Or July, Lips. pp. 205, 6. Yet scarcely so, considering the length which this would give to the Carthaginian Council which met in April, and the unhealthy season to which it would throw the Roman Council.

[4] *Ep.* 50.

Church. He is accused by Cornelius not only of embezzling church funds (which might mean that he had carried sums over to what he held to be the true succession), but also of having defrauded the patroness to whom he owed his freedom[1]. Such reports however easily passed into circulation, and perhaps shew little but that he had funds at disposal, just as the accusations of avarice against Novatus have doubtless to do with the pecuniary organization of the sect[2].

Still more notable delegates were the Bishop Evaristus[3], who had been one of Novatian's consecrators, and to whom his 'Commons' had instantly elected a successor; and lastly Novatus himself, once more on his own ground, fortified by his success at Rome[4].

The ground was however less secure behind him than he trusted. Cyprian does not hesitate to ascribe the next act of the drama in some measure to the withdrawal from Rome of his great influence[5]. The very day after he reached Carthage with his colleagues, the acolyte of Cornelius sailed into the port, and with the warning we have mentioned he delivered a second letter. He had in fact hurried on board 'the very 'hour, the very moment,' says Cornelius, 'of the conclusion 'of a Station in which Maximus, with his fellow confessors

---

[1] *Ep.* 50. The Liberian Catalogue states that he was made bishop in Africa, which is possible, but may be due to a confusion with Maximus.

[2] *Ep.* 50, *avaritia* Hartel for common reading *pravitate*; cf. *Ep.* 52. 2.

[3] See p. 136.

[4] The omission of the name of Novatian, designated only 'hujus scelerati hominis,' led some to regard this (50) letter of Cornelius as a fragment. Coustant however (Routh, *R. Sac.* III. pp. 31—33) shewed that to drop the *name* of objectionable persons was a common practice with popes and others. Routh observes that the name of Novatian is *never mentioned by Cornelius* in any letter. He employs various periphrases, and in one place, to avoid speaking of his baptism, has περιχυθεὶς ἔλαβεν without τὸ βάπτισμα (Eus. vi. 43, Routh, III. p. 67). Cyprian, on the other hand, who had not the bitterness of Cornelius, evidently plays on the concurrence of names and acts, 'Novatiani et Novati novas...machinas' 'Novatus...rerum novarum semper cupidus.' *Ep.* 52. 1, 2.

[5] *Ep.* 52. 2.

III. II.   RESTORATION OF ROMAN CONFESSORS.

'Urban, Sidonius, Macarius and most of their adherents had 'rejoined the main body of the Church[1].'

A rumour had been rife of this return from the Novatianist camp[2]. Cornelius was characteristically the last person to credit it. At some gathering of presbyters, attended by five bishops but not by Cornelius, Urban and Sidonius appeared to express on the part of Maximus and his party a desire for reunion. Some feeling of distrust decided the clergy to decline to treat with representatives, and a large body of Novatianists agreed to attend. The main ground of ill-will against them was the calumnious nature of the circular letters issued so widely and effectively in their name. They disclaimed the responsibility and even the knowledge of these. 'Nothing had been further from their thoughts than 'an abandonment of the Church. They had been led to 'question simply the title of Cornelius.' Their accusation against themselves was the sanction which they had given to the new ordination. It was not in human nature that they should escape without some invective. They however pressed for pardon without needless humiliation.

Nothing further could be determined without the bishop. Upon a second day he convened a full presbytery with the five bishops. Individual opinions were pronounced and re-

---

[1] The date of this must have been before the Roman Council (see p. 163), since otherwise they would have been excommunicated, which it does not appear that they were, and posterior to the Carthaginian Council, since Cyprian makes no allusion to it as sitting, in his letters to or about the confessors, and he read the account of their return (*Ep* 51. 1) to the Church, not the bishops. It must also have been directly after Novatian's second embassy, described in the same bundle of letters from Cornelius; for Novatus was on that embassy, and Cyprian says they returned to the Church upon his departure from Rome.

This date disposes of Ritschl's belief that Novatus himself appeared before the Council. The *auditis eis* which he quotes from *Ep*. 45. 4 refers to the *first* embassy of which Novatus was not a member

[2] Rettberg, who is always assuming intrigues, relates how Cyprian took advantage of Novatus' coming to Carthage to press them to leave Novatian, and succeeded. The notion is simply negatived by possibilities of time.

corded[1]. The confessors, who again appeared, took the same dignified ground as before. Allowances must be made on both sides. They listened to an exhortation to sincerity. But[2] they simply asked to be received back again without penance or disgrace[3]. 'They had been imposed upon. Facts had 'been misrepresented to them. They had never intended to 'set up a second bishop. The essential unity of the episcopate 'was clear to them as to others. They had wished for one 'true bishop, and they had not, until undeceived, recognised 'such an one in Cornelius.' Charity and policy alike forbade harshness towards such sufferers and such penitents; the laity impulsively embraced them, they wept for joy, they broke out into loud thanksgivings. The presbyters opened their circle and took Maximus[4] back to his old place near the

LOCULUS OF MAXIMUS.

[1] Sententias...quas et subjectas leges: *Ep.* 49. 2, verbatim, I believe, like those of the VIIth Council, A.D. 256.

[2] 'Omnibus *invicem* remissis.' 'Desiderantes...ut exhiberent,' singular construction unless *hortabamur*, or some such word, has slipped out, *Ep.* 49. 2.

[3] I can assign no other force to their requests 'ut ea quæ ante fuerant gesta in oblivionem cederent nullaque eorum mentio haberetur proinde atque si nihil esset vel commissum vel dictum,' &c. taken in conjunction with *Ep.* 49. 2, Cornelius' statement, 'omnia ante gesta remisimus Deo,' and the point which the confessors made of it in *Ep.* 53 'omnibus rebus prætermissis et judicio Dei servatis.'

[4] See de Rossi, *Roma Sotterranea*, vol. I. pp. 295, 6, Tav. xix. 5, vol. II. p. 184. Though the name is common, yet it is scarcely likely that another unknown Maximus, also a presbyter, should have found a place, with his name in Greek and in lettering of that age, in the catacomb chapel of, and so close to the side of, the bishop Cornelius, whom the influence of *this* Maximus so largely contributed to establish. The statement that he was martyred under Valerian, Baron. *ad Nov.* 19, Baluze ap. Routh, *R. S.* III. p. 39, is answered by Tillemont, t. III. The Depositio Martirum (Mommsen, *op. cit.* p. 632) has this entry, Mense Julio VI. Id. 'Et in Maximi [sc. cœmeterio]

III. III.   RESTORATION OF ROMAN CONFESSORS.   163

bishop, from whom death itself was no more to part him for ever. The laymen of the schism were desired at once to resume full communion[1].

This generous treatment probably justified the expectations of Cornelius and made recantation easier to others.

The temperate firmness and the serene joy of Cyprian's remonstrance and congratulation to the confessors on their secession and their return place the 46th and 54th letters among the most delicate specimens of the collection, and are alone enough to give Cyprian a foremost rank among wise and loving saints. Nor was Dionysius[2] behindhand in greeting their returning steps. But to Cyprian the return was more than a glad reunion—more than an incident of the Gospel of Peace. It was a conclusive evidence of the truth of his theory. 'This error being gone,' he exclaims, 'light 'is shed in all hearts: it is demonstrated that the Catholic 'Church is One, and admits neither schism nor division. 'Separation has no note of permanence[3].'

III.

Continued action against Novatianism—Roman Council of A.D. 251, *Antiochene of* A.D. 252.

The winding up of the Carthaginian Council brought us (as we saw) to the June (scarcely the July) of A.D. 251[4], nor can any long interval[5] have elapsed before the Roman bishop

A.D. 251.

Silani. Hunc Silanum martirem Novati furati sunt.' There is no cemetery of Maximus. Did the Novatianists attempt to claim him still?

[1] The Nicene Council similarly received Novatianist presbyters back to their full rank and the Collation of Carthage (411) the Donatists.

[2] Euseb. vi. 46 mentions his two letters, τοῖς αὐτοῖς τούτοις μεταθεμένοις ἐπὶ τὴν ἐκκλησίαν.

[3] *Ep.* 51 ad fin.

[4] See p. 159.

[5] The date October given by Pearson (*Annal. Cypr.* A.D. 251, xiii.) and adopted by Fechtrup (p. 139) again depends on the radical mistake as to the time of Cornelius' election. Out

with a Council of sixty others from Italy and with many presbyters and deacons, accepted and promulgated the same decisions, and excommunicated Novatian on account of his inhumane doctrines.

The right direction of Roman and Italian opinion was (as we have seen) aided by the powerful sympathy of Dionysius. He had followed up his bracing advice to Novatian[1] and his reply to Cornelius by a letter, singularly called 'diaconal[2],' addressed to the Romans themselves 'through Hippolytus[3]'; a second direct to them 'on peace and likewise on repentance'—that is, on the Restoration of the Lapsed; one to the Confessors, while still adherents of Novatian[4], and two more after their return.

It seems to require more knowledge than we possess to enable us to decide whether the Hippolytus, through whom the first letter to the Romans was transmitted, was the great 'Elder[5]' and philosopher, whose episcopal work though not

---

of this synod, called by Jerome (who treats it as almost one with the Carthaginian) 'Synodus Romana Italica Africana' (*Lib. de Vir. Illustr.* c. 66), Labbe, I. pp. 865—868, misled by Baronius, has made three. Cf. Zonaras xii. 20, ed. Dindorf, III. pp. 134, 135.

[1] Eus. *H. E.* vi. 45.

[2] See Note at end of this Section.

[3] Eus. *H. E.* vi. 46 ἑξῆς ταύτῃ καὶ ἑτέρα τις ἐπιστολὴ τοῖς ἐν Ῥώμῃ τοῦ Διονυσίου φέρεται διακονικὴ διὰ Ἱππολύτου. τοῖς αὐτοῖς δὲ ἄλλην, κ.τ.λ. Jerome, *de Viris Illustr.* 69 'Dionysius...in Cypriani et Africanæ synodi dogma consentiens (v. p. 356 infr.) de hæreticis rebaptizandis ad diversos plurimas misit Epistolas, quæ usque hodie exstant, et ad Fabium, Antiochenæ urbis episcopum, scripsit de pænitentia, et ad Romanos per Hippolytum alteram, &c.' Jerome (*op. cit.* 61) knew Eusebius' list of Hippolytus' writings and had 'found' (*repperi*) many more of those which Eusebius (vi. 22) said were to be found (εὕροις ἄν). Both name the πρὸς Μαρκίωνα and the πρὸς ἁπάσας τὰς αἱρέσεις 'adversus omnes hæreses.'

[4] Eus. *H. E.* vi. 46 ...ἔτι δὲ τῇ τοῦ Νουάτου συμφερομένοις γνώμῃ.

Mai, *Classicorum Auctt. e Vat. Codd. editorum* t. X. 1838, p. 484, has a fragment of Dionysius which, from its peculiar touches on 'Peace,' indicating a context on that topic, I rather ascribe to *this* letter named by Eusebius than to one of the three treatises 'on Penitence' named by Jerome, to which Mai refers it (viz. *ad Fabium Antioch.*, *ad Laodicenses*, *ad Armenios*). Jerome, *de Vir. Ill.* 69.

[5] See Bp. Lightfoot, *Apostolic Fathers*, pt. I., *S. Clement of Rome*, vol. II., p. 435, ed. 1890.

ascertained by Eusebius, or, more strangely, by Jerome[1], lay among 'the nationalities' in the Port of Rome. If this were possible the idea is historically attractive. For though there is no colour for attributing to him actual Novatianism, yet his former attitude towards two predecessors of Cornelius,—with whom he 'was at daggers drawn[2],' and whom he so relentlessly depicts,—gave ground enough for his being thought not unlikely to take the Puritan side, as afterwards he was believed to have done[3]. That position had been a right but very fierce resistance to a low tone of doctrine and morals. Neither side in Rome would now be prompt to appeal to him, charged as they stood the one with laxity, the other with irregularity; while he, at his great age, with his profound study of the working of sects, was the very man through whom the great Alexandrine would naturally approach the Romans[4]. Nor would any policy be so likely to secure his cooperation, which was of serious consequence, with the Council. It bears the singular title of 'A *Diaconic* Epistle through Hippolytus to them in Rome.'

Cyprian approved the mingled severity and moderation of the language of the Roman Council, and letters of assent came in from many Italian bishops who had not attended it.

Next, in pursuance of its resolutions, (if it had not been rather a subject of the programme[5],) a bishop Trofimus,

---

[1] Eus. *H. E.* vi. 20 ...'Ἱππόλυτος, ἑτέρας που καὶ αὐτὸς προεστὼς ἐκκλησίας. Jer. *de Virr. Ill.* 6: 'cujusdam ecclesiæ episcopus, nomen quippe urbis scire non potui.' See Lightfoot, *op. cit.*, p. 434.

[2] 'At daggers drawn with the heads of the Roman Church.' *Id.* p. 412.

[3] Prudentius, *Peristeph.* xi. 19 'Invenio Hippolytum, qui quondam schisma Novati Presbyter attigerat, nostra sequenda negans.' Cf. vv. 28 ff.

Lightfoot, *op. cit.*, pp. 328, 424, has shewn that Prudentius' account of the Novatianism of Hippolytus comes from the Inscription by Damasus, while Damasus cautiously states that he proceeds only on popular belief. 'Hippolytus *fertur* premerent cum jussa tyranni Presbyter in scisma semper mansisse Novati....Hæc *audita refert* Damasus probat omnia Christus.' De Rossi, *Inscrr. Chrr. Urb. Rom.* II. p. 82.

[4] On Chronological and other Difficulties see Note at end of Section.

[5] It seems to me, though I do not know that the allusion has been noticed, that the words '*tractatu cum collegis plurimis habito* susceptus est Trofimus'

who had offered incense in the troubles and been imitated by his flock, was together with them restored to communion by Cornelius. It is not denied that his people's attachment to him and the assurance that they would follow his return, eased the reception of Trofimus. But Cyprian, who defends the fact against misrepresentations forwarded by Novatianists to Africa, denies on his own knowledge that he was suffered to resume his Orders[1]. It is improbable that a lapsed bishop would be obliged or allowed to do public penance. The statement itself that Trofimus 'with penance *of entreaty* confessed his old fault' is against it, and it is said that he made 'satisfaction,' although it is presently added that 'the return of the brethren made satisfaction for him[2].'

(*Ep.* 55. 11) must refer to this Roman Council of June or July.

[1] 'Sacerdotii,' *Ep.* 55. 11, shews that Trofimus was a bishop not a *priest* (as Fechtrup). *Ep.* 55. 2 '*Trofimo et turificatis*' leaves it short of certain whether Trofimus himself had gone so far in his lapse. And while in the order of this Epistle the case of the *sacrificati* is treated separately from his in another section, and the restoration of his Orders is expressly disproved, Ritschl (p. 79) describes him as *Sacrificatus*, as restored corruptly to his Episcopal place, and asks 'What defence is it to allege, like Cyprian, that Trofimus had after the example of former bishops sacrificed himself for his flock, and lapsed in order to keep them together?' This ridiculous question exhibits Ritschl's rendering of 'conligendis fratribus nostris carissimus frater noster necessitate succubuit' (*Ep.* 55. 11). *Frater* is of course not Trofimus at all but Cornelius himself, and the *necessitas* is the obligation which he felt to receive Trofimus back (though only as a layman) in accordance with precedents, for the sake of recovering with him the whole diocese. In *Ep.* 67. 6 Cornelius is particularly mentioned as concurring with the whole episcopate in the impossibility of reinstating lapsed bishops in holy orders. [He restored one of Novatian's consecrators only to Lay-Communion, Cornel. ap. Eus. vi. 43.] A false argument is usually rested on mistakes rather more subtle than these.

Fechtrup sees in his restitution the 'special occasion' of Novatian's secession. Rather too acute; since (1) it must have been known in Rome that Trofimus was *not* restored to Orders, though it was reported in Africa that he was; and (2) his restitution was after the secession, so far as we can tell.

[2] *Can. Ap.* 25 degrades clerics without excommunication since one act is not twice punished. [Basil, *Ep.* 188 (214), applies this to a deacon as being incapable of restoration to orders.] *Concil. Eliber. can.* 76 fixes penance for deacons, *Neocæs. can.* 1 for priests, without restoration, *Nicæn. can.* 16 involves it for both. Leo I, *Ep.* 167 (2),

As for other great centres, Novatian had announced to them his election as he did to Carthage[1], and not always without effect. His high tone was impressive[2]. Even Alexandria had needed a strong remonstrance from its prudent and gentle chief, Dionysius the Great[3]. To the Egyptian church also at large, and to Conon, bishop of Hermopolis, in particular[4], Dionysius addressed papers on the Lapsed and their Repentance, carefully distinguishing for them the different classes of offending[5]; nor can his letter to Origen on Martyrdom have been unconnected with the discussion. To the Armenians he wrote on the same question with the same precision[6] as to the Egyptians; again to the Laodicenes under Thelymidres.

But about no See was such anxiety imminent as about Antioch. There the Patriarch Fabius had a certain leaning towards the Schism[7]. Dionysius wrote 'much' to him on 'Repentance,' and so free was the East from some of the Western dangers, that he is able to lay great stress on the view taken by the martyrs. 'As they accepted these penitents, 'united with them in prayers, renewed social intercourse with 'them[8], so let us; not constituting ourselves critics and re-'visers of their judgment[9].' 'Christ Himself—as in the case 'of Serapion[10], a lapsed man who was endowed with miraculous 'insight before being restored to communion—has declared His 'acceptance of their contrition.' The arguments of Dionysius were followed up by Cyprian's announcement to Fabius of

---

says custom excludes penance for restoration; he allows it for private discipline. Felix III (483-492), *Ep.* 7, allows it to bishops, priests and deacons who had consented to rebaptization.

[1] *Ep.* 49. 1 'litteræ...frequenter missæ pæne omnes ecclesias perturbassent...'
[2] *Ep.* 55. 1, 2, 3.
[3] Eus. vi. 46 ἐπιστολὴ ἐπιστρεπτική = 'objurgatoria.' Reading, 'causing conversion,' Sophocles, *Lexicon.*
[4] ἰδία γραφή.
[5] τάξεις παραπτωμάτων διαγράψας.
[6] Eus. *l.c.* Hieron. *de Viris Ill.* c. 69 'ad Armenios de pœnitentia et de ordine delictorum.'
[7] Eus. vi. 44 Φαβίῳ ὑποκατακλινομένῳ πως τῷ σχίσματι.
[8] Eus. vi. 42 προσευχῶν αὐτοῖς καὶ ἑστιάσεων ἐκοινώνησαν.
[9] *l.c.* δοκιμαστὰς τῆς ἐκείνων γνώμης.
[10] Eus. vi. 44.

the synodical decision of Africa, then by Cornelius' account both of the Roman and the African Councils, and yet again by a letter from Cyprian urging the general excommunication of Novatian and all his followers[1]. Lastly Cornelius addressed to him that memoir to which we owe our fullest knowledge of the great Puritan's antecedents. His attitude had indeed been so menacing[2] from the first that (as Dionysius himself wrote to Cornelius on receiving his announcement of his election along with the rival missive of Novatian) the three great prelates of Cilicia, Cappadocia and Palestine, Helenus with his bishops, and Firmilian and Theoctistus, had resolved to confer with him in Synod in his own city and invited Dionysius to join them there.

A.D. 252. Fabius died ere they met. His successor Demetrian held the Council in March of the next year, 252 A.D., and, though not without effort, secured the condemnation of Novatus—meaning thereby Novatian—as 'the Friend of Sin[3].' In that same sense Jerome and others call his opinion

---

[1] Eus. vi. 43. The letters of Cornelius were in Greek, those of Cyprian in Latin. Of Cyprian's there were two at least which are not extant if, as we gather from the context, they were addressed direct to Fabius. Eusebius, just as he cannot distinguish between Novatus and Novatian, fails also to perceive that the principles of the legislation originated in Africa. The letters of Cornelius were certainly four in number. Euseb. vi. 43 speaks of *epistles* which gave information about the 'Roman synod, and the opinions of them of Italy, Africa, and the countries there' (these must have been at any rate two): of a *third*, about the determinations of the synod (περὶ τῶν κατὰ τὴν σύνοδον ἀρεσάντων), which is Jerome's *third* epistle of Cornelius 'De Gestis Synodi' (Hier. *de Virr. Ill.* 66, *Cornelius*): and of a *fourth* from which he gives long extracts on Novatian's former proceedings, the confessors, the consecrating bishops, his earlier opinions, baptism and ordination as a presbyter, and condemnation, with a list of the condemning bishops and their sees. This fourth seems to correspond exactly to Jerome's 'fourth very prolix' one on the 'causes of Novatianism and the anathema.' Jerome's first two 'De Synodo, Romana, Italica, Africana,' and 'on Novatian and the Lapsed' correspond well enough to Eusebius' (two) 'Epistles.' Valois argues in vain that Eusebius knew of only three, and Rufinus of two. Tillemont recognises the four. It is singular that Jerome calls the Antiochene patriarch Flavian, whom Eusebius consistently calls Fabius.

[2] ἔνθα κρατύνειν τινὲς ἐπεχείρουν τὸ σχίσμα, Eus. vi. 46.

[3] φιλαμαρτήμων, *Libellus Synod.* ap. Labbe, cf. Euseb. vi. 43; vii. 5, 8, and the Synodicon, Labbe, vol. I. c. 738:

the Cainite heresy—so deadly to the brethren, so desperate in itself.

Difficulties in identifying Hippolytus through whom Dionysius wrote to the Romans with Hippolytus of Portus.

The point really is whether Hippolytus of Portus was living in A.D. 250—1. If this were admitted it would not have been doubted that he was the Hippolytus meant. But it is generally denied, and if one doubts Bp. Lightfoot's conclusions one does it with uneasiness[1]. The denial is because he would have been very old in A.D. 250, that he had been deported to Sardinia in A.D. 235, and that he is not heard of afterwards—unless it is here.

Dates do not forbid us to think of Hippolytus as interested in Novatianism in the year 250.

(1) Bp. Lightfoot holds that it is not possible, because his literary activity began in A.D. 190. Unhappily we have not the promised proof of this date, for the learned and interesting essay was alas! never finished, but even so, 60 years is no unexampled period for such interests to be sustained.

A tradition of old age appears again and again in Prudentius[2] for what it is worth. If he were 25 in 190 A.D. he would in 250 be 85.

(2) Bp. Lightfoot thinks that, having been deported in 235 to Sardinia, which is expressly called *insula nociva*, along with Pontianus, who died there on Sep. 27, Hippolytus was not likely to have survived.

The statement in the Liberian Catalogue is this (Mommsen, *Chronogr. v. J.* 354, p. 635, Lipsius, *op. cit.* p. 266), ' Eo tempore Pontianus episcopus et Yppolitus presbyter[3] exoles sunt deportati in Sardinia in insula nociva Severo et Quintino cons. in eadem insula discinctus est[4] iiii Kl. Octobr. et loco ejus ordinatus est Antheros xi Kl. Dec. cons. ss.' Cf. *Liber Pontificalis*

we must collect that Fabius' intention was to aid Novatianism by his proposed Council, and that Helenus of Tarsus, Firmilian of Cappadocia, and Theoctistus of Palestine, hoped by the help of Dionysius of Alexandria to avert this result; and that Demetrian, successor in the see, but not in the views of Fabius, decided sensibly to hold the Council and promulgate its conclusions against the schism.

[1] I acknowledge the tenderness with which he partly excuses and partly accepts in the essay quoted a juvenile lucubration *On the Martyrdom and Commemoration of S. Hippolytus* in the *Journal of Classical and Sacred Philology*, vol. 1. pp. 188 sqq.: 1854.

[2] Prudent., *ut supr.*, senex vv. 23, 109, senior 78, caput niveum, canities 137, 138.

[3] 'Presbyter,' see p. 165, note 3.

[4] May not the curious expression 'discinctus est' allude to the divestiture of the High Priest Aaron in preparation for death?

(ed. Duchesne, vol. I. pp. 62, 145, and note), which reads *deputati ab Alexandro* and *insula Bucina*. [A.D. 235 was really *sub Maximino*.]

But Sardinia was not universally fatal. And Pontian's death is mentioned, and that of Hippolytus is not. If it be said that Pontian's alone is mentioned because he was the bishop, this would have also checked the mention of their joint exile. The passage has no bearing on the date of Hippolytus' death. Its one suggestion is that Hippolytus did *not* die when Pontian died.

Neither has the *Depositio martirum* any bearing on that date (as G. Salmon in *Dict. Christian Biog*. III. p. 88 *s.v.* suggests). It has 'idus Aug. Ypoliti in Tiburtina et Pontiani in Calisti.' They may have been put together, as Cornelius and Cyprian soon were, on account of their connection in life.

(3) But it is also true that no activity of Hippolytus is mentioned between A.D. 235 and 250, which at first seems strange considering the man he was.

But yet again what documents are there in which we should have expected him to be mentioned as alive? And old age and infirmities after an exile to Sardinia at the age of 60 might have kept him quiet, and nevertheless he might be the right person to transmit a letter of reconciliation.

The first sixty years of this century are like an underground tunnel with two breaks of broad daylight. One is that vivid light which Hippolytus himself throws on the times of Callistus and Zephyrinus A.D. 202—222; the other is that of the Cyprianic correspondence 247—259.

From 222—247 we have really no documents likely to illustrate such a position and life as his. We have remarked in the text that he was not likely to be prominently in request with either Novatianists or Cornelians, and the Cyprianic correspondence only deals with actors; if in fact Dionysius wrote to the Romans through him, we find him at once in a worthy and significant position. *Valeat quantum*. There is no statement that he was alive, none that he was dead. At the same time δι' Ἱππολύτου cannot be explained except in a forced way.

(4) Bp. Lightfoot (p. 372) would take διὰ Ἱππολύτου to mean only 'the delegate charged to deliver the letter.' But surely it would be strange to cite and identify an Epistle to the Romans by the name of the excellent deacon or subdeacon who carried it, as such officers were incessantly doing. Both Eusebius and Jerome mention the 'through Hippolytus,' and only eight paragraphs before Jerome has given a list of the writings of 'Hippolytus.' Eusebius characterizes or quotes more than thirty letters of Dionysius (*H. E.* vi. 40, 41, 44, 45, 46, vii. 2, 4, 5, 7, 9, 10, 11, 21, 2?, 26), and to none other of them does he refer by the name of the bearer.

(5) It is said also (p. 373) that 'Hippolytus is a fairly common name.'

III. III.   COUNCIL AT ANTIOCH.   171

But this I do not find. In 13 of the indexed volumes of the *Corpus Inscrr. Latt.* containing over 63,000 inscriptions there are only fourteen instances of the name Hippolytus and three of Hippolyte. It is a most rare name.

In default of proof that he was dead, a more venerable Hippolytus may still seem to have been concerned in introducing the great man's letter to the great church.

Why is Dionysius' Epistle to the Romans called διακονική?
(Eus. *H. E.* vi. 46.)

1. The bidding prayers and litanies recited by Deacons in the Greek Liturgies, which begin with ἐν εἰρήνη δεηθῶμεν and pray first for the Peace of the World and the Church, are called indifferently διακονικὰ and εἰρηνικά. This has led Bp. Chr. Wordsworth (*Hippolytus*, p. 179, ed. 1880) to interpret διακονική as equivalent to εἰρηνική. See Goar's *Euchologion* (Paris, 1647), p. 65, *Liturg. Chrys.* ὁ διάκονος λέγει...τὰ εἰρηνικά; p. 195, *Liturg. of Presanctified*, λέγονται [τὰ] ταῦτα τὰ διακονικά, and Goar's note, p. 123. Sophocles (*Gk Lex. of Rom. and Byz. periods*) s.v. τὰ εἰρηνικά 'said by the Deacon,' 'called also τὰ διακονικά.' Cp. the προσφώνησις of the Deacon, *Apost. Constt.* viii. 13.   But when one thing is called by two different names for such wholly different reasons, the names do not in serious language, or except in slang, become interchangeable in other entirely different applications. I cannot think this interpretation possible.

2. Bp. Lightfoot thinks it 'a reasonable conjecture' that the letter had some reference to the arrangements of Fabian about deacons (see sup. pp. 67, 68). But Eusebius' notice of this letter is embedded in his notices of the letters on Novatian, and it is not written to Fabian, or even Cornelius, but 'to those of Rome'—to the people. How Fabian's Deacons can have been to such an extent the subject of the letter as to give it the name of a 'Diaconic' letter, I do not see. Again a 'Diaconic' letter no more seems to mean a letter about Deacons than an 'Episcopal' or 'Pastoral' letter is a letter about Bishops or Pastors.

3. Both guesses are those of learned and ingenious men. But διακονική is not a technical word for any kind of letter, and perhaps Dionysius may have himself used it in his own letter as a lively expression, in setting forth that he was not writing to them as bishop, in any authoritative way, but that he simply meant to minister to their deliberation as a deacon rather than a bishop might do—that the ἐπιστολή is not ἐπιστρεπτική like that to his own flock (Eus. vi. 46), nor ἐπισκοπική, nor even πρεσβυτερική, but merely such as a deacon might submit to them. The word might be taken from some such phraseology, as it has seemed to me. [Cf. ἀποδεικτική...προτρεπτικός, ap. Bp. Lightfoot, *op. cit.* pp. 395 and 397.]

4. Nevertheless I rather incline to a suggestion made to me by M. Larpent that the word, which means simply 'serviceable,' in Plato *Gorg.* LXXII. (p. 517 B) οὐδ' ἐγὼ ψέγω τούτους ὥς γε διακόνους εἶναι πόλεως, ἀλλά μοι δοκοῦσι τῶν γε νῦν διακονικώτεροι γεγονέναι καὶ μᾶλλον οἷοί τ' ἐκπορίζειν τῇ πόλει ὧν ἐπεθύμει; Xenophon, *Œconom.* VII. 41 ὁπόταν ἀνεπιστήμονα ταμιείας καὶ διακονίας παραλαβοῦσα ἐπιστήμονα καὶ πιστὴν καὶ διακονικὴν ποιησαμένη παντὸς ἀξίαν ἔχῃς; Aristoph. *Plout.* 1170 ἵν' εὐθέως διακονικὸς εἶναι δοκῇς, may be applied in the same sense to a *Letter* of practical advice.

IV.

Constitutional Results of the First Council.

All these evidences of activity and wide-spread communication are made still more interesting by the observation of certain constitutional points which the decision of the Carthaginian Council involved. We note four such.

First, the submission of the views of the primate himself to his Council. They were substantially modified. The course which he proposed to them in the *De Lapsis* was less lenient than theirs[1] (although even this was to be still more softened in the course of the next year), and he was aware of the change produced in himself[2]. Charged with the inconsistency, he does not deny it. Again the Novatianist deputation appealed from the Council to him as a sympathizer with their rigorism. But in fact purism in him was subordinate to his broader views on Unity. He evoked a spiritual power as wiser, more liberal, stronger and more divine than any solitary utterance, and he remained loyal to it.

Secondly, Cyprian had in his epistolary proposals assigned weight to the verdict and recommendations of the martyrs in procuring reconciliation. The Council wholly ignores these intercessions. Fifty and sixty years later the Letters of Confessors might, by canons of Elvira and Arles, be

[1] *Ep.* 54. 4.   [2] *Ep.* 55. 3.

exchanged for Episcopal letters[1]; value being thus attached to them while the proper regimen of the Church was formally supported. But the Council of Carthage is in its reaction strong enough to pass over in silence the 'merits' which had lately threatened all organization.

For now comes out the unity of their decisions as against both of the schismatical leaders; since it is definitively settled, *thirdly*, against Novatian, that there are no remissible offences which it is beyond the power of the regular organization of the Church to remit,

And *fourthly*, against Felicissimus, that no sanctity[2], conferring authority to assign terms of communion or remit sin, resides in any class or person save in the body of the Church with its authentic administrators[3].

The principles then which had now been solidified into legislation specifically invested the primæval Christian institution of episcopacy with all the functions of government, and accordingly the private sentiments of the metropolitan were, with his cheerful consent[4], overruled, while his past acts as bishop of Carthage were ratified. No representations against a bishop once seated were to be admissible[5]. The Resolutions went forth in the name of the Bishops only.

[1] *Conc. Eliber.* A.D. 305-6, *can.* 25 'omnis qui attulerit literas confessorias, sublato nomine confessoris, eo quod omnes sub hac nominis gloria passim concutiant simplices, communicatoriæ ei dandæ sunt litteræ.' *Conc. Arel.* (314), *can.* 9 'De his qui confessorum literas afferunt, placuit ut, sublatis iis literis, alias accipiant communicatorias.' Hefele has not understood the application of these canons.

[2] Perhaps the miraculous argument in the *De Lapsis* from instances of divine anger against the irregularly admitted is meant to meet the particular feeling which rested on the exceptional sanctity of the martyrs.

[3] We must not say the administrators alone. The function of the laity is repeatedly, though not very explicitly, urged. In *Ep.* 64. 1 it is an objection to one readmission that it was made 'sine petitu et conscientia plebis.'

[4] ...scias me nihil leviter egisse sed... omnia ad commune concilii nostri consilium distulisse...et nunc ab his non recedere quæ semel in concilio nostro de communi conlatione placuerunt.... *Ep.* 55. 7.

[5] Gravitati nostræ negavimus convenire ut collegæ nostri jam delecti et ord nati...ventilari ultra honorem... pateremur. *Ep.* 44. 2.

And now if we remember that each bishop was the representative of a free election, and their assembly a free assembly of equals,—the only free elections, the only free, the first representative assembly in the world—we shall see that Episcopacy had virtually taken its place among Roman Institutions, informed with Roman strength and Roman respect for Law, summing in itself, and disparting to its members powers judicial and executive, reserving to itself all appeals, and originating legislation. It was an Institution not only fraught with the ruin of polytheism but rich with the freedom and the order of the coming society.

V.

Corollaries:—Puritanism: Saint-Merit: Flight from Suffering.   The DE LAPSIS.

Cyprian's Letter to the Confessors on their return contains a passage of about twenty lines which Augustine cites in full no less than three times in separate works[1], as containing the absolute Scriptural answer to Puritan separations. It is the earliest exposition of the parable of the Tares, and of S. Paul's image of the Palace with its Vessels precious or vile as accurate presentments of the lasting conditions of Church Society. No human right exists to eradicate tares, or to break the poorest earthen vessels in pieces. Freedom to become good corn, or make a golden urn of itself belongs to every soul. The forfeiture of light will ever mark assumptions of the divine judgeship.

Against Novatianism, Donatism, and how many long perpetuated species of Puritanism and Calvinism, rudimentary inorganic forms of the first reaction of converted spirits

[1] To Macrobius, *Ep.* 108, c. 10. Against the Donatist Cresconius, ii. 43, and Gaudentius, ii. 3.

against the kingdom of sin, do these few words bear witness.

The Letter was accompanied by an interesting gift:— Copies of his treatises ON THE LAPSED and OF THE UNITY OF THE CATHOLIC CHURCH.

Of the latter we shall speak presently.

To postpone with Bp. Pearson[1] the date of the former to November is to attribute to Cyprian a publication out of date at its appearance, and counsels upon which he had already improved. 'The Avenging' of which he speaks in the opening is no doubt the destruction of Decius in that November[2]. But while large parts of the book, as we have it, wear all the marks of an oration[3], other parts never can have been so delivered, and are plainly to be reasoned out in the study. In fact we have in our hands the edition published some months later; as we have in several of Cicero's orations; and to this edition belongs the actual exordium.

On the other hand the strong and immediate Apology for Fugitives marks the moment when prejudice against his own retirement has not yet died out[4].

It is a work of a high order. Its literary form is excellent, but far beyond that praise is the power with which it lifts the contentions of parties and the vexing questions of the moment into a region in which they can be seen as deductions from leading principles, and determined on high grounds. So to rise, so to uplift is to the full as difficult in church politics as in mundane controversies. And the high aim is effected, and the tone sustained without one failure.

Its outline may be sketched as follows:—

After the close of a persecution an ideal position of *De Laps* ii., iii.

---

[1] *Ann. Cypr.* A.D. 251, c. xv.

[2] There is nothing in the overthrow of Julius Valens or Priscus which would wear this aspect to Christians of the time.

[3] See for example c. 2, when he speaks of confessors as present, and then addresses them.

[4] c. 3.

spiritual influence is occupied by faithful sufferers, even by voluntary exiles for conscience' sake; and by those who had been faithful in danger, although not in actual suffering.

iv.

To the Lapsed sympathy is due; and his sympathy rings as true as his sense of discipline; especially with those who had broken down under intensity of torture. Between these and others he draws a broad line.

v.—xiii.

After shewing that Persecution is not without its good and useful service he proceeds to analyse the causes of Lapse which have been so wide-spread and so operative through the whole Church,—and that in spite of forewarnings, of the unnatural horrors of the very act, of all the given opportunities for avoiding it. He concludes that the secret is to be found in the world-leavened spirit of the Church.

xiv.—xxxvi.

He next enters upon a close argument (1) with the party of lax readmission, (2) with the Confessors who promote it, and (3) with those of the Lapsed who seek it; setting before them deterrent experiences and the dishonesty of the position.

He concludes by an exhortation to honesty of confession, to seriousness of repentance and to activity in good works. High hope is yet in store for them.

The book on the Lapsed has largely contributed to our narrative. Its teachings concerning the Eucharist, and its evidence upon contemporary Supernaturalism will be discussed each in its own place. Upon Penitential Discipline, its views, equally remote from Protestant and Roman standards, have been exemplified sufficiently.

I. Yet we may now further remark on the *singularity* of the relation in which Romanism stands to the Cyprianic view of the influence of interceding saints. Their merit, (Cyprian holds,) may aid sinners in the day of judgment, in the world to come[1]. But they cannot on earth reverse or disturb the organization and working order of the visible Church.

---

[1] *De Lapsis,* c. 17.

Departed martyrs are heard in the Apocalypse still praying to be avenged. How can they in that situation be the defenders of others[1]?

How ingenious then is the Romish combination of a supposed accumulation of meritorious treasure with its official dispensation by visible authorities!

II. His opinion[2] that there might be occasions when a man would not be justified in accepting the offered crown of martyrdom, and that flight from persecution in such circumstances was 'a private confession of Christ as martyrdom is a public one,' must have saved to the Church valuable lives, although the problem of decision in any given case was not the least of the difficulties which arose between Christianity and heathenism.

The eloquence of the *De Lapsis* seems almost perfect. The style has gained in lucidity though still here and there the touches are a little too ornamental. There are few finer passages than the triumphal ode in prose with which he celebrates 'The White Cohort of Christ,'—the Confessors, men, women and children, restored to the Church after their warfare. A touching instance of its felt power is an adaptation of two passages from it on an African inscription[3],

Magus Innocent Child.

Now thou beginnest existence among the Innocent.
How stedfast now is Life to thee.
How joyful thou art to be welcomed by thy Mother the Church
on thy return from this world.
Let the sighing of our hearts be stilled.
Let the weeping of our eyes be stayed.

---

[1] *De Lapsis*, c. 18.

[2] c. 3, cf. c. 10.

[3] Pitra, *Spicilegium Solesm.* vol. IV. p. 536, MAGVS puer innocens | esse jam inter innocentis cœpisti. | quam staviles tivi hæc vita est | quam te letum excipet mater ecclesia de oc | mundo revertentem. conprematur pectorum | gemitus. struatur fletus oculorum. The name *Magus* and a peculiar arrangement of cross and palm branch indicate a Carthaginian origin for the

Another beautiful passage[1] and one which illustrates how the oratory of Cyprian sometimes piles itself up like that of Barrow, is worthy of quotation upon the obliteration of repentance by over hasty communion.

'This is no peace but war. He does not join the Church 'who parts from the Gospel. Why do men call an injury a 'blessing? Why give to impiety the style of "Pity"? How 'do they pretend to give communion, when they interrupt the 'repentant lamentation of those who have need to weep in-'deed? Such teachers are to the lapsed as hail on corn; are 'as a star of tempest to trees; the ravage of pestilence to 'flocks and herds; the wildness of the storm to ships at sea. 'The solace of everlasting life they steal away; uproot the 'tree; creep on with sickly suggestion to deadly infection; 'wreck the ship ere it enter the harbour. Such easiness yields 'no peace, but annuls it; gives no communion but hinders 'salvation. It is a fresh persecution, a fresh temptation. Our 'subtle foe employs it in his advances to assail the fallen yet 'again with unperceived devastations: stilling their lamenta-'tion, silencing their sorrows, wiping out the remembrance of 'their sin, hushing the groaning heart, quenching the weeping 'eyes, drowning the entreaties of long and full repentance 'toward a deeply offended Lord,—and all the while it stands 'written, "Remember from whence thou art fallen and re-'pent.'"

monument itself. The Cyprianic passages are *De Lapsis* (2) Quam *vos lætos* excipit mater ecclesia de *prælio* revertentes, (16) comprimatur pectorum gemitus, *statuatur* fletus oculorum. It has been suggested to correct *statuatur* as in itself absurd to *struatur* by the monument. However *statuatur* is quite Cyprianic; 'Si fontem siccitas *statuat*,' ad Demetr. c. 7. The second and third lines also of the inscription seem quoted, but I know not whence. [Hartel: læto sinu—pectoris.]

[1] c. 16.

Mai's supposed Fragment of Cyprian.

I can find no place among the Cyprianic arguings which could be filled by the fragment ΚΥΠΡΙΑΝΟΥ περὶ μετανοίας (Mai, *Class Auctt. e Vat. codd. editorum* Tomus X. pp. xxix., 485—7), nor, I suppose, could Mai, who says 'videtur hic Cyprianus Antiochenus.' For that however there is no colour. The point of the extract is that equal sufferings have no power to equalise the bad and good. Besides, if we except slight touches on S. Paul (which compare with Cyprian [Hartel], p. 304, 26; 511, 16—18) not one of the Scripture illustrations is Cyprianic in handling. The Fragment adduces Pharaoh, the Penitent Thief, Naboth, Ananias, who are never named by Cyprian; Job is not taken from Cyprian's very distinct point of view; Zedekiah also, not in Cyprian, is curiously dealt with, much as in the spurious *De Pascha Computus* (Hartel, *App.*, p. 258, 22; 260, 19). The contrast between Daniel and Nebuchadnezzar is that the former was consigned to feed beasts and the latter to feed with beasts. The realistic contrast between our Lord and the Thief lacks Cyprian's delicacy. Thus the Fragment's first air of resemblance to Cyprian melts away.

CHAPTER IV.

CYPRIAN 'OF THE UNITY OF THE CATHOLIC CHURCH.'

I.

Time and Substance of the Treatise.

THE two or three leading motives of this victorious essay were sketched at the point where we had to outline the principles on which the Council acted. The flesh and blood, so to speak, the colour and the warmth, claim nearer attention.

The conjuncture at which it was read to the Council[1] is discernible. Allusions to Novatian and to his having assumed the episcopate are plain and numerous[2]. On the other hand there is no reference to Felicissimus and his faction, a subject which in a paper on unity could not have been avoided unless it had been already disposed of. Allusions there are[3] to laxity and dissoluteness on the part of former confessors, but without any reference to methods to be adopted towards them, and only in illustration of the position that confessors (and so Novatian) were not secure from falling away. Thus the publication of the treatise is marked

---

[1] *Ep.* 54. 4. In *de Unitate* c. 5 we have a trace of its original character as a Lecture or Essay addressed to colleagues: 'Quam unitatem tenere firmiter et vindicare *debemus* maxime *episcopi qui* in ecclesia *præsidemus*.'

[2] c. 3, ministros justitiæ *asserentes*... interitum pro salute, &c. c. 8, uno in loco...multos pastores... c. 9, luporum feritas. c. 10, episcopi sibi nomen. c. 13, æmuli sacerdotum (bishops). c. 15, sacramentum profanat. c. 17, aliud altare.

[3] c. 21.

as after the settlement of the question of Felicissimus and before that of Novatian was determined.

The position of Novatian was the problem of the hour. Heresy had hitherto been manifold and fantastic. But Schism,—meaning secession upon questions not originally doctrinal,—had been almost unknown. Now, however, beginning from the central see, the Church reeled with the new possibility of being cleft in twain upon an enquiry as to whether she possessed disciplinary power for the reconciliation of her own penitents.

The rationale of such a separation, its relation to the divinely preconceived economy—'What such a portent meant? How God could suffer it?'—was the question on many lips. 'It is not (they said) as though a new dogma or mysticism 'attracted the speculative and devout. But with teaching 'identical, amid undoubted holiness of life, we see Altar 'against Altar, Chair against Chair, in the metropolis of the 'world and Church.' This is the problem which Cyprian sets out to solve. 'The characteristic danger of the age when 'Christianity is for the first time widely accepted is the 'presentment of old error under Christian forms.

'Such danger can be detected only by distinct concep-'tions as to the abode of truth, clearness as to the Scriptural 'idea of unity. These are not far to seek. When the Lord 'gave Peter his commission, "Whatsoever *thou* shalt bind 'shall be bound," and then renewed the commission to '*all* the Apostles, "Whosoever sins *ye* remit they are 'remitted," it is obvious that He placed all alike on the 'same level[1], yet, by first addressing Peter alone, He indicated 'the Oneness or Unity of the commission[2] itself. So ever

---

[1] Hoc erant utique et ceteri apostoli quod fuit Petrus, pari consortio præditi et honoris et potestatis, sed exordium ab unitate proficiscitur, c. 4. Then follows the famous interpolation, —of which below.

[2] Pacian, *Ep.* 3, c. 11, repeats the illustration with clearness: Ad Petrum locutus est Dominus, ad unum, ideo ut unitatem fundaret ex uno, mox idipsum in commune præcipiens.

'since, this tangible bond of the Church's unity is her one
'united episcopate, an Apostleship universal yet only one—
'the authority of every bishop perfect in itself and inde-
'pendent, yet not forming with all the others a mere agglo-
'meration of powers, but being a tenure upon a totality, like
'that of a shareholder in some joint property[1].'

Such is his statement of the historic and existent conditions as against the threatening schism. He continues,
'The man who holds not this church unity, does he believe
'that he holds the Faith? He who contends against the
'Church, is he assured that he is within the Church? The
'Old Testament and the Pauline teaching harmonize with
'the Gospel as to this unity. And the episcopate above all
'is bound to exert itself in the maintenance of its own
'indivisible oneness.'

Then follows the famous and beautiful passage on the natural analogies of this spiritual unity. 'There is one
'Church which outspreads itself into a multitude (of churches),
'wider and wider in ever increasing fruitfulness; just as the
'sun has many rays but one only light, and a tree many
'branches yet one only heart, based in the clinging root;
'and, while many rills flow off from a single fountain-head,
'although a multiplicity of waters is seen streaming away in
'diverse directions from the bounty of its abundant overflow,
'yet unity is preserved in the head-spring. Pluck a ray away
'from the sun's body! unity admits no division of light.
'Break a bough off a tree! once broken it will bud no more.
'Cut a rill off from the spring! the rill cut off dries up. So
'too the Church flooded with the light of the Lord flings rays
'over the whole world. Yet it is one light which diffuses
'itself everywhere; the unity of the body knows no partition.
'She reaches forth her boughs over the universal earth in the
'richness of her fertility, broadens ever more widely her
'bounteous flowing rivers, and still there is one head, one

---

[1] Episcopatus unus est cujus *a singulis in solidum* pars tenetur. c. 5.

'source, one mother, rich in ever succeeding births. Of her 'we are born; her milk our nurture, her breath our life.'

Scripture, he proceeds to shew, teems with examples and illustrations of this unity. 'The Sons of Christ are the sons 'of his undefiled spouse. He cannot have God for his father 'who has not the Church for his mother.' The Ark of the Flood, the Seamless Coat, the one Flock, the one House untouched in the fall of Jericho, the one House of the Paschal Lamb, the 'one mind in the House' of Israel, the Dove-like form and nature[1] of the Spirit, all are parables illustrating the inferences which we might draw from the Kingdom of Nature, and from the Unity of the Godhead, as well as from the direct injunctions of Christ, S. Paul and S. John[2].

The application is immediately pointed. 'There are now 'those who withdraw from the Church, and build them alien 'homes. This must be recognised as the departure of alien 'spirits.'

A conception of Separatism is now distinctly obtained. 'Heresy itself has its place in relation to unity in the economy 'of God. It is a testing power. It is a præ-judicial separa-'tion.

'Its promoters first assume preeminence among the 'unthinking, then holy orders, and then the episcopal pre-'rogative, of which the essential character is that it is a *given*, 'that it is a *transmitted* power. They take Christ's special 'Blessing on the United "Two or Three" and apply it to their 'own separatist twos and threes[3], as if the Lord meant to 'commend not unity but paucity. They corrupt the Font

---

[1] The gall-lessness attributed to the Dove is brought in from Tertullian, *De Bapt.* 8. It receives interesting illustration from contemporary inscriptions. In the cemetery of Callistus (de Rossi, *Rom. Sott.*, vol. II. p. 185, Tav. xxxvii.—xxxviii. n. 19) a lady is described as PALVMBA SENE FEL, and in the crypt of S. Prassede (*Inscrr. Christ. U. R.* vol. I. p. 421, no. 937) we have PALVM-BVS SINE FEL. Compare *Hamlet*, Act II. sc. 2, 'But I am pigeon-liver'd and lack gall To make oppression bitter.'

[2] *De Unit.* cc. 6—9.

[3] *De Unit.* cc. 10—12.

'of Baptism'—(mark here the earliest appearance of Cyprian's great characteristic error)—'so that its water stains rather 'than cleanses; they erect a rival altar, they offer a rival 'sacrifice, but it is the sacrifice of jealousy, and so their very 'martyrdoms are wretchedly not crowns but judgments. For 'while a Lapse from the faith is purged by the Baptism of 'Blood the religion of the Schismatic is spurious in essence, 'not for any narrower cause but that it fails in the first broad 'principle of Christianity, a Loving Union with the brethren. 'Schism is accordingly more fatal than lapsing, and the 'schismatic's death under the persecutor is no martyrdom, 'only a penalty and a despair.'

He comes to passing events and living persons. The eminent, unnamed, intemperate-tongued, confessor who has established a separate communion, can be none but Novatian. 'Be that confessor who he may, he is not greater, better, dearer 'to God than Solomon once was. Yet he retained God's grace 'only so long as he trode God's path...He is a confessor! 'after confession the peril is more, for the foe is more pro-'voked. He is a confessor! The more should he stand by 'the Gospel, for of the Gospel came his renown....He is a con-'fessor! Let him be lowly and calm, let him be modest with 'discipline in action, like the Christ whose confessor he is. 'He is a confessor—but not so, if afterwards the greatness 'and worthiness of Christ be evil spoken of through him[1].'

There is here an undertone of anxiety for the fidelity of confessors at large, which exactly suits the immediate position of Roman affairs, mingling with his thankfulness for the general loyalty[2], and echoing the personal appeals already cited[3]. He proceeds 'I would indeed, dearest brothers,—I 'counsel, I urge—that, if it be possible, not one of the brothers 'should perish—that the joyful mother should lock to her 'bosom one united people.' If the return of wilful leaders be

---

[1] *De Unit.* cc. 17, 20, 21. [3] *Ep.* 46.
[2] c. 22.

hopeless, it is still conceivable to him that the mass of the misled should see with their own eyes, and extricate themselves from personal complications.

Lastly, he restates the nature and obligation of unity and the causes which underlie disunion.

The unity of the Godhead, of the person of Christ, of the ideal church, of the faith, must be reproduced in the unity of the earthly congregation. Agreement is the medium of that unity. Sections from the living organism must lose vitality. The unity of humanity within itself and with God is that in which alone salvation consists[1].

'As for the real causes of disunion, its origin is not in the 'theory of this or that teacher. Loss of unity is the natural 'outcome of an age of recognised, sanctioned, recommended 'selfishness—selfishness which saps belief and moral force 'together, which undermines that faith whereon rest the 'principles of God-fearing, righteousness, love and hard 'work, and diminishes the awe of things to come[2].'

This was penetrating doctrine; went to the heart of things. Which of the churches will master it earliest?

The suitability of the whole argument to the crisis, and its effectiveness, need no illustration. The beauty of its diction is a fit vehicle for the loving holiness and might of its spirit. It searches alike the deeps of the divine word and of the human heart. Again and again its persuasions and its warnings have availed with spirits nobler than the noblest

---

[1] Stripped of its figures this climax (c. 23) contains the ground of Cyprian's zeal and the essence of his doctrine. The passage almost defies translation— 'unus Deus est, et Christus unus, et una *ecclesia* ejus, et fides una, et *plebs* [una] in solidam corporis unitatem concordiæ glutino copulata. Scindi unitas non potest, nec corpus unum discidio conpaginis separari, divulsis laceratione visceribus in frusta discerpi. Quicquid a matrice discesserit seorsum vivere et spirare non poterit, substantiam salutis amittit.'

Plebs una, Hartel, misled perhaps by false collation, on the authority of *W*, a mistake for *M* (Monacensis); and of *V* (Veronensis); neither MS. of any value on such a point. WGR omit *una* after *plebs*.

[2] c. 26.

which have agonized themselves into separations—yes, and in hours of greater temptation than theirs.

II.

Two Questions on Cyprianic Unity. 1. *Was it a theory of Conviction or of Policy?* 2. *Does it involve Roman Unity?*

Of the Unity of the Catholic Church Cyprian has been suffered—reverently, I hope, and dutifully, so far as a faithful purpose is able to represent him—to speak for himself.

Yet the merest outline reveals the defects as well as the merits of his marvellous book.

The impossibility of harmonizing his theory, as it stands, with some phenomena of church history is owing to its non-developement of one essential principle.

The distinction between a Visible and an Invisible Communion upon earth did not present itself to him—still less the true incorporation with the Visible Church itself of members not entirely sound. We are not called upon to dilate on a topic which has engaged Hooker[1], but we must notice that it is this same deficiency which in his next great crisis placed Cyprian himself in some danger of separatism.

But there arise two further questions which demand candid answers.

1. Was Cyprian's view of the Church as one whole with one proper and characteristic government a sincere doctrine? Had he received it? Had it been a reality to earlier Christian thought? Or, was it only the justification of his practical policy, a tissue of the ingenious suggestions point by point of a difficult position?

2. Did this theory of Unity rest on, contain, or logically

[1] *Eccl. Polity*, B. III.

IV. II. QU. I. WAS THE THEORY A POLICY? 187

lead up to a recognition of a central church authority in the Roman or Petrine see?

The questions are of moment apart from their interest, or their bearing on Cyprian's honesty and on his foresight.

The first enquires whether Cyprian was an Expounder or an Inventor of the Oneness of the Church.

The second enquires whether Roman Supremacy was an outcome of his teaching on that Oneness.

Before the former question can be well answered we must know whether the word *Ecclesia* had until now described only the individual congregation—or, if more, more only by transference. If that were so, the Cyprianic theory was novel— not more than an engine against Novatian. If it were not so, the course of the enquiry would probably reveal the principle on which Oneness was attributed to an Ideal more complex or more abstract than that of 'parishes.'

Now a review of Cyprian's few writings before the Decian persecution is enough to shew in the first instance that the idea then conveyed in the word 'Church' was not limited to the individual congregation, either with or without its chief pastor. That name is from the first used equally and without distinction of the Congregation, of the Diocese, and of the Whole Body of the Faithful. It is not the case that the former senses are earlier in Cyprian than the latter. The latter sense also appears without effort and without explanation, as familiar to all.

Thus in the First Book of Testimonies, the Church is the New People in contrast with the Jewish. It is the Barren Mother of Old Testament figures, proving more fruitful than the fruitful wife. It is the Sara, the Rachel, the Hannah, whose sons are types of the Christ. It is 'She who hath borne the Seven Sons,' for it was to Seven Churches that St Paul wrote as well as St John. In this one passage two of the senses stand clearly out. *Test.* i. c. 19. c. 20.

In the Second Book the 'Church' is the 'Spouse of Christ.' ii. 19.

H. V. 3.　　In the 'Dress of Virgins,' the virgins themselves are 'the glorious fruitbearing of the Mother the Church.'

H. V. 10.　　'The Church had been planted and founded upon Peter.'

In these three passages the larger sense alone is possible.

Ep. 10. 5.　　In the 10th letter, 'Happy is our Church' means specifically the Church of Carthage; but in the very first letter the
Ep. 1. 1, 2. word is used in both the first and second of the three senses. A certain rule of clerical discipline 'in the *Church* of the Lord,' which had been laid down in a Council of earlier bishops, is mentioned in the same passage with the direction that certain offenders are not to be prayed for 'in the Church,' that is in the congregation. In the same epistle, Clerks are to have their time free from private business to serve 'the Altar and the Church,' just as in the 3rd (so numbered) it is said
Ep. 3. 3. that the disobedience of Deacons to their Presbyter leads to the 'forsaking of the Church and the substitution of a profane Altar.'

Ep. 2. 2.　　In the 2nd letter the Christian who has to give up his profession as a Dramatic Tutor is maintained by 'the provision' and 'at the charges of *the Church*,' seemingly the local church to which he belongs, but is urged to 'learn 'saving things *within the Church* instead of teaching deathful 'things outside the Church.'

It cannot be said then that the use of this word in the sense of 'Congregation' or 'Diocese' is earlier than its aggregate sense, and it is needless to point out how, in some of these instances, the eye sees in the Diocese the true image and life of the whole.

It is similarly impossible to say that the earliest idea was that of the *plebes* apart from its governing body. It is no
Ep. 63. 13. 'definition' when Cyprian writes '*The Church*, that is the 'plebes established *in the Church*, faithfully and firmly per-'severing in what it has believed.' It is no definition, for the word to be defined actually recurs within it, and forms part

IV. II. 'THE CHURCH' NOT THE ISOLATED CONGREGATION. 189

of the definition so-called[1]. The question remains, 'What is the Church within which the *plebes* is thus established?' Is it an unorganized, undisciplined, unruled aggregate of individuals? On this the 3rd (so numbered) letter is significant *Ep.* 3. 3. enough when it says that the Apostles constituted the Deacons 'to be the ministers of their own *Episcopate* and of the Church.' This imagined 'Definition' has in it nothing which is inconsistent with other words which really belong to the same period—'they are the Church—a Commons united *Ep.* 66. 8. to a Bishop—a Flock clinging to its Shepherd.'

In the 4th letter, one of his very earliest, we find an *Ep.* 4. 4. exposition of which the hardness and definiteness is never again exceeded. 'If they refuse to be pure in life and habit, 'they cannot be readmitted to *the Church;* they cannot count 'on life and salvation if they will not obey the Bishops. In 'the old Law he who would not obey the Priest was slain 'with the temporal sword. To be cast out of the Church now 'is to be slain with the spiritual sword. For outside the 'Church they cannot live, *inasmuch as the House of God is* '*One, and no one can be safe but in the Church.*'

In the 3rd Book of Testimonies we read, 'Schism not to *Test.* iii. 'be made, even if he who departs remain in the one Faith and c. 86. 'the same Tradition[2].'

It is then uncritical and unhistorical to suppose that the thought of the aggregate Church rose later on Cyprian's mind, or grew up gradually out of the idea of the individual Church. From the first it was impossible not to see literally each in the other. It is also equally uncritical to think

---

[1] *Ep.* 63. Yet Ritschl (p. 91, pp. 241, 242) actually proposes, on account of the supposed simplicity and absence of organization implied in what he is pleased to treat as a 'definition,' to transpose this epistle and place it among the earliest letters before the Decian persecution.

[2] This passage is not necessary to this Catena, if anyone would give a date later than I do to this 3rd Book. See p. 23. But it is clear that this is a general precept on schism, and has no reference to Novatianism, and is therefore earlier than Novatian. Cyprian would not have allowed that Novatian remained 'in the one Tradition.'

that there ever was a time when the Church was contemplated apart from its Ministering Rulers or they from it. Each again was essential to the other. With the passage from the 4th epistle before us, it is impossible to conceive that the Church appeared to Cyprian to have ever carried itself on or subsisted without its episcopal order—or ever to have been anything but a Unity.

We have seen before[1] what the Bishop was to his own Congregation and 'Diocese.' Was there anything which for the whole Church Catholic corresponded to the Bishop's position in respect of his own Diocese? The Cyprianic answer is absolutely clear:—What the Bishop was to his own Diocese that the whole united Body of Bishops was to the whole Church.

When, in his one sarcastic letter—and sarcastic indeed it is—Cyprian writes to Florentius Puppianus, 'The Church, 'which is "CATHOLIC, ONE," is not split nor divided but 'is certainly knit together and compacted by a *cement* of 'Bishops fast cleaving each to each other[2],' this grotesqueness may put more forcibly, but does not express more substantively, the ground which is *assumed* in the earliest epistles.

In the 1st epistle—The Church Law forbidding clerics to engage in secular business 'had been long ago determined 'in the Council of the Bishops'; 'the Bishops, our prede-'cessors, religiously considering and soundly providing for 'this, enacted &c.'; 'that so the decree of the Bishops, reli-'giously and needfully passed, may be observed by us.'

More palpably still than single phrases can state it, the Roman presbyters assume, in the 8th letter, that in the

---

[1] c. II. viii. sup.

[2] *Ep.* 66. 8 quando ecclesia quæ 'catholica una' est scissa non sit neque divisa, sed sit utique conexa et cohærentium sibi invicem sacerdotum *glutino* copulata. The authority for 'catholica una' without *et* is conclusive; and for this reason, and because it is assumed (*quæ est*) as the ground for deduction, I take it to be meant as a quotation from the Baptismal Creed.

IV. II. 'AS BISHOP TO DIOCESE SO BISHOPS TO CHURCH.' 191

absence of both Bishops the two churches have to maintain the brotherhood of mutual counsel.

In the 3rd (so numbered)—An individual Bishop having laid before the body of Bishops a complaint against a Deacon of his own, Cyprian's reply speaks of 'the Apostles, that is the Bishops and Prelates'—a description of a united college surely, if words can describe one.

Lastly—to go no further—the great decision is postponed until all the Bishops of Africa can assemble and make sure of acting in harmony with the Bishops of Italy.

The College of Bishops, then, is the very form and substance of the inherited free government, advising by resolution, commanding by mutual consent, yet not even when unanimous constraining a single dissentient bishop[1]. As the Nicene Fathers did not make but formulated the Nicene Faith, so the characteristic of Cyprian, his merit as some venture to think, is the clear outlining and distinct expression which he gave to the principles which he found in use, and the stedfastness with which he worked the code and submitted himself to it. His characteristic reward was the loyalty of those who felt his loyalty to them,—felt it rendered because they were Bishops in council, though evidently not his peers in learning or in policy.

If then the First Question be, Did Cyprian create his theory of government in the Church in order to solve his own problems? the answer is that it was far older than Cyprian, although in him it was lit and fired by that sense of Love and feeling after Unity which seemed to Augustine the most special characteristic of the man[2].

---

[1] See Cyprian's speech on opening the seventh Council.

[2] Ritschl's incredible remarks on this character having been put on, and assumed by Cyprian as a mere weapon and instrument, may be read in the original (pp. 89, 105, 109). It is worthy of these criticisms that they force him to place the 63rd epistle *very early* (see p. 189 n.), because the simplicity of its language on the Church appears to him inconsistent with Cyprian's later views—only, he ought then also to have placed the earliest Epistles and the

Our Second Question was, Did the theory of Cyprian demand or lead up to or suggest a single Centre of Church Government—at Rome or elsewhere?

Rome could not but be a centre of thought and feeling. It was not merely the largest, richest or strongest city. It was the head of the civilised world, with a practical reality of power and fitness unattributable to and unimaginable of any other head before or since. Was the Christian Church in it similarly not only the foremost church, but was it the head of the world-Church which was already in existence?

We need not stay to enquire whether Cappadocia, Antioch, Jerusalem could so regard it—but was it such to the West? was it such even to Carthage? *Principalis*[1] *Ecclesia* it was. It had a lofty undeniable primacy among all churches which believed it to be the Foundation of Saint Peter, and to have in it S. Peter's *Cathedra*, ascended by his successors. Certainly not less veneration could attach to it than to the Alexandria of S. Mark, or the Ephesus of S. John—say even more—but was it of a different kind or order?

Did the theory of Cyprian either in itself, or as embodying the Western feeling, whatever this was, towards Rome, suggest that this see was a centre of *authority* or *jurisdiction* to the Church at large? We have seen how each Bishop was held to be a centre of authority and fountain of jurisdiction to his diocese. Did the theory of the *Oneness* of the Church involve that there should be One See whose influence embraced all other sees analogously? that there should be a Bishop of Bishops?

The only possible answer is that this conception, so far from being verified or supported by Cyprian's theory, contradicts that theory, has overthrown it in practice, and tends to obliterate it.

Testimonies (which are not at all '*simple*' in his sense) very late. He is compelled further to assert (p. 94) without a vestige of authority that in *de Unit.* 5 the words from *nemo* to *corrumpat* are a later interpolation.

[1] Cyp. *Ep.* 59. 14. See *Appendix* on *Principalis Ecclesia*, p. 537.

1. We shall presently see in detail that in order to adapt even the very language of Cyprian in the passage which they thought the most favourable to their pretensions, the papal apologists have framed, and at all hazards, and against evidence full and understood, have stedfastly maintained the grossest forgery in literature. Without the insertion of their phrases the passage means something palpably different. This does not look as if Cyprian here had ever been felt to be on their side.

2. Does Cyprian's practice exemplify the Roman theory? We shall see how the subsequent history of his intercourse with the Roman see exhibits him sometimes, as we should say, rightly in conflict with it, sometimes wrongly; but in conflict almost always—exhorting the Roman bishop, rebuking him or making excuses for him, or assuring him that he had excommunicated himself by his vain threats of excommunicating others—obeying him never[1].

3. But it may perhaps be said, that great men and saints are not always consistent, that his practice may have been inferior to his theory, or even contradictory.

The answer to this is that the very mention of the supremacy of one Pontiff, or the universality of one jurisdiction, is the precise contrary of the Cyprianic statements. The form of government for the whole Church which these enunciate is that of a Body—its whole episcopate. This is a Representative Body. Its members, appointed for life by free election, represent each one diocese[2]. They give their judgment by suffrages. They have no power of delegation, for Christ constituted *them* to govern,—not to appoint governors. Purity

---

[1] Cyp. *Epp.* 68. 2, 3; 72. 3; 75. (Firmil.) 2, 3, 6, 17, 24, 25.

[2] This is no less the case wherever they are appointed by the Representatives of Representatives. Appointment by Presbyters is less after the first model, Presbyters not being properly representative of their congregations. Cooption by other Bishops is still less satisfactory, while the only intolerable plan is that of their appointment by one superior of their own order appointed by a few of themselves.

of conduct was essential to the continuance of any one of them in his authority[1]. No minority among them could be overborne by a majority, in a matter of administration, even though it were so grave a question as that of Rebaptism. If all but one voted one way, that one could not be overruled in the direction of his diocese. 'These considerations, dear 'brother,' writes Cyprian in the name of his sixth Council, 'we 'bring home to your conscience out of regard to the Office 'we hold in common and to the simple love we bear you. 'We believe that you too, from the reality of your religious 'feeling and faith, approve what is religious as well as true. 'Nevertheless we know there are those who cannot readily 'part with principles once imbibed, or easily alter a view 'of their own, but who, without hurting the bond of peace 'and concord between colleagues, hold to special practices 'once adopted among them—and herein we do no violence 'to anyone and impose no law. For in the administration of 'the Church each several prelate has the free discretion of his 'own will—having to account to the Lord for his action[2].' The prelate who is thus allowed the same freedom as the rest of his order in governing his own diocese is Stephanus, Bishop of Rome. No protest of his in answer claimed the right to direct all or any of the rest.

'It remains for us to deliver each our judgment on the 'particular question,' so said Cyprian, opening the seventh of his Councils, 'without judging any, without removing 'any from our communion, whose judgment may differ from 'our own. None of us constitutes himself a bishop over 'bishops, or makes it imperative for his colleagues to obey 'him, through any despotic awe, inasmuch as every bishop 'by leave of his freedom and office, has a free scope of

---

[1] *Ep.* 67. 3 'Propter quod plebs *obsequens* præceptis dominicis et Deum metuens *a peccatore præposito* (sc. episcopo) *separare* se debet, *nec se* ad sacrilegi sacerdotis sacrificia miscere, quando ipsa maxime habeat potestatem vel eligendi dignos sacerdotes vel indignos recusandi.' Cf. *Ep.* 68. 3.

[2] *Ep.* 72. 3.

'his own, and can no more be judged of another than he 'can himself judge another. We must all alike await the 'judgment of our Lord Jesus Christ, who alone by Himself 'hath the office (*potestas*) of promoting us in the govern-'ment of His Church, and of judging our course of action[1].'

4. In what then consisted in effect the unity of a body so constituted? It was a practical unity, a moral unity, held together by its own sense of unity, by 'the cement of mutual concord[2].' As problems arose they were to consider them each by itself. The first thing was that they should, with as deliberate consultation as could be had, state their several opinions without favour or fear.

If we consider what great effects were produced, what far-reaching and enduring results were secured, through the mere exercise and utterance of this moral, or spiritual, judgment, by men whose divine commission was simply to use this, and to express this, we may perhaps think that an incessant complaining of the unwillingness of imperial assemblies to discuss, decide and give effect to church measures, is at least not primitively church-like. The periods in which the Church has worked its will upon us through civil rule are not times of impressive spirituality. The immeasurably higher enthusiasm and stronger effectiveness which has attended its moral judgments under governments as hostile, or as surly, or as indifferent as mere politicians could wish governments to be towards really Christian matters, might encourage the faith of modern churchmen in the value of their one undisputed prerogative.

A bishop could not then resist their united voice without hardihood, but if he did, he was unassailable unless viciousness or false doctrine were patent in his life or teaching. In

---

[1] *VII. Conc. Carth. Præfat. Cypriani.*
[2] *Ep.* 68. 3. An important passage and often quoted to evince the constitutional character of the body, but not so often to shew the simply moral force of its action—which is what it really shews.

that case the allegiance of his flock was to be withdrawn. He was to be regarded (says the African primate, with a strong local colouring) as a brigand chief who had got possession of a caravanserai[1].

The divine reality of such their unity had been taught typically in the respective charges of the Lord to Peter and to the Twelve[2]. The authority and power committed is the same to each several apostle. But for the sake of shewing (such is Cyprian's interpretation) that many apostles did not make many churches, but one only, therefore the first declaration of the foundation of a universal Church is couched in language addressed to one only—S. Peter. For that one occasion the words are to one, but the meaning is for ever to all.

As nothing limited it in space, but the authority belonged to all the apostles, wherever they went, so in time also, after they were departed, nothing limited that authority to Peter's successors among the successors of them all. Though the charge to Peter appears among the earliest of Cyprian's Christian ideas[3], as does also the obedience due to bishops[4], yet Peter's successors are nowhere mentioned or hinted at by Cyprian as necessary to the Church's Unity[5]. But the successors of the other Apostles are. And of them it is said that the power given by Christ to them, in equal measure with S. Peter, passed on to the churches which they established, and to the bishops who everywhere succeeded them[6].

A headship attributed to the successors of one among them would simply ruin at once the whole theory of the

---

[1] *Ep.* 68. 3.
[2] See Catena of passages on the Unity from Peter, infra p. 197.
[3] *De Habitu Virgg.* 10.
[4] *Ep.* 4. 4, where the spiritual sword is described to be as deadly to the spirit as the material sword was to the life of any who disobeyed the ancient high priest.
[5] This Ritschl himself confesses. It will be understood that he plays the dangerous game of maintaining presbyterianism against episcopacy, by trying to saddle Cyprian's episcopacy with the papacy as its necessary deduction.
[6] *Ep.* 75. 16, see Catena below.

IV.II. THE CYPRIANIC AND ROMAN THEORIES CONTRARIES.

unity and of the authority which subsisted in the *copiosum corpus sacerdotum*—the *episcopatus unus, episcoporum multorum concordi numerositate diffusus*[1]. And this *is* Cyprian's theory.

5. Yet again, as that Body might not rule any one Bishop, it follows *a fortiori* that any one Bishop could not rule that Body. It is plain that such pretension could never be set up without violating the principle and essence of Cyprian's theory. This theory could not even coexist with the theory of a dominant centre. The two views are mutually exclusive.

A singular fate overtook two strong sentences of the early Latin fathers. It is comprehensible how the sentence of Cyprian could be vivisected and injected with corruption till, as we find it, it seemed to yield a sense contrary to its original force, and to the context, and to the whole scheme of the treatise, and to the leading idea of its author. But, that Tertullian's scornful parody of some Bishop of Rome's assumption—'*Pontifex* scilicet *maximus, quod* est *episcopus episcoporum, edicit*[2],'—should have worked round into becoming the actual title and style of his successor, exhibits a feat of that brilliant imagination which even itself could never have realised.

Catena of Cyprianic passages on the Unity signified in the Charge to Peter.

ib. [A.D. 248. Petrus etiam cui oves suas Dominus pascendas tuendasque
1. commendat, super quem posuit et fundavit ecclesiam, aurum quidem et argentum sibi esse negat,...

A rhetorical contrast of the facts in Matt. xvi. and Acts iii. not by itself touching the question of Unity.]

iit. A.D. 251. Probatio est ad fidem facilis compendio veritatis. Loquitur Dominus ad Petrum: 'ego tibi dico' inquit 'quia tu es Petrus 'et super istam petram aedificabo ecclesiam meam, et portae 'inferorum non vincent eam. Dabo tibi claves regni caelorum:

---

[1] In Cyprian this thought and these words are in perennial flow. But *Ep.* 55. 24 is a strong condensed chapter. Cf. *Ep.* 58. 3.
[2] Tert. *de Pudicit.* 1.

198 CATENA FROM CYPRIAN ON THE UNITY OF THE CHURCH

'et quæ ligaveris super terram erunt ligata et in cælis, et
'quæcumque solveris super terram erunt soluta et in cælis.'
Super unum ædificat ecclesiam, et quamvis *apostolis omnibus*
post resurrectionem suam *parem potestatem* tribuat et dicat:
'Sicut misit me pater et ego mitto vos. Accipite Spiritum
'Sanctum: si cujus remiseritis peccata, remittentur illi: si
'cujus tenueritis tenebuntur,' tamen ut *unitatem manifestaret,
unitatis* ejusdem *originem ab uno incipientem* sua auctoritate disposuit. *Hoc erant utique et ceteri apostoli quod fuit
Petrus, pari* consortio præditi et *honoris et potestatis*, sed *exordium* ab *unitate* proficiscitur, *ut ecclesia* Christi *una monstretur.*

Whatever may be the value of the argument or illustration, there can in this
its genuine shape be no doubt as to the meaning of the passage. The Apostles
are all made equal in honour and power by our Lord's commission. Simply to
declare the unity of His Church, He, the first time that He gives that commission,
gives it to one. Afterwards he repeats the same commission (as Cyprian understood it) to all. The *origo, exordium*, of unity starts (*proficiscitur*) from one as a
manifestation or demonstration (*manifestaret, monstretur*) of unity.

The same teaching identically appears, with greater or less compression, but
with no variation of idea, in all other references to whomsoever addressed: as follows

Ep. 43. 5. A.D. 250. (*Plebi universæ*). Deus unus est, et Christus unus et *una ecclesia*
et *cathedra una super Petrum Domini voce* fundata.

The unity is here inferred from the *Lord's voice* speaking to Peter alone, as set
forth in the *De Unitate* published the year after at the same place.

Ep. 45. 3. A.D. 251. (*Cornelio Fratri*). Hoc enim vel maxime, frater, et laboramus et
laborare debemus ut *unitatem* a Domino et *per apostolos nobis
successoribus traditam,* [not *vobis* nor *per Petrum successoribus*,
but to the bishops as succeeding to that equal authority of
the apostles] quantum possumus obtinere curemus, et quod in
nobis est palabundas et errantes oves...*in ecclesia colligamus.*

Ep. 48. 3. „ „ (*Cornelio Fratri*). Communicationem tuam id est catholicæ
ecclesiæ unitatem pariter et *caritatem* [n.b. not *honorem* or
potestatem.]

Ep. 55. 8. A.D. 252. (*Antoniano Fratri*). The see of Rome is *Fabiani locus...locus
Petri* et gradus cathedræ sacerdotalis.

Ep. 59. 7. „ „ (*Cornelio Fratri*). Petrus tamen super quem ædificata ab
eodem Domino fuerat ecclesia, *unus pro omnibus loquens*, et
ecclesiæ voce respondens ait, 'Domine, ad quem imus?'

14. „ „ ...et ad Petri cathedram atque ad ecclesiam principalem *unde
unitas sacerdotalis exorta est.*

Ep. 66. 8. A.D. 254. (*Florentio cui et Puppiano Fratri*). On same passage as *Ep.* 59. 7
'ad quem ibimus &c.' loquitur illic Petrus super quem ædificata fuerat ecclesia, *ecclesiæ nomine* docens.

1. 3. A.D. 255. (*Quinto Fratri*, referred to in *Ep.* 72 *Stephano fratri*). Cyprian here shews what deduction is not to be drawn from the commission of our Lord.

> Nam nec Petrus, quem primum Dominus elegit et super quem ædificavit ecclesiam suam, cum secum Paulus disceptaret, vindicavit sibi aliquid insolenter aut adroganter adsumpsit ut diceret *se primatum tenere* et *obtemperari a novellis et posteris sibi potius oportere*....

I.e. Peter did *not* draw the inference of his primacy from the fact of his selection to be the 'origo' or 'exordium' of unity.

3. 7. A.D. 256. (*Jubaiano Fratri*). Manifestum est autem ubi et per *quos* remissa peccatorum dari possit, quæ in baptismo scilicet datur. Nam *Petro primum* Dominus, super quem ædificavit ecclesiam, et *unde unitatis originem instituit et ostendit*, potestatem istam dedit ut id solveretur [in terris] quod ille solvisset. et post resurrectionem quoque *ad apostolos* loquitur dicens 'sicut misit me pater et ego mitto vos.' hoc cum dixisset, inspiravit et ait *illis* 'accipite spiritum sanctum. si cujus remiseritis peccata....' unde intellegimus non nisi in ecclesiæ *præpositis* et evangelica lege ac dominica ordinatione *fundatis* licere baptizare....

In manner precisely parallel to the *De Unitate* he infers that what was first said to one in token of unity was afterwards said to all as their charter of authority—and to none but them.

5. 16. A.D. 256. (*Firmilianus Cypriano Fratri*). Qualis vero error sit et quanta cæcitas ejus qui remissionem peccatorum dicit apud synagogas hæreticorum dari posse, nec permanet in *fundamento* unius ecclesiæ, quæ semel a Christo super petram solidata est, hinc intellegi potest quod *soli Petro* Christus dixerit 'quæcumque ligaveris, ...' et iterum in evangelic [quando] in *solos apostolos* insufflavit Christus dicens 'accipite spiritum sanctum. si cujus...' potestas ergo peccatorum remittendorum *apostolis* data est et *ecclesiis quas* illi a Christo missi constituerunt et *episcopis qui eis ordinatione vicaria successerunt.*

Here similarly Firmilian (who as is well known echoes Cyprian to the letter) holds the voice to Peter to be the token of unity, and the powers to be shared by the apostles, the churches and the successive bishops all alike.

17. A.D. 256. ...hanc tam apertam et manifestam Stephani stultitiam quod qui sic de episcopatus sui loco gloriatur et se successionem Petri tenere contendit, super quem fundamenta ecclesiæ collocata sunt, multas alias petras inducat et ecclesiarum multarum nova ædificia constituat, dum esse illic baptisma sua auctoritate defendit.

I.e. The present bishop of Rome, *Stephanus*, who so prides himself on his succession, sacrifices the prerogative of himself and all other true bishops by recognising baptism external to the church and them.

III.

The Appeal of the modern Church of Rome to Cyprian on 'The Unity of the Catholic Church'—by way of Interpolation.

Notwithstanding its somewhat technical character, I cannot but present this strange matter as part of the continuous narrative of Cyprian's 'Life and Work.' The conception of his formative influence on the Church of Christ would be at once exaggerated and incomplete without some account taken of an immense power claimed in his name, and exercised through the shadow of his name, by men and societies who have no act or real word of his to shew on their side.

In the year 1682 the Gallican Church held that celebrated assembly which affirmed their ancient Liberties, and described in The Four Articles the limits of papal authority. Yet, as Bossuet in the most eloquent perhaps of his harangues had discoursed to them, 'The object of that assembly was Peace' —Peace with Innocent the Eleventh. 'Conserver l'Unité' was the guiding thought of Bossuet's life[1]. Their Synodical Letter[2] therefore, addressed to the whole French hierarchy, prefaced its protest against that pontiff's usurpations with a confession of their duty to his See. That duty was established and acknowledged by words borrowed from Cyprian's fourth chapter on Unity—the printed text.

It is difficult to exaggerate the effect of those words even amid the universal indignation which then possessed court, Church and people. The authority of that primæval voice was once more as conclusive as it had now been for some centuries. It was alleged as conclusive, and was alleged alone.

And yet the great orator of Meaux, amid his own array

---

[1] Sermon prêché (9 Nov. 1681) à l'ouverture de l'assemblée générale du Clergé de France, 'Sur l'Unité de l'Église.'

[2] Lettre de l'assemblée du Clergé de France, tenue en 1682, à tous les Prélats de l'Église Gallicane. Dupin, *Libertés de l'Église Gallicane* (1860).

of inconclusive authorities, forbore to marshal this capital and decisive text.

That very year there appeared the new English edition from which that text was omitted.

The words are spurious. The history of their interpolation may be distinctly traced even now, and it is as singular as their controversial importance has been unmeasured. It is a history which well may make it the most interesting of literary forgeries. But the Ultramontane is still unconvinced, and as he may long remain so, we lay the evidence before others.

The eloquent Mgr. Freppel, Bishop of Angers, late Professor at the Sorbonne,—in which capacity he delivered his course of lectures on Saint Cyprian, repeats the contention that the giving of the keys to Peter and the charge to feed the flock is 'the charter of investiture of the papacy,' and in support of it asks leave 'to place under our eyes this remarkable passage' of Cyprian. 'Whatever difficulty criticism 'may raise on the authenticity of such or such a word in 'particular' does not affect the argument. 'We have a right 'to maintain a reading which has such numerous and such 'antient testimonies for itself[1].'

I quote this merely as a clear statement of the position which Romish argument has taken and still takes as to the passage and as to its value as it stands[2]. It is easy to allege that 'Cyprian only repeats here what he says so many times elsewhere,' but the tenacity with which this place is reprinted and repeated betokens well enough the misgiving as to the other passages being capable of enduring the required meaning without the comment of this fabrication[3].

---

[1] S. Cyprien. Par M. l'Abbé Freppel, Prof. à la Faculté de Théologie de Paris 1865 (Cours fait à la Sorbonne), pp. 277—291.

[2] See also Prof. Hurter, S. J., SS. Patrum Opusc. 1. p. 72.

[3] Most old copies of Cyprian bear witness to the agitations of spirit over these clauses. Beside me casually is a Maran (Venet. 1758); some lines are erased and references placed at the sides. A Pamèle, clean throughout

The 'numerous and ancient testimonies' consist of (1) the *editions* which contain the passages, and the *manuscripts* on which they are supposed to rest. (2) *Citations* of the passage.

Our simplest method is to give the passage in full, exactly as this author reproduces it (as he says) from 'the editions of Manutius (1563) (who first printed it), De Pamèle (1568), Rigault (1648), Dom Maran (1726)[1].'

" The Lord saith unto Peter, 'I say unto thee that thou art Peter, and upon this rock will I build my Church, and the gates of hell shall not prevail against it. I will give unto thee the keys of the kingdom of heaven: and whatsoever thou shalt bind on earth shall be bound in heaven, and whatsoever thou shalt loose on earth shall be loosed in heaven.' *And to the same (apostle) He says after His resurrection 'Feed my sheep.'* He builds *His* Church upon *that* one, *and to him entrusts His sheep to be fed*. And although after His resurrection He assigns equal power to all His apostles, and says 'As the Father sent me even so send I you, receive ye the Holy Ghost; whosoever sins ye remit they shall be remitted unto him, and whosoever sins ye retain they shall be retained,' nevertheless in order to make the unity manifest, He *established one Chair, and* by His own authority appointed the origin of that same unity beginning from one. Certainly the rest of the apostles were that which Peter *also* was, endued with equal partnership both of honour and office, but the beginning sets out from unity, *and Primacy is given to Peter, that one Church of Christ and one Chair may be pointed out;* and all are pastors and one flock is

---

except for two very soiled pages here with ruffled corners. A Baluze (Paris 1726) has racy passages written out into the margins, and the whole of this so appears. So of the two Pembroke MSS., one has the passage scored with a pencil, the other with a knife.

[1] We must however state that Manutius does *not* give the clause 'he who deserts the chair of Peter on which the Church was founded,' nor Maran the words 'established one chair and.'

shown, to be fed by all the apostles with one-hearted accord, that one Church of Christ may be pointed out. It is this one Church which the Holy Spirit in the Person of the Lord speaks of in the Song of Songs, saying 'My dove is one, my perfect one, one is she to her mother, elect to her who brought her forth.' He that holds not this unity of the Church, does he believe that he holds the faith? He who strives and rebels against the Church, *he who deserts the Chair of Peter on which the Church was founded,* does he trust that he is in the Church? Since the blessed Apostle Paul also...[1]"

The words in italics admittedly must be from the pen of one who taught the cardinal doctrine of the Roman see. If Cyprian wrote them he held that doctrine. There is no disguising the fact. Onofrio Panvinio[2] for instance in his great treatise on the Primacy of Peter places this whole passage from Cyprian 'foremost of the holy Fathers' next after his citations of Scripture, and the words we have printed in italics he has anticipated us by printing in capitals as the crucial and decisive ones.

But the reader will observe that, separated from the italicised words, the passage runs smooth and the doctrine is a different one. It is the doctrine of a catholicity perfect in unity without hint of Petrine or of any primacy. As we have already seen, it exhibits a unity indicated (such is the special argument of the passage) by Christ's committing one and the same charge, first to one and then to all of the apostles as peers or equals of that one.

Now the indictment we prefer is that every italicised word is a forgery; and a forgery deliberately for three centuries past forced by papal authority in the teeth of evidence upon editors and printers who were at its mercy. The recent

---

[1] See Latin Text in *Appendix* (p. 549) with collations.

[2] O. Panvinio, *De primatu Petri et Apostolicæ sedis potestate*, pp. 3, 4. Veronæ, 1589.

labour of Hartel reveals a similar process at work long before upon the manuscripts. The corruptions were always patent, but now we can actually watch the agents.

If proven, the interest of our tale is beyond that of literary curiosity or even literary morality. Dukes and Cardinals, Prelates and Masters of the Palace prevailed over brokenhearted scholars. It was a Battle of the Standard, fought that a forgery might not be (as one of the defenders expressed it) 'ravi à l'Église.' All that energy, all that diplomacy,—the very tone of this moment—are the best witnesses to the value of the Protestant conviction that, although all Cyprian would have to be read by the light of those phrases could they be saved, Cyprian without them is an irrefragable witness against those assumptions. But our business is now with the literary evidence. The reader may point the moral.

We will take the manuscript history of the passage first.

The codices of Cyprian[1] *de Unitate* which are older than the tenth century are as follows:

The Seguier manuscript at Paris; so styled from its first known possessor the great Chancellor, from whom it passed to the Prince Bishop Coislin of Metz, thence to the Abbey of S. Germain des Prés by his gift, thence after the fire of 1793 to the Library of Paris, where it is now. It is a most precious volume of the Sixth or the Seventh century preserving the most genuine readings and oldest forms of words, and it is distinguished in collations as S.

The Verona Codex of the Sixth or Seventh century (V), an uncial MS. which was given to Charles Borromeo by the canons of Verona, used by Latinius in preparing his notes for the edition of Manutius, and further known to us by his collations, copies of which were in the hands of Baluze and Rigault, and another copy is extant at Göttingen. A somewhat inaccurate collation was also made by R. Rigby for Bp. Fell. Latinius was certain that it was of the Sixth century.

[1] Hartel, Præf. ii., iii., v., ix., xii., xiv., xix., xxii., xxiii., lxxx., lxxxiv.

IV. III. THE INTERPOLATIONS AND THE MANUSCRIPTS. 205

The Codex Beneventanus (called also Neapolitanus) was one of the best manuscripts[1]. We are acquainted with it from the collations made by Ant. Agostino Bishop of Alifi and used by Rigault, and those made by Rigby for Bishop Fell.

The MS. of Würzburg (W) of the Eighth or Ninth century, ascribed by some to the Seventh.

The codices Reginensis 116 (R) and San Gallensis 89 (G), both of the Ninth.

In not one of these manuscripts have the italicised words appeared in any shape.

Of Trecensis (Q) of the Eighth or Ninth Century, and of Monacensis (M) of the Ninth, we will speak presently.

The great scholar Latino Latini, Canon of Viterbo, who died at the age of 80 in 1593, tells us he had seen seven manuscripts (integros) of Cyprian in the Vatican in which all these words were wanting[2].

Baluze[3] says that he had himself seen twenty-seven manuscripts without them.

Bishop Fell used four English codices of which none have a trace of our italics[4]; and besides these four English manuscripts (to which we add a Pembroke codex missed by him[5]) all have only the additional Post-Resurrection Charge to St Peter, (a mere parallel text,) without any word at all about the Chair, the Primacy of Peter, the Unity of Peter, or the desertion of the Church founded on Peter. These manuscripts are all of the tenth century or later.

Baluze[6] says that the German manuscripts of the time of

---

[1] Hartel, pp. citatis.

[2] Latino Latin., *Bibliotheca Sacra et Profana a D. Macro (Magri)*, Romæ 1677, p. 179.

[3] *Cypriani Opera.* Baluze. Paris, 1726, p. 545. Comm. in loc.

[4] Viz. Bod. 1, Ebor, New College 2, Sarum. In spite of these Fell kept the interpolated post-resurrection charge to Peter.

For a description and new collations of the English manuscripts see Appendix at end of this volume.

[5] Viz. Bod. 2, Lambeth, Lincoln, N. C. 1, and Pem. 2. [Fell's readings of Voss' MSS. have not been revised.]

[6] *Cypriani Opera.* Paris, 1726, p. 545.

Venericus bishop of Vercelli[1] seem not to have had these words; nor are they found in any of the earlier editions (or their numerous reprints) of Cyprian which appeared before that of Manutius in 1563 and which represent to us many manuscripts which have long disappeared[2].

We must now see what authority there is in favour of the italics against this mass of negative evidence.

In 1568 Jacques De Pamèle, canon of Bruges, brought out his Cyprian. Ignorant of the facts and of Latini's griefs (of which we shall presently speak), he accepted Manutius' edition as representing the famous Verona manuscript. But as Latini hinted 'he had no nose'; he was absurd enough to think the spurious tract 'on Dice-players' was in Cyprian's style, and careless enough to say that its Latin texts were in Cyprianic form. He surrendered himself to a manuscript[3] belonging to the abbey of Cambron[4] in Hainault, which was more interpolated throughout than any known copy. He thought it confirmed the Verona reading.

The corruption according to Baluze was found also in an ancient manuscript of Marcello Cervini, afterwards Pope Marcellus II., and this one was used by Onofrio Panvinio[5]. It was found in a certain Bavarian manuscript which Bishop Fell knew only through Gretser[6], who assures us it was

---

[1] A.D. 1078—1082. Gams, *Series Episcoporum*, p. 825.

[2] Very inaccurate accounts of these editions are prefixed to the editions of Baluzius by Maran and of Fell, and repeated in the Oxford translation of Cyprian, p. 151 (Library of the Fathers). Hartel has examined and given a careful account of them in his ' Præfatio.'

[3] Not that manuscripts caused Jacques De Pamèle unreasonable trouble. Latinius, in one of his polished letters to him (*Epp*. I. p. 309), admires the condition in which we should see ancient authors 'in aliam formam a nativa degenerasse' if they were edited as his friend edits 'contra fidem codicum.'

[4] Codex Cambronensis—'interpolatior interpolatissimis'—Hartel.

[5] Baluze, *Cypr. Opera*, p. 545; Panvinio, *De Prim. Petr.* p. 4, only alludes to 'scripta exemplaria.'

[6] J. Gretser, *de jure et more prohibendi, expurgandi, et abolendi libros*

IV. III. THE MANUSCRIPT EVIDENCE OF THE FORGERIES. 207

of 'the highest stamp.' We shall however presently know more about it if the reader will only bear in mind that this was evidently the Munich manuscript,—Monacensis or M.

The manuscripts which have this passage have it with all the varieties, omissions, and transpositions which universally indicate corruption of text. The oldest which has additions like those in Manutius is one of the tenth century. It belonged to Isaac Voss and is called **h** : it is copied partly from T, and partly from interpolated manuscripts[1]. But we may pass it over as we shall meet the corruption higher up the stream. Similarly we need not here concern ourselves about a manuscript of the fifteenth century in the Bodleian[2] which has a like tale to tell.

But there is one[3] in the Bodleian of the eleventh, or perhaps the tenth century, which exhibits well the most peculiar and interesting phenomenon connected with the manuscripts. There once existed a manuscript of Cyprian of which three others now extant belonging to the tenth and earlier centuries are copies. These three are the Troyes Codex,—Trecensis, or Q, of the eighth or ninth century; the Munich codex,—Monacensis, or M, of the ninth; and the Bodleian just named, of the tenth or eleventh. These three are all copied from copies of one lost manuscript which we may call the Archetype[4].

---

hæreticos et noxios (Ingoldstadt, 1603, Lib. II., c. 7, p. 303.) He says he fell upon this codex 'in Bavarica bibliotheca —membranaceum. .optimæ notæ.' See *Appendix*, p. 549, as to its readings.

[1] Hartel, p. xl. He says '*the same* additions,' pp. x . and xii. n., but it is worse than Manutius in reading 'this unity of Peter's' instead of 'this unity of the Church.'

[2] Fell's 'Bod. 3.'

[3] Fell's 'Bod. 4,' 10th or 11th cent.

[4] The Codex Trecensis, Q, and Monacensis, M, are independent copies of one copy of the lost Archetype (Hartel, p. xxxv). Our Bodleian, which is not described by Hartel, is not copied from that same copy of the lost manuscript, for though it has the interpolations almost the same, still its readings deviate from M and Q, and these deviations are better and more genuine readings. It was copied then from a lost manuscript other and better than the immediate original of M and Q. If with Hartel we call M and Q's lost original <X> we may call the lost

Now it seems almost incredible but it is true that these manuscripts should reveal so minutely as they do the manipulation practised on their forefather. Codices M and Q give the interpolated passage in full, and having come to the end of it with its four inserted clauses they proceed without stop or stay to give the genuine passage without any interpolations at all. First comes the doctored recension which the scribe of the Archetype was intended, by the person who directed him, to substitute for the original. This remodelled paragraph was finished up with an emphatic repetition of the keyword with which it began—'He built His Church upon One[1].' But the thrice-fortunate copier supposed this final repeated keyword to be the cue in the original from which he was to go on. Accordingly having copied out his interpolated pattern schedule he went on from those words in the genuine manuscript before him, and wrote out in his simplicity the genuine passage which began with them[2]. The Bodleian Codex gives first three interpolated clauses only but in its repetition of the whole passage inserts the fourth interpolation.

If any one asks, How copyists could so flagrantly go on giving a genuine and an interpolated text on the same page, we can only be thankful to the fatuous or cynical fidelity which wrote out what was before it. Many and inferior manuscripts give only the corrupt form. But the double form went on being copied for a long time. For example, the third Bodleian MS. of Fell, as we have mentioned, has still the duplicate form[3] as late as the fifteenth century,— and what is still more remarkable the Jesuit theologian

---

original of the Bodleian <X 2>. It is coordinate with Hartel's <X> and <Y>.

[1] 'Super unum ædificavit ecclesiam,' just as others have similarly emphasized by redoubling them the similar words 'That the Church of Christ may be shewn as one.'

[2] See *Appendix*, p. 549. Hartel, Præf. pp. x., xi., xliii., notes pp. 212, 213.

[3] Bod. 3, Laud Misc. 217.

IV. III. INTERPOLATIONS FORCED ON MANUTIUS' TEXT.

Gretser copies it out double word for word in triumphant fury to demolish Thomas James the 'English Calvinian,' to prove as he says that 'papistæ have seen manuscripts[1].'

Thus if there never was a viler fraud than the inventor's, there was never a worse nemesis than the honest obtuseness of his instrument.

We must now enquire how interpolations against which the manuscripts bore such conclusive evidence came to be embodied for the first time in the edition of Paulus Manutius in 1563 after all earlier editions and reprints had escaped them[2].

The son of the great Aldus had been two years settled in Rome, loaded with every kindness, honour, and privilege; his failing health spared by a staff of able correctors who were assigned to him for the great undertaking of the new Papal press in Greek, Latin and the Vernacular. Cyprian was the first author issued from that press. Charles Borromeo had been truly anxious for the restoration of the text of Cyprian to its primitive integrity. The Verona manuscript had been procured by him for the purpose.

The editing of the text was committed to Latino Latini. Besides 'collecting with many watchings and labours' an illustrative commentary on obscure passages, he made accurate collations and prepared a brief critical commentary on the readings[3]. In one of his private letters[4] he complains that after the most conscientious labour upon the text he found that, while passing through the press, not only were Biblical quotations altered to conformity with the Vulgate, but besides, 'whether it was at the mere pleasure of certain

---

[1] Gretser, *l.c.* p. 303 (Ingoldstadt 1603).

[2] Hartel names 10 edd., and there were at least 20 including reprints of Erasmus.

[3] Besides the Verona and Benevento (or Naples) codex, Hartel, p. lxxx., ascertains that he had of our extant ones Vat. (ϕ) n. 199 and prob. Monacensis (μ).

[4] Ad Andr. Masium (Maes) II. p. 109 [Hartel, p. x., cf. p. lxxx.], and Life of Latini prefixed to the *Bibliotheca*.

'persons or of set design, he knew not, *some passages were 'retained contrary to the evidence of the manuscripts, and even 'some additions made.'* Under these circumstances he would not allow his name to be connected with the edition, 'deeming 'it no light crime to conceal the truth or to alter the smallest 'letter,' and withdrew his annotations. In the *Bibliotheca Sacra et Profana*, or collected notes of the same critic[1], he mentions three epistles of Cyprian first discovered by himself in the MS. then at Saint Salvadore's at Bologna, and in two Vatican MSS., of which epistles the arrogant 8th letter from the Roman Clergy which Cyprian treats contemptuously was one. These he says the superior authorities[2] would not allow to be published 'un-emended,' and accordingly the 8th epistle does not appear at all in that edition. They refused also to allow the anti-Roman epistle of Firmilian to be 'brought forth out of darkness'—but in this Latini seems to have acquiesced, 'detesting the man's petulance[3].' Upon a remark of Pamelius[4] censuring a certain reading of Manutius a few lines forward in the *De Unitate*, he observes 'this 'is one of the alterations which were made neither by me, nor 'by Manutius, but by one who had permission to pervert, 'to add, to cut out, or to corrupt whatever he would, against 'my will.'

That our present interpolations were among this personage's manipulations is clear from Latini's statement on the same page, that he *had never seen* these in any manuscript *except* 'in a fragment very recently written at Bologna, '—a small book containing only a few treatises of Cyprian, 'belonging to Vianesius de Albergatis,—and also in a com-'plete copy at Bologna (from which the said fragment was 'copied) which was itself also written in a recent hand.'

There is in the Library at Göttingen[5] a copy (brought

---

[1] *Bibl. Sacr. et Prof.*, p. 174 *b*.
[2] Qui præerant, *l. c.*
[3] *B. S. et P.*, p. 177 *b*.
[4] Pamel., *Cypr.* (Antv. 1568), p. 262 *a*, note 4. *B. S. et P.*, p. 179 *a*.
[5] Hartel, p. xi. and p. 213 n.

from Venice) of the edition of Manutius, with notes written on its margin. Those notes are copies of manuscript notes by Latini. One of these notes says upon this place, '*These 'words* were added out of *a single* manuscript belonging to 'Virosius (a clerical error for Vianesius) of Bologna, now in 'the Vatican, by P. Gabriel the Pœnitentiary with the consent 'of the Master of the Sacred Palace.' So close a chain of evidence leaves no doubt as to the time, manner and performers of the interpolation.

The most competent editor of his age and country felt compelled to resign his work because he was powerless to prevent the Theologues of the Vatican from remodelling his text. But we are not quite at the end of this strange story.

In the Council of Trent in the year 1563 the debate was at its height 'whether Bishops have their powers *of Divine right* or *of Papal right*[1].' The ambiguous canon proposed from Rome, that bishops hold the principal place dependent on the pope, was under discussion with a view to substituting for it, chief under the pope but not dependent. Quotations from Cyprian were rife. About the 20th of June, Carlo Visconti, Bp. of Ventimiglia, the pope's secret minister at Trent, and his spy upon his legates, an experienced diplomatist and 'man of exact judgment,' received letters from Rome telling him that the new Cyprian had appeared, with the passages which the correctors had expunged from the *De Unitate*[2]. The possible effect on the Council itself was serious. Visconti went straight to Agostino, now bishop of Lerida, a great lawyer, diplomatist and antiquarian, who had received the same intelligence and with it a copy of the new book. He could tell Visconti that Latini himself had many days back communicated the facts to Cardinal Hosio (Osius); facts which he thoroughly understood, for it was he who had years before

---

[1] *De jure divino, de jure pontificio.* See Sarpi, Books VI., VII., esp. VII. 52.

[2] Visconti wrote 'de Authoritate.' An apt slip.

made the collation of the Benevento manuscript. The Agent told the one Legate whom the pope trusted there, Cardinal Simoneta, and on June 22nd advised the Vatican that 'before *such an opinion* got established' as that the correctors had been overruled, 'they should find means to remove it; which 'could be done by giving authority to *those words* which had 'been published, authenticating them with the testimony and 'approbation of persons who had seen and confronted the 'antient codices[1].'

So writes one who had just recorded the 'testimony' of the persons who had 'confronted' the antient codices,—the verdict of the correctors.

Even in 1563 it was a little late for such measures. But the note actually attached to the volume is now full of meaning[2]. It ends thus, 'It is not improper if pious and 'catholic interpretations and true senses be applied to the 'writings of the old fathers in order to preserve always the 'unity of the Church which Cyprian in his writings had most 'at heart. Otherwise no end to heresies and schisms.' This must have sounded mysterious to the unsuspecting student of Cyprian; and they were few who knew that they were meant at once to gloze the gloss and to defend the scholarship of the perpetrators.

Such is the history of the interpolations in the edition of Manutius where they first appeared.

Their appearance in the Benedictine edition is no less remarkable.

Baluze had rejected them on the weighty evidence which he states with utmost clearness[3], and had printed off the

---

[1] Epp. Car. Vicecomitis, L. xlv. al Card. Borromeo [Baluze, *Miscell.* III., p. 472 (Mansi), Lucæ 1761—1764]. See *Appendix*, Visconti's Letter, p. 544.

[2] See same Appendix, p. 545.

[3] His witnesses being (as we have indicated) the Seguierian and Veronese manuscripts, Latini's account, the 27 codices, the condition of the text temp. Venerici Vercell., and the citations (see below) by Calixtus II., the cardinals in 1408, and the Roman Correctors (see p. 218, n. 5) p. 545 (Paris ed. 1726).

IV.III. INTERPOLATIONS FORCED ON BENEDICTINE TEXT. 213

sheets without them. His death in 1718 interrupted the work which had been committed by order of the Regent Duke of Orleans to the Royal Press. In 1724 it was resumed for completion by the Benedictines of S. Maur at the request of 'Typographiæ Regiæ Præfectus,' and entrusted to Dom Prudent Maran. Baluze had formerly been banished by Louis XIV. and his property confiscated, for publishing in his History of the House of Auvergne fragments of a cartulary and an obituary which shewed the descent of the Cardinal de Bouillon from a sovereign house in France[1]. He had been placed in the Index by the court of Rome on account of his Lives of the Popes at Avignon. And now his genuine text of this passage in Cyprian was assailed by J. du Mabaret, Professor in the seminary at Angers, in a dissertation[2] which he submitted to Cardinal Fleury, now Minister, to the dominant Jesuits, and others in the interest of the holy see. The minister named a commission to decide the critical question. It was understood that a difficulty with the court of Rome would follow the omission of the passages from an edition issued under the authority of the ministry. It was decided to restore them. The prince of courtiers, the Duc d'Antin, of whom it was said that he acted flatteries which others spoke, was charged with the delicate office. He requested Dom Maran to 'confer' with the abbé Targny[3]. The result of the 'conference' was what printers

[1] The accuracy and honesty of Baluze in that most curious of historical disputes are demonstrated by M. Ch. Loriquet, 'Le cardinal de Bouillon, Baluze, Mabillon et Th. Ruinart, &c.' Rheims, 1870.

[2] Lettre d'un sçavant d'A. aux Auteurs des Mémoires de Trévoux pour reclamer un Passage important de S. Cyprien prêt à être enlevé par de célèbres Editeurs. *Mémoires de Trévoux* for Oct. 1726. See *Appendix*, p. 546.

[3] Targny enjoyed the confidence of the admirable Camille Le Tellier, abbé de Louvois, to whom he was 'Theologian,' and after Le Tellier's early death, the confidence of the Cardinal de Rohan, and died in 1737. See Sainte Beuve, Index de *Port Royal*. The Latin rendering of Chiniac (see p. 216, n. 1) confuses the history by a mistranslation worth noting. 'Cum abbate Targny (theologo Domini *le Tellier* dicti Abbatis *de Louvois*) tunc in rebus ecclesiasticis partes *agentis*.' The Abbé de Louvois had died in 1718 and

call 'a cancel.' The leaf was reprinted with the interpolations inserted, at the expense of typographical as well as moral symmetry, Baluze's note greatly reduced, and a parenthesis incorporated with it stating that 'it had been '*necessary* to alter much in Baluze's notes, and that more 'would have been altered if it could have been *conveniently* 'effected.' The double sense of the words can scarcely be missed[1]. The sole ground alleged for the reintroduction is that the 'words had appeared in all French editions for 150 years, even in that of Rigault'—the truth being that Rigault in his foot-notes repudiates them and prints the uncorrupt text in full.

I perceive—and anyone who will look in the first edition published at Paris in 1726 may perceive—in that magnificent volume the traces of this sad story. On page 195 the interpolation has been introduced. In order to make room for it this and the next page have been reprinted with forty-seven lines of type, there being through the rest of the volume only forty-six lines to a page. On these or on the adjoining pages he will find also the traces of the binder's 'guards' by which the separately printed pages have been inserted.

The Index seems to yield the same evidence. It fails to register 'cathedra, primatus, pastores, grex' from page 195, apparently because the clauses containing them were foisted into it after the Index had been printed off, although it gives the same words abundantly from other passages, and though other words from the genuine part of that page are given copiously: *e.g.* 'apostoli' is quoted from it twice, but not from the forged part.

---

his éloge was delivered at the Académie des Sciences at Easter 1719. The French is 'conférer avec l'abbé Targny (Théologien de le Tellier, dit l'Abbé de Louvois) qui jouoit alors un rôle dans les affaires de l'Église.' The parentheses are as I give them.

[1] 'Quin etiam *necesse fuit* in Baluzii Notis non pauca mutare, ac plura essent mutata, id si *commode* fieri potuisset'—Maran's parenthetic note p. 545 (ed. Paris 1726) on p. 195.

ORIGIN OF THE FORGERIES.

Dom Maran's preface betrays the very moment of the change. For it was made after that preface was actually in print. He there cites the passage with only the early and honest addition 'et iterum eidem post resurrectionem suam...[1]' and proceeds 'I quote this testimony [of Cyprian's] 'just as it is contained in this edition of Baluze's, but the 'words of Cyprian are read differently in the editions of 'Manutius and Pamelius[2].'

In the notes which are placed in this Paris edition at the end of the volume, it has been found necessary to cancel what must have been far the largest part of Baluze's original note. A whole sheet, a pair of leaves, printed off before his death, had to be entirely removed, viz. pages 545 and 546. In order to preserve the continuity of the paging two leaves which precede and follow the abstracted ones, and which also had to be reprinted, have two page-numbers on each of their two pages. Thus, page 543 is now numbered also 544; what would have been 544 is now 545 and 546, and so on until page 551, when the single numbering of the pages is resumed. Similarly, at the foot of the same leaves, the notations Ggggg and Ggggg ij which designated the filched sheet have been affixed additionally to their neighbours Fffffij and Hhhhh.

Professor Mabaret *now* had a sight for the first time of Baluze's original note, upon which he penned some elaborate[3]

---

[1] It is necessary to observe also that Baluze wrote: Super *illum* unum ædificat...&c. Præf. p. x.

[2] Præf. p. x. 'Hoc testimonium ita protuli ut habetur in hac Baluzii editione. Sed Cypriani verba aliter leguntur in editionibus Manuti ac Pamelii.' In the mutilated note the Benedictine editor has left one sentence without a verb— 'sed tamen scriptura, quam in contextu sequimur non solum editionibus Manutiana antiquioribus sed etiam codicum manuscriptorum auctoritate' (Paris ed. 1726, p. 545). The Venice ed. 1758 (p. 461) adds 'confirmatur.'

[3] '...l'apostilla de point en point,' Chiniac, as note 3. Mabaret's paper had the grand title 'Baluzii in Cypriani locum *Primatus Petro, &c.* primigenia Observatio censoriâ virgulâ castigata.'

annotations which the editors did not consider worth printing[1].

III. 1. What, lastly, is the Origin of the interpolated passages themselves? It will be observed that they are four. To the first, namely 'And to the same apostle, &c.' applies the remark of Latinius that the corrections have crept in from marginal summaries, not all at once but from time to time. This is the oldest of all, occurring in manuscripts which have no other trace of addition. It is simply a second text adduced and affirmed to be illustrative of that which Cyprian had quoted. The word *illum*, 'upon *that* one' apostle, is alone later and polemic.

2. The second interpolation 'established one chair' apparently exists only in the most corrupted manuscripts[2]. It is omitted even by Maran when replacing the forgeries. It makes nonsense of the argument as regards its order, but *may* also have been a marginal note.

3 and 4. The opening words 'and the Primacy is given to Peter' of the third interpolation had a similar origin. For in that state, in the form namely, '*Here* the primacy is given to Peter,' Cardinal Hosius[3] mentioned that they existed still in a manuscript of his own, where they found place immediately before the first interpolation.

But the rest has a very different origin.

The Bishops of Istria had from the time of Vigilius onward contended against the authority of the second Council

---

[1] The history of the Paris edition is given in the *Catalogus Operum Steph. Baluzii* by P. de Chiniac prefixed to Baluze's *Capitularia regum Francorum* Paris 1780, I. pp. 73, 74, and in his *Histoire des Capitulaires* 1779 (the same essay and Appendix in French), pp. 226—228.

[2] MQ., B3B4 Pem. and Pamelius's Cambronensis. On the source of atque rationem B2 Pem., atque rationem sua B3B4, atque orationis suae M after originem, see Appendix on the Interpolation, p. 550.

[3] Ap. Pamelii adnot. (Cypr. 1568, p. 261) and Lat. Latinius *Bibl. S. et P.*, p. 178. Latinius here writes Hosius, but in his Letters he writes Osius.

of Constantinople as having virtually censured that of Chalcedon. In A D. 585 Pelagius the Second invoked the effective authority of the Exarch Smaragdus of Ravenna and in an Epistle to the Bishops appealed to the 'terrible testimonies of the fathers'—as he may well call his own quotations. Among them Pelagius alleges a passage from Augustine which has never been identified and bears small resemblance to the views of that father. Then, four centuries before its appearance in any known or any evidenced manuscript of Cyprian, Pelagius produces the passage from the *De Unitate*, with the interpolations which we are now considering, and without the citation from the Canticles. Thus,

> Aye and Blessed Cyprian too, that noble martyr, in the book which he called after the name of Unity, among other things says thus: 'The beginning sets out from unity: and Primacy is given to 'Peter, that one Church of Christ and one Chair may be pointed 'out: and all are pastors, but one flock is shewn, to be fed by the 'apostles with one-hearted accord,' and a few words later, 'He that 'holds not this Unity of the Church does he believe that he holds 'the faith? *He who deserts and rebells*[1] *the Chair of Peter, on 'which the Church was founded, does he trust that he is in the 'Church?*'

These interpolations can never have been meant as honest paraphrases. The manipulation is too much. However here they appear for the first time, and the inspection of the passages side by side will shew how, down even to their omission of the verse of Canticles, the later recensions of the manuscripts have been formed upon this Epistle of Pelagius.

The omissions are as evidence of design no less instructive than the insertions. 1. The text which assigns to *all* the

---

[1] Observe the retention with an impossible construction of the genuine *resistit* which better scholars dropped out of their remodelled Cyprianic text. This one fact also prevents our acceptance of the possibility that the solitary manuscript of the 10th century which contains the letter of Pelagius may itself have been interpolated from manuscripts of Cyprian. Pelagii Papæ ii. *Ep.* 6 (2 *ad Epp. Istr.*) Labbe (ed. Ven. 1729), vol. VI. c. 632.

See with 'Note on the Citation from Pelagius II.,' p. 220, Appendix on the Interpolation, p. 551.

apostles the remission of sins is left out, and that which gives the Feeding of the Flock to Peter is substituted for it. 2. Those expressions are left out which indicate that unity *begins* from one apostle, as being to the corrector's mind inadequate. 3. So also, as irrelevant to his purpose, is the text of Canticles.

After this we have the awkward introduction of 'Paul's unity' because at Rome the later watchword became 'Peter and Paul'; and the reading *hanc et Pauli unitatem* is the attempt to invoke Paul also after *Petri* had been already adopted.

We must also note the force of the earlier interpolation *illum* before *unum*. The contention of Cyprian was that the Church was built on *one*. For the corrector's purpose it must be '*that* one.'

Mgr. Freppel's last argument for the interpolations is that they are cited in the Acts of Alexander III.[1], in the *Decretum* of Gratian[2], and in the *Decretum* of Ivo of Chartres[3].

If such quotations in the twelfth century possessed any importance, it would be more worth while to observe on the other hand (with Baluze) that Pope Calixtus II. in a Bulla to Humbald of Lyons[4], that the Cardinals of Gregory XII. assembled at Leghorn in A.D. 1408[5], and that the Roman

---

[1] Baron. *Ann. Eccl.* A.D. 1164, xxix. 'Hanc igitur unitatem non tenens Fridericus Imperator tenere se fidem credidit. Qui Cathedram Petri deserit super quam fundata est ecclesia quomodo se in Ecclesia esse confidit.' But he does *not* give the 'phrase entière' as Mgr. Freppel (p. 279 n.) states.

[2] A.D. 1151.

[3] A.D. 1090–1116, Ivo *Decr.* pars v. c. 361, where it is thus quoted, '*Petri* unitatem qui non tenet, tenere se fidem credit? Qui *cathedram Petri* super *quam* fundata est Ecclesia deserit, in Ecclesia se esse confidit?'

[4] Baluze, p. 545, and others mention this, but the text is first published in *Bullaire du Pape Calixte II.* by U. Robert, Paris, 1891 (I. p. 307; B. 212, 5 Jan. 1121).

[5] Ep. Cardinalium Greg. xii. ad Episcopos A.D. 1409 (1408), Labbe, vol. XV. p. 1159. Nearly all of c. 4 and 5 of Cyprian are quoted without one trace of corruption, although the interpolations would have so precisely suited their purpose that in default of them they in fact introduce a new one of their own inserting 'Episcopatus, ergo *summus*, unus esse debet.' [In *Bibliotheca Max.*

Correctors, with the edition of Manutius before them, all gave the passage pure of corruption.

And as to the appeal to Gratian who, in the 93rd Distinction[1], quotes as from Cyprian the 4th interpolation thus, 'He who deserts the chair of Peter whereon the Church 'was founded, let him not trust that he is in the Church,' it actually yields us a fifth instance of the singular fatality which has haunted the dealers in this forgery, for in another passage Gratian[2] cites the 4th and 5th chapters entire from 'the Lord saith to Peter,' not only omitting the phrase he elsewhere cites but absolutely without any trace whatever of any even the earliest corruptions.

Singular, hateful, and in its time effective, has been this forgery as a Papal aggression upon history and literature. Its first threads may have been marginal summaries in exaggerated language. Then came an unwarrantable paraphrase and a deliberate mutilation for a political purpose. Then it appeared in manuscripts of the author with its indictment round its neck, side by side on the same page with the original which it caricatured. Then it was forced into two grand editions with an interval of a century and a half between them, first by the court of Rome itself, then by the court of France with the fear of Rome before its eyes.

Tantæ molis erat Romanam condere Sedem.

This is the true 'Charter of the Investiture of the Papacy' and as authentic as other documents in that cartulary.

How to make the best of the forgeries now.

The surrender by some of so important a help suggested to others the endeavour to do without it by weaving together different texts from

Pontificia, Rom. 1697, tom. VI. p. 905, the interpolations are not only not omitted but specially insisted on.] See however, Baluze, pp. 545, 546.

[1] *Decreti* Pars I. Dist. xciii. c. iii.
[2] *Decreti* Pars II. Causa XXIV. Quæstio I. c. 18.

Cyprian to shew that this one (in its corrupt state) represented what after all was his real teaching:—an attempt which would never have been thought of if this spurious passage had not first caused him to be thought so powerful a support. This is done with the utmost special pleading by P. Ballerini A.D. 1766 *de vi ac ratione primatus Romm. Pontiff.* XIII. iii. ed. Westhoff 1845. But a Catena of the passages is given sup. pp. 197 sqq. To any fair mind, Roman or other, I commend them.

It is nothing to say that they also have scholars as alive to the forgeries as we are. These forgeries have been important steps in their ascent to power and maintenance of claim. Unreproved and honoured scholars of theirs still uphold their genuineness and reprint them in text-books. Others with superior art like the Rev. L. Rivington avoid quoting the intruded words, but force the whole gist of them, and infallibility besides, if he had been so understood antiently, into the genuine words. If such had been the meaning of Cyprian, the forger would have had no occasion for his craft.

Note on the 'Citation' from Pelagius II. (p. 217).

The 'Citation' from Pelagius II. is of course the *decus et columen* of the Roman proof of the genuineness of the forgery. But there are three alternatives (i), (ii), (iii), which have to be faced. I will call the text (as it stands) of Pelagius II. P, as seeming less to insist upon his personal responsibility for it.

We have no external evidence to the authenticity of the first two epistles of Pelagius II. to the Bishops of Istria, beyond the fact that the third alludes to some earlier 'epistles' and 'words of admonition.' Paulus Diaconus (Warnefridus), *de gestis Langobardorum* III. 20, mentions 'an Epistle' of his (written for him in fact by Gregory when a deacon) on the *Tria Capitula*, and Gregory *Epp.* II. 36 mentions 'a Book' (*liber*) of Pelagius, on the subject. The 'Book' is no doubt our long third 'Epistle.' Hence

Alternative (i). If the second Epistle were not authentic of course its testimony to the interpolation would be valueless.

But assume it to be authentic. There being only one MS. of the Three Epistles[1] and that of the xth century; and codex M of Cyprian being of the ixth century; we ought to consider whether P can have been interpolated from M or its relations. Hence

Alternative (ii). In that case again Pelagius would yield no evidence.

---

[1] Given to Baronius by Nicolas Fabre, Baron. *Ann. Eccl.* A.D. 586, Pelag. IX., xxviii. Labbe [Mansi IX. Florent. 1763, cc. 434, 891, 895], and now in Paris. See *Catalogus codd. MSS. Bibl. Reg.* P. 3, t. 3, Paris 1744, p. 170.

IV. III.   THE 'CITATION' FROM PELAGIUS II.   221

However I think that the reading of the Cyprianic interpolation which stands in *P* is not derived from the interpolation which appears in codex *M*. Reference to the Texts in Appendix will make the facts clear.

It was of course not sufficient for the argument, as it stands in *P*, to rely on *Ecclesiæ* without express mention of *Cathedra Petri*. Therefore for *Ecclesiæ renititur* the manipulator has put *Cathedram Petri deserit;* but he has left *et resistit* coupled to *deserit*, thinking this connection of *resistit* with the accusative over the body of *deserit* might pass. But the scribe of *M* knew this coupling to be inadmissible in a good style, and smoothed the difficulty, as any good grammarian would, by leaving out the genuine *qui Ecclesiæ renititur et resistit* and replacing it by *qui cathedram Petri super quam fundata ecclesia est deserit.* This seems to be the genesis of the wording in the interpolated part of *M*. And so *P* remains the fount of the phrase.

Alternative (iii). Whether the text is Pelagius' own or not, its wording convicts it of awkward but intentional manipulation. *M* had *P* before him and corrected it.

The 'Citation' is indeed a valuable one. Its presence in this Epistle suffices to shew that *either* 1, the Epistle is not genuine, or that 2, it has been corrupted since it was written, or that 3, Pelagius himself adulterated the 'Citation'—a 'Citation' of much value in establishing the text of Cyprian—but to whom?

CHAPTER V.

THE HARVEST OF THE NEW LEGISLATION.

I.

The softening of the Penances.—SECOND COUNCIL.

IN spite of all the care and circumstance which had waited on it, the Rule of restoration for the Lapsed was the work of a class, the most austere and in reality the least tempted.

For we must recollect that, although the clergy were most exposed to persecution, yet the sorest of all tempters, reputation, position, and even (if they ever expected a cessation of persecution) worldly advantage, called on them to stand firm as strongly as the same motives invited many of the laity to yield. The Rule was too rigid to be a real aid to human nature and it was therefore injurious to the Church.

A.D. 252.
A.U.C. 1005.
Coss.
Imp. Cæs. C. Vibius Trebonianus Gallus P.F. Aug. II.
Imp. Cæs. C. Vibius Afinius Gallus Veldumnianus L. Volusianus P. F. Aug.

The Persecution of Gallus (as it may be called for convenience) was a general movement of popular feeling against those who refused to perform the sacrifices ordered by edict for the averting of the spreading Pestilence of the time. Street cries demanded 'Cyprian for the lions[1].' Manifestations and visions to him and to others gave warning—not wholly justified by the event[2]—of sufferings at hand more severe than ever[3]. Of the libellatics condemned to indefinite suspension many were living in penitence, 'never quitting

---

[1] *Ep.* 59. 6. Cf. edicta feralia, 58. 9. In *ad Novatianum* 6, Hartel, Appendix p. 57, it is spoken of as a *secundum prælium*, in which they who had been 'wounded' *prima acie id est Deciana persecutione* recovered themselves.

[2] *Ostensiones, Ep.* 57. 1, 2, 5; and this non-fulfilment is a fair chronological note that such anticipations are not a forgery later than the persecutions.

[3] ...non talem qualis fuit sed multo graviorem et acriorem, *Ep.* 57. 5; cf. 58. 1.

the threshold of the Church¹'; some, where the clergy had a Novatianist bias, died unaneled²; some clerical delinquents had quietly resumed their posts, whence no material power was able to dislodge them; many persons had resumed with the name of Christians their old unchristian lives³, and many families of those who despaired of practical restoration to the blessings of the Church had been lost to heresy and even to gentilism. The examination into individual cases had revealed unexpected palliations; men had sacrificed to save families and friends from the 'question'; or had without reflection allowed themselves to be registered as 'sacrificers,' while simply intending to purchase exemption. Cases where there was less excuse deserved no less compassion.

At or near to Capsa⁴ three men named Ninus, Clementian and Florus, after enduring much violence from their own magistrates and the angered populace, were thrown victorious into prison. Dragged out on the arrival of the Proconsul upon his progress⁵, and submitted to repeated tortures in which life was carefully guarded, they 'could not endure till the crown came⁶.' They fell. Then they crept back as miserable penitents to the Church. More than two years after⁷ their

---

¹ *Ep.* 57. 3.
² *Ep.* 68. 1.
³ *Ep.* 65. 3.
⁴ *Ep.* 56. 1. Capsa (Gafsa) lay a little north of the Tritonian Lake in the proconsular province; a rich and very antient town in a beautiful oasis; had been strongly national, suffered horrors under Marius for loyalty to Jugurtha, the Capsitani were still in Pliny's time 'as much a clan as a Roman town' (*non civitas tantum sed etiam natio*). Then it was raised to the rank of a 'Colony'; and was one of the two capitals of the Byzacene province under Justinian. See *Corp. Inscrr. Latt.* VIII. i. p. 22. Pliny's *Capsitani* refers rather to the *natio*, Cyprian's *Capsensis* to the city.

⁵ The halt at Capsa of an earlier proconsul, C. Bruttius Præsens, father of the unhappy wife of Commodus, consul in 153 and 180 A.D., seems to be marked by the epitaph of his wife. *C. I. L.*, VIII. i. no. 110.

⁶ *Ep.* 56. 2 'coronam non potuisse perferre.' Note use of *perfero* with an object of the thing to be attained. *Corp. Inscrr. Latt.* VIII. i. 2803 a, at Lambæsis, 'conjugis absentis reditum perferre nequisti' of a lady dying before his return.

⁷ Triennium (*Ep.* 56. 1), a good instance of the inclusive reckoning in vogue. This was before Easter (Apr. 11) A.D. 252, so that even if the proconsul had visited Capsa (which is not

SECOND COUNCIL OF CARTHAGE.

bishop Superius presented them to the new bishop of Capsa, Donatulus[1], and the five colleagues who had assembled for his consecration, and asked whether their pitiable exclusion might not now be closed. It was agreed to refer the question to the Council which Cyprian had convened for after Easter. And Cyprian on receiving their application did not hesitate to express in warmest terms his conviction in their favour.

In very many cases sympathy and policy united their claims for mitigation, and the SECOND COUNCIL, which assembled at least two-and-forty bishops in the May of this year[2], ruled 'that all who had so far continued stedfast in penance should be at once readmitted.' Cyprian penned the Synodical Letter which announced the decision to Cornelius[3].

May 15, A.D. 252.

---

likely) as early as January 250, two years and three months is the longest time possible. See p. 41, n. 2.

[1] The meeting at Capsa was for the purpose of ordaining a new bishop. Donatulus is among the Fratres saluted. In A.D. 256 he appears as Bp. of Capsa at vii. Conc. Carth., and was therefore no doubt the person now ordained.

[2] Easter fell in A.D. 252 on Ap. 11. The SECOND COUNCIL UNDER CYPRIAN *De pace lapsis maturius danda* is dated ID. MAIJ, May 15.—*Ep.* 59. 10.

[3] Mr Shepherd (*Letter ii.* p. 10, following the wake of Lombert ap. Pearson, *Ann. Cypr.* A.D. 253, ix.) argues that the censure passed upon Therapius (*Ep.* 64) for readmitting the lapsed presbyter Victor to communion could not have been consistently passed after the relaxation granted by the Second Council, and that accordingly the Council which censured him, which we count Third, placing it about the September of 253 A.D. (*Ep.* 64), must have preceded our Second Council of May 252 A.D. which issued *Ep.* 57. This is so poor an attempt at harmonizing that we can only wonder why for a moment Mr S. should seem to drop his universal scepticism in its favour. We must briefly observe (1) with Pearson that the Conciliar Epistle 57 makes reference to *one* previous Council, and emanated therefore more probably from a second than a third, but Pearson's (second) observation that it is improbable that so many as 66 bishops should have again met before Easter 252 after their session of A.D. 251, has nothing in it. (3) In *Ep.* 57. 1 the relaxation is granted in anticipation of the persecution under Gallus 'necessitate cogente,' but *Ep.* 64 is written in a calm, such as set in when Æmilian's seizure of empire in April 253 withdrew attention from Christian progress, and was continued by Valerian from June onward upon principle. (4) *Ep.* 64. 1 distinctly speaks of the *conditions* of relaxation granted by the Second Council as having been neglected in the act of Therapius. He had received Victor not only '*nulla infirmitate urgente,*' the plea allowed by the First Council, but also '*ac* (*nulla*) *necessitate cogente,*' *i.e.* the relaxation granted by the Second. The very words are borrowed from *Ep.* 57,

It may be described as an able answer to his own once sterner language. To his former argument that restitution was 'superfluous in the case of men ready to seal their sincerity 'by martyrdom, since the Baptism of Blood was higher than 'Ecclesiastical Peace,' he replies that 'it was the Church's 'duty to arm such combatants for that last encounter with the 'protection of the Body and Blood of Christ.' 'Men might 'well faint (he says) who were not animated by the Eucharist.'

He remained the guiding spirit of the movement although his policy had so altered,—rather perhaps because it had so altered—and even when its working had evoked one antipope in Rome and two in Carthage. The letter of Antonian exhibits commonplace bewilderment at the change. At the results of the change Cornelius gazed in horror, Cyprian with an unaffected though not careless contempt[1].

II.

The Effect on Felicissimus and his Party.

It happened thus. The effect of the late amnesty upon the Puritans would be to confirm them in their austerity. At the same time their numbers were increased by new

and are again expanded in the words '*nunc non infirmis sed fortibus pax necessaria est.*' (5) Some time then after Easter 253, and before Autumn 254 when the 4th Council was held, we must place the 3rd Council which replied to Fidus. Autumn or September of 253, which is Pearson's conjecture, seems a reasonable time. The 4th and 7th Councils were certainly held at that time of year. Maran's (§ xxiv.) notion (adopted by Hefele) that Fidus was answered by 66 bishops on Id. Mai 252 in the second Council seems unreasonable, for why should only 42 of them have concurred in the Synodic Epistle? It was this Synodic Epistle which actually laid down the conditions for neglect of which Therapius was censured: surely not by the same Council.

[1] Satis miratus sum te...aliquantum esse commotum. (*Ep.* 59. 2.)—Quod autem tibi de Fortunato isto pseudepiscopo non statim scripsi, frater carissime, non ea res erat quæ, &c....nec tamen de hoc [Maximo pseudepiscopo] tibi scripseram quando hæc omnia contemnantur a nobis...(*Ep.* 59. 9). To conceive (Rettberg § 13, p. 152) that Cornelius repaid the services which Cyprian had rendered him, and now in turn upheld the tottering throne of Carthage, is indeed to misunderstand the circumstances and mistake the men.

converts from heathenism, and what would be the relation of these to the Church whenever the enlargement of their dogmatic views should incline them to the Catholic body[1] was sure presently to become a serious question. They now cast off their last hope of Cyprian and elected and consecrated the head of their first legation, Maximus, to be their anti-bishop (or more accurately 'anti-pope') at Carthage[2].

Meantime the laxer party perceived that the ground was cut from under their feet, and their leading adherents, never having done penance, found themselves as far as ever from readmission to the Church; their numbers also had been swelled by disciples who wished for communion on easy terms[3], and all these clamoured for some action on the part of their heads which would give them a tenable position[4]. They had been taunted as the 'only unepiscopal body' among professed Christians[5]. Accordingly, when Privatus, once bishop of the new great colony of Lambesis[6], but some years since

---

[1] *Ep.* 69. 1, *Ep.* 71. 1, 2.

[2] I think this cannot have been done earlier. In *Ep.* 52. 2 Novatus has not yet made a Bishop in Carthage. In *Ep.* 59. 9 Maximus is spoken of as sent *nuper* (viz. A.D. 251) and consecrated *nunc, i.e.* in A.D. 252 (that letter having been written this year after the Ides of May, *Ep.* 59. 10, 13). But in *Ep.* 55. 10 ad Anton. we find they had appointed bishops in many places before the second Council. If therefore this step was delayed in Carthage, it may have been because hopes were still entertained of some declaration in their favour by Cyprian. Nor can I think that the hope, though misplaced, was unnatural.

[3] *Ep.* 59. 15.

[4] *Ep.* 59. 15, 16.

[5] *Ep.* 43. 5.

[6] *Lambæsis* more often in inscriptions, and (Hartel) 'in the codices of Augustine' (*Sentt. Epp.*), but in some inscriptions, as uniformly in the manuscripts of Cyprian, *Lambese* (*Sentt. Epp.* 6; *Ep.* 36. 4; *Ep.* 58. 10). The history of this striking though much spoiled place, now Lambessa, is beautifully worked out by Wilmanns from its inscriptions, above 1700 in number (*Corp. Inscr. Latt.* VIII. i. p. 283). It was a wholly modern military town, sprung from the great camp of the Third Legion, which, after A.D. 123, Hadrian fixed on the north slope of Aurasius or Middle Atlas, to keep the continent quiet. In A.D. 166 it was but a *vicus*, but the leave given to the legionaries to have families increased it immensely, and by A.D. 208 it was a *municipium* and capital of Numidia. Its streets and great structures began shortly before that. Even its temples remained under military authority, exempt from civic magistrates. Analogy leads Wilmanns to believe it was made a Colonia when Gordian removed the Legion. That would be between A.D. 238 and 244. I should infer

V. II. THE INDEFINITE IN DOCTRINE AND DISCIPLINE. 227

condemned of heresy in a Council of ninety bishops holden at that place[1], and severely censured by letters from Donatus of Carthage and Fabian of Rome, applied for a fresh hearing by the Council of 252 A.D. and was refused, this party too repaired its own defect by procuring his adhesion in the heat of his mortification. A new coalition of Five[2] created one of Cyprian's oldest opponents, Fortunatus[3], into a second anti-bishop of Carthage.

The fault was fatal[4] and it was followed by instant collapse. Whatever presbyteral standing they had was gone. Whatever hopes they had cherished of a grand general reconciliation with the Church were gone. Their followers were not in the main prepared to accept a new Church and a new bishop. They had thrown away the advantage which numbers gave them; although those numbers were up to that moment scarcely a minority as compared with the Cyprianic church[5]. The announcement in Carthage that twenty-five bishops were expected from Numidia to consecrate Fortunatus in Carthage,

---

from Cyprian's wording that it was a Colonia not only when he wrote in A.D. 252, but many years before when Privatus its bishop was condemned, 'Privatum veterem hæreticum in Lambesitana colonia ante multos fere annos condemnatum' (*Ep.* 59. 10). As that was in Fabian's time, between 236 and 250, this casual Cyprianic date exactly fits in with Wilmanns' observation. Next year 253 the Legion was restored, and the greatness of the place, with its 60,000 people, continued till Constantine made Cirta the capital and gave it his own name. Then Lambesis collapsed. In A.D. 364 it had no bishop. I may observe that in 252 its bishop was probably Januarius, as he is a very senior bishop (6th) in 256. *Sentt. Epp.*

[1] *Ep.* 59. 10 'nonaginta episcoporum sententia condemnatum, antecessorum etiam nostrorum. Fabiani et Donati literis severissime notatum.' Thus conscientiously expressed by an Ultramontane, 'Privat s'était vu condamner ...par une assemblée de 90 évêques, dont *le pape* saint Fabien avait *confirmé la sentence*.' Freppel, p. 295.

[2] They were Privatus himself; Felix, a pseudo-bishop of Privatus' appointment; Repostus, a lapsed bishop probably of Tuburnuc (see p. 80, n. 5); Maximus and Jovinus, convicted of lapse and sacrifice, who (from their having been first condemned by nine bishops there by the first Council) were doubtless bishops.

[3] Dean Milman took Fortunatus for a *Novatianist* anti-bishop. It apparently escaped his observation that there were *two* anti-popes in Carthage. *Lat. Christianity,* I. I.

[4] *Ep.* 59. 15.

[5] If I rightly understand *Ep.* 59. 15.

15—2

the announcement in Rome that they had actually done so, failed to accredit him[1]. Felicissimus sailed for Rome in the capacity of legate to his new chief[2] or instrument: Cornelius and the milder party might yet be willing by a recognition of Fortunatus to drive Novatianism off the field with numbers. They represented Cyprian's cause as lost. 'They were pre-'pared to bring him to trial before the church of Carthage. 'His flock were ready to expel him tumultuously from the 'city. If Cornelius refused to hear the documents which 'they submitted, they should feel bound to communicate them 'to the Roman laity[3].' Cornelius was disconcerted by the violence of Felicissimus though not imposed upon. He repelled him with spirit, but wrote tartly of Cyprian's neglect in not informing him of the movements of the party. Cyprian in his long-practised tone of business indicates a certain defect in the memory of Cornelius, and apologizes for unavoidable delay on the part of his messenger, the acolyte Felician. His advice is keen and stimulating, and though he opens half sarcastically he is profoundly affected by the prevalent disorders. 'If Sacrificers and deniers of Christ are to be proposed, 'admitted, and then to terrorize, the Church may as well sur-'render to the Capitol at once; Bishops may be gone and take 'the Lord's altar with them; idols and images may transfer 'themselves and their altars into the assemblage of the clergy.' 'No priest of God is weak enough, abject or prostrate enough, 'nor so enfeebled by the imbecility of mortal incompetency, as 'not to rouse himself against the enemies and assailants of God 'in godlike wise, and feel his lowness and feebleness inspirited 'by the valour and vigour of the Lord.' The best refutation however was that Cyprian himself was almost worn out by the

---

[1] *Ep.* 59. 11. Clear it is that among the allusions to schism and pseudo-bishops in the *de Unitate* none bear on the incidents of the two Carthaginian pretenders. It is Novatian himself who (in all the chapters viii. to end) is distinctly before the eye of Cyprian as the divider of the flock. This alone might fix the date of the treatise.

[2] *Ep.* 59. 1, 16.

[3] *Ep.* 59. 2, 3, 18.

labour of examining and readmitting the fast-recanting adherents of Felicissimus and by the anxieties of rejecting those whom the flock (for every case was formally put to them[1] and considered in their presence) absolutely refused to receive. The Christian public witnessed singular pictures of the brutal insistence of some, the tearful thankfulness of other candidates for restoration[2]. Mistakes were made. Cyprian confesses that he had disastrously in more than one instance overruled protests against false penitents. It is well worth remarking that in this age the claim for stricter penitential discipline was not sacerdotal or official, but popular. In epochs of suffering it will be always so.

These causes then, the decision of the Council, the suicidal policy of a rival episcopacy with no moral basis, and the popular demand for discipline, acted rapidly to break up the party. Cyprian estimated that at the moment when its emissary was intimidating Cornelius at Rome it had suddenly shrunk in Carthage to a congregation inferior in number to the clerical members of the first Council[3]. Presently all trace of them is lost. They vanished before more earnest questioners. But Novatianism contained no such seeds of speedy dissolution. Although Cornelius represents to Antioch, to Alexandria[4] and to Carthage in terms stronger than Cyprian

---

[1] *Ep.* 59. 18, *rogari*, cf. rogare legem, magistratum.

[2] *Ep.* 59. 15. The statement of Socrates (v. 19) that this was the moment at which Penitentiary Presbyters were instituted to hear private confessions is counter to the whole view of the time. Sozomen (vii. 16) gives an interesting picture of the Roman method of penance at a much later date in which the bishop is himself the fellow penitent and the absolver. And this direct contradiction of his own statement that Penitentiaries were an institution in the West as well as in the East shews how little was known of the date or origin of such officers.

[3] *Ep.* 55. 15, *i.e.* than the bishops, presbyters and deacons who had been their 'judges.' Eighty-eight bishops from all parts of Africa are scarcely likely to have been attended on the average by more than two clerics each at the outside. If we add forty as a possible number for the presbyters and deacons of Carthage—it may give us rather more than 300 as the relics of the Congregation of Felicissimus.

[4] Eus. *H. E.* vi. 43, 46.

uses of Felicissimus, that Novatian was almost abandoned, still his sect with its episcopal successions endured throughout Christendom far into the sixth century,—a stern Puritan relic of the Decian persecution. It has been well said that 'like 'all unsuccessful opposition it added strength to its triumphant 'adversary, and only evoked more commandingly the growing 'theory of Christian Unity.'

III.

The Legacy of Clerical Appeals under the Law of the Lapsed.— THE THIRD AND FOURTH COUNCILS.

The Spanish appeal against Rome.

From this point we may with advantage carry our view forward to certain illustrative cases which arose in the course of the next two years, after the main work of reconciliation for such as returned was over. We have notices of three appeals made to the See of Carthage. They are clerical cases. For the clergy, as they were less tempted to fall, so found it harder to return. It was easy for them to achieve a new position in some aggressive sect; and it was not the wisdom of the Church to confer its functions on the timid or vacillating. We cannot with confidence assert that terms for them were separately considered at the Second Council, yet we find it immediately and generally accepted that lapsed Bishops and Clerks could never be restored to Orders[1]. Cyprian rests his argument for this[2] not on injunctions of the Council but on Scripture, drawing the rule from the Levitical institutions, and from visions vouchsafed to himself. Yet elsewhere[3] he says that, in common with himself and all the bishops of the world, Cornelius had concluded this. Not for four years more, until the second Council on Baptism, was the principle of degradation

[1] *Ep.* 55. 11.   [2] *Ep.* 65.   [3] *Ep.* 67. 6.

extended to any presbyters and deacons who had taken part in a heresy or a schism[1]; and it presents a singular and contradictory appearance of laxity that only Novatianists and Donatists held the mark of orders to be so indelible that bishops returning to them after lapse resumed their functions[2].

Late in the summer of the next year one of the African bishops, the same Fidus, who, as we shall learn, counted infants under eight days old too impure for christening[3], reported to the primate that a lapsed presbyter, Victor by name, had after an insufficient period of penance been admitted to communion by their colleague Therapius of Bulla[4]. A few words of this worthy, who spoke in his place of seniority as sixty-first bishop in Cyprian's last Council[5], give an idea of one whose fancy might outrun discretion. 'He who concedes 'and betrays to heretics,' he then said, 'the Church's (right of) 'baptism, what is he but the Judas of Christ's Spouse?' But if Therapius thought an unsound opinion within the Church a worse betrayal of the Church than apostasy from her, the uncharity of Fidus is in contrast to the spirit of Cyprian. Fidus evidently desired that a new excommunication should overtake Victor.

A.D. 253.
A.U.C. 1006.
Coss. Imp. Cæsar C. Vibius Afinius Gallus Veldumnianus L. Volusianus P. F. Aug II.
...[Valerius?] Maximus.

At his good fortune the THIRD COUNCIL of sixty-six bishops, who met Cyprian probably[6] in September A.D. 253, were less offended than at the autocratic manner in which

A.D. 253, Sep.

[1] *Ep.* 72. 2.
[2] *Cod. Cann. Eccl. Afr.* 27 (C. Justellus, Paris 1614, I. p. 98 ; II. p. 41). L'Aubespine, *Observat. V. in Optat.*
[3] V. infra ch. VIII. v. 2.
[4] *Ep.* 64. Baluze (copied by Routh, *R. S.* vol. III. p. 144), and Morcelli (*s.v.*), take Bulla without sufficient reason to be a different place from Bulla Regia. It was in Numidia Proconsularis, near where the boundary crosses the Bagradas, and over 50 miles from Hippo Regius on the road to Carthage—now Hammam Darridji. *C. I. L.* VIII. i. p. 157, ii. p. 934.

It was a small old (Oros.) Free-Town (Plin.) above the vast rich plain of the Bagradas (Procop. *de Bell. Vand.* i. 25). It cannot have been, as Mommsen seems to suggest, the same as Bulleria, since a bishop from each attended the summons of Huneric to Carthage in A.D. 484. A sketch in A. Graham's *Tunisia*, p. 188.
[5] We cannot attach weight to the statement of the later MSS. of the *Sententt. Epp.* that he was a confessor.
[6] On the date of this Council see notes 2, 3, p. 224.

even the now lenient conditions of restoration had been ignored. They would not withdraw the boon which a 'Priest of God' had granted, but a vote of censure was passed upon Therapius (who may be supposed to have been present in his place in Council[1]) for giving a gratuitous indulgence which the Laity had neither requested nor sanctioned[2].

The second case came from Assuras[3]—a populous inland town, whose ruins lie widespread over height and ravine. The Temple and the Christian Church, which are still, after its gates of the Antonines, the most marked objects there, may well have witnessed the incidents which brought on the appeal. The diocese had already elected Epictetus to the Chair vacated by the idolatrous sacrifice of Fortunatian[4], when this traitor bishop, supported by a party of fellow-lapsed, reclaimed the function and emoluments[5] as his right. Cyprian, whose characteristic mistake was to consider every office of a church vitiated to nullity if discharged by an unworthy minister, urges that view more than the broad ground of order, in answer to an appeal to him from the disquieted flock, and counsels a resort to individual canvassing, if necessary, in order to knit the church firmly together under their authentic bishop.

A.D. 254.
A.U.C. 1007.
Coss. Imp. Cæs. P. Licinius

Far the most important to us however of all cases of appeal is one which did not come before Cyprian until about September A.D. 254. Its importance lies in the principles which it reveals as already regulating the intercourse

---

[1] The form of expression may seem to warrant this: 'satis fuit *objurgare* Therapium collegam nostrum...et *instruxisse.*' *Ep.* 64. 1.

[2] *Ep.* 64.

[3] *Ep.* 65. Also, like Bulla, in Numidia Proconsularis. See N. Davis, *Ruined Cities within Numid. and Carth. Territories*, p. 69, and Sir G. Temple's *Excursions*, vol. II. p. 266. Colonia Julia Assuras: *Sentt. Epp.* 68 'ab *Assuras*'; *Corp. Inscrr. Latt.* n. 631 inhabitants Assuritani *passim;* now *Zanfur*, but its plain *B'hairt Essers*. Bruce's drawing of the Temple and arch is in Col. R. L. Playfair's *Travels*, p. 208.

[4] Pamelius erroneously treats this man as a Novatianist. Fell follows.

[5] *Ep.* 65. 3 'stipes et oblationes et lucra.'

V. III. SPANISH APPEAL TO CYPRIAN AGAINST ROME. 233

of churches or dioceses. But, reserving for the present the development of these principles, we will here relate only the striking circumstances of the Lapse and the immediate action taken upon it. It is a wild tale, so to speak, of the old Border Life between Christianity and Paganism.

<small>Valerianus P. F. Aug. II.
Imp. Cæs. P. Licinius Egnatius Gallienus P. F. Aug.</small>

The Bishops of Leon and Merida in Spain had accepted testimonials to their orthodoxy as pagans[1]. The former, Basilides by name, repented and formally abdicated his see when the persecution lulled. He then confessed not only his crime of Lapse, but how in the superstitious terror of some illness he had blasphemed the God of his faith. After this confession he thankfully accepted the position of a Layman.

Martial of Merida had long ago enrolled himself in one of those religious colleges which, besides their other celebrations, performed the funeral ritual of their members with all pagan solemnities in cemeteries secured to them by law[2]. With such rites he interred children of his own.

The Chairs of these two men had been filled by other two elected by their own churches and approved by the neighbouring prelates. Basilides afterwards recovering from his dejection paid a visit to Rome, and there he and, we must infer, Martial also[3], by some fraudulent means procured a declaration from the new pope Stephen that he would hold them still to be the lawful occupants of the two sees.

Against this sudden and monstrous utterance the Spanish churches appeal to Cyprian. A FOURTH COUNCIL of seven and thirty bishops, assembling under him at Carthage[4], accept the appeal, reverse the Roman sentence[5], and instruct the churches to keep to their righteous course. There is no further reference to the Roman see in the matter.

<small>A.D. 254 ?Sep.</small>

---

[1] *Ep.* 67. See above, p. 82.

[2] Renan, *Les Apôtres*, ch. xviii. p. 354, gives some interesting details of these colleges.   [3] *Ep.* 67. 5.

[4] *IV. Concil. Carth.* sub Cypr. (September?) A.D. 254. *Ep.* 67, Synodica.

See more fully on this appeal and on the affair of Martian of Arles in the chapter on Stephen, p. 311.

[5] Simply, 'our colleague Stephen was a long way off and ignorant of the facts and of the truth.' *Ep.* 67. 5.

It is obviously of extreme interest and importance to observe principles not created but unquestioningly acted upon in this cause. The action taken is quite compatible with the thought of Rome as *Principalis Ecclesia*[1] as a centre of 'unity,' but irreconcilable with any view of that see as a centre of legislation or jurisdiction, or even as a centre of reference.

Meantime we may remember that while the legislation provided for the Lapsed was temporary, the principles which it first brought into strong relief are for all time. And we may still regard our possession of them as our inheritance from the Decian persecution.

A less happy forecast attends the case of a 'contumelious' Deacon and a Layman abetting him, which is referred to Carthage by the Bishop Rogatian[2], in all likelihood the same who figures in the Councils, Bishop of Nova, deep in Mauretania[3].

The tone of the letter indicates that he was known to Cyprian; 'Let no man despise thy old age,' he says. He writes however not for himself only but in the name of 'colleagues,' so that his systematic consultations were at work. The idea of authority is developed and fortified, but it is the same idea as in the fourth epistle, resting on the same precept in Deuteronomy[4] of reverence and obedience to the High Priest. That means simply, that details had taken time to work out, but that from the first Cyprian held that view which he held last of the identity of internal relations in the two polities of Israel and the Church.

The case, says Cyprian, might have been properly dealt with by excommunications on the part of Rogatian himself alone.

This is the course which, with his 'colleagues who were

---

[1] See p. 192, and *Appendix*, p. 537.
[2] *Ep.* 3.
[3] See *Appendix on Cities*, p. 575.
[4] Deut. xvii. 12, 13. It was probably this quotation which determined Pearson.

present,' he recommends in the last resort, but he would rather rely on an appeal to good sense and feeling[1]. It is well and sincerely urged. But here we see excommunication, instead of being kept as the discipline of sin, already looming as an engine for managing the Church.

---

[1] O. Ritschl pointed out (p. 239) that argument and allusion in *Ep.* 3, as Pearson counted it, are not of an early stamp; and I would further observe on the close verbal resemblance between *Ep.* 3. 1, 2 and *Epp.* 59. 4; 66. 3; and *de Unit.* 17, 18, which connects it with the time we are discussing.

If the 'colleagues present' are a Council, and not rather the Occasional Board, it was probably the Third Council, for Rogatian attended the Second and Fourth.

CHAPTER VI.

EXPANSION OF HUMAN FEELING AND ENERGY.

I.

The Church in relation to Physical Suffering.

1. *Within itself—The Berber Raid.*

EVEN whilst the Council sate news arrived that many Christian maidens, wives and children[1], had been kidnapped from Numidia by the Berbers. The frontier tribes, quieted last by Severus, were in movement this year and were carrying terror into the provinces.

Faultily[2] and fatally these indigenes[3], ages ago rolled back by settlers from Asia and Europe, were being now ruled by fortresses, military colonies, farmers holding by service-tenure, absolute magistrates, without any attempt to interest or incorporate them. Their raids were really waves in their steady return.

A.D. 252.
Coss.
p. 222.

In the year 252 there was a concerted general advance. Mauretania felt them. They broke out of Aures[4] through the grand chain of fortress settlements, harrying the domains

---

[1] *Ep.* 62. 5. Cyprian appeals to fathers and husbands as necessarily sympathizing. It was a raid on persons. In c. 3, p. 699, l. 21, I demur to Hartel's reading 'vinculi maritalis amore' from the Rheims MS., which Baluze here sets aside for the better expression '*pudore* vinculi maritalis' of the editions which represent lost MSS. The Rheims MS. is not a good text, Hartel has to set it aside constantly.

[2] F. Lacroix in the *Revue Africaine*, vol. VII. p. 363.

[3] There are and were traces of their name over all North Africa. Tissot, *Géogr. de la Prov. d'Afrique*, I. p. 394.

[4] See *Appendix on Cities*, p. 575.

VI.I.I. THE CHURCH AS TO SUFFERINGS OF HER MEMBERS. 237

of the strongest towns, Thubunæ on the Salt Marsh, and the vast soldier-colony of Lambæsis. From the Sahara they came right through the Province itself into the terebinth woods of Tucca and to the great centre of traffic Assuras, little more than a hundred miles from Carthage.

The Christian population of at least eight sees was thus lacerated[1].

As memorials of transactions so fatal ultimately to the church of Africa and to all the civilization which depended on it, clearing the ground as they did for Vandal and for Saracen, there remain in explanation of each other only scattered notices, a few inscriptions, and the sixty-second epistle of Cyprian which went with a ransom[2].

This must have been a serious time for the dominion of Africa, though we know nothing direct about it. Not Cyprian but two or three unburied marbles[3] tell us how

---

[1] In the fourth century children were constantly redeemed from the Berbers and baptized if unidentified, *V. Conc. Carth.* c. 6, A.D 398, Labbe II. 1455 (*Brev. Conc. Hipp.* A.D. 393, c. 39, but see also nn. on cc. 38, 39, Hefele, *H. d. C. B.* VIII. 509), *Cod. Cann. Eccl. Afr.* 72, Justell p. 198 (ed. 1614), Labbe, II. 1308. (? *pro* hinc *leg.* huic.) In A.D. 409 we mark them kidnapping still further north at Sitifis itself, Aug. *Ep.* cxi. (cxxii.) *.

[2] An affecting inscription given in *Rev. Afr.* VII. p. 359 belongs to the year A.D. 247 (Anno Provinciæ Mauretaniæ 208) A P CCVIII D M HAVE SECVNDE PARENTIBVS TVIS DVLCISSIME FLOS IVVENTVTIS AN V A BARBARIS INTEREMPTVS MVCIA AMAR [the last four letters from Wilmanns' cast, who has s after D M, and for V a small L (?), *C. I. L.* VIII. ii. 9158]. A forgery claiming to be of year 254 with a curious story is given *C. I. L.* VIII. i. p. xxxvii., 30. Other inscriptions, belonging to the next 30 or 40 years, relate to the defeats of FARAXEN · REBELLIS CVM SATELLITIBVS SVIS, *C. I. L.* VIII. ii. 9047, the chieftain from whom the *Fraxinenses* hod. *Fraoucen* are said to be called, of the QUINQUEGENTANEI REBELLES at Bougie, *Saldæ*, *C. I. L.* VIII. ii. 8924 (*Rev. Afr.* IV. p. 434), and of Babari at Cherchel, *Cæsarea.* ERASIS FVNDITVS BABARIS TRANSTAGNENSIBVS *C. I. L.* VIII. ii. 9324 (*Rev. Afr.* IV. p. 222. Mus. Alg. No. 74).

The Quinquegentanei disappear soon after their overthrow by Maximian (Eutrop. ix. 23). The Berbers between Sitifis and Cirta are by Pliny v. 30 (4) and Ptolemy iv. 3 (p. 111 B) called Sabarbares, Σαβούρβουρες, which is said to contain the Numidian prefix *Zab* (*Revue Africaine*, vol. VII. p. 27, &c.), but in either case with v. l. Sababares, Σαβούβουρες, as in one of the above inscriptions. In *Ep.* 62. 3 Barbarorum, &c. would correctly have a capital letter.

[3] *Index, Corp. Inscrr. Latt.* II. p. 1081 (published since the previous para-

a year or two later the Bavares under four united native princes wasted Numidia as far up as Milev. There, and again on the Mauretanian frontier, they were violently checked by C. Macrinius Decianus, propraetor. He defeated at the same time other great leagues or clans[1] of them, as the Quinquegentanei, who fell on Mauretania itself; and while he claimed the credit of the capture and execution of Faraxen[2], almost a chieftain of romance,—like the present Berber chiefs, 'who look as if thawed out of marble statues of Roman emperors[3],'—it would seem that the actual seizure of him and his whole staff was the exploit of Gargilius Martialis, an officer who had served in Britain and now commanded the loyal Moorish cavalry. Still further west Auzia, now *Aumale*, must have been in peril, for when, in A.D. 260, Gargilius himself was destroyed by a Berber ambush, Auzia commemorated by a statue his former act of 'valour and vigilance.'

The redemption of captives, like the portioning of orphans, had long been among the Romans a favourite work of liberality—'most worthy of the gravity and greatness of the senatorial order[4].'

There was nothing specifically Christian, nothing novel in the collection which was promptly made at Carthage for

---

graph and its note 1 were written), considers that the victories of Decian belong to the years 253 and 254. He was 'Legatus duorum Augustorum Numidiæ,' *i.e.* of Valerian and Gallien, in A.D. 260, to which year the movement itself belongs. See the inscriptions, *C. I. L.* VIII. i. 2615 (at Lambesis), ii. 9047 (Auzia), and compare ii. 9045. Mark the expressions 'provinciam Numidiam vastabant,' 'insidiis Bavarum *decepto.*'

[1] Gen. Creuly shews that Babares included Quinquegentanei and Fraxinenses, *Rev. Archéol.* 1861, p. 51. See also Tissot I. 458, II. 790.

[2] The *Dux famosissimus* (full of legends) of the Fraxinenses must be Faraxen himself. Col. R. L. Playfair, *Travels in the Footsteps of Bruce* (p. 72), says that in the Aures mountains over Lambesis is a high wooded and secluded valley called *Ti Farasain.* Its name, perhaps, may be a record of this raid.

[3] Col. R. L. Playfair, *op. cit.* p. 70.

[4] Redimi e servitute captos...vulgo solitum fieri ab ordine nostro...Hæc (consuetudo) est gravium hominum atque magnorum. Cic. *de Off.* ii. 18. 63; cf. 16. 55.

VI. I. I. THE CHURCH AS TO SUFFERINGS OF HER MEMBERS. 239

the victims, except the number and poverty of the contributors. But this novelty was Christian. The motives which they had found irresistible were 'that the captives 'were living shrines of deity; that Christ was in them and 'they in Christ; that such an event was a probation not only 'of sufferers but also of sympathizers; that all looked for a 'Judgment in which sympathy would be the main subject of 'enquiry.' If He will then say 'I was sick and ye visited me,' much more will the Redeemer say 'I was captive and ye redeemed me.' How full Cyprian's mind was at this moment of these topics we shall recognize as we proceed.

Nearly eight hundred[1] pounds was subscribed by the community, and by the sitting bishops; by these partly on behalf of their poor churches. The list of donors, sent into Numidia, was accompanied by the request that they might be commemorated at the sacrifices and in private prayers, and with an assurance of further help should the need, as was too likely, recur.

Of Genuineness Geographical.

A beautiful incidental proof of the genuineness of our documents comes out here. The relief is sent from Carthage to eight Numidian bishops, Januarius, Maximus, Proculus, Victor, Modianus, Nemesianus, Nampulus, Honoratus, but there is no mention of their sees. Now in the list of the Council of 256 four of these reappear as bishops of two Numidian sees which are named and two Provincial; viz. Januarius of Lambæsis and Nemesianus of Thubunæ, Victor of Assuras and Honoratus of Tucca. These towns with Auzia give the geographical line I have indicated, which is itself a sign of accuracy. What forger of another age and country could have marked for himself upon his map a line of barbarian advance and then have forborne to indicate it, but in a wholly unconnected document have attached to the sees which marked that line the names of some of his fictitious bishops? Behind this line toward Mt. Aures

---

[1] *Ep.* 62. 4 'sestertium centum millia nummum. Gronov. lib. de sest. n. 18' Hartel. The two xvth century extant MSS. of this epistle scarcely justify Hartel in reading 'sestertia centum milia nummorum,' nor do Baluze's quotations prove it to be possible.

lie several Cyprianic sees, such as Thamugadi, Mascula, Theveste, and beyond it Gemellæ, Badias, and others; some of these no doubt were the other four sufferers. In another place I shall shew how the order of the names in Councils (a matter of seniority) corresponds with other indications.

2. *The Church in relation to Heathen Suffering.—The Plague.*

And now the formation and compacting of the Christian community have for some time engrossed us. Meanwhile changes have passed over the aspect which that community presented to the world. That community owed and owned a duty to all unconverted humanity—not only a duty to absorb it with all possible rapidity into itself—but a duty also towards the part not within any given time likely to be absorbed. That enquiry into social morals which most taxed the philosophical power of paganism had been overtaken by a code, or the principle of a code, which exempted no man from active benevolence. The doctrine of Grace operating upon and cooperating with the human will to reconstruct character, the embracement of eternal life and reward, the earthly pattern of Christ and the passion of reproducing it, above all the experienced and attested union of the individual spirit with Him during the present existence, placed the Christian, so soon as he began to realize this new range of Ideas, in an attitude of fresh and unexpected energy towards every person and every contingency with which he came in contact.

This realization had been to the practical comprehension of the convert Cyprian an affair of perhaps a few weeks[1]. This realization was what he excelled in impressing on other men. Even the East appreciated this action of his on the community. 'He educated the whole moral tone, dissipated 'undisciplined ignorance of doctrine, brought order to the lives 'of men[2],' says Gregory of Nazianzus. We have watched him

[1] Pont. *Vit.* 3.
[2] Greg. Naz. *Or.* xxiv. 13. ...ἦθος ἅπαν ἐπαίδευσε καὶ δογμάτων ἀπαι- δευσίαν ἐκάθηρε, καὶ ἀνδρῶν βίους ἐκόσμησε.

VI. I. 2. THE CHURCH AND HEATHEN SUFFERING. 241

awhile as the Organizer. We return to follow him through the same period as the Master of Doctrine reduced to Life.

If we can vividly place this work before our eyes as it went on in one great city of the old world, we shall stand close to the fountain-head of the movement. It was in the cities that it burst out, as it was in the busiest Galilean towns that Christ Himself had preached most attractively. While each of the great cities had its own part, Alexandria the more profound and speculative and Rome the more political, Carthage, in some respects so like England, with its blended races, its contracted home, world-wide intercourse, and ready interest in theories which had their birth elsewhere, attained its own truest historical eminence through Christianity, and that eminence the most instructive of all for us.

The field on which first opened out the Christian strength in contrast to heathen helplessness was a terrible one. In the year 252 A.D. the Great Plague reached Carthage. The epoch was one of those periods of physical disturbance which, rightly or not, have been noted in connection with plagues. Famine, protracted drought, tornadoes and unexampled hail-storms[1] prevailed. The pestilence had descended two years before from Æthiopia[2] upon Egypt; a pestilence differing specifically from the third visitation in the reign of Justinian[3], which was strictly analogous to the modern plague, but travelling the same route and exhibiting a somewhat similar character with its predecessor of the fifth century before Christ. Whether these were different disorders, we cannot distinguish. Both were of the class of malignant typhoid fever. The absence at Carthage of those pulmonary complications, which Thucydides describes as one of the most distressing symptoms, may be attributable to the dry atmosphere of

A.D. 252.

---

[1] *Ad Demetr.* c. 7, 10.
[2] Zonaras, xii. 21. Cedrenus, p. 258 A. Compare Thuc. ii. 48 ...ἐξ Αἰθιοπίας... ἔπειτα δὲ καὶ ἐς Αἴγυπτον, κ.τ.λ.
[3] Procopius appears to me to have embellished his long account of this by many particulars from other pestilences. *De Bell. Pers.* ii. 22 (Dind. vol. I. p. 249).

B. 16

Tunisia, but neither does Cyprian mention the red and livid blistering eruption, nor yet the brain affection, which among the Athenian sufferers had frequently resulted in the extinction of memory. If Eutropius is accurate, it also differed from that pestilence in not extinguishing like it all other disorders, but was on the contrary attended by a multiplicity of them[1]. Other symptoms, perhaps the most general, are identical—the diarrhœa, the ulcerated mouth and throat, the congested eyes, the internal fever and incessant sickness; the loss to survivors of the feet or other extremities, the lameness, blindness, or total deafness. Both were preceded by the intense nervous depression which induced the premonitory symptom of threatening spectres[2].

This plague went on for a term of twenty years ranging the civilised world, returning once and again to countries which it had desolated and to cities in which it seemed to have stricken every house[3]. In A.D. 261 its recoil on Alexandria was worse than its first assault, and in four years more it had reduced the population by above one half[4]. It fell on the armies of Valerian and delivered the East up to Sapor. In 262 five thousand persons died in Rome, and the same number in Achaia, on a single day[5]. In 270 the emperor Claudius died of it while it was serving as his most effective auxiliary against the Gothic hordes in Thrace. It had run but half its course when Dionysius quotes and affirms the remark that of all the wars and miseries which oppressed the race

---

[1] Sola pestilentia et morbis atque aegritudinibus notus eorum principatus fuit. Eutr. ix. 5.

[2] Greg. Nyss. *vit. S. Greg. Thaum.* § 12. Procop. *l.c.* p. 251 φάσματα δαιμόνων...παίεσθαι ᾤοντο πρὸς τοῦ ἐντυχόντος ἀνδρός.

[3] Dionys. ap. Euseb. vii. 22.—Continuatas per ordinem domos...Pont. *Vit.* c. 9. So Orosius, vii. 21.

[4] At Alexandria the whole sum of claimants for corn between the ages of 14 and 80 was after the reign of Gallienus equal only to the former number of those between 40 and 70. Gibbon hence deduces the above fact, ch. x. ad fin.

[5] That is if I comprehend the odious obscurity of Trebellius Pollio (*Gallieni Duo* 5). Gibbon takes it that during some time 5000 died in Rome daily.

VI. I. 2. THE CHURCH AND HEATHEN SUFFERING.

of man the plague alone had outrun the darkest anticipations.

This was the horror and the misery which fell like an unnatural night on the Christians' dawning hopes of peace and order.

In our present year it carried off the young emperor Hostilian[1], and the emperor Gallus and his son Volusian were winning golden opinions by their care for the interment of the meanest victims[2]. To confess to any sanitary motive, such as we hope we may suspect, would have been impiety. Avowed measures of relief were limited to edicts for universal sacrifices which exposed Christianity to fresh persecution from populaces which furiously marked its non-compliant attitude, and also to an unprecedented issue from the imperial mints of coins dedicated to 'Healthful Apollo[3].' These remedies marked the limits of antique self-devotion to populations sick

---

[1] Aur. Victor, *Epit.* c. 30. All MSS. here read Hostilianus *Perpenna* or *Perperna*, an Etruscan name originally which occurs on no coin of him. Hints seem latent under both names of his brother, made emperor with him, and lost with Decius, viz. Herennius Etruscus, son of Herennia Etruscilla. Zosimus, i. 25, lays this death to the jealousy of Gallus.

[2] Aur. Victor *de Cæs.* c. 30 'tenuissimi cujusque exsequias curarent.' Earlier we have in Petronius *Satyric.* c. 116 'tanquam in pestilentia campos, in quibus nihil aliud est nisi cadavera quæ lacerantur aut corvi qui lacerant.'

[3] The story of the invocation is tragic. Caracalla sick in mind and body after Geta's murder struck his denarius bearing APOLLO SALUTARIS with other coins of similar allusion (see Stevenson, *Dict. Rom. Coins*, 1889, p. 67). Then Gallus in this plague about A.D. 254 (so Eckhel) struck large brass and other metals and forms, APOLLINI SALUTARI (Stevenson, p. 67). In the British Museum are two 'Antoniani,' an aureus and a half-aureus of the type. Also (Grueber and Poole, *Roman Medallions in Brit. Mus.*, pp. 57, 60) a brass medallion of Gallus and one of Volusian, which bear Apollo with radiate head standing on rocks holding in his right a laurel branch, in his left a serpent, legend ARN AZI. These refer to the same tutelage and the need of it, even if Pellerin's clever interpretation of *Arna* and *Asisium* erecting a Colossus is not certain (Stevenson, p. 82). See H. Cohen (not quite accurate), *Monnaies frappées sous l'Empire Romain*, 1885, vol. v., pp. 238, 239, 268.

Similar types are continued through the next reign with revivals of the Di Majores and (it is said) the first appearance of Diana (also a healer) on coins. Many are found in England. *Leicestersh. Archit. Soc. Trans.* XI. i. p. 193.

unto death. That the greatest happiness of the greatest number is best secured by the devotion of the individual to his own, was not then a floating theory. It pervaded society as a living principle. When physical terror became the dominant chord in life 'egoism' perfected its melody. Instant flights, the desertion, the exposure of the dying, the barred gates of the house-courts, the hasty flinging out of the dead, street assassinations and drugged possets, the spoliation of unprotected fortunes, the last corruption of the judicature, marked the opportunity and the successes of Self let loose[1] upon society. Every natural, every acquired scruple broke down[2].

But the entrance of self-sacrifice upon the scene does indeed difference the plague in Carthage, in Neo-Cæsarea, or Alexandria from the plague of Athens. In each of these cities the Bishop of the Christians was a leading citizen. The earliest-dated though but passing mention of this plague is in connection with the deaths of several[3] Egyptian Deacons. The behaviour of Gregory in Pontus secured the faith of that region. Nor had the wearing persistence of the misery any power to abate zeal. In Alexandria ten years later, when half the town had perished[4], there was still in rendering the last offices almost an excess of tenderness, such as scarcely could be justified except by the moral effect of intrepidity upon a population. For it so subjected the Church to contagion, and swept away such crowds of faithful lives, that the Christians owned that now at length was verified the soubriquet with which by an ungenerous perversion that Parisian-like populace had long stigmatized them—they were become 'the Offscouring' of all.

At Carthage, so soon as the usual street-scenes and house-scenes began, Cyprian summoned his community, and in a

---

[1] Pont. *Vit.* 9 ; *ad Demetr.* 10, 11.
[2] Prædandi dissimulatio nulla, *ad Demetr.* 11.
[3] *I.e.* assuming that there were only seven according to Conc. Neocæs. A.D. 314, can. 15.—Euseb. vii. 11. Cf. 22.
[4] Page 242, n. 4.

VI. I. 2. THE CHURCH AND HEATHEN SUFFERING. 245

speech which his deacon wished the whole city could have heard from the rostra, developed the duty and divineness of prayer and labour on behalf of persecutors. In this light he appealed to their Christian belief in their veritable Sonship to God[1]. His epigrammatic '*Respondere Natalibus*' is a nobler version of *Noblesse oblige* and no less defies rendering. He then, with the facility which marked his arrangements, forthwith proposed and carried a scheme for the systematic care of the city. With a few marked exceptions[2] the whole society, rich and poor alike, partly from motives like his own, partly under the spell of his personal influence[3], responded to the appeal, undertook the parts he assigned them, raised an abundant fund, and formed an adequate staff for the nursing and burial of sufferers and victims, without any discrimination of religious profession[4].

Of this organization probably little or nothing transpired before the heathen. We see to-day how the wide organizations, much more the self-sacrifice, of the Church's work in obscure London can escape the philanthropic novelist and even the religious sects of more prosperous quarters. The slow, vast effect of those unsuspected forces on Carthage may cheer the sacrificers and organizers of to-day. It was not likely to be recognised in that old tortured and torturing city that the new enthusiasm of humanity was fired by Christianity. Or if this partly emerged, still nothing could overcome the natural disgust with which citizens regarded such stolid

---

[1] Pont. *Vit.* 9 'Respondere nos decet natalibus nostris.'

[2] I infer that there were exceptions from *De Op. & El.* 12 '*quosdam in ecclesia videmus...de quibus mirari non oportet quod contemnant in tractatibus servum*' which evidently refers to unanswered appeals made by himself upon this subject.

[3] Sub tanto doctore ... placeret et Deo patri, et judici Christo, et interim sacerdoti. Pont. *Vit.* 10.

[4] ...exuberantium operum largitate, quod bonum est ad omnes, non ad solos domesticos fidei. Pontius, *Vit.* 10, desires the forgiveness of the Jewish Saint Tobias 'once, twice and frequently,' for rating his 'incomparable piety,' which collected only the remains of his own fellow-believers, lower than that of Cyprian. 'Fulness (he adds) belongs to the times of Christ.'

enemies of the emperor and the empire. How else account for the erect coldness with which their sect looked on at the propitiations and tears presented to Health, to Apollo, and to Cælestis Queen of Heaven? None however was so obnoxious as the 'Overseer' of the Christians—for the populace knew well that title. The publication of the sacrificial edict had been once more a signal for the Circus to demand that Cyprian should be fetched and matched with one of their lions, and he was officially proscribed by name and office[1].

His terrible work was not over, and grave political complications had gathered round him, when five years later, A.D. 257, he was banished. This, says his biographer, 'was 'his reward for withdrawing from living sight a horror like 'that of hell' and for 'saving his country from becoming the 'empty shell of an exiled population.' Allow the utmost for partiality, that effort to grapple with a Plague-city must have been as energetic as it was novel.

3. *The Theory.—Unconditional Altruism.*

Cyprian's mode of organizing had this merit and this ruling spell, that he took those who were to be organized into his full confidence. He filled them with the ideas which had carried himself to the point of action. 'Il parle, il parle beaucoup, il fait tout ce qu'il a dit' was the witty description of a novel diplomacy which converted a province into an empire. It was in the highest sense of that description that Cyprian educated his followers into the schemes of duty which rose before him.

We may look on his little treatise, his 'Letter,' as Augustine calls it, 'OF WORK AND ALMS-DEEDS,' as the expansion of his noble motto *Respondere Natalibus*, as a lengthened

---

[1] *Ep.* 66. 4 'Siquis tenet possidet de bonis Cæcili Cypriani Episcopi Christianorum'—quoted from the document referred to in *Ep.* 59. 6 'adplicito et adjuncto episcopatus sui nomine, totiens ad leonem petitus, in circo, in amphitheatro,' &c.

echo perhaps of that last speech of his on the approach of the plague. It is an unreserved statement of the Theory which he carried through without reserve. The strokes which were falling on the Christians turned the affluence of many into poverty. Yet such strokes were partial in their effect, and left many untouched. So too the horrors of Pestilence do not bring the same universal impoverishment as Famine; and even Captivities and Confiscations had only their selected victims. There were patrimonies still; there were old hoards of bullion, which it was time to unlock to the thronging misery; there were matronly jewelleries and all the extravagances of fashion; the barrenness, the dulness, the darkness of wealthy luxurious life oppressed the mind[1]. It was a time to build any freshly gained ideas into the social code, and his own splendid use of wealth gave him a right to utter them.

Christ then had treated the sacrifice of wealth as a note of enrolment in His supernatural society, as a grade in perfection, as a reality which would accompany the soul into immortality[2].

Christ had not merely overlooked mundane considerations. He had personally pledged Himself to convert losses so incurred into gain, and faithless gains into loss. He had charged Himself with the anxieties of the liberal; in short for His followers He had identified Himself with Providence[3].

Socially He had declared Himself to be the new power in the world for the elevation of the masses; He had minutely described how in the close of the world's history He will look back on efforts made for the amelioration of their conditions[4].

Domestic claims cannot really compete with the needs of the poor; both the interests and the characters of Christian families are best provided for by practical demonstrations of

---

[1] *De Opere et Eleemosynis* 11—13; 14, 15; 23.
[2] *De O. et E.* 7, 8, 14.
[3] *De O. et E.* 9, 10.
[4] *De O. et E.* 16, 23.

real faith in immortal recompense, in daily providence, in the fatherhood of God[1].

Once more the whole theory of Christian worship, centering as it does on the Eucharist, is nullified for the rich and selfish. Without personal sacrifice there can be no union with the Divine sacrifice. What an irony to see a gorgeous lady before an altar receiving her communion out of the offerings of the poor[2].

In a nearly contemporaneous letter[3] Cyprian represented Christian endurance by metaphors almost overbold, as a gladiatorial combat fought for crowns before Emperor and Cæsar. He now carries his figure farther. The wealthy who will bestow his means in supporting such combatants is like the Munerarius[4]—the man of rank or ambition who lavishes a fortune to provide a worthy spectacle. With a Goethesque audacity Satan himself is introduced to confront the throned Christ. He points out the glorious shows which his servants ruin themselves to exhibit with unfruitful unselfish splendour in his honour. 'Where, O Christ,' he sneers, 'are *your* 'Munerarii? Where your capitalists, who will do even self- 'remunerating works on such a scale upon your principles,— 'either through gratitude for your loving Passion, or in hope 'of your bright reward?'

But our account of the motives for generosity which Cyprian expands before the Church, would not be complete without his peculiar and less satisfactory development of the relation of Almsgiving to Sin. Not only do prayer and fasting lack substance and reality apart from such alms and work[5], but when past sinfulness has been obliterated by the blood of Christ in Baptism, the effectiveness of that Baptism is prolonged and subsequent frailties continually abolished, through

---

[1] *De O. et E.* 16, 20.
[2] *De O. et E.* 15.
[3] *Ep.* 58 'plebi Thibari consistenti.'
[4] Note the popular word invented by Augustus, Quintil. viii. 3, and note the near resemblances of language between *De O. et E.* 21 and *Ep.* 58. 8.
[5] *De O. et E.* 5.

the maintenance in all its freshness of the state of mind in which we leave the font by a constant flow of working and almsgiving[1]. There can be no better illustration than this teaching (in which a distinct propitiatory value is assigned to our own action) of the combined results, in the development of doctrine, of resorting to the Jewish Apocrypha, relying on a Version, and constructing a theory from a word[2]. When this thread of erroneous, or at least ambiguous, theory was presently after woven in with Tertullian's new forensic language on satisfaction being made to God by penance[3], a commencement of much mediæval trouble was made.

On the other hand for this very treatise the first Council of Ephesus was grateful, when they could quote, with other 'chapters' from the Fathers, against the confusions of Nestorius[4] its clear-toned opening 'The Sent Son willed to be the Son of Man.'

And Augustine with quite a burst of love brings up its eloquent truths as against the Pelagian thought that some men in this life are sinless. 'So didst thou teach, so didst thou admonish, incomparable teacher and glorious witness[5].'

II.

Resentment.

Such was the preparation which the Christians of Carthage were receiving for their conflict with the misery of a heathen

---

[1] *De O. et E.* 2.

[2] Such are most distinctly the sources of the idea—Sicut *aqua* (*i.e.* Baptism) extinguet ignem (*i.e.* gehenna) sic eleemosyna *extinguet* peccatum (Sirach iii. 30), and again Prov. xvi. 6 'Misericordia et veritate redimitur iniquitas' (xv. 27 'per misericordiam et fidem purgantur peccata'), which in the African version was '*Eleemosynis* et fide delicta purgantur.'—*De O. et E.* 2.

[3] *De Pœnitentia* 5.

[4] Labbe, vol. IV., p. 67 (202), A.D. 431. It was read again at the second Council A.D. 449, and again at Chalcedon A.D. 451. *Ibid.* p. 1134. Vincent. Lirin. *Common.* II. 30.

[5] Out of this short treatise Augustine quotes part of its third chapter twice, viz. in *Contra duas epp. Pelagg.* B. IV. c. x. 27, and *Contra Julian. Pelag.* B. II. c. viii.; part of ch. i. in *Contra duas epp. Pelagg.* B. IV. c. viii.; and part of chap. xxii. in the same passage.

city. Meantime the rancour of its population which had laid wars and drought and pestilence at the door of the tolerated Christians found a more emphatic voice than usual in the utterances of an aged magistrate, Demetrian. After having been freely admitted in the character of an enquirer to Cyprian's house, he was now, with one foot in the grave, acting on the tribunal the part not merely of a harsh enforcer of the penal statutes, but of an ingenious inventor of tortures. He was open to the further suspicion of having himself put the most exciting imputations against the accused into circulation[1].

'The indignation raised by cruelty and injustice and the 'desire of having it punished, which persons unconcerned— 'and in a higher degree those who were concerned—would feel, 'is by no means malice. It is one of the common bonds by 'which society is held together...a weapon put into our hands 'by nature...which may be innocently employed....one of the '*instruments of death* which the author of our nature hath 'provided....not only an innocent but a generous movement 'of the mind....a settled and deliberate passion implanted in 'man for the prevention and remedy of wrong[2].'

It is thus that Butler characterizes *Resentment*. It is thus that Cyprian exemplifies it, as precisely as if his words had been weighed to comply with the philosopher's subtle and original distinction.

'We may hate no man.' '*Odisse non licet nobis*[3].' He could know no greater joy than that Demetrian should be partaker of his own blessing, but 'he makes a way for his

---

[1] Sub ipso exitu, *ad Demetr.* 25; cum frequenter ad me venires, 1; novas pœnas, 12; quos tu forsitan concitasti, 2.—Confiscation, chains, execution, the circus and fire (cf. Tert. *ad Scap.* 4 'cremamur') were all in vogue against Christians at this time. *Ad Demetr.* 12. Pearson exposes the older statement that Demetrian was proconsul. His power and his intimacy with Cyprian may suggest that he was one of the Five native *primores* associated with Roman officers for Christian investigations.

[2] Bishop Butler, Sermon VIII. *On Resentment.*

[3] *Ad Demetrian.* 25.

indignation.' So long as Demetrian had 'bayed and raved at God' it would have been 'an easier, lighter effort to beat 'rising waves back with shouts than to curb such fury by 'accost,' but it is time to speak when a double and triple injustice is perpetrated with every accompaniment of cruelty.

Tertullian had in his day confronted a persecutor[1]. Strange to say, in this one instance 'The Master's' spirit is more gentle than the gentle prelate's. There are points of contact shewing the appeal to Scapula to have been studied by the author of the appeal 'TO DEMETRIAN.' In both we have the remonstrance against the suppression of the One Natural Worship; both point to the quietude of the prevailing Sect[2]; to the power of their prayers in exorcisms and of their suffering example in conversions. But here the resemblance ends. Tertullian's exordium is almost affectionate; he has no denunciations; no word of the Eternal Doom of persecutors nor of the new philosophy of Divine Probation. He is mainly occupied with relating warnings that have befallen severe governors, and blessings that have attended lenient judges and ratified Christian Prayers. The aim of Cyprian is quite different and much wider. Demetrian and he represented face to face the popular and the new or advanced answers to the question, 'Whence all this political and all this physical misery?'

The Heathen cry was, 'The progress of Christian opinion 'is refusing to the immortal gods the institutions which ac-'knowledge and represent them,—temple, pageant, art, drama, 'circus, arena, private homage, oath, vow, even incense and 'blood; all that we know of sacred is to them execrable; the 'same opinion denies to our human constitution its own satis-'factions, its own necessities.' 'Nature is chastising our 'tolerance of the unnatural.'

The new reply is very grave. For Cyprian too nature and

---

[1] *Ad Scapulam.*
[2] Pars pæne major cujusque civitatis, *ad Scap.* 2; nimius et copiosus noster populus, *ad Demetr.* 17.

humanity were at present dark of aspect. But his explanation of the phenomena of suffering was threefold. First, he believed that on general grounds a decrepitude of universal life, corresponding to that of individual objects, must be expected and is begun. The opinion of the old age of the world, which Columella so long since had rejected[1], gained ground with the decline of virtue. Christians in particular fancied that it accorded with their then scheme of prophecy. This was a hypothesis more obvious, in the silence of economics, than to trace the decay of enterprise, of production, of art-skill[2] to the universal expulsion of free labour by slave labour, the artificial appreciation of corn, and the consolidation of real property in hands incredibly few.

The second answer regarded political convulsions. These Cyprian concurred with his antagonist in regarding as divine judgments—and upon impiety.

But impiety where? In illustration he points to the system of slavery—to the absolute conviction which that institution implied of the accuracy with which duty ought to be rendered by one set of mortal lives to the other[3], and of the unlimited chastisement due to disobedience. 'Was it 'reasonable to suppose that the universal profligacy of disobe-'dience to acknowledged moral laws should receive no check 'from the Master of Man? or was it wonderful that civic strifes

---

[1] *De re rustica*, Præf., l. ii. 1.

[2] Agricola...nauta...in artibus peritia, *ad Demetr.* 3.

[3] *Ad Demetr.* 8. This argument shews that the idea that slavery was unchristian had not penetrated even Cyprian's humane nature. At the same time his indignation about the atrocities shews what was coming, and he plainly does not treat slavery as a *natural law*. The passage is well worth quoting. 'Ipse de servo tuo exigis servitutem, et *homo hominem* parere tibi et obœdire compellis, et cum sit vobis *eadem sors nascendi, conditio una moriendi*, corporum materia consimilis, animarum ratio communis, æquali jure et pari lege vel veniatur in istum mundum, vel de mundo postmodum recedatur, tamen nisi tibi pro arbitrio tuo serviatur, nisi ad voluntatis obsequium pareatur, imperiosus et nimius servitutis exactor, flagellas, verberas, fame, siti, nuditate, et ferro frequenter et carcere adfligis et crucias. Et non agnoscis [miser] Dominum Deum tuum, cum sic exerceas ipse dominatum.' *ad Demetr.* 8.

'and aristocratic savagery should beckon the Goth to the 'frontier? That deaths should avenge an aristocratic and com-'mercial rapacity which inflicted worse famines than nature? 'That pestilence should linger in cities where its warnings had 'only evoked fresh rebellions against morality[1]?'

Here he introduces with force a fact of which Demetrian had already heard something—that *such* scourges had been unerringly foretold by Prophets as visitations upon *such* sins, and foretold with this remarkable supplement to their predictions, that reformation would be *adopted only by* the few and scorned by the mass. 'And yet,' he finely exclaims, 'ye are indignant at the indignation of God[2].'

Thirdly. He retorts the causes of that divine indignation in a more sounding strain—'You and your courts are labour-'ing for the eradication of the only rational and spiritual 'worship extant; labouring to conserve the adoration of inept 'figments and animal monsters. Full of this zeal you actually 'invert the usages of law[3] against us. But argue with us, con-'vince us by reason;—or only come and listen to your own 'demon deities confessing, screaming, flying[4] from our prayers. 'Then set the unmeaning meanness of your cringing prostra-'tions against the open-browed, manly, sensible devotions of our 'assemblies. Do you think it conceivable that brute force should 'move us from our position to yours? Do you doubt our 'sincerity? The certainty of our conviction as to this world 'and the unseen is best evidenced by our perfect acquiescence 'in your inflictions. Vast as our numbers are in the empire, 'we have never turned on an oppressor. The last persecution 'has indeed for our sake collapsed in the 'crash of empire' 'when treasure, forces and camp were lost with Decius[5],— 'but without our act or wish. Once more our conviction is

---

[1] *Ad Demetr.* 10.
[2] *Ad Demetr.* 9
[3] See above, II. 1, p. 61.
[4] See p. 10, n. 3.
[5] We must read *ruinis rerum* not *regum* (17), but the touches leave no doubt of the event. The death of the Decii immediately suspended persecution.

'evidenced in our acquiescence in the heavenly chastisements
'which we fully share with you. For think you that we claim,
'as spiritual worshippers, exemption? Surely no,—on us, with
'our eternal trust, chastisements fall light. To us they come
'in an aspect new-born with us into the world's thought, as a
'*probation*, as a discipline of strength. In the flesh we are but
'men liable to all things human. We dwell in one house with
'you; we fare as you do; we bear willingly what God in our
'records said long since He must inflict for the wicked's sake.
'Our prosperous days are not here. They are to come. For
'you we grieve and with you, and we intercede unfalteringly
'for your worldly happiness. But the present interruptions of
'that happiness are not only fulfilments. They are forewarn-
'ings also. There is in the distance a divine day; when we
'who in this world are Re-born, and signed with a certain
'sign in a certain blood, shall part from you, and never rejoin
'you. The pleased tormentor of to-day must then become
'the spectacle of the tormented[1]. By that fear, by the abun-
'dant time and occasion offered for your change, by all the
'dear hopes which, as we know, centre on that change, the
'persecuted appeal to the persecutor in his own behalf.'

Such is in brief what I have called the '*Resentment*' of
Cyprian. Throughout there is a transparent consciousness
that the struggle between Christian and Roman will ere long
be contested on more equal terms[2]. Already the former are

---

[1] *Ad Dem.* 24. Gentle as the upshot of the peroration is, and infinitely differenced from the wild threat of Tertullian (*De Spectac.*), the bitterness of the sights which Cyprian knew of, 'Qui hic *nos spectavit*...Crudelium *oculorum* brevis *fructus*,' rankles too much here. So also candour cannot pass over Cyprian's comment on the threat which the fifth Maccabee hurls at Antiochus—a comment which in this century would not be possible in the catholic Church 'Quale illud levamentum fuit martyri, quam magnum, quam grande solacium, in cruciatibus suis non tormenta propria cogitare, sed tortoris sui supplicia prædicare,' *ad Fortunat.* 11. Eternal punishment and the eternal preservation necessary to make it possible are stated in awful terms 'Servabuntur, cum corporibus suis animæ infinitis cruciatibus ad dolorem.' *ad Demetr.* 24. Romans under persecution might be reckoned on to discover this doctrine.

[2] We may compare this with the

proud of their numbers[1]; already there is hope in speaking out: already there is a conviction that the masses are ready to hear reason[2]: a perception that persecution is the grandest opportunity for the missioner[3].

Jerome[4] has echoed a criticism of Lactantius that Cyprian might have met the heathen magistrate more convincingly upon general grounds than by Scripture texts[5]. It is necessary to differ from the prince of critics because (1) the texts, where used as arguments, are alleged, after description of the tokens of Divine anger, only to shew that the visitations had been predicted[6]. The argument is this. They who could predict them might be presumed to have a key to the right explanation of them. They did predict them as punishments upon idolatry and oppression. This kind of exhibition of prophecies is surely a legitimate allegation to produce before an unbeliever. (2) It is visibly the sequel of arguments which had been touched upon and but half developed in conversations. Cyprian shews himself[7] aware that Scripture texts are not producible for every purpose. (3) Having to meet just such unfamiliar knowledge as would have adhered to a Demetrian, Cyprian, I observe, does not once quote to him any author of Scripture by name,—always 'a prophet,' 'another prophet saith,' 'God in the Holy Scriptures.'

The man's acquaintance with the elements of Christian argument justifies Cyprian precisely in the ground he takes,

---

more passionate conviction of Tertullian in the *De Corona*.

[1] Nimius et copiosus noster populus ulciscitur (*ad Demetr.* 17).

[2] *Quos tamen sermonis nostri admittere credo rationem* (*ad Demetr.* 2). Disceptatione vince, vince *ratione* (13).

[3] ...dum me christianum *celebri loco* et *populo circumstante* pronuntio et vos et deos vestros clara *et publica prædicatione* confundo... *ad Demetr.* 13.

[4] *Ep.* 83 (70) *ad Magn.*; Lactant. *Divin. Institutt.* v. 4.

[5] Rettberg, p. 266 f., taking occasion by Jerome and conceiving further an *impolicy* in addressing a magistrate in language so strong, concludes Demetrian to be a fictitious personage. But the trait of his visiting Cyprian professedly to enquire, actually to declaim, his advanced age, the peculiar mode of citation and other slight fitnesses are against this.

[6] Hoc scias esse *prædictum* (*ad D.* 5): Ipsum audi loquentem (*ad D.* 6).

[7] *Ad Demetr.* 3.

while it further verifies to us the reality of the circumstances.

Of the Style of the 'Demetrian.'

The style of this brochure is elevated, pure and strong. Some of the expressions finely terse and epigrammatic. 'Veneunt judicaturi.' 'Deus nec quæritur nec timetur.' 'Quasi, etsi hostis desit, esse pax inter ipsas togas possit.' Somewhat of a relapse into the early floridity is perceptible in the third and seventh chapters. Twice Cyprian moulds a line of Virgil into his prose (*Georg.* i. 107) 'herbis siccitate morientibus æstuans campus' (20), and (*Georg.* i. 154) 'in agro inter cultas et fertiles segetes lolium et avena dominetur' (23).

III.

The Interpretation of Sorrows.

Exercitia sunt nobis ista non funera. *De Mortalitate* 16.

Difficulties which arose from within the community were scarcely less perplexing. It seemed as if the Pestilence might work a new lapse of its own. Numbers were dismayed that the scourge of Christ's persecutors should light no less heavily on His friends[1]. Others shewed the first symptoms of the fanatic spirit, so fatal afterward to Africa, and chafed when death threatened to forestall their martyr-crown[2]. Others still liable to be summoned to the tribunal shrank from the cross. To preserve their faith by deluding the tyrant was not an extinct temptation. What was the church of Carthage? It was an unpopular yet important section of a great city population, overmastered by powerful ideas, unfamiliar as yet with their manifold applications; dragged daily into contact with bitter social hardships, then suddenly made sharers in the world-wide terror of the Plague, then accounted responsible for its mysterious origin; flung back thus on the old enigmas of

---

[1] *De Mortalitate* 8.   [2] *De Mort.* 17.

VI. III. THE INTERPRETATION OF SORROWS.

existence and not exempted from new enigmas in their faith, —such a body needed indeed that some broad and Christian view of this physical calamity should be opened before them.

The work of mercy had been organized, but to control these cross currents of feeling required yet greater skill and delicacy. To beard a slanderous tormentor was perhaps a duty, but a harder one was to maintain in a people so tried the gentleness and tranquillity of spirit, the intelligence of devotion, the sense of unity with God which marked the line between the Church and polytheism. In quick succession came out three more of Cyprian's finest Essays. The topics of the pungent pamphlet 'on Demetrian' are reviewed from the positive side in the encouraging address 'on the Mortality.' Then we have the noble joyous treatise 'on the Lord's Prayer.' The later 'Exhortation to Confession,' a Scripture manual for Martyrs, must be treated with these as his last teaching in this region.

It was in answer to actual calls that the pen of Cyprian was thus busy amid such distractions. Few of the bishops could make adequate answers to the questionings of the times. The laity of the distant[1] town of Thibaris entreated his presence among them. Edicts of Gallus for sacrifice had reached them. Torture had recommenced. There and elsewhere

---

[1] *Longe, Ep.* 58. 1. Unnamed by geographers, and not identified until 1885 when an inscription GENIO THIBARIS AUGUSTO SACRUM R P THIB D*d* (*Respublica Thibaritanorum Decreto [decurionum]*) was found near where a small tributary of the Medjerda leaves the hills on the south of the plain of Bulla and of the road to Cirta, at *Henchir Hamâmet*. The ruins of its basilica stand out. (Tissot, pl. 18; vol. II. p. 367.) It is just in Zeugitana where Fell, p. 120, by some accident places it; p. 237, he identifies it with *Tabora* in Mauretania Cæsariensis. Morcelli says Hardouin places it in the Byzacene because its bishop votes among these provincials in the Council of Carthage (*Sentt. Epp.* 37). I may mention that there is no geographical order of voting there. He adds that their bishop Victorian appears twice in the Collation of Carthage A.D. 411; *Cognit.* I. 133 and 187. (Labbe, vol. III., pp. 202 and 222.) The name in Cyprianic codices is also read *Thebaritanos* and *Dhibari*. At Mohammedia, 'once Tabaria' (?), 9 miles from Tunis, *i.e.* in Zeugitana, the name *Thibbure* has been read on a slab (*Rev. Afric.* v. I. p. 378).

congregations ceased to assemble, and the bishops to preach[1]. Their own bishop Vincent four years later was the most fanatical of all the speakers in the Council of that date, holding heretics to be so much worse than heathens as to need not only Baptism, but a previous Exorcism, if they joined the Church. At present the bishop is only alluded to as silenced. The Lapsed were still unrestored, and no restoration but that of martyrdom was yet recognised[2]. Harassed and unsupported many Christians buried themselves in the solitudes of the adjacent Tell, many escaped by sea. And then many were haunted by the apprehension that a lonely death in exile was no true confessorship of Christ.

A.D. 252, March?

The 'urgency of affairs' in Carthage rendered a visit from Cyprian hopeless. But he wrote to THIBARIS an affectionate and reassuring LETTER[3], which contains in germ the scheme of the essays which he next undertook, and some few thoughts which he does not repeat. Had his 'Mortality' and his 'Lord's Prayer' been already composed he would have sent them these as he sent the 'Unity' and the 'Lapsed' to the Roman Confessors. The multiplication of practical needs for his counsel was ever the motive of Cyprian's literary work. In words almost identical with those of his Second Synodical Letter, which followed immediately, having told the Thibaritans of the warnings which made him feel that they were but at the beginning of sorrows, he reminded them that stages of history which have been predicted in Scripture ought when reached to create no difficulty to Christians. He sketched out for perhaps the first time the full doctrine of probation, and the preparation for a final judgment which it afforded. And then while, as to Demetrian, he insists that endurance without an attempt at retaliation is characteristic of the Christian life

---

[1] *Ep.* 58. 4. [2] *Ep.* 58. 8.
[3] Appropinquante jam, imo imminente Galli persecutione, is Pearson's date for the epistle (*Annal. Cypr.* A.D. 252, ix.). The tortures and flight had however recommenced (*Ep.* 58. 4), and as yet the lapsed had not been relieved by the second council (*Ep.* 58. 8). I should date the letter March A.D. 252. By April the council would have been planned.

on earth¹, still the hope of eternal triumph is with real inconsistency heightened by the meditation of eternal vengeance.

We have no right to slur this trait of the thought of the time, but if we think a truer lesson might have been early learnt, yet the succession of ages which have not learnt it should impress on us what is the hardest lesson which Christ set to man.

The Lapsed are invited to rearm, and regain their loss. The loneliest Death for Christ is witnessed by Him, and is as glorious as any public martyrdom. We have spoken before of the fine image which in this letter he borrows from the gladiators fighting and dying before the Emperor and the Cæsar. 'A combat high and great! guerdoned gloriously 'with a heavenly crown! That God should be our spectator! 'should open His eyes on men whom He has deigned to 'make His sons, and enjoy the spectacle of our contending! 'We give battle; we fight in wager of the faith; God our 'spectator, His Angels spectators, Christ a spectator too².'

Nothing however is more eloquent than this practical closing application of the Christian armoury from S. Paul. 'Take we also as a covering for our head the Helmet of 'salvation, to fence our ears against the deadly Edicts, our eyes 'from the sight of the abhorred Images; to fence our brow that 'the Seal of God may be safely kept on it, our lips that the 'victorious tongue may acknowledge its Lord Christ. Arm we 'our right hand too with the spiritual Sword—sternly to repel 'the deathly sacrifices, that, unforgetful of the Eucharist, it may, 'as it has received the Lord's Body, so also clasp Himself³.'

From such needs then grew the address⁴ 'ON THE MORTALITY.' Cyprian says it is intended to fortify the more

---

¹ Quibus occidere non licet, occidi necesse est. *Ep.* 58. 4.

² *Ep.* 58. 8. Did Cyprian know the Carmina Sibyllina? See C. Alexandre, *Oracula Sibyllina* (1869, pp. 52—54).

³ *Ep.* 58. 9.

⁴ The 'Epistle' as Augustine calls it (*Contra ii. Epp. Pelagg.* IV. viii. 22 and x. 27). He cites it in six places, *Contra Iulian.* II. viii. 25, *Op. impf. c. Iulian.* VI. xiv., *Ep.* 217. 22, and in *de Prædestinatione Sanct.* xiv. 26 as librum ...multis ac pæne omnibus qui ecclesiasticas literas amant laudabiliter notum. See Pearson (*Annal. Cypr.* A.D. 252, xvii.) on the references to it in *Chron. Euseb.* and in Possidius.

timid minority of his flock; and he makes tender excuse for their misconceptions. But it served a far wider purpose. It taught the teachers.

The new leading thoughts in the Demetrian were (1) the evidence which Prediction might afford to heathens that the Christian interpretation was true, and (2) the idea of Probation by trouble, as characteristic of Christianity. To his own people he presents the converse of these thoughts. Predictions of chastisement fulfilled are a pledge that promises of joy will be accomplished. The idea of Probation, unrevealed to Plato, unpreached by Cicero, is brought home now as the philosophy of suffering, the interpretation of sorrow. Job, Tobias, Abraham[1] are the new masters of the ruined, the oppressed, the bereaved. One stroke of Providence effects both the Discipline of Love and the Censure of Sin. In the present calamity, the noisome repulsiveness of the plague deepens the trial, and yet what pure woman, what innocent boy would not shrink from this less than from the torturer's polluting fingers[2]? (3) Cruelty and hardness have been denounced already as the main provocations of paganism. And now 'the service of the 'sick, the kindness of kinsfolk, *pitifulness to sick slaves*, the 'self-devotedness of physicians,' these, says he, are among the first subjects 'which the dread and deadly-seeming pestilence comes to look into.'

The ecclesiastical belief in a speedy dissolution of the world, the illustrations which it drew from prevailing famines or pestilences, and the class of motives to virtue which it suggested are sometimes treated as retrogressions in philosophy, hindrances to the political efficiency of citizens, and interferences with the Hellenic sense of 'Beauty.' But in fact this belief was (as we have seen) carried into the Church from the thought of the day. What the Church really contributed was a new way of regarding that belief. The interpretation which Cyprian and others proposed for universal physical disasters excluded probably all the conceptions with

---

[1] *De Mort.* 10, 11.   [2] *De Mort.* 15.

which contemporary intellects, whether popular or cultivated, invested these terrific crises, and to us that interpretation offers crucial tests of whether the Church was advancing thought and sentiment, and elevating courage, or was parting with a glorious view of nature.

Such frightful ills were traced to one or other of about five general causes; to a dualism of conflicting deities, good and malevolent; to a dualism of the beneficent spirit and of matter instinct with mechanic laws; to a necessity controlling deity and matter alike; to fortuitous conditions and fixed sequences in matter itself; to the personal displeasure of deity which willed its own recognition by traditional rites and under popular titles, although such names might not be strictly identified with divine personalities. This last was the more refined version of the popular creed which felt the action of beings vindicating a right to material offerings and to the extermination of atheists.

The despair and apathy which these beliefs engendered in the presence of universal suffering are commonplaces with the Greek historian and Roman poet. But the first Christian who touches the subject is led by the Mortality into a region of sublimity and tenderness.

On him it enforces (1) absolute confidence in a Paternal care, which through visible correction[1], through acknowledged probation[2], through resignation to yet uncomprehended purposes[3], elevates and purifies and calms.

(2) It enjoins on him utmost activity, organization, self-devotion in the alleviation of suffering and of bereavement[4]. These effects on Christian thought and practice are deduced from distinctly Christian grounds.

These same grounds create in him (3) the conviction that moral causes in society[5] have an effect on the conditions

---

[1] *De Mort.* 15.
[2] *De Mort.* 1, 9, 15.
[3] *De Mort.* 11, 18.
[4] *De Mort.* 16.
[5] *De Mort.* 15.

accorded to humanity, not only immediately by the recompense earned by the individual's vice or virtue, but mediately by affecting general laws, exterior and physical, through exercise of the moral judgment of God. Not only is a world in order a field for human excellence to expand on and an external instrument for it to utilise, but a world in physical disorder is an instrument of correction, converting selfish and abject thoughts to interior and to wider considerations[1], vivifying the hypothesis of an existence independent of physical decrepitudes[2], and exciting in those who believe the divine Fatherhood an almost emulous beneficence[3]. There are germs of further social advance in Cyprian's teaching. Could it have been demonstrated to him that pestilence is (irrespectively of interposition) a direct result of the uncivilised squalor which dogs the feet of luxury, he must have emphatically replied by an application (not perhaps yet visible to him) of the doctrine which underlies all his teaching. He would have said that luxury and squalor are both expressions of hideous moral errors. 'Enterprise, administration, humane intercourse, skill in arts[4],' are to him the signs of an advancing, progressive, youthful world. Waste of the world's resources, content in sordidness, disregard of natural ties, indifference to the meanest, the crushing of small industries, the abolition of small holdings for the sake of grazing farms and deer forests[5], are to him so many crimes against the world's life. And it is a familiar thought to him that there is so exact an appropriateness in the observed consequences of accumulating evils, that believers in Providence do not err in calling these consequences 'decisions'—*judicia*—judgments[6].

---

[1] *De Mort.* 4.
[2] *De Mort.* 2, 21—26.
[3] *De Mort.* 26.
[4] *Ad Dem.* 3. Cf. *de Mort.* 4, 24.
[5] Egentem et pauperem *non vident* oculi superfusi nigrore. *de Op. et El.* 15. —Suffocationes impotentium commerciorum (paraphrase of Isai. lviii. 1). *de Dominica Orat.* 33.—Continuantes saltibus saltus et de confinio pauperibus exclusis infinita ac sine terminis rura latius porrigentes. *ad Donat.* 12.
[6] Cf. *de Laps.* 1, *ad Dem.* 5, 7, 17.

VI. III. THE INTERPRETATION OF SORROWS.

Not the respect only but the adherence of many a heathen was ere long compelled by the attitude of the Christians[1], and yet failures of faith there were 'in the Home of Faith,' and their bishop marked many incredulities against 'our Master in believing[2].' Minds fresh from paganism took unexpected turns. He meets them with brightness. 'You, 'who because you are Christians expected immunity from this 'visitation, will you, as Christians, claim exemption from the 'scirocco, from ophthalmia, from stranding ships[3].'—'You who 'fret to think that plague may cut you off from martyrdom, '—know that it is not the martyr's blood but the martyr's 'faith that God asks[4].'

To others death was dreadful still. These then have yet to fill their imagination with realities which they have coldly accepted. 'Nor are we now without special helps.—A col-'league of mine, a fellow bishop, lay at the point of death. He 'prayed for a respite. At once a young man stood at his side, 'noble, majestic, of lofty stature and bright countenance,—no 'eye of flesh could have endured to look on him, save eyes 'which were closing to this world. There was indignation in 'his spirit, and his voice shook, as he said "Ye fear to suffer. 'Ye are unwilling to depart. What shall I do unto you?" It 'was the voice of one who heeds not our momentary desires 'but our lasting interest. Not for himself, but for us, the 'dying man heard that.'

To this tale Cyprian adds what we may well believe, how many times he had himself, 'little and last' though he was, heard the prompting to preach publicly the glorious verities of death[5], as it comes by the will of God.

'Let us realize what we mean by the presence of Christ, 'and the eternal society, the increasing hosts of our friends, the

---

[1] Gentiles coguntur ut credant. *de Mort.* 15.
[2] *De Mort.* 6.
[3] *De Mort.* 8.
[4] Nec enim sanguinem Deus nostrum sed fidem quærit. *de Mort.* 17.
[5] *De Mort.* 19, 20.

'loved, the revered, the sainted who are there[1].' His voice swells to lyric fervour, and preludes the most majestic of odes[2]. For him the cheering certainties of exalted life are dashed by no pagan reminiscence, no anticipated mediævalism. He cannot mourn the departed though much he misses them like distant voyagers[3]. He cannot brook even the assumption of black garments as a memorial of those who wear immortal white.

'Put the terror of death out of doors: dwell on the Undyingness beyond it[4].'

It may be difficult to revive the early freshness with which feelings and thoughts, now long grown usual, began to mingle in the older talk along street and quay in Carthage. But it is not hard to say whether the city and the world gained by the change.

The 'EXHORTATION TO MARTYRDOM,' or rather 'TO CONFESSORSHIP[5],' is a Manual of Scripture passages, connected by brief remarks, and arranged under thirteen heads for reflexion. It was compiled five years later, after Valerian's Edict for persecution, at the request of a layman, Fortunatus by name, and it is, says the author, 'No discourse, but material for discoursing[6].'—'Not a garment, but

---

[1] *De Mort.* 26.

[2] *De Mort.* 26. It is difficult to resist the impression that the Cyprianic 'Illic *apostolorum gloriosus chorus*, illic *prophetarum* exsultantium *numerus*, illic *martyrum* innumerabilis populus' is something more than a coincidence with the Ambrosian 'Te *gloriosus apostolorum chorus*, te *prophetarum* laudabilis *numerus*, te candidatus *martyrum* laudat exercitus.' These are among those clauses of the Te Deum which Dr Swainson counts as 'closely connected with the Eucharistic hymn of the liturgy of Jerusalem' (*Dict. of Christian Antiqq.*, s. v.). But the resemblance here lies in the triple parallelism of the clauses, and the use of such words as *chorus* and *numerus*, which are not points of the liturgy.

[3] Non amitti sed præmitti...ut navigantes solent, desiderari eos debere, non plangi. *de Mort.* 20.

[4] *De Mort.* 24.

[5] The original title was *Ad Fortunatum* simply.

[6] ...non tam tractatum meum videar tibi misisse quam materiam tractantibus præbuisse. *ad Fortunatum*, 3.

Wool and Purple of the Lamb Himself' ready for the weaving[1].

Its purpose is to assist himself and others in preparing persons for their Second Baptism—'the Baptism stronger in 'grace, loftier of effect, more precious in honour—the Baptism 'wherein angels are the baptizers, at which God and His Christ 'are joyful—the Baptism, after which no man sins[2].' The very existence of a practical little book like this answers the question whether martyrdoms were very few and scattered. The cheerfulness of Cyprian's own spirit appears in his inference that the very number of the sufferers shews that such endurance cannot be over-difficult or too severe[3].

The place which the book has in the progress of Cyprian's thought may be recognised. In his 'Unity of the Church' he had accumulated every Scriptural illustration, apt or otherwise, of that doctrine. In this book he developes rather laboriously a new one. The Seven Maccabees whose history he details (as Origen does on the same subject)[4] are not only patterns to individuals, but also present an image of the Totality (Septenary) of all the Churches, their Mother being 'the First and the One,' 'the Beginning and the Root,' that is to say the Catholic Unity, which was founded by the word of the Lord, and gave all Churches birth[5].

Again, experience has now carried him beyond that flattery of Confessors which marked former years. Among other applications to the circumstances of the time are these: he observes (1) that when a question arose whether the youngest Maccabean brother should save his life by an act of conformity, no suggestion was made that the merits of the Six Martyrs could plead for him. Again (2) in warning his people against a resort to *Libelli*, he shews that Eleazar

---

[1] *Ad Fortunat.* 3. This metaphor makes certain, I think, the conjecture of Scaliger on Tert. *de Monog.* 7, 'Summus sacerdos patris et *agnus* de suo vestiens.' Codd. *magnus*.

[2] *Ad Fortunat.* 4.
[3] *Ad Fortunat.* 11 fin.
[4] Orig. *Exh. ad Mart.* 23.
[5] *Ad Fortunat.* 11.

declined to do what all the Libellatics had done: (3) he says the true martyrdom is in the spirit ready for martyrdom, whether it be consummated or no; and the tract closes with the observation that the crown which under persecution is assigned to Martyr-warfare is in 'time of Peace' bestowed on Conscientiousness.

But not even on this sensible moderation rests either the merit of this pamphlet or the indication it gives of what the everyday Cyprian really was like; still less on its own assumed grounds—the nearness of the End, the Advent of Antichrist, the accomplished skill of the Arch-enemy accumulated (as it is grotesquely put) in his six-thousand-years conflict with man[1]. More broad and strong are the well conceived theses; and marvellous, considering the blankness of all secondary aids, is the command of Scripture.

That some degree of conformity to the worship of the vulgar may be allowed to mingle with the higher light is a notion admitted only in churches in which a genuine struggle with the essence of polytheism is not maintained. Cyprian makes the very substance of the martyr-spirit to be a perfect sense of the heinousness of Idolatry under every species, of the aggravated 'difficulty' which it raises in the way of its own forgiveness as sin, and of the necessity for absolute genuineness in all relations with Deity.

---

[1] The quaint idea is caught from Tertullian, *de Vel. Virgg.* 1, 'diabolo...adjiciente cottidie ad iniquitatis ingenia.' The totaling of dates in Hebrew Scriptures gives, according to Clinton, 4138 B.C. as a date for Adam. But the LXX. makes it, according to Cunninghame, 5478 B.C. Iulius Africanus shortly before Cyprian's time had brought this to 5500, which would make the date of the edict of Valerian to be the 5757th year of the world; 'Sex millia annorum jam pæne complentur,' *ad Fortunat.* 2. In the beginning of the fifth century Anianus also computed 5500, and Panodorus 5493. Sulpicius Severus, who brings his history down to A.D. 400, also has 'Mundus a Domino constitutus est abhinc annos *jam pæne sex millia*.' *Chron.* i. 2. The significance of the 'six thousand years' lay in the Rabbinic belief, which, until the time had long gone by, coloured and usually distressed the Christian mind, as to the week of millennia and the consummation of all things. See Lactantius *Div. Inst.* vii. 14 and the citations in notes there. And see Clinton *F. R.* v. II. p. 220,

The next most important themes of this text-book are that probationary aspect of suffering, which his mind had long realized; the certainty of a supporting Providence, and faith as the measure of the support it yields.

IV.

Intelligent Devotion.

'ON THE LORD'S PRAYER.' It was not enough to arm the confessor, to nerve the timid, to silence the calumniator.— Common life needed building up. Cyprian saw no nearer or better road to edification than to fill with intelligence the universal Devotion. The recitation of the Prayer of Christ might become mechanical even when times of trial call it not unfrequently to the tongue. They who have seen abroad great naves empty for noble vespers and crowded for the rosary may thence draw the nearest notion of what antient 'Battology' was with its lullaby of spiritual contentment[1]. The Essay ON THE LORD'S PRAYER is written with precision and with a visible delight. The freshness of his thoughts, the sweetness of his words, the fulness and fitness of his use of Scripture are a delicate fruit indeed to have been produced under the flaming heat of controversy, amid the whirl of organization, in the atmosphere of a plague-stricken city[2]. There are points where the commentary very closely touches both the historic facts and the spirit of which the facts were a product. We see too how the little treatise both enshrined

and Dr Salmon's articles *Africanus* and *Panodorus*, in *Dict. Christ. Biogr.*

[1] Matt. vi. 7.

[2] Mgr. Freppel (p. 341) says well in comparing this with Tertullian's treatise On the Prayer,...'une onction douce et pénétrante, une nature plus ouverte aux impressions de la piété donnaient au disciple un avantage sur le maître, dans un sujet où le cœur doit parler de préférence à l'esprit'; although some of the Master's most famous and stirring words are found in that treatise, and few passages of spiritual poetry can exceed his last two sections.

But it is curious to note how he not only omits the word 'noster' but, I think, forbears to dwell anywhere on the *plural* character of the prayer which means so much to Cyprian.

and foreshadowed some of the most beautiful phrases of familiar liturgy.

The special development from the words '*Our* Father' of the essential character of Unity and of the inexpiableness by martyrdom of the stain of schism incline me to place this Essay in date close to that 'On Unity,' which in almost the same words states conclusions which only four years later Cyprian expresses in quite other language[1].

In applying the petition for Bread to the Daily Eucharist the author dwells on the danger of those from whom it is withheld[2]; 'martyrdom' or confessorship is a familiar thing; it is also a temptation to arrogant assumption[3]. These thoughts mark the very crisis of the time.

The recommendation to '*every single man* to prepare himself to surrender worldly wealth' comes with a special force from one who was parting with his all[4].

It is the time too when the idea seems ever present to his spirit by which he nerved himself and the rest to meet 'the Mortality'—the inborn power of Christian sons to resemble the Divine Father—a sonship and a resemblance wrought through Baptism. 'We ought to know that when we call 'God "Father" we ought to live as if Sons of God'—'We that 'ought to be like our Father'—'What He made us by Second 'Birth such He would have us, as reborn, to continue—born 'of water and Spirit[5].' These belong to the period of *Respondere Natalibus*.

---

[1] Compare *de Unitate* 14 'Tales etiam*si occisi* in confessione *nominis fuerint*, macula ista nec *sanguine abluitur; inexpiabilis et gravis culpa discordiæ* nec passione purgatur,' with *de Dominica Oratione* 24 'nec *si pro nomine occisus fuerit crimen dissensionis fraternæ poterit* evadere,&c....Quale delictum est quod nec baptismo *sanguinis* potest *ablui!* quale crimen est quod martyrio non potest *expiari!*' The same doctrine is stated in *Ep.* 73. 21—but in very different phraseology. ...ut quis coram hominibus Christum confiteatur, ut sanguine suo baptizetur? Et tamen nec hoc baptisma hæretico prodest, quamvis Christum confessus extra ecclesiam fuerit occisus, &c.

[2] *De Domin. Orat.* 18.
[3] *De Domin. Orat.* 26.
[4] *De Domin. Orat.* 20.
[5] *De Domin. Orat.* 11, 12, 17, 23.

The Essay of Tertullian on Prayer has been the model after which Cyprian worked, although in the freest manner. Saint Hilary, while he omits to comment on the Lord's Prayer in the course of the fifth chapter of S. Matthew, preferring to send his readers to Cyprian's Essay, does justice Tertullian's 'most apt volume,' regretting that the unhappy position of its author—'the later aberration of the man'—should have prejudiced its acceptance[1].

Its method and interpretations have been followed by Cyprian into a mysticism unusual to him. And indeed, where Tertullian had only taught that we should, besides the Morning and Evening Prayers, pray thrice daily as debtors to THE THREE, Cyprian has a mystical expansion upon the perfect trinity of the Three 'Hours' with their three-hour intervals—'a sacrament of the Trinity which was to be revealed in the last days,' and this is the earliest passage in which the Latin word 'Trinity' occurs in this sense[2].

What effect Tertullian's book had taken in the interval between is traceable in the difference of the correctives employed. It is still indeed necessary to check the '*tumultuous loquacity*' of persons praying aloud 'when we assemble with the brethren and celebrate the Divine Sacrifices with the Priest of God,' but several superstitions have disappeared, which Cyprian could not have failed to rebuke had they still prevailed. Such was the practice of washing the hands before prayer[3] in strange commemoration of Pilate's surrender of the Lord; the putting off of the woollen cloak[4] at the same time;

---

[1] Hilar. *in Matt.* v. 1.
[2] By Tertull. *adv. Prax.* 2, 3, it is not applied as a name of Deity though the sense approaches it. In the 7th council (A.D. 256) Eucratius of Thenæ uses it in the distinctest manner in his phrase '*blasphemia Trinitatis*'; *Sentt. Epp.* 29. The earliest Greek use of Τριάς is where Theophilus of Antioch A.D. 180 (*ad Autolych.* ii. c. 23) calls the first three days of creation before the emergence of the sun and moon an emblem of the Trinity.
[3] See Tert. *de Orat.* 11.
[4] The pænula, φαινόλης or φελόνης.

the sitting down after prayer in imitation of Hermas[1]; the disuse of the Kiss of Peace when fasting, and the abstaining from the Liturgy on Fast days. The disuse of veils by maidens had continued, as we have seen. It was also probably still a question whether it was correct to kneel on the Sabbath, although Cyprian does not notice it. If we consider these ritualistic questions of the Early Church, we need scarcely despair of our own working their own solution.

It is characteristic of the tempers of the two authors that Tertullian hailed the Confusion of the Nations as a phase of the Kingdom to come. Cyprian omits this, and, while his note on the second word of the Prayer is his well-known beautiful phrase 'To us, prayer is of the people, and is common to all,' Tertullian who comments on S. Matthew's form of the prayer, here, with S. Luke, drops the word 'Our' and does not even allude to it.

Although in reading Cyprian's treatise after his 'Master's' a softened echo of strong words is audible, and the writing out of his riddling epigrams in limpid sense is frequent and deliberate, there is little transcription, as in earlier days, of sentence or phrase. The Scriptural illustrations alone shew markedly the originality of Cyprian's work in a point in which it must have been actually difficult to avoid repetition. Tertullian quotes about sixty places, and Cyprian seventy, and of these latter only about seven seem to be suggested by Tertullian's use of them[2]. Even these are differently rendered into the vernacular[3].

[1] Tertull. *de Orat.* 16. *Herm.* Ἀποκάλυψις ε′— Προσευξαμένου μου...καὶ καθίσαντος.

[2] *I.e.* judging by the marginal references and doing the best one may with Öhler's indices, which for inaccuracy almost rival Dr Routh's. However *Das Neue Testament Tertullian's* of Roensch appears to bear out the statement.

[3] They are these; *Isai.* 1. 2, ap. Tert. *de Orat.* 2, filios genui et illi me non agnoverunt; ap. *de Dca. Orat.* 10, filios generavi et exaltavi, ipsi autem me spreverunt. *Mt.* 23. 9, ap. Tert. *de Orat.* 2 ne quem in terris patrem *vocemus nisi quem* habemus in caelis; ap. *de Dca. Orat.* 9, ne *vocemus* nobis patrem in terra, quod *scilicet* nobis unus pater qui est in caelis. *Mt.* 26. 41 (*Luc.* 22. 46),

Both give and comment upon the third petition as 'Thy will be done in heaven (the heavens) and in earth,' which form also, Augustine says, was more in use, and to be found in a majority of manuscripts[1]. Accordingly neither annotator finds in this clause any reference to either angelical or physical order. They are obliged to understand heaven and earth as symbols for spirit and flesh within us, or again for heavenly and earthly-minded men.

Cyprian expands and somewhat dilutes Tertullian's splendid phrase, '*We* are heaven and earth.' He closes thus, 'At Christ's bidding we pray; and we ask that we 'may make our prayer be to the salvation of all, that as 'God's will was done in heaven—that is in us through our 'faith, that we might belong to heaven; so God's will may 'be done also in earth—that is in them, on their believing[2]; 'that so they who are by their first birth earthy may begin 'to be heavenly by being born of water and of the Spirit.'

ap. Tert. *de Orat.* 8, orate ne temptemini; *de Dca. Orat.* 26, ne veniatis in temptationem. *Mt.* 18. 32, ap. Tert. *de Orat.* 7, dominus debitum remisit; ap. *de Dca. Orat.* 23, dimissum sibi...omne debitum. *Mt.* 6. 34, ap. Tert. *de Orat.* 6, nolite de crastino cogitare; ap. *de Dca. Orat.* 19, nolite in crastinum cogitare. For *Lc.* 22. 42, ap. Tert. *de Orat.* 4, Pater, transfer (παρενέγκαι, om. εἰ βούλει) poculum istud (om. ἀπ᾽ ἐμοῦ), nisi quod mea non sed tua fiat voluntas. *de Dca. Orat.* 14 puts together *Mt.* 26. 39 Pater, si fieri potest, transeat a me calix iste, with *Mc.* 14. 36 (ref. om. by Hartel) verum tamen non quod ego volo sed quod tu vis ('Ἀλλ᾽ οὐ τί, *Mt.* πλὴν οὐχ ὡς). *Jo.* 4. 23, ap. Tert. *de Orat.* 28, veniet hora cum veri adoratores adorabunt patrem in spiritu et veritate; ap. *de Dca. Orat.* 2 (ref. om. by Hartel), horam venire quando veri adoratores adorarent, &c. *Jo.* 6. 38, ap. Tert. *de Orat.* 4, non suam sed patris facere se voluntatem; ap. *de Dca. Orat.* 14, non descendi de cælo ut faciam voluntatem meam sed voluntatem ejus qui misit me.

To illustrate panis cottidianus Tert. *de Orat.* 6 quotes *Jo.* 6. 33, 35, and *de Dca. Orat.* 18; *Jo.* 6. 51. Abraham is Tertullian's example of 'probation,' *de Orat.* 8; Job is Cyprian's, *de Dca. Orat.* 26.

[1] Aug. *de dono persev.* iii. 6. P. Sabatier, *Bibl. Sacr. Lat. Vers. Antiq.* Reims, 1743—49, v. III., p. 33, says that Cyprian has 'sicut' like all other authorities except Tertullian. But this is a mistake due to the text of all the printed Cyprians in his time. All the great MSS. have 'fiat voluntas tua in cælo et in terra.' *de Dca. Orat.* 14.

[2] See *de Dca. Orat.* c. 17 'In terra, hoc est in illis credentibus.' Hartel, under a misconception explained more fully below (*Note on Characteristics, &c.*), changes the unvarying reading into 'credere nolentibus.'

The clause '*Lead us not into temptation*' is explained by Tertullian as 'Suffer us not to be led[1],' and without a hint of the genuine form Cyprian uses the Master's gloss as his own text of the prayer[2]. Apparently he was the first, though not the last to do so; and it illustrates his excessive love of lucidity. Augustine notices his reading, and observes 'and thus do some pray'—among them probably his revered S. Ambrose; and he adds that he 'had nowhere found this in a Greek Gospel,' but that it was in many Latin manuscripts of Africa[3].

From his words on '*Deliver us from Evil*[4]' it is not clear whether he gives *Evil* a personal sense—The Evil One. '*A* '*Malo*—we comprise all adversities which the Enemy devises 'against us in this world'; 'We ask God's protection against '*Evil;* that gained, we stand quiet and guarded against all 'works of Devil and World.' It looks rather the other way. But scarcely so if we take into account his previous words on the clause about Temptation. 'Here is shewn that the Foe 'hath no power against us, except first God give him leave, 'that so all our fear, devotion and observance may turn 'toward God, seeing that *the* Evil One (*Malo*) hath no licence

---

[1] *Id est* ne nos patiaris induci ab eo utique qui temptat. Tert. *de Orat.* c. 8. Elsewhere only Ne nos inducas. *de Fug. in Persec.* 2.

[2] *De Dca. Orat.* 25. See Roensch, *N. Test. Tertullian's,* p. 600. His references are taken from Sabatier.

[3] Aug. *de dono persev.* vi. 12. Sabatier (*op. cit.*) gives it thus as his text of the Versio Antiqua of S. Matt. vi. 13 from the Colbert MS. (*c*, cent. xii., Paris, *Fonds Lat.* 254) in the form 'ne passus nos fueris induci,' and from the second S. Germain (cent. ix. or x., *g.* 2, *Fonds Lat.* 13169) and the S. Gatien MS. (cent. ix., Paris) as 'ne patiaris nos induci.' ['Ne patiaris nos induci,' Book of Armagh and the Rushworth Gospels (also Irish), centt. viii., ix., J. Wordsworth and H. J. White, *Nov. T.* I. xi., xiii. 60.] Sabatier cites this latter form also from Arnobius, *de Deo Trino,* 233 d, S. Ambrose, *de Sacram.*, ll. v. vi. col. 377 a, 385 c, and S. Augustine, l. ii. *de Serm. Dom. in m.* col. 206 a, 212 a, who treats it as an embodied explanation (videlicet exponentes) and who himself constantly uses *inferas*. J. Wordsworth, *Old Lat. Bibl. Texts*, I. p. xxx., xxxi., describes *g.* 2 as not really an Old Latin MS. but a vulgate text interpolated or mixed, and *c* as more distinctly an Old Latin MS. [They here represent both Ambrose and the older Africans?]

[4] *De Dca. Orat.* 27. Cf. 25.

'in the matter of temptations, except power be given him
'from God...and power is given to *the* Evil *One* (Malo)
'against us according to our sins (Is. xlii. 25), and again
'"the Lord stirred up *Satan*" (1 K xi. 23,) "an adversary,
'" Rezon," against Solomon himself[1].'

The fulness and the value of this Essay to Church thought are well illustrated not only by Hilary's estimate of it, but by the practical account to which it was soon turned.

A century and three-quarters later[2] the monks of Adrumetum were affected with Pelagian leanings. Three of them visited Saint Augustine and spent Easter with him. As evidence of what catholic doctrine really was, he read them this book, and recommended the study of it to the Monastery, which possessed a copy of it. By it, he says, 'as by some 'invincible dart were transpierced heretics who were yet for to 'come.'

Of the three points which catholic truth held fast against Pelagius he found two distinctly laid down in it, (1) That all holiness is a free gift of the grace of God, and (2) That actual sin is committed by the holiest of men. For Cyprian's exposition, Augustine shews, sets forth how gifts of grace are to be sought for them that have none, and power to persevere for those who have received them.

The third point (3)—That all men are originally sinful— he shews to have been catholic from Cyprian's Epistle to Fidus.

The freedom of that Epistle and of this Treatise from technical language (even the expression *original sin* not occurring in them) vouches for their early date. No fabricator could have extricated himself from terms in which all around him clothed their thoughts. Augustine, with all his fluency and ease, could never have so expressed himself, and as his conceptions hardened and narrowed in his years of contro-

---

[1] *De Dca. Orat.* 25. [2] A.D. 427. Aug. *Ep.* ccxv.

versy[1] his own language and that of his contemporaries became too rigid to allow their ideas to be expressed as once they had been. Yet whilst the phraseology familiar since that controversy is wholly wanting, nothing can exceed the strength and depth and definiteness with which (as brought out by Augustine's analysis) one truth breathes from every line—that truth tacitly so forgotten in ever new forms of error—'That all things which relate to character, by which 'we live rightly, are to be asked of our Father in heaven, and 'that to presume on (the strength of our) free-will is to fall 'from grace.' This is but a solitary instance however of the importance of literal and accurate exposition. No less than thirteen times[2] in his treatises against Pelagians is Augustine able to cite this one small work of him whom, in his high spirits, he calls 'victoriosissimus Cyprianus.'

Lastly. The simplicity of its thought as well as of its diction seems fraught with hints for the preacher as to the true method of doctrinal teaching. As to its substance may we not hope that we are ourselves somewhat nearer to Cyprian than to Augustine? At least we recognise how much of spiritual conflict and misery might have been spared if only the early recognition had lasted on that all good is of God 'the Father of lights,' that 'all holy desires,' even in their first stir, 'proceed from Him,' that all works 'pleasant' to Him are wrought by the grace of Christ and the infusion of His Spirit, that His presence and action are essential to every existence even which we can believe to be real and substantive; that only that subsists which subsists by Him.

---

[1] See Dr W. Bright's Introduction to *Select Anti-Pelagian Treatises of St Augustine.*

[2] In the Benedictine Index (Venet. 1735) add these references: 486 d, 815, 826.

TABLE

SHOWING THE VERBAL DEBTS

TO

TERTULLIAN

IN

CYPRIAN'S TREATISE
DE DOMINICA ORATIONE.

TABLE *shewing the verbal debts to Tertullian*

Tertullianus de Oratione.

XVII. Deus autem non vocis sed cordis auditor est.
   The rest of the chapter of Cyprian strongly, but hardly verbally, resembles Tertullian.

,, ne ipsis quidem manibus sublimius elatis sed temperate ac probe elatis [*sed qu.* levatis], ne vultu quidem in audaciam erecto.
justificatior pharisæo procacissimo discessit.

II. 'Dominus'..præcepit ne quem in terris patrem vocemus nisi quem habemus in cælis.
hoc est quod Israeli exprobratur.. (Es. i. 2)..et oblitos patris denotamus.

III. non quod deceat..quasi si sit et alius de quo.. nisi optemus.. Ceterum quando non sanctum et sanctificatum est per semet ipsum nomen dei cum ceteros sanctificet ex semet ipso?... Id petimus ut sanctificetur in nobis qui in illo sumus..

V. VENIAT QUOQUE REGNUM TUUM...in nobis scilicet. Nam deus quando non regnat?... regni dominici repræsentatio...optamus...non diutius servire.

IV. non quod aliquis obsistat quominus voluntas dei fiat..sed in omnibus petimus fieri voluntatem ejus.... Quæ ut implere possimus, opus est Dei voluntate.

,, Dominus quoque cum substantia passionis infirmitatem carnis demonstrare jam in sua carne voluisset, Pater, inquit, transfer poculum istud ; et recordatus, Nisi quod mea non sed tua fiat voluntas (Lc. xxii. 42).

,, est et illa Dei voluntas quam Dominus administravit prædicando, operando, sustinendo.
ex interpretatione figurata carnis et spiritus nos sumus cælum et terra... sensus petitionis ut in nobis fiat voluntas Dei in terris ut possit scilicet fieri et in cælis. Quid autem Deus vult quam incedere nos &c.

VI. PANEM .. spiritaliter potius intellegamus. Christus enim panis noster est, quia vita Christus et vita panis. Ego sum, inquit, panis vitæ...Tum quod et corpus ejus in pane censetur ; Hoc est corpus meum. Itaque petendo panem quotidianum perpetuitatem postulamus in Christo et individuitatem a corpore ejus.

in Cyprian's Treatise De Dominica Oratione.

Cyprianus de Dominica Oratione.

4. quia Deus non vocis sed cordis auditor est.

6. non adlevatis in cælum inpudenter oculis nec manibus insolenter erectis.

,, cum sibi pharisæus placeret sanctificari hic magis meruit.

9. Dominus..præcepit ne vocemus nobis patrem in terra quod scilicet nobis unus pater qui est in cælis.

10. quæ vox Judæos etiam perstringit et percutit..(Jo. viii. 44; Esai. i. 2)..in quorum exprobrationem..quia eum dereliquerunt.

12. non quod optemus Deo ut sanctificetur orationibus nostris, sed quod petamus a Deo ut nomen ejus sanctificetur in nobis. Ceterum a quo Deus sanctificatur qui ipse sanctificat?...Id petimus et rogamus ut qui in baptismo sanctificati sumus in eo quod esse cœpimus perseveremus.

13. regnum etiam dei repræsentari nobis petimus..'nam Deus quando non regnat'..ut qui in sæculo ante servivimus postmodum..regnemus.

14. nam Deo quis obsistit quominus quod velit faciat? sed quia nobis a diabolo obsistitur quominus per omnia &c.

,, quæ ut fiat in nobis 'opus est Dei voluntate,' id est ope ejus et protectione, quia nemo suis viribus fortis est, sed &c.

,, Dominus infirmitatem hominis quem portabat ostendens ait, Pater, si fieri potest transeat a me calix iste, et...addidit dicens: Veruntamen &c. (Mt. xxvi. 39 *with* Mc. xiv. 36).

15. voluntas autem Dei est quam Christus et fecit et docuit,—then follows an extremely beautiful passage, Cyprian's own.

16. cum corpus e terra et spiritum possideamus e cælo ipsi 'terra et cælum sumus' et in utroque, id est et corpore et spiritu, 'ut Dei voluntas fiat' oramus...hoc precamur et in cælo et in terra voluntatem circa nos Dei fieri : quia hæc est voluntas Dei ut ...

17. petimus...ut quomodo in cælo, id est in nobis, per fidem nostram voluntas Dei facta est ut essemus e cælo, ita et in terra, hoc est in illis credentibus, fiat voluntas Dei.

18. quod potest et spiritaliter et simpliciter intellegi, nam panis vitæ Christus est, et panis hic omnium non est sed noster est...quia Christus eorum qui corpus ejus contingimus panis est. Hunc autem panem dari nobis cottidie postulamus ne qui in Christo sumus et eucharistiam ejus cottidie ad cibum salutis accipimus.... abstenti et non communicantes...a Christi corpore separemur.

VI.	illius hominis, qui provenientibus fructibus ampliationem horreorum et longæ securitatis spatia cogitavit, is ipsa nocte moritur.
VII.	consequens erat, ut observata dei liberalitate etiam clementiam ejus precaremur. Quid enim alimenta proderunt, si illis reputamur revera quasi taurus ad victimam?
	nisi donetur exactio; sicut illi servo dominus debitum remisit.. Idem servus ...tortori delegatur.
VIII.	adjecit ad plenitudinem tam expeditæ orationis... Ergo respondet clausula...
IX.	compendiis pauculorum verborum quot attinguntur... Quid mirum? Deus solus docere potuit quomodo se vellet orari. Ab ipso igitur ordinata religio orationis &c.
I.	..Dei sermo..Jesus Christus dominus noster nobis discipulis Novi Testamenti novam orationis formam determinavit. [Cyprian drops the ambiguous phraseology about Christ being Dei Spiritus.]
XXV.	observatio etiam horarum quarumdam... quæ diei interspatia signant tertia sexta nona quas sollemniores in scripturis invenire est. Primus spiritus sanctus congregatis discipulis hora tertia infusus est. Petrus qua die visionem communitatis omnis in illo vasculo expertus est, sexta hora orandi gratia ascenderat in superiora..ut quod Danieli quoque legimus observatum..
	exceptis utique legitimis orationibus quæ sine ulla admonitione debentur ingressu lucis ac noctis.

IN CYPRIAN'S TREATISE DE DOMINICA ORATIONE. 279

20. sæculares copias cogitantem et se exuberantium fructuum largitate jactantem ... nocte moriturus.
22. post subsidium cibi petitur et venia delicti ut qui a Deo pascitur in Deo vivat..

,, si peccata donentur quæ debita Dominus appellat.
23. qui servus.... in carcerem religatur [*sic H. sed qu.* relegatur?].
27. post ista omnia in consummatione orationis venit clausula universas petitiones et preces nostras collecta brevitate concludens..
28. quid mirum ... si oratio talis est quam Deus docuit qui magisterio suo omnem precem nostram salutari sermone breviavit?... Nam cum Dei sermo Dominus noster Jesus Christus omnibus venerit et colligens doctos pariter et indoctos omni sexu atque ætati præcepta salutis ediderit, præceptorum suorum fecit grande compendium ut in disciplina cælesti discentium &c.

34. in orationibus vero celebrandis invenimus observasse cum Daniele.. horam tertiam sextam nonam ... quæ horarum spatia jam pridem spiritaliter determinantes adoratores Dei statutis et legitimis ad precem temporibus serviebant.. hora tertia descendit Spiritus sanctus.. item Petrus hora sexta in tectum superius ascendens signo pariter et voce Dei monentis instructus est, ut omnes ad gratiam salutis admitteret...
35. .. recedente item sole ac die cessante necessario rursus orandum est.

On the Characteristics and Genuineness of the De Dominica Oratione.

IT has been contended that the treatise 'Of the Lord's Prayer' is later than Cyprian, on grounds which I hope to extricate fairly from the discursive handling the question has received. The reply might be scarcely worth making but for the interesting characteristics which come out by the way.

It has been alleged

I. That the treatise betrays an acquaintance with the commentary of Chromatius of Aquileia who died about 406 A.D.

II. That its language on 'Daily Bread' is more 'Sacramental' (i) than that of Chromatius, (ii) than that of Gregory Nyssene or Chrysostom, who probably represent the prevailing view of the fourth century, (iii) and than is consistent with Augustine's doubt as to the sacramental force of the petition[1].

III. That Venantius Fortunatus, Bishop of Poitiers in the sixth century, who uses Tertullian's treatise on the Lord's Prayer, does not use that of Cyprian, which his predecessor Hilary had commended[2].

I. On the first head, I will accept for comparison the passages, printed after this note, from Tertullian (*de Orat.* c. 4), Chromatius (*Tractat.* xiv. 4 *in S. Matt. Ev.*), and Cyprian (*de Dca. Orat.* 14—17), on the words 'Fiat Voluntas Tua,' &c. The selection (however undesignedly) is an unfavourable test-passage. Resemblances are likely to be fewer on this petition than elsewhere, since Chromatius is expounding the common reading 'As in heaven so in earth' while the Africans explain their own form 'Thy will be done in heaven and in earth.' The comparison however yields abundant evidence that Chromatius had studied Cyprian, not Cyprian Chromatius. A question is put which, if accurately worked out, would lead us right. 'How could Chromatius, if he were making use of 'Cyprian, have escaped introducing ideas that Cyprian had taken from

---

[1] E. J. Shepherd's *Fourth Letter to Dr Maitland*, 1853.

He further observes that if his 'arguments are cogent and conclusive,' Cyprian becomes 'an important witness against *many* Augustinian writings.'

That is true. For example the following works of Augustine would be forgeries in whole or in part—*Contra duas Epistolas Pelagianorum; Contra Julianum Pelagianum; De Correptione et Gratia; De dono perseverantiæ; Ep.* 215, which accompanied his book *De Gratia et Libero Arbitrio; De Prædestinatione Sanctorum,* and *Ep.* 217, in which books at least 14 passages of our treatise are quoted, woven in, and commented on in a way often essential to the structure.

[2] Hilar. *Comment. in Matth.* c. v. 1; Venant. Fortunat. *Miscell.*, lib. x. c. 1, *Exposit. Orationis Domini.*

'Tertullian? How account for the elimination of so much that is Ter-
'tullianistic?' The answer is that, condensed and prosaic as Chromatius
is, he does *not* 'escape.' Of the rich profusion of Tertullian's ideas
Chromatius reproduces few. But some few he has; and *each one* of these
has adhering to it something which Cyprian had added. Again not one
'Tertullianistic idea' is reproduced in Chromatius which is not in Cyprian,
or without Cyprian's stamp on it. It follows that Chromatius has been
acquainted with Tertullian's treatise *through Cyprian's*—at least, through
some treatise which has handled Tertullian on the same subject in the
same manner exactly as our *De Dominica Oratione* does.

To confine ourselves for proof to this one short and unfavourable
passage:

1. Tertullian is shewing how it is we can sensibly *pray* for God's
irresistible will to be done: 'Fiat Voluntas Tua...non quod aliquis *obsistat
quominus* Voluntas Dei fiat...sed *in omnibus petimus* fieri Voluntatem
Ejus.' Cyprian generally tries to make Tertullian more elegant and more
clear. There was an inartificial imperfectness in merely repeating,
instead of incidentally explaining, the words *Voluntas Dei fiat*, while
the rough *in omnibus* left the difficulty where it was. For the difficulty lies exactly in apprehending how the Divine Will can fail to be
operative *in all*. Cyprian therefore has 'Nam Deo quis *obsistit quominus*
quod velit faciat?...sed quia *nobis* a diabolo *obsistitur quominus per omnia*
noster animus atque actus Deo obsequatur, oramus et *petimus* ut fiat *in
nobis* Voluntas Dei.'

Now Chromatius comes in; takes Cyprian's *quod velit faciat;* and
whereas Cyprian, with *in omnibus* before him, had written *per omnia in
nobis*, Chromatius finds the *per omnia* unnecessary, drops it; retains
(Tertullian's and) Cyprian's *obsistere* and Cyprian's *oramus*, but gives
of all Tertullian's context not a syllable which is not in Cyprian. Says
Chromatius 'Non *enim* quisquam est qui *obsistere* et contradicere Deo
possit, ne *quod velit faciat*...sed ut *in nobis* voluntas Ejus fiat *oramus*.'
Anyone of the slightest skill in composition sees that Cyprian is the
middle term between Tertullian and Chromatius.

2. Tertullian says God's Will is 'that we should walk after His
discipline.' He says nothing about Faith or Believing. Cyprian introduces it among many other points,—'stabilitas in fide,' 'per fidem,'
'credentibus,'—of which last more presently. Chromatius makes it the
first point in his definition 'Voluntas Dei est, ut *toto corde ei credentes*
hæc quæ fieri præcipit impleamus,' and more. Any master of style would,
I think, pronounce that a writer working *from* Chromatius must have
made more distinct use of his *credere* and *credulitas* than the book we
ascribe to Cyprian has done. It is absent in Tertullian, oblique in
Cyprian, express in Chromatius. And it is so important that once stated
it must have been re-stated.

3. Tertullian has here the truly Tertullianesque expression 'ex inter-

pretatione figurata carnis et spiritus nos sumus cælum et terra.' There he leaves it, downflung for readers to think about. What did he mean by *nos?* Each individual, compounded of flesh and spirit? or the world of carnally minded and spiritually minded men? Cyprian explains the petition on the first hypothesis, to mean 'That God's will may be done in our body and in our spirit.' He then gives the other alternative (potest et sic intelligi), viz. that 'quomodo in cælo, id est in nobis, per fidem nostram Voluntas Dei facta est,...ita et in terra, hoc est in illis credentibus, fiat Voluntas Dei,' gliding thus into an explanation of the other meaning. 'That they whom just before he describes as *qui* adhuc *terra* sunt et *necdum cælestes,* &c. may begin *esse cælestes* ex aqua et spiritu nati.'

Now both these mystical interpretations have arisen from the Africans' form. To pray that God's Will 'might be done in heaven' implied to them that Heaven was a region where it was not yet done to perfection. Hence it could not to them (as we saw) mean the Heavenly Hosts, but rather the highest part of man, his regenerate spirit, or else the converted part of the world. This interpretation could not have arisen where the reading 'sicut in cælo' prevailed—'cælum' being then the region where it is done exemplarily in contrast to earth.

How does Chromatius proceed? He has the true reading and he has Cyprian's comment. To him Cyprian's first alternative is out of the question. No man could apply it to the true reading. No man could pray 'that God's will may be done in his flesh *as it is in his* spirit.' He is obliged to omit this. But the second alternative of Cyprian will fit well enough. Therefore to his own sensible explanation as to the Angels he adds 'Vel certe... 'ut sicut in cælo, id est in sanctis et *cælestibus* hominibus, Dei Voluntas 'impletur; ita quoque in *terra,* id est in his *qui necdum crediderunt,*' &c.

Here again it is impossible to doubt that Cyprian is the *middle term,* and that it is owing to no one but him that Chromatius has dropped the first and true idea of what Tertullian meant by making '*heaven and earth*' a figurative equivalent for '*us,*' and taken a less harsh suggestion of what it could mean.

Tertullian gives his mystic rendering of 'cælum et terra' second of his five points on this petition. Cyprian moves it to last. There Chromatius has it also, and expunges the poetry which Cyprian had left in.

4. The reader has no doubt noticed a singular variant in the last clause. Where Cyprian has *in illis credentibus* (undoubtedly the true reading—our three manuscripts of this treatise which are of the first order have no negative), Chromatius has *in his qui necdum crediderunt.* It is something singular that just this passage should have been lighted on, for did a shadow of doubt linger as to which was the original writer, the evidence that Chromatius has here marked an obscurity in what was before him and avoided it by a turn of expression, would suffice to dispel it. Clearly the two passages are not independent. Whichever is original, the other is a copy.

Now, no one could have misapprehended the Chromatian prayer that 'God's will may be done *in his qui necdum crediderunt.*' No one would have reproduced it in the Cyprianic form '*in illis credentibus.*' But the Cyprianic form *might* cause hesitation—'Ut quomodo in cælo, 'id est in nobis per fidem nostram, Voluntas Dei facta est, ut essemus e 'cælo, ita et in terra, hoc est in illis *credentibus*, fiat Voluntas Dei.' It was natural to see how Cyprian's participle might be misunderstood; how it might not be perceived that by *in illis credentibus* Cyprian meant 'in '*them* (as opposed to *in nobis*), upon their believing, being converted or 'beginning to believe,' and since at present they are *not believers*, simply to express that one point first. Chromatius accordingly puts it into unmistakeable form 'qui necdum crediderunt.' Augustine similarly has explained by paraphrase the expression of Cyprian, which would have been needless if a negative had been there. Of course *before believing*, when men 'become heavenly,' they are non-believers; accordingly he has '*ita et in eis qui non credunt et ob hoc adhuc terra sunt.* Quid ergo 'oramus pro nolentibus credere nisi ut Deus in illis operetur et velle[1].' H. Grave was actually misled as to the participial use and inserted *nondum*, F. Morel *non*, as if 'in illis credentibus' did or could mean 'in those believing,' and Hartel has given us the startling conjecture 'in illis cred*ere nol*entibus'—which comes indeed from Augustine, but not from the sentence which paraphrases Cyprian.

Cyprian uses participles familiarly in this appositional condensed way, and in the same phrase has 'cælestes ex aqua et spiritu nati.' There is no indication that Augustine or Chromatius missed the Latin, like the editors; but since no one would have altered the clear Chromatian into the difficult Cyprianic, it is certain that Chromatius either applied to the Cyprianic the same remedy which other creditable men hit upon, or (if anyone thinks *necdum* or *nol*entibus genuine) that he had before him an older text than we have a trace of, in which case Augustine, his contemporary, had it too. In either case our *De Dominica Oratione* is older than Chromatius and was before his eyes as he wrote[2].

II. We now come to the second objection to the genuineness of Cyprian on the Lord's Prayer—The strength of the Eucharistic language.

(i) This is admitted to be quite in consonance with the 'other

---

[1] *De Prædest. Sanct.* viii. 15.

[2] I must not drag my readers through a refutation of Mr Shepherd's secondary difficulties. Can he be himself serious when he asks us to account for Chromatius not having reproduced two particular passages of Tertullian? However they are two which Cyprian has transferred from their context to new heads (*de Orat.* 3 and 5, which are to be found in *de Dca. Orat.* 17 and 19). There are scores of Tertullian's ideas in Cyprian for which Chromatius finds no room. The point is, Chromatius knows no Tertullian except what has been restamped by Cyprian.

writings' attributed to Cyprian and with 'that of the suspicious Firmilian.' If Chromatius were less strong (which is not so evident) this would not at that stage of thought be conclusive as to mere earliness of date.

'Christ is our Bread of Life.' 'Our daily Communion is a daily Reception of Him.' 'We pray that we may not through the coming in (*intercedente*) of any grievous sin be separated from the Body of Christ'—*a corpore Christi separemur*. Such is the Cyprianic gloss on Tertullian's forceful word 'in asking daily bread we claim continuance in Christ and undividedness from His Body'—*individuitatem a corpore ejus*. Now Chromatius repeats Cyprian almost word for word, substituting *interveniente* for *intercedente*, a word of double meaning, and *peccato*, as more general, for *graviore delicto*. Augustine surely echoes the same gloss when he has '*Sic vivamus ne ab illo altari separemur*.' Here as before Cyprian's place in the chain is distinct[1].

(ii) To pass to the 'conjecture from the commentaries of Gregory of Nyssa and Chrysostom, that in the Oriental church the petition was considered as originally intended by our Lord to express *only what it primarily means*, and that such was the prevailing interpretation in the fourth century,' which probably 'was the case in the West also.'

The truth is that the fathers of the Antioch school had nothing but the realistic explanation to offer, because they accepted Origen's erroneous derivation of ἐπιούσιος as meaning 'Bread for our Substance,' but rejected, as their wont was, his spiritualised mystic view of 'Substance' as the Essence of Our Being. The Bread prayed for necessarily was to them only the Nurture of our Material Substance[2].

The Western current of interpretation steadily kept to the rightly derived rendering 'Daily.' It also never from Tertullian (our earliest witness) onward failed to see an Eucharistic reference here. Jerome's rendering 'supersubstantial' was long before it partially displaced 'daily,' but it was Eucharistic still.

Thus then while the Eastern view was realistic in the fourth century only under a reaction from a mysticism far exceeding that of the West, the view in this treatise occupies the very position which Cyprian should occupy in the universally Eucharistic interpretation of the West.

(iii) Augustine's view would be stated accurately thus. In his treatise 'Of the Sermon on the Mount' he will not *limit* the petition to either earthly subsistence or to the Eucharistic gift; his reasons for not confining it to the latter being that Orientals do not receive It 'daily,' and that Occidentals use the prayer many times a day *after* reception. Nevertheless he allows this as one of the three senses which we may combine; that which he prefers being God's Spiritual Word. Yet in

---

[1] Chromatius' words are: ne aliquo interveniente peccato a corpore Domini separemur. *Tract.* xiv. 5.

[2] Dr Lightfoot on ἐπιούσιος, App. to *Fresh Revision of New Testament*, p. 209 &c. (2nd Ed. 1872).

three different sermons[1] he gives the prominence to the Eucharistic sense. 'The Faithful know what it is that they receive in the Eucharist' —'so then the Eucharist is our Daily Bread.' The handling of Augustine, more analytical and yet more mystical, is distinctly in a later mood than the simply moral tone of Cyprian.

On this head it is added[2] that 'It is natural to suppose that the 'Sacramental Interpretation [of Daily Bread], when first introduced, 'would follow, not precede, the Primary Meaning; and when it is found to 'precede it, that the stream of time had rolled further down—' *i.e.* as the 'Primary Meaning' precedes the 'Sacramental Interpretation' in Chromatius and follows after it in the Cyprianic treatise, therefore the latter is a later work. This assumption would make Chromatius early indeed, for Tertullian's authorship of his *De Oratione* is not disputed, and Tertullian gives *first* the Spiritual and the Sacramental sense and then what he calls the 'Carnal' sense which is Mr Shepherd's 'Primary Meaning.'

III. Why so late an author as Venantius Fortunatus (whose references would prove nothing as to date) does not, in his unfinished treatise on the Lord's Prayer, refer to Cyprian's expressly, I cannot say, nor need we enquire. He was not bound to use the same materials as his predecessor. And if Hilary's reference to the treatise is no argument for its genuineness, surely the silence of Venantius is no argument against it. But I think Venantius is *not* untinged with Cyprian. On such a subject coincidences are natural, but some resemblances here seem to be more than coincidences. It must be remembered that Venantius' *object* is different. He writes very compressedly, but more theologically. For instance, he says in speaking of the word Father, 'we be not sons in the mode of the 'Person of our Lord Jesus Christ, because He was born of His Own 'Substance,...yet through grace of the Only Begotten we have attained to 'be made Adoptive.' So again when Cyprian says the Jews are not Sons[3], Venantius says 'the Arian, the Jew, the Photinian, the Manichee, the Sabellian, and other plagues'; and when speaking of the Will of God, goes at length into the question of the erroneousness of the 'Human Will.' Compare however what both say as to the petition 'Hallowed be Thy name' being a prayer for *Perseverance*. Or compare the words of *de Dca. Orat.* 13 on 'Thy Kingdom come,' Potest...ipse *Christus esse regnum Dei quem venire cottidie cupimus, cujus adventus* &c. quia in illo *regnaturi sumus*, with Ven. Fortunatus (col. 317 A, Migne, *Patr. Lat.* v. 88) Adveniat *regnum tuum, hoc est Christus Dominus* nobis adveniat quem *quotidie* sanctorum chorus veneranter *expectat*, in cujus promissione se confidunt justi *regnare*. Or on 'fiat Voluntas Tua,' *de Dca. Orat.* 14 Nam Deo quis *obsistit quominus quod velit faciat?* sed quia *nobis a diabolo obsistitur*...opus est Dei voluntate, id est ope ejus et protectione, quia

---

[1] Aug. *Serm.* 56, 57, 58.   [2] Shepherd's *Fourth Letter*, p. 37.
[3] *De Dca. Orat.* 13.

nemo suis viribus fortis est sed Dei indulgentia et misericordia tutus est, with Fortun. (col. 317 A and col. 318) Non id fit quia aliquis potuit *resistere* ejus voluntati *ut non faceret* aliquando *quod voluit* omnipotens...sed ut in nobis impleatur ejus voluntas ut operetur, *quoniam, adversario resistente*, nos voluntatem ejus implere non possumus nisi patrocinio ejus muniamur.

Or again, observe how in commenting on *cælum et terra* we have, besides the usual interpretation, the further one that the flesh may do the works of the Spirit, and the expression 'nos videmur facti esse *cælestes* per baptismum'—purely Cyprianic and introduced with a softening phrase. In these passages the order of the thoughts is Cyprian's, the peculiarities are Cyprian's, and the Tertullianesque handling of the third petition is recast after Cyprian. There can be little doubt that Fortunatus was in some shape acquainted with Cyprian, though his aim and his touch are different.

I may observe further that Ambrose[1] in his commentary on S. Luke passes in silence the first four verses of chapter xi., omitting the Lord's Prayer altogether. This would seem to be inexplicable except for the existence of some standard treatise. Whether there was such a treatise appears from Hilary's *Commentary on Matt.* v. 1, 'De orationis sacra-'mento necessitate nos commentandi Cyprianus vir sanctæ memoriæ 'liberarit.'

It is easy with a careless sponge to stain a Numidian Marble. It may take a month's work to extract that stain. And when it is done a fanciful retina may see the blur still. In the history of scholarship I know nothing (more honest and nothing) more wanton, than the sharp guesses and insinuations which, without real devotedness in research, without delicacy of perception, only with an imitative ring of criticism, have been syringed over some of the noblest essays of a great author.

[1] Ambros. *Exposit. Evang. sec. Luc.*, lib. vii. 87.

Comparison elucidating the dates.

[*The asterisks, obeli, &c. call attention to the more detached similarities of phrase.*]

Tertullianus, *de Oratione*, c. 4.	Cyprianus, *de Dominica Oratione*, cc. 14—17.	Chromatius, *Tractat.*, xiv. 4.
1.] Secundum hanc formam subjungimus: Fiat voluntas tua in cælis et in terra, non quod aliquis obsistat, quominus voluntas Dei fiat, et ei successum voluntatis suæ oremus, sed in omnibus petimus fieri voluntatem ejus;	1.] Addimus quoque et dicimus: Fiat voluntas tua in cælo et in terra, non ut Deus faciat quod vult, sed ut nos facere possimus quod Deus vult. nam Deo quis obsistit quominus quod velit faciat? sed quia nobis a diabolo obsistitur quominus per omnia noster animus adque actus Deo obsequatur, oramus et petimus ut fiat in nobis voluntas Dei: quæ ut fiat in nobis* 'opus est Dei voluntate,' id est ope ejus et protectione, quia nemo suis viribus fortis est sed Dei indulgentia et misericordia tutus est.	1.] Dehinc ait: Fiat voluntas tua sicut in cælo et in terra. par quoque et hic intelligentiæ ratio est. non enim quisquam est qui obsistere et contradicere Deo possit, ne quod velit faciat; cum voluntate ejus et in cælo et in terra cuncta consistant; sed, ut in nobis voluntas ejus fiat, oramus.
2 = C. 5.] Ex interpretatione enim figurata carnis et spiritus nos§ sumus cælum et terra. quanquam, etsi simpliciter intellegendum est idem tamen est sensus petitionis, ut in nobis fiat voluntas Dei in terris, ut possit scilicet fieri et in cælis. quid autem Deus vult quam incedere nos secundum suam disciplinam**? petimus ergo substantiam et facultatem voluntatis suæ subministret nobis, ut†† salvi simus et in cælis et in terris, quia summa est voluntatis ejus salus eorum quos adoptavit.	2 = T. 5.] Denique et Dominus† infirmitatem hominis quem portabat ostendens ait: pater, si fieri potest, transeat a me calix iste, et exemplum discipulis suis distribuens, ut non voluntatem suam sed Dei faciant, addidit dicens: verumtamen non quod ego volo sed quod tu vis. et alio loco dicit‡: non descendi de cælo ut faciam voluntatem meam sed voluntatem ejus qui misit me...	Cyp. 2 = Tert. 5. Not in Chrom.]
3.] Est et illa Dei voluntas quam Dominus administravit prædicando, operando, sustinendo. Si enim ipse pronuntiavit‡ non suam, sed patris facere se voluntatem, sine dubio, quæ faciebat, ea	3.] Voluntas autem Dei est quam Christus et fecit et docuit. humilitas in conversatione, stabilitas in fide, in factis justitia, in operibus misericordia, in moribus disciplina**, injuriam facere non nosse et factam posse tolerare...	3.] Voluntas autem Dei est, ut toto corde ei credentes hæc quæ fieri præcipit impleamus. de qua voluntate Dei Apostolus testatur dicens: *Voluntas Dei est sanctificatio vestra ut abstineatis vos a*

Tertullianus, *de Orat.*, c. 4.

erat voluntas patris, ad quæ nunc nos velut ad exemplaria provocamur, ut et prædicemus et operemur et sustineamus ad mortem usque. quæ ut implere possimus* opus est Dei voluntate.

4.] Item dicentes, fiat voluntas tua, vel eo nobis bene optamus, quod nihil mali sit in Dei voluntate, etiam si quid pro meritis cujusque secus inrogatur. jam hoc dicto ad sufferentiam nosmetipsos præmonemus.

5 = C. 2.] Dominus† quoque cum sub instantiam passionis infirmitatem carnis demonstrare jam in sua carne voluisset: Pater, inquit, transfer poculum istud, et recordatus, nisi quod mea non, sed tua fiat voluntas. ipse erat voluntas et potestas patris, et tamen ad demonstrationem sufferentiæ debitæ voluntati se patris tradidit.

(*Reifferscheid.*)

Cyprianus, *de Dca. Orat.*, cc. 14—17.

exhibere ... in quæstione fiduciam qua congredimur, in morte patientiam qua coronamur: ...hoc est præceptum Dei facere, hoc est voluntatem patris implere.

4.] Fieri autem petimus voluntatem Dei in cælo et in terra...nam cum corpus e terra et spiritum possideamus e cælo§ ipsi 'terra et cælum sumus,' et in utroque, id est et corpore et spiritu, ut Dei voluntas fiat oramus. est enim inter carnem et spiritum conluctatio...et idcirco cottidianis immo continuis orationibus hoc precamur...

5 = T. 2.] Potest et sic intellegi...ut quoniam mandat et monet Dominus etiam inimicos diligere et pro his quoque qui nos persecuntur orare. (cf. Tert. 3.) petamus et pro illis qui adhuc terra sunt et necdum cælestes esse cœperunt ut et circa illos voluntas Dei fiat...ut precem pro omnium †† salute faciamus ut quomodo in cælo, id est in nobis, per fidem nostram voluntas Dei facta est ut essemus e cælo, ita et in terra, hoc est in illis credentibus, fiat voluntas Dei, ut qui adhuc sunt prima nativitate terreni incipiant esse cælestes ex aqua et spiritu nati.

(*Hartel*[2].)

Chromatius, *Tractat.*, xiv. 4.

carnalibus concupiscentiis (1 Th. iv. 3). de quo et Dominus in Evangelio locutus est dicens: *Hæc est voluntas patris mei qui misit me ut omnis qui videt Filium et credit in eo habeat vitam æternam* (Jo. vi. 40).

4.] Cum ergo dicimus: Fiat voluntas tua sicut in cælo et in terra: hoc oramus, id est ut sicuti Dei voluntas ab angelis fideliter custoditur in cælis ita quoque a nobis religiosa ac fideli devotione [1] semper servetur in terra. quæ voluntas ut in nobis rite possit impleri, sine intermissione[1] divinæ dignationis auxilium postulandum est.

5.] Vel certe Fiat voluntas tua sicut in cælo et in terra; ut sicut in cælo, id est in sanctis et cælestibus hominibus, Dei voluntas impletur; ita quoque in terra, id est in his qui necdum crediderunt, per credulitatem fidei et veritatis cognitionem, ut Dei fiat voluntas oramus.

[1-1] Three lines omitted *absque sensu*, apparently by a printer's slip at first in Grynæus, *Monum. P. Orthodoxographa*, v. II. p. 1214, 1569; La Bigne, *Max. Bibl. Vet. Patr.* v. v. p. 987, Lugd. 1677; and Galland. *B. V. P.* vol. VIII. p. 348, Venet. 1772; but given in first Basle Edition 1528, in Braida, Utini, 1816, q.v. and Migne.

[2] Hartel's text, except in his infelicitous conjecture *credere nolentibus* for *credentibus*, see p. 271, n. 2.

V. *Ritual.*

1. *The Mixed Cup.*

The last question[1] which comes within the present cycle of Cyprian's activity was that of Ritual.

He has worked out the application of the new Christian principles to the treatment of Suffering; to the purification of the passions of Resentment and Sorrow; and to intelligent Communion with the Father. Time brought also round some necessities for clearness in the Ritual in which the new principles had tacitly embodied themselves. A little later, and it assumed such proportions as to dwarf for a time the rest, and to leave the one blot on Cyprian's glory.

A material change had been introduced some time before

---

[1] Probably not 'last' chronologically, though Rettberg (p. 145, n. 1) wishes to transfer *Ep.* 63 to a date as late as the last persecution, since the expression 'cum mediocritatem nostram *semper* humili et verecunda moderatione *teneamus*' *Ep.* 63. 2 postulates time for the exhibition of such qualities. Ritschl, pp. 241, 242, thinks the claim to modesty and humility more characteristic of the beginnings of an episcopate. There is nothing in this. And in an admittedly late letter, *Ep.* 66. 3, Cyprian makes the same claim, 'humilitatem meam et fratres omnes et gentiles quoque norunt et diligunt'; which also the confessors in almost the last letter of all declare to be true; 'omnibus hominibus...in obsequio humilior...' *Ep.* 77. 1. Ritschl's theories drive him to put *Ep.* 63 early, because of its supposed definition of 'ecclesiam,' as 'plebem in ecclesia constitutam,' c. 13—but we have seen that this is no definition.—Cyprian is merely interpreting the water in the mixed chalice to signify the 'ecclesia' 'plebs' or 'populus,' (here including of course the Ministry,) in contradistinction to the wine, as representing the Divinity of the Lord. The truth is that the letter bears no note of date except that the *semper... teneamus* implies *some* time, (as Rettberg,) and that ch. 17 'ad collegas nostros litteras dirigamus ut ubique lex evangelica...servetur et ab eo quod Christus et docuit et fecit non recedatur' implies a well-established position. Persecution seems to be in a simmering state. The doctrine of the sacraments and of the priesthood has been very fully thought out. Si Christus Jesus Dominus et Deus noster ipse est summus sacerdos Dei patris &c....utique ille sacerdos vice Christi vere fungitur qui id quod Christus fecit imitatur &c., (14) si sacerdotes Dei et Christi sumus non invenio quem magis sequi quam Deum et Christum debeamus (18). He speaks in obedience to distinct vision and command. On the whole Pearson's opinion of the place of the Epistle is not ill-founded.

by a number of bishops, and among them perhaps a bishop of Carthage[1], into the Eucharistic offering—the adoption of water instead of wine. There is in this no trace[2] of religious antipathy to wine, such as had been taught ninety years before by Tatian. Not to say that there is no other indication of such teaching hitherto in Africa, the present was, we clearly learn, the mere social timidity of a simple people[3]. Christian wives of heathen husbands, many dependents, and others incurred unworthy suspicions from having the scent of wine about them at an early hour[4]. A compassionate evasion had suffered them to communicate in water.

When scarcity of wine was found to have occasioned the same irregularity at Regensburg, Saint Wolfgang wept so profusely that his recovery was despaired of[5]. The statement that the Norwegians in the fifteenth century received permission from Innocent the Eighth to celebrate in water,

---

[1] *Ep.* 63. 1 '...quidam...non hoc faciunt. 14 in præteritum...ante nos...' 17 'si quis de antecessoribus nostris...non hoc observavit et tenuit.' This word (*quidam*) must be the ground of Pearson's statement that the custom originated with 'some bishop of Carthage,' *Ann. Cypr.* A.D. 253, iii. But if we consider the very official form of the letter, and its address to the senior bishop of the province, the inference is not, I think, so certain. The mood indicates some particular person.

[2] As supposed by F. Münter, *Primord. Eccles. Africanæ*, p. 127; compare M. Leydecker *de Statu Eccles.* v. *de cultu*. Münter quotes, as if it illustrated the point, the 'appendix' c. 52 of Tertullian's *Præscriptio Hæreticorum*—which appendix is a separate work, not African. The Hydro-parastatæ, Aquarii, or 'Water-offerers' were in the 4th century a branch of Tatianists, or Encratites; an Apocrypha-collecting, ascetic, Judaic, Docetic School; see H. L. Mansel, *Gnostic Heresies*, pp. 136, 7. Tillemont, v. II. p. 410. Not one of those unmistakeable marks occurs in Cyprian's account.

[3] *Ep.* 63. 17, 18 simplicitati, simpliciter.

[4] Suspicions not unjustified, if there were many of those who (as Novatian says) held it un-Christian to drink after eating, 'Videas ergo tales *novo genere* adhuc jejunos et jam ebrios,' and possibly at the Eucharist, as he speaks of their 'osculum.' This curious passage leaves it uncertain whether (1) they drank overmuch wine at fasting communions, or took stimulants before them, or (2) whether Novatian himself inclined to the use of water in communion, or (3) whether this was simply a foolish defence of actual vice. Novatian, *de Cibis Jud.* c. vi.

[5] *Acta S. Wolfgangi Ratisponensis* c. 24, ap. Edm. Martène, *de Ant. Eccles. Rit.* I. iii. Art. vii. 32.

on account of the liability of their wine to sourness, is not only denied but quite improbable[1].

Cyprian felt impelled to issue an official letter to Cæcilius of Biltha, not as an offender, but as senior bishop of the Proconsular Province. Cæcilius was one of the most regular attendants in Cyprian's Councils. He had formerly been employed in the suppression of grosser irregularities[2]; and his speech, crossed perhaps with aged virulence, is the first of the unhappy verdicts of the great Council on Baptism.

In the letter now addressed to him by Cyprian the wildness, it must be admitted, of the Biblical interpretations and the looseness of the logic, is equalled only by the quiet insinuating beauty of its style[3], the soundness of its conclusions and its value in evidence[4]. The substance however is to this effect:—

That Wine in the Chalice is essential to the evangelical tradition; to the symbolic sense of the Last Supper; to the fulfilment of antient types; and to the faithful representation of the Lord's own act. It is further apparent that Cyprian and his contemporaries would have regarded the admixture of water as being not indeed equally essential with the presence of Wine, yet in its place essential for the fulfilment of those four necessary conditions. 'Drink ye the Wine which I have mingled for you' he quotes from the Book of Proverbs[5], and then proceeds 'Wisdom declares her Wine to be mingled;

---

[1] Baluze (p. 477) appears to accept it on authority of Raphael Volaterranus, l. 7, p. 150, though even Bp. Jewel states it hesitatingly on the same. Controv. w. Harding, vol. I. pp. 137, 222 Park. Soc. See Baronius, *Annal. Eccles.* A.D. 1490, c. xxii.

[2] p. 47.

[3] Aug. *de Doctrina Christiana*, B. IV. c. xxi. quotes it as a model of the 'submissum dicendi genus.'

[4] *Ep.* 63. Pearson's reasons for assigning it to A.D. 253 are that some expressions indicate a time of persecution, and that Cyprian had been long in office. Dom Maran (*Vit. Cypr.* xxxiii.) rightly thinks them not cogent. But I cannot agree with him that it is to be placed after the controversy on Baptism had broken out. Cyprian's whole soul was then so charged with that subject that he could not have gone so near without allusion to it far plainer than Maran extricates.

[5] Prov. ix. 5.

'foreannounces, that is, with prophetic voice the Lord's Cup 'mingled of Water and Wine, that it may appear that in 'the Lord's Passion that which had been foretold was done[1].' Again 'the Lord taught us by the pattern of His instruc-'tions that the chalice was mingled by conjunction of Wine 'and Water[2]'; and again 'we find that what He ordered is 'not observed by us, unless we too do the same things which 'the Lord did, and similarly mingling the cup, depart not 'from His Divine instructions[3].'—Still such passages cannot fairly be cited as exhibiting a direct decision of Cyprian's that Water absolutely *must* be used as well as Wine, because the immixture of Water was not the exact question before him; and incidental judgments ought not to be alleged in controversy as if they were direct. This is clear from another clause of the last cited section. 'In respect of which' (the incidents of S. Matt. xxvi. 28, 29) we find it was a 'mixed 'chalice which the Lord offered, and that it was the *wine* 'which He called *blood*. Hence it appears that Christ's blood 'is not offered if there be no *wine* in the chalice.'

It is true that he plainly says 'wine alone *cannot* be offered,' and again 'the cup of the Lord *is not* water alone nor wine alone,' but he gives his reason for this assertion, so that the assertion will not be valued (except as distinct evidence of practice) by those to whom the reason does not commend itself. This reason is that the water signifies the People (according to the interpretation of the Apocalyptic Seer that the waters are peoples[4]) while the wine signifies the blood of Christ Himself with Whom His People[5] are blended in inseparable union and conjunction.

---

[1] *Ep.* 63. 5.
[2] *Ep.* 9.
[3] *Ep.* 63. 10.
[4] Apoc. xvii. 15.
[5] *Ep.* 63. 13. This account is adopted by the Council of Tribur A.D. 895, can. xix. and that of Florence A.D. 1439, *Decret. ad Armenos* (Labbe, Mansi, vol. XVIII., Venet. 1773, col. 142, vol. XXXI. 1798, col. 1056), but it is combined by them with the reason attributed to Alexander Bp. of Rome A.D. 109 (*Ep.* 1. 4, spurious of course, Labbe, Mansi, vol. I. Florent. 1759,

The same union is expressed in the Bread itself to which no consistency could be given but by the use of water. The many grains represent the multitudinous partakers who only receive their unity in the one Loaf, the Bread of Heaven[1].

coll. 638, 9), namely the miraculous outflow from the side of Christ. The Council of Trent adopts the interpretation of the *water* meaning the *people*, but judiciously drops the appeal to Saint Alexander. (Session 22, ch. 7.)

'In most liturgies, when the water is mixed with the wine some reference is made to the blood and water which flowed from the Lord's side.'...'The same reason is given generally by the liturgies': Cheetham, who specifies Roman, Mozarabic and Ambrosian as instances. This statement may so easily cause important mistakes that it is well to observe that ten principal liturgies, among them the *Roman*, which direct the mixture, have no allusion to this text. The Syriac Liturgy of S. James, the antient one of Lyons, the Carthusian (perhaps as a survival of antient Lyons) may be added to the other two which have it. The Liturgy of Constantinople pointedly avoids it, for it recites the text (Jo. xix. 34, 35) where the Priest, in the little play which goes on at the Prothesis, stabs the Host 'with the Lance'; the mixture of the chalice follows after this. The Æthiopic pointedly avoids it; its illustration is Cana, and though 'the Blood shed on Golgotha' is named the Water is not. The Gregorian and Gelasian and the Nestorian (Adæus and Maris) do not actually name Water, though the mixture was made, nor do five minor ones given in Renaudot's second volume, pp. 126—163; two others do, pp. 170, 177; but in none of them, I think, is there any allusion to the Effusion.

The parallel must surely have presented itself to Cyprian's '*memoriosa mens*' and so can scarcely have approved itself to him as being true symbolism. He does not however, among the innumerable passages which he bends that way, apply it to Baptism either, as our own Rite does, following the Sarum *Benedictio Fontis* (Maskell, *Mon. Rit.* I. p. 19) which comes from the Gelasian Sacramentary. Muratori, *Lit. Rom. Vet.* t. I. cc. 569, 570. Tertullian thrice applies it to the distinct baptisms of Water and Blood, *de Bapt.* 9, 16, *de Pudic.* 22.

The prayer at the mingling in the Roman Missal carries the symbolism to a higher region—from the congregation to humanity itself, but does this by dressing up the beautiful *Mattins and Vespers collect* of the Nativity in the Gelasian Sacramentary. Muratori (*op. cit.*) I. col. 497 'Deus qui humanæ substantiæ dignitatem et mirabiliter condidisti et mirabilius reformasti; da quæsumus *ut ejus efficiamur in divina* consortes qui nostræ humanitatis fieri dignatus est particeps Christus Filius tuus.' The Missal alters the great words italicised into 'per hujus aquæ et vini mysterium ejus divinitatis esse.'

Whichever symbolism be accepted the act itself of *mingling* seems not to be suitable to any time after the presentation is begun by placing the elements on the πρόθεσις or credence, or at any rate after their removal from it for the oblation.

[1] *Ep.* 63.13'...ut quemadmodum grana multa in unum collecta et conmolita et conmixta panem unum faciunt, sic in Christo qui est panis cælestis unum sciamus esse corpus cui conjunctus sit

Nevertheless, though Cyprian has not given even in these words a declaration on the subject, yet since he lays down[1] that 'the Lord's sacrifice is not celebrated with legitimate conse-'cration except our oblation and sacrifice correspond with His 'Passion,' and as 'legitimate consecration' is assumed to consist in doing what our Lord did, preserving the tradition, representing the Passion, or following its points in symbol, we are compelled to conclude that, although he allowed that the blood of Christ was received through communion in the wine, yet he would not have held that the consecration of wine without water was 'legitimate,' but would have included that practice, however long-standing in any church, under the category of Human Tradition followed in place of Divine Example[2].

Other corollaries of a not unimportant character are immediately inferrible from this Letter-Treatise. The Communion of the Congregation is essential. The absence of the Congregation prevents the Commemorative Mixed Chalice which may be offered in the Family after the Evening Meal from being anything of a true *Dominicum*.

Again, the Morning Hour is the only hour at which the Resurrection[3] (which is the power of the Eucharist) can duly be celebrated; Christ Himself had offered in the

---

noster numerus et adunatus.' This image, which was as his lovers know so favourite and constant an image with Dean Stanley, is the most antient symbolism we have. See the beautiful Eucharistic prayer in the *Teaching of the xii. Apostles*, c. 9, Ὥσπερ ἦν τοῦτο [? τὸ] κλάσμα διεσκορπισμένον ἐπάνω τῶν ὀρέων καὶ συναχθὲν ἐγένετο ἕν, οὕτω συναχθήτω σου ἡ ἐκκλησία ἀπὸ τῶν περάτων τῆς γῆς εἰς τὴν σὴν βασιλείαν. Cf. *Constt. Apost.* vii. c. 26 which omits ἐπάνω τῶν ὀρέων and has εἰς ἄρτος for ἕν.

[1] *Ep.* 63. 10.

[2] *Ep.* 63. 14. Baluze, p. 477, cites an instructive rubric from an antient use of S. Martin's at Tours. 'If by mistake the priest has consecrated unmixed wine, or water without wine, the wine is held to be sacrament, but not the water.' It seems natural that the Monophysite church of Armenia (Martène) should consecrate wine only, but their antiently alleged reason was a passage of Chrysostom *Hom.* 82 (83) in Mt. 26, c. 2. For this usage they were reproved (with a proper explanation of their Chrysostom) in the 32nd canon of the Quini-Sextine Council A.D. 692, but keep it still.

[3] *Ep.* 63. 16.

VI. V.   RITUAL.—THE AGE OF BAPTISM.   295

Evening solely in order to mark the close of the old order and to merge the Passover Ritual into ours.

Thus in the Celebration of the Eucharist no less than in the Theory of Orders points arise in which no modern community can be strictly said to be at one with the Cyprianic Church.

2. *The Age of Baptism.*

The Ritual of another Sacrament was also now coming into the field, though not yet in all its import. In September A.D. 253 or late in the summer of that year[1] it was considered safe to hold the Bishops' meeting omitted at Easter. The tumult of military faction and perhaps the succession of Valerian, whose household is described as a 'Church of God'[2], so leavened was it with Christianity, gave this breathing-space. Sixty-six bishops met in Carthage.

A record of two of their deliberations is preserved in their letter to Fidus a Bishop. He had found it in his heart to petition that an excommunication prematurely removed from a repentant presbyter might be renewed[3]. He also found it in his heart to request that a canon might be passed prohibiting the baptism of infants under eight days old. The mind of the Bishops, Cyprian replies, was 'far other' than his; 'not a man agreed with him'; they 'judged that God's pity and grace could be denied to no child of man.' Fidus shrank from bestowing the Kiss of Peace on so young a babe, as if it were yet unclean. Cyprian replies that the fresh handiwork of God claims only deeper reverence: in it we discern, we kiss His own creative hands. It is only to our sight that birth begins existence. To God the soul has lived before. Judaic forms of uncleanness were but types, and are for ever

A.D. 253.
A.U.C. 1006.
Coss. Imp. Cæsar C. Vibius Afinius Gallus Veldumrianus L. Volusianus P. F. Aug. II.
...[Valerius?] Maximus.

---

[1] The date of *Ep.* 64 is discussed p. 224.
[2] Dion. Al. ap. Eus. vii. 10.
[3] Sup. p. 231.

at an end. Perhaps this Eighth Day itself had been assigned to circumcision in order to give to a carnal rite some touch of spiritual association with the Resurrection Day, the First of the New Week. The first weeping of the 'helpless new-born babe' sounded to the heathen like a foreboding of the misery of living, to the Christian ear it was a prayer and an appeal.

These beautiful thoughts helped the straightforward reasoning to shatter in Christian spirits the petty pleas of Fidus, with whatever of Judaizing lay behind them.

With this letter in his hand[1], at Carthage upon S. Gaudentius' day, a hundred and sixty years later, in the Basilica where lay Perpetua and Felicitas[2], Augustine defended against Pelagius the principles of Infant Baptism.

And we may remember in a yet earlier essay how there can be nothing broader and freer than Cyprian's recognition that Christian Baptism is truly a re-assertion of our human Childhood and Sonship to God. "*All* who by the hallowing "force of baptism come to the gift and *patrimony* of God, "there, by the healthful laver's grace, put off the 'old man,' "are remade by the Holy Spirit, and in a second nativity are "cleansed from the old infectious plague spots[3]."

---

[1] Aug. *de Gestis Pelagii* xi. § 25. See also *contra ii. Epistolas Pelagg.* lib. IV. c. viii. § 23.

[2] Basilica Majorum ? Majorini ? Major. The MSS. of Victor Vitensis *Hist. Persecut.* i. 3 have *Majorum*, except W (Vindobon. sec. xi.) and L (Berolin. sec. xii.), but Petschenig has thought fit to prefer in this place the reading of these two, *Majorem*. The titles of Aug. *Sermm.* 34 *Ad Majores* and 165 and 294 support *Majorum*, but 258 has *Majorem*. It is impossible not to remember the recently explored great Basilica of Carthage close outside the walls, with its nine aisles, its large baptistery and vast semicircular narthex and trilobate 'martyrium.'

[3] *De Habitu Virgg.* 23 '*Omnes* quidem qui ad divinum munus et *patrimonium* baptismi sanctificatione perveniunt *hominem* illic *veterem* gratia lavacri salutaris *exponunt* et innovati Spiritu Sancto a *sordibus contagionis antiquæ* iterata nativitate purgantur.' Compare also *De Habitu Virgg.* 2 'scientes quod templa Dei sint membra nostra *ab omni fæce contagionis antiquæ* lavacri vitalis sanctificatione purgata.' I must with most editions and seven of Baluze's codices, in spite of S, W, D and Hartel, maintain *patrimonium*, which Goldhorn restores and Baluze (p. 533) allows. 'Divinum munus et patrium' is not Cyprianic order or sense.

Objection to Council III on account of its Antipelagianism.

It has been ironically observed that the question of Fidus 'gives 'Cyprian the opportunity of making a thoroughly antipelagian dis-'course'—a wild statement and misleading to those incapable of following it up. The letter has been treated as spurious on the alleged grounds, first that it resembles the later Canon CX of the African Code, and secondly that its language shews it to be later than the Pelagian controversy[1].

Now, that CXth canon is against those who object to Infant Baptism, or hold it to be a sort of dramatic fiction, on the ground that there is no original sin[2].

But Fidus has not a word either for or against the doctrine of Original Sin. He approved of Infant Baptism; only, for certain small reasons, not till the infant was eight days old. And the answer observes that besides the irrelevance and unkindness of his ideas, the innocent child was at least as worthy of acceptance as a sin-laden man: a not very antipelagian doctrine.

Then, as to the language; it is impossible that it can have been penned after the Pelagian controversy. There is not one technical term in it[3]. So far as verbal likeness goes the Cyprianic fathers might have almost seemed rather against the Augustinian thought. This defines original sin to be '*both* another's *and* our own.' They say 'The sins remitted to the infant are the sins of others, *not* his own.' Thus nothing can be more different than the purview of the canon and the epistle except the language itself; and while no forger after the controversy could have helped using recognised terms, we have in the language of Cyprian just the clear but untechnical style which marks the catholic doctrine in an age prior to a controversy[4], but which cannot perhaps for ages afterward be recurred to as adequate and used accordingly.

---

[1] Shepherd, pp. 31, 32, and p. 11, letter 2.

[2] προγονικὴ ἁμαρτία —ὅπερ ἤλκυσαν ἐκ τῆς ἀρχαιογονίας Justel. *Cod. Cann. Eccles. Afric.* 110

[3] No 'Originale Peccatum,' 'Peccatum originis' or 'Contagium Peccati.' *Contagium mortis antiquæ* is the true but *untechnical* consequence of our first birth.

[4] Precisely the same treatment of the same doctrines with the same freedom from technicality exists in the *de Op. et Eleem.* and *de Mortalit.* ap. Aug. *Contra ii. Epp. Pelagg.* l. IV. c. viii. § 21, and see the list of ancient authors to the same effect quoted by Routh, *R. S.* vol. III. pp. 148, 9.

CHAPTER VII.

THE ROMAN CHAIR.

I.

The End of CORNELIUS.

WE have anticipated by three months at Carthage a great change which had occurred at Rome. Cornelius had been suddenly[1] banished to Centumcellæ—that Città Vecchia which has been so fateful for his line. The first intention had been to isolate him. But his apprehension was the signal for a crowd of the Lapsed[2] to revoke and expiate their Denial. They thus justified Cyprian's policy of penance with hope of restitution[3]. They were hurried away with him as were also the Confessors who had lately escaped to him from the influence of Novatian. Their numbers were such as to impress at least themselves, and perhaps the government, with the idea that, if they had been so minded, they might have made something at least of a stand. 'It was a confessorship of the whole church of Rome[4].' Such an exile then was a happy reunion of extreme factions, and breathing

---

[1] Repentina persecutio...sæcularis potestas subito proruperit, *Ep.* 61. 3. Cf. *Ep.* 60. 2 'quasi minus paratos et minus cautos.'

[2] Quot illic Lapsi gloriosa confessione sunt restituti...nec jam stare ad criminis veniam sed ad passionis coronam, *Ep.* 60. 2. Confessorem populum, *ibid.* 1. Compare the *Liberian Catalogue*, '...confessores qui se separaverunt a Cornelio cum Maximo presbytero, qui cum Moyse fuit, ad ecclesiam sunt reversi. Post hoc Centumcellis *expulsi*. Ibi cum gloria dormicionem accepit.' There is no ground for accepting Lipsius' alteration to *pulsus*, p. 123. On the contrary a banishment on a large scale is intended, such as Cyprian describes.

[3] Ipso dolore pænitentiæ facti ad prœlium fortiores, *Ep.* 60. 2.

[4] Adversarius ... intellexit ... Christi milites...nec repugnare contra impugnantes, cum occidere innocentibus nec nocentem liceat, *Ep.* 60. 2. Ecclesia omnis Romana confessa, *Ep.* 60. 1.

this consolation Cornelius died 'with glory' in June A.D. 253[1].

The Antipope was too inconspicuous to the Magistracy to be in danger. In Cyprian's eyes his immunity otherwise unexplained ought to have been to him evidence of his Divine rejection. *Quid ad hæc Novatianus?* The outburst was the open seal of heaven's favour and hell's hostility to the true priest and people, and was clearly designed for this very end[2].

Cornelius has been ranked as a martyr by the church of Rome since the middle of the fourth century, and his festival kept with Cyprian's on the 14th of September. The statement is first found in Jerome[3] that 'they suffered on the same day though not in the same year.'

In the contemporary sense of the word a Martyr he was, as dying in exile[4]. Cyprian who in writing to him speaks of his 'glorious witness,' afterward speaks of him and Lucius (who was not a martyr either in our sense of the word) as

---

[1] That the month of his decease must have been *June* is shewn above (chap. II. p. 127 note). Pearson (who is however misled by the traditional *September* of his legendary martyrdom) argues justly that the events and changes which occurred after May 15, 252, and before his death could not have been crowded into the June of 252—viz. the ordination of Fortunatus, his voyage, rejection and fresh attempt, with all the letters which passed between Cyprian and Cornelius, the latter in security at Rome, the former in daily expectation of death. Again Dionysius of Alexandria mentions in a letter to Cornelius the death of Fabius of Antioch, and the consecration of his successor Demetrian. (Eus. *H. E.* vi. 46.) According to the *Chronicle* of Eusebius this was in the consulship of Valerian and Gallienus I., or in the year 2272 after Abraham, A.D. 253—4 (Lipsius, *op. cit.* p. 210). This is a strictly independent testimony in support of the most accurate catalogues which, giving to his seat 2 years 3 months and 10 days, bring the year of his death to 253 A.D. Jerome makes the strange statement 'Rexit ecclesiam *sub Gallo Volusiano duobus annis.*' *De Viris Ill.* 66.

Pearson (*Annal. Cypr.* 252, xiii.) accuses the Roman Breviary of placing his death under Decius. At present however it reads *Gallo et Volusiano consulibus* which though incorrect is Pearson's own. He relied on the faulty (Lipsius, *op. cit.* p. 209) consular list of the Liberian Catalogue.

[2] *Ep.* 60. 3. *Ep.* 61. 3 'tota cordis luce perspicimus, &c.'

[3] *De Viris Ill.* cc. 66, 67.

[4] Sup p. 91.

'planted together in glorious martyrdom,' and again styles him a Blessed Martyr[1].

However, these terms are familiar enough to us as used of living prisoners or exiles, and by no early authority is he said to have been put to death. His name is not on the Liberian martyr-roll, nor yet in the Deposition of Bishops. All accords with the more modest antient record 'There with glory he took sleep[2].' His remains were carried to Rome, and were laid near to the older bishops but not among them[3]. He rested amid the ashes—so it must seem—of his patrician house[4], and with his name cut in Latin, and not like his predecessors in Greek[5].

Salonina, the wife of Gallienus, whom his father Valerian immediately associated with himself, in this[6] October was both a Cornelia and a Christian[7]. We might without over-

---

[1] *Epp.* 60 init.; 68. 5; 61. 3; 67. 6; 69. 3.
[2] Mommsen, *op. cit.* p. 636.
[3] The old *Salzburg traveller* notices this. Rossi, *R. S.* I. p. 180.
[4] See Northcote and Brownlow, *Roma Sotterranea* I. pp. 352—363.
[5] Sup. p. 124. Rossi, *Roma Sotterranea*, tom. I. p. 274 ff., tav. iv., 2. All before him and those for fifty years later down to Eutychian are Greek like their liturgy.
[6] *Corp. Inscrr. Latt.* VIII. i. 2482.
[7] Of the many coins of Cornelia Salonina some remarkable types have on the obverse her throned, sceptred figure, holding in her right hand an olive branch, and with the legend AVGVSTA IN PACE.

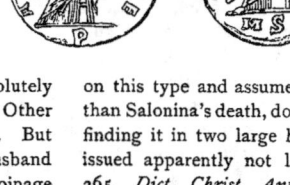

This *In Pace* is elsewhere absolutely limited to Christian memorials. Other coins of hers bear common types. But it is observable that though her husband Gallienus was much given to coinage 'Consecrations' of his predecessors and of his family except of Valerian, there is no pagan apotheosis of Salonina. De Witte, who first commented on this type and assumed it to be later than Salonina's death, doubted this after finding it in two large hoards of coins issued apparently not later than A.D. 265, *Dict. Christ. Antiq.* 'Money'; Stevenson, *Dict. Rom. Coins*, p. 711. The doubt is, I suppose, because of the incident of 'the Empress's' danger in A.D. 268 at the Siege of Milan. C. W. King

boldness perhaps conjecture that such a princess was not unconcerned in the locality or the adornment of his repose.

This chamber is said in a later story to have been first prepared for him in a crypt on her own estate, on the Appian Way, hard by the cemetery of Callistus, by the lady Lucina called afterwards the Blessed, who was also incorrectly said to have aided Cornelius himself in laying the body of S. Peter in the Vatican and of S. Paul on the Ostian Way. But it was delicately done, whoever brought to his side in death the Presbyter and Confessor Maximus whom Cornelius had brought back to the Catholic Church in life[1]. The sepulchre of Cornelius 'is with us to this day,' still rich in architectural appointments and shewing trace of some grand sarcophagus to which his bones had been transferred from a simpler but not unnotable grave.

We may add that in the fourth century Damasus in his last illness opened the old chapel more to the light and began a staircase for pilgrims[2]. Injured by Lombard invaders it

---

does not see why she should be supposed to have been then alive (*Early Christian Numismatics*, p. 47) but I think he cannot have noticed that incident; for Zonaras would be worse than he is if he did not mean to connect it with that siege. But on the other hand it seems to me not impossible that Pipara, his German princess, 'quam perdite dilexit,' and in honour of whom he and his court wore their hair yellow (Treb. Pollio, *Gallieni duo* c. 21), may have been the Βασίλισσα of this camp-story. At any rate, whether in life or death, Salonina's is a Christian legend, without pressing the MS. on some of the exergues to mean *Memoriæ Sanctæ*. Other indications of a Christian influence on this incomprehensible emperor occur in the text.

Gallienus once sent a mass of valuables to propitiate Claudius, among them 'trientes *Saloninianos* trecentos' perhaps of his Empress, perhaps of his son (Treb. Poll. *Claud.* 17).

[1] Sup. page 161. Rossi, *Roma Sotterr.* tom. I. p. 291, tav. xix. 5. Lucina, a rare surname, is found in the Cornelian gens. Rossi, *R. S.* t. I. p. 314.

[2] Aspice descensu exstructo tenebrisque fugatis
Corneli monumenta vides tumulumque sacratum.
Hoc opus ægroti Damasi præstantia fecit,
Esset ut accessus melior, populisque paratum
Auxilium Sancti, et valeas si fundere pure
Corde preces, Damasus melior consurgere posset
Quem non lucis amor tenuit mage cura labcris.

This recovery, from several fragments

was restored by Leo III. in the ninth century, and then the tall commanding figures of the brotherly Cornelius and Cyprian were painted on its walls[1].

It is impossible not to be led a little aside by what has been of undying interest to so many generations. But to return to the facts of Cornelius' death and burial. The inferences from them are clear enough. Dying quietly at Cività Vecchia his death-day had for a time no very marked commemoration. When a festival was sought for him as a Martyr he was conjoined with his friend and brother Cyprian whose day had been long observed at Rome. For so, without any mention of Cornelius, Cyprian's actual death-day appears in the Kalendar of A.D. 354.

'Fourteenth of September, commemoration of Cyprian, Africa. It is kept at Rome in the cemetery of Calistus[2].'

---

and from Damasus' familiar tags, of the original inscription placed over the tomb at Damasus' restoration is one of De Rossi's most ingenious and perfect triumphs. *R. S.* i. p. 289—291.

[1] Rossi, *R. S.* t i. tav. vi.

[2] A.D. 354 'XVIII. KL. OCTOB. CYPRIANI AFRICÆ ROMÆ CELEBRATUR IN CALISTI.'

With extraordinary violence Rossi wishes to insert *Corneli in Calisti* before the name of Cyprian, and Mommsen (*Abhand. d. k. S. Ges. d. Wissensch.* II. p. 633, note 2, über den Chronograph vom Jah. 354) would take *cele-* *bratur* to be a corruption of *Corneli*. To such lengths will determined critics even now proceed. The unfortunate suggestion is borrowed apparently from Muratori, *Lit. Rom. Vet.* I. col. 39, n. c. (See *Appendix* on S. Cyprian's Day, p. 610.)

The *Felician Catalogue* says Cornelius was beheaded at the Temple of Mars, and gives the story of Lucina, of which the untruth will appear in the history of Xystus. This catalogue is accordingly obliged to omit the older words 'Ibi cum gloria dormicionem accepit.' Lipsius, *op. cit.* pp. 125, 275.

II.

The Sitting of LUCIUS.

The whole chronology with its perplexities is unravelled by this disengagement of the decease of Cornelius from its liturgical connection with the fourteenth of September, and its certain replacement, in June A.D. 253. A few days may perhaps be assumed to have elapsed before the twenty-fifth of that same month, on or near to which his successor Lucius came to the Chair for a brief eight months and ten days[1].

He was immediately banished[2] though without deprivation of property or rights[3], and directly afterwards recalled or allowed to return; with him came home apparently the great mass of exiles. Whether this was some experiment in the working of terror and leniency, or whether it was a result of the divided sentiments of the imperial households we cannot tell. Valerian became severely anti-Christian, but we have just seen that Salonina, the wife of his son Gallienus, who at this juncture, succeeded with him to the honours of Consul, Imperator, Cæsar and Augustus, was probably a Christian and of the same great house as the last Bishop; and Gallienus in his rescript of toleration published when he began to reign alone in A.D. 261[4], speaks of having already *long ago made concessions to the Christians.*

[1] Cyprian's solitary letter to Lucius (*Ep.* 61) indicating only one other, and this lately written and anticipating martyrdom for him besides, would mark the pontificate as probably short. But Lipsius has shewn independently that the 'iii years' which the Liberian chronologist prefixes to his 'viii months and x days' is a mere blunder, and that Eusebius *H. E.* vii. 2 μησὶ δ' οὐδ' ὅλοις οὗτος ὀκτώ... is right. Lipsius, *op. cit.* p. 210. The *Felician Cat.* has 'sedit annos iii menses iii dies iii.'

[2] No ground for stating that he had been also previously banished with Cornelius.

[3] Relegationem...relegatus (*Ep.* 61. 1), used unquestionably with precision by the Old Legist.

[4] Clinton, *Fasti Romani,* vol. I. pp. 286, 7. Euseb. *H.E.* vii. 13 'The relief was to be universal: they are not to be kept out of their places of worship (ἀπὸ τόπων τῶν θρησκευσίμων): they may exhibit as their warrant this form of rescript: no one is to molest them: καὶ τοῦτο ὅπερ κατὰ τὸ ἐξὸν δύναται ὑφ' ὑμῶν ἀναπλη-

Certainly the persecution was not supposed to be over with Lucius' recall. Cyprian had visions of coming evil and tells him that he may and ought to expect to be 'immolated before the eyes of the brethren' in Rome. The Church was itself unaware of the reason of the change; and long afterwards referred it simply to the 'will of God[1],' just as Cyprian, at the moment, referred it to the favour of God investing his episcopate at once with Confessorship. He pictures his return as a scene of such joy that it was a foretaste of Christ's near return[2], and Lucius the likeness of His forerunner.

More than this is not to be known of his character. Cyprian seems to write to him as to a manly kind of person, but it would be pressing his phrases too far to be sure that they describe the person rather than the protective office.

An early ritual tradition ascribes to him the 'precept' that the bishop of Rome should be accompanied in every place by two presbyters and three deacons[3]; a tradition which perhaps echoes some facts of his exile.

But what is most important is that, in his view as to the right treatment of the Lapsed and their restoration after penance to peace and communion, he was at one with his predecessor Cornelius,—that is firmly against Novatian and with Cyprian—and that he had issued documents upon that subject[4].

On the 5th of the following March he was laid beside Fabian in the cemetery of Callistus. The day is given us in Mar. 5, A.D. 254. A.U.C.

ροῦσθαι ἤδη πρὸ πολλοῦ ὑπ' ἐμοῦ συγκεχώρηται.' C. W. King, *Early Chr. Numis.* p. 47, interprets κατὰ τὸ ἐξὸν 'according to what was right'— but I do not see the point of that, and would suggest that the clause may mean 'what you may perform in accordance with this leave, I have conceded practically long since.'

[1] *Catal. Liber.*: Hic exul fuit et postea nutu dei incolumis ad ecclesiam reversus est. *Catal. Felic.*: Hic in exilio fuit 1007. postea natudi incolomis. Coss. Imp.

[2] Cyprian seems to be rhetorically betrayed into this unfit image simply from having used the word *adventus* twice. *Ep.* 61. 4.

[3] Hic precepit ut duo prisbī et III diaconi in omni loco cum epō non desererent. *Catal. Felic.*

[4] Litteris suis signaverunt, *Ep.* 68. 5.

Cæs. P. Licinius Valerianus Pius Felix Aug. II.
Imp. Cæs. P. Licinius Egnatius Gallienus Pius Felix Aug.

the entombment-list not of martyrs but of bishops[1]. His original sepulchral slab with Greek characters, and no mention of martyrdom, adds simply the most interesting of the examples of the vulgar termination, common in Greek, Jewish, or Græcizing-Latin Inscriptions during the third century, but almost extinct before the end of the fourth[2].

The incidents of the last few pages, difficult, and almost fretful, for criticism to elicit and to combine with so much certainty, will not seem trivial to those who perceive through them, how firm and subtle were the new threads which were now being drawn through all society, securing the allegiance of imperial antient houses, drawing to the centre of influence men who had not even a family

---

[1] III NON. MAR. LUCI IN CALISTO. Mommsen, *op. cit.* p. 631. III NON. MAR. CONS. s͞s. *Catal. Liber.* Lipsius, *op. cit.* p. 267. The Liberian list is not only wrong in carrying this date into the 3rd consulship of Valerian and 2nd of Gallienus (A.D. 255) under whom it puts down also the death of Stephanus over four years later, but irreconcilable with its own date of 3 years 8 months 10 days which it counts from Gallus II. Volusian I. (A.D. 252).

[2] We have ΛΙΤΟΡΙC A.D. 263, ΑΥΡΗΛΙC temp. Anton. P. From the Jewish cemetery at Rome ΓΑΙC, ΚΑCΤΡΙΚΙC, ΑCΤΕΡΙC, ΝΟΥΜΕΝΙΣ. Ritschl by such examples as *Cæcilis*, *Clodis* shews it not to have been a wholly modern corruption, and thinks it archaic. The latest instances we have are ΤΑΡΑCΙC A.D. 461, and ΟΥΡΑΝΙC vith or viith. cent. Rossi, *R. S.* vol. II. pp. 66, 8. From Felician Catalogue, Lipsius, p. 275, quotes CORNILIS.

name, knitting together classes that had been apart since Roman law began;—how a new moral magistracy grappled with the sins which underlay crimes;—how possible it was to fall out of such an association, and then—how men would give all things—health, wealth, connection, honours—to be restored to it.

III.

STEPHANUS.

The Church not identified with or represented by Rome.

Cyprian's relations with Rome soon afterwards underwent a great change. It takes effort to view with candid and clear vision, so as to see them in their first meaning, such facts and expressions as controversies have since coloured and shaded. Yet the truth is that what was confused and beclouded while nothing but amity existed was made distinct by variances. The dignity of the Roman See was in Cyprian's eyes that of an inherited precedency and presidency, and not due merely to the fact that, if Carthage was the second city of the world, Rome was its mistress[1].

But that even its more moderate claims to spiritual supremacy are a doctrine unknown to Cyprian is evidenced, as we have seen, by the definite alterations which Roman divines have introduced into his language and maintain there[2].

Exemplifications of his real theory are 'writ large' in his corrections of the successor of Lucius. Long before the bitterness of theological difference arose between them, in dealing with moral cases of Lapse, we had to look onward, and we saw how the church of Africa received appeals against two

---

[1] Milman and others assign rather too much weight to this. Cf. *Ep.* 59. 14. See pp. 195, 196 above.

[2] See a very profligate blazon of that theory as a historic fact in Freppel, pp. 128—130 and 218—20.

ecclesiastical judgments of the Roman Bishop and reversed them[1]. Presently we shall find him admonished of his duty toward a Novatianist and desired to transmit an account of his discharge of it to Carthage[2]. The Christian world contemned his arrogance, while it confirmed his practice in Baptism. Modern Rome outdoes his pretensions and freely uses the Rebaptism he rightly condemned.

It might at first sight seem as if only one common link could hold together alliances so inconsistent with each other, alliances with Lapsed, with Novatianists, who stood equally aloof from Lapsed and from Heretics, and with the Heretics themselves,—a consistent opposition to Cyprian. It might seem as if nothing but uniform contravention of Cyprian's policy in its three branches could evolve such variety. Stephen might wish to abolish out of Rome the influence to which his predecessor had yielded; Cyprian's Petrine unity, he might say, was but theoretical, his practical Episcopal unity threatened the Roman unity. But if he could force Cyprian into opposition to his See and its Traditions, that Petrine theory of his would serve to put Cyprian in the wrong, and leave him on his own shewing no better than a Novatianist[3].

But mortal opponency surely never ran so wild a length. At any rate, of this low subtlety there is no appearance on the part of Stephen. Indeed at Rome, where Cornelius was so much more of a presence than Cyprian, the effect to the eye of the Church would be that of an onslaught upon Cornelius and his councils rather than on Cyprian. Besides it had virtually been Cornelius who modified Cyprian's puritanism. When Stephen restored peccant bishops he was following Callistus; when he condemned Rebaptism he was appealing to tradition older than Callistus[4]. In all the letters

---

[1] Pp. 233, 234 above. *Ep.* 67.
[2] *Ep.* 68.
[3] So Ritschl.
[4] Hippolytus, *adv. omnes Hæreses*, ix. 12, cf. 7.

to and about him Cyprian never writes as if Stephen were making capital out of his own Petrine unity; he repeats the theory[1]. He shews no consciousness that his view of episcopal unity is disputed or is likely to be disputed by Stephen. He strongly states[2] his conviction of the truth and antiquity of the African discipline, but acknowledges in Stephen as in other bishops the right and the responsibility of differing. Thus there is no trace of that diplomacy with which Stephen is ingeniously credited by moderns: nor yet of the mere obstinacy of which he is accused by his contemporary[3].

The business of history is not to be reviving blots which have faded from the world's mind, but to mark and trace all life which was ever true and all truth which ever lives.

Our material is sufficient to indicate that from the first Stephen had no leaning towards rules which his predecessors and Cyprian had laid down for themselves. His temper (which so often corresponds to, even if it does not interpret, a policy) was that of a man averse to strictness, and severe only with those who wished to see him so. His policy may be characterized as roughly anti-Novatianist or anti-puritan, and in Cyprian himself there was, as we have seen, an undertint of puritanism not invisible to Stephen, whose ruling that a lapsed or a perjured bishop might, without over severe conditions, resume his see, or even a Novatianist retain his, were strong anti-Novatianist examples of tolerance. But in fact he may be rather said to have inaugurated, or at least to have been an early type of the regular Roman policy of comprehension on easy terms saving as to the one article of submission: ready in Spain to restore semi-pagans to the Episcopate; ready in Gaul to uphold the harshest repeller of penitents; ready anywhere to receive Marcionites without Baptism to Communion. And although the issue of his long severe Baptismal controversy with Cyprian has been determined by the Church catholic in Stephen's sense; although the practice

---

[1] *Ep.* 73. 7.   [2] *Ep.* 72. 1.   [3] *Ep.* 75. 2, 6, 17.

he maintained has been accepted as true wisdom and true charity; although Cyprian's theory has been rejected as well-nigh unchristian, yet few moral triumphs have equalled the ascendency of the vanquished Carthaginian. It arose solely upon the nobility of tone, the magnanimous gentleness, the postponement of self to the Church, in which he conducted his unhappy cause. The never broken veneration entertained for him is an answer to the calumny that theologians cannot forgive an opponent, or spare the memory of the defeated. It was the victorious Stephen who did not recover the shock of that conflict. While Cyprian and Cornelius are companion saints in Kalendar and Collect[1], beside the altar of the Catacomb[2] and in the mosaic heaven of the Basilica[3], Stephen rested for centuries in the unpraised silence into which Pontius[4] dismisses him. Not until in the ninth century a catacomb yielded a marble chair with an inscription over an unnamed martyr pope, did the church of Rome assign saintship to Stephanus' disengaged name. How he has lost both chair and legend again will be narrated hereafter.

Jeremy Taylor sets an uncharitable seal to the popular church view of his 'uncharitableness. Stephen was accounted a zealous and furious person[5].' Still we need not forget that his portrait is made up of traits etched in scraps by the pen of an adversary, and that he was not solitary (as Florentius evinces) in his aversion to the power which Cyprian was now wielding[6]. Dionysius the Great makes

---

[1] Leonian Sacramentary, Muratori, *Liturg. Rom. Vet.* tom. I. col. 404; Gelasian Sacramentary, c. 668; Gelasian Kalendar, c. 49; Gregorian Sacramentary, t. II. c. 119; Gothic Missal, t. II. p. 629, an entirely different office for Cornelius and Cyprian, but still together. On the variations of the day here and in other rituals, see *Appendix*, p. 610.

[2] See Rossi as above, pp. 302, 3.

[3] As at Ravenna in S. Martinus in Cælo Aureo (afterwards S. Apollinare Nuovo).

[4] Without mentioning Stephen he markedly proceeds 'Iam de Xysto bono et pacifico sacerdote.' Pont. *Vit.* c. 14.

[5] Of Heresy 22, *Liberty of Prophesying*, vol. v. p. 396 (ed. Eden, 1853).

[6] *Ep.* 66 Florentio Puppiano.

thankful mention of his liberality to the churches of Syria and Arabia[1]; and to Vincent of Lerins[2] there floated across two centuries a tradition of modesty as well as zeal, of faith as well as dignity[3].

It was about the twelfth of May, A.D. 254[4], when Stephen succeeded to the Chair of Lucius. Cyprian's first extant letter to him was not so much in a tone of equality as in the spirit of direction, if not of dictation. He anticipates no differences, but plainly expects to be on the same terms with him as had existed with Cornelius. His language is rather peremptory, but with a peremptoriness which feels it may reckon on compliance.

May 12, 254.

In the next letter Cyprian has already given Stephen up. He makes a faint apology for him on the ground of his 'unacquaintedness with the facts and truth' of the case, makes allowance for his 'inattention[5],' and proceeds to lay down principles and give directions in absolute reversal of Stephen's.

Elsewhere[6] we have given the outline of the heathenish Lapse of two Bishops in Spain and of the action taken about them. We reserved till now a consideration of the principles that reveal themselves in that intercourse of churches or dioceses. We must enter a little more into detail.

1. *The Spanish Appeal.*

It will be recollected that Stephen on the personal application of Basilides gave judgment that such men as he

---

[1] Eus. *H. E.* vii. 5.

[2] Vinc. Lirin. *Commonit.* I. 6.

[3] Tillemont, vol. IV., p. 32, quotes Augustine *de unico Bapt. c. Petil.* 14 as averring that the Donatists confessed Stephen's 'administration' to have been 'sans reproche'; 'gessisse episcopatum illibatum.' This may only mean that they admitted him to be a genuine bishop, a true member of a true line.

[4] Lipsius, *op. cit.* p. 214.

[5] Ritschl's view that *Ep.* 68 is earlier than 67 is just. There is no mistaking the change of tone towards Stephen from an affectionate confidence to a self-restrained coldness. Afterwards it was exasperated.

[6] P. 233 above.

and Martial should on recantation be restored to their sees[1]. The church of Leon with Astorga thereupon appointed its presbyter Felix, and the church of Merida its deacon[2] Ælius, to compose an instant appeal to the great church of Carthage. Merida sent by the same bearer an epistle from Felix of Saragossa. Whether this Felix was the bishop of that place, or some representative layman, does not appear, but the historians of Arragon have debated the question with interest[3]. Sabinus, who had been unanimously elected to succeed Basilides and confirmed by the neighbouring bishops, and Felix, who had replaced Martial, carried the three Letters.

The reply of Carthage to the churches is the composition of Cyprian. It closes with his own nominal salutation. It is written in the name of seven and thirty prelates who assembled in Carthage in the autumn of A.D. 254[4]. It punctiliously exempts Stephen from further blame than that of negligence in accepting Basilides' mere assurance of repentance, and ratifying his episcopal tenure, when even to absolve him would have been a strong measure. It assumes that if he had investigated he would have decided as they—Cyprian's Fourth Council—decided, namely that the two men had for

---

[1] It is not expressed that Martial approached Stephen, but *fallacia* (*Ep.* 67. 5) is attributed to him, and these respectable Spaniards are treated as both on one platform.

[2] The Spanish deacons bore an important part in the administration of churches. See Concil. Elib. *Can.* 77 *Si quis diaconus plebem sine episcopo vel presbytero, &c.* Neander, *op. cit.*, vol. I. 324, et sup. p. 114. Diaconal presumptions are restrained A.D. 314 at Arles, *Cann.* 15, 18.

The Abbé Duchesne, *Fastes Épisc. de l'Anc. Gaule*, t. I. p. 40, cites from the Letter of Vienne and Lyons A.D. 177, Eus. *H. E.* v. 1 '*le* (sic) diacre de Vienne, τὸν διάκονον ἀπὸ Βιέννης' as an early sample 'd'un diacre chargé du gouvernement spirituel d'une chrétienté éloignée de la Mère-Église.' But the true reading is Σάγκτον διάκονον κ.τ.λ.; the letter is here giving a list of *names*; and even in this age the phrase in that sense would have been τὸν ἀπὸ Βιέννης διάκονον.

[3] See Baluze's not. in loc.

[4] The Council of 254 A.D. must have been held towards autumn. Easter day was on the 23rd April, Stephanus was ordained about May 12. *Before* the Council was held Basilides had already been at Rome, seen Stephen, and been assured by him of the propriety of his resuming his see; the Churches of Leon and Astorga had received the decision and appealed to Cyprian against it.

ever surceased from the episcopate. To Stephen himself the Council submits no representation of its opinion. They make not the most distant allusion to any inherent prerogative of his office as Bishop of Rome[1]. There is no request that he would reconsider his judgment, or recognise theirs. They simply reverse his verdict and regard their reversal as final. Their long epistle, estimating the many points at issue, treats the decision of the Bishop of Rome as simply and gravely mistaken, and therefore to be set aside. There are then no less than four accounts upon which this Synodical Epistle of A.D. 254 on the affair of Basilides and Martial is important as a witness to the relations subsisting within the congregations and between the congregations of the Church. It creates none. And it does not imply, but distinctly states these relations.

I. Its main purport is the distinct accepting and absolute deciding of an appeal from the church of one nation to another in reversal of an ecclesiastical decision by the Bishop of Rome[2]. The sole rule to be recognised in the judgment is that of Scripture. 'There can be no acceptance of person, 'no dispensation can be granted by any human indulgence, 'in matters where divine prescription interposes a veto and 'appoints a law[3].'

II. It assigns to the Laity the right, and insists on their duty, of withdrawing from the communion of a 'sacrilegious' or 'sinful' bishop. 'The Laity mainly have the power in

---

[1] The Donatist Congregations A.D. 313, in fear of the factions of the Italian Church, appeal to be heard by the Bishops of Gaul. They were finally only allowed three, fifteen others being Italians. Optat. i. 23.

[2] *Ep.* 67. 1 and 6.

[3] *Ep.* 67. 2 *intercedit...præscriptio.* Mark the hand of the Civilian in all the terms. We have to choose between *Perscriptio* Q and the original L, and *Præscriptio* C, R and the corrector of L: all these are of cent. ix (Q cent. viii—ix?); all editions had *præscriptio* until Hartel, and his choice seems perverse. *Præscriptio* is used elsewhere by Cyprian, and *perscriptio* beyond its common use for a fair copy or for a cheque relates rather to the *terms* of a document than to its *authority*, which is what is required by *tribuit legem.*

'either choosing worthy Bishops or in rejecting unworthy 'ones.' 'The Laity must not flatter themselves with the idea 'of being untouched by the contagion of his offence if they 'communicate with a Bishop that is a sinner.' 'They must 'sever themselves from a sinful prelate[1].'

III. It marks (beside other things) the presence and testimony of Laity as required, or, as it is here expressed, as 'a thing of divine tradition and apostolic observance,' in the appointment of a Bishop,—'that he may be chosen in the pre-'sence of the Commons under the eyes of all, and be approved 'as worthy and meet by public judgment and testimony.' 'In the presence of the Commons which fully knows the life 'of each, and has discerned everyone's line of action through 'intercourse with him[2].'

IV. It marks the sense that there resided no power in a Christian congregation which could assign episcopal authority over itself, or commit the celebration of sacramental acts to any nominee lacking the note of regular apostolic Orders. The custom is kept for 'the nearest Bishops of the province to meet and the Bishop to be chosen' not by, but 'in the presence of the Commons.' 'Upon the 'judgment of the Bishops the Episcopate was conferred on 'him, and the hand laid upon him[3].'

2. *The Gaulish Appeal.*

The majestic Romanesque portal of the Cathedral of Arles ranks the noble image of her Founder and Patron Trophimus the Ephesian with the protomartyr and the apostles. From at least the ninth century onwards it was unquestioned

---

[1] *Ep.* 67. 3. Routh, *R. S.* vol. III. pp. 151, 2, correctly, after Erasmus, treats the passage as referring to sins which were Ecclesiastical disqualifications. It also lays down that *freedom from moral defect* is essential at ordination in order to the *virtue of the ministration*, and herein we see the growth of Cyprian's one characteristic confusion.

[2] *Ep.* 67. 4, 5.

[3] *Ep.* 67. 5.

history that he had been installed there by S. Paul on his way to Spain, after consecration to the Bishopric by S. Peter at Rome[1].

In the middle of the fifth century fewer particulars had been extant. The position of Constantinople made it convenient in the West to begin to rank Metropolitans not by the political importance of their province, but by the supposed antiquity of its conversion. Still when Zosimus in A.D. 417 declared the scandalous Patroclus to be the Metropolitan of the Provinces of Vienne, Narbonensis Prima and Narbonensis Secunda, he only affirmed without naming a date that Rome had sent out Trophimus as Chief Bishop, and that from 'his fountain all Provinces of Gaul received the rills of the faith[2].'

The Bishops of this Province in an appeal to Leo, A.D. 450, framed on Zosimus' words, still claim no more than that it was known at Rome, and generally, that Trophimus had been sent by 'the Blessed Peter the apostle'; but that is the then usual phrase for the See of Rome[3]. So far, all that stands before us from the fifth century is a local tradition of a Roman Missionary Bishop as Founder. But again there were old diptychs of the church of Arles in which Trophimus was only the second name on the list of Bishops; and thus, even

---

[1] Stephano V. Papæ tributa Epistola ad Selvam, &c. Labbe, XI. 550. Ado, *Chron. Æt. VI.* 59.

[2] 'Summus antistes &c.' Zosimi *Ep.* v. *ad Epp. Galliæ*. The successors of Zosimus, it may be observed, Boniface, Celestine, and Leo the Great, did not feel the necessity, and admitted the old rank of Vienne. Symmachus once more rehabilitated Arles. Gregory the Great speaks of Arles as the channel of all Gallic Christianity. See Greg. Magn. *Epp.* v. 53, note c; ed. Bened. (p. ii. c. 781, Ven. 1744).

[The Abbé Duchesne shews that the ties of the 3rd century between Arles and Rome were decayed in the 4th, and that Transalpine Gaul in practical affairs was drawn to Milan. Zosimus' act was in counteraction to this. The 'Vicariate' of Arles in cent. vi. was isolated and transient, and not effective. Duchesne, *Fastes Épiscopaux de l'Ancienne Gaule*, 1894, I. p. 86.]

[3] Quesnel, note on Leon. Magn. *Ep.* LXV. 'Preces missæ, &c.' But has 'ab apostolis' the same sense? See Tillemont, *Note* I, *sur S. Denys de Paris*, vol. IV. p. 707.

if those diptychs were not accurate, it appears that there had been a time when the name of Trophimus was not impressed on the mind of the church of Arles as its Founder[1].

In Gregory of Tours[2], A.D. ? 573—594, we come on an intermediate view of the story. Seven Presbyters were ordained Bishops at Rome in the consulship of Decius and Gratus, and sent to the great sees of Gaul, to Tours, Narbonne, Toulouse, Paris, into Auvergne, to Limoges, and among them Trophimus to Arles. The consulship of Decius and Gratus corresponds to the year A.D. 250, in which year Fabian was martyred on the 20th of January, and the see was vacant all the rest of the year. Gregory might have been sure that Fabian had as little to do with Trophimus and Arles as S. Peter and S. Paul had[3].

But in fact a letter from Cyprian to Stephen[4] lets us know who the real Bishop of Arles was at that time and for some years after. It is earlier than the Baptismal Controversy which began in A.D. 255, Stephen's second year[5]. But it implies the passage of earlier letters, a period of waiting for answers and for action, such that it cannot have been written until well on in his second year. Again Cyprian remarks in it that 'many brethren had died at Arles without being restored to 'communion (by their puritan bishop), *in these past years*[6].' Such a phrase can scarcely mean much less than *three* years. Novatianism began only in June A.D. 251. Accordingly this

---

[1] Mabillon ap. Tillemont, IV. p. 703.
[2] *Hist. Franc.* I. 28.
[3] Pearson shewed that Sulpicius Severus and the Passion of Saturninus lend no countenance to these statements. *Annal. Cypr.* A.D. 254, viii., ix. Tillemont endeavours to save the credit of Gregory as a historian of the reign of Decius by suggesting that Trophimus might have come on a mission to Provence then, and been consecrated years after. But he has also placed under Decius the rise of Novatian, the rise of the Valentinians, and the martyrdom of Xystus. However there was no bishop of Arles, we may be sure, before the death of Irenæus about 203 A.D., and the see was otherwise occupied in A.D. 250. The Greek name which Pearson treats as against his coming from Rome would rather tell in favour of it.
[4] *Ep.* 68.
[5] Lipsius, *op. cit.* p. 213 ff. Pearson, *Annal. Cypr.* A.D. 254, vi.
[6] *Ep.* 68. 3 '...annis istis superioribus.'

Novatianist bishop, whose name was Marcian, must have governed the church of Arles from 251 at latest to 254.

Marcian not only exercised the harshest puritan discipline in the perpetual exclusion of the most sorrowing penitents even in their last hours, but he openly renounced communion with the other bishops and took the extremest Novatianist tone that the whole Church, by readmitting the Lapsed, un-churched itself[1]. The general condemnation of Novatian, his doctrine and adherents[2], did not affect the position or the conduct of Marcian, until Faustinus, bishop of Lyons, laid the facts before Cyprian, and together with his fellow bishops represented the case to Stephen. Stephen took it in silence. His broad anti-Novatianist tone would not allow him to be hard even on a Novatianist, and Cyprian attributed this *laisser passer* policy to carelessness.

Faustinus complained of Stephen in a second letter to Cyprian. And Cyprian took upon himself to address Stephen in strong terms as to his duty.

So much has been and still is made to turn on the very phrases of this letter that in fairness the debated sentences must be reproduced.

We are to observe *what* Cyprian recommends to be done: *who* to be the doer or doers: especially to note what part the Roman is urged to take, and on what grounds.

'It is,' says Cyprian, '*our* duty to consider this affair and 'to remedy it; thinking on God's clemency as we do, and 'holding the balance of the Church's government, and so 'exercising severity toward sinners as not to refuse the 'Divine healing to the Lapsed.'

---

[1] ...collegio nostro insultare...a communicatione nostra se segregaverit...de majestate ac dignitate ecclesiæ judicare. *Ep.* 68. 2.

[2] ...quod *necdum videatur* a *nobis* abstentus, &c., *Ep.* 68. 2, finding himself not even yet excommunicated by us, Marcian says, 'Stephen and Cyprian do not and cannot excommunicate me. I withdraw from them.' His master Novatian on the other hand was excommunicated at once, prayed to be admitted, and was told that the only terms were submission. This is the connection of *Ep.* 68. 2.

He therefore urges Stephen to write 'a very full letter' to the Gallic bishops. What he recommends him to advise is 'that *they*,' the bishops, 'should no longer allow Marcian to trample upon our (Episcopal) College.'

As an example of what they might do, and in consistency ought to do, he quotes the refusal of the assembled African bishops to hold communion with Novatian after his spurious celebration of Divine worship and assumption, of office in separation from Cornelius. The parallel is distinct: as the African bishops excommunicated Novatian, so let the Gallic bishops excommunicate Marcian.

By his excommunication the see would be at once vacant. So far is clear. Cyprian proceeds, 'Let letters be dispatched 'from you into the Province and to the Laity who stand faith-'ful at Arles, whereby[1], Marcian having been excommunicated, 'another may be appointed in his room, and the flock of Christ, 'which for to-day, broken up by him and wounded, is lightly 'esteemed, may be gathered together.' Does Cyprian mean that *by virtue of the letter itself* Marcian would be excommunicated, and his successor appointed? or were the receivers of the letter intended to perform those acts? The wording alone might admit the former alternative as easily as the second (though not more easily) *in respect of the substitution of the new bishop*. In respect of the excommunication the Latinity is against the idea that the letter would effect it.

But we observe that this second letter is to be addressed *to the Laity*. The first letter which Cyprian recommended Stephen to write was to the Bishops[2], urging them to action. This is to be to the Laity; because to the Laity[3] belonged the filling of the see, voided upon Marcian's excommunication, by their election of a successor. Nomination by Laity was,

---

[1] ...litteræ *quibus abstento* Marciano alius in loco ejus *substituatur*. *Ep.* 68. 3. The abstention would have been already effected by the bishops, according to the tenor of the first letters: and with this the construction of this phrase agrees.

[2] ...plenissimas litteras ad coepiscopos nostros in Gallia constitutos. *Ep.* 68. 2.

[3] ...ad plebem Arelate consistentem litteræ. *Ep.* 68. 3.

VII. III.   2. THE GAULISH APPEAL.   319

we have already seen, the rule of the Cyprianic age, and needful for a true appointment[1].

Stephen is not requested by Cyprian to take any part beyond the writing of letters in the same sense in which he had himself presumably answered Faustinus, namely by counselling the Bishops of the Province and the Laity of the City to perform their several duties in respect of the Novatianist prelate[2].

He proceeds, 'It is for this end, dearest brother, that the 'Body of the Bishops is great and large, knit fast with glue 'of mutual concord and bond of unity, that so, should any of 'our college attempt the forming of a heresy, the rending and 'wasting of Christ's flock, the rest may come to the rescue, and 'like serviceable compassionate shepherds gather the Lord's

---

[1] Supra pp. 35 ff., 135.

Dr J. Peters, Theological Professor at Luxemburg (*Cyprian von Karthago*, Regensburg, 1877), writes, p. 478, this shameless comment on this same passage:—' According to this, each bishop, as a successor of the apostles, is responsible for the whole: yet since their multitude is bound together in the unity of the One Chief Head, the mode of affording help in extraordinary cases is clearly ascribed to The One. If the "cement of mutual concord" is *not strong enough* for the maintenance of that bond of unity which is to encircle all, then comes The One, according to his answerableness for the whole throughout.'

The very point of Cyprian's remarks is that the united Episcopate *is* 'strong enough.'

But Dr Peters continues, 'So that, elsewhere, as Cyprian told us, *he sets sail to the Chair of Peter, and the Head-Church from which priestly unity took its beginning*,' p. 479. I dare not undertake to say *whom* or what manner of person Dr Peters *intended* his readers to understand by him 'who set sail.' Some good authority, one would suppose. In point of fact it was a group of 'heretics who dared' so to do! And Cyprian marvelling at their audacity, asks 'what purpose could they have for doing so?' and after arguing that there was no real end to be answered, adds 'unless perchance that handful of desperate ruined things counts the authority of the bishops in Africa established to be *less*.' Can perversion do more? And if amazed one asks 'Where is all that about The One to be found?' Dr Peters replies 'that it was not necessary to explain to the Pontiff his own authority.' Surely, it was still less necessary to tell him that the authority was in the Bishops, if it was in himself.

[2] In the teeth of a letter which recognises that the bishops will excommunicate and the laity re-appoint, Pamelius, Du Perron (ap. Baluze), and Baronius collect from this passage 'that the Roman bishop had power even thus to excommunicate, nay to deprive (any) bishops, and to substitute fresh ones.'

'sheep into the flock[1].' Would not this be strange, incomprehensible language, if Cyprian had held that the remedy, and the application of the remedy, throughout the world lay in an over-arching supreme pontificate of Rome? Unity is oneness of a number, and so Cyprian invariably writes.

Cyprian next, after picturing the state of Marcian's people with two fine images sketched from his own familiar African scenery,—from the half-ruined coasting-harbour, and from the caravanserai occupied by brigands—proceeds thus. 'We, 'dearest brother, must take to ourselves our own brethren; 'escaped from the rocks of Marcian, and making for the 'Church's harbour of safety. We must provide them such an 'hostelry as the gospel speaks of, where the Host may take 'care of them.' With the person of the Pope full in view before him, and directly addressing him, he describes the remedy as being in the hands of many, not of one, in 'our' office, not 'thine.' 'For,' he continues, after citing Ezekiel's denunciation of the heedless shepherds, 'albeit we are many shepherds, yet we have but one flock to feed.' Is this the language of one who held that on earth there is one shepherd, as well as one flock?

'We have to maintain the honour of our predecessors 'Cornelius and Lucius,...whose memory, much as *we* revere 'it, ought to be much dearer to you, their representative[2] 'and successor. Full of God's spirit, planted in the glory of 'martyrdom, they decided for Restoration (of penitents)... 'And this is what all of us altogether everywhere decided,... 'for among us in whom was one spirit there could be no 'diversity of sentiment. And so, it is plain that one whom 'we see entertain different sentiments does not hold the truth 'of the Holy Spirit as the rest do.

'Intimate to us distinctly who is put into Marcian's place 'at Arles, that we may know to whom we must commend 'our brethren, and to whom we must write.'

[1] *Ep.* 68. 3 '...copiosum corpus est sacerdotum...ut...subveniant cæteri.'   [2] Vicarius, *Ep.* 68. 5.

2. THE GAULISH APPEAL.

So ends the letter: a letter as independent as it is deferential. Not such as an Archbishop of the Roman obedience could by any possibility address to his Pope. That there was such a thing as a patriarchal Primacy; that the Bishop of Carthage acknowledged the one chair in the West which apostles had planted; that he counted it a duty of that see to be to other sees a remembrancer of duty and purity; that the Roman see had naturally close relations with the sees of 'The Province,' all this is true. It is not perfectly exact to say with Pearson, 'Cyprian asks nothing of Stephen which he is not ready to discharge himself,' without the addition that he held it Stephen's duty to move first. Cyprian, even in his ill-repressed indignation at Stephen's indifference, gives him a place and name before his brethren. But—without entering now into the infinitely graver questions of uncorrupt truth, pure worship, and paramount Scripture as essential to the validity of rights and tenure of any see—such primacy was not historically a dominion either secular or spiritual. Of control in things of faith, of jurisdiction to be exercised administratively, executively, or legislatively in another see, of sole or immediate supremacy without appeal, this letter presents no least trace.

And now, lest it should be imagined that Romish claims are such as find any countenance in the concessions of impartiality or in the analysis of truth-seeking, we may finally contemplate Professor Dr Peters's summary of this Letter.

'Cyprian here concedes and ascribes to the Successor 'of Peter "the ordinary and immediate Jurisdiction" over 'foreign Dioceses; and consequently over the whole Church[1].'

Mgr. Freppel alone could outdo this; and he does. Cyprian...'sees in the Roman pontiff the guardian and the 'defender of the *canons* for the universal Church; the bishop 'whose jurisdiction, far from expiring on the confines of a

[1] Dr J. Peters, *Cyprian von Karthago*, p. 479.

'province or a country, extends to the entire universe.' "Use," 'he writes to him, "the plenitude of your authority; address 'to the bishops of Gaul and to the people of Arles letters, '*plenissimas litteras*, in virtue of which Marcian may be 'deposed and another elected in his place." I ask any 'honest man,' cries Mgr. Freppel, 'how should Cyprian have 'proceeded in order to affirm more highly the primacy of 'the pope? For the deposition of a bishop is the gravest act 'of jurisdiction one could point to[1].'

Not only are such terms as 'ordinary and immediate jurisdiction,' 'defender of canons for the universal Church,' ridiculous in their anachronism; not only is the phrase 'use the plenitude of your authority' an invention of Freppel's own, which he prints as a citation, and comments on as original; but the whole language of both authors is in the teeth of the text. The text assigns the function of excommunication, involving deposition, to one authority, the duty of substitution to another, and neither of these offices to Stephen, who is simply urged to press their duty, as became his place, upon the Bishops and Laity of Provence.

---

[1] Freppel, p. 367.

These writers cannot be regarded as other than faithful exponents of the Roman doctrine. The Bull *Unam sanctam* concludes with the words 'Subesse Romano Pontifici omni humanæ creaturæ declaramus dicimus definimus [diffinimus] et pronunciamus omnino esse de necessitate salutis.' Baronius *Annal. Eccles.* tom. xiv. p. 34, Bonifac. Pap. viii. Ann. 8, iv., A.D. 1302; *Corp. Iuris Canon.* Richter et Friedberg, pars 2, col. 1246 (ed. 1881). *Extravag. Comm.* l. I. tit. viii. c. 1 'de majoritate et obedientia.'

The Vatican decree '*De vi ac ratione primatus Romani Pontificis*' runs thus: Si quis itaque dixerit Romanum Pontificem habere tantummodo officium inspectionis vel directionis, non autem plenam et supremam potestatem jurisdictionis in universam Ecclesiam, non solum in rebus quæ ad fidem et mores [morem P.], sed etiam in iis quæ ad disciplinam et regimen Ecclesiæ per totum orbem diffusæ pertinent; aut eum habere tantum potiores partes, non vero totam plenitudinem hujus supremæ potestatis; aut hanc ejus potestatem non esse ordinariam et immediatam sive in omnes ac singulas ecclesias, sive in omnes et singulos pastores et fideles; anathema sit.' *Constitutio Dogmatica prima De Ecclesia Christi, cap.* III. (V. Pelletier, *Décrets et Canons*, Paris 1871, p. 150; *Collectio Lacensis*, 1890, vol. VII., p. 485).

INTERCALARY.

PRESBYTERS AS MEMBERS OF THE ADMINISTRATION.

SOME enquiry was promised[1] into the part borne by the Clerus of antient cities, the Ordo, the Consessus or Bench of Presbyters, in the administration of church business. It would have been almost meaningless to map this out before becoming familiar with the kind of transactions amongst which their office was to be used. But some principles of its exercise can now be readily drawn out. The later correspondence of Cyprian passes into other lines, so that the indications we seek cease before the great controversy with Stephen begins.

The first epistle presents a certain Body at Carthage 'taking notice of' a Christian's will at Furni; a will, which, in violation of a *forma* or rule passed, with a prescribed penalty, by a previous Council of bishops, appointed a cleric to a legal function. This Body is not a Council, and does not either make a rule or affix a sanction, but acts as a Court in deciding that *ipso facto* the penalty has been incurred and must take effect[2].

This Body then exerts in another town of the province, which had a bishop of its own, authority over the clergy, and

---

[1] P. 21.
[2] ...*cum cognevissemus*, *Ep.* 1. 1, the law term for magisterial enquiry. The ruling is '*ideo...non est quod* pro dormitione eius apud vos fiat oblatio,' &c. *Ep.* 1. 2.

so virtually over the laity, through the carrying out of the sentence by the clergy. Its members are the Bishop of Carthage, some bishops who were in Carthage at the time and attended the meeting, and 'our compresbyters who were assessors to us[1].' There is an ambiguity as to whether '*our* compresbyters' were the *Consessus* of the city, or included others who came with their bishops.

It is not then a corporate body; it is not limited to certain persons, but to a certain class or classes. The nucleus and main part of it is the Consessus, the Presbytery of Carthage, with the Bishop for its head; it includes other bishops then in Carthage, and possibly (but this is not clear) other presbyters.

Its authority, which amounts to jurisdiction, is evident. In the epistle to Lucius he says that persecution has been the test not only of the true bishop but also of the true consessus. It has shewn which 'presbyters were united with their bishop in his sacerdotal office[2].' Had the presbytery then this authority, or something like it, inherently and apart from the presidency of the bishop? or, if not, could it by delegation of the bishop be invested with such authority?

The occurrence of Cyprian's long retirement brings some significant facts into unexpected salience, and the concurrent vacancy of the Roman see remarkably illustrates the case.

In three several letters from his retreat[3], addressed to the presbyters and deacons of Carthage, Cyprian requests them to supply his place:—'There discharge ye both your own parts and mine'; 'Your diligence must supply[4] my office'; 'Discharge my function about the conduct of things which the religious administration requires.'

He had arranged for some amount of money to be

---

[1] ...ego et collegæ *mei* qui præsentes aderant et compresbyteri *nostri* qui nobis adsidebant, *Ep.* 1. 1.

[2] *Ep.* 61. 3 'sacerdotali honore.' Both words technical.

[3] *Epp.* 5, 12, 14.

[4] Repræsentare, 'make to be present.' Sed officium meum vestra diligentia repræsentet, *Ep.* 12. 1.

realised and distributed to the clerics that there might be means in several hands. He had left in the hands of Rogatian, his commissioner, 'a little sum realised' apparently by some recent sale, and sent him a further portion afterwards[1]. Out of these funds he requests the presbyters and deacons to care for the poor, the sick and strangers, for Christians in prison, and for the bodies of those who die under torture or confinement[2]. He begs them to make such arrangements for visiting prisons as will least provoke suspicion, and to calendar the dates of martyrdoms and confessors' deaths and communicate them to him for remembrance in his daily Eucharists.

In common with the Plebes, this clerical body was usually consulted by Cyprian on the merits of persons proposed for Ordination. They were thus fixed upon 'by counsel in common,' but exceptions, at least during his absence from Carthage, were frequent. He sends to them the names of several men whom without such consultation he had admitted to Orders, some of them to a seat in the Consessus, to daily allowances and the monthly dividend[3].

He urges them to promote among the people habits of fasting and prayer for the internal reformation of the Church, and for its outward deliverance; to instruct the ignorant,

---

[1] Summula...redacta, *Ep.* 5. 1. De quantitate mea propria...aliam portionem, *Ep.* 7. *quantitas*, technically a lump sum, in *C. I. L.* VIII. i. 262 capital as opposed to *usuræ*. In *Ep.* 39 (n. 3 inf.) it has no sense of allowances, but is simply even sums.

[2] *Ibid.* and *Ep.* 12.

[3] *Epp.* 20, 38, 39, 40. *Ep.* 39. 5 '...presbyterii honorem designasse nos illis jam sciatis, ut et sportulis idem cum presbyteris honorentur, et divisiones mensurnas æquatis quantitatibus partiantur, sessuri nobiscum provectis et corroboratis annis suis....' 'Every presbyter had his standing allowance out of the church-treasury; besides the same allowance called *sportula* [cf. *Ep.* 1. 1 'sportulantium fratrum'], some also had their portion in that dividend which was the remainder of the month's expense; thirdly, out of the presbyters under him the bishop as then had a certain number of the gravest who lived and commoned always with him,' Hooker VII. xxiii. 9. *Sessuri nobiscum,* &c. means not this (though the fact may be so) but their future place in the consessus, as 'nobiscum sedeat in clero,' *Ep.* 40.

but especially those confessors, in or out of prison, whose spiritual self-satisfaction made them not very amenable[1].

So far, nothing is enjoined on the Body except a faithful performance of their individual clerical duties. He regrets their imperfect performance of their prison-duties, especially with regard to religious instruction,—duties always hitherto recognised, he says, as their proper work[2].

Strenuous admonition on their part, he insists, was required. And in virtue of the episcopal energy (*sacerdotii vigor*[3]) which he had now to exercise from a distance, he endeavoured through them especially to prevent the breaking down of discipline.

Do we here find duties of a more governmental character?

He declines in the fourteenth epistle to take a step which had been suggested by four of the presbyters, without first receiving counsel from the Body of the presbyters and deacons and being also informed of the judgment of the laity. This step was the restoration of some of the Lapsed to communion. When in spite of his message the four admitted them, he considered that the Body had failed in its duty of repressing them, and he appeals to the laity to keep the Lapsed quiet[4]. Later on[5], writing to the laity, he commends the special activity of three of the presbyters, and of the deacons as a body, in encouraging or in deterring the lapsed.

There is still no exclusive authority recognised as inherent in the consessus. The disciplinary duties here particularised are of the moral order, and can scarcely amount to more than persuasion. They are capable of being discharged by the laity, failing trustworthy clerics.

The only authority which, in Cyprian's opinion, could, as we have seen, decide on the whole wide policy to be pursued was a gathering of *co-episcopi*, and further they too must have

---

[1] *Ep.* 14. 1, 2, 3.
[2] *Epp.* 15, 16.
[3] *Ep.* 20. 2.
[4] *Ep.* 14. 4; *Ep.* 17. 2, 3.
[5] *Ep.* 43. 1.

a common understanding with the bishops of other countries. The only authority which could under that policy decide on the reinstatement of individuals was an assemblage in which both the clergy and the laity of their own Church should with the bishop at their head examine and conclude each case[1]. In this function the weight of the laity was such that they vetoed some whom Cyprian and others would have restored[2], while elsewhere he expresses regret at having in some cases overruled them. Their right as laymen to abstain from communion with a Lapsed or a Novatianist Bishop is affirmed again and again[3].

We found no particular authority assigned to the Clerus in the election of a Bishop. Their part was to bear testimony to the life of the person proposed for election. The laity elected; the neighbouring bishops assented and ordained[4]. Cyprian's letters to Cornelius, in which the principles of the coming legislation were discussed, were 'always read aloud' by Cornelius to the clerus and the laity together —'to the most flourishing clergy which sits with thee in 'the foremost rank, and to the most holy and most honour-'able commons[5].'

Whilst therefore its counsel was of the greatest weight and import in the deliberation with the bishop on all the greater affairs of the Church, we find no trace of authority or jurisdiction belonging to the Consessus as such.

The level of moral influence which belongs to it stands markedly apart from the way in which, for instance, excommunication was inflicted.

In Cyprian's absence excommunication was imposed directly by a commission appointed by himself, consisting of three bishops and two presbyters[6]. It is true that he commended the presbyters and deacons of Carthage for resolving

[1] *Ep.* 17, &c.
[2] *Ep.* 59.
[3] *Epp.* 65, 67.
[4] *Ep.* 55. 8; *Ep.* 67. 5.
[5] *Ep.* 59. 19.
[6] *Ep.* 42.

not to communicate with Gaius of Dida, a presbyter, and his deacon, after these had anticipated the Church's making of rules for re-admission, but it must be especially observed that this resolution was taken upon the *counsel of colleagues of mine*, who had frequently warned Gaius against the step, who were now *præsentes* in Carthage, and thus completed a body like that which Cyprian had presided over in the first Furni case, namely, the clerics of the city (*clerici urbici*) and bishops, whether of the Province or from beyond seas[1]. He then adds his own episcopal direction that any, whether home or foreign clergy, who in like manner anticipate the Church's own ruling are to be similarly withdrawn from.

To these bishops *præsentes* he desires that what he writes on the course to be followed may always be communicated at once. They evidently clothe the presbyters and deacons, in the absence of their own bishop, with a sufficient episcopal authority. We may just mark (though without stress) the distinctness with which they are mentioned as contributors to the subscription raised for the Confessor Bishops in the mines[2]; but an apt instance occurs in the second city of the province, Hadrumetum. Its presbyters and deacons had, in the absence of their bishop, placed themselves in communication with the new Bishop of Rome[3], before his title was cleared. Cyprian and another bishop arrive, and are *præsentes*. Upon their authority communication is suspended.

We are now in a position to gain a clearer view of the principles on which the presbyters and deacons of Rome had acted in the vacancy of the see, after Fabian's martyrdom.

Even in the eighth letter, in which they describe themselves as 'we who seem to be set over them, to lead the

---

[1] *Ep.* 34. 1. *Dida*, otherwise unknown. Morcelli's conjecture 'Idensis' not likely. It was too far off in Mauretania.

[2] *Ep.* 62. 5. Cyprian with his own *quantitas* sends them a list of subscribers at Carthage, 'sed et collegarum quoque et sacerdotum nostrorum, qui et ipsi, cum præsentes essent, ex suo plebis suæ nomine, quædam pro viribus contulerunt, nomina addidi.'

[3] *Ep.* 48. 1, 2.

flock in place of shepherds,' the extent of what they claim to have done is only to have been active in keeping people from lapsing, and in recovering the Lapsed to repentance—their due spiritual ministration in time of danger. Their statement in the thirtieth letter that all they had done was done with the help of the Confessors shews that they had no idea of a constitutional power devolving to themselves in the vacancy. But when they have officially to resolve that the adoption of a permanent system must wait for the determination of a new bishop in consultation with themselves, with the Confessors, and with the laity, this constitutional conclusion is formed in a meeting at which are present neighbouring bishops, bishops then visiting the city and bishops exiled from their dioceses.

Again, afterwards, when the Novatianist Confessors wished to return to the unity of the Church, the course taken was this. Delegates of theirs seek an interview with the Presbytery. The presbytery desire the attendance of the whole number, examine them, and report to Cornelius full particulars[1]. Cornelius next summons the presbytery, and with them five bishops, then *præsentes*[2]. They determine on their course, each opinion being recorded. Then the Confessors are introduced, and make their petition orally. The 'people' are admitted in large numbers, to hear the confession, and resolve upon it. The scene has been described above.

The result is this. When the see was vacant, or the bishop absent, the episcopal functions of hearing, judging, ruling (quite apart from the sacred offices of ordination, &c.) did not pass into commission in the hands of the clerus, but were reserved whenever it was possible. And by the attendance of other bishops, any steps of discipline which had to be immediately taken received an episcopal sanction. Hadrumetum, Rome, and Carthage, as well as the minor cases of Assuras[3] and Furni yield one result.

[1] Omni actu, *Ep.* 49. 2. qui et eo die præsentes fuerunt. *Ep.* 49. 2.
[2] Adfuerunt etiam presbyteri quinque [3] *Ep.* 65.

The contrast is manifest between what could constitutionally be done by the largest clerus in the most influential position, and the power and responsibility attaching to the least prominent bishop. It is no account of the facts to say that the scheme carefully examined yields no trace of presbyterian government. It is an absolute negation of the presbyterian idea. It is an equally complete negation of the papal idea. Scarcely less does it contrast with that modern sharpness which would fence off each diocese as a preserve in which neighbour bishops have no concern or interest. The true capitular idea is there, but with a flexibility and width of which we are not yet capable again.

> The Epistle of Firmilian (*Ep.* 75. 4) has to some seemed to speak as if in the general Councils of the East bishops and presbyters sitting together regulated church affairs in common, '...apud nos 'fit ut per singulos annos seniores et præpositi in unum con-'veniamus ad disponenda ea quæ nostræ curæ commissa sunt.' Ritschl, however, points out (p. 157) that the Greek original must have been οἱ πρεσβύτεροι οἱ προϊστάμενοι, and the *et* due to a misunderstanding of the translator. Similarly (*Ep.* 75. 7) '...quando 'omnis potestas et gratia in ecclesia constituta sit ubi præsident '*majores natu qui et* baptizandi et manum imponendi et ordinandi '*possident potestatem.*' He compares Hermas (*Vis.* ii. 4) where οἱ πρεσβύτεροι οἱ προϊστάμενοι τῆς ἐκκλησίας is in the Latin version 'seniores qui præsunt ecclesiæ,' and Eusebius *H. E.* vii. 5. 1: 5. 5: 29. 1, from which it is clear that bishops alone formed the Eastern Councils.

CHAPTER VIII.

THE BAPTISMAL QUESTION.

Veri similitudine aberrantes a veritate.
AUG. *de Catechizandis Rudibus*, c. 8.

THERE is an early and rather graceful martyr-tale which Baronius welcomes as history, and which Tillemont smiles at himself for admitting to some consideration on account of its honest mien[1]. It is called the 'Acts of Hippolytus, Eusebius, and their Fellow-Martyrs.' Hippolytus is a Roman recluse who lives in a sandburrow in the Crypts, or Catacombs[2], and there conceals for some time his converted relations. The difficulties of maintenance in such a place, the unhistorical details, and later features shew the story to be pure romance.

The principal personage is Pope Stephen, who is introduced to baptize the multitudes whom Hippolytus Christianizes. The well appropriated by the story to his use is yet near the old entrance from the sandpit-road to the Cemetery of Domitilla on the Via Ardeatina[3]. This character in which

---

[1] Baronius, *Annales*, A.D. 259, vii—xii. Tillemont, *Note ii. sur S. Estienne*, v. IV. p. 593.

[2] In cryptis...in arenario.

[3] J. H. Parker, *Archæology of Rome*, p. xii. *The Catacombs*, sect. VI. p. 89. On one side of the original entrance and like it built of beautiful

332   THE BAPTISMAL QUESTION.

Stephen appears, as the Great Baptizer, is the rude form which the main episode of his life assumed among the simple.

It is with that episode that our next group of letters and documents is concerned. This group includes Epistles 69 to

brickwork is the arched recess with the deep well. The well-top is of white stone, two feet high; on either side above, the holes for the beam on which the pitcher hung; in the wall on our right, the conduit and basin to receive the water. On the other side of the entrance a vestibule with seats of stone. The baptismal arrangements throughout deserve more notice than, I believe, they have received.

VIII.   THE BAPTISMAL QUESTION.   333

75 and the 'Judgments of the Eighty-seven Bishops.' They belong to the years 255 and 256 A.D. Their exclusive subject is 'Rebaptism.' For although Cyprian protests[1] against the application of that term to his view, catholic teaching insists on the assertion which it involves.

The simplest lines on which our investigation can advance will be—I. to give what we perceive of the earlier opinions forming Cyprian's tradition; II. next to describe the positions of the two leaders and the action and documents of the contest; III. then to group together the reasonings urged on either side of this great argument.

A great argument it is, in spite of its narrow form. The first questioning was 'How can profane waters bless?' It means at least this:—'A Soul longs to be baptized into 'Christ. A mistaken, erring, even an immoral believer does 'in intention baptize it into Christ. Is that Soul in fact 'baptized into another than Christ, or into a society other 'than His Church? Or, is the baptized proselyte of a 'heretical sect a baptized Catholic in spite of circumstance?' The decision which the wise and loving Cyprian formed and laboriously propagated was to deny the reality of all such baptism. This is that grave anti-catholic error of his which not only struck unperceived at the root of the spiritual constitution of the Church, and threatened to number her among her own sects, but in principle withdrew the virtue of the Sacrament from the immediate ministering of Christ present, and attached it to the human agent.

The difference was great. Yet not for a moment did Cyprian dream of severing the connection between his own church and the churches which he conceived to be in error. Not for a moment has the Catholic Church ceased to revere him as one of her most authoritative fathers. *O si sic*

---

[1] *Ep.* 73. 1. However, the Nicene Council, canon 19, adopts ἀναβαπτί-ζεσθαι as a word without a sting, for the church baptism which it orders for returning Paulianists.

omnia. The bounds which of necessity, as men now believe, part many sects at present from the Church are like low lines of hill in comparison with that mountain-range of difference on fundamentals which lay between Cyprian and those from whom he dissented.

The distance between their possibilities and ours is the distance between a great age of construction and an age of minute criticism. But have we for ever lost the power of acting as they acted? of seeing with the 'larger, other eyes'?

To Cyprian himself in his ingenuous moderation it seemed but an obvious course to desire 'every man to speak his 'thought: to judge no man: to remove no man from the 'right to communion, if he dissents...': 'to wait for Christ's 'own judgment[1].' The Donatists, perplexed like us by this liberality in one whom they chose to look on as their patron, imagined it to have been a ruse to elicit free expression of opinions; on which Augustine's comment is that this would have been a morality far worse than any heresy[2]. Equally simple the course seemed to Augustine: 'Put me down as 'one of those whom Cyprian failed to persuade. Never may 'I attain his glory; nor compare in authorship with him; for 'his genius I love him, in his eloquence I delight me; I 'marvel at his charity, and I venerate his martyrdom,—but 'this, his strange doctrine, I do not accept[3].' The great lesson in fact which Augustine is perpetually enforcing by Cyprian's example is the lesson of our 'liberty without losing our communion-rights to think diversely[4].'

Hooker's famous apophthegm, 'The teacher's error is the 'people's trial,—harder and heavier to bear, as he is in worth 'and regard greater that mispersuadeth them,' no way qualifies his appreciation of him 'whom the world did in his life-'time admire as the greatest among prelates and now honours

---

[1] *Sentt. Epp. Proem.*
[2] *Contra Crescon.* iii. 2.
[3] *c. Crescon.* II. xxxii. 40.
[4] Salvo jure communionis diversa sentire. *De Bapt. c. Donatt.* VI. vii. 10.

'as not the lowest in the kingdom of Heaven[1].' Taylor vigorously sums the moral, 'Saint Cyprian did right in a 'wrong cause and Stephen did ill in a good cause. As far 'then as piety and charity is to be preferred before a true 'opinion, so far is Cyprian's practice a better precedent for 'us, and as an example of primitive sanctity, than the zeal 'and indiscretion of Stephen. S. Cyprian had not learned 'to forbid to any one a liberty of prophesying or interpre-'tation if he transgressed not the foundation of the faith and 'the creed of the Apostles[2].'

I. 1. *The Tradition of Africa.*

We now proceed to consider, as one source of Cyprian's teaching, the tradition which he inherited :—

The religious sympathies of the Africans flowed ever in deep impetuous narrow courses like the streams of their own Atlas. To make separations sharp and unkind was not the aim of a Tertullian only or a Donatus. Cyprian himself is not unaware of the tendency of his church to narrow its own limits. 'Certain predecessors of ours among the bishops here 'in our own province,' he writes, 'have utterly refused any 'place of repentance' to offenders who in other churches 'were forgiven after penance.' Nay Augustine, broader churchman as he was, had rather a shivering trust in even the Divine charity towards those whom his particular breadths did not comprehend.

The 'first of all mortals,' as Vincent of Lerins puts it, to rule that they who had been baptized by schismatics must be baptized anew ere they could become catholics was Agrippinus of Carthage[3]. Augustine points out often that Cyprian

---

[1] *Ecclesiasticae Polity*, B. v. lxii. 9.   *Of Heresy*, 23.
[2] *Liberty of Prophesying*, Sect. 2.   [3] Vinc. Lir. *Common.* i. 6.

is unable to adduce any earlier authority than his against 'universal, sturdy custom[1].' As regards the Western churches the reader may accept the statement. Agrippinus was the bishop next but one before Cyprian in his see. Under him a Council of seventy[2] African and Numidian[3] prelates decided in his sense.

In the Roman Church on the contrary the tradition was clear and continuous against Rebaptism of schismatics. Some have understood a passage of Hippolytus, which covers the ground up to that time, to accuse Callistus[4] of rebaptizing them[5]. But not only is the passage not susceptible of that meaning, but the distinct unchallenged declaration of Stephen that his church had never allowed such a practice

---

[1] Universalis...robusta consuetudo. Aug. *de Bapt. c. Donatt.* III. i. 3; xii. 17; II. vii. 12; IV. vi. 8.

[2] Aug. *de unic. Bapt. c. Petil.* xiii. 22.

[3] *Ep.* 71. 4.

[4] Sedit A.D. 217—14 Oct. A.D. 222.

[5] Hippolytus, *Ref. Hær.* ix. 12 Ἐπὶ τούτου [τοῦ Καλλίστου] πρώτως τετόλμηται δεύτερον αὐτοῖς βάπτισμα. The words should have accurate attention: it is not said τετόλμηται αὐτῷ, but ἐπὶ τούτου αὐτοῖς 'by that party during his bishopric.' It is not πρῶτον αὐτοῖς τετόλμηται as though *they* were the inventors; but ἐπὶ τούτου πρώτως 'primarily in his time.' The perfect τετόλμηται indicates that *their* practice existed still at Rome when Hippolytus wrote, and so probably in Stephen's time, without in the least affecting church tradition. The passage proceeds, Ταῦτα μὲν οὖν ὁ θαυμασιώτατος Κάλλιστος συνεστήσατο. Ταῦτα refers to all the list of doctrines and practices which Callistus was supposed to patronise. The careful reader of the whole story will not conceive that the word συνεστήσατο is intended to state that Callistus himself taught Rebaptism, but will rather admire the skill with which Hippolytus avoids asserting it. Nor will he have any doubt that αὐτοῖς means a corrupt and evil faction who for a time were too near the papal chair, but fell (some at least) into the Elchasaïte delusions.

To so much exculpation Callistus is entitled, but it is positively scaring to mark the modes and motives of Roman Catholic scholars. Even Hefele, B. I. c. II. § 4, not seeing how to deliver Callistus from the scandal of a practice (which is not really imputed to him in the words) or how to disentangle him from his party (which is more difficult) represents Hippolytus as saying, 'Rebaptism was introduced under Callistus *in some churches* in communion with him'; adding, 'one can scarcely doubt that he has in view Agrippinus and his Synod of Carthage.'

On the other hand, for want of attention to these same points Fechtrup (p. 194 and n. 1) renders 'unter Kallistus sei das Wagniss der Wiedertaufe *in der Kirche auf*gekommen,' and fixes the Council of Agrippinus in the middle of the Episcopate of Callistus A.D. 220, a date which suits none of the conditions.

from the apostles down is incontrovertible[1]. Hippolytus however, though Callistus' bitter enemy, certainly avoids ascribing the practice to him personally. 'In *his time* first hath second baptism been ventured on by *them*,' that is, by the worldly, lax and perhaps licentious party which was named after that liberal and versatile prelate. All doctrines and practices found their way sooner or later to Rome. This practice came to Rome in Callistus' time, and was adopted during his administration by the party with whom he had been connected before he became pope, and who were called Callistians by his enemies and theirs[2]. Only, whereas in its native province that practice bore a Puritan character, drawing the sharpest line between church and sect, it received in the Capital the quite opposite stamp; being intended by the Callistians to open an easier way than that of penance to the restoration of gross sinners. The reception of schismatics followed easily, but the Church never accepted this, nor is there evidence that Callistus himself did.

If we allow four or five years for the practice to have been in use elsewhere before it came in at Rome, we might infer that the unknown date of Agrippinus' Council was about 213[3]. In the Council of September A.D. 256 was present one Novatus who had been bishop of the rich and beautiful city of Thamugadi so long that he was now one of the very oldest prelates there, fourth by seniority out of the eighty-seven. If our date for Agrippinus' Council be correct we can under-

---

[1] Ap. *Ep.* 75. 5, 6, 19; ap. *Epp.* 71. 2, 3; 73. 13. What Bunsen means by saying 'Döllinger has demonstrated that Zephyrinus (A.D. 199—217) admitted rebaptism of those who had been heretics, and as such had committed carnal mortal sins' I cannot divine. *Hippolytus and his age*, v. 1. p. 271 (ed. 1854).

[2] Τὴν τοῦ ὀνόματος μετέσχον ἐπίκλησιν καλεῖσθαι διὰ τὸν πρωτοστατήσαντα τῶν τοιούτων ἔργων Κάλλιστον Καλλιστιανοί. Hippolytus, *Ref. Hær.* IX. 12. They especially affected the style of 'Catholics,' ἑαυτοὺς οἱ ἀπηρυθριασμένοι καθολικὴν ἐκκλησίαν ἀποκαλεῖν ἐπιχειροῦσι, as was natural.

[3] This date best fits all the circumstances of the text. I am sorry that I once wrote differently: Article on 'Agrippinus,' *Dictionary of Christian Biography*.

B. 22

338   THE BAPTISMAL QUESTION.

stand how this old man could just speak of the members of that Council, forty-four years before, as 'colleagues' while he also calls them 'men of holiest memory[1].' We can understand how Cyprian, talking of a long-standing custom, says 'many years have passed and a long period since Agrippinus' Council,' while Augustine, thinking of the whole tenor of church practice, says 'the novelty had prevailed but a few years before Cyprian[2].'

An interesting question has arisen as to whether this Council had felt the influence of Tertullian, since in a treatise commonly accepted as catholic, and if so probably prior to the year 200, he not only declares the rebaptism of heretics to be necessary, but says he had written a Greek treatise to that purpose[3].

I can feel only surprise that his pamphlet on Baptism should ever have been looked on as catholic work[4]. Its singularities, not to say frivolities, are as striking as its power and grasp and goodness, and they have the Montanist tinge. When a Catholic he did not write in the character of a Montanist, but as a Montanist he often wrote like a noble Catholic.

Neander thinks that, when under the influence of Montanism, he could scarcely have spoken as he does here of the visible Church. But his Montanist mind is a strange stormy study. This dogma, we should remember, was quite in the Montanist vein[5], and his belief in continuous revelation did not obliterate respect for a solemn church utterance, though it made him hold churchmen cheap.

He observes that 'it would be improper to rehandle the

---

[1] Morcelli's date A.D. 197, sixty years before, would make 'decretum *collegarum nostrorum*' meaningless.

[2] Cf. Firmilian, *Ep.* 75. 4, speaking of Valentinus and Basilides as having lived *post apostolos et post longam ætatem. Ep.* 71. 4. Aug. *de Bapt. c. Donatt.* IV. vi. 8.

[3] Tert. *De Baptismo*, c. 15.

[4] Bp. Kaye doubts if he is right in following the majority of commentators in so classifying it.

[5] In a pamphlet which he hurled at the Church as a Montanist, the Heathen baptized by a Heretic has to be cleansed of 'both the men,' his ethnic self and his heretic self: *De Pudicitia* c. 19.

'question of what should be observed as concerning heretics, 'for it has been published to us.' His word is *'published'* not *'handed down'* to us[1]. This expression can, I believe, only refer to the Council of Agrippinus. It cannot refer, as some wish, to the voice of Scripture, for Tertullian is the most patient and pertinacious arguer upon texts, and never passes Scriptural warrant with so vague an allusion. He can only have in view some well-known, recent, authoritative sentence, and the great Council of Seventy under the Bishop of Carthage is fitly alluded to by the Carthaginian presbyter in those terms.

Later on in the controversy we become suddenly aware from the lengthy Epistle of Firmilian, Bishop of Cæsarea in Cappadocia, that there had for long past been some interchange of influences on this subject between Africa and the Eastern regions of Asia Minor. We therefore look to what we know of the judgment of these last.

I. 2. *The Tradition of Asia Minor East.*

In his furiously Montanist treatise 'On Fasting' Tertullian speaks with reverence of the 'councils' habitually held 'throughout the Græcias' as an impressive image of the whole Church. He would fain see them, with their preliminary fastings, introduced into the West[2]. We may readily assure ourselves that, when so speaking, he had not in view councils which specially subjected Montanists to Rebaptism as an apostolic institution for the restoration of heretics[3]. This would have been

---

[1] *Editum* not *treditum*. *De Bapt.* 15. The difference is an accurate one.

[2] If this suggestion of Tertullian's *de Jejun.* c. 13 reasonably indicates that the First Council of Carthage under Agrippinus had not yet been held (Hefele, *H. des Concíles*, B. I. c. ii. § 4), this helps us to fix the date of that pamphlet as towards 210 A.D. And if the previous reasoning is accurate we should further determine the date of the *de Baptismo* to about A.D. 214 or 215.

[3] *Ep.* 75. 5, 7.

more than flesh and blood, particularly Tertullian's, could endure to eulogize.

The Council of Iconium there held for Phrygia, Galatia and the neighbouring districts is one which thus ranked Montanists with heretics needing baptism. There is no reason for fixing its date earlier than A.D. 230[1]. Firmilian, writing in 256, says he had been one of the 'very many' who there so ruled it[2], and Synnada[3] which dealt with the same subject in the same sense was probably near the same time. One of these two is probably that 'Council of Fifty' which Donatists alleged against Augustine[4]. The large number of Fifty Bishops gathered in that small locality is a note of truth. For in Phrygia Towns and Bishoprics were identical[5]. A system of Rector-Bishops, which commends itself to some imaginations now, prevailed there. Power vested in an aggregation of necessarily second-rate men proved to be powerless against those elements of faction, passion and superstition which S. Paul foresaw might rend and end those churches.

The religious tone of Phrygia was peculiarly likely to lead to some difficulty as to Baptism. Everything initiatory, that is

---

[1] The date of Tillemont, IV. p. 140, and Valois on Euseb. vii. 7.

[2] Plurimi simul convenientes in Iconio diligentissime tractavimus et confirmavimus, *Ep.* 75. 19.

[3] The site of Synnada was unknown until 1876, when M. Perrot found it in the highlands of Phrygia. It was an assize-town (*conventus*) and the central office of the imperial *procurator marmorum*, manager of the quarries and vast transport of bath-slabs, monolith columns and capitals of the purple-flecked Phrygian marble called Docimites or Synnadic. After A.D. 160 the office was merged in the new one of *procurator Phrygiæ* who took the woods and lands also. Strabo speaks of its great ἐλαιόφυτον πεδίον, but there must be some mistake (conj. ἀμπελόφυτον), as olives will not grow at 3400 ft. (W. M. Ramsay, *Journal of Hellenic Studies*, vol. VIII. pp. 481, 2). As to points connected with the Council, it suits Dr Peters' arguments to call Synnada the capital of Phrygia, but it never was so until after 300 A.D., and then capital only of the Division 'Salutaris.'

'Why does Firmilian *not mention* the Council of Synnada?' is an unanswerable question. Döllinger arbitrarily takes one out of many possible replies and thereupon dates the same Council. Hefele does not even quote his reasons.

[4] Aug. *c. Crescon.* iii. 2, 3.

[5] W. M. Ramsay, *The Cities and Bishoprics of Phrygia, J. of H. S. l.c.*

VIII. I. 2. THE TRADITION OF ASIA MINOR EAST. 341

everything exclusive, was dear to the native mind. But while Augustine remarks that fifty oriental bishops were no evidence, though backed by seventy Africans, against the unity of the tradition elsewhere, Iconium and Synnada must both be numbered among the series 'held long ago' and 'in many districts,' of which Dionysius the Great tells[1] his namesake (as yet a presbyter) of Rome that he had heard, and which took the same view as to the reception of Heretics in general.

The firm belief which these Councils entertained that they were continuing apostolic usage, while the very need for them is the best evidence that the usage was far from being clear or accepted, may connect itself with the fact that two canons, based, to say the least, on their decisions, appear in the Apostolic Canons. It would not be strange if one of these two were the actual utterance of Iconium[2].

---

[1] Before A.D. 258; ap. Eus. vii. 7, which is given in full in Note on 'Dates,' p. 347.

[2] *Apost. Can.* xlv. (Dionys. Exig. xlvi.), Ἐπίσκοπον ἢ πρεσβύτερον αἱρετικῶν δεξάμενον βάπτισμα [ἢ θυσίαν] καθαιρεῖσθαι προστάσσομεν. Τίς γὰρ συμφώνησις τοῦ Χριστοῦ πρὸς τοῦ Βελίαλ; ἢ τίς μερὶς πιστοῦ μετὰ ἀπίστου; The manifest interpolation ἢ θυσίαν has no place in the Latin rendering of Dionysius.—*Can.* xlvi. (D. xlvii.) Ἐπίσκοπος ἢ πρεσβύτερος τὸν κατ' ἀλήθειαν ἔχοντα βάπτισμα ἐὰν ἄνωθεν βαπτίσῃ, ἢ τὸν μεμολυσμένον παρὰ τῶν ἀσεβῶν ἐὰν μὴ βαπτίσῃ, καθαιρείσθω, ὡς γελῶν τὸν σταυρὸν καὶ τὸν τοῦ κυρίου θάνατον, καὶ μὴ διακρίνων ἱερέας τῶν ψευδιερέων.

45. 'Bishop or Presbyter admitting baptism of heretics we appoint to be deposed. For what is Christ's consent to Belial, or what the faithful man's part with the faithless?'

46. 'Bishop or Presbyter, if he baptize anew him that hath a Baptism according to truth, or if he baptize not him that hath been polluted of the impious,—let him be deposed, as one that mocketh the Cross and the Lord's Death, and discerneth not priests from the false priests.'

These canons are plainly the work of different legislators. One clause of the second covers the whole ground of the first. They allege different specimens of the then popular arguments. Only the first of the two appears in the Coptic Code (Bunsen, *Hippolytus and his age*, vol. II. p. 228, ed. 1854). We might have fancied that, were they actual canons of Iconium or Synnada, they would not have escaped some allusion to Cataphrygians. But Firmilian shews (*Ep.* 75. 19) that the Iconium Resolution was made *general* on purpose; 'repudiandum esse omne omnino baptisma quod sit extra ecclesiam constitutum,' and thus it is possible that the very words of Iconium may be contained in Canon xlv. Pearson considers them earlier than Iconium, but if so, why should they not have been

Evidence there is none to enable us to answer the interesting question whether Tertullian's Greek Treatise had influenced the decision of the Greek Councils[1]. If it were so his weapon was strangely turned against him.

One far-fetched theory is that Tertullian actually condemned Heretical Baptism with the aim of procuring an oblique sanction for Montanism from the Catholic Church, which he expected not to condemn its advocate: nay, that he was so far successful that Synnada left Montanism in consequence untouched. This view, not baseless only, but contrary to the facts of the documents, is worth noticing only as an instance of the modern Roman determination to trace every anti-Roman fact to condemned or suspected sources outside the Church. Tertullian is to be the great 'First 'cause of the Innovation introduced as well into Africa as 'into the East.'

II. 1. *Position of the Leaders.*

Tertullian then, whether he contributed or no, through his treatise on Fasting, to popularise in Africa the idea of Councils, cannot, at least by his treatise on Baptism, have affected the Agrippine decision. Tertullian with his spiritual allies and Agrippinus with his Bishops were alike carried on by a rising wave of rigour, which swept across Asia Minor and Africa, was observed from Egypt as it passed, and just reached Rome, there to affect only a miserable sect. In the more tenacious Asia the practice of Rebaptism, once ratified,

---

appealed to as still more important? Firmilian appeals to that Council's decision as final, and Dionysius to both it and Synnada as most weighty.

[1] Fechtrup, p. 195, alleges no evidence except the writing of that treatise in Greek. Unhappily such things well expressed pass for evidence. Dr Peters (p. 498) rejoices to think the notion is his own. 'Diese Behauptung ist neu!' We will lament for him that Döllinger should have anticipated him (see Döll. *Hipp. und Kallist.* p. 191), only Döllinger observes its fearful effect on the longevity of Firmilian and dates Iconium about A.D. 231.

quietly held its ground. In busier Africa it quietly went much out of use, so that Cyprian, while he declares that 'thousands of heretics have thus become churchmen through 'the Laver of Life,' has nevertheless to meet the argument that numbers of them had been received without it, and had fallen asleep in the bosom of the Church[1]. It had continued in Numidia since the old Council, but a change of feeling forces her bishops to consult Carthage afresh[2]. And Augustine confesses that he 'scarcely knows what Cyprian means 'by saying that the practice had prevailed from Agrippinus' 'day to his own; for,' he rationally asks, 'what occasion was 'there for Cyprian's three Councils if all Africa had but one 'custom? or why should Cyprian have argued to Jubaian 'that he was making no change, since Agrippinus had deter-'mined it before? or why should so many of the Bishops 'have advised [in the Third Council on Baptism] that reason 'and truth must be preferred to custom[3]'—if the fact were not, as Firmilian allows, that, while Asia had maintained the doctrine and the practice, the practice of Africa had diverged from the theory[4]?

We have seen all along that Cyprian's most brilliant characteristic was that he quickened anew every languishing organ of church life and inspired with fresh forces each doctrine which worldly peace was holding lightly. In the most vigorous time of life he first received both doctrines and ordinances into a vivid intellect logically trained. He could not accept them merely. They must live. They must be lived. To such 'late-learning' leaders of great movements it has not unfrequently happened that some one point bursts out of its desuetude upon their imagination with disproportioned power. In his case the exceeding delight of his own reali-

---

[1] *Ep.* 73. 3 and 23. Dr Peters points out, p. 437, note 5, that Tertullian, *de Pudic.* 19, seems to say that Rebaptism was among the Montanists ('*et apud nos*'), as in contrast to the Catholics whom he is disparaging. But the bearing of the words is arguable.
[2] *Epp.* 70, 71.
[3] Aug. *de Bapt. c. Donatt.* III. xii. 17.
[4] *Ep.* 75. 19.

sation of the blessing and illumination of Baptism[1] gave intense meaning to the old ruling, when he first read it, that even believers in Christ, unless once baptized into the catholic fulness of the one Church, need still to be baptized. Every reader of the *De Unitate* is startled at the vehemence[2] with which he so early recorded this conviction. Then although the Novatianist exclusion of the whole Church from the Church provoked no mere retaliation, it is impossible to think that it did not stimulate the sense that the schismatics were themselves excluded by an earlier flaw; point the observation that they had suffered so much less in the persecution; and awaken a confidence that the neglected church duty would, if revived and insisted on, exhibit to all men the fact that Novatianists were not church people at all. A half-worldly temptation strangely reinforced the spiritual enthusiasm.

When therefore the question arrived in simple form 'Are we of Numidia right in rebaptizing, or are you of Carthage right in ignoring the standing order?' it was not a crotchet which Cyprian took up. The whole man was on fire.

It is only through these facts that we can account for what we have now to study and lament; the precipitation and the passion which possessed him and the many men whom he had by this time moulded to be like him. It was inevitable that sooner or later the broad and the purist theories should collide, because they were theories embodied in daily usages.

Some indication on the part of Stephen in favour of heretical baptism was the occasion of the conflict. Whether the incident was to his honour or no, it is thankless to aggravate the failings of an unpopular personage, from whose

---

[1] See sup. p. 15, *ad Donatum*.
[2] Peters, p. 510 n., speaks of a different interpretation proposed by himself and not approved.

conduct nothing but good has resulted. His tolerance of Novatianism, and his patronage of lapsed bishops, may make it probable that personally he was biassed, though in the right direction, by little else than his vague liberality. But it is at least possible that his motive was the exact contrary of this; that he interposed with a necessary correction of the Callistian Liberals, who doubtless were prepared to purge errors of belief as they purged errors of life, by second baptism.

'It must move our wonder,' says Cyprian in his first letter on the subject[1], 'nay rather our indignation and grief, 'that there are Christians found to take the side of antichrists; 'that shufflers in the faith, and traitors to the Church, take á 'stand within the Church herself against the Church. Now, 'since these allow (notwithstanding their usual pertinacity and 'indocility) that heretics and schismatics alike do not possess 'the Holy Spirit, and that accordingly, though they can 'baptize, they cannot impart the Holy Spirit,—here we con-'vict them;—namely, by pointing out that such as have not 'the Holy Spirit cannot baptize at all.' In enquiring who his earliest adversary was, it is noteworthy, though not in itself sufficient index, that 'pertinacity and indocility' are the particular virtues which Cyprian steadily assigns to Stephen.

Next, an Italian localisation is given to these asserters of the obnoxious doctrine by another passage in the same letter[2]. 'Since the Church alone has the water of life, and 'power to baptize and to wash man, he that says one can 'be baptized and sanctified in Novatian's hands, must first 'prove and convince us that Novatian is in the Church, or a 'prelate of the Church. The Church is one. As one she cannot 'be both inside and outside. If she is with Novatian, she was 'not with Cornelius. But if she was with Cornelius, who

---

[1] *Ep.* 69. 10.   [2] *Ep.* 69. 3.

'succeeded to Bishop Fabian by legitimate ordination,...
'Novatian is not in the Church, and cannot be counted
'a bishop, seeing that he, in contempt of evangelical and
'apostolic tradition, being in succession to no one, is self-
'produced. For in no wise can he hold or keep the Church,
'who has not been ordained in the Church.'

The personality of the gainsayer next becomes clear (though as yet no name has been mentioned) when in the seventy-first letter[1] we read, 'We must not go by prescription 'of custom: we must prevail by reasoning: for neither did 'Peter, whom the Lord chose first of all, and on whom He 'built His Church, when afterward Paul disputed with him on 'Circumcision, insolently claim or arrogantly assume anything 'to himself, declaring "that he himself held the primacy and 'ought the rather to be obeyed by novices, and men (called) 'later than himself"; neither did he look down on Paul, as 'the Church's former persecutor, but he adopted the counsel 'of truth, and readily assented to the legitimate system that 'Paul maintained; giving us thereby a lesson in unity and 'patience, not to hug our own fancies with *pertinacity*, but, if 'our brothers and colleagues offer upon occasion useful and 'wholesome suggestions, rather to make those our own, if 'they are true and regular.'

Although he may in these passages include other and nearer neighbours; whether bishops who in the first Council dissented from his views, or that remarkable Unknown Author (he may have been one of these) from whose pen we have the fine contemporary tract 'Of Rebaptism[2]'; yet plainly the one prominent figure before him, in whose opposition all other opposition was merged, is none other than the Bishop of Rome. And in Stephen's tone there had evidently been some personal disparagement, as well as some uncalled for measuring of the popedom of Rome against that of Carthage.

---

[1] *Ep.* 71. 3. [2] Vid. infra p. 352.

VIII. II. I.   POSITION OF THE LEADERS—STEPHEN.   347

Then flowed in upon Cyprian (not, one would infer[1], without something of concert with himself) a series of formal letters, known to us only by his replies, requesting him to deliver his opinion upon the subject. The original enquiry was whether a baptism among the adherents of Novatian, the accuracy of whose creed was unimpeached, might be accepted as valid, when such persons turned to seek admission among the Catholics. The question then ran through degrees of misbelief until the case of Marcionites, and perhaps even of Ophites, was debated[2]. Stephen made no difficulty about including, Cyprian about excluding, one and all. But for the ordinary African bishop who felt the puritanic tendency of his people towards Novatianism, (a tendency which had already surged up in Montanism, and was to break over them yet more terribly in Donatism,) and who now saw Rebaptism used in this alone of all heresies as its characteristic initiation, it was no slight dilemma which presented itself in the question, Was the adherence to this almost isolated tradition of Africa itself a dangerous, a puritanic, a practically Novatianistic departure from the breadth of catholic use?

Dates (Council of Iconium and other).

Eus. *H. E.* vii. 7. (1) Lipsius (*Chron. d. Römischen Bischöfe*, pp. 219, 20) argues that the Synod of Iconium was *later* than the Synod of Antioch A.D. 253, because it appears from comparing Euseb. vi. 46 with vii. 4, 5 that after the unexpected harmony at Antioch they felt anxious lest the question of baptism should divide them. But surely this is no argument for dating any one *particular* Synod. For we might equally well apply it to others, one by one, and conclude that *all* Baptismal decisions were later than the Council of Antioch. (2) Lipsius argues that since Cyprian was πρῶτος τῶν τότε (Eus. vii. 3) who held this particular opinion (ἡγεῖτο), therefore Cyprian's rupture with Stephen *preceded* the Council of Iconium.

[1] The series is so complete as to suggest this. As the three Councils represent, 1. Africa, 2. Africa and Numidia, 3. Africa, Numidia and Mauretania, so the letters are, 1. from an African Layman, 2. From the Bishops of Numidia, 3. From two Bishops of Mauretania.

[2] *Ep.* 73. 4.

which he accordingly dates 255 A.D. But certainly Eusebius does not mean to contradict the statement which he quotes (vii. 7) from Dionysius who in A.D. 256 writes that Rebaptism had been held 'long ago,' πρὸ πολλοῦ, κατὰ τοὺς πρὸ ἡμῶν ἐπισκόπους, ἐν ταῖς πολυανθρωποτάταις ἐκκλησίαις καὶ ταῖς συνόδοις τῶν ἀδελφῶν ἐν Ἰκονίῳ, καὶ Συνάδοις καὶ παρὰ πολλοῖς τοῦτο ἔδοξεν, nor yet can he mean to deny that the Council of Agrippinus had so ruled in Carthage itself. But if πρῶτος τῶν τότε affects the date of Iconium it must affect the date of Dionysius' Councils, and that of Agrippinus too. Mark too that the τῶν τότε is in the very next sentence to his distinct expression (vii. 2) ζητήματος οὐ σμικροῦ τηνικάδε ἀνακινηθέντος.

The fact is, Eusebius means exactly what he says. Asia Minor had quietly continued, Africa had in many parts quietly dropped the practice, and Cyprian was the first τῶν τότε, *i.e. of his contemporaries*, to moot its reaffirmation.

Lipsius is driven by his own special pleading to say that there were *two* synods at Iconium 'which must not be confounded,' one of A.D. 255 mentioned by Firmilian, and the other much earlier named by Dionysius; both about the baptism of heretics ; both making only the same declaration, at considerable interval. Sufficiently improbable. Besides, Firmilian attended the one he mentions, and he, writing in 256 A.D., speaks of it (*Ep.* 75. 7) as having been held *jam pridem*.

Of Roman writers, Baronius and Labbe[1] were anxious to believe this synod was held in Stephen's time, and thereby to justify his behaviour to the East. Dr Peters on the same side[2] places it 'not in the second, but very early in the third century' in order to enable it to have been misled by the pamphlets of Tertullian, and this induces him to put Synnada earlier still, and at the same time as Agrippinus' Council.

The order in which Dionysius names the two synods is rather against the general assumption that Synnada preceded Iconium.

The following then are the approximate dates which appear probable in respect of the conditions with which we are acquainted.

Zephyrinus Bp. of Rome	A.D.	199—217.
Tertullian becomes Montanist	*circ.*	200.
,, writes *De Jejunio*	*circ.*	209, 10.
Council of Agrippinus	*circ.*	213.
Tertullian's *De Baptismo*	*circ.*	214, 15
Callistus Bp. of Rome		217—222.
Council of Iconium	*circ.*	230.
Council of Synnada		? 231.

[1] Baron. *Ann.* A.D. 258, xiv.; Labbe A.D. 258, in spite of Pagi and Harduin whom he quotes; *Conc.* t. I. p. 769.
[2] P. 498.

II. 2. *Acts and Documents.*

Our clearest method will now be first to describe the Documents, and then to draw out by themselves the Arguments, which are so often repeated that chronological analysis of the letters would be wasted here[1].

Magnus, a layman, whom Cyprian treats with respect and affection, writes the first letter—an enquiry whether Novatianists should be accounted as other heretics in the need of church-baptism on recantation. In Magnus' circle the old canon was plainly not forgotten, and the plausibility of an exception is obvious.

Then followed an application from eighteen bishops of Numidia. These had continued the practice which they and their predecessors had helped Agrippinus to establish[2]; but the movement of the times, especially perhaps among the laity, required fresh consideration. The reply to Magnus came from Cyprian[3]; that to the Numidians from a Council which he soon convoked, of thirty-three bishops of Africa with the presbyters of Carthage[4].

This is CYPRIAN'S FIFTH COUNCIL OF CARTHAGE and FIRST ON BAPTISM, A.D. 255.

The seventieth epistle is their conciliar declaration, confirming that of the old Council of Agrippinus, That neither the baptism nor the confirmation of heretics has any value: That converts from a heresy can only through baptism enter into the faith and unity of the Church.

This decision seems to have been not unanimously arrived

A.D. 255.
A.U.C. 1008.
Coss. Imp. Cæs. P. Licinius Valerianus Pius Felix Aug. III. Imp. Cæs. P. Licinius Egnatius Gallienus Pius Felix Aug. II.

---

[1] We may repeat that the group includes *Epp.* 69—75 and the *Sententiæ Episcoporum* of the Third Council, and belongs to the years A.D. 255 and 256.

[2] *Ep.* 70. 1.

[3] *Ep.* 69. Rettberg (pp. 190—192) assigns to this letter the same date as to that which answers Pompeius, *Ep.* 74, on account of the same 'Ideenkreis' apparent in it. But as his reply to Magnus is rested upon his own view and arguments without reference to councils, it certainly precedes all the councils. That to Pompeius alludes (*Ep.* 74. 12) to the first Council (*Ep.* 70. 1) if not to the second.

[4] *Ep.* 71. 1.

at. Cyprian describes it as the judgment of 'very many fellow-bishops'; but he laments the fact that 'certain of our colleagues are guided by some strange confidence' to the other opinion[1].

Next comes a Mauretanian bishop, one Quintus[2], enquiring through a *compresbyter* Lucian; he is answered by the seventy-first letter, with the seventieth, already in wide circulation, enclosed[3]. The tone of Cyprian is as of one who has suffered slights. It is clear that the tone of the Roman bishop was already becoming injurious; clear also that unanimity had not yet prevailed in Carthage.

At this time, without one allusion in it to the embittering controversy, Cyprian published his tract, 'Of the Excellency of Patience,' to be a calming note in the awaking storm. Very little later in date, and similar in purpose, is his 'Jealousy and Envy'; equally reticent on passing circumstance, except for one slight touch upon Novatian. These shall be examined later. Now we need only name them as further illustrations of Cyprian's vision of a new philosophy of moral feeling, adjusted to the new doctrine and proportioned to its standard. And we may think of the angelic spirit of the man who, when passions were rising on every side, read to himself and his combatants lessons so sweet and so stern.

---

[1] *Ep.* 71. 1 *plurimi...censuerimus* here seems to be not equivalent to 'a numerous body and all of them,' because the phrase describing the objectors, *quidam de collegis nostris* (which is repeated in *Ep.* 71. 1), is not apparently a mere plural equivalent for *qui hoc illis patrocinium de sua auctoritate præstat*, who must be Stephanus, and who is again meant in *Ep.* 71. 3 *primatum*, &c. (see note 5, p. 351).

[2] *Ep.* 71. 4. Quintus and his *coepiscopi* are spoken of as *illic*, and informed of the state of things in Africa and Numidia which followed Agrippinus' Council. I doubt not that Quintus is the Bishop of Buruc who spoke in the Seventh Council, whom extant MSS. call Quietus, *Sentt. Epp.* 27 (see *Appendix* on *Lists of Bishops*, p. 565). Morcelli thought so but merely through misreading, for there is no *var. lect.* Fechtrup confounds him (p. 202) with Quintus of Aggya which was in the Proconsular Province.

[3] *Epp.* 72. 1, 71. 4. What does Peters mean in view of the last reference by saying on p. 513 that we might have expected Cyprian to appeal to the Council of Agrippinus and rely on that as proof of custom, and that Cyprian's not doing so shews that he was aware the canon was not acted on?

Next year, A.D. 256, the question occupies the Bishops in their Council before Easter; the SIXTH UNDER CYPRIAN and SECOND ON BAPTISM. They were seventy-one in number[1]. They formulate into a kind of Canon, applicable to clergy who had joined heretical or schismatical bodies and then recanted, the same practice which they had adopted as to lapsed Clerics, namely to restore them simply to Lay-Communion. They decide that baptism is necessary for all converts from the sects. They adopt the terrible phrase of 'the stain of profane water bespotting' those baptized with it[2].

A.D. 256.
A.U.C. 1009.
Coss. L. Valerius Maximus [II?] M. Acilius Glabrio.

We must note that now the prelates of Africa and Numidia[3] are sitting together, and are unanimous under Cyprian in re-affirming the old decision of their own predecessors under Agrippinus. A synodical letter from them was forwarded to Stephanus at Rome. The letter to the Numidians and the letter to Quintus were enclosed with it. It is an unconciliatory document, and hints consciousness of the offence which it will give[4].

Stephen had however among Cyprian's bishops those who sympathized with him[5]: one of these, or, as it has been surmised, Stephen himself through them, circulated an authoritative paper, recognising the baptism of even Marcion[6] by name. A copy of it, with some other arguments, was

---

[1] *Ep.* 73. 1.

[2] *Epp.* 72. 1; 73. 1. Cyprian had used the expression in its fullest strength in *De Unitate*, c. 12, and adhered to it in his first letter, to Magnus (*Ep.* 69. 16). Optatus endorses it, solely with reference to the Patripassians, Bk v. c. 1.

[3] In A.D. 312 the relations of Numidia to Carthage were not held to be definitively settled. Hefele, B. I. c. iii. § 14.

[4] Augustine does not seem to have seen this letter, which is strange. Jerome mentions it *adv. Luciferian*, 25.

[5] Quidam de collegis nostris, *Ep.* 71. 1. Cf. Quidam de collegis, *Sentt. Epp.* 59. Quidam nostri prævaricatores veritatis, *Sentt. Epp.* 38, and see note 1, p. 350.

[6] *Ep.* 73. 4. Cf. Aug. *de Bapt. c. Donatt.* VII. xvi. (30). Rettberg, p. 178, cites Coustant, *Epp. pont.* p. 226, and agrees that this document was a copy of Stephen's letter to the East. No evidence. Peters thinks that it was the extant tract *De Rebaptismate*, which renders it doubtful whether he can have read that tract through.

forwarded to Cyprian by Jubaian, a prelate of Mauretania, who felt himself much exercised by their strength. The Mauretanians had not been represented in the old Council of Agrippinus, and the opening now occurred for securing them upon a new one. Cyprian answered these, and in so elaborate a form, that at the final Council he read his answer as the complete exposition of his views, supplementing it with Jubaian's grateful and convinced reply. This letter was accompanied to its first destination by copies of the documents that had been sent to Stephen, and a codex of 'The Excellency of Patience.'

A deputation of bishops from Cyprian now went to Rome and waited upon Stephen, as bearers either of the last-named or of some separate epistle. Some little graciousness might have made much of so conciliatory an act. But (so at least Firmilian relates the incident amid his condolences[1]) no audience was allowed them either public or private; and the Roman congregation was desired to shew them no hospitality or attention[2].

Nevertheless, the letter was answered[3], and that in terms appreciative of the importance of the situation and of the greatness of the baptismal gift[4], large in charity towards Separatists, and not deigning to argue at length. Stephen asserted in it the apostolic authority of a distinct tradition for the Roman usage[5], magnified the chair of Peter[6], and vituperated Cyprian as 'a false Christ, a false apostle, a treacherous worker[7].'

Lamentable language: yet Cyprian's qualification of dissentient colleagues as 'Fautors of Antichrist' and 'Traitors to the Church[8]' laid him open to it.

---

[1] *Ep.* 75. 25.
[2] Labbe, *Conc.* t. I. p. 771, makes this an embassy of excommunicated Oriental bishops. But the reference of the *a quibus* is to *vobiscum* (*Ep.* 75. 25), the Africans; or else to both the Orientals and the Africans together, a theory not yet ventured on.
[3] *Ep.* 74. 1.   [4] *Ep.* 75. 17.
[5] *Ep.* 75. 5, 6 (compare *Ep.* 73. 13).
[6] *Ep.* 75. 17.
[7] *Ep.* 75. 25.   [8] *Ep.* 69. 10.

Stephen however had by this time issued a paper[1] which awakened a universal storm of indignation and dispute[2] among the Bishops of the East[3], or, according to the more guarded statement of Dionysius the Great, among the Bishops of Asia Minor[4]. He threatened to withdraw from their communion.

To assume that Stephen had already rebuked these Bishops of the East when Cyprian first mooted in Africa the question of rebaptism[5] is one of the Roman modes of at once exhibiting his vast jurisdiction and of softening the blameworthiness of his asperity towards so great a saint. But this was not so. The thought contradicts all our documents upon critical examination[6]. Stephen quarrelled with Cyprian first, and then turned on those who were sure to side with him. No doubt the relations of the Roman bishop with the East must have been somewhat complicated by the propension which the late patriarch of Antioch had exhibited

---

[1] 'Επεστάλκει μὲν οὖν πρότερον, Euseb. H. E. vii. 5.

[2] *Ep.* 75. 24 'Lites enim et dissensiones quantas parasti per ecclesias totius mundi?'

[3] *Ep.* 75. 25.

[4] Euseb. vii. 5.

[5] So Maran and Hefele, B. I. c. ii. § 6. Rettberg agrees.

[6] Apart from the erroneous date 253 which Maran (*Vit. Cypr.* xxix.) and others have assigned to Stephen's denunciation of the Orientals in order to bring it earlier than his controversy with Cyprian (since we now know that Stephen's accession was not earlier than about May 12, 254), the conclusion is against the whole tenor of our documents. 1. How Eusebius writes we have seen (Note on *Dates*, p. 347). The opening strife is seen by him in Cyprian's movement and Stephen's indignation. 2. Dionysius in the fragment of his Second Letter preserves a fragment of his First. In this the words ὡς οὐδὲ ἐκείνοις κοινωνήσων διὰ τὴν αὐτὴν ταύτην αἰτίαν clearly shew Stephen to be already for the same Baptismal cause in collision with some other church: and none but the African is possible. 3. Dionysius' series of letters has one to Stephen in his three years' seat and three to his successor who sate one. It may fairly be inferred that the close of Stephen's time saw the commencement of the correspondence. These points are brought out by both Peters and Fechtrup. On the other hand Maran urged a rhetorical phrase of Firmilian's (*Ep.* 75. 25) 'Stephen quarrels now with the Easterns, now with you' as if it were a chronological note of the order of events. And Peters instead of dealing rationally with the words suggests that probably the vanity of Firmilian caused him the subjective sensation of having been assailed first.

toward Novatian, nor was it a meaningless anxiety which lurked under Stephen's complaint of 'treachery.' But it was a weakness and an error to urge upon such men an unreasoned conformity; to threaten that he would hold no communion with bishops who used second baptism. They had what they thought immemorial usage[1] and their recent Councils behind them; and he but smote a rock. The most conspicuous Churchman of the day, Firmilian, metropolitan of Cappadocia, replied 'Thou hast excommunicated thine own self.'

Did Stephen excommunicate the Bishops of the East?

Our only original materials for settling whether Stephen carried his threat further are *Epp.* 74. 8; 75. 24; Dionys. ap. Eus. vii. 5. There is, I think, just critical light enough to arrive at the fact. Supposing Dionysius had written that Stephen ἐπεστάλκει ὅτι οὐ κοινωνήσοι (as Thucyd. 8. 99 writes ἐπεστάλκει...ὅτι οὔτε αἱ νῆες παρέσοιντο κ.τ.λ.) even this would not have said more than that he threatened. But he writes ἐπεστάλκει ὡς οὐ κοινωνήσων, and this subjective ὡς marks a distinct subtraction from the actuality of the verb [being used as Henri Estienne says '*cogitationis* vel *consilii* indicandi causa quo quis aliquid facit vel facere se simulat vel aliis videtur.' *Thesaurus G. L.* ed. Hase, and Dindorf VIII. col. 2085. L.] (Winer, *Gr. Gr.* Part III. 65. 9.) Also Cyprian says Stephen 'sacerdotes...*abstinendos putat*' (*Ep.* 74. 8) and Firmilian '*putas* omnes a te abstineri posse' (75. 24). Both imply that the note had been sounded, but not that the deed was done. If these passages proved the excommunication they would prove it to be earlier than the Third Council, but Cyprian's speech (*Sentt. Epp. Proem.*) shews that 'compliance' had not then 'been enforced by terror.' '...quisquam *nostrum*' there cannot of course mean Africans as against Romans.

Dionysius the Great.

Two of Stephen's leading presbyters, Philemon and Dionysius a learned[2] successor of his own, in the first instance shared his views and supported his action. Later on they

---

[1] 'A Christo et ab Apostolis,' *Ep.* 75. 19.
[2] λόγιός τε καὶ θαυμάσιος, Eus. vii. 7.

consulted the great Dionysius at Alexandria[1]. He replied, as he himself observes, at first briefly and then at some length. In the fragment of his letter to Philemon, which Eusebius has preserved, he mentions that from his predecessor Heraclas he had received it as a rule, not to rebaptize returning heretics: but he is here speaking only of such as had been baptized before their error: an exception which even Cyprian allowed[2]. Clement of Alexandria had however more than doubted the reality of heretical baptism, for he glosses one of the strange phrases interpolated by the Seventy in the ninth chapter of Proverbs 'so wilt thou cross over the water of strangers' by the words 'Wisdom here accounteth the heretic baptism to be no native, genuine water[3].' But no Egyptian synod had then taken up the question, and determined it. So far from this, that Dionysius of Alexandria in his letter to Xystus of Rome[4] relates a moving story of his own resistance to the entreaties, tears and prostrations of an aged Catholic who discovered his own Baptism to have been utterly heretical. He encouraged him to have no scruples; his long life in the Communion of the Body and Blood of Christ countervailed every incompleteness. He failed to persuade the old man, who dared not communicate and scrupled, as if unbaptized, even to attend the prayers. Yet, although ready to be advised by Xystus, Dionysius could not upon his own convictions give way: so important did he deem it that the relations of communions to each other should not be at the mercy of the weak and scrupulous. Again we must remember

---

[1] I am not clear that they did not write to Dionysius even in Stephen's lifetime. ...συμψήφοις πρότερον Στεφάνῳ γενομένοις, καὶ περὶ τῶν αὐτῶν μοι γράφουσι...Euseb. *H. E.* vii. 5. The latter participle in the absence of any limiting particle (and if they had just written he would have said γράψασι) is rather imperfect than present—'were correspondents of mine.' But it is in his letter to Xystus that he mentions the fact, and the *fuller* letters (which remain) are written in Xystus' time.

[2] Euseb. vii. 7. *Ep.* 74. 12.

[3] On Prov. ix. 18 διαβήσῃ ὕδωρ ἀλλότριον—τὸ βάπτισμα τὸ αἱρετικὸν οὐκ οἰκεῖον καὶ γνήσιον ὕδωρ λογιζομένη (Σοφία). *Strom.* I. xix.

[4] His 5th on Baptism, Euseb. vii. 9.

that his severe language about Novatian is extracted from one of his Baptismal Letters, namely the fourth to his namesake at Rome; that it is severe on account of the hard separatism of the sectarian, and that one trait of this separatism is that by Rebaptism 'he sets at nought the Holy Font[1].' It seems clear then that he agreed, as did the two Roman presbyters, with Stephen's theory. But he was shocked with his want of delicacy, and addressed to him an earnest entreaty not to be severe upon a practice resting on such authority of old bishops and councils[2]. We know also that he admitted the Baptism of Montanists, at which Basil[3] expresses surprise, considering this to be a distinct Heresy about the Godhead. But here Dionysius was better informed.

It is difficult then to reconcile with these fragmentary facts which we know, Jerome's statement that Dionysius 'consented to the dogma' of Cyprian[4]. Still it may be argued that Basil would not have been so surprised as he was at Dionysius, if his view of Montanism had not seemed an exception to his view of other heresies, and that he would have been more surprised if he had admitted the baptism of all. For Basil is mistakenly persuaded that a difference had been already at that early date defined between heretical and schismatical baptism and that the latter was admissible.

Perhaps we may infer from all that is before us that Dionysius held a policy not unlike Basil's own about the Kathari: and would have had every country observe its own tradition. While he himself would have accepted Stephen's clientèle, he was not willing that Africa and Asia should be interfered with. Such a policy suits the broad and tolerant character of Dionysius' mind and the hypothesis harmonizes the various statements.

---

[1] Euseb. *H. E.* vii. 8. By the light of his fifth letter and Cyprian's 'Novatianenses rebaptizare,' *Ep.* 73. 2, it is plain that Rebaptism is meant.

[2] σκόπει τὸ μέγεθος τοῦ πράγματος, Euseb. vii. 5.

[3] *Epist.* 188, *Canon* 1.

[4] *De Vir. Illustr.* c. 69.

His middle position is not that of one who is not strict or whose mind is not made up[1]. His information increased with his enquiries, but his views and his conduct were consistent throughout. His view was that heretics may be validly admitted without second baptism, but that churches which ruled otherwise must not be overruled from without. His conduct was very decisive. Thanks to Eusebius we possess the outlines and fragments of five Letters which he wrote 'On Baptism' to Rome[2]. His First was to Stephen; a full[3] letter, called forth by one from Stephen, of which the address is not given, but the subject was 'about Helenus of 'Cilicia and Firmilian of Cappadocia and all (the bishops) 'of their provinces and of all the neighbouring tribes.' 'About them he repeated the censure and the threatening with which he had already approached Cyprian, declaring 'that he would not communicate with them either,' and 'for the self-same cause.' Dionysius addressed him in the interests of peace. He delineated the restored tranquillity of the Eastern church. Persecution past; the Antiochene Patriarch who had leaned to Novatian succeeded by one of comprehensive sympathies; Jerusalem, Cæsarea and Tyre, the Syrias and Arabia grateful for Roman beneficence; Mesopotamia, Pontus, Bithynia—all exulting in brotherly concord. The chord which plainly he hopes to touch in Stephen's heart is the near fulfilment of the Pentecostal foreshadowing. Of Saint Luke's list are wanting only Parthia and Persia, for Egypt and Rome are the correspondents and Africa is the unnamed subject. 'How grievous,' is Dionysius' evident inference, 'that such unity should be vexed by threatenings.'

Of the three next letters we have spoken already.

The candid and enquiring mind of him who was not afraid

---

[1] As Rettberg.
[2] Euseb. *H. E.* vii. 2—9.
[3] πλεῖστα...ὁμιλήσας, Euseb. vii. 4. Cf. 2, 5. This 'The First on Baptism' must be the same which he himself describes in his 'Second on Baptism' addressed to Xystus, Stephen's successor. Euseb. vii. 5.

of studying the attractive literature of heretics, because (as he tells the Roman presbyter) the Divine voice reminded him that he was 'capable of criticizing and that such fearless study had brought him to the faith at first,' comes out in delicate touches. His earliest letter urges on Stephen the general ground of the peace of the Church, without reference to authority. Of the Rebaptizing Councils he then seems to know nothing. But to Xystus he writes, 'I *find by enquiry* that decrees have been made in this sense in the 'greatest episcopal synods,' and to Dionysius 'I *have learnt* this too,' meaning the copious precedents, and particularly the Councils of Iconium and Synnada[1].

Greatly then to be regretted is the loss of a sixth Letter—written in the name of the church of Alexandria by their bishop and containing his final discussion[2] of the whole question. We may nevertheless be assured that his conclusions were the same pacific and truthful ones to which he pointed all through. Had he really decided either for Rebaptism (as Jerome heard) or against Cyprian, this would have been the most important factor in the controversy; and Eusebius could not have failed to record it. His silence implies that he had already indicated sufficiently the lines laid down by Dionysius the Great.

To return to Carthage. One last enquirer now appears, Pompey, the bishop of Sabrata upon the Syrtis, in the later province of Tripoli. He had received the circulated documents and was anxious to learn how Stephen had replied to them. Cyprian sends him Stephen's epistle to himself, with an antidote of his own[3]—a fine letter though not moderate[4].

---

[1] πυνθάνομαι Euseb. *H. E.* vii. 5, μεμάθηκα vii. 7. I must here justify Peters (p. 502) against Fechtrup (p. 232) in laying stress on the expressions of Dionysius. Fechtrup says that Dionysius mentions the Councils in his account to Xystus of his First Letter; which is true, but not as from the letter itself, only in his account of it.

[2] διὰ μακρᾶς ἀποδείξεως. Euseb. vii. 9.
[3] Pompeio Fratri, *Ep.* 74.
[4] *Dial. c. Luciferian* § 27.

One of those which Jerome calls 'a rending of Stephen and of "*the error*" of inveterate tradition.' In the course of it he lays down the principles of a true Reformation (and such he conceived his own measures to be) in lines which the historian of our own Reformation might adopt for his proëm. 'Reli-
'gious and single-hearted minds have a short method to dis-
'burden themselves of error, and to discover and develop
'truth. For if we turn back to the fountain-head and source
'of the Divine tradition, the human error disappears; the plan
'of the heavenly mysteries is perceived, and all that lay
'darkling under the gloom and mists of darkness opens out
'into the light of truth. If some aqueduct, whose stream was
'ever large and copious before, fails suddenly, do we not pro-
'ceed to its fount, there to learn the nature of that failure;
'whether its flow has dwindled at the source through the
'drying up of the veins, or whether indeed it gushes thence
'in full unshrunken volume, but has failed in mid course?
'that so, if it is the fault of a broken or porous channel that
'the water does not run in uninterrupted flow, unceasingly
'and perpetually, the channel may be repaired and strength-
'ened, and the collected waters be delivered for the use and
'drinking of the city in all the self-same richness and purity
'with which they issue from the spring. Even so God's priests
'must deal now, and keep the Divine charge; so that, if in
'aught truth totters and wavers, we turn back both to its
'source in the Lord, and also to its delivery by evangelists
'and apostles, and our plan of action takes its rise where rose
'alike our order and our beginning[1].' Considering that in these words Cyprian is laying the plan of a campaign against

---

[1] *Ep.* 74. 10 'et ad originem dominicam et ad evangelicam adque apostolicam traditionem.' The length and detail of the simile may seem to point to some recent incident of management on the wonderful Aqueduct of Carthage. From the 'heads' in Zaghouan and Djougar (Mons Zeugitanus and Mons Zuccharus) through channels sixty miles long, part buried, part on the surface of the slopes, part on vast arches, it poured in Cyprian's days seven millions of gallons daily into the city and neighbourhood, the '*civitas*.'

Rome, it is clear that Rome was not to him the 'fountain' or the 'beginning' of either doctrine or order.

He closes his letter with a canon framed as an amendment on that of Stephen with which he opens. Pompeius if he had wavered was convinced, and his proxy is presented by his neighbour, Bishop Natalis, of Œa, at the next Council[1].

That there is no reason to suppose Letters are missing from the Correspondence with Stephen.

The above is a simple and sufficient account of the circumstances of the correspondence. Rettberg (pp. 181 sqq.) admires Mosheim's 'discovery' of other letters, and thus arranges the extant and supposed documents. 1. The Synodal Letter, Cyprian to Stephen, Epistle 72. 2. Stephen's reply, *lost:* Cyprian mentions it in Ep. 74 to Pompeius, 'in moderate terms as a moderate paper'; and 'would have written more 'harshly if he had been characterized in that letter as he was in the one 'seen by Firmilian': to Pompeius he also uses metaphors and arguments not used in the Synodal Letter, but quoted by Firmilian as occurring in Cyprian's letter to Stephen; whence is inferred 3. A reply from Cyprian to Stephen *lost*, moderate of tone, and *resembling* that to Pompeius in argument and illustration. 4. Stephen's second reply to Cyprian, *lost;* inhuman in character; the one described by Firmilian. 5. The Legation-letter from Cyprian to Stephen, &c., *lost.*

The detection of lost documents is a diversion for critics. But I see no evidence of any of these having existed except of course the Letter of Stephen. Evidently that which Pompeius saw was the same which Firmilian saw, even if not the same that was sent to the Oriental bishops; and the Legation probably presented the Synodal Letter only. For (1) Firmilian nowhere alludes to a letter from Cyprian to Stephen as enriched with those metaphors, &c. The Garden, the Fountain, the Ark, the Apostolic tradition of Rebaptism, are plainly taken from Cyprian's letter to Firmilian himself. (2) The Synodal Letter was Cyprian's ultimatum. It left the question thenceforward in the hands of the bishops. Accordingly the next declaration is 'The sentences of the bishops' one by one. The force of that declaration is thus accounted for. (3) As to the argument that Cyprian would in writing to Pompeius have been stung to sharper retaliation on Stephen if he had seen what Stephen, according to Firmilian, said of him, we may consider that Augustine was impressed by the 'moderation' of Cyprian; and that there is surely strength enough in such phrases as 'everything else,

---

[1] *Sentt. Epp.* 84.

'whether haughty, irrelevant, or self-contradictory, which Stephanus 'ignorantly and unadvisedly wrote' (*Ep.* 74. 1). Then, seeing that Stephen's supposed '*moderate*' letter is described as evincing 'eagerness for presumption and contumacy,' and made Cyprian in his 'moderate' reply exclaim that, if such principles prevail, 'we must give up to the Devil the 'ordinance of the Gospel, the dispensation of Christ, the majesty of God... 'The Church must give place to heretics, light to dark..., hope to despair..., 'reason to error .., immortal life to death..., truth to fiction..., Christ to 'Antichrist' (*Ep.* 74. 8); seeing also that the same letter of Stephen's went the length of saying that dissentient bishops should be excommunicated (*sacerdotes abstinendi*), we may allow that it was probably in its personal parts strong enough to have been the one which Firmilian saw.

That the Epistle to Pompey (Ep. 74) and Stephen's Epistle quoted therein are earlier than the Third Council on Baptism.

It has been maintained (O. Ritschl, pp. 113 f.) that Cyprian's opening address to the Third Council on Baptism, leaving liberty of action to all bishops, is a kind of offered compromise or conciliation to Stephen; and that therefore the letter to Pompey (*Ep.* 74), shewing relations with Stephen to be at an end, must be dated after that Council; and therefore also the letter of Stephen, which is criticized in it, must be a rescript of Stephen's after his receiving the Report of that Council from Cyprian.

But the speech of Cyprian is no olive-leaf. It states the position of tolerance which he takes as against one who wants to make himself a bishop of bishops, and who by 'tyrannous terror' seeks to force obedience on colleagues. (*Sentt. Epp. Proem.*)

Again the extracts from Stephen's Letter, contained in *Ep.* 74, are mainly *arguments*, from practice of heretics, from traditions, backed by a threat of excommunication—the very point touched in Cyprian's speech—arguments embodied to be refuted in a long argumentative letter from Cyprian to a neighbouring suffragan who enquires 'what reply Stephen has sent him to our document'—*quid mihi ad litteras nostras...rescripserit*[1]. They belong to the progress of the discussion; and wear no semblance of a Roman ultimatum answering the ultimatum of a Council of three provinces; and the letter which contains them makes no allusion whatever to a Council so important, as settling the whole question for all Africa, that, if it had sate and reported before that letter was written, it could not but have been mentioned.

If the contents of one letter ever established its place in a series, the 74th letter to Pompey and the letter of Stephen which it quotes preceded the Third Council.

[1] *Ep.* 74. 1.

That Ep. 72 to Stephen is rightly put down to the Second Council on Baptism not the Third.

It has been ingeniously maintained (O. Ritschl, pp. 114 ff.) that Epistle 72 is the Synodal Letter not of the Second but of the great Third Council: (1) *Because* it takes that standpoint as to the liberty of bishops which Cyprian takes in his address to the Third Council. *Answer.* It is the same view which Cyprian uniformly takes. Cf. *Ep.* 55. 21; 69. 17; 73. 26. (2) *Because*, if the Spring (or Easter) Council had already sent so decisive a letter to Stephen as this 72nd no third Council need have been specially convened, as this was for September the same year. *Answer.* Stephen's reply to the Second Council-letter was so truculent, as its relics in *Ep.* 74 shew, that it was essential to present to him the strongest African front possible. It was therefore necessary to convene the Mauretanians, as well as the Africans and Numidians who formed the Second Council. And Ritschl himself thinks this was so important that he actually believes (p. 117) that the determining to convene the Mauretanians was a solid part of the business of the Second Council. [He believes also that he has shewn that *Ep.* 74 and its quotations from Stephen's letter, are later than this Council; but there he fails. See last note.] (3) *Because* the mention of the Second Council in *Ep.* 73. 1 does not imply that a letter was sent to Stephen. *Answer.* It was not absolutely necessary to say so in telling Jubaian what the resolution was, even if a letter went to Stephen. But the position of the Third Council is rather that of a tremendous demonstration, by an utterance obtained from every single bishop, upon Stephen's threat of excommunication. Their mere opinion had been sent to Stephen before, more than once, and it does not appear that any letter was sent by the Third Council. The *Sententiæ* were enough. (4) *Because* (p. 116) letter 72 itself states that the Council from which it emanated was a specially convened one '*Ad quædam disponenda necesse habuimus...cogere et celebrare concilium*,' whereas the Second Council was the ordinary Easter (or Spring) Meeting of Bishops at Carthage. *Answer.* Ritschl's quotation is unconsciously not quite candid. If the words which he represents (and does not represent) by dots are inserted the sentence is '*Ad quædam disponenda* et consilii 'communis examinatione limanda *necesse habuimus*, frater carissime, con- 'venientibus in unum pluribus sacerdotibus *cogere et celebrare concilium*: 'in quo multa quidem prolata adque exacta sunt. Sed de eo vel maxime 'tibi scribendum, &c.' (*Ep.* 72. 1) (viz. the baptismal question). Now here Cyprian plainly seems to say that he felt obliged to take the *opportunity* of 'many bishops meeting' to hold 'a Council' in order to arrange, *examine*, and *formulate* certain things, and that besides the one subject on which he wrote to Stephen, there were 'many' others 'brought forward and disposed of.'—It seems as if a more accurate account could scarcely be given of the annual episcopal meeting of the year A.D. 256

being turned into the Second Council of Carthage under Cyprian on Baptism. The letter says it came from such a body[1].

To this I must add that the description of Council II. in *Ep.* 73. 1 answers almost in words to the description in *Ep.* 72 of the Council from which itself emanated. Thus

| *Ep.* 72. 1 convenientibus in unum pluribus sacerdotibus..de eo vel maxime tibi scribendum...quod magis pertineat....et ad ecclesiæ catholicæ unitatem..eos qui sunt.. profanæ aquæ labe maculati, quando ad nos...venerint, baptizari oportere....Tunc enim demum plene sanctificari...salutaris fidei veritate servatum. | *Ep.* 73. 1 cum in unum convenissemus...episcopi numero septuaginta et unus..hoc..firmavimus statuentes unum baptisma esse quod sit in ecclesia catholica constitutum...non rebaptizari sed baptizari a nobis quicunque ab.. profana aqua venientes abluendi sint et sanctificandi salutaris aquæ veritate. |

(5) *Because Ep.* 73. 1 says nothing about the *multa* which *Ep.* 72. 1 says were handled in its Council. *Answer.* No. For *Ep.* 73 is answering Jubaian's question as to what had been done on *one* point.

(6) I add that it is a very strong point indeed that *Ep.* 72 mentions as documents issued by Cyprian prior to its own Council only *Epp.* 70 and 71 (to the Numidians and Quintus), and does not name 73 (to Jubaian) which Cyprian, after it was written, used quite as a manual (as it is) of arguments on his side, and read as such to the Third Council. If *Ep.* 72 had emanated from the Third Council it must have mentioned this *Ep.* 73. Ritschl tries to meet this by saying that *Ep.* 73 was too rude to Stephen to be sent to him—which is feeble, considering the language which was undoubtedly sent. Besides, how could that hold when the Epistle had been already read to the whole Council?

I know how troublesome all this detail of restoring the documents to their right order is, but what else can be done when such a scholar as Ritschl takes such infinite pains to dislocate them?

That Quietus of Buruc who spoke 27th in the Seventh Council is Quintus the Mauretanian, recipient of Ep. 71.

Hartel gives the name of the bishop of Buruc who spoke in the Seventh Council (*Sentt. Epp.* 27) without various reading as '*Quietus.*' So do most editions. But Pamèle in his text, Morcelli, and Labbe, I. 810, xxvii., and Index, have '*Quintus.*' Here is perhaps an indication

---

[1] For younger readers may I observe that *firmare consilium* does not by itself imply an affirmation of a previous decision? In *Ep.* 73. 1 it is the word *denuo* which gives that sense; but in *Ep.* 71. 4 *firmavit* is the word used with *statuit* of Agrippinus himself.

that there were some MSS. which read 'Quintus.' But however that may be, observing the verbal and material correspondences between this short speech and Cyprian's letter to Quintus the Mauretanian Bishop (*Ep.* 71), I cannot doubt that the speaker was Quintus himself. There are these— (*a*) The passage Qui baptizatus a mortuo in *Sirach* 34. 30, and the strange argument about baptism by the dead (p. 411 inf.), are nowhere used by Cyprian except in his letter to Quintus; and in the Council no speaker except this (Quietus or) Quintus employs it. (*b*) *Sent.* 27 qui ab hæreticis intinguuntur. *Ep.* 71. 1 qui apud hæreticis tincti sunt. (*c*) *Sent.* 27 uno vitali baptismate quod in ecclesia catholica est, et sanctificari debere....*Ep.* 71. 1 unum baptisma esse: quod unum scilicet in ecclesia catholica est...et sanctificandi hominis potestatem. (*d*) *Sent.* 27 cur ad ecclesiam veniunt?...cognito errore pristino ad veritatem cum pœnitentia revertuntur. *Ep.* 71. 2 ad ecclesiam revertentes et pœnitentiam agentes...peccato suo cognito et errore digesto. (*e*) *Sent.* 27 si enim qui aput illos baptizantur per remissionem peccatorum vitam æternam consequuntur, cur ad ecclesiam veniunt. *Ep.* 71. 3 sciamus remissam peccatorum non nisi in ecclesia dari posse.

Labbe noticed a resemblance. I have shewn elsewhere [*Appendix on Cities*, p. 607] that Buruc was more likely than not in Mauretania. I should venture to read *Sentt. Epp.* 27 QUINTUS A BURUC.

The SEVENTH COUNCIL UNDER CYPRIAN AND THIRD ON BAPTISM was held on the First[1] of September, A.D.

[1] Mr Shepherd, *Letter ii.* p. 14, comments: 'This Council wonderful to say has a date.' He might have wondered also that the Second (his own Third) has a date (*Ep.* 59. 10). He further thinks 'it would have been far more natural to have said A.D. 180 or some such date,' for another event. This certainly would have been an interestingly early use of the Christian era. This was introduced by his favourite Dionysius Exiguus, 'whom he would rather have called Magnus.' He may be excused for not knowing that Baronius had used up that minute *mot*, but has he noticed how far it was usual for letters and events to be carefully dated in those times and countries? For instance, Augustine's letters or Tertullian's historical allusions? Yet doubtless the paucity of dates of any kind is remarkable. It is connected with that intense African hostility to even civil forms that had been solemnly used by heathenism, which comes out in Montanism, Novatianism, Donatism, and so fiercely in Tertullian. It is hard to impugn a council's genuineness for wanting a date, when the Council of Cirta (A.D. 305) is questioned by the Donatists (in 411 A.D.), who must have known something of African Christianity, solely on the ground that it *has* a date. The Catholics had to reply that, though Donatist councils and documents were undated, Catholics did not eschew dates. Yet it may be that Donatism preserved a Puritan tradition and that the Catholics

256[1]—an assemblage of no less than eighty-seven bishops 'from the provinces of Africa[2], Numidia and Mauretania'—a proportionate representation of course they could not be—with[3] presbyters and deacons, in presence of a vast laity.

Sep. 1, A.D. 256.

A great vision was fulfilled. It was given to Cyprian to see in actual presence that 'copious body of bishops' in which he had long ago declared that the safety and purity of the Church lay.

The bishops, it will be borne in mind, were the elected judges, overseers and teachers of the Christian section of as many African towns. No part of the Empire was more full than Africa of intellectual, civic and financial life. The Christian section was the army of advance in things social, moral and religious. It was the section which at present found it hardest to assert its rights, whether individual or corporate, in the Empire. Yet it was developing new institutions theoretically and practically. It was already creating a new literature, and it had in its bosom the constitution and legislation of the future. Brought up themselves in daily sight of justice and of rule the bishops had been elected

---

had come to use them more freely by degrees. On the whole we might be content to admit for an undated Council the excuse which the Catholics allowed for one that the Donatists relied on. 'It is not dated, either year or day. But we do not mean to dispute it for that. It is more likely to be due to unbusiness habits than to fraud.' See Augustine, *Brev. Collationis cum Donatistis*, tertii diei, cc. xiv, xv. §§ 26 and 27. Cf. Neander (*op. cit.*), vol. III. p. 263 note.

[1] Firmilian's letter was not received until the Council was over.

[2] *Sententiæ Episcoporum, Proem.* Fifty-five suffrages were from Proconsular Africa (twelve of them from within a circle of 45 Roman miles of Carthage)—this disposes of O. Ritschl's (p. 117) view that Cyprian found it necessary to secure the help of Mauretania before venturing his step against Stephen;—twenty-eight from the larger region of Numidia; Mauretania can have sent only two suffrages, those namely of Nova and Buruc, and half an interest in the see of Tucca. See *Appendix on Cities*, p. 575, and Note on p. 363, 'Quietus or Quintus.' *Ep.* 71 and *Sentt. Epp.* 27.

[3] Dr Pusey, *Councils of the Church*, p. 73, lays stress on those presbyters and deacons being stated in the Acts to be the presbyters and deacons of the respective bishops, '*their* presbyters and deacons.' But the word is not in the text. The laity are described as *maxima pars plebis*.

to their presidencies because in them was recognised the true spirit of rule, of instruction, of sensible converse with men. The special saintliness of asceticism, which might have procured election later on, had not yet come into vogue. A new spiritual power had 'come into the world' and it was committed to them to exercise it in a world of realities.

The towns from which they came, and through which they travelled, presented the social life of the age in almost every aspect—as simple 'municipia,' as 'free and exempt' cities or 'republics,' or as 'colonies' loaded with titles and privileges, and splendid with buildings which, like the amphitheatre of Thysdrus, rivalled or outdid the similar structures of Rome. Their elaborate official organizations and their administrations, fiscal and agrarian, are as well known to scholars as modern finance is to the officials of our Treasury. The list of towns[1] shews how immediately the early Christians faced their problems by laying hold of the centres of life and activity. The policy of the Christian Church was in all respects unlike that of the modern Missionary Society. It handled christianisation as the state handled civilisation. It began with strong focal centres. It threw out fresh centres as fast as it could make them strong and safe. It left no new focus unsupported. It gave each bishop the utmost independence consistent with unity.

Nothing can exceed the variety of the social situations. Some of these cities were primæval settlements of Canaanites, which still used and occupied their rock-cisterns and half-solid citadels or Bozrahs of gigantic stones; which with all their accretions were yet governed by Sufetes, the 'Judges' of Palestine, stamped their Phœnician names on their coinage until late in the Empire, and served Baal and Ashtoreth in Imperial Temples.

---

[1] See Appendix on the Lists of Bishops attending the Councils (p. 565), and Appendix on the Cities from which the Bishops came to the Seventh Council on the first of September A.D. 256 (p. 575).

The Homeric Lotus-land, the large low Isle of Meninx, just then beginning to call itself Girba, maintained, as it does to-day, a pure Berber stock which had learnt of these Canaanites to grow the best dates and dye the brightest and costliest purples[1]. They have been impartially receptive of all the successive faiths of the masters of the mainland.

The island rock of Thabraca, whose peak rose some three or four hundred feet above its busy little port and the forests of the mainland, was own daughter to Tyre, and mother of all the coral fisheries of the Western Mediterranean. And while the peculiar Punic fish-craft was then the wealth, as it is still the subsistence, of Hippo Diarrhytus and other towns, the bishop of Carpos was bishop of a bright and fashionable seaside spa.

Of many seaports represented some were still the insecure little roadsteads which had for centuries shipped off the precious yield of Numidian mines, and the homely produce of Kabylian farms. Other immense elaborate harbours had grown up as factories of Carthage; others enclosed a vast precinct for the chief corn-markets of the world, and depots for the grain which fed the proletariat of Rome. Of these some had once saved their commerce by offering themselves to the Romans, as their cousins the Gibeonites offered themselves to Joshua, or had risen again on such a flood of exports and imports that they despised even the cruel impost which still avenged their resistance to Julius Caesar himself.

Tripolis and the Emporia were rich and luxurious amid unceasing wars with the invading tribes and the advancing sands of the Sahara.

Other cities were seated among illimitable slopes of corn, or overlooking the High Plateaux, or among the forests through which ran chains of villages and lines of road still

---

[1] Their bishop Monnulus is interesting, not only for his sad grammar, but as using, to express 'the *stain* of error,' a very technical term of Dyeing, and that in a form nowhere else existing. (*Sentt. Epp.* 10.) See *Appendix on Cities*, p. 575.

marked by broken oil-mills, dry fountains and post-stations. Crystal rivers, which after short courses now plunge in sands, were then banked and quayed and at last led off into a thousand channels of irrigation.

Cirta, the old capital of Numidia, on earth's most perfect City-throne, was with consummate wisdom long allowed to maintain with four antient surrounding burghs a sort of unity or republic of their own.

The vast region of Mount Aures with its rich uplands and inaccessible lairs of restive tribes was girdled with a ring of strong and brilliant towns and was held chained, as it were, to Carthage and its orderly powers by Hadrian's great work, the new straight road of near two hundred miles to Theveste. To that ring belonged the military centre of Lambæsis, the beautiful Thamugadi, the most antient mart of commerce, and Theveste, the centre of communication. And these were model cities also, each a miniature Rome with every appliance of domestic, civic and luxurious existence that could keep legions and tribes engaged. Not only theatre and amphitheatre for their dissipated and ferocious amusement, temples to the gods and genii of Health and Commerce and Fatherland, whether Tyre or Rome, baths, with all their amusements, triumphal arches which set forth the conquests of the Emperors and the motherliness of Empresses, ample basilicas ready to become churches, forums and mimic curiæ in which business was discussed by orators with all the semblance of freedom. Here soldiers had unusual privileges of marriage, and their children were enrolled in an honourable tribe.

Along the Theveste Road itself, constructed by the Third Legio Augusta, was a line of fresh thriving stations, with here and there an antient town renewed, so populous that before long there was a Christian See every thirteen miles or so.

Farther off huge frontier fortresses, like Capsa 'fenced with sands and serpents,' held the key of Sahara for the whole

Tell, and controlled the caravans which laboured up and down and across the enormous basins of the salt lakes, or like Gemellæ[1] created their own oasis and there held the utmost bastion of civilisation against the Spirit of the Desert—who after all is master.

In safer districts lay what were simply the adorned and noble cities of Peace—Thuburbo, Assuras, Thelepte, Mactharis, and many others,—above all, Sufetula, which was not even walled.

In short, the material spectacle of these African cities was not unworthy of their setting in Nature. And what more can be said? There is no measuring them by our small and sombre ideas of market towns and appropriate public works.

Yet many heathen knew that all the brilliance was darkened by a reckless using up of life and hopelessness in death. The Christian Bishop in each knew that he and his were armed with a message of reality. To the delivery of it it was vital that they should be of one mind about this 'entering into life.' Therefore they met at Carthage about Baptism.

For the present we regard the record of the Council simply as 'a Document.' The arguments which prevailed in it will come later under review. Its proceedings were opened by the reading of the Jubaian correspondence, and of the letter to Stephen[2], with a very few words from the President, which Augustine justly eulogizes for their large pacific spirit[3] and indomitable tolerance. Diversity in diocesan practices had no terrors for him, although the responsibility of creating diversity seemed to him appalling. Of creating it himself he was all unconscious. 'Our present business,' he said, 'is to state individually our views of the particular subject

---

[1] Its desert of Mokran is all intersected with channels, cross dykes and ditches. Its bishop, Litteus, proves his case by a metaphor from 'the blind leading the blind into the ditch' (*Sentt. Epp.* 82).

[2] *Sentt. Epp.* 8.

[3] Aug. *de Bapt. c. Donatt.* VI. vi. (9); perseverantissima tolerantia, ii. 5.

'before us, judging no one, nor removing from his rights
'of communion any who may hold different views from our-
'selves. For there is none of us who constitutes himself
'Bishop of Bishops, or pushes his colleagues with a tyrannous
'terror to the necessity of compliance; since every Bishop
'according to the scope of the liberty and office which belongs
'to him has his decision in his own hands, and can no more
'be judged by another than he can himself judge his
'neighbour[1], but we await one and all the judgment of
'our Lord Jesu Christ, who One and Alone has the power
'both to prefer us in the governing of His Church, and
'to judge our conduct therein[2].' Then every prelate in his seniority[3] delivered his opinion. We cannot doubt that we

---

[1] Mark Cyprian's studied use of *alio* and *alterum*. In the next clause I think the punctuation of all the editions is wrong. The *expectemus* depends on *quando*. *Sentt. Epp. Proem.*

[2] The old papal way of handling these thorny phrases was to turn them to account like Baronius by saying that Cyprian 'though not over-respectful' 'alluded of course to the Decree published by Stephen's Supreme Pontific authority and headed as usual *more maiorum* with the said title of Bishop of Bishops.' (*Ann.* A.D. 258, xlii.) The middle mode was that of the Franciscans R. Missori (1733) and M. Molkenbuhr (1790) and hapless Archbishop Tizzani (1862), rent by those who fawn on him as 'savant prélat' and 'docte critique' (Freppel, p. 429 sqq. Peters, p. 504). According to this mode the controversy is a romance and the records forgeries.

The third or modern ultramontane mode is Mgr. Freppel's. He declares with truth, 'It is *impossible for me* to see any allusion to Stephen in these words.' He then artlessly remarks that Cyprian's 'absolute silence' about Stephen at this Council 'deserves all our attention' and is a 'chose étonnante'—evidently a token of 'dernier hommage' (p. 425) to the 'Sovereign Pontiff.' So too Dr Peters (pp. 515, 516) can see no allusion at all to Stephen. He however happily elucidates for us what Mgr. Freppel left dark—viz. 'who then *is* the object of Cyprian's allusion?' It is Cyprian himself. He, as 'the born President of the Assembly and " Obermetropolit" of all Africa,' merely disclaims any purpose of using *his own* position, which actually was that of a 'Bishop of Bishops,' to check freedom of expression.

He further remarks that the Synod was not at all designed to reply to Rome, but was summoned solely to stem the growing opposition of the African bishops to Cyprian—an opposition which exhibited itself in the universally and individually expressed coincidence of their views with his.

[3] See Routh, *R. S.* vol. III. p. 191.
Erasmus and Manutius. Corrupt MSS. Cambron. ap. Pamèle. In the editions of Erasmus (the first of this Council) and Manutius, and in the much interpolated *cod. Cambronensis* (Pamèle), the

have the very words of each of those eighty-seven men[1]: from some a telling argument; from some a Scripture; from some an antithesis, an analogy, or a fancy[2]. Here a rhetorical flourish, there a solœcism, or an unfinished clause[3], a re-statement of the opinion in terms of an argument[4], or a personal virulence or fanaticism far outshrieking the usual tone[5]. Two of the juniors adopt the judgment of the majority[6], pleading their own inexperience. Such weaknesses (except perhaps the last) still appear occasionally in

title of 'Confesso-' is prefixed to the names of twelve of the bishops, viz., 42, 47, 48, 49, 52, 54, 58, 61, 62, 68, 79, 82; that of 'Martyr' to 72, 76, 80; and 'martyr de schismaticis' to 70, Verulus; that of confessor et martyr' to 45 and 87. These titles are not in our manuscripts. Baluze omitted them (Baluze, p. 329 and p. 601), so Morcelli (1. pp. 151, 226), as not belonging to the 'gesta,' as of course they could not, and as not given by Augustine. But though not authentic, they perhaps preserve an independent tradition. For example, only four appear of the confessor-bishops named in *Ep.* 76, and the designation of Verulus is interesting.

[1] Shepherd doubts. But Cornelius sent in *Ep.* 49 (2 the sentences of an episcopal conference to Cyprian, 'quas subjectas leges.' In Eus. vii. 29 we have the discussion between Paul of Samosata and Malchion taken down in shorthand, ἐπισημειουμένων ταχυγράφων.

[2] See Polycarp of Hadrumetum, *Sentt. Epp.* 3. Nemesian, the martyr-bishop of Thubunæ, says, 'This is the Spirit which from the beginning moved upon the face of the waters, for neither the Spirit can operate apart from water, nor water apart from the Spirit.' *Sentt. Epp.* 5.

[3] *Sent.* 73 'unum habet esse et baptisma,' 'there has to be also one baptism.'

Hartel thinks this a corruption, but it is African use, and even with passive infinitive. *Ep.* 52. 3 '...ejici de ecclesia et excludi habebat'; *Ep.* 63. 6 'laudari et adorari haberet.' *Testim.* i. 11 'quod ...et Novum Testamentum dari haberet,' &c. Mark again the entirely broken construction of the end of *Sent.* 7, and the *viva voce* doubling of 'illos' in *Sent.* 25. *Sent.* 4 'Debemus ergo fidem nostram exprimere *ut* hæreticos et schismati*cos* ad ecclesiam venientes, qui pseudo-baptizati videntur, debe*re eos* in fonte perenni baptizari.' [Cf. *Ep.* 72. 2 'addimus *ut...eos* suscipi.' *Ep.* 70 fin. 'et *eis...*dare *illis*.']

[4] So Pomponius of Dionysiana: 'It is evident that heretics are not able to baptize and give remission of sins, who have no power either to loose or to bind anything on earth,' *Sent.* 48. The pomposity of Felix of Uthina again is unmistakeably genuine, *Sent.* 26.

[5] *Sent.* 37. Vincent of Thibaris; 'we *know* Heretics to be worse than Heathens.' Wherefore he recommends that they should be exorcised before being baptized; a view accepted also by Crescens of Cirta. *Sent.* 8. Cf. *Sent.* 10 'ut cancer quod habebant et damnationis et iram...sanctificetur'; on this remarkable speech see *Appendix on Cities*, p. 598.

[6] *Sentt.* 71 and 78.

debate. On the whole we can but admire the Roman pith and terseness of epigram, the ability and even more the temper of so great a number of speakers to a conclusion which we dissent from. Augustine points out the quiet intention to adhere to unity which appears not only in Cyprian's own words, but in such expressions of the rest as 'so far as in us lies,' 'with all our powers of peacemaking we must strive.'

Cyprian in a sentence of six simple lines closed the discussion. 'My own opinion is quite expressed in the letter to 'our colleague Jubaian—that heretics being by formal declara-'tion[1] of apostles and evangelists styled adversaries of Christ 'and antichrists, must, when they join the Church, be bap-'tized with the Church's one baptism, in order to become 'of adversaries friends, Christians of antichrists.' That was the unanimous sense of his Council.

Firmilian and his letter.

Our next 'Document' is one of singular interest, 'THE LETTER OF SAINT FIRMILIAN TO CYPRIAN.'

It would be in contradiction to the whole of his policy if we supposed that Cyprian condescended to bring to bear upon the Council the pressure of any external influence whatsoever. If he had desired to do so, it was within reach. After the Council had decided, immense weight must have been added to its resolutions by the confirmation which they received from Asia Minor. Directly after the meeting, and so not early enough to announce an answer, Cyprian had written to the bishop of Cæsarea, metropolitan (so to speak) of Cappadocia, a very copious letter, and accompanied it with copies of two others[2]. These he had sent by Rogatian, one

---

[1] *Contestatio. Sentt. Epp.* 87. Note the old jurisconsult's natural use of the law-term.

[2] The copious references made in Firmilian's letter to Cyprian's arguments are all to be found in the two

of his deacons, who brought back the reply before the winter[1].

Cæsarea was a memorable place. Its four hundred thousand upland people[2] were even now in some unconscious way preparing for a heroic stand within three years from this time[3] against foes at present undreaded and undreamed of.

epistles 73 and 74. Careful examination will convince the reader that nothing is quoted from 69 (as Ritschl p. 129 supposes), which does not appear in 73 or in 74.

Of these *Ep.* 73, addressed to Jubaian, was, as we have seen, used as a full manual of the question, containing all earlier arguments rearranged, with others added. And *Ep.* 74 was written to Pompey immediately after the judgment of the Council, and contained the latest view of the whole question, and also of Stephen's present position.

These two letters therefore gave the gist of all questions and arguments on which his judgment was required and were for this reason sent to the great Asian authority.

This answers Ritschl's question, Why, if not all, yet at any rate the simpler epistles were not sent to Firmilian instead of the later most elaborate ones, in order to obtain his judgment which was required with speed.

[1] *i.e.* the winter of A.D. 256, for before the next Stephen died and Cyprian was in exile; and the report sent from this Council would not have been kept back a year.

Here this difficulty is raised, viz. that Firmilian, speaking of the persecution of Maximin which followed the earthquakes in Pontus '*post Alexandrum imperatorem,*' who was killed in February, A.D. 235, says it was '*ante viginti et duos fere annos*' (*Ep.* 75. 10), which if literally exact would date the letter at the beginning of A.D. 257. But the end of 256 A.D., especially with *fere*, and considering their inclusive mode of reckoning, is sufficiently near.

Dr Peters (p. 516) thinks that the delegation rudely repelled by Stephen was that which took similarly to him the news of this same Third Council. Anyhow Firmilian has had the account of that rejection from Cyprian. Supposing the delegates to have left Carthage about the end of the first week of September, there were eight weeks for them to go to Rome, to return to Carthage, then for Rogatian to make his way to Cæsarea and be back in Carthage '*before winter,*' which, for navigation purposes, began at this era about November 3. This would be time enough. Pearson, Rettberg, Lipsius think the letter to Firmilian went off before the Council, but *Ep.* 74 is after the Council and it was enclosed.

[2] Zonaras, xii. 23. Cæsarea is between 3000 and 4000 feet above the sea.

[3] There can be no doubt that 260 A.D. is the real date of the capture of Valerian (see *Appendix on Chronology, Valerian,* p. 552). Cæsarea fell very near to that time. See the notes of Gibbon's editors. It is totally impossible that Firmilian's letter can have been written soon after so fearful an event without an allusion to it, considering his style; and if it were after, it must have been *immediately* after. Consequently we may be sure that the sack of Cæsarea was between 257 and 261.

Their walls, like those of most inland towns remote from frontiers, had long since decayed or been removed[1]. They fell by thousands, choking up their own ravines before the Persian Sapor. By thousands they were driven like cattle to watering[2]. They lost all things; and then they recovered themselves as Paris only in our own days has done.

Their present native bishop, predecessor of their native Basil, was a memorable man. Firmilian, conspicuous by his family, had already, five-and-twenty years before this, become more conspicuous in that position[3]. His eminent character ennobled a race so noble that fifty years later under Diocletian, the judge entreated a Christian martyr not to tarnish its record by a criminal death. 'But its best nobility,' Capitolina replied, 'is that Firmilian was a scion of the house.' 'Him will I follow: after him I fearlessly confess that Jesus Christ is King of kings[4].'

He had paid Origen prolonged visits in Palestine, so best to deepen his intimacy with 'things Divine[5]'—no common student of no common master. To one of these times belongs perhaps his introduction of the awakened pagan lawyer Gregory, afterwards the Thaumaturge, to Origen for his many years of study in all that was knowable. He had prevailed on Origen to come and lecture from church to church among the towns which hung about the vigorous plateaus of Cappadocia[6]. And there later on, still in Firmilian's time, sheltering from persecution, Origen apparently found fresh material for his lifelong study[7]. Firmilian

---

[1] Niebuhr, *Lectt. Rom. Hist.* tr. Schmitz, vol. III. p. 295.

[2] Zonaras xii. 23.

[3] In A.D. 231 'the 10th year of Alexander.' Διέπρεπεν δὲ ἐν τούτῳ, Euseb. *H. E.* vi. 26.

[4] Tillemont, vol. IV., p. 309.

[5] τινὰς αὐτῷ συνδιατρίβειν χρόνους τῆς εἰς τὰ θεῖα βελτιώσεως ἕνεκα, Euseb. vi. 27.

[6] εἰς ἐκκλησιῶν ὠφέλειαν, Euseb. vi. 27.

Jerome, *De Virr. Ill.* 54, says all Cappadocia concurred in the invitation.

[7] Euseb. vi. 17. But we must take care not to make Eusebius say more than he meant, for he too seems to have a little exceeded his authority. After speaking of Symmachus as combating (ἀποτεινόμενος πρὸς) the narrative of S. Matthew, he proceeds 'Origen indicates (σημαίνει) that he received from

was admired 'for the trained exactitude of his intellectual faculties in philosophy and theology alike[1]';—'an illustrious man,' says Nicephorus. But so Dionysius the Great[2] had ranked him long before with 'the more illustrious bishops whom alone I name.' The great historian of Armenia speaks of his many works, among them a 'History of the Vexations of the Church' under Maximin and Decius[3]. He was among the earliest thinkers who touched with precision the facts of Original Sin[4], and S. Basil appeals to the treatises[5] of 'our Firmilian' in evidence of the exactness of his own teaching concerning the Holy Spirit.

one Juliana these notes (ὑπομνήματα) with other interpretations (ἑρμηνεῖαι) of Symmachus on the Scriptures, and he says also that she received the books by succession from Symmachus himself.' The expressions are so similar, and the σημαίνει is so cautious that Eusebius must be building on a Note which Palladius also saw (*Hist. Lausiaca* c. 147, ed. Ducæus, *Bibl. Vet. Patr.* Paris 1624. t. II. p. 1049) in Origen's own handwriting in a very old book which was written in sense-lines (παλαιοτάτῳ βιβλίῳ στιχηρῷ), and had thus been inscribed by Origen: 'This book I found in the possession of Juliana, a virgin in Cæsarea, when I was in hiding at her house. And she used to say she had received it from Symmachus himself, the interpreter of the Jews.' There is mention here only of one book, and that not named. Origen's word was εἰληφέναι, not διαδέξασθαι on which any idea of relationship rests. As to modern observations— Ὅπερ ἐγέγραπτο means 'which book had been inscribed' with the words given, not that the book was a manuscript by Origen. Στιχηρός does not mean 'a poetical book,' but a book written in sense-lines. Although Eusebius says nothing of a second sojourn in Cappadocia, there is no ground to question the truth of Palladius' quotation, but the contrary. Origen then was probably in shelter there during the two years (A.D. 235—7) of Maximin's persecution of Christian Teachers (Doctores, vel præcipue propter Origenem, says Orosius, *Hist.* vii. 19 rather boldly) ; or else, being there already at work, he may have been forced into hiding by the measures of Serenian, proconsul. Palladius calls Juliana λογιωτάτῃ καὶ πιστοτάτῃ. The text followed by Meursius, Lugd. Bat. 1616, and the translator Hervetus confuses the story by hiding the Book instead of Origen.

[1] περιφανὴς ἀνὴρ καὶ ἑκατέρας γνώσεως ἠκριβωμένας ἔχων τὰς ἕξεις. Nicephorus Callist. *Hist. Eccl.* vi. 27 (*valeat quantum*, but his word is from Dionysius).

[2] τοὺς γὰρ περιφανεστέρους, μόνους τῶν ἐπισκόπων ὠνόμασα, Dion. ap. Euseb. vii. 5.

[3] Moses of Khoren (†c. 390—c. 487) calls him *doctrinarum mirifice studiosus*, but desiderates more precise detail of persons and places in his accounts of Armenian and other martyrdoms. *Hist. Armen.* l. ii. c. 72.

[4] Routh, *R. S.* III. p. 149.

[5] οἱ λόγοι οὓς καταλέλοιπε. Basil, *de Spiritu Sancto*, c. xxix. 74.

His name stands first in Eusebius's roll of the great contemporary Church-rulers;—before Gregory and Athenodorus of Pontus, before Helenus of Tarsus, and Nicomas of Iconium, Hymenæus of Jerusalem, Theotecnus of the Palestinian Cæsarea, and Maximus of Bostra[1]. This was after the death of Dionysius, who may have been greater in speculative power, whilst Cyprian had left him no room for originality in his Baptismal thesis,—the only document of his that we possess. But his sense of the need of action was the wider; his was the more 'choragic' spirit, so to speak.

Dionysius wrote against Novatian. He wrote against Paul of Samosata. Nay, he wrote to the diocese of Antioch itself in a tone as if their wild prelate had already been deposed. But Firmilian was in both instances a foremost influence in assembling the churches for fair hearings of the questions[2]. He was President of the Third Council of Antioch (Second against Paul of Samosata) and there determinedly accepted, against the sentiments of the Council, the apologies and promises of Paul, 'trusting and hoping,' and leaving him room for repentance. When this charity of his proved as useless as it was in those days remarkable, the Fourth Council of Antioch assembled, and whilst they tarried for him as necessary to their deliberations Firmilian died at Tarsus on the journey.

This was the man to whom Cyprian wrote; not because, as Romanists have hoped, the cause in his hand was prejudged, but because he was the foremost church-ruler of the East.

His Letter, extant in a contemporary Latin version of his Greek, is the most enthusiastic of the series. It has many points of strong interest. Of the claims of the great See of the West to guide the Catholic Church he does not write with either awe or scorn. It is plain he had never heard of

[1] Eus. *H. E.* vii. 28.
[2] He was connected with Four Councils of Antioch, the first in A.D. 252, against Novatianism, and three on Paul of Samosata (1) in 264, (2) at an uncertain date between 264 and 269, and (3) in 269. Euseb. *H. E.* vi. 46, vii. 30.

them[1]. It affirms the apostolic antiquity of the custom of rebaptism in Asia; it touches on the annual synods of that region, on the fixed and extempore portions of the Eucharistic liturgy, on the clerical function with regard to 'penitence' being not to bestow remission of sin, but to awaken conscience and promote reparation; the quasi-supremacy of Jerusalem, the unity subsisting under wide division. The conduct of the Roman towards the Carthaginian Pope he compares without a misgiving to the act of Judas. For arguments on the Baptismal question he relies on Cyprian, of two of whose letters this is to a great extent an approving digest with illustrations. It is in fact an 'open letter,' a restatement of the case from the beginning, a contribution to the controversy on Cyprian's side, the very force of which consisted not only in affirming the concurrence of East Asia Minor with Africa, but in showing how completely the arguments were adopted there, which were urged in vain on Italy. He says himself he had those letters by heart.

On the Genuineness of the Epistle of Firmilian.

Questionings of the genuineness of Firmilian's letter are so mere an episode in the criticism of it and in the history of Cyprian that it would be waste of space to discuss any but the most recent. Others shall be just enumerated first.

As if early doubts had existed, Rettberg (p. 189, note) under some

---

[1] It is almost worth while to direct attention to Baronius on Firmilian (*Annal. Eccl.* A.D. 258, xliii.—l.) as an example of his powers in statement and in criticism. Cyprian (he says) tried to procure the adherence of the Oriental bishops; *For* since he wrote to so remote a region as Cappadocia he cannot have omitted to write to the nearer bishops: Firmilian stands convicted of a 'patens mendacium' when he says that Stephen styled Cyprian a 'pseudo-christ and pseudo-prophet'; *For* neither Cyprian nor Augustine mention those epithets: Firmilian made 'insurrection against' the Church of Rome in judaizing with Montanists and Quartodecimans, but was 'restored to Catholic communion' and 'died in the peace of the Church'; *For* he is in the Greek Kalendar—28th Oct. 'Let no man think Firmilian persevered in his excommunicate condition'; *For* with others he sate in the Council of Antioch: Finally, all the Oriental bishops who were of his opinion about baptism recanted next year and gave in their adhesion to Stephen.

strange misconception, writes 'Augustine was inclined to recognise the 'genuineness of the letter as it could be used against the Donatists! 'truly a fine critical canon.' Augustine seems nowhere to make any explicit reference to the letter.

The Epistle did not appear in the Editio Princeps of Cyprian or its repetitions (A.D. 1471—1512) because it was not in the poor manuscripts employed, although before 1726 twenty-six MSS. were known containing it. Again, it was not in the editions of Erasmus (A.D. 1520—1550) because not in the Corbey MS. of the Epistles which alone he employed in correcting the old text. But Manutius had the epistle in two of his manuscripts, yet did not print it at Rome in 1563: 'the authorities,' says Latino Latini, his editor (*Bibl. Sacr. et Prof.* p. 174 b), 'not approving of that hitherto unpublished epistle being brought out of its darkness.' Not that he entertained the slightest doubt of its genuineness. For Pamèle having observed that prudence would have dictated its continued suppression, '*on account of its unepiscopal vehemence and bitterness* which had led Manutius to omit 'it,' Latini comes forward (p. 177 b) to correct him: 'It was I, and not 'Manutius, who left it out, following my predecessors[1], and because I 'detested the petulance of the man [Firmilian][2].' He did not know that previous editors had never had his opportunities. Morel first printed it in 1564; and then Pamèle in 1568, criticizing Morel's imprudence, but thinking the letter too important to be omitted, and administering an antidote.

The first person supposed to have questioned its authenticity was Christian Lupus in his Scholia on Tertullian's *de Præscriptionibus* (Bruxell. 1675), on the ground that it could not be true, as stated in the letter, that Stephen had called Cyprian 'a False Christ':—'An inane sort of conjecture,' says Baluze, p. 513, 'against which no monument of antiquity is safe.' Poor Lupus however never doubted its authenticity. Baluze misunderstands his rather clumsy expression '*De cujus tamen veritate hæsito*'; which meant only that he questioned whether Stephen could really have so miscalled Cyprian. Lupus elsewhere also uses Firmilian's epistle as genuine. (Chr. Lupus, *Opp.* t. IX. Venet. 1727. Tertull. *de Præscriptionibus*, Scholia, capp. 4, 5, pp. 67, 93.)

In 1733 Raimond Missori, a Franciscan, published at Venice two dissertations in which he assigns the whole of the Baptismal Documents to a race of Donatist forgers; and in 1734 R. J. Tournemine, a Jesuit, printed some 'Conjectures sur la supposition de quelques ouvrages de S. Cyprien et de la lettre de Firmilien,' in the *Mémoires de Trévoux* for 1734, p. 2246. Rettberg characterizes both by saying the latter is 'etwas

---

[1] *Majorum exempla* [?antient codices]. to break off his transcript (at *positis*
[2] Hartel thinks the same feeling c. 3).
caused the scribe of codex O, sæc. xii.,

besonnener obgleich eben so absprechend' as the other. Missori was answered by G. G. Preu in an academical disputation, Jena, 1738; as well as by Joh. Hyac. Sbaralea, Bologna 1741[1]. Routh, *R. S.* III. p. 186, inscribes over him only 'quam infeliciter, quam ridicule.' To Tournemine a 'sehr gründlich' refutation was given by D. Cotta, Tübingen 1740[2].

Routh (*R. S.* III. 186) records that Matthias Dannenmayr, *Institutiones*, p. 115, Vienna 1788, mentions authorities repudiating the scepticism as Romanists; and Weismann, *Introd. Hist. Eccl. N. T.* [Halæ Magd. 1745], vol. I. p. 249, and Koch, *De Legationibus Ecclesiast.* § xviii. p. 94, others as Protestants: he refers also to T. M. Mamachi, *Origg. et Antiqq. Christian.* [Rom 1749—55] II. p. 316. In 1790 and 93 another Franciscan revived the attack, viz. Marcellinus Molkenbuhr in two Latin Dissertations; he was laboriously refuted by Lumper (Migne, *Cursus Patrolog.* Tertullian, vol. III.; P. G. Lumper, *Historia Theologico-Critica*, vol. XIII. pp. 797 sqq.).

In 1795 Giov. Marchetti in his 'Esercitazioni Cyprianiche,' Roma [1787, *Nouv. Biogr. Gen.*], also attacks the genuineness.

In 1817 Morzelli in his great *Africa Christiana* (v. II. p. 138) strangely rejects it, only because he cannot think that so saintly a person can have denounced the Pope, and on the same grounds he denies the Epistle of Cyprian to Pompey.

In 1853[3] Mr Shepherd 'added to and moulded' Molkenbuhr. His idea is that the documents which the Romanists held so injurious to their cause had been forged in the Roman interest.

In 1862 V. Tizzani, Archbishop of Nisibi, brought out 'La celebre contesa fra s. Stefano e s. Cipriano' (Roma, Salvincci). Him we leave to the very tender mercies of his ashamed Romanists Dr Peters (p. 504), and Mgr. Freppel (pp. 429 sqq.).

Mr Shepherd's restatements and arguments, disengaged from their liveliness, are these:

1. That Firmilian's letter is not spoken of by antients like Eusebius, Augustine, Jerome, Optatus, &c., though it might have been expected of them; especially because 'depraved human nature' would delight in its 'ridicule, sarcasm and abuse.'

Several treatises which Mr S. says ought to have cited Firmilian's letter if it were genuine, are themselves, according to him, not genuine, so that he can scarcely argue from their omissions. But no one doubts Eusebius's ignorance of the West, or Augustine's of the East. Eusebius's knowledge of Cyprianic transactions comes only from Dionysius' letters, while Augustine is as ignorant of Clemens Alexandrinus, of Dionysius

---

[1] Rettberg, p. 190 n. [2] Rettberg, *ibid.*
[3] Rev. E. J. Shepherd's *Fifth Letter to Dr Maitland.*

himself, of Helenus of Tarsus, and all the great prelates whom Eusebius ranks with Firmilian, as if they had never lived. Shepherd argues as if ignorance of an author's existence was knowledge of his non-existence. Nevertheless Augustine seems quite aware that some Orientals had mingled in this controversy—*quorundam orientalium litteris* (*c. Crescon.* iii. 1, 2)—and been influenced by '*epistolare colloquium*' (*De Bapt. c. Don.* iii. 2), although the accuracy of his information may be gauged by his doubts as to whether many of them had held to rebaptism, and by his statement that they had recanted (*c. Crescon. l.c.*). Why Shepherd thinks that 'Eusebius records none of the facts of the quarrel 'between Stephen and the Oriental churches, the probable convening 'of one or more large Synods, and the cutting off of a large portion of the 'East from the Roman Communion' (p. 18), is hard to say. He records them all. It cannot be necessary to discuss why Jerome or Optatus do not name Firmilian's letter. But Basil knew and used it. See note, p. 388.

2. 'Cyprian *can* only have written to Firmilian *because* Firmilian 'was, like himself, under the Roman ban, and yet the letter shows no 'evidence of Cyprian's knowing this (p. 20).' Such a fact would have been good ground for a forger's selection of a correspondent, and a forger would for certain have brought out the point. The silence then favours genuineness. But the real reason for Cyprian's writing to Firmilian is quite different and fully brought out in the text.

3. 'Cyprian does not even whisper the name of Firmilian in his great Council (p. 21).' How should he? on his own responsibility he wrote to him explaining his own position, but independently of and after the Council.

4. The deacon Rogatian who carried the letter 'would not have been in such a hurry to return (p. 19).' It was important that he should not only convey the reply, but also that he should anticipate the winter at sea, beginning as we have seen on Nov. 3.

5. 'The journey of 2000 miles in a direct line' could not be performed 'between the end of September and beginning of November' even 'if at that season there was a vessel sailing at all' (p. 25). About 1400 miles is the real distance, and Mr S. has not realised either the rate of Roman travelling, or the number of Roman vessels, which for obvious reasons covered the Mediterranean more numerously than those which trade to the port of London itself, and especially before the open season ended. He talks about sailing to Ephesus or Antioch, but the valley of the Sarus readily brought the people from the port of Tarsus to Comana, within fifty miles of Cæsarea.

It is well just to note how the incidents of those objections 3, 4, and 5 support each other,—the speed of Rogatian's journey on the verge of winter, the haste of Firmilian to reply, and the silence at the Council about his letter.

6. Some other 'arguments' are beneath notice, but the boldest is that "the 'Hellenisms' of the letter are not Hellenisms," and that there is 'no trace of the translator in the *rest* of the letter.' Of course none if the 'Hellenisms' are not such. As to this however *judicent periti*. In the translation it is impossible not to recognize touches of Cyprian's style. Mr Shepherd admits it to be in the easy natural style in which the author of the rest writes his own letters.

It is equally impossible not to see the Greek:—

A.   In some of the compound phrases and coupled epithets:

1. magnam voluntatis caritatem in unum convenire:—πολλὴν τοῦ θέλειν προθυμίαν (cf. 2 Cor. viii. 11) εἰς ἓν συνελθεῖν. No occasion for *alacritatem*, the conjecture of Routh, who points out the reference.

3. ...a Domino missi sunt unitatis spiritu velociter currentes (ταχυδρομοῦντες).

4. quoniam sermo divinus...distribuatur, the whole clause.

B.   In the literal and sometimes awkward rendering of words:

3. fratribus tam longe *positis* (κειμένοις).

4. seniores et præpositi for πρεσβύτεροι οἱ προεστῶτες, Ritschl. Cf. sup. p. 330 n.

In c. 7, præsident *majores natu*, where age is nothing to the point, but the translator could not have used *presbyteri*, which would ascribe to presbyters the power of confirming and ordaining.

5. inexcusabilem sententiam (ἀναπολόγητον).

6. *eos qui* Romæ *sunt*,...nec observari illic omnia *æqualiter quæ* Hierosolymis observantur (ὁμοίως καί).

7. possident potestatem (κεκτήνται).

10. nec vexari *in aliquo*.

11. quamvis ad imaginem veritatis *tamen* (κατ' εἰκόνα ὅμως τῆς ἀληθείας).

ib. dæmonum fallacia *ipsa* est (αὐτή). (Noticed by Hartel, Præf. pp. xl., xli. n.)

12. *dividuat* (the true reading for *induit*). Cf. ἀποχωρίζοντες τὸ ἅγιον πνεῦμα ἀπὸ τοῦ πατρὸς καὶ τοῦ υἱοῦ, Theodoret, *H. E.* 4. 9, p. 314, ed. Gaisf. (Hartel *l.c.*).

17. *quid aliud quam* communicat (τὶ ἄλλο ἤ). (Hartel *l.c.*; correctors inserted *agit*.) Cf. 23 *quid aliud quam*...bibis.

22. *nos* etiam *illos quos hi qui* prius in Ecclesia Catholica Episcopi fuerant cannot be an original Latin clause. [? ὅσους οἱ κατ' Ἐκκ. Κ. ἐπισκοποῦντες ποτὲ ἐβαπτίσαντο.) Cf. S. Luc. ii. 49 Vg. 'in *his quæ* Patris mei sunt,' ἐν τοῖς τοῦ Πατρός.

25. *ut quid* illos hæreticos...vocamus (ἵνα τί). (Hartel *l.c.*)

Note also

3. *quod totum hoc* fit divina voluntate.
23. volentibus vivere.
24. ...consilii *et sermonis* (βουλῆς καὶ λόγου, should be *rationis*).
25. quæ ipse *ac merito* audire deberet (καὶ ἀξίως).
25. bene te valere *omnibus nobis*...optamus, ut...habeamus nobiscum *etiam de longinquo* adunatos.

C.   Instances in which the Greek seems scarcely understood:

2. sed non *enim* si=ἀλλ' οὐ γὰρ εἰ, where Hartel (p. xli. n.) would after Noltius improve the Latin at the expense of the Greek by *etiam* conjectural.

8. nisi si his episcopis *qui nunc* minor fuit Paulus (τῶν νῦν).

22. ut per eos qui *cum* ipsi: *cum* unmeaning, and Hartel would omit *qui*. (? οἴους read as οἱ ὥς.)

There is room for differences of judgment, but the above instances to which many might be added are fair, and together evince a Greek original.

In c. 10 we may further notice the applicability to the conditions of Asia Minor, and of no other region perhaps, of the use of such words as *patrias suas* about *local* persecutions.

The remarkable translation in c. 24 of Eph. iv. 2, 3 'sustinentes invicem in dilectione, satis agentes servare unitatem Spiritus in conjunctione pacis' is in the same words as in three places of Cyprian, and differs from every other known rendering. *Ep.* 55. 24; *De Unit.* 8; *De Bono Pat.* 15 (wrongly cited by Sabatier as from *De Op. et El.*). This seems to indicate the use of a version which Cyprian used or made. It is worth observing that even the African Nemesian (*Sentt. Epp.* 5) quotes the passage as '*curantes* servare.'

The other quotations in the Epistle are either not marked enough to be conclusive, or may have been borrowed from Cyprian's own Baptismal letters.

Ritschl has undertaken to dissect the Epistle with a view to shewing that parts of it have been added in Latin by Cyprian or his party to the original letter of Firmilian. Even if the operation had been performed with success, what would survive of the Epistle so much more than suffices for the utmost support of Cyprian's views, that any motive for forgery is latent. But the destruction of literary monuments by conceits is so much to be deprecated that it is right to see how baseless the allegations are.

Chapter 12. Ritschl decides that this is 'von anderer Hand angefügt' (p. 132)

(1) because the question of the effect of unworthiness is deduced in c. 11 from the story of the demoniac woman.

(2) because the last words of 12 merely repeat the last words of 11. Now this parallel form belongs to the stating of the Three Dilemmas pointed out below, and the beginnings also are parallel.

c. 11. Numquid et hoc Stephanus......quando apud illos omnino Spiritus Sanctus non est.

c. 12. Illud etiam quale est quod vult Stephanus......non sit autem illic Spiritus Sanctus.

c. 13. Sequitur enim illud quod interrogandi sunt......apud quos Spiritus Sanctus non est.

(3) because (pp. 128, 9) c. 12 is closely modelled on *Ep.* 74. 5 only (...sich übrigens ganz geschickt zu verstecken) and *tincti* is used for *baptizati* in order to vary the words. (On this see 'Quotations,' p. 387.) Again for the same reason 'si non mentitur apostolus' is used instead of 'dicit apostolus.' But 'non mentitur' takes S. Paul's words (Gal. i. 20) from the same Epistle here quoted (Gal. iii. 27). And thirdly, *quasi possit ...separari* is varied with *nisi si...dividunt* and expanded. This varying however runs through nearly the whole Epistle; only the words are usually *more* varied. The phenomena are throughout precisely those of a retranslation of a translation, not checked by comparison with the originals. They are familiar to classical tutors. The points are kept, the emphasis is different, the wording sometimes very near, sometimes far away. In this last instance the original force of *quasi possit...a Christo Spiritus separari* is increased by the retranslation *nisi si a Christo Spiritum dividunt.* (May I here observe that *Nisi si* with the Indicative is used in a *reductio ad absurdum* when it is meant that the opponent is logically *proved* to be actually in an absurd position, and is not merely warned off his ground by a sight of the consequences? Compare 75. 11 nisi si...contendunt, 75. 14 nisi si...parit, 73. 21 nisi si...prædicant.)

To pass from wording to substance. In cc. 11, 12 and 13 Firmilian puts Three Dilemmas to Stephen against his principle that 'baptism in heresy was Christian baptism':

(1) Would Stephen say that baptism by a person possessed by a demon was Christian baptism, if administered in regular form? (c. 11).

(2) The baptized, if S. Paul is true, have 'put on Christ.' According to Stephen, they must still receive imposition of hands within the Church in order to receive the Holy Ghost; will Stephen then say that Christ is where the Holy Ghost is not? (c. 12).

(3) Will Stephen say whether the baptism of heretics is 'of the flesh' or 'of the Spirit'? If it is of the flesh, how does Christian baptism differ from Jewish baptism? If 'of the Spirit,' how is it that they cannot impart the Spirit? (c. 13).

Or briefly (1) Is there absolutely no limitation to efficacy through unworthiness? (2) If heretics impart Christ, why not the Spirit? (3) If their baptism is spiritual, what defect in their spiritual status?

Of these Three Dilemmas Ritschl proposes to drop out (2), that is ch. 12, on the above frivolous grounds.

Chapters 23—25 are also charged as a fraudulent addition to Firmilian's original. They form, it is said, 'a whole' by themselves; the Epistle ended with chapter 22, and chapter 23 begins with introducing a text of Proverbs that has no connection (unvermittelt) (p. 133) with what precedes. Further, certain words in the end of 22 are echoed in the end of 25 (I suppose to create a deceitful similarity, but am not sure why).

Now these are the passages:

c. 22....'And Stephen is not ashamed to maintain this; so that he says remission of sins can be given through them, though they are involved in all manner of sins, as if the Laver of Health could be in the House of Death. c. 23, What place then will there be for that which is written "Keep thee from the strange water, and from a strange fount drink thou not[1]," if leaving the "sealed fount[2]" of the Church you take[3] 'strange water' of your own instead, and pollute the Church with profane founts?'

Even if a letter could have ended so abruptly, yet a complete 'whole' does not begin as c. 23 begins. The Proverb certainly has a connection. It is itself the link. It is quoted to support by Scripture the argument that the Laver or Font can be only in the Church. It is quoted by Cyprian in the same connection in *Ep.* 70. 1 and thence (like so many other texts) adopted by Firmilian. It is quoted again in the same connection by Nemesian, *Sentt. Epp.* 5.

Again the end of 25 is no repetition of the first words of the above extract, but a strong advance upon them.

c. 25...'it is manifest that neither can we have baptism in common with heretics with whom we have nothing at all in common. (That is the point reached in 22 and he proceeds) And yet Stephen is not ashamed to afford to such his patronage against the Church, and for the sake of maintaining the cause of heretics to cleave the brotherhood asunder, and, over and above that, to say Cyprian is a false Christ and false apostle and teacher and worker; and conscious that all these flaws are in himself, forestalls them by falsely laying to another's charge what he should quite deservedly have said of himself.'

---

[1] The strange (African?) addition to Prov. ix. 18 which appears in LXX. and in *Ep.* 70. 1, in *Sentt. Epp.* 5, in Aug. and in Ambrose, but not in the Vulgate.

[2] Cant. iv. 12.

[3] I must read *suscipis* with the early corrector of Q. There is no v. l. as to the other Presents.

The objection to c. 24 (p. 133) that its expositions are built up out of *Epp.* 73. 15 ; 74. 4 and 73. 20 would be of no weight if true. Firmilian's open letter uses up for the purpose of reaffirming them most, if not all, of the arguments contained in the two epistles which were submitted for his confirmation. But it does not happen to be true except in mere verbal coincidence, as to the first two passages. The substance of *Ep.* 73. 15 is the apostolic definition of heresy. That of *Ep.* 74. 4 is the handling of Stephen's argument derived from the practice of heretics. Neither of these reappear in c. 24. That of *Ep.* 73. 20 is that Stephen actually misleads the poor heretic who would fain enter the Church by rightful steps. This is repeated (not in c. 24, but) in c. 23 of *Ep.* 75.

It is asserted (Ritschl, p. 134) that c. 25 contradicts c. 6 as to the course of Stephen's action ; and as c. 6 is interesting in other particulars it may be given so far in full.

c. 6. 'That the Roman church does not in all things observe the primitive tradition, and alleges the authority of the Apostles to no purpose, anybody may know from seeing that about the celebration of Easter, and many other "sacraments" of religion, there exist with them some diversities, and all things are not observed there in the same way (*æqualiter quæ*) as they are observed at Jerusalem, just as in the other numerous provinces too there are many things varied to suit local and tribal differences (*locorum atque hominum*), and yet on this account the peace and unity of the Catholic Church have not at any time been departed from. Stephen has now dared to do this, breaking (that) peace with you which his predecessors have ever kept with you in love and mutual honour.'

The supposed contradiction to this is found in the opening of c. 25. 'How diligently hath Stephen fulfilled these the Apostle's commands 'and salutary monitions (those namely of Eph. iv.) keeping "lowliness 'and meekness" in the first rank ! For what is more "lowly and meek" 'than to have differed with so many bishops throughout the whole 'world, breaking the peace with each in various kind of discord, one 'while (*modo*) with Eastern bishops, of which (fact) we are confident that 'you too are aware, another while with yourselves who are in the south.'

c. 6 then, it is said, makes the breach with Africa the first, while c. 25 places it later than the Eastern quarrel. c. 6 however touches no question of time but only says that the Africans are themselves a living instance of Stephen's quarrelsome pretensions; and c. 25 does not say that his Oriental quarrel preceded in point of time his African quarrel. But if Dionysius and Eusebius (Euseb. *H. E.* vii. 5) satisfy the reader that the Oriental difficulty was the earlier he will scarcely find his opinion contradicted in 25, and in that case the error would be in Ritschl's genuine chapter.

B.

The linguistic objection, that the last word of the epistle *adunatos* is there applied to the union of Episcopal equals among themselves, whereas Cyprian uses it only of the union of inferiors to superiors, as of the people to their bishops, or of the Church to Christ, absolutely breaks down. *Adunatus* and *adunatio* are used by Cyprian of the unitedness of his own action with that of the Roman presbytery, and specially of the equal relation and union among themselves of the congregation[1], of the sons of God[2], of the true people of Christ. Thrice in chapter 2, which the critic himself calls genuine, of this very epistle, it is used in the same sense, and once even of the union of angels with the Church. Similar is Cyprian's application of the word *adunatio* to the mutual bond of churches[3], and to the 'many grains' of the sacramental loaf[4].

Lastly, it must be observed that the marks of translation from the Greek are as rife in Ritschl's condemned chapters as in any others.

Conclusion. These then are the fruits of (what I believe to be) thorough examination of the objections pushed against the genuineness of Firmilian's epistle. The more general questions raised either prove pointless or lead to further confirmations.

The diction is manifestly that of a translation from Greek; the style rings with Cyprian; the arguments are Cyprian's own. All fits precisely the conditions of a letter translated under Cyprian's hand or eye from the original of a Greek writer who had studied Cyprian's arguments.

The chapters which have been distinguished by a superfine acumen as insertions either cannot be detached from the context without violence to the argument, or are provably not liable to the special charges made, whether historically or linguistically; and they have the same marked character as the rest.

No literary document bears clearer stamp of authenticity and genuineness than this interesting translation from such an author by such an author.

Quotations of Scripture in Firmilian.

Another test may be applied. There are quoted in *Ep.* 75 (Firmilian) some 21 passages of Scripture. Twelve of these are also quoted

---

[1] ...plebs adunata, *De Dca. Orat.* 23.
[2] ...filii Dei...respondeant adunati, *De Zel. et Liv.* 18.
[3] *Ep.* 62. 1.
[4] *Ep.* 69. 5; cf. *Ep.* 60. 1.

VIII. II. 2. ACTS AND DOCUMENTS—FIRMILIAN.

in Cyprian's writings. If the renderings of them in *Ep.* 75 differed appreciably in form or words from Cyprian's renderings, we might doubt whether the translation of the epistle was produced by Cyprian, under Cyprian's direction, or in Africa at all. If on the other hand the renderings in *Ep.* 75 corresponded to those given by Cyprian, this resemblance would confirm the other indications of time, place and authorship. We will examine all those citations in *Ep.* 75 which recur in Cyprian.

A. The following quotations appear in the Latin version of Firmilian's letter in precisely *the same* wording in which they occur in Cyprian's writings not only (as two of them do) in the two letters which Firmilian had read, but in his other writings.

Ep. 75. 9 quotes Marc. xiii. 6 verbatim as *de Unit.* 14, and *Ep.* 73. 16.
,, 75. 14 ,, Lc. xi. 23 ,, ,, *Ep.* 69. 1 and *Ep.* 70. 3.
,, 75. 15 ,, Cant. iv. 12, 13 ,, ,, *Ep.* 69. 2 and *Ep.* 74. 11.
,, 75. 23 ,, Prov. ix. 18 ,, ,, *Ep.* 70. 1 (Nemesian differently, *Sentt. Epp.* 5).
,, 75. 24 ,, Eph. iv. 1—6 (a long quotation).
                viz. 2, 3   *Ep.* 55. 24 and *de B. Pat.* 15; *de Unit.* 8.
                4, 5   *de Unit.* 4 (except that *de Unit.* consolidates 'sicut vocati estis in una spe' into 'una spes' as does Cæcilius, *Sentt. Epp.* 1. It is not in fact a '*reading*': our Common Prayer Book does the same).
                3, 5   quoted by Nemesian, *Sentt. Epp.* 5, except *curantes*.

B. In the following, the variations are such as might occur in different MSS. of the same version. The reader may observe that in 1 *Cor.* xi. 27 the Firmilian form is nearer to each of two differing forms than they are to each other: *Gal.* iii. 27, *tinguere* for *baptizare* is common both in Cyprian (*e.g. Epp.* 73. 5; 71. 1; 75. 13 which last Ritschl thinks genuine),—and therefore could not serve in 75. 12 as Ritschl says, for a disguise,—and also in Tertullian. The two passages which differ significantly are both from the *Testimonia*, which generally presents most variety. Nemesian, *Sentt. Epp.* 5, quotes two passages which *Ep.* 75 quotes and in both differs alike from it and from the version in Cyprian.

Ep. 75. 12	quotes	*Gal.* iii. 27 with tincti. *Epp.* 62. 3 and 74. 5 baptizati.	
,, 75. 14	,,	*Ps.* xliv. 11...*populi tui, quia desideravit.*—*Testim.* ii. 29 ...populum tuum et domum patris quoniam concupivit.	
,, 75. 15	,,	1 *Pet.* iii. 21 sic et nos (*v. l.* vos). *Ep.* 69. 2; 74. 11 quod et vos.	
,, 75. 16	,,	*Mt.* xvi. 19 quæcunque (first). *Ep.* 33. 1; *de Unit.* 4 quæ.	
,, 75. 16	,,	*Jo.* xx. 23 et si cujus. *Epp.* 69. 11; 73. 7; *de Unit.* 4 all omit 'et.'	
,, 75. 20	,,	*Phil.* i. 18 adnuntiatur (*v. l.* annuncietur). *Ep.* 73. 14 adnuntietur (*v. l.* -atur).	
,, 75. 21	,,	1 *Co.* xi. 27 quicumque ederit panem aut. *Epp.* 15. 1; 16. 2 qui ederit panem aut. *De laps.* 15 quicumque ederit panem et. *Test.* iii. 94 quicumque manducaverit panem et....	

The facts are alike whether the passages occur in *Epp.* 73 and 74, or in other writings of Cyprian.

It seems obvious on careful consideration of all the facts that the quotations are not rendered anew from Firmilian's Greek text, but are simply given from texts then in use in Africa.

This independent and minute test then again supports the idea of the version being Cyprianic.

Basil and the Letter of Firmilian.

If the following clauses of Basil, *Epp. Classis II.*, *Ep.* 188 *canonica Prima* (*Amphilochio*), and of Firmilian *Ep.* 75. 7, 8 are read side by side, as suggested to me by M. Larpent, I believe it will be felt that they are not independent. The resemblances are closer and more parallel than mere treatment from the same point of view could create.

VIII. II. 2. BASIL AND THE LETTER OF FIRMILIAN.

Οἱ τοίνυν Πεπυζηνοὶ προδήλως εἰσὶν αἱρετικοί·

εἰς γὰρ τὸ Πνεῦμα τὸ ἅγιον ἐβλασφήμησαν,

Μοντανῷ καὶ Πρισκίλλῃ τὴν τοῦ Παρακλήτου προσηγορίαν .. ἐπιφημίσαντες... οἱ Καθαροὶ καὶ αὐτοὶ τῶν ἀπεσχισμένων εἰσι ... * οἱ δὲ τῆς Ἐκκλησίας ἀποστάντες οὐκέτι ἔσχον τὴν χάριν τοῦ ἁγίου Πνεύματος ἐφ' ἑαυτοῖς· ἐπέλιπε γὰρ ἡ μετάδοσις τῷ διακοπῆναι τὴν ἀκολουθίαν. Οἱ μὲν γὰρ πρῶτοι αναχωρήσαντες παρὰ τῶν πατέρων ἔσχον τὰς χειροτονίας, καὶ διὰ τῆς ἐπιθέσεως τῶν χειρῶν αὐτῶν εἶχον τὸ χάρισμα τὸ πνευματικόν· οἱ δὲ ἀπορραγέντες, λαϊκοὶ γενόμενοι, οὔτε τοῦ βαπτίζειν οὔτε τοῦ χειροτονεῖν εἶχον τὴν ἐξουσίαν, οὐκέτι δυνάμενοι χάριν Πνεύματος ἁγίου ἑτέροις παρέχειν, ἧς αὐτοὶ ἐκπεπτώκασι. Διὸ ὡς παρὰ λαικῶν βαπτιζομένους τοὺς παρ' αὐτῶν ἐκέλευσαν...τῷ ἀληθινῷ βαπτίσματι τῷ τῆς Ἐκκλησίας ἀνακαθαίρεσθαι.

...quod etiam illi qui Cataphrygas appellantur .. nec patrem possunt habere nec filium

quia nec spiritum sanctum, a quibus si quæramus quem Christum prædicent, respondebunt eum se prædicare qui miserit spiritum per Montanum et Priscam locutum... Sed et ceteri quique hæretici, si se ab ecclesia Dei sciderint, nihil habere potestatis aut gratiæ possunt quando omnis potestas et gratia in ecclesia constituta sit, ubi præsident majores natu qui et baptizandi et manum imponendi et ordinandi possident potestatem, hæreticum enim sicut ordinare non licet nec manum imponere, ita nec baptizare nec quicquam sancte et spiritaliter gerere, ... quod totum nos jam pridem in Iconio...collecti .... confirmavimus tenendum ... 8 *fin.* .... nisi eos prius etiam ecclesiæ baptismo baptizasset.

The correspondences are the more striking because they are so little verbal. There is the constructive heresy of the Montanists; there are the two classes of heretics and schismatics; the loss of the power of imparting the Holy Spirit through the loss of the Apostolic Succession; there is the reference in Basil to some earlier canon, in Firmilian to his contemporary Council of Iconium; and there is the marked phrase 'The Baptism of the Church.' And all these topics are in the same order.

A. Harnack, *Gesch. d. alt-Chr. Litteratur bis Euseb.* I. p. 409 refers to this passage, but does not notice the parallelism. It has been mentioned above (p. 375) that in *de Spiritu Sancto* xxix. 29. 74 Basil appeals to Firmilian's doctrine as a standard. The words omitted at the asterisk * couple *Cyprian* and 'our *Firmilian*' together as antient authorities who required the baptism of schismatics equally with heretics. Πλὴν ἀλλ' ἔδοξε τοῖς ἀρχαίοις, τοῖς περὶ Κυπριανὸν λέγω καὶ Φιρμιλιανὸν τὸν ἡμέτερον τούτους πάντας μιᾷ ψήφῳ ὑποβαλεῖν, Καθαροὺς ....

The Nameless Author 'ON REBAPTISM.'

The interest centering on the champion of the winning yet lost cause must not make us forget that so far he alone has registered what of record there is against himself. There must be facts a champion could not record. His councils cannot have been so unlike all others as not to have been scenes of controversy; his signataries not the only prelates who had opinions; his bishops not more docile than his presbyters[1]. He regrets himself that not all, though so many, were with him. In his last Council he seems to absolve some dioceses from compliance. In his opinion worldliness accounted for the disuse of Agrippinus' rebaptismal statute; but we are well able to see that that effect was at least also producible by thought, by charity, by comprehension of Apostolic principle; and if a contemporary of this stamp, one who differed 'by a whole sky' from Cyprian, not traditionally or overbearingly but philosophically, should have survived, how valuable might be his separate illustration of the Christian reason and spirit in that age.

Such a writer, I entertain no doubt, exists for us in 'THE AUTHOR ON REBAPTISM.'

> His pamphlet was found and copied by the Père Jacques Sirmond from a 'very antient manuscript' of Cyprian in the library of S. Remi at Rheims,—where it exists no more. It there followed Cyprian's letter to Pompeius[2] and was subscribed *Cæcilii Cypriani finivit de rebaptismate*. Rigaut first printed it in 1648 seeing its value, and from its diction concluding it to be *ab ævo Cyprianico parum distans*. Then Labbe in 1672 in the *Concilia*, vol. I., and, after making a new collation, Baluze. Hartel has no other materials to edit from (Præf. p. lxii.).

[1] *Ep.* 71. 1 '*plurimi* coepiscopi...*quidam*.' 69. 10 'intus in ipsa ecclesia.' 73. 26 'collegis et coepiscopis.' *Sentt. Epp.* 59 '*quidam* de *collegis* nostris.' *Sentt. Epp.* 38 '*quidam nostri* prævaricatores veritatis.' Compare 'episcopos plurimos' and *quidam* in *Ep.* 63. 1 and *de Mort.* 1 'etsi aput plurimos...tamen... quosdam.'

[2] *Ep.* 74.

Labbe says (*Synopsis Conc. Apparat.* tom. I. p. 83) a MS. of it in the Vatican attributes it to 'Ursinus the Monk an African,' and so names it. Pearson accepts this. Baluze also, because the interval between its writing and the Apostles is called (c. vi.) *tot sæculorum tanta series*, a phrase inapplicable in the age of Cyprian. Oudin (*qui fourmille d'erreurs*, as Tillemont says), besides Routh (*Rell. Sac.* vol. V. p. 283), who quotes Labbe as saying *Three* manuscripts, accept Ursinus. Such names claim an otherwise superfluous answer. What we know of Ursinus is from Gennadius, presbyter of Marseilles (*ob.* A.D. 496), in his continuation of Jerome, *De Viris Illustribus*, c. 27. 'Ursinus (Ursicinus *Sirmond*) Monachus scripsit adversus eos qui 'rebaptizandos hæreticos decernunt, docens nec legitimum esse nec 'Deo dignum rebaptizari illos qui in nomine simpliciter Christi, vel 'in nomine Patris et Filii et Spiritus Sancti quamvis pravo sensu 'baptizantur: sed post Trinitatis et Christi simplicem confessionem 'sufficere ad salutem manus impositionem catholici sacerdotis.' It is hard to see how this can have been taken for an account of our author. He is plainly not a monk but a bishop. The words *legitimum* and *Deo dignum* point to express reasonings turning on (1) authority, (2) analogy, which are not touched in this book: nor yet the distinct on of baptisms in the name of Christ and of the Trinity, nor the possibility of the latter being validly bestowed although *pravo sensu*, which is an intelligible ground dealt with by Cyprian (*Ep.* 73. 5). Neither is a preliminary confession insisted on. Again, would 'Catholicus *Sacerdos*' have been used in this abstract unless it were in the treatise described? our author always speaks of *Episcopi*.

Cave (*H. L.* I. p. 131) suggests that the Vatican subscription is due to some reader of Gennadius, and Tillemont that it would be well to ascertain that the MS. is one of this treatise. I do not know whence comes Cave's account of Ursinus as 'gente Afer' except from the subscription, or his date 440 A.D., but at any rate Ursinus must have written (from Gennadius' statement) at a much later period of the controversy, and probably in its Donatist stage.

As to Baluze's remark on the 'tot sæculorum tanta series' indicating a later date, the phrase is not of course more literally accurate in 440 than in 250. It belongs to their general leaning to large numbers: the expectation of the end of the world had something to do with making the Christian past seem long; but apart from that, this very treatise calls the few years of Peter and Paul's mutual knowledge 'tanta tempora'; Cyprian speaks of 'tot hæreticorum milia' having entered the African church by rebaptism (*Ep.* 73. 3); Optatus, B. v. c. 5, speaks of John as baptizing 'infinita milia hominum.'

Fleury was absurd enough to think Stephanus a possible author.

Tillemont (in his clever discussion vol. IV. note xl., see also note xxxix.), Du Pin, Maran, Galland, Neander, Hefele, recognise the early date. Cave also, partly on the ground of references to contemporary persecutions; but of these, says Oudin, *De Scriptt. Eccles. Ant.* v. I. p. 1006, Lips. 1722, truly, there is *ne γρὺ quidem*. The position of the treatise in the Rheims manuscript is not without its bearing on the date.

As literary tokens of his antiquity we may mark the genuine reading of S. John vii. 39 '(The) Holy Ghost *was not*' before Christ's exaltation. No Latin father reads this uncorrupted. Again, 'The Holy Ghost,' he says, 'came down... not of His own will,' a paraphrase, which heresy early rendered impossible, of '...He will not come unto you...I will send Him unto you,' combined perhaps with 'He shall not speak from Himself[1]....'

From a doctrinal point the higher value set upon the Imposition of Hands than on the Baptism itself is a mark of early and not far from Tertullianesque age[2]. Again, the familiar use of 'Baptism in the name of Christ' as equivalent to perfect baptism would have been impossible when the distinction had once been thought out between that form and the Invocation of the Holy Trinity. No one could have used the terms as equivalent after Cyprian's correspondence with Stephanus was known.

---

[1] Jo. vii. 39 (ap. Auct. *de Reb.* c. 14) and xvi. 7, 13 (ap. Auct. c. 6). Tillemont, who does not recognise either quotation, says (to some extent rightly) (v. IV. note xl.) that the fourth century 'would not have tolerated such expressions.' It had in fact already inserted δεδομένον, δοθέν or *datus*. No Latin fathers omit the word *given* except the translator of Origen, if he may be treated as independent. The true reading was preserved extensively in Latin MSS. Thus it is found in Dunelm. (Δ [Bentl. K] sæc. vii., viii.), Fuld. (F 541—546 A.D.), Sangerm. (G sæc. ix.), Stonyhurst (S¹ sæc. vii.), Lindisfarn. (Y sæc. vii., viii.), Harl. (Z¹ sæc. vi., vii.). Cod. Bezæ (d sæc. vi.), though it has not *datus*, has *in eos*, Brix. (sæc. vi.) not *datus* but *in eis*. See Bp. Wordsworth of Sarum and H. J. White, *Nov. Test. Latine*, vol. IV. p. 559 (Oxon. 1895).

Routh remarks on the second passage 'dictum illud non intelligo.' His 'edition,' *R. S.* vol. v. p. 291, is in the main a wretched reprint of Fell's wretched copy, reproducing even nonsensical punctuations.

[2] Auctor c. 6 ad fin. Cf. Tert. *de Bapt.* 6, 7, 8.

There is a yet nicer indication. We shall presently see that the Author's theory of the visible Church was in itself adequate to solve Cyprian's difficulty. Yet the Author has no more than an instinctive sense of its truth and of its applicability. He does not drive it home. This is a phenomenon which can only occur in contemporary arguments. Two theories exist side by side; in the next generation one of them will have yielded. At first the discoverer of the true one has rarely learnt its full speculative value: he applies it merely as a test to points of practice.

Again, the Author does not meet the great doctrine of 'Unity' on which every argument of Cyprian's is based. When once a theory has passed out of the essay-stage, in which others as yet compete with it; when once it has possession of the field, no eye can stir without seeing it. No one could have written on Cyprian's subject even a few years later without knowing of this key to his whole position. The absence of any allusion to the doctrine of Unity assigns the Treatise on Rebaptism to the first years of the controversy. How could it have been excluded ever so little later when the forms in which it was cast and the Scriptural symbols in which it was expressed were so taking, so popular, so numerous, and so assailable[1]?

Acute in disputation[2] and fresh in language he writes as one who hopes still to influence the controversy[3]. He is one

---

[1] It must be remembered that they occur in the 'Unity' as emphatically as in his Letters.

[2] As an instance of his ability and desire to look at facts as they are, note how, anticipating 'your usual' answer (which Cyprian does use in the case of the Samaritans, *Ep.* 73. 9) viz. that 'the disciples held the right faith when they were baptized long before receiving the Holy Ghost,' he works out how their Messianic beliefs were then Judaic as to cardinal points, and not imperfect only but erroneous, at the very time when they were not only baptized but baptizing others.

[3] '...et turbulentis hominibus ut *vel nunc* suum negotium agere *incipiant persuadere: consecuturis* plurimum etiam *nobis* si hoc quoque *consilio sano tandem voluerint* acquiescere.' 'Ut agendi in ecclesia formam...*universis* fratribus *insinuemus.*' [*Agendi* conjecimus, Hartelius et multo ante egomet. Accendi MS., *alii* tacendi, accedenti, attendi. *Routh* accenseri.] Auctor c. 1. In c.

of the bishops[1]. To him Cyprian's proposal is in effect a new question, an attempt to alter, to reform very widely the usage of the churches, a step to Novatianism[2]. He is not an Italian. No Italian could have avoided as he does an appeal to Roman tradition and the Roman pope. His speech is African[3]. His adversaries are not heretics like the Donatists; they are churchmen and bishops. There is no other date possible for him, unless it can be shewn that there was some other at which there raged a second tempest like ours within the Latin-speaking church, yet one in which there was no recurrence to either the arguments or the refutations of Cyprian. It would indeed be necessary to create a second Cyprian. For no one else can be represented in the unkind sketch which the Author gives of his antagonist, as he sees him abetted by his bishops in imputing their own faulty inventions irreverently to the Church their mother. To set against all the heart-burnings and separations that will arise, the sole fruit of the new question is, he says[4], the exaltation 'of one single person, whoever that is, so that he may 'be vaingloriously proclaimed among the thoughtless as a 'man of great insight and consistency; and that, whilst

19 he calls the controversy *præsentem altercationem*.

[1] He contrasts baptism administered '*per nos*' and confirmation following immediately, with baptism administered '*a minore clero per necessitatem*.' c. 10.

[2] Super hac nova quæstione c. 1. Nunc primum repente ac sine ratione insurgere c. 6. Hæreticorum... c. 1.

[3] A few of these idioms may be quoted. Datives, alio (c. 4); solo (c. 12);—præstaturus (c. 9); devotans (c. 9); flumina de ventre ejus currebunt (c. 14), this (African) future is demanded by the sense and the citation though Routh and Hartel have 'currebant'; existimarent ut...perseveret (c. 9), *think that he would continue* (cf. Optat. iii. c. 4 expectantes ut venirent, iii. c. 8 dicebatur ut negaretur Christus, *it was ordered that he should be denied*). As peculiarities of version note '*absconsa hominum*' (c. 13), Ro. ii. 16 (not noted by Hartel); propitius sit tibi (c. 9), Mt. xvi. 22; neque novi te (c. 9), Mt. xxvi. 70.

May I here suggest an emendation of c. 2, viz. $\overline{\text{IE}}$ (=Joanne) for SE? 'ait enim Dominus...baptizandos esse non quemadmodum a *se* in aqua ad pœnitentiam sed in Spiritu Sancto.'

[4] Auct. c. 1.

'enjoying the admiration of heretics[1], whose solitary comfort 'in perdition is to be seen sinning in company, he may be 'extolled among his copyists and compeers, for having set 'right the errors and defects of all the churches.' This pursuit of logical issues, this tendency to Puritanism, lust of remodelling, extended ambition are contemporary accusations, not so acrimonious as those of Puppian[2], but as surely aimed at Cyprian. The charge of imitating Novatian is exactly what angers Cyprian into the retort that 'Novatian is the Ape of the Church,' and that the way to harden heretics is to patronise and imitate them[3]. The Author's sneer that 'want of humanity' is what makes his opponent undervalue *custom* is familiar[4]. In the frequent interchange of singular and plural addresses we see the large party, and the leader who is himself the party. Cyprian's use of a favourite text is sharply touched. 'Whereto perhaps you, with your 'novelty, may forthwith impatiently answer, as you are wont, 'that the Lord said, Except a man be born again, &c.[5]' Even the exquisite writing does not escape. 'How,' he asks sarcastically, 'must the line of disqualification be drawn? 'Why should it be drawn at heresy, more than at immorality? 'and then why not at erroneous views—at virtual heresy? 'at want of skill in imparting these rudiments? You must 'at last come to enforcing your '*denuo*' baptism if the 'catechising bishop has been imperfect in expression—not 'so ornate and precise as you are[6].'

Finding ourselves then so close to Cyprian in this treatise,

---

[1] Hæreticorum stupore præditus, Auct. 1.

[2] *Ep.* 66.

[3] Cyp. *Ep.* 73. 2 'simiarum more'; 3 'nos non demus stuporem hæreticis patrocinii et consensus nostri....'

[4] Auct. 16.

[5] Quoted four times in Cyprian's Epistles, but of course the remark cannot be limited to them only. Also Nemesian, *Sentt. Epp.* 5, Auctor c. 3.

[6] ...sed non tam ornate ut tu et composite, isti quoque simpliciores homines mysterium fidei tradant. Dicturus es enim utique *pro tua singulari diligentia* hos quoque denuo baptizandos esse. Auct. c. 10. It appears to me as certain that Cyprian is here meant as that it can never have been written after his martyrdom.

it is natural to ask, Was the Author acquainted with Cyprian's full writings on the subject? or Had Cyprian himself read the Author? The questions seem capable of answer. And as answers are deducible from facts lying aside of that main stream of the Argument on which we have not yet embarked, we may intelligibly complete our review of the Book as a document by producing them here.

(1) Did then the Author know Cyprian's later writings on the subject?

There is scarcely a semblance of this. He nowhere attacks his very assailable typology. For example Cyprian asks, 'If heretic baptism be so safe, why any church 'reception? If that baptism is a reality, heretics may be 'holy martyrs.' And the Author meets these questions; but it is simply as floating arguments without any appearance of setting treatise against treatise. He was acquainted with Cyprian's line of action, with his treatment of the ordinary texts, and with certain pamphlets on both sides[1]. But he does not fasten on Cyprian's specialities as we know them. His treatise must therefore come quite early in the movement[2] of his day.

But another strong personality, besides Cyprian's, seems to be before him, when, analysing Christ's prediction of 'false prophets with miraculous powers,' the Author speaks of 'certain powers,' and of 'the false prophesying[3],'—the term for Montanism—in his own day, and then goes on 'but 'certain it is that, because they are not Christ's, they have 'nothing to do with Christ: just as if any one draw away from 'Christ, cleaving only to the Name of Him, he is not much 'helped thereby, nay rather is actually borne down by this 'Name; although he *were before time* most strong in the faith,

---

[1] His use of '*ut soles*,' cc. 3, 8.— '*Scripta atque rescripta*,' Auctor c. 1.

[2] I am unable to see what Fechtrup, p. 207, n. 2, sees: that *de Rebapt.* 13 is an answer to Cyp. *Ep.* 73. 21 on the profitlessness of martyrdom to heretics.

[3] *Falso prophetare—fidelissimus—clero aliquo honoratus.* Auctor 12.

'or most upright, or held some rank among the clergy, or had 'attained the dignity of confessorship.' Can there be much question as to who was the original of this sketch? And if it is Tertullian the early date is still more distinct.

Our impression of the Author's place in the controversy is supported by what appears to be the answer to the next question:—

(2) Had Cyprian read the Author?

When the Author proposes with the air of a new dilemma 'What place can you consistently give to the unbaptized confessor?' and when Cyprian describes this exact question as 'the human argumentation of certain persons,' his reference seems to be distinct[1] and express.

When Cyprian says that the apostolic motto 'unum baptisma' must not be construed as a rubrical direction but is a declaration of the oneness of the Christian bond, he seems to assail some such interpretation as the Author adopts, that 'to repeat baptism was contrary to *a decree* of the Apostles.' Stephen himself had not gone beyond saying 'what we have received from the Apostles,' meaning by tradition[2].

Again, the specialness of Cyprian's warning against the idea that heretics will be kept away by the required repetition, whereas they will rather be attracted, has the appearance of a reply to some such representation as that in which the Author paints the responsibility of a church which would by

---

[1] Auctor 11 '*Quid autem* statues in personam ejus *verbum audientis qui* forte *adprehensus* in *nomine* Christi statim *confessus ac priusquam baptizari aqua* permittererur ei fuerit punitus, &c. ...quia Dominus...eum...*ut pollicitus* est exornet...martyrum autem nonnisi in ipso et per ipsum Dominum possit *consummari*.' Compare *Ep.* 73. 22 '...quidam quasi evacuare possint humana argumentatione praedicationis evangelicae veritatem, *catechuminos* nobis opponunt, *si quis* ex his *antequam* in ecclesia *baptizetur* in *confessione nominis adprehensus fuerit* et occisus, an spem salutis...amittat eo quod *ex aqua* prius non sit renatus...Sanguine autem suo... *consummari* et divinae *pollicitationis* gratiam consequi declarat...Dominus.' The resemblance is verbal as well as mental.

[2] *Ep.* 73. 13, Auctor 10.

needless demands deter from spiritual baptism those for whom she holds material baptism to be essential[1].

If then these are fair indications that Cyprian knew the Author's work, can it perhaps be the actual epistle which Jubaian enclosed to Cyprian[2]? There is a singular touch here. Cyprian, scouting the idea that one baptized outside the Church need not be baptized into it, as baptized already in Christ's name, says to Jubaian that he will not pass over 'a mention of Marcion' which he observes in that enclosure[3]. 'Marcion does not hold the same Trinity we hold, the same 'Creator-Father, the same Son in true flesh, and therefore 'Marcion's baptism is not in the true Christ's name[4].' Now this is precisely the ground which the Author takes in denying to the (Marcionite) heretic the possibility of martyrdom. 'It is an empty appearance of martyrdom, when the 'man believes in a different God, a different Christ; not the 'omnipotent Creator of Scripture nor the Son of Him[5].' This seems to be the 'mention of Marcion' which Cyprian takes up. To the Author's acceptance of heretical baptism he simply opposes his rejection of Marcionite martyrdom.

If it be thought that, supposing this to have been Jubaian's enclosure, Cyprian would not have passed silently over its main issue,—namely, that while Baptism proper is a 'Water-Baptism,' like that of John, accompanied by Invocation which has a certain power, 'Spirit-Baptism' accompanies the Laying on of hands,—the answer is simple. It is because this theory in no way entered into the controversy with Rome.

---

[1] *Ep.* 73. 24 compared with Auctor 10. Not to accumulate passages, we may add Auct. 2, John 'desciscens *a lege* id est *Moysi antiquissimo baptismate*' compared with *Ep.* 73. 17, the Jews '*legis* et Moysi antiquissimum baptisma fuerant adepti.' And one very interesting instance is the comparison of Auctor c. 6 where he is apparently correcting an extreme opinion on his own side as to the naked solitary invocation of Jesus' Name sufficing for salvation with Firmilian, *Ep.* 75. 9, who calls the invocation of the name of God or of Christ alone a 'mendacium.'

[2] So Dr Peters, pp. 517 sqq.
[3] *Ep.* 73. 4.
[4] *Ep.* 73. 5.
[5] Auct. 13.

The view is as remote from Stephen's as it is from Cyprian's opinions.

The Treatise then seems to yield these interesting facts about itself; that Cyprian was acquainted with it; that its Author, while certainly acquainted with Cyprian's action and view, was not acquainted with his later or more elaborate writings on the controversy; that consequently he handled it in its early stage; that it was not improbably the treatise which Jubaian submitted to Cyprian.

Its interest lies not in Cyprian's being careful to answer it. It is a fresh specimen of the life in which he lived. Its arguments although they lie aside of the thread of the controversy yet are produced in defence of the prevailing practice. In its way it helped to widen the bond of Christendom at a time when the greatest Christian man living was for contraction. Its interpretation of isolated texts was such as no modern could employ or be affected by. The forced subtle exegesis evolved by an acute mind whilst intent on the letter is in contrast with the large anti-superstitious view which the same mind, rich with Evangelic teaching, took of the most sacred rite. His letter perished, his spirit prevailed. The frequency with which this phenomenon repeats itself in Theology is a great witness that there truly abides in Theology a living spirit, from age to age using, and then dropping, that 'letter' which to the eyes of subsequent generations may seem to have been all of which their fathers were capable.

III. *The Arguments.*

We may open our review of the Arguments with a fuller statement of that which, at the time when Cyprian began to give his support to the revival of the old discipline of Agrippinus by requiring a Second Baptism, defended the prevailing practice of receiving returned schismatics by

THE BAPTISMAL QUESTION.

imposition of hands. The Author on Rebaptism, though his particular arguments faded, yet contributed to maintain opinion on the side which finally prevailed. The theory he alleged may have been too subtle to be of popular service at any time, too fanciful to have captivated the solid reason of the Church for any period, and yet in fragments, in scattered lights, by side-strokes, such theories do substantial work. In one sense nothing really dies of which the spirit has entered into the life of the Church, however she may have outgrown the stage at which the form was accepted.

This is the line of reasoning by which the Author maintained the *status quo*:—

'I. The preaching of John distinguished two baptisms, the one of Spirit, the other of Water. These two are separable. When separated they are still integral; not unmeaning fragments[1]. The essence of Water-Baptism is the Invocation of the Name of Christ; even after the gift of the Spirit, that Invocation is a *Power;* prior to it, a Beginning which in due time may be completed[2]. It has a virtue[3] which intellectual error cannot destroy; which may revive after dormancy; to which mistaken doctrines cannot in its ministrants be worse hindrances than immoral lives. It remains ineffective until the Imposition of Hands gives the Baptism of the Spirit; although for such as never attain this it must be completed by the Divine Goodness. The Baptism of Blood, again, cannot be less salutary than that of water, although to the heretic it is nothing, because he suffers not in Christ, but only under Christ's Name[4].

II. Invocation then, or Water-Baptism, must in order to become effective be *completed* for the heretically baptized by the Spirit-Baptism of the Laying on of Hands[5].

---

[1] Auctor cc. 2—5, with illustrations from Scripture and from daily life.
[2] cc. 6, 7.   [3] c. 10.
[4] Auctor c. 11.
[5] Thus he developes Acts xv. 13—

[17] 'Those Gentiles on whom Christ's *name* has been *invoked*...have still to "seek the Lord." The case of the heretically baptized is here contemplated.' c. 12.

VIII. III. THE ARGUMENTS—CYPRIAN'S I. OBJECTIVE.

III. Both the species of Baptism were represented on the Cross in their Unity, but *two* baptisms of *one* species would be unendurable[1].

IV. There are then three Baptisms—of Water, of Blood, of the Spirit; and these three are recognized by S. John[2]. And the Holy Spirit willingly imparts Himself even to the unworthy for certain ends. We should therefore trust Him so to do, adhering to the true rite; and not doing violence by a second Baptism either to the Invocation of Christ or to venerable custom[3].'—Such is his thesis[4].

In examining the views of Cyprian, we have to avoid making him responsible for the arguments of his partisans, whose handling in the Seventh Council is at times very discrepant from that of his letters. Firmilian, on the other hand, is a fair representative and sensible summariser.

Cyprian's arguments are of remarkable range and fulness. He ignores but one aspect of the question. And that one is capital.

The objective entity of the Church, the objective presence of the sanctifying Spirit, the subjectivity of the baptizer and of the baptized are discussed; historic evidence, biblical declarations, casuistic difficulties are tested.

His *objective* grounds may be arranged thus :—

(1) *The unity of the Church* demands (re)-Baptism. The question with him broadened at once, as we have seen, from the consideration of schism to the consideration of heresy. In the critical point these were identical. The demarcation of

---

[1] Auctor c. 14.
[2] 1 Jo. v. 6—8.
[3] c. 15.
[4] The exception which follows is interesting in illustration of what some sects were. 'The conjuring fire' which is shewn upon the water at Simonian Baptism is an imposture sufficient to invalidate the rite and make it deadly. It becomes 'another Sacrament.' The fire mentioned in John's Baptism is metaphoric. But at the first effusion of Pentecost fire was symbolic, just as physical 'salus' is the symbol of spiritual in miracles of healing. c. 16.

Church from non-Church was distinct[1]. The representation of sacred acts outside the Church was no equivalent for the reality of sacred acts within it. The inviolate oneness had no outlying dependencies. Although the schismatic[2] might own 'One Lord' and claim 'One Faith,' yet the 'One Baptism' was not his, for the One Baptism implied the One Church, which he renounced.

(2) He could not however claim even *Unity of Belief*, 'One Faith,' whilst the Apostles' creed stood in its African form. 'Dost thou believe the Forgiveness of Sins and the Life Everlasting *through Holy Church?*' was on his lips null in the very hour of baptism[3].

(3) The remissory virtue of the rite in respect of sin shewed it to be a *function of the Holy Orders* which had no being outside the Church[4]. So that from the ecclesiastical side it might be said that the whole episcopal authority as the bond of unity, and the whole dignity of the Divine economy and organisation were involved in the question whether the baptism of heretics was to be recognised[5]. If it were, then the Church had many centres, and rested not upon one Foundation-rock but upon several[6]. And if that baptism were recognised, untruly and untruthfully, then the unforgiven sins of these strangers must be shared by those who received them[7] into a communion which behind the earthly scene knew them not.

---

[1] *Ep.* 69. 3.
[2] *Ep.* 75. 14, 15, 24, 25.
[3] *Ep.* 69. 7; *Ep.* 70. 2.
[4] *Ep.* 73. 7, a view which the mind of Fortunatus of Thuccaboris developes into 'Jesus Christus...potestatem baptizandi episcopis dedit,' *Sentt. Epp.* 17. Tertullian held the authority to baptize to be derivable from bishops, but as a matter of order not of essence; Tertull. *de Bapt.* 17.
[5] *Ep.* 72. 1.
[6] *Ep.* 75. 17.
[7] *Ep.* 73. 19 '...se alienis immo æternis peccatis communicare.' Augustine properly observes that Victor of Gorduba (*Sentt. Epp.* 40) goes far beyond Cyprian in alleging that such sins must permeate the whole communion with defilement [Aug. *de Bapt. c. Donatt.* VII. iv. (6, 7)], but it is scarcely an illegitimate extension of Cyprian's view, though inconsistent with other principles of his.

VIII. III. THE ARGUMENTS—CYPRIAN'S I. OBJECTIVE.

The separatist teacher has surrendered[1] the animating, unifying Spirit, and no personal earnestness of his own could convey that Spirit to his followers by baptizing them[2]. He illustrates his principle by the ingenious remark that in order to the exercise of this function John Baptist received the Holy Ghost in his mother's womb[3]; but since John did not impart the Holy Ghost to his baptized crowds, he has to limit the application to his baptism of our Lord; and similarly he says that the Apostles received the Spirit by the breathing of Christ, that they might be enabled *to baptize and give remission of sins.*

(4) The *admission of* reconciled *separatists* to the Church by imparting to them the Holy Ghost *by imposition of hands*, which is the usage of even those who recognised their baptism, was a practical declaration that they had not received, but still needed to receive, that Holy Ghost. For the usage can never be defended from the Apostles laying their hands on the baptized Samaritans, since that was a confirming of work initiated by their own Deacon[4]. But if the schismatic admittedly had not as yet received the Holy Ghost, how should he sanctify the very water for baptism? or the unction of confirmation[5],

---

[1] ...amiserit Spiritum Sanctum, *Ep.* 70. 2.

[2] *Ep.* 69. 11. 'Qui non habet quomodo dat?' became a catchword of the Donatists. The reply of the Catholics was 'Deum esse datorem': see Optatus, who solves the question with laughter.

[3] *Ep.* 69. 11 ¹ *..adhuc esset...in* utero matris constitutus.' Cf. Luc. i. 15 ἔτι ἐκ κοιλίας μητρός.—Jo. xx. 21—23.

[4] *Ep.* 73. 9, in connection with *Ep.* 69. 6.

[5] Oportet mundari et sanctificari aquam prius a sacerdote ut possit baptismo suo peccata hominis qui baptizatur abluere...quomodo autem mundare et sanctificare aquam potest qui ipse im-mundus est et apud quem sanctus spiritus non est?...ungi quoque necesse est eum qui baptizatus est ut accepto chrismate, id est unctione, *esse unctus Dei* et habere in se *gratiam Christi* possit. Porro autem eucharistia est unde baptizati unguntur oleum *in altari* sanctificatum. Sanctificare autem non potuit olei creaturam qui nec altare habuit nec ecclesiam, *Ep.* 70. 1, 2. Cf. Sedatus, *Sentt. Epp.* 18 'in quantum aqua *sacerdotis prece in Ecclesia sanctificata* abluit delicta, in tantum hæretico *sermone* velut cancer infecta cumulat peccata.' In Tertullian (*de Bapt.* 7) the unction gives the Christian his priesthood. On Aug. *de Civ. Dei* xx. 10, *Enarr.* II. (2) in Ps. xxvi., *Enarr.* in Ps. xliv. 19, and

which is the sign of the Royalty and Priesthood of every Christian man? Above all, how should he give the New Birth[1], which as the essence of the sacrament is essentially the act of the Spirit?

(5) *Nor* yet could their Baptism be regarded as *an inchoate Sacrament*, begun without the Spirit, but completed in Him[2]. The washing of water *without* the Spirit is a mere *carnal Judaizing*[3] *rite*. Nay, applied as a deceiving semblance, it must be worse. It is a material pollution[4]. Under sentence, and void of merit, the pretenders can neither 'justify nor sanctify' their baptized[5]. Who but the holy can hallow[6]? Who but the living give life[7]?

Jerome, *Comm. in Joel* ii. 28 sqq., making it confer our Kingship and Priesthood, see Dr A. J. Mason, *Relation of Confirmation to Baptism*, 1893, pp. 87, 171. And popularly Prudentius, *Psychomachia*, v. 361, 'unguentum *regale*.' See Bunsen: 'to the (catechumen's) vow for life and death corresponded the unction as Priest and King...The seal of a free pledge, of a responsible act,' *Hippolytus and his age*, vol. II. pp. 120, 1 (1854). Observe however that in the *Apostolic Constitutions*, bk. vii. c. 23, it is said that if there is no oil for the anointing before the baptism, nor chrism (μύρον) for the subsequent anointing, water suffices for both; ἀρκεῖ ὕδωρ καὶ πρὸς χρῖσιν καὶ πρὸς σφραγῖδα. It is with Water that the English Church seals the baptized with the Signaculum Crucis, although the Royal Priesthood of the Laity would be more plainly expressed and taught if we used the primitive anointing.

As to the account of Theodoret, *Hæret. Fab.* iii. 5, that the Novatianists used no unction, it is possibly due to the fact that Novatian himself had not received it in his 'clinical' baptism (Routh, *R. S.* vol. III. pp. 69, 70), for we must include this among τὰ λοιπὰ 'ὧν χρὴ μεταλαμβάνειν' which were omitted on that occasion, and which are distinguished from his neglect of confirmation by Cornel. *Ep. ad Fab.* Euseb. *H. E.* vi. 43. If it were true the argument of Cyprian would have been futile.

[1] *Ep.* 74. 5, 6.
[2] *Ep.* 74. 5.
[3] *Ep.* 75. 13. Cf. Tert. *de Bapt.* 18.
[4] Profanæ aquæ labes, *Ep.* 72. 1; adultera et profana aqua, *Ep.* 73.1, cf. 21; profana aqua polluuntur, *Ep.* 69. 16. In words this becomes more revolting in the Vote of Sedatus (*Sentt. Epp.* 18, above p. 403, note 5), but the sense is nowhere stronger than in Cyprian's earliest declaration on the subject 'men are not cleansed in that baptism but rather are defiled; nor are their sins purged away but indeed are heaped higher.' *De Unit.* 11.
[5] *Ep.* 69. 10, *sanctificare* is here rather to *consecrate* than technically to *sanctify*. The effect of it is to make a man a temple of God. *Ep.* 73. 12.
[6] *Ep.* 69. 2.
[7] *Ep.* 71. 1.

(6) Is it maintained that for an earnest though misinformed convert the *Presence and Sanctity of Christ* Himself countervail the unworthiness of the ministrant? Then, if Christ be there, how should His Spirit be wanting? And if the Spirit be absent, as our Imposition of Hands affirms, how can we affirm that Christ is present[1]?

We have thus approached the *subjective* basis of the Cyprianic argument.

(1) If *Faith of the Recipient*[2] is urged as the ground of the blessing, a mere faith in his own faith cannot be adequate. To be effective a faith must be a true faith. But while the faith of the schismatic is deficient in a cardinal point, namely, the remission of sins through the Church, the faith of the heretic is false and often blasphemous[3].

(2) But must not the *Invocation* of God in the Lord's own words be effective? There seem to have been in Africa some who understood baptism 'in the Name of Christ' to be sufficient without the Trinal Invocation. This was evidently very rare, if ever it was more than an exception. Augustine[4] says that although still in his day many honest clergy prayed ignorantly, and many erroneously, through their having possessed themselves unwittingly of copies of heretical devotions, yet that it would probably be easier to find some non-baptizing sect, than people baptizing with a mutilated formula.

Stephen bestows no consideration, still less any approval, upon such a form. When he defends baptism 'in the Name of Christ' he is using the words in a Scriptural sense, of persons who at least intended to be baptized into the *Faith* of Christ. He assumes the ordinary correctness of baptisms in such respects. Cyprian it is true argues against the validity of *some*[5] kind of baptizing 'in the Name of Christ,' but only

---

[1] *Ep.* 75. 12.
[2] *Epp.* 73. 4; 75. 9.
[3] *Epp.* 73. 4, 5; 74. 2.
[4] Aug. *de Bapt. c. Donatt.* VI. xxv. (47).
[5] *Ep.* 73. 18.

just as he argues against the validity of *some* baptizing in the Name of the Trinity, namely because *another* Christ and *another* Trinity are understood by the baptizers.

Baptism in the Name of Christ alone.

It is necessary to look into this question with some care on account of A. Neander's bold assertion (*General Hist. of the Christian Religion and Church*, sect. iii., vol. I. pp. 446, 7, and notes, Bohn) that from Cyprian's letters and from the (contemporary) book *De Rebaptismate* it is undeniably clear that the *Roman party* maintained, 'in a more liberal Christian spirit' than his, the objective validity of baptizing in Christ's name alone, without the Invocation of the Holy Trinity.

It is in the first place unfair to attribute to Rome the views of the Author on Re-baptism who is certainly an African. But there is no sign of his having held such a view.

1. What the Author on Rebaptism says is (c. 7) that, while the Trinal Invocation was not only *verum et rectum et omnibus modis in ecclesia observandum* but was *observari quoque solitum*, 'we should con-'sider that Invocation of the Name of Jesus ought not to be looked on 'by us as *futile*' (a *nobis futilis* videri): 'it might have a sort of initial virtue capable of subsequent completion.' debet invocatio hæc nominis Jesu *quasi initium quoddam mysterii Dominici commune nobis et ceteris omnibus* accipi, *quod possit postmodum residuis rebus impleri.*—He does not say what the *residuæ res* are, but since the 'Name of Jesus' is the only thing as yet 'common' to the Church and these persons, the *residue* of the Invocation, the communion of the Father and the Spirit, cannot be excluded from them.

In the title and first chapter of the book the expression 'semel *in nomine Domini Jesu Christi tincti*' is equivalent to 'Christian baptism,' and does not mean one class of baptisms only, for it comprehends those who already were baptized in the name of the Trinity.

2. What the 'Roman party' maintained can be gathered from the arguments against them, but especially from certain clauses imbedded in those which are recognisable as fragmentary quotations from Stephen. Such passages are these. Stephen, *Ep.* 73. 16, is represented as saying, 'In nomine Jesu Christi ubicumque et quomodocumque baptizati gratiam baptismi sunt consecuti,' and *Ep.* 73. 18 'extra ecclesiam immo 'et contra ecclesiam modo (*i.e.* provided that it be) in nomine Jesu Christi 'cujuscumque et quomodocumque gentilem baptizatum remissionem pec-'catorum consequi posse': which is a version of the same citation, '*cujus- cumque*' (*sic lege*) being Cyprian's paraphrase of Stephen's own word *ubicumque*, and meaning 'whatever doctrine of the Person of Christ be

VIII. III. THE ARGUMENTS—CYPRIAN'S 2. SUBJECTIVE. 407

entertained by the sect.' The same passage Firmilian-Cyprian (*Ep.* 75. 18) quotes thus: 'sed in multum' inquit 'proficit nomen Christi ad fidem 'et baptismi sanctificationem, ut quicumque et ubicumque in nomine 'Christi baptizatus fuerit consequatur statim gratiam Christi.' And again the same passage is quoted *Ep.* 74. 5 'qui in nomine Jesu Christi ubicumque et quomodocumque baptizantur.' Now this one harped-on quotation (for it is only one) would have carried Neander's sense, had the question been one of *comparing the value of two* forms. But there is no such question stirring. The question is whether a schismatic *person can baptize*, all else being equal. Stephen uses 'baptized *in the Name of Christ*' in the New Testament sense as equivalent to Christian baptism —as Origen explains Rom. vi. 3, 'baptized into *Christ*,' by reference to the context to mean ordinary Christian baptism, 'cum utique non habeatur legitimam baptisma nisi *sub nomine Trinitatis*[1].' And that it was only in this form that Stephen considered the 'Name of Christ' to be applied in baptism is plain from Firmilian's other quotation from him, *Ep.* 75. 9 'non quaerendum esse quis sit ille qui baptizaverit eo quod qui 'baptizatus sit *gratiam consequi potuerit invocata Trinitate nominum* '*Patris et Filii et Spiritus Sancti.*' Firmilian indeed expressly assumes, *Ep.* 75. 11, that Stephen would require the *symbolum Trinitatis*, even though his principles would (as he supposes) allow, if it were correct in that point and in the interrogations, a baptism by a demoniac or a demon.

Looking then even to the letter of what Stephen wrote (though so little remains to us), Neander's account of it is not justified. If we consider how strong Cyprian (*Ep.* 73. 18) was on this point,—*Ipse Christus jubet baptizari gentes in plena et adunata Trinitate*, following his Master who says *Lex tinguendi imposita est et forma praescripta* (Tert. *de Bapt.* 13)—we shall see that had he conceived 'Baptism in Christ's Name' to imply the disregard of Christ's 'form,' he would have been armed with an argument against Stephen which he could not have failed to use. We shall also observe, with Tillemont (Tom. IV., *Note* 39 *sur S. Cyprien*), that neither Eusebius, Augustine, Vincent of Lerins or Facundus ever perceived in Stephen such false 'liberality' as Neander would fain discover in him.

In this view of Stephen, Fechtrup agrees, pp. 221—224. Tillemont, attaching impossible force to the title of the pamphlet, thinks the Author's position was that which Neander takes. On the ground of the passage of Augustine, quoted in the text, it has been doubted whether all the sects named by Gennadius (*de Ecclesiast. dogmat.* cap. lii.) really did disuse the form.

While therefore Cyprian regards this Form of Christ's

---

[1] Origen, *Comment. in Epist. ad Rom.*, lib. v. c. 8.

Institution 'in the full and united Trinity' to be essential[1], he appeals beyond this to common reason to decide whether one can be *truly* baptized into the Son, who denies the truth of the Son's humanity, or one who is taught to believe the God of Creation and the God of Israel to be an evil deity[2].

Granting then that the true formula has been uttered by people of such tenets[3], he argues with force and dignity that the rite is not a question of words: that the absent Christ, the absent Spirit are not bound by them, as by a spell, to bless untruth, unfaith, broken charity. Thus then an effective faith on the part of the recipient *cannot be secured by the formula*.

(3) Again, what may be effective faith outside the Church is *incapable of definition*. It is no part of the Church's duty or prerogative to graduate degrees of departure from the truth. Since a death suffered in persecution for a spurious creed ought clearly not to rank as martyrdom for the truth, how can there be ascribed to erroneous baptism a virtue that is denied even to the Baptism of Blood[4]?

But it is when he comes to the handling of the *Historical Proof* that for a time Cyprian seems to have his adversary in his grasp.

(1) He had pleaded 'Usage,' and Cyprian, with a fire

---

[1] *Ep.* 73. 18.

[2] *Ep.* 73. 5 and *Ep.* 74. 2. The first appearance of his argument is in his 'Master' (Tert. *de Bapt.* c. 15), who in his Greek treatise had drawn it out more fully still. 'Our God and theirs is not the same; nor is our Christ *one*, that is to say, not the same: accordingly their baptism and ours is not *one*, because not the same; for as they have it not duly and properly, they have it not at all; and that cannot be taken account of which is not had; and as they have not they cannot receive.' The Author on Rebaptism follows the same line of thought. c. 13.

[3] *Ep.* 75. 9.

[4] *Ep.* 73. 21. *De Dca. Orat.* 24. *De Unit.* 14, 19. The universality of this judgment can scarcely be illustrated better than by the fact that the broad churchman who wrote the Tract *De Rebaptismate* in cc. 11, 13 disclaims any doubt on the subject: 'as the sufferer believed on another God and on another Christ, he is a confessor not of Christ, but in an unsubstantial (*solitario*) name of Christ.'

caught from Tertullian[1], argues that no lapse of time, no extent of use can countervail Truth. Newest found Truth is more precious than the most venerable error[2]. Usage may be an apology for ignorance while ignorance lasts, but it cannot be a reason against Reason[3].

(2) Moreover the argument is two-edged. The use of Rome was not the universal use[4].

(3) Again, it was argued that seceders from the Church were not rebaptized upon their return to it, why then should they in whose fellowship they had lived meantime be differenced from them? He replies that they had once received that one Baptism which was ever-availing to them as penitents for any sin. Their case was not parallel to that of a heathen who had been made not a churchman at first but a heretic[5].

(4) It was argued that the original practice of the Church was attested by the fact that the most divergent heretical bodies recognised each the baptism of the others, and required no renewal of the sacrament upon transitions: and so still (it was said) the Church when they came home to her, had nothing to require but a true confession[6]. Cyprian replied that the Church had nothing to learn from heresy; and to the objection that his own theory was in fact Novatian's, who rebaptized even his Catholic adherents, he answered[7] on a sound principle[8] that accidental coincidence with heresy invalidated

---

[1] Tert. *de Vel. Virgg.* 1.

[2] This meets the plea of Dr Peters (p. 538) that Stephanus relied not on Usage but on Tradition. Cyprian required that Usage should be verified by Reason and by Scripture before he would allow it to be Tradition at all.

[3] *Ep.* 71. 3.   *Ep.* 73. 13.

[4] *Ep.* 71. 4, which was also true, as Firmilian remarks, in other matters, *e.g.* in the celebration of Easter, *Ep.* 75. 6.

[5] The Novatianists and the Donatists, in the spirit of true Puritans, treated Catholic Baptism as null. The former appealed to churchmen with such expressions as 'Estote Christiani,' 'Cai Sei, Caia Seia, adhuc paganus es, aut pagana.' (Optatus iii. 11.) Optatus speaks of the horror which affected him at the re-exorcism of Christians, 'vos ...dicitis Deo habitanti Maledicte, exi foras!' iv. 6.

[6] *Ep.* 74. 4.

[7] *Ep.* 73. 2.

[8] So Aug. *de Bapt. c. Donatt.* III. xi. (16).

no Church usage, and that indeed the Puritanic mimicry[1] was good as evidence of what Novatian had learnt in the Church.

(5) *Casuistic difficulties* are met by him with genuine breadth. For example, he is asked, 'If *regeneration within 'the Church* is thus essential, what is the position of those for 'whom either term has failed?—of catechumens martyred 'before baptism[2]? of heretics received in time past without 'baptism and so deceased[3]?'

His theory, like his Master's, was in this one point less narrow than the more liberal party might have fairly expected. Things essential to earthly order would not (he knew) bar the goodness of God; the most glorious of baptisms sanctified such as having lived by the light they had fell asleep in the Church, though unbaptized; no man should fear their being parted from her eternally. 'Simplicity like this is enough for me,' says Augustine at this, in the midst of his refutations[4].

Ready with an answer like this, Cyprian could yet more effectively press the abandonment of error when detected, and despise mere scruples of conscience as to the unknown consequences[5] of Rebaptism 'should the first baptism have been perchance valid in the sight of God.' As for casuistic difficulties, such could be propounded on either side. What for instance could even now be said as to the validity of baptisms performed by a demoniac woman with every Christian solemnity?—a professed prophetess who foretold and claimed to have caused the earthquakes which led to the persecutions of A.D. 235, who traversed frozen snows barefooted and unhurt, who had trains of followers for whom she celebrated the eucharist with a form of 'invocation not to be discredited[6],' and seduced a deacon and a country presbyter? Were her unexceptionable rites valid or no?

---

[1] 'Simiarum more,' *Ep.* 73. 2.
[2] *Ep.* 73. 22.
[3] *Ep.* 73. 23.
[4] *Contra Crescon.* ii. 33. (41).
[5] 'Invidia quadam.' *Ep.* 73. 25.
[6] *Ep.* 75. 10. A Cappadocian case given by Firmilian. Cp. the liberty given to the wandering Prophets, τοῖς

VIII. III. THE ARGUMENTS—CYPRIAN'S 4. BIBLICAL.

The liberal Author on Rebaptism, though he calls a certain Simonian Baptism, in which fire was exhibited upon the surface of the water, 'an adulterine, nay internecine' rite, does not absolutely declare rebaptism necessary even then[1].

Of Cyprian's *Biblical arguments* the more familiar need scarcely more than simple mention. There is the 'One Loaf,' 'One Cup,' 'One Ark,'—to which the Donatists added 'One Circumcision,' 'One Deluge.' There is the schismatical (note, not heretical) gainsaying of Korah. There is the inference that if the Apostle baptized the household on whom the Spirit had fallen[2], how much more should those be baptized on whom it was confessed by the imposition of hands at their reception that He had never fallen.

A neat ingenuity appears in his dealing with some of the passages;—as when he explains[3] the omission of the Father's Name from S. Peter's injunction of Baptism (Acts ii. 38) by observing that these neophytes were Jews who needed but the Son's Name to supplement their antient Baptism: or when, on Philippians i. 18, which was quoted[4] as shewing that even an Apostle recognised the evangelizing work of his opponents, he points out that their work was within the Church and their enmity personal not doctrinal.

Some of his most constant and conclusive quotations are strangely erroneous. He perhaps started the interpretation of *Qui baptizatur a mortuo quid proficit lavatione ejus*[5]*?* 'He that is 'washed after touching a dead body *and toucheth it again*, what 'profiteth he by his washing?' as if it meant 'He that is baptized by one that is dead,' *i.e.* by a heretic. This is quoted in his sense by Quintus (Quietus) in the Council[6]; and constantly by Petilianus, Cresconius, and other Donatists, against Augustine,

---

δὲ προφήταις ἐπιτρέπετε εὐχαριστεῖν ὅσα θέλουσιν. Διδαχὴ τ. ιβ' Ἀπ. 10.
Unum de Presbyteris rusticum (? *sic l.*).
[1] Auctor c. 17.
[2] *Ep.* 72. 1.
[3] *Ep.* 73. 17.
[4] *Ep.* 73. 14.
[5] Sir. 31 (34). 30. *Ep.* 71. 1.
[6] *Sentt. Epp.* 27.

who at first was only able to reply that 'the Dead' baptizer is a heathen priest, or a deified hero, rather than a heretic[1], not observing the omission of 'and toucheth it again.' When he saw it he thought Donatus a 'Fur divini eloquii,' and yet again discovered that in most of the older African manuscripts these words were wanting, and retracted his strong language[2].

A spurious passage as well as a genuine one may have a spurious sense assigned to it, and run as mischievous a course. Cyprian in the First Council on Baptism, quotes the Alexandrine addition to Proverbs ix. 18, *Keep thee from alien water, and of the alien font drink thou not.* Since the Alexandrine Clement had already applied the further spurious context *So shalt thou cross alien water* to 'heretical baptism,' and *pass beyond an alien river* to 'the ethnic and disordered waves to which their pervert would be hurried,' it is possible that Cyprian or one of his bishops (Tertullian does not quote it) thence learnt the application. Firmilian adopts it from them, and in the Third Council Nemesian of Thubunæ (whose unusually long speech shews that he read Tertullian as well as Cyprian) makes the passage his own. Augustine's common sense is not misled as to the meaning, but its authenticity he does not question[3].

Then again favourite passages are Jeremiah xv. 18 and ii. 13. *Deceiving water* and *Broken cisterns* are to Cyprian plain

---

[1] *c. litt. Petiliani* I. ix. (10), cf. *c. Crescon.* II. xxv. (30). *Retractt.* i. 21, 3.

[2] They are in some editions wrongly inserted in the citation by Quietus *Sentt. Epp.* 27. LXX. βαπτιζόμενος ἀπὸ νεκροῦ καὶ πάλιν ἁπτόμενος αὐτοῦ.

[3] *Ep.* 70. 1. Clem. Alex. *Strom.* B. I. c. xix.; his second clause not even in LXX. *Ep.* 75. 23. *Sentt. Epp.* 5. Aug. *c. Donatt. Ep. de Unit. Eccl.*, c. xxiii. (65). The Benedictine editors have not observed that the forgery is quoted, but treat the words as a version of Prov. v. 15. They are not in the Vulgate. Cyprian and Firmilian of course give them in the same form 'ab aqua aliena *abstine te* et *a* fonte, alieno ne biberis'; Nemesian 'ab aqua *autem* aliena *abstine nec de* fonte *extraneo* biberis'; Augustine 'ab aqua aliena *abstine te et de* fonte alieno ne biberis.' The varieties of early Latin Versions are illustrated here. Compare *Tables* in Bp. Westcott's article 'Vulgata' in Smith's *Dict. of the Bible*.

prophecies of heretical baptism. We may apply to him almost literally the address of Optatus to Parmenian, when after refuting his Cyprianic use of the 'broken cisterns' he proceeds 'You batter the Law to such purpose that wherever you 'find the word *Water* you conjure out of it some sense to 'our disadvantage[1].' By the same verbal handling Cyprian furnished the Donatists with their pet absurdity, 'Let not the sinner's oil anoint my head,' as being David's denunciation of heretical unction[2].

There is no denying the poetic aptness of his favourite application of 'The Garden enclosed..the Fountain sealed.. the Paradise with its pomegranates[3],' from the Canticles, nor of his bold pressure of the New Birth[4] and Sonship of the Christian—who in Heresy can no more find a Mother, than Christ can find in her the spotless spouse[5].

The Answer of Stephanus to this last was noble; that Heresy was indeed an unnatural mother, who exposed her children as soon as they were born, but that the Church's part was to find and bring them home and rear them for her Lord[6].

Still the argument was on neither side a matter of simile. Whilst a glance through the references above given will shew that Cyprian's scheme is not fully developed in any one place, but has to be worked out from his correspondence, it did not lie in fragments in his mind, but was to him intelligible, coherent, logical—and was *revealed*.

Against such a piece of Christian philosophy, held and promulgated by one of Cyprian's powers and Cyprian's

---

[1] Optatus iv. 9.
[2] Ps. cxl. (cxli.) 5. *Ep.* 70. 2. Optatus iv. 7.
[3] Cant. iv. 12, 13; *Epp.* 69. 2; 74. 11; 75. 15.
[4] *Ep.* 75. 14.
[5] *Ep.* 69. 2; 74. 11; 75. 15, answered by Aug. *c. Crescon.* I. xxxiv. (40). How poetry may be turned into cast-iron mark in Felix bishop of Bamaccora (*Sentt. Epp.* 33) who says that 'Christ has given us his security (*cautum*) that ours is a *private* fountain (*privatus*).' Cyprian at least kept *signatus*. Hartel (small blame to him) has not even noticed that Felix is quoting.
[6] *Ep.* 75. 14.

character, backed by an army of prelates whom he rather restrained than stimulated[1], moving as one man to his direction yet with an independence which threw each upon himself for his argument, how great was the triumph of Stephen!

No council assembled to support him. Alexandria remonstrated: Cappadocia denounced[2]. His good cause was marred by uncharity, passion, pretentiousness. Yet he triumphed, and in him the Church of Rome triumphed, as she deserved. For she was not the Church of Rome as modern Europe has known her. She was the liberal church then; the church whom the Truth made free; the representative of secure latitude, charitable comprehensiveness, considerate regulation.

This question she decided on one grand principle,—rather a grand instinct as yet, to be informed later into a principle. For Stephen's theology was not sufficiently advanced to define it. Nor was it formulated until Augustine's time. It was the principle which all the four western doctors contributed to establish in the analogous case of ordination. It was the same for which the Church must ever be content to set aside her ever-recurring temptations to discountenance error by denying the grace of those who err, to assert her dignity by increasing severity, and to attract mankind, as Cyprian said she would[3],—and this is hardest to forego,—by her very exclusiveness.

'As there was much for a learned Cyprian to teach, so there was something too for a teachable Cyprian to learn,'

---

[1] This must be our inference from his opening speech; they would have liked well to 'pass judgment' on the Bishop of Rome: some would not only have baptized but exorcized returning heretics: Vincent of Thibaris (*Sentt. Epp.* 37) exclaimed 'we *know* heretics to be *worse* than the heathen.'

[2] Firmilian sprinkles over him such flowers as 'Animosus, iracundus...quin immo tu hæreticis omnibus pejor es... audacia, insolentia, imperitia.' 'His inhumanity was welcome; it had brought out the faith and wisdom of Cyprian, even as the perfidy of Judas had brought—!' 'A budding title of Episcopus episcoporum [it had already provoked the sarcasm of Tertullian] protrudes itself.'

[3] *Ep.* 73. 24.

says Augustine[1], criticizing his reproof of Stephen's indocile temper. The fallacy which underlay Cyprian's convictions was really that which had deceived Tertullian; which later moved and maintained[2] the Donatists in extending to what they held to be 'Treason' in an orthodox cleric the grace-debarring power which their fathers had attributed to schism; which made Wyclif[3] deny the validity of Sacraments or Orders given by a Bishop or Presbyter whilst in sin; which led Calvin and Knox to refuse baptism to the infant children of 'papists,' or the divines of Geneva to allow it upon a charitable hope that the 'grace which had adopted...the great-grandfathers might not yet be so wholly extinct' as that the infants should have 'lost their right to the common seal[4].'

Although in Cyprian[5], and even as it would seem in the Donatists, there is no trace of such teaching as that the moral character of the priest affects the efficacy of the Sacrament, yet the Puritan dogma (compared with which any other sacerdotalism is but shadowy) That the minister is of the substance of the sacrament[6] may be considered to lie implicitly

---

[1] *De Bapt. c. Donatt.* v. xxvi. (37).

[2] 'To confront us with Cyprian's writings as if they were bases of canonical authority.' Aug. *c. Crescon.* II. xxxii. (40); cf. Aug. *Ep.* 93. c. 10 (38), ad Vincent.; Aug. *Ep.* 108. c. 3 (9), ad Macrob.

[3] '...*Si episcopus vel sacerdos existat in peccato mortali non ordinat, conficit, nec baptizat*' is a Wyclifite proposition which some of his disciples renounced at the Council of London, A.D. 1382, and which was condemned at Constance; see Labbe (Mansi), vol. XXVI. col. 696—vol. XXVII. col. 1207. Venet. 1784.

[4] Hooker, B. III. i. 12.

[5] Routh (vol. III. p. 151) strangely accuses Erasmus of having written that 'Cyprian seems (in *Ep.* 67) to feel that the sacrifice of a wicked priest avails nothing but rather defiles the people,' for Erasmus continues 'But he means, I think, in the case of a bishop *appointed by heretics*, who is *not a real bishop:* his rites do not profit those who support his impiety.' Erasm. *ad loc. Cypr.*—The Donatist limitation of disqualification to the *Traditores* seems arbitrary, but apparently existed in an unthought out fashion. For Augustine seems always able to reduce them to a dilemma by asking whether 'secret murders and adulteries were not an equal disqualification.' They therefore had not so *stated* it. There is a special case too in his *c. lit. Petiliani* III. xxxv. (40) 'You (Donatists) *do not deny* that the people (whom a criminal priest baptized) really *were* baptized.'

[6] Hooker, V. lxi. 4 1.

in that one proposition in which Cyprian differed from the rest of the West. It was not until Augustine's time that a categorical answer was developed soundly to each separate argument of Cyprian and his bishops: so long did they retain their seeming convincingness almost unbroken, nay had become 'like Scripture'[1] to their maintainers.

Yet the true solvent had evidently been perceived at once by his opponents, although the minute fragments of Stephen's own language which Cyprian gives us do not contain the exact statement. 'The grace of Baptism' they said was 'of Christ, not of the human baptizer.' He who baptized did 'not give being or add force' to the Sacrament. This had been almost on the lips of the Numidians when they first told Cyprian of their difficulty as to rebaptizing, 'because,' said they, 'Baptism is *One*.' That oneness is of the One Lord: but they had allowed themselves to be put off with the superficial reply that its oneness was of the one Church, and that to admit non-Church baptism was to admit two baptisms or to recognise more[2].

The Author on Rebaptism states it with even scornful force, so that it is surprising that he should have let slip for so many subtleties this real answer[3]. 'Let us, excellent

---

[1] P. 415, note 2.

[2] Fechtrup, p. 201, n. 2, in trying to answer Peters is misled by Peters' wrong reference (p. 512) for his perfectly right statement. Peters should have cited *Ep.* 70. 1 and *Ep.* 71. 1. On the other hand Peters is wrong in thinking that Cyprian himself has this key to his own error in *Ep.* 69. 14. There he does not speak of Christ simply, but of 'Christ in his Church' as giving equal grace to every member of it in Baptism. See also 13 of the same Epistle. He guards himself carefully.

[3] Auctor 10 'virorum optime, reddamus et permittamus virtutibus cælestibus vires suas, et dignationi divinæ majestatis concedamus operationes proprias, et intellegentes quantum in ea sit emolumentum libenter ei adquiescamus.'

This is well expressed by Optatus, lib. v. c. 1; 'Has res unicuique non ejusdem rei operarius sed credentis fides et Trinitas præstat.' c. 4 '...omnes qui baptizant operarios esse, non dominos, et sacramenta per se esse sancta, non per homines....' Optatus answers by implication many of Cyprian's arguments. But it is visible how the power of his great name forbade direct attack. Augustine first both meets him full and reads the true lesson of his life, Conformity amid Differences.

'sir,' he writes (as I believe against Cyprian himself), 'render 'and allow to the Powers of Heaven a might of their own, 'and suffer the condescension of the Divine Majesty to have 'its independent operations.'

His conception of the visible Church is indeed higher than Cyprian's, and had he learnt how to apply it, would have been of more value than all his arguments besides. 'What,' he asks,—' unless some higher principle modify the rigidity of 'your strict formula—What is the portion reserved for the 'Christian multitude[1] which dies without the imposition of 'hands?'—'What for those bishops themselves,' his irony adds, 'who fail to visit and confirm such as sicken and die in 'the outlying districts of their dioceses[2]?'

Thus on every side, he infers, even within the acknowledged pale, even within the entrenched lines of saints and martyrs, there lies a vast verge beyond the operation in full measure of that simple sacerdotal unity, which is nevertheless essential to the general effectuation of the gospel.

And what lies beyond the pale?[3] It is in the solemn consensus which exists as to the adequate and complete sanctification of that admitted verge or margin that we are to look for analogies which shall solve the new-rising problems suggested by the existence of heresy. We cannot subject all truth to the conclusions of a theory which is true up to its limits, but which has limits beyond which nothing is clear save the Love and the Power[4].

Cyprian's demand for a sanctity in the baptizer in order to 'justify and to sanctify' the baptized[5], may well have revolted the Church of Rome as it does the Church of England. Doubtless he took the terms in a weaker sense than we.

---

[1] Auctor, c. 4 plerique.
[2] Dispersis regionibus, c. 5.
[3] Compare Aug. *de Bapt. c. Donatt.* IV. c. vii. (10) 'If within the closed garden of God there are thorns of the Devil, why may not the Spring of Christ flow out beyond it?'
[4] 'Salvation is of the Church': True. 'Nulla salus extra ecclesiam': True, if the definition of Ecclesia be so wide as to have no *constitutional* value.
[5] *Ep.* 69. 10.

But they at least make Stephen's invective intelligible. The structure of the Church, the apostolic teaching, the personal work of Christ seemed to him endangered[1]. And they were so; had not theological science arisen to refrain such careless modes of speech.

Stephen taught that as one who separates from the Church does not forfeit his own church baptism by his wandering, but when he returns will return in its validity, so neither in the meanwhile does he lose the 'power' which as a baptized man he possessed of imparting Baptism to others[2].

And he taught that the child or the heathen who learns Christ through the teaching of the heretic cannot be charged with 'defect or disorder' in the reception of that sacrament to which he comes with fullest faith[3], and which it is the will of God to impart to every creature. Though he is excluded from 'fellowship in holy duties with the visible Church,'—the *beata vita* as Augustine truly calls it—yet of that visible Church he is still a member. Its true image is the great House with all its variety of vessels, and the Cornfield, capable of including for awhile, nay even of producing, not misbelievers only, but misdoers[4]. These teachings of Stephen on the lasting virtue of Baptism were reaffirmed by Augustine with overflowing illustration, but there is no thought in either that Baptism has in it any spell to countervail separation. That would be not liberality but superstition.

Whatever evil is in heresy or schism, or in any form or origin of them, is no more purged by Baptism than any

---

[1] *Ep.* 75. 25 '...pseudochristum, pseudoapostolum, dolosum operarium....'

[2] Usurpare eum potestatem baptizandi posse, *Ep.* 69. 7.

[3] '...homo ad Deum veniens, dum sacerdotem quærit, in sacrilegum fraude erroris incurrit.' A quotation (from Stephen probably) which ought by its very wording to have softened Cyprian. *Ep.* 70. 2.

[4] Although these illustrations are not quoted among the fragments of Stephen yet they were already in use. Cyprian had perceived their bearing on the case of the Lapsed, though he now failed to apply them more widely. *Ep.* 55. 21.

unrenounced sin. As it is no step to salvation, but away from it, if one obtains baptism by a feigned or inconsistent repentance[1], so if another is baptized a foe[2] to Unity, to the Peace of Christ, to Charity with His Church, these are not conditions for realising the Remission of Sins. The innermost power of baptism is in both men let and hindered, until it matures in fellowship and unity regained. Both need a change[3]. Both alike must make a more truthful confession[4]. But both alike have received a consecration, and a 'Stamp of the Lord[5],' which protests to them, which makes for reconciliation. The change they need is not another Consecration, but a fulfilment of the former. With that it begins not to be present, but to be profitable, to minister to salvation[6]; their sins melt away as they enter within the bond of love[7].

If policy, convenience, interest, taste, jealousy, self-will, carelessness or the like take a man who knows there is but 'One Baptism' to seek it from a separatist or to continue with him in his separation, those errors of the soul will work their proper effect; his knowledge will not excuse his indifference to unity. His Baptism is not for his soul's health[8].

But the faithful believer who receives Baptism from the outside teacher when his only other choice is to die unbaptized against Christ's word, has remission of his sins and all other benefits. He loses nothing.

The symbols are lucid. The flood which upbears the ark is deathful to the despisers. Heaven's rain feeds thorns and tares for destruction as well as wheat for the garner[9]. Yet

---

[1] Aug. *de Bapt. c. Donatt.* VII. v. (8) 'verbis non factis renuntiantes.' I. xii. (18) 'quid, si ad ipsum Baptismum fictus accessit?'

[2] *Ibid.* I. xiii. (21).

[3] *Ibid.* VI. xiv. (23).

[4] *Ibid.* I. xii. (18) 'verax confessio.'

[5] Aug. *Ep.* 98. 5 (ad Bonifacium) 'quæ consecratio reum quidem facit hæreticum...habentem dominicum characterem.'

[6] *De Bapt. c. Donatt.* VII. liv. (103) 'non incipit adesse quod deerat, sed prodesse quod inerat.' I. xii. (18) 'ad salutem.'

[7] *Ibid* VI. v. (7).

[8] *Ibid.* VII. iii. (5).

[9] *Ibid.* VI. xl. (78).

Euphrates was not hedged in by Paradise. The river of Eden flowed out into the world[1].

The Church has within every separated communion a something which is all her own[2]. By that something she bears sons in them to herself. They are not born to others. When they turn homeward they are wholly hers.

The only real blot which Cyprian struck was the vulgar, perhaps we ought to say the African, explanation of the laying on of hands in the act of restoration to the Church. If it had meant a first imparting of the Holy Spirit which schismatics could not impart by their own imposition of hands (for unquestionably they too used this rite), then it might be fairly reasoned that their Baptism equally needed renewal. But in reality it had no such meaning. Stephen explains it clearly as a rite 'unto penitence[3]': even Crescens of Cirta as 'a reconciliation in penitence[4].' It was not the imparting of the Spirit for the first time; it was a renovation by the Spirit, an introduction to Communion of a repentant and enlightened 'Child of God.' For 'a Son of God' throughout, in spite of his theological errors, Stephen declares such an one to have been in the full sense[5]. And it is this very expression which was most offensive at Carthage, and which is cavilled at even in the synodic letter of their second Council[6] on baptism.

There were three intentions (besides that of ordination) with which the imposition of hands was used. It was used 1. for what we call Confirmation. 2. for the Reception of Penitents[7]. 3. for Exorcism. The second of these is what Stephen clearly brings out as its true meaning in the

---

[1] *De Bapt. c. Donatt.* VI. xxi. (37).
[2] *Ibid.* I. x. (14).
[3] In pœnitentiam, *Ep.* 74. 1.
[4] *Sentt. Epp.* 8.
[5] *Ep.* 74. 6. Compare 75. 17.
[6] Tunc enim demum plene sanctificari et esse '*filii Dei*' possunt si sacramento utroque nascantur, *Ep.* 72. 1: 'filii Dei' is evidently a quotation. The two sacraments are baptism and laying on of hands.
[7] In which sense it is used in the *Apostolical Constitutions* viii. c. 9 tit. χειροθεσία καὶ εὐχὴ ὑπὲρ τῶν ἐν μετανοίᾳ.

reception of schismatics, while Cyprian maintained that it meant the first, and thereon built a logical claim to have Baptism repeated as Confirmation was repeated. Of his extreme partisans, some would even have made it mean the third[1], and so treated the schismatic as a demoniac.

To some it has seemed not clear that Stephen meant to exclude 'Confirmation' from the idea. Still he shews no intention whatever to include it; and he uses terms which give to it the other sense. The doubt arises only from the fact that Cyprian[2] endeavours to fasten that sense upon him, and that we have no reply from his side. Similarly Firmilian infers unfairly, and quite contrarily to Stephen's actual principle, that if Baptism with its gracious gifts were communicable by heretics, no imposition of hands need be used, but that we might unite with them in their prayer-meetings and at the altar and its sacrifice[3].

Note on force of Stephen's 'Nihil innovetur nisi.'

Questions have arisen upon the phrase of Stephen 'Si qui ergo a 'quacunque hæresi venient ad vos *nihil innovetur nisi quod traditum est*, 'ut manus illi imponatur in pœnitentiam....' *Ep.* 74. 1. Does Stephen here (1) contemplate a 'Renewal' (innovetur) of *something for the convert*, but only such a renewal or repetition as Tradition warrants? or (2) does he forbid 'Innovation' *in the rites*, and require Tradition to be maintained against it?—Does the *innovari* mean 'renovation' or 'innovation'? Mattes (*Tübing. Quartalschrift*, 1849, p. 636, ap. Peters, Fechtrup and Hefele) adopts the first, and argues that as *Penance* has not occurred before, the thing to be renewed is *Confirmation*. So Hefele declares (B. I. c. i., § 6) that the second could not have been expressed grammatically

---

[1] *Sentt. Epp.* 7, 8, 31, 37.

[2] *Ep.* 73. 6, and so Nemesian, *Sentt. Epp.* 5, and Secundinus Bp. of Carpos, *Sentt. Epp.* 24.

I may remark that Tissot t. I. p. 164 would correct the name of this place (which was nearly opposite to Carthage on the gulf) to Carpi: but one of his citations from the maritime Itinerary has *a Carpos Carthaginem*... and the others prove nothing. The MS. authority in Cyprian offers Carpos, and an inscription A.D. 350—361 has KAR · POS which Wilmanns would wrongly correct. *C. I. L.* VIII. i. n. 994. See *Appendix on Cities*, p. 575 infra. Greek geographers Κάρπη and Κάρπις. Adj. Carpitanus, Morcelli, I. p. 121.

[3] *Ep.* 75. 17.

except by 'Nihil innovetur, *sed* quod traditum est *observetur*.' Peters takes *innovetur* to mean renewal in the convert, answering to what is implied in laying hands on the sick, in exorcism, and in penance, and holds that it is called 'innovari' because of the imposition of hands used already in Baptism. This he says is 'Grammatical.' Fechtrup (p. 225), who sees that the clause 'ut manus imponatur *in pœnitentiam*' is the expansion of '*quod traditum est*,' and yet the act cannot be said 'to be renewed,' having never been done before, feels obliged to say that in the '*nisi quod* traditum est' there is an incorrectness of expression, and that even the best authors often write incorrectly. Fortunately it is only the commentators who fail in grammar. Both in Latin and Greek, particles denoting *exception* introduce not merely what is an exception under some rule laid down, but also any contradiction of it, even the most positive. Thus in Vulg. Matt. v. 13, 'ad nihilum valet ultra *nisi* ut mittatur foras' does not mean that vapid salt *has* a value for the one purpose of being thrown away, but that 'it is of *no* value *and can only* be treated so.'—'Et multi leprosi erant *in Israel* sub Elisaeo propheta : et *nemo eorum* mundatus est *nisi* Naaman Syrus' (Luc. iv. 27), '*no* Israelite was cleansed, *but* a non-Israelite was.' So Cyprian *Ep.* 63. 13 '...Sic vero 'calix Domini non est aqua *sola* aut vinum *solum nisi* utrumque sibi 'misceatur, quo modo nec Corpus Domini potest esse farina *sola* aut aqua '*sola nisi* utrumque adunatum fuerit.' 'Each element is *not* one substance *but* a compound.' Hence the passage before us 'nihil innovetur nisi quod traditum est' means, in accordance with usage, 'No innovation is to be made, only tradition must be kept to.' Eusebius (*H. E.* vii. 3) also had these very words before him when he described Stephen as μὴ δεῖν τι νεώτερον παρὰ τὴν κρατήσασαν ἀρχῆθεν παράδοσιν ἐπικαινοτομεῖν οἰόμενος ; and Cyprian thus sets them aside, 'quasi is *innovet* qui unum 'baptisma uni ecclesiæ vindicat, et non ille utique qui...mendacia profanæ 'tinctionis usurpat.' Vincent of Lerins (*Commonit.* i. 6), who gives the phrase as 'nihil novandum *nisi quod* traditum est,' explains it '*non* sua posteris tradere *sed* a majoribus accepta servare.' We conclude therefore with certainty that *innovetur* does not refer to *the renewal* of anything, but to *innovations* in the rite, and that the Imposition of Hands which 'tradition' required was that which appertained to the Reception of a Penitent alone.

Hefele, in spite of his view of 'grammar,' admits (in a footnote) that this is the interpretation of Christian Antiquity and that the words so understood became a dictum classicum.

IV. *Ecclesiastical Results.* 1. *The Unbroken Unity.*

Of all the legacy of lessons which this remarkable story leaves us, none more strike home than those which spring from the observation that Cyprian had a real point of contact with Novatianism. We have already seen that the Novatianists perceived it.

The central idea with both was that the Church must be attainted by, and therefore cannot tolerate, the admixture of elements foreign to her spirit. Such inadmissible element the Novatianists found in those who, having tasted all her gifts, forsook her and forswore them. In the case of the Lapsed, however, Cyprian detected the fallacy. He would not, like Novatian, leave them to be reconciled in some unpenetrated region. To him they were still the Church's reconcilable children; not really such aliens as many wilful offenders within her[1].

To himself however the bounds of the visible Church were marked by historic lines—lines divinely drawn with perfect definiteness and unfailingly preserved for the guidance and security of all. Without the action of the Catholic ministry of the one episcopate there could be no effective Communion, and no admission within even her outer courts. For who was to admit? The moral qualities or the correct beliefs of the individual were irrelevant to the solely constitutional question, Has he been made a member of the visible Church?

According to Novatian, Renouncement of Communion annulled membership for ever. According to Cyprian, uncatholic Baptism never conferred it. We are not required to appraise the two errors. But the grand difference is here. Cyprian's historic lines, which misunderstood had baffled him, when rightly interpreted corrected him. Novatian with his unsoftened character broke from them without remorse, laid new ones down, and made all converge upon himself. The

[1] *Ep.* 55. 21.

Divine idea which Cyprian saw in History, the Unity and Love which underlay the scheme of it, would not suffer him, though opposing the claims of heretics, to dissolve the ties with one single diocese, much less with all. However erroneously any see and its prelate might decide, it was inconceivable that he should break with the brethren. The heart of Love kept him straight where the logical mind went astray.

So Novatian became a sect; not untruthful, but hard and barren: died after a while and left no seed.

The great Church held her way, and every generation as it swept its sands over Cyprian's error bore stronger witness to the power of Cyprian's passion for unity. Whilst he seems almost dearer because he could not be perfect, the perfectness of that passion of his is still unrealised, and too often unfelt.

Although the Roman Church took wider views than Cyprian of so great a matter as Man's Sonship to God, yet, as to the possibility and duty of union in diversity, he held a practical theory which Rome never mastered.

Augustine, who says he never wearied of re-reading the 'peace-bestowing utterances'[1] of the end of the Epistle to Jubaian[2], draws out the noble independence of thought and action which Cyprian willed to maintain without bigotry or exclusion—Every bishop free to judge for himself; none to suffer separation for their thoughts; therefore everyone to be tender of the bond of peace. *Salvo jure communionis diversa sentire.*

2. *The Baptismal Councils failed doctrinally—and why?*

Unity then was not broken. Yet what is the conclusion to be drawn from the spectacle of these Carthaginian assemblies? To some it might seem discouraging.

Can it be accounted for by the incidents of these assemblies?

---

[1] *De Bapt. c. Donatt.* v. xvii. (22).   [2] *Ep.* 73. 26.

A Province may be too large to form a real Synod. There are Provinces of to-day whose very extent, forbidding even attendances, throws decisions into the hands of a metro-political party.

Bishops may be too numerous for the area. There may be more positions of influence than there are men born or drawn to fill them. In such cases the numbers outweigh the able men, or they fall under the power of politic men. A leader who combines fervour with policy sweeps them head-long.

But the degree in which these causes as yet existed at Carthage is not sufficient to account for the doctrinal failure. They were exceptionally modified by the independence ex-pected of the bishops and by the earnestness of the times.

The Councils were neither deficient nor excessive numeri-cally, nor were they created for the sake of their suffrages, nor were they packed. They were under no State pressure. They were not recalcitrating at any state tribunal. The question was a broad one. They were not trying a teacher or judging a leader. They were looking for principles. Seldom could personal elements be so nearly eliminated. Again, they were really representative. Each bishop was the elect of his flock. None of the Councils was senile or too youthful. The members were not drawn from seminary or cloister. They were men of the world, who in a world of freest discussion had become penetrated with Christian ideas: seldom ordained, sometimes not Christianised till late in life. Their chief was one in whom mental and political ability were rarely blended; rarely tempered with holiness, self-discipline and sweetness.

Such was that house of bishops. The result it reached was uncharitable, anti-scriptural, uncatholic—and it was unanimous.

A painful issue. Yet in another respect, the moral is for us encouraging. The mischief was silently healed and perfectly. And how? By no counter-council—for later decrees merely register the reversal—but by the simple working of the Christian Society. Life corrected the error of thought.

Is there then no need of Christian assemblies? no hope in them, or of them? Is the Church a polity unique in this sense, that without counsel it can govern itself, without deliberation meet the changing needs of successive centuries? To how great an extent even this may hold true we read in the disappearance of the Cyprianic judgments. Nor can anything be more consonant with our belief in the indwelling Spirit of the Church; nothing more full of comfort as we look on bonds still seemingly inextricable, and on steps as yet irretraceable.

But nevertheless if no reasonable mind questions the necessity of Councils, in spite of the gloomy moral and doctrinal history of whole centuries of them, may it be the case that their constitution has been incomplete, and that the so early ill success of Cyprian's Councils in particular was a primæval warning of the defect?

The Laity were silent. Yet we cannot but deem that it was among them principally that there were in existence and at work those very principles which so soon not only rose to the surface but overruled for the general good the voices of those councillors. Each Council was a parliament of head officials; a governing body composed of provincial governors, whose irresponsibility, save in the forum of their own conscience, had more and more become Cyprian's axiom and theirs.

Were these bodies divinely constituted for the great object of 'guidance into truth'? were they the very Church in its 'doctrinal capacity,' the living Church to which The Presence was promised? It has been held that they were and ever are. Yet whatever false strands have been inwoven with Catholic doctrine have been introduced by such bodies alone. These particular judgments were, according to the whole Church

Catholic, greatly perverse. They were even then contrariant to the Church opinion which surrounded them and quietly prevailed over them. That this was so may be inferred from several considerations: 1. from the determined unanimity of the Council: the eighty-seven sentences voiced only one oracle. 2. from the avowal of two among the number that they were incompetent to form an opinion, yet they did not abstain from voting, but voted with the majority. 3. from the evidence which the Book on Rebaptism gives of a powerful and informed opinion existing yet unrepresented. 4. from the silent reversal of the decision.

It is true that in and from the second century Synods of Bishops were the rule. But all that we know tends to the conclusion that it was no 'derogation of antient custom to admit others than bishops to be members of a synod[1].' The custom of admitting laity was dying out under Cyprian[2]. It had been no new experiment of his. The second and even the third centuries preserved traces of their old admission. The intrusion of the words '*and the*' into the text of the Conciliar letter of Jerusalem, 'The apostles and the presbyters *and the* brethren greeting...,' shews that at the time when they were added[3] it did not seem so impossible that the laity should have consulted even with apostles; that they had in reality been consulted appears from the narrative, 'It was determined by the apostles and the elders *together with the whole Church*,' unless this is thought to be rhetoric. Irenæus writes a very grave decision on the keeping of Easter 'in *the name of the*

---

[1] Hefele's assertion. *Introd.* § 4, 5.

[2] It seems that in later African Councils *seniores plebis* were at times consulted. This may be a relic of the early usage, but the shadowy character of the facts only illustrates its practical disappearance, and does not support Münter's view of the democratic aspect of that church. *Primordia Eccl. Afr.* (Hafniæ, 1829) pp. 41, 51. See *Cod. Cann. Eccl. Afr.* c. 100, cf. c. 91. *Acta Purgationis Felicis* ap. Optat. ed. Ziwsa (Vienn. 1893), *Appendix* p. 198.

[3] Acts xv. 23. Tischendorf although he retained καὶ οἱ in Ed. 7, omits it in Ed. 8, and it is omitted by Lachmann, Tregelles, Westcott and Hort, and Revised Vers., with ABℵ*CD, Vulg. *all.* ἔδοξε = Decretum est, Placuit, Acts xv. 22.

brethren whom he presided over throughout Gaul[1].' Is it supposed that he had not obtained their judgment? A very early writer[2] speaks of the formal condemnation of Montanism by Councils, '*The faithful* throughout Asia 'having met for this purpose, many times, and in many places 'in Asia, and having examined the novel arguments, and 'demonstrated their profanity, and having rejected the 'heresy.' It seems impossible that 'the faithful' should not include the laity, and the question is of doctrine, subtle doctrine. Origen, in a passage which would not be conclusive if it stood alone, uses an expression which, side by side with others, hints that the consultation of the laity by the bishops, though disused in his day, had its place in the traditions of the past as well as in reason. 'Moses sought the counsel 'of Jethro, though an alien to the Jewish race. But *what* '*bishop* in *the present* day.. condescends to take the counsel 'of an *inferior priest* even, much more of a *layman*, or a 'Gentile[3]?' He has been showing that the 'counsel of the Gentiles' was to be learnt from their great authors, and apparently some practical way of consulting presbyters and laity was not unknown to him.

But the earlier Cyprianic letters themselves are distinct as to the propriety and duty of recognising and including a not silent laity in the Councils of the Church.

It cannot be admitted that Cyprian meant to consult the laity on only personal, individual questions, such as enquiries into the fitness of private persons to be restored to communion[4]. That is very far from what he says when, for

---

[1] Euseb. *H. E.* v. 24 ἐκ προσώπου ὧν ἡγεῖτο κατὰ τὴν Γαλλίαν ἀδελφῶν ἐπιστείλας, παρίσταται τὸ δεῖν κ.τ.λ. ἀδελφοί throughout the context means the Christian body not the bishops.

[2] Cited by Dr Pusey (*Councils of the Church*, c. II. p. 53) mistakenly as Apollinarius of Hierapolis. Valesius on Euseb. v. 16 made this clear.

[3] Orig. *Hom. xi. in Exod.* c. 6 'Quis autem hodie eorum qui populis præsunt...' The version no doubt represents προεστώτων. Cp. note on p. 310.

[4] Dr Pusey, *Councils of the Church*, c. III. pp. 74 sqq.

instance, he thus addresses the presbyters and deacons of Carthage: 'I could give you no reply at all by myself, for 'from the first outset of my episcopate I resolved to transact 'nothing on my own private judgment without your counsel, 'and without the consent of the laity. But when by God's 'grace I am come to you we will treat in common of things 'either transacted or to be transacted, as the honour due 'from each to other requires[1].' At the commencement of his episcopate the question of restoration had not arisen.

Again, when he asks the laity to persuade the Lapsed to patience until, 'convening our fellow-bishops, we may in good 'numbers—deferring to the discipline of the Lord and the 'Confessors' presence and your own opinion also—be able to 'examine the letters and express desires of the blessed 'martyrs[2],' it is the determination of the broad principle, not the application to particular cases, in which the Laity are called to assist. Yet if we narrowed to the utmost the questions proposed, it would be little to the purpose; we should still have to ask where even this measure of consultation with the veritable laity appeared in the later Councils[3]?

It was no mere question of the application of rules, no investigation of individual cases, which was in view. That function is not necessarily conciliar. It is judicial. That function may be committed to delegates, it may be concentrated in a metropolitan, according to the constitution or the use of the several churches. It was not this which Cyprian had in the early days of his episcopate, and seconded as yet

---

[1] *Ep.* 14. 4.

[2] *Ep.* 17. 3.

[3] Hefele, *Introd.* 4. 12, gives a thin list of Councils in which laity have a serious place, and he attaches quite as much weight to them against his own opinion as they deserve. The most notable is Orange [Arausicanum II.] A.D. 529 in which 14 bishops and 8 illustres viri sign with the same formula *consentiens* or *consensi et subscripsi* (Labbe, tom. v. c. 814).

Note also the just complaint made in January 1436 to Sigismund that at the Council of Basle the decrees are being made by the lower clergy and the laity, there being scarce 20 bishops present among 500 or 600 members. [Cp. Eugenius IV. *Ep. ad Nuncios*, Baronius (Raynald), June 1436, i.—xvi.] Ambr. Traversari, *Ep. ad Sigismund.*

by the Roman clergy, set out as the conciliar office of the laity.

'In so vast a business' writes the Roman Presbytery to him, 'we approve what you also have yourself recommended, 'first to await the restoration of peace to the Church, and so 'after that, by united counsel with the bishops, presbyters, 'deacons, confessors as well as the faithful laity, to consider 'the treatment of the Lapsed[1].' It is not the treatment of the individuals which is in question here, but the greatest question of discipline which had ever arisen, the terms of the restoration of apostates to the communion of the Church. The Roman Confessors state in precisely the same way the views of Cyprian and of themselves as to the body which has power to determine principles so great. It is *because* 'the offence is so great' *because* it 'affects almost the whole world' that 'it ought not 'to be, as you yourself write, handled except with caution and 'moderation after counsel taken with all the bishops, presby-'ters, deacons, confessors, and the faithful laity themselves, as 'in your letters you yourself too testify, lest through our ill-'timed wish to patch up ruins we may prove to be preparing 'other and greater ruins[2].'

It cannot be argued with these passages before us that the laity, though present, were originally meant to be present only, and not to be consulted[3]. It was Cyprian's purpose to

---

Cecconi, *Stud. Storichi sul Conc. di Firenze*, Part I. docum. 76, p. cxcv. (Firenze, 1869).

[1] ...quanquam nobis in tam ingenti negotio placeat quod et tu ipse tractasti, prius ecclesiæ pacem sustinendam, deinde sic conlatione consiliorum cum episcopis presbyteris diaconis confessoribus pariter ac stantibus laicis facta lapsorum tractare rationem. *Ep.* 30. 5.

[2] *Ep.* 31. 6.

[3] *Ep.* 19. 2 'This is what befits both the modesty (*verecundia*) and discipline and the very life of us all, that we bishops assembling with clergy, the faithful laity also being present, who themselves too are to be had in honour in proportion to their faith and fear, may be able to arrange all things with strict regard to common deliberation (*communis consilii religione*).' The Bishops will decree but not without common determination. To interpret '*præsente* etiam stantium *plebe*' as of by-standers only is to contradict the other passages and this also. Yet Hefele can write 'The laics were scarcely more than spectators.' (*Introd.* § 4. 5.) But if so,

consult them and a purpose which the Roman clergy strongly supported, not upon the administration of principles in individual cases, but on the formation and enunciation of those principles. The question was 'the terms of communion' for those who had lapsed from Christianity to heathenism : a question as great in itself as the 'terms of communion' for those who had been schismatically baptized.

It has been said that the first question was 'the restoration of those who had denied the faith,'—a practical matter ; and the second question, 'that of heretical Baptism,—a matter of doctrine[1].' But it is not fair thus to formulate one of the topics in the abstract and the other in the concrete. It would be equally correct to reverse the phrases and to say the latter was a practical matter, namely 'the admission of schismatic penitents,' and the former a more awful doctrinal point, 'Apostatical Communion.' But in truth two questions could scarcely be more analogous as questions of dogmatic discipline.

'The contrast (it is said) is very striking.' That is most true. Cyprian's first view disappeared from his mind. His early pledge was not redeemed. But when we look to the ennobling success of his former Councils, and the collapse of the later ones rescued only by the sweet grandeur of the man from creating wide disunion, we cannot but think the change disastrous[2]. The course of History affirms this conclusion of Christian reason.

---

what becomes of his other plea, viz. that earlier precedent was departed from in Cyprian's admission of them, *ibid.*

[1] Dr Pusey, *Councils of the Church*, c. III. p. 87.

[2] It may be difficult to be sure of the exact meaning of Hefele's assertion that 'Bishops *alone* have the assistance of the Holy Spirit to govern the Church of God' (*Introd.*, § 4, 11). He speaks however in reference to Councils, and he distinguishes the *votum decisivum* which belongs in them to Bishops only from the *votum consultativum* which may be assigned to others. Yet upon that developed theory what becomes of the authority of so many Councils, in which abbots, archdeacons, cardinal priests, cardinal deacons, generals of religious orders, doctors in theology, doctors in canon law, have admittedly exercised the *votum decisivum*? (See

3. *The Catholic and the Ultramontane estimate of Cyprian.*

...τὸ μεμνῆσθαι τοῦ ἀνδρὸς ἁγιασμός.
GREGORY NAZIANZEN.

It is of importance in the history of Christian character and of the gradual building up of that character, as the spiritual expression of the consciousness formed by doctrine, that we should have a clear idea of the conduct of Cyprian through the controversy—Worthy or unworthy? behind or in advance of his contemporaries? in his attitude in relation to Rome catholic or uncanonical?

His language is not always free from severity, yet when most severe it is in such contrast with Stephen's hard statement and arrogant threat; in such contrast with the common style, that Augustine seldom refrains at mention of Cyprian's name from some epithet of mildness, gentleness, sweetness, placability, peacefulness. His influence on Augustine's own controversial tone is probably inestimable. How different it would have been if Tertullian and not Cyprian had been his pattern, and yet we largely owe our very possession of Tertullian to Cyprian's appreciation of him, and rendering of his thoughts 'into so quiet and so sweet a style.' It was this which made the dark half-heretic intelligible and acceptable to Catholics who, but for the scholar, would have shunned 'the Master.' His moderation much exceeds that of Firmilian and is equal with that of Dionysius, whose very

Hefele, *Introd.* § 4. 11, 12.) If these be held, as they are, to be Councils as good and valid as any, then the Divine Right of the Episcopal Order exclusively to form conciliar decisions is given up. But if so, what lines separate those particular ranks from the laity or the rest of the clergy? The dilemma is fatal either to the authority of all those Councils or to the *jus divinum* in Councils of a solitary episcopate.

[At the Council of the Nidd it is not clear whether the Archbishop of Canterbury and Ælfleda voted. It is said that with the Bishops who held the Council separately, were *aliquando cum eis Archiepiscopus aliquando vero sapientissima virgo Ælfleda*. Ex Malm. *de gest. Pontif.* lib. III.]

office was the peacemaker's, not the combatant's. But it is in his conduct of business and in his public appearance that he rises to the highest tone. Among the causes of the extraordinary unanimity of the Councils we must reckon the candour and immediateness with which he appeals to a larger and larger circle of judges as the strife waxes hotter; judges neither named by himself nor naturally biassed towards him; bishops first of one, then of two provinces, then from beyond their border.

'If my sins do not disable me, I will learn, if I can, from 'Cyprian's writings, assisted by his prayers, with what peace 'and what consolation the Lord governed His Church through 'him [1].'

'The very remembrance of the Man is a sanctification [2].'

Such were the judgments of Augustine and of Gregory.

Such has been the judgment of the whole Church. The East, which knew little of him personally, accepted his tenet as a sort of inspiration. For the simple detail of his conversion it substituted a supernatural tale, and it assigned him a supremacy all his own. 'Not over the Church of Carthage alone does he preside,' says Gregory Nazianzen in an oration delivered at Constantinople, 'nor yet over the 'Church of Africa alone, famous until now from him and 'for him, but over all the Western Church, nay and almost 'the Eastern Church itself, and over the bounds of south 'and north, wheresoever he came in admiration. Thus 'Cyprian becomes our own [3].' But where the man was well and thoroughly known, there even while this his doctrine and discipline were fading away, his excellent political wisdom and energy, and still more his integrity and rare union of

---

[1] Aug. *de Bapt. c. Donatt.* v. xvii. (23).

[2] Greg. Naz. *Or.* 24, vii., *De S. Cypriano.*

[3] Greg. Naz. *Or.* 24, c. xii. (οὐ γὰρ τῆς Καρχηδονίων προκαθέζεται μόνον Ἐκκλησίας); compare other expressions of his ...τὴν κοινὴν Χριστιανῶν φιλοτιμίαν... τὸ μέγα ποτὲ Καρχηδονίων ὄνομα νῦν δὲ τῆς οἰκουμένης ἁπάσης, c. vi.

zeal and love, activity and moderation, made him at once and for ever the delight of the West[1].

For ever—in spite of the new malevolence, which since the dogma of Infallibility has made it necessary for papal advocates to bespatter each whitest robe that has not walked in the Roman train. We must justify Stephen, both act and method, is their deliberate language. 'If we can succeed 'in this by representations drawn from the documents, we 'will not without irrefragable arguments treat the letter of 'Firmilian as a forgery or a romance[2].'

We have done justice to Stephen's correct judgment on the particular point, and to the soundness of his reasons. But that he claimed an authority which the great fathers and churches disdained rather than discussed; that he placed the just custom of his church in an uncatholic form against the tradition of other churches, that his best reasons were unreasonably presented, that his reception of accredited doctors was unchristianly harsh, has scarcely been questioned till of late[3]. It is the burden of the evidence.

For be it first observed that of all who asked Cyprian's counsel, of all his own councillors, of prelates assembled from Africa, Numidia, Mauretania, of Firmilian and Dionysius the Great, not one *suggests* the least deference to the Roman See[4], nor mentions its estimate of itself as an element in the question, or as a scruple to be borne in mind. Augustine, who marshals every argument in refutation of his opinion, never suggests that obedience to Rome's speaking would

---

[1] 'Doubtless present,' says Augustine, 'through the unity of the spirit' with the Council which set aside his error. See the whole of the beautiful language of *de Bapt. c. Donatt.* v. xvii. (23).

[2] Peters, p. 540.

[3] See for example Tillemont, *S. Cyprien*, Artt. xlvii. xlix., vol. IV. pp. 149 f., 155 f.

[4] In *Ep.* 70. 3 the reference to the foundation upon Peter of the one Church having in this place no relation to Rome, corresponds with the absence of any such reference in the genuine part of *De Unitate* c. 4. And the word *ratione* here occurring perhaps gave rise to the *rationis* and then the *orationis* of the forgery.

have saved him from his error. Gregory the Theologian had not a suspicion that any authority could have been higher than Cyprian's, 'he presides over West and East.'

The sole and the full evidence shews Stephen's claim as ungrounded and his manner of stating it as intolerable.

But now the Ultramontane contention is 'that Stephen 'can never have contented himself with mere declaration, '*because* such a course would be so evidently ineffective to 'dispel prejudice[1]. The fragments which lie in Firmilian's 'letter must represent some elaborate refutation[2]. Augustine, 'unacquainted with that letter and with the treatise on Re-'baptism, excuses Cyprian ignorantly, as if Stephen had 'appealed only to custom[3]. Cyprian's hard words shew that 'he presumed on victory[4]: his third Council of 87 bishops 'was summoned in the confidence produced by his triumph 'over Jubaian[5]: his arguments exhibit partly wantonness, 'partly a determined adroitness in avoiding the point[6]: his 'vindication of the independence of each bishop in unbroken 'unity is a mere "turn" to forestall the expected prohibition 'of his practices from Rome[7].'

This wily worldly politician—for he was no better if his doctrine of unity was not the very pillar of his belief—' may 'or may not have retracted his error formally. He *must* 'have done all that Rome required or she would never have 'placed him in the roll of saints, much less have com-'memorated him in the canon of the mass. *Probably* he 'desisted from his practice without retracting, and this but 'shewed how holy Stephanus had taken the mildest way 'of bringing back the venerable wanderer to the truth. How 'great the guilt of Cyprian had been is known only to God. 'His other services, his martyrdom, atoned for it. But who

---

[1] Peters, p. 532.
[2] *Id.* pp. 540—549.
[3] *Id.* p. 538.
[4] *Id.* p. 511.
[5] *Id.* p. 515.
[6] *Id.* p. 535 'mit welch vornehmer Gewandtheit...: vorbeizuschiffen.'
[7] *Id.* p. 514.

'would rely on what Cyprian in his hours of passion and
'of error thought of the papal supremacy, a doctrine which
'Firmilian, though he tries to be sarcastic, does not seriously
'question? And oh what a warning to us, who have not
'Cyprianic merit, to shun Cyprianic opposition to that
'doctrine! *We* perhaps might never be allowed the oppor-
'tunity of recanting[1].'

What an exquisite picture! Stephen smiling benevolently from his throne on the passionate prodigal seated at his feet, reclaimed by his gentleness, clothed and in his right mind.

And what love for historic truth and method! Countless known facts rejected for hypotheses constructed backwards from the present Roman position.

And what oneness with the Catholicity of old!

That these writers cannot be regarded as other than faithful exponents of the doctrine, see p. 322 note.

[1] Peters, pp. 549, 550.

CHAPTER IX.

EXPANSION OF CHRISTIAN FEELING AND ENERGY (RESUMED).

The Secret of Conduct.

I. 'OF THE GOOD OF PATIENCE.'

AUGUSTINE well-nigh adored Cyprian's 'Heart of overflowing love.' He dwells on how he extended to worldly or immoral colleagues the same loving patience that he used 'in tolerating those good prelates who in turn tolerated him' when through 'human temptation he was "otherwise minded" on an obscure question[1].' Experience since Augustine's finds antagonists on obscure questions harder to bear with than worldlings—especially when one is oneself on the subtler side. But whichever alternative is the harder, Cyprian merits all the honour which even Augustine could bestow.

In an earlier chapter we saw how soon Cyprian recognised that the new standing-point required a readjustment of ethical views of old problems, whilst the position of the new people daily created new problems. Persecution could not do its unequal work and rouse no Resentments. Old riddles of Sorrow and Suffering grew still harder to the called and chosen whose choice and calling landed them in the loss of all things. The whole philosophy of Probation had blossomed

---

[1] Aug. *de Bapt. c. Donatt.* IV. ix. (12).

out. The philosophy of Spiritual Worship was in bud. On each of these he had written, we have seen how.

But now the seething tumult of Christian opinions on questions of intense interest to the faith, demanded, in supplement to his philosophy of Unity, some Theory of Right Feeling and Action amid Divergences apparently scarce less vital than those which separated catholic and heretic together from their joint oppressors.

Cyprian did not find himself involved as by surprise in these considerations. He had understood Christianity to be the doctrine of a new and true School—the last and everlasting. Here was 'the Method of a heavenly Learning 'whereby our School (*secta*) directs itself to the attainment 'after a Divine manner of the reward of faith and hope¹.' The scope of Paul's mission had been to '*form* the nations'; that Apostle of Nations had expressly witnessed 'against 'their philosophy and empty fallacy, self-evolved and mater-'ialistic—*secundum traditionem hominum, secundum elementa* '*mundi*'—in contrast to that reality which 'rested on the person of Christ indwelt in by the fulness of deity².'

To develop and apply the influences of this fresh and powerful factor to thought and action was a pressing necessity. And now, at the outset, what was befalling the very fountain of the new morality, the Spirit of Charity or Love? To say nothing of the threatening masses of heresy, was this new controversy with Italy only a new field, such as heathenism had never known, for Intolerance, Jealousy and Hate? Evidently the supremacy of a Power actively antagonistic to those Church-passions must be affirmed and enforced. The old riddles were world-riddles of life. The Church-riddles injected no less perplexity into faith.

Cyprian found the danger strong in himself. It grew among his partisans as fast as among his adversaries. His own action had awakened it. It was his to find the remedy.

---

[1] *De Bono Patientiæ* 1.   [2] *De B. Pat.* 2.

IX. I.   SECRET OF CONDUCT—'*DE BONO PATIENTIÆ.*'   439

Accordingly, writing to Jubaian[1], he says, 'So far as in 'us lies, we are not, for the sake of heretics, going to contend 'with colleagues and fellow-bishops: with them I keep 'Divine concord and the Lord's peace.... In patience and 'gentleness we hold fast by charity of spirit, by the honour 'of our college, by the bond of faith, by concord within the 'episcopate.

'To this end I have just composed a small book on '*The Good of Patience*, to the best of my small powers, under 'the permission and inspiration of the Lord.'

Under this simple heading, which appears in the pamphlet itself also[2], and which is caught up from a passing touch of Tertullian's[3], he develops his new chapter of Christian Ethics. Were it not thus dated and motived by himself[4], its determined exclusion of the least provoking allusion—an example of its own teaching not always to be reckoned on in eirenica—might have left both motive and date doubtful. That his auditors are subject to persecutions not only from Jews and Gentiles but from separatists also is its nearest reference to circumstances[5]. No word about the 'college of bishops' here, nor of any discord within it.

But what is the '*Patience*' which Cyprian desires to evoke?

Patience was that element which Cicero combines with the Realisation of High Ideals, with Self-Reliance and with Perseverance, to complete the notion of Fortitude. And he thus defines it[6]: 'It is the voluntary and long-continued 'endurance of hardship and difficulty for ends of honour and 'usefulness.'

Was this what Cyprian longed to see becoming a more

---

[1] *Ep.* 73. 26.
[2] *De B. Pat.* 15.
[3] Tert. *de Pat.* i. '*Bonum ejus (patientiæ)* etiam qui cæci vivunt summæ virtutis appellatione honorant.'
[4] Pontius alludes to it in a single word. 'Unde sic Patientiam disceremus?' *Vit.* c. 7.
[5] *De B. Pat.* 21.
[6] *De Inv.* ii. 54 'Fortitudo...ejus partes: Magnificentia, Fidentia, Patientia, Perseverantia.'

active principle in the Church? No. Martyrdom and Confessorship had more than fulfilled this ideal.

The Tracts and Epistles of Seneca are not unlike Cyprian's in their purpose of raising the moral tone of society. And in Seneca a certain humanity, a certain spirituality, breaks in upon his Stoic paradox on all sides. He sees 'a kinship and a likeness' between God and good men. He regards the originally good as 'a true progeny' of God, and their worldly afflictions as 'a lovingly severe education.' It is in their 'power of Patience' (endurance) that the 'might of virtue is shewn'; and it is 'by Patience that the spirit comes at last to contemn the power of evils[1].' But Seneca finds the perfection and the reward of Patience in a habitual joyous Pride in self, with a pleasant contempt for undisciplined minds[2]. He attains to the paradox that herein man has the advantage of God—that while God stands only 'outside the endurance of evils, man stands above that endurance[3].'

It was something more than this antique virtue that Cyprian perceived. There was a new thing in the world, a gift of God, the impartment of a something out of God's own nature, and so a certain seal of Sonship[4]. Patience is of the Father, and 'the sons must not degenerate[5]. The perfection ' of the sons is the restoration of the original likeness of the ' Father in the manifestation of His patience.' 'Perseverance in Sonship' is the imitation of the Father's patience.

What then is the new spirit which now enters into the old word[6]?

---

[1] Seneca, *Dial.* I. i. 5; ii. 4, 7; iv. 6, 13.

[2] Sen. *Dial.* II. ix. 3 'inde tam erectus lætusque est, inde continuo gaudio elatus.' xiv. 1 'o quantus inter ista risus tollendus est; quanta voluptate implendus animus ex alienorum errorum tumultu contemplanti quietem suam.'

[3] Sen. *Dial.* I. vi. 6.

[4] Cum Deo virtus ista communis... Deo auctore, *De B. Pat.* 3;...Dei res, 5.

[5] *De B. Pat.* 3, 5, 20.

[6] Dr Peters gives a wordy, incompetent account of this treatise, which he characterizes as very easy to understand,—as it is, if the exceeding diffi-

Cyprian does not verbally distinguish the aspect of the virtue regarded as *the power which bears* from that of the *power which forbears;* the sufferance of calamity from the repression of the desire to avenge oneself. Both unite in his PATIENTIA.

In the New Testament we commonly have two words for these two aspects, 'endurance' (*hypomone*), for the former; 'long-suffering, tolerance' (*macrothymia*), for the latter.

'The former is opposed to cowardice or despondency, the other to wrath or revenge. The former is closely allied to hope, the latter is commonly connected with mercy[1].'

But in Aristotle the former is the child of unmanliness or cowardice; and Cyprian points out that the philosophies, whether Stoic or Cynic[2], which exercised it did not, in theory or in practice, aim at either *humility* or *mildness*, but were essentially self-satisfying and severe[3]. But humility and mildness are to the Christian grace essential[4].

The second aspect of Patience (*macrothymia*) places itself

---

culty, which Cyprian himself points out, of correlating heathen and Christian virtues, is ignored.

[1] Bp. Lightfoot on Col. i. 11, adding that the distinction is not without exception.

[2] It is Cynicism which Tertullian has in view in the parallel passage of his *De Pat.* ii. 'affectatio humana caninæ æquanimitatis stupore formata.'

[3] *De B. Pat.* 2.

[4] Arist. *Rhet.* ii. 6 ἀπὸ ἀνανδρίας γὰρ ἢ δειλίας ἡ ὑπομονή...and classical *patientia* was never clear of the slur. See Tac. *Agric.* 16 '(Britanniam) unius prælii fortuna veteri *patientiæ* restituit.' Cyprian (*De B. Pat.* 2) derives both these ideas, of the *falsa sapientia* and of the essential thought of Christian Patience as *humilis* and *mitis*, from Tertullian's passing observations in his c. xvi. and c. xii. Let me here quote in support of the view of Cyprian that Humility is thus essential to its idea a delicate analysis from Prof. H. Sidgwick's article on Ethics in *Encycl. Brit.* (IXth ed.), v. VIII. p. 591 a: 'The far greater prominence (of Humility) under the new dispensation may be partly referred to the express teaching and example of Christ; partly, in so far as the virtue is manifested in the renunciation of external rank and dignity, or the glory of merely secular gifts and acquirements, it is one aspect of the unworldliness which we have already noticed; while the deeper humility that represses the claim of personal merit even in the saint belongs to the strict self-examination, the continual sense of imperfection, the utter reliance on strength not his own, which characterize the inner moral life of the Christian. Humility in this latter sense 'before God' is an essential condition of all truly Christian goodness.'

in no contradiction to Justice. Theophylact[1] describes 'The Long-suffering man' as inflicting justice 'after abundant deliberation, not in sharp haste, but tardily'—a view which we may illustrate from Plutarch's beautiful book 'Of God's tardy judgments,' where he says that, as a means of producing likeness to God, the contemplation of God's gentleness will not be ineffective, as one observes 'how lingeringly 'and leisurely He does justice even on the wicked, not 'that He is afraid lest He should Himself chastise over 'hastily and have to repent, but because He would cure our 'savagery and vehemence of vengeance, and teach us not 'to spring in anger on those who hurt us, whilst our wrath 'burns and throbs and is convulsed, as if we were glutting 'thirst or famine; but, imitating His mildness and delays, 'orderly, regretfully, and taking into our counsels Time, who 'is least likely to be visited with repentances, so to set our 'hands to justice[2].'

By this excellent passage we see that what Cyprian adds to the idea is the resolution which, when we ourselves suffer for conscience' sake, commits the whole cause unreservedly to God; and this it is which makes of Christian patience an active power and an attribute of deity. Tertullian, while giving the same counsel, ends his treatise with one glance at 'the fire beneath' which awaits 'false patience' as it awaits all other falsities. But to Cyprian such a thought is not a hope but a dread certainty, and the God to whom he bids the Christian commit his cause is, as he reminds him, One Who has not yet thought it necessary to avenge either Himself or His Slain Son or His persecuted Church.

We proceed to speak of the Form in which was brought out the necessity of this fresh Virtue to the Church's life.

---

[1] Theophylact. Bulgar. *Ad Galatt.* v. 22.

[2] Plut. *de sera numinis vindicta,* v. ...ἀλλὰ μιμουμένους τὴν ἐκείνου πρᾳό- τητα καὶ τὴν μέλλησιν, ἐν τάξει καὶ μετ' ἐμμελείας, τὸν ἥκιστα μετανοίᾳ προσοι- σόμενον χρόνον ἔχοντας σύμβουλον.... Cf. Thuc. iv. 18.

IX. 1. SECRET OF CONDUCT—'DE BONO PATIENTIÆ.'

Although it comes to us in the shape of an Essay for devotional study it bears marks of having been originally an Address to some audience[1].

It begins with thoughts and illustrations derived from his 'Master's' tract on the same subject, shuns his harsh views, avoids his mistakes, and misses his picturesqueness. It is charged with sweeter and truer notions of Life in God. And in a way quite unlike the specimens of remodelling which we have examined hitherto, it avoids verbal coincidences even when they seem inevitable.

While Tertullian starts from himself with a sharp gird at his own feverish impatient nature[2], which disqualifies and yet fits him to discourse on the topic, Cyprian begins with his audience, and with the occasion for the virtue of which he is to speak, which they will find in listening to himself.

Cyprian proceeds (as we saw) to indicate the need of a new and Christian doctrine concerning a virtue lauded and misrepresented in other systems—a fact about them which Tertullian in one breath accepts as homage and resents as impertinence[3]. c. 2.

But ours is a Patience of Life, of Action, not of Speculation—a part of God's own Nature and Self which passes with His Divine Being into all His Sons, and belongs to the restoration of the lost likeness. c. 4. c. 5.

Respondere Natalibus is still Cyprian's motto as in the days of the plague[4], and as he lovingly presses home our

---

[1] If any editor has noted this it escapes me. Even Augustine calls it an Epistola, *c. Duas Epp. Pelagg.* IV. viii. (22). Yet the opening phrases indicate that it was orally delivered. They are too full, and would be too flat, for a metaphor to readers. 'De patientia *locuturus*, fratres dilectissimi, et utilitates ejus et commoda *prædicaturus*, unde potius incipiam, quam quod nunc quoque ad *audientiam* vestram patientiam *video* esse necessariam, ut nec ipsum quod *auditis* et discitis, sine patientia facere possitis. Tunc enim demum sermo et ratio salutaris efficaciter discitur, si patienter quod *dicitur audiatur*.' *De B. Pat.* i.

[2] Semper æger caloribus impatientiæ. Tert. *de Pat.* i.

[3] Tert. *de Pat.* c. i.

[4] Pont. *Vit.* 9.

Sonship and its obligation, he shews himself a better master of motive than his Master, who, at this section of the subject, only represents to us the obedient patience of our slaves and our animals, and the suitableness of our rendering the like to the Giver of such comforts[1].

c. 4.
c. 6.
c. 7.
c. 8.

c. 9.

c. 10.

The Patience of the Father is displayed through ages in the gifts of nature to the idolatrous nations, in all the delays, all the opportunities He allows: the Patience of the Son is shewn in His eternal preparation for man's salvation, in every act of His manhood and passion, full of power as of suffering,—power which (in exorcism) still visibly tames the spiritual foe—and is displayed too in the opening wide of His Church *to the return of the sinfullest*. In this last clause we have not merely an allusion to his own controversies, but a deliberate broadening out of the spirit of Tertullian, from whom this argument 'Of the Patience of God' is wholly derived[2], though much expanded. He concludes this section by alleging from S. Peter and S. John the immense necessity of an Imitation of Christ along with the personal Types of His patience offered by Abel and the Patriarchs, by Joseph and Moses, by David in his 'great and marvellous and *Christian* patience' with Saul, and by the Martyrs and Prophets of the old Covenant. Here then we must not miss his doctrine that, while ethnic patience before Christ was worse than nothing, Jewish patience was perfect to the full extent to which types can be perfect: Theirs was a prefiguring of His.

cc. 11—17.

The next main division of the subject is the Necessity and Utility of Patience under the conditions of Humanity

---

[1] Tert. *de Pat.* iv.

[2] Details of imitation crop up in the statement of our Lord's baptism 'a servo' (*De B. Pat.* 6) in the remark that He never betrayed Judas' name throughout his discipleship (6); perhaps in the expression that He was led '*ad victimam*' (7). Tert. *de Pat.* iii. (which however appears elsewhere in Cyprian's reading of Es. liii. 7 [*Testim.* II. 15], cf. *De B. Pat.* 23. Hartel with Cod. Seg. reads *ad crucem*).

IX. 1. THE 'PATIENCE' OF TERTULLIAN AND CYPRIAN.

in its fall[1]. The tears of the new-born child initiate a state c. 12.
of troubles in which the Christian has the fullest share;
Patience is his one prospect of dealing with them; nor can
he find any other road to such special 'Truth' and 'Freedom' as are promised him, nor into that Faith, Hope, and
Perseverance, which form the subjective part of his religion;
nor yet find any other rampart of the Purity, Honesty, and c. 14.
Innocence which he guards.

Of Charity which is Christianity in essence, and of the c. 15.
Peacefulness, which so palpably differences Christian from
heathen society[2], Patience and Tolerance are the substantial
substratum[3].

This section of Cyprian's is also built on Tertullian.

Far less orderly and regular but far more picturesque and Tert. de
striking is Tertullian's handling. Tertullian finds the Necessity Pat. vi.
for Patience in the obligations of accepting Christ's view of
riches, bearing our losses and distributing our largesses
Christianly; in the necessity of taking Christ's view of in- viii.
juries, though here his hot spirit cannot forego a distinct
satisfaction in the surprise and disappointment with which
our patience must afflict our enemies; in the necessity of ix.
a nobler view of the death of friends; in the necessity for x.
surrendering all vengeance into the hand of God. We have
to bear alike the results of our own misdoing, the plots xi.
of the Evil One[4], and the corrections of God; we have to
become 'humble and mild.'

---

[1] Augustine, c. Duas Epp. Pelagg. IV. viii. (22), points out the irreconcilableness of this passage (c. 11) and of c. 17 as shewing what Cyprian understood by 'all have sinned' with any Pelagian opinion.

[2] Compare Cyprian's first experience of this in ad Donatum, 14, with this which is his last.

[3] ...patientiæ et tolerantiæ firmitate. (De B. Pat. 16.)

[4] Tertullian uses Malus as the equivalent of ὁ πονηρός. Certemus igitur quæ a Malo infliguntur sustinere. Again: Quaqua ex parte, aut erroribus nostris, aut Mali insidiis, aut admonitionibus Domini intervenit usus, ejus officii magna merces.... De Pat. xi., cf. xiv. 'dissecabatur Malus.' On the use in general see Bp. Lightfoot on Revision of the N.T. (ed. 3), App. II. p. 294.

446 EXPANSION OF CHRISTIAN FEELING AND ENERGY.

Tert. *de Pat.* xii.

Peacefulness[1], Forgivingness, *The continuance of Single life after Divorce*, Earnestness in Repentance, are the steps of the climax which, like his scholar, he finds and dwells on with delight in S. Paul's perfect analysis of Charity[2]. And then each has his characteristic corollary: Tertullian strangely—that we have so far spoken only of 'a simple uniform Patience, merely in the heart'; but that she further has a 'multiform function in the body—toiling to deserve the Divine favour.' This function is Asceticism. 'The 'afflicting of the flesh is a placatory victim unto the Lord 'through the sacrifice of humiliation; offering squalor with 'stint of rations[3] to the Lord; content with plain food 'and pure water, joining fast to fast, *growing into* sackcloth 'and ashes.'

xiii.

Of this satisfaction Nebuchadnezzar was an example, though not of the highest order; and throughout every stage of pain, self-inflicted or enforced by the persecutor, patience is the minister of power.

This chapter with its extravagant teachings finds no counterpart in Cyprian, and while it indicates its author's tendencies even in his orthodox years, it instances also how uncatholic fashions in the Catholic Church arise not from her true fathers, but are the inventions of sectarian geniuses.

While Tertullian's corollary is the very wildness of self-maceration, Cyprian's is that noble doctrine of Probation of which the English Church philosopher has been the chief exponent[4].

c. 17.

---

[1] Tertullian (xii.) speaks of the difficulty which a son of impatience finds in forgiving seventy times seven times. Cyprian (16) passingly alludes to the need for forgiving not numerically but universally.

[2] *Caritas* is Cyprian's rendering, *Dilectio* Tertullian's in 1 Cor. xiii. 4.

[3] Tert. *de Pat.* xiii. 'cum sordes cum angustia victus domino *libat*.' '*Libare* sordes' would surely be too violent for Tertullian, even if he tolerated the heathen metaphor of *libation*, which he nowhere does, and surely could not. I venture to suggest *litat*. Compare Tert. *de Pat.* c. x. 'Quem autem honorem litabimus Domino Deo'; *adv. Valent.* ii. 'Infantes testimonium Christi sanguine litaverunt.'

[4] Cyprian's *examples* of patience are

IX. 1. THE '*PATIENCE*' OF TERTULLIAN AND CYPRIAN.

The 'Necessity of Patience' is in Tertullian prefaced, T. *de P*. v. and in Cyprian followed up, by an enquiry into the 'Origin,' *De B. P.* or, as Tertullian has it, the 'Parentage,' of Impatience[1]. c. 19. Both assign its genesis to the same cause—The Devil's Envy of Man. The older writer dwells with acerbity on woman's part in the Fall. All falls are traced to the same source down to Israel's choice of 'profane guiding gods[2],' to the massacres of prophets, and (says Cyprian) to all the falls of the heretics in his own day. But Tertullian has a T. *de P*. vi. beautiful contrast of the genesis of Patience in the Faith of Abraham and of her perfecting in Christ's doctrine of the Love of Enemies.

Yet again Cyprian, rarely borrowing his words[3], follows *De B. P.* and enlarges his Master's list of the Effects of Patience in 20. T. *de P*. xi. generating the altruism of the Christian communities and their persevering work for the world through every keen discouragement—as 'sons of the Father.'

At the last, the Master rises into the most beautiful T. *de P*. xv. passage in all his writings, impersonating her beauty like a Catherine of Raffaelle. 'Her countenance still and calm, 'brow pure, no wrinkledness from mourning or from anger 'to pucker it, eyebrows evenly smoothed for joyousness, eyes 'downcast in lowliness not unhappiness, lips sealed with all 'the dignity of silence; her complexion that of free hearts 'and innocent; she shakes her head at the Accuser, her smile 'threatens him; about her bosom her amice lies white and 'folded close, unpuffed, unruffled; for she sitteth upon the

the Lord's pacific calm, Stephen, Job, and Tobias; Tertullian's (*De Pat.* xiv.) are the Esaias of tradition, Stephen, and Job. Tertullian's details of the wife and the *bestiolæ* are borrowed by Cyprian, but not his strange mistake that Job's children were never replaced, and that he ascetically preferred to live alone. Cyprian cannot refrain from supposing that Satan's success through Eve encouraged him to employ Job's wife. But with fine pathos, after calling him 'Dives in censu dominus, et in liberis pater ditior,' he says 'nec dominus repente nec pater est.' *De B. Pat.* 18.

[1] Exordia, Cyprian; Natales, Tertullian.

[2] Profanos deos...itineris sui duces.

[3] T. divitem temperat.—C. coercet potentiam divitum.

'throne of that gentlest, kindest Spirit who rolls not in the
'whirlwind, nor blackens in the cloud, but is ever of a tender
'clearness, open and singlehearted, the Spirit whom in his
'third vision, Elias saw. For where God is, there also is His
'foster-child, even Patience.'

So he writes, and then, as if impatient of Patience herself,
he dashes suddenly into a wild invective against the 'patience
T. de Pat. xvi. 'of the Gentiles of the earth—a false, a criminal patience, taught
'them by Satan's self, emulating God. Patient of every shame
'for gold's sake, patient of rivals, plutocrats, dinner-givers—
'impatient of God alone...' For this patience there waits
only fire. ...'We, we must offer the patience of the spirit,
'the patience of the flesh. We believe in the resurrection of
'flesh and of spirit.'—He ends.

Cyprian's conclusion is as different as may be and as
characteristic. 'All retributions to be let alone by man. They
De B. Pat. belong to God, saith Prophecy. *I have held my peace: shall
cc. 21, 22. I hold my peace for ever*[1]?... The silent Lamb of the Passion
cc. 23, 24. is the Judge who *will not keep silence*. He who avenges
not Himself, who so long avenges not His slain Son—shall
His servants, with unscrupulous, unblushful precipitation
vindicate themselves before He is vindicated? Rather, work
on, stedfast in tolerance, and in the "Day of Wrath[2]" stand
with the just and the godfearing.'

2. 'OF JEALOUSY AND ENVY.'

The Tractate 'of Jealousy and Envy,' which long remained
abroad as well as at home a famous and popular 'epistle[3],'

---

[1] Isai. xlii. 14. *E. V.* 'I have long time holden my peace; I have been still and refrained myself.' *H. Ewald:* 'Ich schwieg—soll ich auf ewig verstummen an mich halten?' *Die Propheten d. Alt. Bundes.* (1840), v. II. p. 420.

[2] '*Ille Iræ* et vindictæ *Dies*' is the earliest theological use of this title. Is it taken from Rom. ii. 5?

[3] Epistola populis nota, Aug. *d. Bapt. c. Donn.* IV. viii. (11).—'...librum... valde optimum,' Hieron. *Comment. in Ep. ad Galatt.* l. iii. c. 5.

IX. 2. SECRET OF CONDUCT—'*DE ZELO ET LIVORE.*' 449

belongs to nearly the same time; but as it is unmentioned in the letter to Jubaian it came out probably a little later, although before the recommencement of persecution[1]. This too is motived by the dread that in the official life of the Church fresh fields were opening to commonplace passions. Their outer activity might be checked by the rules of the society, yet the religion would miss its end if it left Christian hearts to be ridden over so secretly by that mysterious Being whose energy Cyprian recognised in the constant depravation of good as fast as it arose[2].

These are some now visible effects of 'blinding jealousy.' 'There is a breaking of the bond of the Lord's peace, a 'violence done to brotherly charity, there is a corrupting 'of truth, a dividing of unity, a dashing into heresies and 'schisms, (and it will continue) so long as there is this cavil-'ling at chief priests, this envying at the bishops,—any man 'complaining aloud at not having been preferred for conse-'cration, or disdaining to submit to another's prelacy. Hence 'one "lifts up the heel"; hence one rebels, proud out of jealousy, 'crooked out of rivalry, a foe through enmity and envy not to 'the man but to his office.' Maximus, Felicissimus, Novatus, still more Novatian, may have passed before his mind's eye as he wrote[3]; but it was the general condition of factiousness which had to be probed in order to be healed. Such is the motive.

The purpose then is in continuance of his plan of analysing and developing the new school of life. And in this his last treatise he boldly feels after a more searching and more formative discipline of the conscience than hitherto. He goes to the foundations of spiritual self-knowledge.

---

[1] This may be fairly inferred from the character of the exhortation in c. 16.

[2] Observe in this treatise the constant reference of phenomena to a Living Will of Evil.

[3] This passage (c. 6) and that in c. 12 (p. 454) below must I think be taken as a grave incidental judgment on Novatian's motives.

c. 1.
c. 3.

It is upon the 'dark and hidden devastation' which 'lurkingly affects unwary *minds*' that he focuses the new light. 'The darts rain thickest from the ambushes. The more 'hidden and clandestine the archery the more fatal it is. Let 'us awake to understand it.' And so through the whole treatise.

c. 6.
c. 7.
c. 9.

It is to 'the recesses of the mind,' 'the unhappiness which is 'in the secret places of the heart,' 'the wounds deeply lodged 'within the hiding-places of the conscience,' that he directs men's own observation. And so with the course of remedy which he applies. It is the inner life of the conscience to which the great organizer addresses himself in the last issue.

c. 15.

It is the 'Deifica Disciplina'—the 'Discipline that divinises' —which must, which only can, complete our soul's 'Birth unto God.'

c. 16.

The first question, 'How am I to hold the grace once given against the most secret and fatal of inner assaults?' he answers thus :—By meditations—by exercises spiritual— Reading, Thought, Prayer, Works of Charity. 'For not the 'days of martyrdom alone are the days of coronation for

c. 17.

'God's warriors. *Peace too has her crowns*[1].' 'But how to attain them' is the next question, 'if Jealousy and Envy have been long dominant in me[2]?'

'It is possible still,' he replies. 'The inner accurate searching and weeding of the heart.. The sweetening of bitterness. The Sacrament of the Cross, with its food and wine.. *The imitation of good men*, or, if at present that seems impossible, sympathy with them, and *delight in the happiness* of others.'

c. 18.

So nearly and so effectively does he reach the idea of an enchiridion that he concludes with suggesting topics for frequent reflection, and especially that one which in all times has been found most potent, 'The Practice of the Presence of God.'

---

[1] Divina nativitas. Deifica disciplina (c. 15). Corroborandus, firmandus animus (c. 16).

[2] ...tu etiam possis qui fueras zelo et livore possessus... (c. 17).

IX. 2. SECRET OF CONDUCT—'DE ZELO ET LIVORE.'

Superficially unlike, this is in some respects the most Cyprianic of Cyprian's tracts. It is broadly practical, and it is defective in scientific analysis of the passion to be subdued, though he rightly, like Clement of Rome, detects it to be the most fatal of all to Church-life.

We will now ascertain his notion as to what *Zelus* and *Livor* are, and conclude with his ideal of the opposite temper: an ideal perhaps never more perfectly realised (never certainly by any controversialist) than in himself[1].

The Title 'De Zelo et Livore' leads us to expect something of logical distinction. But the 'et Livore' proves to be rather a substitute for an epithet to explain in what sense he means to use '*Zelus*[2].'

For in Aristotle *Zelos* has none but a good sense—'a reasonable quality in reasonable men,' for it is 'a kind of 'pain at a visible presence of good and precious gifts, possible 'for oneself to attain; a pain not because another hath them, 'but because oneself hath not[3].' It is this classical sense which Œcumenius well puts when he[4] calls it 'an enthusiastic move-'ment of soul towards something, with some attempt to 'resemble what it so earnestly affects.'

But such noble emulation may be depraved in two ways, by a desire to engross the perceived good, or by the mere base wish that the owner had it not. This antiently was *Phthonos*, the 'mean passion of the mean,' 'pain at another's good,' 'apart from any hope of obtaining it[5]'; or, as Plutarch,

---

[1] Augustine has caught this. Cyprian says (c. 13) 'eum posse *caritatem tenere*, quisque magnanimus fuerit et benignus et *zeli* ac *livoris alienus*.' Augustine says, Vere decuit Cyprianum de zelo ac livore et arguere graviter et monere, *a quo* tam mortifero malo cor ejus penitus *alienum* tanta *caritatis* abundantia comprobavit: qua vigilantissime custodita, &c.' *De Bapt. c. Donatt.* IV. viii. 11.

[2] D. Brutus, who was a lover of unfashionable words, is seemingly the only præ-Augustan who uses *livor* (Cic. *Epistt. ad Fam.* xi. 10, 1).

[3] *Rhet.* ii. 11.

[4] Œcumen. *Comment. in Ep. Cath. Jacob.* iii. 14.

[5] Aristot. *l. c.*, and ii. 10, μὴ ἵνα τι αὐτῷ, ἀλλὰ δι' ἐκείνους. Cf. ...λύπην ἐπ' ἀλλοτρίοις ἀγαθοῖς. Diog. Laert. VII. i. (111).

'simply against those who seem to prosper,...against those who seem to advance in excellence[1].' Again Cicero, who proposed for clearness' sake to call the active feeling *invidentia*, further cleared the definition by adding that the envied well-being is such as to be unhurtful to the envious[2].

But amid the falling esteem which the new ethics introduced for all qualities which tended to emphasize or even pronounce that *Ego*, which had hitherto been the world's centre, the idea that was in *Zelus* declined. At once in S. Paul its workings take rank with those of enmity and contention[3]. Jerome still notes the double use, the noble and the base. But Cyprian had placed it wholly on the level of *Phthonos*. He begins by coupling it with *Livor* and his first words run thus, ' To be jealous (*zelare*) of the good you see, 'and to envy (*invidere*) better men is held by some a slight 'and trivial crime[4].' In reality it is one of the deadliest because one of the most secret of our temptations. Its origin, he proceeds, like that of Impatience[5], is in the will of Satan. It was the sight of the Image of God in Man which gave the occasion. 'He, throned in angel majesty, he well-pleasing 'and dear to God, he was foremost to perish and to destroy... ' He brake out into Jealousy (*zelus*) through malevolent Envy '(*livor*)...He snatched from man *the grace of his imparted* '*immortality*, and himself lost all that he once had been.'

c. 4.

c. 5.

Man had caught the infection; yet, as Cyprian seems to mean, it was not in the first-fallen that its power appeared. It was in the 'primal hatreds of fresh brotherhood'; and down from Abel to the delivery of the Christ 'through envy,' Cyprian touches the great Jewish instances.

---

[1] Plut. *de Odio et Invidia*, vi. ...τοῖς μᾶλλον ἐπ' ἀρετῇ προϊέναι δοκοῦσι.

[2] *Tusc. Disp.* iv. 8. 17 'ægritudinem susceptam propter alterius res secundas quæ nihil noceant invidenti; nam si quis doleat ejus rebus secundis a quo ipse lædatur, non recte dicitur invidere.'

Cf. iii. 9. 20.

[3] ἔχθραι, ἔρις. Gal. v. 20, on which see Bishop Lightfoot.

[4] *Zelare* is applied indifferently to things and persons, *fratrem* (c. 11), *virtutem...felicitatem* (c. 7).

[5] *De B. Pat.* 12, 19.

IX. 2. SECRET OF CONDUCT—'*DE ZELO ET LIVORE.*' 453

Then come the evils of which, in the Church and in the world, Jealousy is the 'root'; and here there is again a trace of classification. They are (1) hate and animosity, (2) avarice and ambition, (3) irreligion, as overpowering the consideration of the Fear of God, the School of Christ and the Day of Judgment, (4) pride, (5) cruelty, perfidy, impatience, discord, wrath, (6) Church Divisions[1]. c. 6.

Lightly to sketch the remainder of the treatise:—It dwells on the self-torment of envy, on its physical symptoms[2], the difficulty of eradicating it, the self-contradictions of the situations it creates[3], its contrariety alike to the Lowliness and to the Light of Christ[4], and to the whole Imitation of Him. Yet is it curable by one master-thought of His duly learnt. He, when He taught that *least* is *greatest*, 'lopped 'emulation away, removing the material[5] cause of envy 'itself.'

It outlines next the pattern of a Christian as drawn by our Lord and Saint Paul, and this may well be quoted at length on account of the perfect ideal which, in its 'reality and its healthfulness[6],' Cyprian set before himself. It is scarcely possible that a closer parallel could be found to the very

---

[1] It would seem from the above that Cyprian, as a moralist, uses *zelus* as the most comprehensive term, *livor* (unkind) or *invidia* (mean) as its immediate development, and *æmulatio* as a specific activity. The following are illustrations. Satan's first emotion was *zelus:* then *invidia* grassatur on earth, and man *livore* periturus...diabolum qui *zelat* imitatur (c. 4). Ab *invidis* nunquam livor exponitur...*Invidus* in majus incendium *livoris* ignibus inardescit (c. 7). Zeli tenebræ, nubilum *livoris, invidiæ* cæcitas (c. 11). *Zelus* is the opposite of *magnanimitas, livor* of *benignitas* (c. 13). Again, (1 Cor. iii. 1—3) *zelus* is found only in infants in Christ: accordingly it is the ruin of *pax* and *caritas*, and is the contrary of the *unanimis* et *mitis* character.

[2] Vultus minax..pallor in facie, in labiis tremor.... c. 8.

[3] Perseverans malum est hominem persequi ad Dei gratiam pertinentem, calamitas sine remedio est odisse felicem. c. 9.

[4] Is the rather singular phrase Quæ sunt Christi gere quia *lux et dies Christus est* (c. 10) the germ of the hymn *Christe qui lux es et dies*?

[5] Omnem causam et materiam. c. 10.

[6] Per quem (Cypr.)...Dominus veracissima intonuit et salubria præcepit. Aug. *de Bapt. c. Donatt.* IV. viii. (11).

character which Pontius and Augustine from acquaintance and study describe as his own.

c. 12.

'We must remember by what name Christ calls His own people, by what title He designates His own flock. Sheep He names them, that Christian innocence may match the innocence of sheep. Lambs He calls them, that their simplicity of mind may copy the lamb's simple nature. Why lurks a wolf under sheep's clothing? Why does one calling himself a Christian falsely defame Christ's flock? To take upon one Christ's name and not walk by Christ's way,—what is this but the counterfeiting of a Divine name, an abandonment of the road of salvation? Forasmuch as Himself saith in His teaching, "he cometh unto Life who keepeth the commandments," and "he is wise that heareth His words and doeth them," and "he too is called the chief doctor in the kingdom of heaven who teacheth and so doeth,"—shewing that, what the preacher preacheth well and serviceably shall then profit the preacher, if what is delivered by his lips be fulfilled by deeds following. But what did the Lord oftener instil into His disciples? what, among saving warnings and heavenly precepts, hath He bidden us more observe and keep than that "with the same love wherewith He loved His disciples, we should also love one another"? Now how doth he keep either the peace of the Lord or charity, who through the coming in of jealousy can neither be a peacemaker, nor be in charity[1]?'

From this remonstrance he rises still in his delineation of the unearthly spiritual idea of the Christian Life, of the change actually wrought by the New Birth, and of our true

c. 13.

Sonship to God. He weaves together the Apostle's sayings about the 'mortifying of the deeds of the flesh,' the 'being led by the Spirit,' and being 'God's sons'; he argues from them, 'If we have uplifted our eyes from earth to heaven, and

c. 14.

'raised to things above and things Divine a heart full of God

---

[1] See p. 449, n. 3.

IX. 2. SECRET OF CONDUCT—'DE ZELO ET LIVORE.' 455

'and of Christ, let us be doing nothing but things worthy of 'God and of Christ.' Again he quotes 'Risen with Christ... 'minded of things above...life hid with Christ in God...Christ 'our life one day to appear, and we with Him,' and again he argues, 'We then, who in baptism died and have been buried as to the fleshly sins of the old man, who by heavenly regeneration have risen with Christ, think we and do we the things that are Christ's! The Apostle tells of "the first man of the earth and of the second man from heaven," of our "bearing the image of the one first, and afterwards of the second." That heavenly image we shall never wear *unless we present Christ's likeness in what we have already begun to be.* *This it is to have changed what you once were and to have begun to be what you were not*; namely, that a Divine nativity shines out in you, that a deifying education responds to your Father God, that, in the honour and praise of *living, the God brightens in the man*...Unto this brightness the Lord shapeth and prepareth us, and the Son of God enwindeth this likeness of God His Father into us.' Then follow his favourite passages in which the Sonship of the Christian is worked out. c. 15.

Then the questions—How to adapt in ourselves the world's necessary life to such a life as this in the world? How to set about it, if nothing yet has been effected?

Of his answers to these we have already spoken.

So in these two Papers Cyprian lets the world see what he held to be at once the Secret of Conduct, the true way of Church-Reform, and the Church's Work for the Empire.

CHAPTER X.

THE PERSECUTION OF VALERIAN.

I. 1. THE EDICT AND ITS OCCASIONS.

'WE stood together linked in a band of love and peace against heretical wrong and Gentile pressure.'

This is Cyprian's reminiscence of the Council a year afterwards. It indicates that externally there had been difficulties in its way which have left no other trace in the correspondence. From indignant words of Pontius we must also infer that some relics of the plague and the gallant service of the Church had lasted through the Council up to the moment of Cyprian's banishment[1]. But it comes as a surprise to find Cyprian's next letter written from exile to exiled brothers of the Council.

A sudden blow has fallen upon a large proportion of the Christian population—a renewal of persecution under which some died early, the heads of the society were expelled, and the youth of neither sex was spared.

Dionysius the Great was already in exile too, sent to Kephron by Æmilian himself[2]. Just when Africa was the least troubled part of the world, the success of the Third Council on Baptism seems to have been a prelude to destruction.

We will shortly speak of the confused circumstances which attended the outbreak.

---

[1] Pontii *Vit.* 11.
[2] The Acta Publica are quoted very fully by Dionysius ap. Euseb. *H. E.* vii.

11. See Note *on Kephron and the Lands of Kolluthion*, p. 463.

The new persecuting phase of Valerian's life was ascribed to the influence of Macrian[1]. These were two remarkable men. Valerian's purity and dignity of character had endeared him to Decius. At Decius' fantastic revival of the censorship, the senate, even if primed to choose him, did it with such acclamations as 'Pattern of old times,' 'Censor all his life,' 'Censor from a boy.' Trebellius adds that he would have been elected imperator by universal suffrage if such voting power had existed[2]. The Christian population honoured him. There were so many of themselves safe in his household, that they affectionately called it 'a Church of God[3].' In spite of a languid temperament he had been always admired for a characteristic insight in selecting men for great posts[4]. We have his own sketch of Macrian whom he chose to fill the closest place to himself[5].

He was made *Rationalis*, Chancellor of the Imperial Exchequer[6]. Though delicate in health, of luxurious habits, and perhaps crippled in person[7], Macrian was a man of the highest force of character and fertility of resource, of distinguished soldiership and influence with the armies in several countries, among them Africa, and of immense wealth. His martial sons were patterns of discipline. Like other agnostics of his time he was deeply impressed by the mysteries of the Egyptian 'Magi,' and is called by Dionysius their 'Archisynagogus,' which must at least mean an intimate and a patron[8]. The family had long kept up a kind of cultus of Alexander

---

[1] Zonaras xii. 24 says his name was Macrinus and his son's Macrianus. But the coins with the old bearded head have MACRIANUS as well as those with the young smooth face.

[2] Trebell. Pollio, ed. Peter, *Valeriani duo*, c. 5.

[3] Dionys. ap. Euseb. vii. 10.

[4] Treb. Poll. *Regilianus*. Nearly all his generals became emperors.

[5] Treb. Poll. *Macrianus*.

[6] ἐπὶ τῶν καθόλου λόγων βασιλέως (Dion. ap. Euseb. vii. 10), *i.e.* a Rationibus or Rationalis.

[7] ἀναπήρῳ τῷ σώματι, Dionysius ap. Euseb. vii. 10. Zonaras xii. 24 says θάτερον πεπήρωτο τῶν σκελῶν which perhaps is not a mere version of Dionysius as he has independent information about the family.

[8] Dionysius, ap. Euseb. vii. 10, says he did not recognise any Divine πρόνοια or κρίσις. As Dionysius was his contemporary and lived in Egypt he may have known what he was saying; which is very unlike Gibbon's version 'As

the Great, wearing his portrait in their embroideries and embossing it on their plate. As there was at Alexandria a ceremonial cultus of Alexander, this perhaps may indicate a traditional connection with Egypt. There was bitter war between the 'Magi' and the Christian Exorcists with their anti-dæmoniac powers. They enforced the common interpretation of the deepening calamities of the Empire, and Macrian prevailed on Valerian to be initiated in their mysteries[1]. His later effect on the reputation of Gallienus himself is compared rather stiltedly by Dionysius to that of a cloud hiding for awhile the sun[2].

Valerian's son Gallienus, or the conception of him, was a terrible product of the times. A polished rhetorician, and elegant composer, devoted personally to Plotinus[3], a scientific gardener withal, and a portent of heartless frivolity and sin. His clever wicked face on the medals[4] is in utter contrast to his father's clean massive head. Yet he had early received such impressions, strengthened possibly by a Christian marriage[5], that the language of Dionysius about him, immediately on the disappearance of Macrian, seems more than gratitude for his instant action in the repeal of Valerian's edict[6].

The persecution thus begun by the virtuous and stayed by

Macrian was an enemy to the Christians, they charged him with being a magician.'

[1] προέμενος in Dion. *Ep. ad Hermammon.*, ap. Euseb. vii. 23, means no other betrayal of Valerian by Macrian than the projecting him on the evil policy which led to his fall. The mistake arises from mixing up with it a spurious sentence in Trebellius '*ductu cujusdam sui ducis*' and fancying Macrian to be meant. His other expression ὑπὸ τούτου προαχθείς (ap. Euseb. vii. 10) has the same sense; Syncellus quoting it has ὑπὸ θεοῦ προαχθείς. Ed. Dind. p. 719.

[2] Euseb. vii. 23.

[3] ἐτίμησαν δὲ τὸν Πλωτῖνον μάλιστα καὶ ἐσέφθησαν Γαλιῆνός τε ὁ αὐτοκράτωρ καὶ ἡ τούτου γυνὴ Σαλωνίνα. Porphyr. *Vit. Plot.* xii.

[4] See plate xlviii. Grueber and Poole's *Roman Medallions in British Museum.*

[5] Sup. p. 280 n. Orosius (vii. 22) attributes his action to a sense of the Divine judgment on Valerian. According to Trebellius he was gratified by the event.

[6] Euseb. vii. 23 gives not Gallienus' original edict but the rescript applying it to Egypt. Ὁσιώτερος καὶ φιλοθεώτερος, in the light of the rest of the letter to

the infamous emperor fulfilled for Dionysius, by help of the key furnished in its exact apocalyptic duration of three and a half years[1], the vision of the Dragon's wrath against the Woman. To Optatus afterwards it seemed to be in connection so close with Decius' persecution that together they made up the terrific 'Lion' Vision of Daniel[2].

It is not common to find so total a revulsion from a tolerant policy except towards the end of a career, or unless some strong personal influences concur with some public difficulty. We see both elements at work when without warning or inquiry edict and rescript fell upon the Church.

The calamities which Macrian explained in his own way were indeed appalling. In the first *triennium* of Valerian (254—257) were felt the first death-pangs of the Empire.

This was 'The Uprising of Nations[3],' as Zonaras says truly,—raiders no more, but Peoples in irresistible advance. The confederate Franks who had been first met some years before by Aurelian at Mayence, and from there to the sea held all north of the Rhine, had streamed across Gaul, heeding no defeats, and were entering Spain. And now the whole vast moat of the Empire formed by Rhine and Danube, with Hadrian's wall and foss between them, then continued by the Black Sea and the Don, was overleapt and overswum at every point. The 'All-men' and the 'March-men' poured countlessly in, the former soon to reach Milan thirty thousand[4]

Hermammon, goes beyond official style. It is possible that Dionysius knew nothing of the personal life. It remains, I believe, problematical how far the scandalous chronicles of the emperors represent more than brutal popular imaginings.

[1] Dr Peters, p. 574, thinks Dionysius is speaking only of the East and that there was no persecution there until the 'second edict' (? the rescript) in A.D. 258, and infers that therefore the Eastern persecution lasted until the death of Macrian. It is most natural to suppose that Dionysius counts from the 'first edict' until Gallienus' edict of toleration, middle of 257 to end of 260. Besides, being himself banished to Kephron A.D. 257, he might fairly count the persecution to have begun by that time.

[2] Optat. iii. 8.

[3] Zonaras xii. 23 ...ἐθνῶν οὖν καὶ ἐπὶ τούτου γενομένης ἐπαναστάσεως....

[4] Zonar. xii. 24.

strong before any check came. The Goths imperilled Thessalonica[1]; a general defence of Greece had to be organized; Athens was refortified, the Isthmus walled across.

To Generals who mostly became Emperors in their day Gallienus committed Italy itself, Illyricum, and Thrace. These were infiltrated with tribes which left 'nothing unravaged' as they passed[2],—Borani, Gotthi, Carpi, Orugduni. He went himself to the protection of the Celtic tribes and found it expedient to marry a Teutonic chieftain's daughter[3], and to surrender part of Pannonia, making the first Roman cession[4] to Barbarism.

A.D. 257.
A.U.C. 1010. *Coss.*
Imp. Cæsar P. Licinius Egnatius Valerianus P. F. A. Germ. Max. IIII.
Imp. Cæsar P. Licinius Gallienus P. F. A. Germ. Max. Dac. Max. III.

About the middle of 257 Valerian marched to the East; for the same enterprising otherwise unknown Borani, whose sole contribution to civilisation was the overthrow of the past, came from the Dniester to Byzantium in flat boats which they there exchanged for Bosporan vessels, and scaring all the settlers of Pontus into the midlands and highlands struck straight for the rich city of Pityus. With all the resources of the great fort and harbour the baffling of them for a single year was a great feat on the part of Successianus. Next year they were to take it, and to take the populous Trapezus, to their own amazement, and they were followed up by tribe after tribe bent only on the annihilation of 'all beauty and all greatness.'

From the East the Persians or Parthians were not like the Northerners driven on from behind, but with a spontaneous lust of rapine they swept Mesopotamia and Syria for captives and spoil.

Africa for all its Berber raids was the safest portion of the Roman world.

---

[1] Zos. i. 29, Zonar. xii. 23, Sync. (Dindorf) p. 715. Whether the fortification of Thermopylæ was a fact seems to me questionable.

[2] μέρος οὐδὲν τῆς 'Ιταλίας ἢ τῆς 'Ιλλυρίδος καταλιπόντες ἀδῄωτον..., Zosim. i. 31.

[3] Sup. p. 300, n. 7.

[4] Gallus in 252 had promised annual subsidies to the Goths (ὑπέσχετο, Zosim. i. 24; exaggerated into σπένδεται by Zonar. xii. 21), but in 238 the Goths had already been receiving annual *stipendia*. See T. Hodgkin, *Italy and her Invaders*, (1892) vol. I. pp. 46 sqq.

The whole Empire was girt as with an ever-contracting ring of fire. No worse time of misery has ever hemmed in civilisation. The barbarian might at any moment be anywhere and the plague was everywhere. Macrian then was not the one persecutor. He was the voice and spirit of the Empire.

The essence of the Empire was unity. One army, one law, one senate. The adoration of the majesty of the Emperor with which no national or local worship interfered, was a necessity which grew more vital as the danger from without grew universal. The most tolerant of emperors could not deny that in the midst of all there was an ever-multiplying power, which defied the central unity. Another unity was growing up and growing everywhere which, as it would not adore Cæsar, could not, men thought, but make common cause with the violators from without. The very usurpers were less traitorous because their aim was at least to perpetuate in themselves the imperial unity. Whenever any stir directed imperial or popular attention to the Christians, there was visible in them an anti-Roman and therefore anti-human unity which was believed to compact itself by the darkest and most compromising bonds.

In every district it had its local chief about whom adherents rallied. Everywhere, even when they obediently abandoned their social evening meetings[1], even when the old theory of an 'illicit religion' could not be pressed consistently any longer, still everywhere unexplained 'conventus' met; any individual who obeyed the magistrate by sacrificing to the Majesty of Augustus evidently ceased to be a member of their corporation; and everywhere the cemeteries had a weird fascination for them; especially if there lay in them agents who had suffered the extreme penalty of the law.

---

[1] *Plin. et Traj. Epp.* 96 'Soliti stato die ante lucem convenire...rursusque coeundi ad capiendam cibum...quod ipsum facere desiisse post edictum meum, quo secundum mandata tua *hetaerias* esse vetueram.' See W. M. Ramsay, *Church in Roman Empire*, ch. x.

It was June 257 when Valerian set out for the East, a propitious moment for an able and popular minister of Macrian's views political and spiritual. By a despatch to the senate Valerian committed to him the military dispositions of the State[1]. In his hands was placed an Edict which emphasized the common law of the Empire, by enforcing these crucial particulars. The Christians were to be parted from their chiefs, to give up their meetings and never to visit the cemeteries.

Its operation was at first intended to be bloodless[2]. It was thought that the removal of their influential men from among them would leave the people to fall back into their old-fatherly natural ways[3]. Particulars were sent to the governors as to who should be separated. Dionysius, who was brought before the Præfect of Egypt[4], observed that Æmilian did not at once order him to hold no meetings[5], but in his simplicity desired him to give up being a Christian—as a ready way of ending the Christianity of the masses[6]. The Proconsular Acts record that when the Præfect had dwelt without effect on the unusual leniency with which the

---

[1] 'Ego bellum Persicum gerens Macriano totam rem p. credidi quidem a parte militari,' Treb. Pollio, *Trig. Tyr.* 12 ff. The appointment is made from the scene of war, not before Valerian's departure. It does not seem to have weakened Gallienus.

[2] Lactantius says Valerian 'shed much blood in a short time' (*De mort. Persecut.* v.). But in the first years 257, 8 it seems doubtful whether any blood was shed.

[3] It is quite touching to see in the Acta of the early trials how the magistrates always think the pantheon gods are the natural ones for all men.

[4] διέπων τὴν ἡγεμονίαν, Euseb. *H. E.* vii. 11, the viceroy in whose hand was the whole civil and military power. It was only in title that he was lower than proconsul or procurator, because Egypt was incorporated abnormally in the Empire, and was administered by the personal staff of Augustus and his successors.

[5] Αἰμιλιανὸς δὲ οὐκ εἶπέ μοι προηγουμένως μὴ σύναγε. Euseb. vii. 11.

[6] With him were convened (according to the *Acta Publica*) the presbyter Maximus, who succeeded him in the see, Faustus a martyr in extreme old age under Diocletian, Eusebius afterwards Bishop of Laodicea, Chæremon, three Deacons who had survived their terrific service in the plague (sup. p. 244) and Marcellus, probably one of the Romans whom he mentions (Euseb. *l.c.*). These seem also to have accompanied his exile.

Emperors were ready to condone his past if he would conform, he gave him a final injunction to convene no assemblies, and to enter no 'so-called cœmeteries[1].' Meantime without a day's respite for his malady he was to convey[2] himself to Kephron—a wretched place, whose very name was new to him, on the edge of the Desert. There his people were at first chased and pelted, but out of the unpromising elements around them, with the help of a confluence of visitors from Egypt, they formed a fresh mission. He was then brought nearer Alexandria, to be within reach if wanted again. This was to 'The Lands of Kolluthion,' a disreputable place on the high road, worried with caravans and freebooters—on which account Dionysius calls it 'more Libyan' than Kephron[3]. But he was also more accessible to friends from the city, who came and stayed with him. They held regular 'Synagogues' there, as in other outlying posts, and so opened yet another mission. These details and contrasts fill up for us what happened about the same time to Cyprian[4], though there is no mention of the month in which Dionysius was sentenced.

On Kephron and The Lands of Kolluthion.

These places, unnamed by geographers, may be too insignificant to be ever identified, but points about them which can be made out from Eusebius (*H. E.* vii. 11) are of interest as touching life. *Kephron* was outside Mareotis, which in Roman times was a nome (Böckh, *C. I. G.* III. p. 316), and its chief place, Marea (*Meri*), on the west of the lake. Kephron was εἰς τὰ μέρη τῆς Λιβύης. A poor village, so far from Alexandria that people who wanted to follow Dionysius (ἀδελφῶν ἑπομένων) had to take

---

[1] Euseb. *l.c.*: οὐδαμῶς δὲ ἐξέσται οὔτε ὑμῖν οὔτε ἄλλοις τισὶν ἢ συνόδους ποιεῖσθαι, ἢ εἰς τὰ καλούμενα κοιμητήρια εἰσιέναι. In this phrase he possibly objects to the old-fashioned word, as much as to the fact that (as he knew) the cemeteries were to them much else.

[2] On the penalty *Deportatio* see infr. note on 'Cyprian's treatment.' The penalty was death for not going to exile at the appointed time. *Digesta*, 48, 19, 4.

[3] Εἰς τὰ Κολλυθίωνος.

[4] It is curious that Eusebius vii. 11 assigns to this Valerian persecution the rough transportation and rescue of Dionysius which he has himself quoted rightly under the Decian visitation, vi. 40.

up their abode there (...πολλὴ συνεπεδήμησεν ἡμῖν ἐκκλησία). It was convenient for other parts of Egypt. 'The Lands, or Parts, of Kolluthion,' Τὰ Κολλουθίωνος, were within the Mareotes. It was no place for residents; 'rougher and more Libyan' than Kephron; which refers less to mileage than to wildness. For it was nearer Alexandria (...γειτνιᾷ μᾶλλον τῇ πόλει, &c.), and a frequented station (probably a night station) ὁδοιπορούντων ἐνοχλήσεσι on a high road, so that the Præfect could readily re-arrest him, and his visitors could come easily and stay the night (ἀναπαύσονται). He compares it to προάστεια, which were often miles from the head-place (Valesius, *note on Euseb. l.c.*). It was γνωριμώτερος καὶ συνηθέστερος than Kephron to the Exile. Now in the Decian persecution he had been exiled to a 'dismal, dirty' place (ἐρῆμος καὶ αὐχμηρὸς) three miles east of Parætonium, and, though Eusebius confusedly quotes his letter about that exile as if it referred to this one, yet this fact suggests that the 'Lands of Kolluthion' may lie somewhere on the same 'road' from Alexandria to Cyrene. Nicephorus, *H. E.* vi. 10, has muddled Eusebius more.

Koluthus, Kolluthus, Kephron were Egyptian personal names (Giorgi, *Fragm. Copticum ex actis S. Coluthi*, 1781; *de Miraculis S. Coluthi*, 1793. Epiphan. *Hær.* 69).

It is curious that a pyramid is called from Kephren, while a paw of the Sphinx bears the inscription Τὸ Κολλυθίωνος προσκύνημα (Letronne, *Inscr. Gr. et L. de l'Égypte*, II. p. 478, D. xxxix.). That neighbourhood seems too far off.

2. *Treatment of Cyprian.*

Aug. 30. At Carthage Cyprian was sent for on the 30th of August (the day before the accession of Xystus at Rome) to the Proconsul's private office or *Secretarium*—a room of audience which for less popular trials now generally superseded the noisy forum and crowded basilica. What was afterwards secured as a right to distinguished provincials, that they should be seated, during their trial, in the *secretarium* of the judge[1], was

[1] *Cod. Justin.* 3, 24, 3. Of all the Christian trials up till Cyprian's in Ruinart's *Acta Sincera* in which the scene of the trial is named, it is always the forum, the tribunal, or before the multitude. Only in the case of the Scillitan martyrs, a later Christian account says that the trial was held in the Secretarium, while the Proconsular Acts say that it was 'statuto forensi conventu' and 'Proconsul...sedens pro tribunali.' Montanus and his companions, a few months after Cyprian, are taken to and fro in the Forum till the 'Præses' decides to hear them in the Secretarium. (Ruinart, *Passio SS. Montani, Lucii*...vi.)

no doubt conceded much earlier by usage. Cyprian was at any rate heard in this less public way,—though probably with open doors. An undoubtedly genuine document of the Proconsular Acts reports the following spirited and mutually somewhat sarcastic conversation which was held there[1].

The Proconsul Aspasius Paternus opened thus:—

The most sacred Emperors Valerian and Gallien have done me the honour to send me a Despatch in which they have directed that persons not following the Roman religion must conform[2] to the Roman ceremonies. I have in consequence made enquiries as to how you call yourself[3]. What answer have you to give me?

Cyprian the Bishop said:

I am a Christian, and a Bishop. I know no other Gods but the one and true God who made heaven and earth, the sea, and all that is in them. He is the God whom we Christians wholly serve. Him we supplicate night and day for ourselves and for all men and for the safety of the Emperors themselves.

Paternus. In this purpose then you persevere?

Cyprian. That a good purpose, formed in the knowledge of God, should be altered is not possible.

Paternus (*sneering at Cyprian's last word*). Well, will it be 'possible' for you, in accordance with the directions[4] of Valerian and Gallien, to take your departure as an exile to the city of Curubis?

Cyprian did not condescend to meet the sneer with more than one word—I depart.

But Paternus wished to know something else.—They have done me the honour of writing to me not about bishops only,

---

[1] Pontius does not report this, observing 'sunt acta quæ referant,' *Vit.* 11.

[2] *Recognoscere:* prefix *re* does not at this stage of language imply *return to*, as the Oxford translator has it.

[3] *De nomine tuo;* explained by the answer.

[4] *Præceptum. Act. Proc.* 1 C. '...immutari non potest. P. poteris ergo secundum præceptum...' *præcipere* and *præceptum* the constant term. So *Passio SS. Pionii et sociorum ejus*, iii. (Ruinart).

but about presbyters too. I would therefore know from you who are the presbyters that reside in this city.

The old jurist had his turn. *Cyprian.* You have by your own laws made good serviceable regulations against the very existence[1] of informers. Accordingly it is not in my power to discover and delate them. However they will be found in their several cities.

Paternus. My question refers to this day and this place.

Cyprian. Inasmuch as our discipline forbids any to offer themselves spontaneously, and this would also go counter to your legislation, they are unable to offer themselves; but if you search for them, they are to be found.

Paternus. I shall have them found—and he added 'They 'have directed further that no assemblies are to be held, and 'that they are not to enter cemeteries. So if any one fails to 'observe this salutary direction he will be capitally punished.'

Cyprian the Bishop replied, Do as you are directed.

Thereupon Paternus sentenced the Blessed Bishop Cyprian to be 'deported' into exile[2].

This was a sentence which carried with it loss of citizenship[3]. Provincial Governors could not inflict it without special

---

[1] Trajan in his Rescript to Pliny (*Plin. et Traj. Epp.* 97) allows Christians to be delated (though not by anonymous accusation) and punished. But Pliny *Panegyr.* 34, 35 gives an account of Trajan's vengeance on *delatores* in general.

Hadrian *ad Minuc. Fundan.* orders *delati* to be punished if guilty, but calumnious *delatores* more severely. Otto, *Justini mart. opera*, vol. I. p. 192— Euseb. iv. 9.

M. Antoninus Pius, *Ep. ad Commune Asiæ* (fictitious, possibly preserving a fact), orders the *delator* to be punished and the *delatus* to be pardoned. M. Aurelius *Ep. ad Senatum* (also spurious) similarly and more strongly. Both are attached to Justin Martyr's *Apologia*: Otto, vol. I. pp. 244, 246. See Euseb. iv. 13, who says Melito quoted the former, but?

An instance of the punishment of a *delator* occurs in the martyrdom of Apollonius A.D. 188 under Commodus. Ruinart, *de S. Apoll. Martyre*, iv.

[2] Jussit in exilium deportari, *Act. Proc.* 2.

[3] Ulpian ap. *Digesta*, 48, 19, 2; 48, 22, 6. I hesitate to understand Ulpian in 48, 22, 14 'Deportatio et civitatem *et bona* adimit' to mean that Deportatio in every case involved forfeiture of goods *ipso facto*. For not only does Marcian, *Dig.* 48, 22, 15, say

direction from the Emperor. Paternus quoted the 'præcept' of Valerian and Gallien for assigning him to Curubis, just as we saw that Æmilian did for sending Dionysius to Kephron[1]. Deportation meant properly to an island. But, as in the case of Relegation, isolated places might be named as well as islands, and in Egypt an oasis, for the scene of exile[2].

Cyprian was allowed time for his arrangements and on September 14[3] reached Curubis, an out-of-the-way, clean, pleasant, well-walled little coast town, about fifty miles from Carthage[4], in a lonely, not savage district, at the back of the great eastward promontory of the Gulf of Tunis. It crowned a low hill, sunny and green, a quarter of an hour's walk from the shore[5]. A torrent beside it scooped out a little harbour, since silted up[6]. In front glowed the island of Kossyra, set in illimitable blue. Its amenities were completed by an aqueduct, which still strides across the torrent bed.

Colonia Julia Curubis. Κουροβὶς Ptol. Libera Curubis Plin. Kourba.

The isolation however was great[7]. The town was some twenty miles from Clypea to its north and twelve from Neapolis

'libertatem retinet, et jure civili caret, gentium vero utitur. Itaque emit, vendit, locat, conducit, permutat, fœnus exercet aliaque similia,' but in the two former passages Ulpian himself does not say as much, but speaks of citizenship only; and I do not see how that could be reconciled with Cyprian's condition, which is an excellent case. He while in '*deportatio*' largely relieved other sufferers (*Epp.* 77, 78, 79), and by order he returned to his own *Horti*, which had therefore not been confiscated during his year of absence. *Acta proc.* 2; Pont. *Vit.* 15. In his dream also, Pont. *Vit.* 13, he asks leave 'res meas legitima ordinatione disponere.' Cyprian's own expression in *Ep.* 76, which is likely to be as technically precise as the Acta, is 'relegatum.'

[1] τοῦτον γὰρ τὸν τόπον ἐξελεξάμην ἐκ τῆς κελεύσεως τῶν σεβαστῶν ἡμῶν, Euseb. vii. 11.

[2] Sed et in eas partes provinciæ, quæ sunt desertiores, scio præsides solitos relegare. *Digesta*, 48, 22, 7.

[3] Eo die quo in exilii loco mansimus, Pont. *Vit.* c. 12. eo die post exactum annum, *id.* 13. die octava decima Kal. Oct., *Act. Proc.* 3 and 6, *i.e.* 14*th Sep.* In the Roman Kalendar, the feast of Cyprian is now Sept. 16th. See p. 620.

[4] One does not know where Dr Peters thinks it was; 'er hatte zur Reise von Karthago bis hieher ungefähr vierzehn Tage gebraucht,' p. 577. Two very short days at the most sufficed. Cf. infr. p. 479, note 3.

[5] Tissot, vol. II. p. 134.

[6] Sir Grenville Temple, vol. II. p. 13.

[7] The Bishops, *Ep.* 77. 2, call it 'in deserto loco' for all its pleasantness.

to the south. It had with them followed the lead of Hadrumetum, and made terms with the Roman invaders at once, and been dignified therefore as a Julian Colony. People of the Freedman class rose easily to its chief magistracy[1], and have left tokens of their loyalty in its improvements.

But beyond such loneliness as this, and of course entire uncertainty as to the future, Cyprian had no hardship to complain of. Some of his household accompanied him, and his devoted grandiloquent deacon Pontius, who tells us through many affected lines that, though as Christians they would have equally enjoyed some place like Kephron, yet he found the shore not too rocky nor too lonely nor too pathless, the woods green and the waters wholesome, as sunny and as adequate a retreat as he could desire even for so great a man's privacy, while constant visitors rejoiced to supply every need[2].

He cannot nevertheless forbear from remarking that although to themselves exile was no felt penalty yet the guilt was extreme[3] of those who inflicted it as a severe punishment on the innocent.

Among these odd observations we catch flashes so like Cyprian's language that we may count them as fragments of his conversation. To the heathen 'their country and their ' uniting name are exceeding dear—*we* recoil even from parents ' if their counsel is against the Lord.' 'To the Christian all this world is one house.' 'The sincere servant of God is a stranger in his own city.' Maxims which, misunderstood, went far to explain why Christians were fancied to be bad patriots. It was not possible yet for them to be at home in a pagan polity as religious as their own. But Pontius himself dwells excellently on Cyprian's sense of civic obligation[4].

---

[1] *Corp. Inscrr. Lat.* vol. VIII. i. pp. 127 ff. It seems to have had one so-called 'Duovir.'

[2] Loci gratiam, &c., Pont. *Vit.* c. 11; apricum et competentem, 12 &c. Murum oppidi totum ex saxo quadrato. *Corp. Inscrr. Lat.* VIII. i. 977.

[3] Ultimum crimen et pessimum nefas. Pont. *Vit.* 11.

[4] Pont. *Vit.* c. 11 'illis patria nimis

His love of conversation was strong as ever. He wished he might die talking—talking of God[1].

One conversation Pontius gives word for word. And a singular story it is—the authentic narrative of one of those visions which he himself regarded, and not unnaturally, with deep reverence.

It is not surprising that on the first night on which he slept in Curubis he dreamt about the Proconsul.

'The day we stopped at the place of banishment, before I went fast asleep there stood before me a young man of immensely superhuman stature. He led me as if to the Prætorium[2], and I thought I was brought up to the Tribunal where sate the Proconsul. As soon as he looked up at me, he at once began to note down on his tablet some sentence of which I knew nothing, for he had not asked me anything in the usual way of enquiry. But the young man who stood behind him read with great attention whatever it was that was entered there. And as he could not speak with me from where he was, he set forth by significant gestures what was going on in the way of writing upon that said tablet. He opened out his hand quite flat like a broadsword blade[3], and imitated the stroke given in an ordinary execution. He expressed what he meant me to understand as well as with the clearest speech. I understood it

---

cara et commune nomen est [cum parentibus]: nos et parentes ipsos, si contra Dominum suaserint abhorremus.' H. The reading is interesting. Some dull African, not catching the construction of the former clause and thinking that 'et parentes ipsos' required a previous mention of parents, inserted *cum parentes* after *est*, in bold native syntax, which is the reading of all the MSS. A duller than he amended it into *cum parentibus*. Cf. *De montibus Sina et Sion*, c. 8 'cum imperatorem et regem suum,' c. 9 'tabulam cum nomen regis Judæorum.'

Pontius in recalling his organization to meet the plague dwells most markedly on Cyprian's zeal 'pro civitatis salute' and for the good of 'respublica' and 'patria.'

[1] ...cupido sermonis, Pont. *Vit.* 14.

[2] The site of the Prætorium at Carthage is fairly to be identified on the eastern slope of the Byrsa. See Tissot, vol. I. pp. 649 ff.

[3] Spata, spatha (Pont. *Vit.* 12), the broad sword used in executions—so called from its shape like the σπάθη of the loom. Thence all Romance words spada, espada, épée, and our spade.

would be sentence of death. I began to ask and sue without stopping, that I might have even one day's reprieve allowed me, till I could arrange my affairs with due method. And after I had frequently renewed my entreaties, he began again to make some note or other on his tablet. However from the calmness of his expression I gathered that my Judge's mind was moved as feeling mine a reasonable approach. And besides, that same youth who awhile back had given me the token of my passion[1], by gesture rather than language, now nodding again and again on the sly, hasted to convey to me, by twisting his fingers together one behind another, that the reprieve for the morrow which I asked for was conceded. I must say that though no sentence had been read I recovered my senses with a very glad heart of rejoicing over the reprieve I received. And yet through the dread of uncertainty as to the interpretation I trembled so, that the remains of the terror made my heart still throb with absolute quivering.'

His candour about the fright it gave him shows a trustworthy witness to a really remarkable dream, for *that very day* year it came to pass. 'The Morrow' became a household word with them—meaning the day when he should suffer—borrowed from the dream[2]. For the present his waking was to a day of very stern suffering and business cares.

There is no doubt that Cyprian's rank procured him special exemptions, while it is also certain that as yet there was no general persecution, but rather a Roman confidence in moral decapitation; a belief that the removal of the Bishops and the making examples of them would be the extinction of Christian life. The 'artistic cruelty' is commented on with which two years later, even before they had to suffer, the Clergy were shut up while various temptations and

---

[1] Passionis, Pont. *Vit.* 12.   crastinus'; 15 'sed crastinus dies ille...
[2] Pont. *Vit.* 13 'proximabat dies   vere crastinus.'

terrors were applied to the layfolk[1]. Cyprian must have felt much sorrow—even if it was an exultant sorrow—over the miseries and courage of brethren upon whom he had drawn so much attention both by his Councils and by his constant magnifying of their office.

3. *Numidian Bishop-Confessors.*

Whether others were exiled at the same time, or what happened to the Presbyters for whom Paternus asked, we have no record[2]. If it was difficult to be severe when the Bishop of Carthage had fared so differently at his hands from even the Bishop of Alexandria, under the Præfect of Egypt, the lenity was made up for to the extreme when the Province after the Proconsul's death fell under a Deputy. And the President of Numidia had no such scruples[3].

Nine[4] of the thirty-one Numidian bishops who had sat in

---

[1] Ruinart, *Passio SS. Jacobi et Mariani...*, x. This document, written by the friend who received these martyrs with others in his villa near Cirta, where their commemorative inscription is still on the well-known rock, and the Passion of Montanus and Lucius and other Clergy of Carthage, partly written by themselves just after Cyprian's death, are full of points of greatest interest. Ruinart, *Passio SS. Montani, Lucii et all. Mm. Afr.*

[2] As Theogenes of Hippo was martyred, as well as Successus of Abbir germaniciana and Paulus of Obba, after Cyprian (cp. Aug. *Serm.* 273, and *Passio Montani* xii. with *Sentt. Epp.* 14, 16, 47 and *Epp.* 76, 80), they had most likely been exiled previously. These identifications may not amount to certainty.

[3] *Passio Montani* ii., iii., vi.

[4] 'Nemesiano, Felici, Lucio, alteri Felici, Litteo, Poliano, Victori, Iaderi, Dativo,' &c., *Ep.* 76, cf. *Epp.* 77, 78, 79. These nine confessor bishops were, I think, probably all from Numidian sees. Nemesian of Thubunæ, Litteus of Gemellæ, Polianus of Mileou, Iader of Midili and Dativus of Vada certainly were. Besides these, two were named Felix, one Lucius and one Victor. Of seven named Felix in the Council two had Numidian sees, Bagai and Bamaccora. Two Lucii attended it, and one of these had the Numidian see of Castra Galbæ. There were two Victors, one of whom was bishop of Octavu(s), and there was a see of that name (or Octava) in Numidia, where was the massacre by Circumcellions (Optatus iii. c. 4), as well as an Octavum or Octavum in the Byzacene. Mark also that Felix Jader and Polianus in *Ep.* 79 send greeting to Eutychianus who was a Numidian, *Ep.* 70. The writers of

the Council are seen a little later at chained labour in the mines. Their treatment had been severe and ignominious. Some had died under it[1], some were in prison. They had been beaten with cudgels, which gives the estimate of their rank as below the middle class of society[2].

Others were brought to Cirta for execution two years later after having been a long while in banishment[3].

Those to whom with presbyters and others Cyprian now writes toiled in the dark at piles of ore, choked with the smoke[4] of smelting furnaces, half-fed, half-clothed, half their

Ep. 77, Nemesian, Dativus, Felix and Victor, also speak as having been tried before the Præses, *i.e.* of Numidia, whereas Cyprian had been before the *Proconsul* of Africa.

The use of *Præses* here illustrates what Mommsen calls 'Nominum inconstantia.' The title *Præses* of Numidia was used in this third century under Septimius Severus (or Caracalla), *C. I. L.* vol. x. i. 6569, and also under Alexander Severus, vol. VIII. i. 2753, 8328 (cf. Index, vol. VIII. ii. p. 1067). Previously Numidia had been under a *Legatus Augusti* of consular or highest prætorian rank. From Gordian to Gallus it was governed only by a *procurator*, a knight. Again in our time under Valerian and Gallien the old status was restored; we have VIII. i. 2615 *Leg. Augg. pr. pr.*; and 2634 *Leg. Auggg. pr. pr.* in A.D. 253 (according to date in Mommsen's Index, if this does not rather belong to the time of Septimius Severus). *Præses* was again in use under Constantine, with consular rank, VIII. i. 2729. See VIII. i. pp. xvi, xviii. It is then interesting to find *præses* here used as the habitual name, though not appearing officially on the monuments of this time.

In the Province itself the *Procurator* (referred to in the text) who administered it for a time after the death of Galerius Maximus is called *Præses* in the contemporary *Passio SS. Montani, Lucii...*,ii., iii., vi. *Passio SS. Jacobi, Mariani...*, iii. (Ruinart).

[1] *Ep.* 76. 1 'martyrii sui consummatione.'

[2] Fustibus cæsi, *Ep.* 76. 2.—Non omnes fustibus cædi solent, sed hi dumtaxat qui liberi sunt et quidem tenuiores homines: honestiores vero fustibus non subjiciuntur...*Dig.* 48. 19. 28. *Flagella* used for slaves only, together with *pœna vinculorum, Dig.* 48. 19. 10. As Cyprian speaks of *traversaria* simply as making the feet *cunctabundi*, these are perhaps some kind of moveable stocks. Ducange in his 19*th Dissertation on Joinville's Life of S. Louis* (Glossarium, [Niort. 1887, vol. x. p. 63]) describes it as a beam through holes in which the feet were drawn wide apart in the torture of the cippus.

[3] Secundinus probably of Cedias *Sentt. Epp.* 11 and Agapius 'jamdudum in exsilia submotos...ab exsilio perducebantur.' *Passio SS. Jacobi, Mariani...* iii.

[4] *Ep.* 77. 3. Cyprian seems to have imagined them as gold and silver mines, *Ep.* 76. 2, but none such are traced in that region. Copper there may have been. See Tissot, vol. I. p. 258.

hair clipt off, sleeping on the ground. Dragged too from the bright towns elsewhere described, the cleanly Romans sadly missed their baths[1].

They were somewhat more than kept alive by the liberality of Cyprian, in his banishment, and of his lay-friend Quirinus for whom he compiled and classified the *Testimonia*.

The sub-deacon Herennianus[2], with three acolytes, Lucan, Maximus and Amantius, conveyed his letter and distributed the help. They brought back answers from three separated groups of confessors. One, the seventy-eighth, is dated from the mine of Sigus about five-and-twenty miles south-south-east of Cirta, in Numidia. The place is well known though it was never important, but the mines have not yet been rediscovered[3].

The lessons of the former persecution seem not to have been lost. There is no lament as yet over lapsed brethren, though here at least the persecution was general[4].

Parts of Cyprian's letter to them are less happy than anything he has written since the high-flown language addressed to the Decian martyrs. Humour seems to fail him when he finds himself amid practical pathos. It surely was grim comfort in the stocks to have their suffering feet apostrophized, to be bidden forget the labour of extracting silver or gold ores because they were themselves vessels of silver and gold, and so were at home in a gold mine. But once free of such fashionable quips, he is himself in his contrasts of 'captive body and kingly heart,' the 'body of this humiliation and the

---

[1] A characteristic touch, *Ep.* 76. 2.

[2] *Ep.* 77. 3. The same no doubt through whom a year later Lucian supplies the Carthaginian prisoners with food, *Pass. Montan.* ix.

[3] Respublica Siguitanorum, *hod.* Ziganieh; Playfair, p. 113, near Bordj ben Zekri. *C. I. L.* VIII. i. p. 552. Several roads met there, it has yielded many inscriptions, and has megalithic monuments which probably are not very ancient. *Ann. Arch. de Constantine*, 1863, p. 21.

If *metallum Siguensem* is right which Hartel gives from a right valuation of MSS. we have an African form.

[4] *Ep.* 76. 6. Later on some fell, repented and were treated on Cyprian's lines. *Passio Montani* xiv.

body of His brightness,' the impossibility of binding the free mind, or spoiling the shrines of the Spirit. And nothing is nobler than the breadth with which he bids them not be moved at their inability to 'offer and celebrate the sacrifices of God,' seeing that in their own persons they actually are 'His holy immaculate victims.'

Their grateful answers are in a simple strain except when they echo his. They feel his intense sympathy, they value his exposition of 'hidden sacraments,' they tell him how they had been fortified for their own hearing before the Præses, by reading the *Acta* of his trial and behaviour before the Proconsul[1]. At present they know him to be 'in a desert place in exile[2].'

4. 'OF ENCOURAGEMENT TO CONFESSORSHIP.'

One occupation of the forced leisure of Curubis, I think, we may trace with fair certainty. The Book commonly called OF ENCOURAGEMENT TO CONFESSORSHIP[3], but originally TO FORTUNATUS, has been already considered in its place in Cyprian's philosophy of life[4]. As to its form it will be remembered that he calls it 'no treatise but material for treating.' It is to meet the wants of teachers. It is a Manual to sustain faith and fortitude in persecution—as in placid times there are Manuals of Communion. He calls it a *Compendium* of *Capitula*, passages arranged under *Tituli*. These 'Titles' are most systematic, but the handling of them is not uniform nor compact. At first the texts are neatly and briefly woven together by a clever thread of connection and comment. But the comments grow longer and more

---

[1] *Ep.* 77. 1, 2.
[2] *Ep.* 77. 2.
[3] DE EXHORTATIONE MARTYRII like Tertullian's *De exhortatione castitatis*. It is quoted by Jerome, *Ep.* 48 *ad Pammachium* c. 19, but in the older editions is attributed to Hilary by an odd traceable blunder.
[4] Sup. c. VI. iii. p. 264.

diffuse and pass into argument and rhetoric, until on the Maccabees, we have almost a sermon with a prefatory note on the number 'Seven.'

It contains no single expression which implies that the storm of persecution had burst. But the atmosphere throughout is charged with the feeling that persecution is imminent and certain[1]. The false certificates of having sacrificed, *libelli*, are spoken of in the way of warning, without mention of people having accepted or refused them[2]. These conditions together seem to fit only the time after the first edict of Valerian when, after a long peace, the persecution which had begun with the bishops, could not be expected to confine itself to them; when there was need of a vigorous and substantial monition, but no opportunity for a very finished one. Again, this is the last-mentioned subject of Cyprian's pen in the quasi-catalogue of Pontius[3].

Accordingly, we attribute this 'Compendium' to the respite of Curubis with its daily increasing danger.

5. *Rome—Accession of XYSTUS and his immunity.*

On August the 2nd Stephanus had died at Rome, after the Edict was out; a circumstance which fell in with the later notion that he was martyred[4]. On the 31st, the day after Cyprian's trial at Carthage, he was succeeded by XYSTUS[5].

Aug. 2, A.D. 257.

Aug. 31.

---

[1] *Ad Fortunat. Præf.* c. 4. The Church is an army in camp before battle. Cf. c. 1 *incumbit*, c. 2 *præparare*.

The *ad Demetrianum*, which has been edited in juxtaposition with the *ad Fortunatum*, was written under raging persecution (*ad Demetr.* 12, 13). The 'recent lesson' of defeat (*ad D.* c. 17) fits the catastrophe of Decius, but not of Valerian whose overthrow was followed by the cessation of persecution.

[2] Libelli, *ad Fortun.* c. 11.

[3] Pontii *Vit.* c. 6.

[4] The notion has indeed come down so late as to possess Mgr. Freppel, pp. 473, 477, and Dr Peters, p. 503.

[5] Aug. 31. In *Acta Stephani* (Bolland) the date given is viiii. *Kal. Sept.*, Aug. 24. But this is inconsistent with the more valuable *Liberian Catalogue* which (corrected by the omission of the 'two years' arising perhaps from

The traditional image of Xystus in hymn, prayer and memorial is a distinct one. An Athenian, a philosopher, a great Teacher[1]. It is acutely and learnedly maintained by the eminent scholar Dr Adolph Harnack that we have a hitherto unrecognised example of that teaching in the nameless Epistle TO NOVATIAN. The theory if just would throw such light and colour upon his figure, although not upon the immediate crisis we are in, that it is necessary to reserve the question for separate discussion[2]. In his eleven months Dionysius wrote Xystus three epistles on Baptism; one representing the sentiments and decisions of the Eastern Bishops and the unreasonable conduct of Stephanus towards them; again, asking his counsel[3] rather earnestly in a case of heretical baptism which he himself had not thought well to repeat; and lastly giving him a long dissertation on the whole question[4].

Xystus no doubt followed Stephen's opinion, but as Pontius, not without a thrust at the dead lion, calls him 'a good and pacific Priest[5],' it is clear that he did not hold Stephen's language about Cyprian.

How it befel that all the time of the removal under the Edict of other Bishops into banishment or degrading

---

'Xystus ii.') gives xi *m* vi *d* for his episcopate. There is no doubt of the day of his death, Aug. 6, 258. See Lightfoot, *Apostolic Fathers*, P. I. S. *Clement of Rome*, vol. I. p. 290 (ed. 1890).

[1] Thus the *Sacramentarium Leonianum* viii. id. Aug. III. (Muratori, *op. cit.* I. 390) 'qui ad eandem gloriam promerendam doctrinæ suæ filios incitabat et quos erudiebat hortatu præveniebat exemplo.' 'Ambrosian' Hymn (H. A. Daniel, *Thesaurus Hymnolog.* 1855, I. no. XCI.) 'Ortus Athenis et altus Philosophorum studiis Mutavit artem artium Præceptor apostolicus.' The *graffito* in the cemetery of Prætextatus represented him in his chair with a hearer at his feet, and in the chair he died (infra p. 490).

[2] *Ad Novatianum*, Hartel, vol. III. p. 52. See Appendix below, p. 557.

[3] συμβουλή.

[4] His second, fifth and sixth Baptismal letters, Euseb. *H. E.* vii. 5, 9.

[5] Pont. *Vit.* 14. Dr Peters, with ultramontane penetration, thinks the expression must be due to Xystus' having informally reconciled Cyprian to the Church, an event which must have occurred, though our documents are all so defective as to omit it, or else Cyprian could never have been canonised.

X. I. 5. ACCESSION OF XYSTUS AND HIS IMMUNITY.

confinement Xystus was unmolested at Rome, is more than we know. Concealment was then a part of church life. Can the magistracy have lain so long under the impression that, through terror of the law whose appearance coincided so nearly with Stephen's death, the See remained unfilled as it had done for a longer interval under similar circumstances after Fabian's death? It is difficult to think that Gallienus had sufficient influence in Macrian's presence to keep the edict so long suspended. Yet when he afterwards repealed Valerian's laws we observe that he took credit for some previous protection of the Church[1]. However that may be Xystus was untouched, and even at Rome not inactive, as we shall see, until a new order was fulminated.

II. 1. THE RESCRIPT.

Fragments of two very different imperial documents belonging to the year 258 are in our hands. One was drawn at Byzantium, the other is generally, it may be groundlessly, said to have been issued on the same occasion.

The year before Valerian had promised to make Aurelian and Ulpius Crinitus consuls on May 22, in the room of himself and Gallien his son. At a brilliant review which he held at Byzantium he did make Aurelian consul, addressing him in the great Thermæ in a fulsome yet deserved panegyric, and conferring on him in the presence of his troops and the 'Palatine Staff[2]' decorations quadrupled and quintupled, to match the allowances previously assigned him to enable him as a poor man to support the consular burdens. For Ulpius

A.D. 258.
A.U.C. 1011.
Coss. Memmius Tuscus...Pomponius Bassus.

---

[1] I have pointed this out, p. 304, n. 4.

[2] *Officium Palatinum*, Fl. Vopiscus *Aurelianus* c. 13. [Organized by Hadrian, Aurel. Vict. *Epit.* xiv. Ap. Scrr. Byzz. τάξις βασιλική, Theophan. Contin. iii.

43. So also τάξις ἐκκλησιαστική.] An intermediate sense of the word *officium* occurs in Pliny *Epp.* i. 5, 11, 'me convenit in prætoris officio,' *i.e.* 'office, business room.' Cf. *Act. Maximiliani M.* c. i. (Ruinart).

Crinitus, the richest man of his times, he did nothing that day except make him adopt that great soldier of fortune, then fresh from his Gothic victories, as his son.

There is no subsequent interval in which Valerian could have kept great state there, either when he was resettling Antioch or while he was dragging about upon the chance of lighting on 'Scythians.' But in fact Memmius Tuscus was with him there as Consul Ordinarius[1], and as he entered on his office on the first of January that year, there is no doubt about the year[2]. If Valerian kept to the day he had named our First Fragment is the 'Court Circular' of May 22. Vopiscus extracted it from the Act Book of Acholius, Master of Presentations[3], or Lord Chamberlain, to the Emperor.

It was an extraordinary levée of great captains, who might scarcely have been expected to leave their tremendous charges even to receive Valerian. Upon his right sat the Præfect of the Prætorium, who as Principal 'Secretary of State' or medium of communication, and second person in the Empire ever since Titus held the office under his father[4], was always with the Court. This was now Bæbius Macer. Next to him sat the Præses of the East, Q. Ancarius.

On the left sat in the russet tunics of their office[5] the great Wardens of the Marches, the *Duces* or special commanders of the *Limites* or fortified frontiers. There was the *Dux* of the Scythian frontier, Avulnius Saturninus; of the frontier of the East, Iulius Trypho; of the Illyrian and Thracian frontier, Ulpius Crinitus himself; and Fulvius Boius of the Rhætian: above Trypho however sat the Præfect

---

[1] As distinct from the honorary consuls.

[2] Fl. Vopiscus, *Aurelianus*, c. 11.

[3] Magister admissionum, Vopisc. *Aurelianus*, c. 12.

Other indications seem to put the day later, and Ulpius Crinitus speaks of himself as having already become what Aurelian was now to be made, a *Vir consularis*. Neither of them appears in consular lists, and Valerian and Gallien did not resign. However the custom already existed of creating *consulares* who had not been consuls.

[4] Aurel. Victor, *de Cæsar.* 9.

[5] ?tunicas ducales russas, Vopisc. *Aurel.* c. 13.

Designate of Egypt, Murrentius Mauricius, and next below him Mæcius Brundisinus, Præfect of the Corn-Supply (*Annona*) of the East.

It has been usually concluded that this Court at Byzantium had something to do with altering the character and increasing the severity of the persecution[1]. Why, is hard to see. This was not business which concerned a great Review. The Emperor's own Rescript could equally well emanate at any point of his marches or halts. It was not till a week after the 6th of August that Cyprian, who had people at Rome on the watch for information, was able to learn that a new and cruel Rescript had arrived there and had instantly been put in force[2]. Certainly then if the Byzantine pageant was held on May 22, we cannot suppose that a decree then made did not reach Rome until well on in August[3]. Whether the date is good or not for the former event, the earliest date which we could allow for the dispatch of the Rescript by the Emperor would be the first half of July.

The process would be this. Something happens at Rome, or the idea is somehow motived there that the Edict is not acting strongly enough to reform the Christians. A request is moved in the Senate and sent to the Emperor, wherever he

---

[1] Pearson, *Annal. Cypr.* A.D. 258, iv.

[2] He obtained the information while the document itself was yet only on its way to Africa, *quas litteras cotidie speramus venire, Ep.* 80. 1.

[3] R. L. Friedlaender, *Darstellungen aus der Sittengeschichte Roms*, Leipz. 1881, vol. II., pp. 17, 199, gives instances of extraordinary travelling at the rate of 100 miles or more a day for six and eight days. Travellers who put up for the nights travelled from 30 to 36 miles a day. If we count the distance from Byzantium to Rome by Dyrrhachium, Brundisium and the Via Lavicana as 1222 or 1233 Roman miles (by Via Prænestina 1240 or 1251), according to the *Itinerarium Antonini*, that gives 17 or 18 days' journey at 70 miles a day, which is not excessive for the transmission of posts as compared with travelling. A rescript which reached Rome on Aug. 4 need not have left Byzantium before July 18 or 19.

Despatches were carried by the legionary *speculatores*, hemerodromos vocant Græci ingens die uno cursu emetientes spatium,' Livy xxxi. 24.

may be, that he would interpret, comment on, or, as he may think fit, assert the principle of the Edict. It was thus that Pliny asked Trajan to express his mind as to how the common law should be worked. Valerian writes back to the Senate. And his said Rescript, our 'Second Fragment,' called also an Oration[1], as representing the oration which the Emperor, if present, would have addressed to the Senate, runs as follows:

'That Bishops and Presbyters and Deacons be incontinently punished with death[2]. Senators however and men of high rank and knights of Rome forfeit their dignity[3]: be, further, divested of their goods; and if after being deprived of their means[4] they persist in being Christians, be also capitally punished; that matrons[5] be deprived of their goods and relegated into exile; and that all Cæsarians who have either confessed before or confess now, suffer confiscation, be put in bonds, entered in the slave-lists[6], and sent to work on Cæsar's estates[7].'

Whoever inspired these novel orders meant them to be final. Rank or sex were no longer to protect any one. It is plain that the higher ranks were felt to be honeycombed by Christianity, while the special provision about the Cæsarians[8],

---

[1] *Ep.* 80. 1. Cf. *Dig.* 24, 1, 3 *Ulpianus*, 'Hæc ratio et *oratione* imperatoris nostri Antonini Augusti electa est: nam ita ait,' &c.

[2] Animadvertantur = capite damnentur. 'Habere gladii potestatem ad animadvertendum in facinorosos homines,' ap. Dirksen, *Manuale, s.v.*

[3] *Egregii* already 'a dignity.' Senators had long been styled 'Clarissimi.' Later on the rank of 'Perfectissimatus' was inserted between 'Clarissimatus' and 'Egregiatus.'

[4] *Ademptis facultatibus.*

[5] *Matronæ* as used in law apparently still means wives not in the power (*manus*) of the husband. See *Dict. Gk. and Rom. Antt. s.v.* 'matrimonium.'

[6] *Descripti*, sic lege, not *inscripti* 'branded,' Mart. viii. 75, 9.

[7] It was a punishment even for slaves to be removed from the *familia* urbana and sent into the *rustica*.

[8] Cæsariani were not '*Palastbeamten*' (as Schwarze p. 115, Peters p. 574, Freppel '*officiers de sa maison*,' p. 485, say), but inferior officials of the Fiscus under the Rationalis or Procurator Cæsaris. In *Cod. Justin.* 10, 1, 5 they are employed in distraints. They had

or lower officials of the Revenue, illustrates the kind of employments into which, as free from idolatrous taint, the Christians crowded. Cyprian notes the inclusion of the whole body of the clergy[1].

But his intelligence comprised more fearful news. The Prefects in the city[2] had without a moment's pause begun the confiscations and the executions[3]. Not only so, Xystus[4] himself had on Sunday the sixth instant been found in the forbidden 'cemetery' and then and there put to death along with four out of the seven Deacons of Rome.

2. *Romae.—The exclusion from the Cemeteries.*

Archæology has few episodes able to compare for unexpected interest with the light and confirmation it throws upon and receives from Cyprian's direct news about the Rescript. This we shall see presently with the assistance of De Rossi as to the martyrdom and memorials of Xystus.

But first there are two points on which we may ourselves look for some elucidation from facts. Why was the entrance of Cemeteries—areas hitherto secured by legal rights—made capital? It was not merely to stop their assembling for worship. They had many *Basilicæ* and other *Fabricæ*, as

---

opportunities of enriching themselves oppressively and were under checks, *e.g.* they might not, while they held office, be admitted to the rank of perfectissimatus, ducena, centena, egregiatus, but might if they retired with spotless character; so Constantine enacts, *Cod. Theod.* 10, 7, 1; cf. 10, 7, 2.

[1] *Ep.* 80. 1, 'universi clerici sub ictu agonis constituti.'

[2] *Ibid.* 'Præfecti in urbe.' I suppose 'præfectus urbanus' and a 'præfectus prætorio.' Under Augustus, who instituted the latter office, there were two. As its civil importance grew vast, there were from time to time three, and at last four. There was sure to be at least one at home, while Valerian had one in attendance so long a time and so far away.

[3] The mere 'si qui sibi oblati fuerint animadvertantur,' *Ep.* 80. 1, looks as if enquiry were not too minute.

[4] 'Xistus' in *Ep.* 80, and Pontius *Vit.* 14 (Hartel).

we know from the history of Fabian. And why the sudden access of severity in the Rescript?

Caius (whom in an early essay Bp. Lightfoot shewed reason to believe to be Hippolytus himself) says, in the Dialogue with Proclus, 'But I can shew you the trophies 'of the Apostles. For if you will go to the Vatican or to the 'Ostian Road you will find the trophies (tombs) of those who 'founded this Church[1].' This is the earliest account we have of the remains of the two Apostles. It belongs to the time of Zephyrinus A.D. 199—217.

The same critic observed much later that the two Apostles together 'appear in connection with the Roman Church in the 'earliest document emanating from, as well as in the earliest 'document addressed to, the Roman Church after their death[2].'

The historic certainty of their martyrdom there, and the identity of their relics is a non-Cyprianic question which I forbear to judge. Until more is known two opposite conclusions will be maintained, mainly upon religious considerations remote from the matter in hand. Should the facts ever grow clearer, one of the two parties will discover that religious opinion has no place in the discussion. There is however no doubt that at that early period the remains of S. Peter were believed to be on the Aurelian Way and those of S. Paul on the Ostian.

There is no more doubt that shortly afterwards they were believed to be together in the 'Catacombs[3],' under the apse of S. Sebastian, three miles along the Appian Way. The Salzburg Itinerary in the first half of the seventh century and the

---

[1] Ap. Euseb. *H.E.* ii. 25. See Lightfoot in *Cambridge Journal of Philology*, vol. 1. p. 98, 1868.

[2] Clem. Rom. *ad Corinth.* v., Ignat. *ad Rom.* iv.; see Lightfoot's note on the latter passage.

[3] *Catacumbas*, properly two words, *cata cumbas*, *i.e.* 'at the sleeping places,' was (as is well known) not a general term as yet, but was long the name of this particular cemetery. It was of course indeclinable and its cases were falsely formed. Gregory, *Epp. lib.* iv. *indict.* xii. 30, correctly 'in loco qui dicitur Cata Cumbas.'

X. II. 2. SS. PETER AND PAUL MOVED TO CATACUMBAS. 483

rather later Epitome, 'Of the places of the Holy Martyrs,' speak of S. Sebastian's[1], *i.e.* the Catacombs, as the place where the two Apostles rested forty years—a symbolic date.

There were eccentric stories to account for this fact. Eastern Christians had tried shortly after the martyrdoms to convey the bodies to Palestine, had been arrested by God and man, and had left them here on the way[2]. Long after they had been replaced in or near their first homes Gregory the Great refused relics from them to the Empress Constantina on the plea of other phenomena and particularly of these stories. But they are attempts to account for the relics having certainly been there, when both before and after they were elsewhere.

Another curious early attempt to decipher what happened is the account in the *Vitæ Paparum* of the Felician Catalogue[3], that Cornelius took the bodies from the 'Catacombs,' and that Lucina (a standing name of Christian ladies in legends) restored S. Paul to the Ostian Way, while Cornelius laid S. Peter once more on the Vatican. This is a great anachronism, but it shews that it was well known that there was a time when they rested in the 'Catacombs.'

Damasus (366—384) adorned the half-underground chamber called Platonia[4] under the apse of S. Sebastian. It is irregular in shape, and has a stone settle. In the middle of it is a pit

---

[1] So also William of Malmesbury in the 11th century: Rossi, *Roma Sotterranea Cristiana*, I. pp. 180—1. L. Duchesne, *Liber Pontificalis*, I. civ—cvii. thinks the 40 years might represent from A.D. 258 to soon after Constantine's defeat of Maxentius, 313. The apocryphal Acts of Peter and Paul and the Pseudo-Marcellus give a year and seven months for the time during which the new tombs were preparing in their first resting-places.

[2] Acta Petri et Pauli, Tischendorf, *Acta Apostt. apocryphæ*, 1851, pp. 38, 39. Pseudo-Marcellus, *de Actibus Petri et Pauli*, ap. Fabricium Cod. Apocr. N.T. v. iii. p. 653. Florentini, *Vetustius Martyrol.* (Lucæ, 1668), p. 111.

[3] (A.D. 530) — Lipsius, *op. cit.* p. 275.

[4] Damasus...'et in Catacumbas ubi jacuerant corpora sanctorum apostolorum Petri et Pauli, in quo loco platomam (platoniam) ipsam ubi jacuerunt corpora sancta versibus exornavit,'... Duchesne, *Lib. Pontific.* vol. I. p. 212. 'Rivestimenti di lastre marmoree.' '*Platonia*, cioè grande lastra marmorea;' Rossi, *Rom. Sott.* II. pp. 22, 33.

31—2

six or seven feet square, and of about the same depth, with an opening into it through the pavement. Damasus paved this chamber, and lined the sides with marble,—still adhering a yard high to the walls. There remains also a large marble slab dividing the pit into two, making it a '*locus bisomus*[1].' For this place he wrote one of his Inscriptions. It exists in several antient collections, as copied from here, and here it began to be replaced by a thirteenth century hand, but breaks off before the last word of the third line[2]. It begins

> Here thou must know the saints beforetime dwelt,
> Whoe'er dost ask for Peter and for Paul[3].

We now understand why the Ambrosian Hymn for the Festival of S. Peter and S. Paul speaks of it as kept in Rome at three places on the same day.

> Through the great city's round the dense crowds stream along.
> Upon Three Roads they keep the sacred Martyrs' Feast[4],

---

[1] There is an interesting paper by H. Grisar, translated by Lanciani, *Le Tombe Apostoliche di Roma* (Typ. Vat. 1892), see p. 36.

[2] A photograph of it is in Parker's *Catacombs*, plate xxi.

[3] Hic habitasse prius sanctos cognoscere debes,
Nomina quisque Petri pariter Paulique requiris.
Discipulos oriens misit quod sponte fatemur.
Sanguinis ob meritum Christumque per astra secuti,
Ætherios petiere sinus regnaque piorum.
Roma suos potius meruit defendere cives.
Hæc Damasus vestras referat nova sidera laudes.

De Rossi, *Inscriptiones Christianæ Urbis Romæ*, vol. II. pp. 32, 65, 89, 105. Duchesne, *Lib. Pontific.* I. p. civ. S. Damasi *Opuscula et Gesta*, ed. Merenda, Rome 1754, pp. 226, 136, 249.

In *v.* 5 *regnaque* need not be amended. It would not have offended the ear of Damasus. Cf. *Carm.* 3, Angelus hæc verba cecinit. *Carm.* 4, In rebus tantis Trina conjunctio mundi.

On *v.* 6 Bp. Lightfoot thinks that it meant only that Rome claimed them as Roman citizens in spite of their Eastern origin, and that the story of the Greeks defeated in the attempt to appropriate them arose from these words being misunderstood. Lightfoot, *Apostolic Fathers*, part I. S. *Clement of Rome*, vol. II. p. 500. See a similar cause and result p. 491, n. 2.

[4] Tantæ per urbis ambitum Stipata tendunt agmina. Trinis celebratur viis Festum sacrorum martyrum. H. A. Daniel, *Thesaurus Hymnologicus*, I. xc. Lips. 1855.

the Three Roads being the Aurelian and the Ostian, where they suffered, and the Appian which passes Catacumbas.

And now we come to the interesting link which rivets these facts to our story.

One of those entries in the Kalendar called Hieronymian, which exhibit the Use of Rome in the fourth century, is this:

> On the twenty-ninth of June at Rome,
> Birthday of the Holy Apostles Peter and Paul,
> of Peter on the Vatican the Aurelian Way,
> but of Paul on the Ostian Way,
> of both in Catacumbas;
> they suffered under Nero,
> Bassus and Tuscus being Consuls[1].

The day seems at first as if it were that of their joint martyrdom. But in the early mentions of their deaths no day is named, much less the same day for both. It then suggests itself at once that it is the day of a Deposition, afterwards supposed to be the day of martyrdom. The *Depositio Martirum* of A.D. 354 registers the day correctly as a Deposition; though the scribe, probably thinking that Catacumbas applied to the Vatican, and knowing that now again S. Paul was on the Ostian Way, has confused the entry by inserting the word *Ostense*[2]. The Consulship named shews that it could have nothing to do with the deaths. But it is the very year 258 A.D., when the severe Rescript appeared following the Edict about the Cemeteries. We may be tolerably sure then that June 29, A.D. 258, was the

---

[1] 'III kal. jul. Romæ natale sanctorum apostolorum Petri et Pauli: Petri in Vaticano via Aurelia: Pauli vero in via Ostensi: utriusque in Catacumbas: Passi sub Nerone, Basso et Tusco consulibus,' Duchesne, *Lib. Pontif.* I. p. cv.

[2] 'III kl. Iul. Petri in Catacumbas et Pauli *Ostense* Tusco et Basso cons.' *Liberian Catalogue—Depositio martirum.* Mommsen's *Über den Chronographen vom Jahre* 354 (Abhandl. d. philolog.-hist. Classe, Königl. Sächsisch. Gesellsch. d. Wissenschaften Leipz. 1850, p. 632), called *Liberian, Filocalian* or *Bucherian catalogue* (*calendar*) from the Pope who ordered it, the compiler and the first editor. It is edited by R. A. Lipsius also: *Chronologie der Römischen Bischöfe* (1869); and the List of Popes is revised from all the published material by Bp. Lightfoot, *Apostt. Fathers,* part I. *S. Clement of Rome,* I. p. 201 sqq.

day when both were removed to their temporary hiding-place in the Catacumbas.

It scarcely is venturing into too minute a coincidence should we observe, that, if a fortnight sufficed, as it probably did, for the government couriers to transmit dispatches between Rome and Byzantium, there was a good margin of time between June 29 and August 6 to communicate to Valerian, even if he were further afield, what the Christians were about, and to receive his reply. The removal from their place of execution of the remains of notorious leaders of a dangerous section, which it was always necessary to suspect and impossible to understand, was probably noted, and invested, as it would be in Europe to-day, with political significance. The graves of those criminal Jewish agitators had not ceased to be visited, and now the modern leaders were somehow turning the old names to account. Xystus in this same year translated to the Cemetery of Callistus the Virgin Lucilla and her father Nemesius the Deacon, who had been laid on the Via Latina by Stephen in 257[1]. It is tempting to think that the Emperor may have been induced to sharpen his decree by tidings of the translation. It could not be unknown that the 'trophies' and the cemeteries were tampered with by the Christians after they had been warned off from places dear and long legally secured to them. 'You know even the days of our 'meetings,' says Tertullian[2], 'and so we are laid wait for and 'apprehended and in these actual secret congregations we are 'arrested.'

The whole proceeding wears the aspect of precaution. There was no knowing what violence might be at hand. And if it could be shewn that the blocking up of passages, the breaking away of staircases, the opening of secret galleries out into the sandpits, which are such marked facts in the history of the cemeteries, belonged partly to the days of Valerian's

---

[1] J. H. Parker, *Archæol. of Rome*, vol. XII. *The Catacombs*, p. 73.

[2] *Ad Nationes*, l. I. c. 7.

persecution, as well as to those of Diocletian, there would be little or no doubt of the meaning of that proceeding.

However this may be we cannot doubt that the Bishop of Rome would have his share in directing the removal of the sacred forms and any other measures of precaution or reverence. And as legislation about cemeteries could nowhere apply to anything like the extent that it did at Rome, we may feel sure that such legislation had its origin in Roman difficulties.

3. *Memorials of Xystus and his Martyrdom.*

We have learnt, from Cyprian's own letter, that Xystus was martyred in a cemetery on the sixth of August[1], and with him four[2] (of the seven) Deacons of Rome.

There is no uncertainty now as to the place of this tragedy. De Rossi's researches, and what he himself calls his 'extended and complicated comment,' a masterpiece of knowledge, insight and patience, have cleared up endless difficulties[3].

1. The earliest list of Roman cemeteries calls that of Callistus 'Coemeterium Callisti *ad S. Xystum* Via Appia[4].' There still stands above ground a small chapel, originally a *Schola*, in plan a square, with large apses on three sides; its front, open antiently like an exhedra, to the Via 'Appia-

---

[1] Xystus sat 11 months 12 (? 6) days, Lipsius, *op. cit.* p. 213. Eusebius, *H. E.* vii. 27 has (in the same error noticed already in other instances) assigned him as many years. So in vii. 14 he seems to speak of him as overliving the edict of restoration. Another error is repeated from him by Jerome, who assigns eight years to Xystus. (*Interpret. Chronic. Euseb.* ad Ann. D. 258.)

[2] *Ep.* 80. 1. Quartus for quattuor, unwarrantable alteration adopted by Pamele, Fell.

[3] The following are the chief references to De Rossi, *Roma Sotterranea Cristiana*: vol. I. p. 247, Xystus' chapel in Cemetery of Prætextatus; vol. II. p. 4, 'S. Sistus and S. Cecilia'; vol. II. p. 20, Crypt of S. Sistus; vol. II. p. 87, Sepulchre, monuments and companions of S. Sistus; vol. III. p. 468, Tricora of S. Sistus and S. Cecilia. See Lanciani, *Pagan and Christian Rome*, p. 117.

[4] *Rom. Sott.* vol. II. p. 6.

Ardeatina[1].' The lower masonry and the fact that it has been rased nearly to the ground and rebuilt under Constantine make it probable that it was one of the 'many fabrics' placed 'throughout the cemeteries' by Fabian[2], and removed as a *conventiculum* by Diocletian. From very early times it has been called the Church of S. Xystus, of S. Cæcilia, or of both. Pilgrims halt at it before descending one of the two flights of steps which lead to the crypt of S. Sisto[3], in which the popes of the third century were usually buried, and to that of S. Cæcilia. Xystus became the chief and central sanctity of this crypt. The plaster over the door of the crypt is scored with invocations of 'Sustus,' *graffiti*[4] so early that they are mutilated by the changes made by Damasus in the fourth century, although Celerinus and Lucianus in the beginning of our story would, with all their exaggerations about martyrs, have revolted from them. Within it was placed the very chair in which he was teaching when he was martyred.

For the whole cemetery Damasus wrote an inscription in his best hexameters, and cut it on marble in this chapel, where De Rossi found almost the whole in above 100 fragments and with surprising skill refitted them together into the appearance of some delicate net[5].

They are to this effect:

> Here closely lie a crowd of Holy ones;
> The awful graves their sacred Bodies keep
> Heaven's palace hath caught up the soaring souls.

---

[1] The Cross-road which connects the Appia and Ardeatina (see map) is so called by De Rossi. The names of these roads are as yet matter of controversy. Sign. Lanciani names, as having lately thrown some light on the question, the memoirs by Christian Huelsan, *sulla porta Ardeatina* in Mittheilungen, 1894, pp. 320—327, Taf. ix. (Roemische Abtheilung), and by Gius. Romassetti, *Scoperte Suburbane*, in Boll. della Commiss. Arch. comunale di Roma, 1895, p. 162.

[2] *Liberian Catalogue*, Mommsen, *op. cit.* p. 635; Lipsius, *op. cit.* p. 267.

[3] *Rom. Sott.* II. p. 27, headed 'La cripta di S. Sisto fu il sepolcreto ordinario dei papi nel secolo III.'

[4] 'Sante Suste in mente habeas in horationes Aureliu Repentinu.' 'Suste san . . . . . utæ Libera . . .' 'Sanc . . . . . . e . . . . . . te abe in oratione . . .', &c. *Rom. Sott.* II. p. 17.

[5] *Rom. Sott.* II. tav. ii.

> Here Xystus' comrades—who the trophies won,
> Here many Peers—who at Christ's altars watch.
> Here lies the Priest who lived a lengthened Peace,
> Here the Confessor Saints whom Græcia sent,
> Here Youths, old men yet boys, and grandsons pure
> Who willed to keep their Virgin Modesty.
> Here would I Damasus have laid my limbs
> But feared to vex the ashes of the Just[1].

This epigram itself witnesses to the pre-eminent honour of Xystus[2], as does likewise the inscription placed above the Chair by Damasus, of which also minute fragments were found.

Its purport was as follows:

> What time the sword pierced through the Mother's heart,
> Set here as Pilot I taught heaven's decrees.
> Sudden they came and took me as I sate.
>
> The peoples gave their necks to the soldiery.
> The Elder marked one who would fain have snatch'd
> His palm; but first he offered his own head,
> Not suffering savagery to strike at large.
>
> Christ with His bounteous gifts of life assigns
> The Shepherd's wage, and folds the flock Himself[3].

---

[1] Hic congesta jacet quæris si turba piorum
Corpora sanctorum retinent veneranda sepulcra
Sublimes animas rapuit sibi regia cæli
His comites Xysti portant qui ex hoste tropæa
His numerus procerum servat qui altaria Christi
His positus longa vixit qui in pace sacerdos
His confessores sancti quos Græcia misit
Hic juvenes puerique senes castique nepotes
Quis mage virgineum placuit retinere pudorem.
Hic fateor Damasus volui mea condere membra
Sed cineres timui sanctos vexare piorum.

Text preserved in *Sylloge Turonensis*, 23, and *Corp. Laureshamensis Sylloge*, 4ta, 43, ap. Rossi, *Inscr. Chr. Urb. Romæ*, II. pp. 66, 105. View of Crypt of S. Xystus, *Rom. Sott.* II. tav. i.

[2] He is said to be the only Roman martyr admitted into the Syriac Kalendar.

[3] Tempore quo gladius secuit pia viscera matris
Hic positus Rector cælestia jussa docebam
Adveniunt subito rapiunt qui forte sedentem.

2. Yet this solemn place of his sepulture is not 'the little church where Xystus was beheaded[1],' though often confused with it.

Opposite to the Cemetery of Callistus along the Appian Way a little further south, and towards the antient temple of Ceres, now St Urban's Church, was found in 1848 the Cemetery of Prætextatus. Prætextatus is the name of a great family who were not all Christians when they began to let Christians use it.

Here is a painting of 'Sustus' with his name. Here was a *graffito* of a Cathedra, another of a Doctor seated in a Cathedra with a hearer at his feet. Here is seen still the inscription

...mi refrigeri[2] Januarius Agatopus Felicissimus martyres[3].

The *Liber Pontificalis* records that with Xystus were slain six Deacons, Felicissimus, Agapitus, Januarius, Magnus, Vincentius, Stephanus, also that the Deacons were buried here on VIII *id. Aug.*[4], while Xystus was laid with his predecessors

Militibus missis populi tunc colla dedere;
Mox sibi cognovit senior quis tollere vellet
Palmam, seque suumque caput prior obtulit ipse
Impatiens feritas posset ne laEDere quenquam.

Ostendit Christus, reddit qui PRæmia vitæ
Pastoris meritum numerum gREGis ipse tuetur.

Text in Duchesne, *L. P.* v. I. p. 156: preserved in *Corp. Lauresh. Sylloge*, 4ta, 60. Rossi, *Inscr. Chr. U. Romæ*, II. p. 108. For probable situation of Chair and inscription, see *Rom. Sott.* II. tavv. 1. and 2. The fragment found in the crypt is indicated by capitals.

The fragments of a third inscription, *R. S.* II. tav. iii. no. 8, no doubt belong to a Damasian epigram on the events, though the letter cutting is less beautiful.

[1] 'Ecclesia parva ubi decollatus est S. Xystus.' Salzburg Itinerary, *Rom. Sott.* I. p. 180.

[2] Refrigeri = refrigeret.

[3] Rossi, *Boll. Arch. Crist.* 1863, p. 3. —*R. S.* I. p. 251, II. p. 89, Agathopus is the form for Agapitus in apparently all codices of the Hieronymian Catalogue. *R. S.* II. pp. 41, 47.

[4] Duchesne, *L.P.* I. p. 155. Cyprian's date is VIII id. Aug.

in the Cemetery of Callistus[1], just across the road. His Chair went with him.

Over two of the Deacons Damasus wrote for the Cemetery of Prætextatus

> Comrades and Servers of the unconquered Cross
> They followed their pure Pastor's Faith and Works.
> Damasus to Felicissimus and Agapitus[2].

A dialogue of some dramatic power with some shreds of authenticity is recited by Ambrose, as having been held with Laurentius[3], another Deacon, by Xystus on his way to execution.

This story seems at first sight irreconcilable with the account of his beheading in the Chair. But we cannot set aside the observation of De Rossi[4] that it is impossible that seven Romans should have been simply murdered without trial by a gang of soldiers; that they must have been taken before the judge, and may have been sent back to the place where they were apprehended as law-breakers to be put to death[5]

---

[1] 'Sepultus est in cymiterio Calesti via Appia nam VI diaconi ejus in cymitirio Prætextati via Appia VIII id. Aug.' Duchesne, *Lib. Pont.* I pp. 68, 9 (*i.e.* first edition of *L. P.* as represented in Felician abridgment).

[2] Hi crucis invictæ comites pariterque ministri
Rectoris sancti meritumque fidemque secuti.
Felicissimo et Agapito Damasus.

Rossi, *Inscr. Ch.* II. p. 66. This epigram probably (as Lipsius suggests, *op. cit.* p. 223) gave birth to the line of legends in which Xystus himself is crucified. Ambros. *de Off. Ministrorum*, I. xli. 'Ambrosian' Hymn ap. H. A. Daniel, *Thes. H.* I. xc. I. Prudent. *Peristeph.* ii. 21—26.

[3] Lipsius regards Laurence as historical, though *archidiaconus* (not in Ambrose) is an anachronism, *op. cit.* p. 120.

The fine story of Laurence, with the circle of heroes who gathered round it, obliterated after a time the recollection that the Chair belonged to Xystus, whose name was not mentioned in the epigram of Damasus placed over it. It was transferred with the story of a Pope's martyrdom in it, enriched by the account of blood shed over it, to Stephen as the nearest unmartyred pontiff, in spite of his not appearing in the *Depositio Martirum* but in the *Depositio Episcoporum* in the Liberian Catalogue (Mommsen, *Chron. v. Jahre* 354, *op. cit.* p. 631), IIII *non. Augustas Steffani in Calisti.* The Chair was bestowed by Innocent XII. on Cosmo III. and taken to Pisa (Merenda, *Damasus*, p. 1).

[4] *R. S.* II. pp. 91, 92.

[5] *Lib. Pontif.* (1st ed.), Duchesne, p. 69, 'truncati sunt capite'—solemn Roman

for a warning to those who persisted in frequenting the cemeteries. Upon the road, he suggests, some such conversation may have been held. He urges the '*rapiunt*' of Damasus.

This conjecture is supported by a passage which De Rossi does not notice. The second edition of the *Liber Pontificalis*[1] says 'Xystus was apprehended by Valerian['s officers] and '*led away* to sacrifice to the demons. He scorned the precepts 'of Valerian and was beheaded[2].'

There is no reason to doubt the incidents which Damasus carefully notes—how he was found teaching in his Chair, how the people offered themselves to die for him or with him, how his anxiety was to prevent them from provoking the soldiers, and how the old man anticipated the self-devotion of one faithful follower by stretching out his own neck to receive the blow.

The relics of the history, the monuments, the epigrams, the letter, are wonderfully yet not too absolutely in accord[3]. And as to the scene itself what more natural than that the quieter and more protected chapel of Prætextatus should have been resorted to by the bishop, deacons and people, when the larger and less private ones were made dangerous by the edict?

---

execution. Cyprian's word *animadversum* is more often than not used of decollation, and there is Damasus' '*caput obtulit*.' The Leonian Sacramentary also preserves 'intrepida cervice,' Muratori, *op. cit.* I. c. 390. This has seven *missæ* for his day.

[1] Duchesne, *Lib. Pont.* I. p. 155; cf. p. 69.

[2] *Ductus* ut sacrificaret.

Præceptum, technical word, as in *Acta Proc.* ap. Hartel, p. cx, l. 24; cx, l. 12; cxi 8 præceperunt, 11 præceptum est, 18 sacro præcepto; cxii 10 præceptum, &c.

[3] The *Lib. Pontif.* entry of all six Deacons as buried in *Cæm. Prætextati* cannot apparently be reconciled with Damasus' epigram saying that '*comites Xysti*' were in *Cæm. Callisti*. De Rossi, II. p. 91 ff. gives it up with distress and says *Lib. Pont.* needs amendment. But only three are claimed for Prætextatus by the Invocation and Damasus, whose epigram for this place shews that he did not understand *all* 'the comrades of Xystus' to be at Callistus. It is not worth while here to pursue the question through the Kalendars. Perhaps Cyprian's statement that four Deacons died *with* him (*cum* eo) may lend a ray. If there were six two suffered later.

XI.   THE BIRTHDAY.   495

to the Governors, and presently he sent two of his military clerks[1] to fetch the Bishop quietly over to Utica.

But now acting with the coolness of a person used to take his own course in details, even with magistrates, Cyprian was not to be found. He was gone to one of the offered concealments—there to stay until the Proconsul should be able to come to Carthage. He was sure that the summons to Utica meant death. And although he had no fear of death, Cyprian had deliberate views as to the scene of his death. This was no new impulse, no new prudence. Years before he had congratulated Lucius on his return from exile to Rome[2], most likely to die there, on this very ground because 'the victim which has to set before the brother-'hood the pattern of manliness and of faith ought to be 'offered up in the presence of his brethren.' So now from his retreat he writes to his Presbyters, Deacons and Commons, that he only awaits the Proconsul's visit to Carthage, because 'the City in which he presides over the Church of the Lord is 'the place where a Bishop ought to confess his Lord and to 'glorify his whole Commons by the confession of their own 'prelate in their presence.' So to confess, there to suffer, thence to take his departure to his Lord, was now his constant prayer[3]. Beyond this, he fully felt that something Divine might be breathed into the last words of a Confessor-Bishop. Confession was more after God's mind than the best

---

[1] *Commentarii* or *Commentarienses* were military clerks in the Proconsul's Office who kept the journals of proceedings. Their position was among the highest *Principales*, or officers below the rank of Centurion. One of their duties was, as we see by later laws (A.D. 371, 380), to schedule prisoners, their offences, rank and age; and they were responsible for their safe-keeping. (*Codex Justin.* 9, 4, 4, 5). If any difficulty had been apprehended a centurion would have been sent, and this was done the second time, after the present failure. Cf. Ruinart, *Pass. Jacobi et Mariani,* iv. At Lambæse an altar is erected by ...*i*VS. SEVER*us a co*MMEN*T*A*riis m. val*ERI ETRV*sci leg.* AVG. PR. P*r* (A.D. 152); another names the *Commentarius* of the IIIrd Legion there. *Corp. Inscrr. Lt.* VIII. i. 2613; cf. 2586.

[2] *Ep.* 61.

[3] *Ep.* 81.

professions. The indwelling God Himself might perhaps use such a moment[1].

Doubtless the Decian persecution had known such inspirations, and there are striking contemporary examples of what they were understood to be. In the year after Cyprian's death Marianus at Cirta, waiting blindfold with many others for the stroke, and 'now filled with the prophetic spirit,' 'strengthened the envy' with which these holy deaths were viewed, by foretelling the approach of God's avenging scourges.

When, at that same time, the clergy of Carthage suffered, Montanus cried with prophetic voice, ' He that sacrificeth to any Gods but the Lord alone will be rooted out.' He then charged Heretics to mark the abundance of her Martyrs as a sure note of the true Church; he charged the Lapsed to submit to the Cyprianic discipline; the Virgins to maintain their constancy; all to be in obedience to the Bishops; the Bishops to maintain among themselves the Cyprianic Unity as the one true bond of the laity. He ended, 'This is the true suffering for 'Christ's sake, namely, to copy Christ in discourse, and *to be* '*in one's own person the great proof of the faith.*'

Now, should God give Cyprian any such message it would be not for Cyprian's sake but for his people's, and they should hear it. Whenever therefore the Proconsul came, then he would be found. The Proconsul came, and Cyprian was at home in his Horti at once. The Proconsul of course knew nothing of the motives of his movement, and naturally determining not to be again eluded, ordered a sudden descent[2] upon the house.

The Thascian gardens, as they would be called, lay doubtless in the vast beautiful quarter which has been all gardens

---

[1] *Ep.* 81. It is to this dying inspiration, and not to the apologia at the trial, that in the Epistle to Thibaris 58, 5 Cyprian applies Matth. x. 19 'in illa hora.'

[2] Pontius *Vit.* 15 has a platitude on his own 'repente subitavit' and the Proconsular Acts c. 2 give the 'repente.'

XI. THE BIRTHDAY. 497

and villas, Roman, Arab, European, ever since the 'rare,' 'sparse' native kraals called *Mapalia* disappeared from it, yet left their name behind. Its rich trees and flowers have seen the great bare hill piled with marble Carthage, then stripped to build Tunis or shipped to Pisa, and they are still there in their glory. The Thascian gardens then cannot have been very far from the Villa of Sextus where the sick Proconsul lay.

Early on the 13th September an unexpected chariot drove through them to the villa door, while a guard of soldiers prevented other egress[1]. The chariot brought two '*Principes*,' as they were styled,—chief centurions. One was a very important officer of the legion, and was, besides, the Proconsul's own *strator* or equerry. The other was attached to the prison department. They quietly fetched Cyprian out, lifted him into their chariot and drove away with him between them[2].

---

[1] This only can have been the use of bringing soldiers to the villa.

[2] ...principes duo unus strator officii Galerii Maximi proconsulis et alius equistrator a custodiis ejusdem officii. *Acta Proc.* 2.

Anyone must be struck with the exactness of the terms used in the *Acta* 2, and the more general but quite correct usage in Pontius. The second centurion of a legion was called *primæ cohortis princeps prior* or *princeps prætorii*, C. I. L. III. i. 2917, ii. 5293, or simply *princeps*. His duties required the assistance of an *adjutor*, a *librarius* and an *optio*. C. I. L. VIII. i. 2555. The *tabulæ militares* were in his hands. He was an officer of much consideration. C. I. L. VIII. i. 2676, the Princeps of the 3rd Legion builds a temple to Invictus Augustus 'ære suo a solo' at Lambæse. *Ibid.* 2841, the Princeps of the 3rd legion 'vix. an. LX...' and built a mausoleum at Rome 'in prædiis suis.' Here we find him able to receive Cyprian and his friends in his house for the night.

A *strator* originally saddled (*sternere*) the great officer's horse and assisted him to mount. The Governors of imperial provinces and the Præfect of the prætorium had *stratores* personally attached to them; but not so Proconsuls, who were required to employ *soldiers* in that capacity. (Ulpian, ap. *Dig.* 1, 16, 4, 'Nemo proconsulum stratores suos habere potest sed vice eorum milites ministerio in provinciis funguntur.')

Inscriptions shew that the dignity of *strator* was valued and the title retained after the function was laid down. Compare Gruteri, *Corp. Inscrr.* I. p. 631, n. 8, 'strator consulis.' C. I. L. VII. 78, 'strator consularis'; VIII. i. 2748, 'præsidis stratores,' 2957, 'istrator legati'; VIII. ii. 9002, 'strator ejus,' sc. of the Præses of both Mauritanias.

Everything had fallen in with Cyprian's plan. He should die among his people. As he left his door for the last time his usual 'serious joyousness' of expression was transfigured by 'the manful heart' to a lofty eagerness and almost mirthfulness[1]—which was indeed to break out, like Sir Thomas More's, as the hour drew near.

When they reached the Proconsul's they found he was again too ill to proceed with the case[2]. He remanded the prisoner till next day, but would not risk his returning to his home or even going upon bail to friends. He was committed to the courteous 'free custody' of the first Princeps himself, and in his house within the city[3] spent the evening as usual with his Deacons and with the higher members of his own household—the household of a Roman gentleman as well as Bishop of Carthage—and with other intimate friends[4].

In *Bollett. dell. Instit. di Corrispondenza Archeol.* 1860, p. 22, a monument is erected 'J. Flavio Sereno perfectissimo viro a cognitionibus Augusti...' by his 'amici et stratores.' *C. I. L.* VIII. i. 2792, a 'signifer' erects a monument to his brother, a 'strator.'

With this Princeps...Strator...Officii came another, *princeps Equistrator a custodiis, i.e.* attached to the department of prisons. So *Codex Justin.* 9, 4, 1, describes those 'qui *strator*um funguntur officio' and 'ministri eorum' as able to inflict suffering on prisoners and to protract their detention. This one was however in a very different position from the first, and Pontius only mentions the first, in whose house he was entertained for the night.

[1] Compare Pont. *Vit.* 6 and 15, 'hilaritatem præferens vultu corde virtutem.'

[2] The sequel shews that Pontius, *Vit.* 15 was hard upon him in setting down to laziness or caprice the remand in which he saw a special providence.

It was expressly assigned to the proconsul to settle (*æstimare*) whether persons after arrest should be imprisoned, committed to sureties, to soldiers, or to their own houses, and he was bound to take into consideration the office, estate, or dignity of the person as well as the character of the charge. *Digesta*, 48, 3, 1.

[3] 'In vico qui dicitur Saturni, between the Via Venerea and the Via Salutaris.' *Act. Proc.* 2. We ought indeed to be able to identify a site noted for us so carefully and near to two if not three of the chief temples of Carthage. But the construction of a vast precinct on the crown of the Byrsa and the pursuit of museum objects, even if the advertisements of 'Terrains à vendre, à bâtir' are fruitless, must long preclude the development of sites.

[4] 'Receptum eum tamen et in domo principis constitutum una nocte continuit custodia delicata, ita ut convivæ ejus et cari in contubernio ex more fuerimus.' Pont. *Vit.* 15. Several interesting points

The first convoy had passed so quickly through a quiet quarter to the Proconsul's, that none were aware of it, until Cyprian was again on his way to the house of the Princeps. Then the rumour ran fast. Thascius the famous orator, the benefactor in the plague[1], was in custody. It was a spectacle of regret to the pagans, of veneration to the faithful. A vast multitude assembled. The whole Christian 'Commons,' so it was said, watched the house lest the least movement should escape them. Afterwards they realized that they had been keeping the Vigil of the Martyr. One message they received from within in the course of the night, a charge that the maidens who were abroad should be well cared for[2].

The morrow rose with the broad pure blaze of the African sky without fleck of cloud. The bay was a sea of glass mingled with fire. A wonderful walk lay before him as he turned away to the north-west. The crush of public buildings on the High Byrsa, the narrow streets of tall houses falling down from it on all sides, the mass and the fierce colouring of the immense temples, the vast palaces of base and savage amusement—how long would this order of things last? what would become of it, face to face with the Bishops and Councils when they should come to their strength, as even now they represented a New Order well begun? The City of God rose before him more solid than those material amazing bulwarks, grander than the majesty of Roman Law, more real than the immeasurable force behind it.

His path led across the Stadium. As he crossed it his

---

appear. *Receptum* (technical word) *in carcerem* (*Digesta*, 48, 3, 1, 2) or as here *in custodiam* (*ibid*. 10). Not merely '*libera* custodia' but *delicata*, which refers to the entertainment. *Conviva*, in its post-classical sense, of the higher rank of the people of a great household. *Ex more*, the style and habit of Cyprian.

[1] Pont. *Vit.* 15; cf. 11, ille qui fecerat boni aliquid pro civitatis saluti.

[2] This was the subject within half a century of a special canon. Conc. Eliberit. can. xxxv. Labbe, Mansi, Flor. 1759, t. II. col. 11. Aug. *Serm.* 309, 4, treats this as a marked instance of 'pastoral wakefulness.'

companions thought, if he did not, of a race run and an expectant crown. He had left the Chief Centurion's threshold, looking like a Chief Centurion himself[1] with a Diviner commission[2]. He moved in the centre of the guard of officers and soldiers, followed by an endlessly gathering army, who looked, says the eyewitness, as if they were 'on the march to take Death by storm.'

The Proconsul had actually summoned the populace to the villa of Sextus[3], so resolved was he that a great blow should be struck, a great example made.

The smooth paved road was deep and silent with dust, as they emerged from the dark close streets on the luxuriant plain. Among the date palms ripening for the gathering, and high above the silver olives, on whose fruit the final bloom was just appearing, the cypresses towered black and still. The stubble of the reaped corn was standing deep, the vines had been relieved of their burdens, the grassy slopes were white with the long summer, and the vast carpets of dazzling flowers had faded, all but the invincible dark green asphodel.

Beyond the wide and peerless tract of vegetation were the glowing hills, dense with brushwood of cistus and cytisus, myrtle and lentisk, gaps opening into the world's cornfields, and the solemn aqueduct bringing rivers of living water from mountains leagues away.

How much of natural things filled the old man's eye we know not—he was beyond caring for little things, but no man knows whether those things are little. Certainly he had not lost that humorous observation which has sometimes caught us unexpectedly in gravest moments.

---

[1] Egressus est domum Principis sed Christi et Dei Princeps, Pont. *Vit.* 16; compare 18.

[2] Ex omni parte *vallatus*, Pont. *Vit.* 16.

[3] *Acta Proc.* 3, multa turba convenit ad Sexti, secundum præceptum Galerii Maximi proconsulis.

This became later on, as in Bede's *Martyrology* (18 Kal. Oct.) and elsewhere, 'sexto milliario a Carthagine juxta mare.'

XI.   THE BIRTHDAY.   501

They reached the Prætorium. The crowd was great. The hearing was appointed for an open colonnaded court called *Atrium Sauciolum*[1]. Again the Proconsul was unable to receive him at once and a more retired room was at his service to rest in. The seat, so it happened, was covered with a white linen cloth like a bishop's chair in the apse. His clothes were soaked through and through with perspiration from such a walk. One of the officers[2] whose business was to carry the Proconsul's passwords to the posts, offered him a change of clothes. Humanely but, Pontius thought, not quite disinterestedly. He was a Lapsed Christian and knew the yet innocent store set by Relics[3]. Cyprian himself only replied, 'Cures for complaints that will be over maybe in the day!'

At last the Proconsul asked for him. He was hastily ushered in and was face to face with the great governor sitting in his civil dress between the high officers of his staff and leading provincials who formed his council; behind him six lictors with the rods and axes[4]; before him a small tripod, or a chafing dish with live coals in it, and a box of incense. It was a brief trial, for Roman courts were rational. He was arraigned on the one count of Sacrilege. As Sacrilege legally covered every violation of or careless

---

[1] *Atrium Sauciolum. Acta Proc.* 3. The only illustration I know of this mysterious name was pointed out by Bp. Fell. In the great Frankish Council at Macon under king Guntramn, A.D. 585, any Cleric is forbidden to attend 'ad locum examinationis reorum'—(*i.e.* place of torture, cf. Tert. *Scorpiace*, 7, martyria fidei examinatoria)—'neque intersit *atrio sauciolo ubi pro reatus sui qualitate quispiam interficiendus est*.' Conc. Matisconense, ii. can. xix. ap. Labbe, Mansi, Florentiæ, 1763, t. IX. col. 956. No Roman court would bear a name meaning 'place of execution'; Galerius's 'atrium sauciolum' was clearly not such a place. Criminals would not be beheaded within the house. The appropriation of the name to a death-chamber must have been altogether later.

[2] 'Quidam ex Tessenariis,' Pont. *Vit.* 16; see *Dict. Gk. and Rom. Antt.* vol. I. pp. 377, 801.

[3] Pontius too, *Vit.* 16, 'sudores jam sanguineos' is a curious exaggeration.

[4] *Acta Proc.* 3, 4. Pont. *Vit.* 16. Cf. *Digesta*, I, 16, 14.

On the curious insignia ('symbola') which belonged to the Proconsul of Africa, see *Revue Africaine*, vol. VIII. p. 323.

offence against the Divine Law, which Law included expressions of the Emperor's will, no Christian lawyer would quibble at the term or pretend that he was not daily and wilfully guilty of it[1].

The imperial note had as before particularized Cyprian.

Galerius spoke.   You are Thascius Cyprianus?

Cyprian. I am.

Galerius. You have lent yourself to be a pope to persons of sacrilegious views.

Cyprian. I have.

Galerius. The most hallowed emperors have ordered you to perform the rite.

Cyprian. I do not offer.

Galerius. Do consider yourself.

Cyprian. Do what you are charged to do. In a matter so straightforward there is nothing to consider[2].

That was all. The Proconsul conferred with his council to make the process technically correct[3]. And then, a reluctant and a very ailing man, he with difficulty yet with sternest concurrence, explained the new criminality and justified the new and necessary penalty. It was simply for being the Bishop of the modern and spreading union that he was to suffer[4].

---

[1] Qui Divinæ legis sanctitatem aut nesciendo confundunt aut negligendo violant et offendunt sacrilegium committunt...Disputari de principali judicio non oportet: sacrilegii enim instar est dubitare an is dignus sit quem elegerit imperator. *Cod. Just.* 9, 29, 1, 2. This is a later exposition of the principle (*Gratian*), but the well-known earlier definitions are more severe.

[2] Consule tibi...nulla est consultatio, *Acta Proc.* 3. Quod caro et sanguis diceret stolide (noverat) hoc diabolum dicere subdole, Aug. *Serm.* 309, 5.

Certain translations seem to make it well to offer these merely grammatical observations.—*Facio* is the sacrificial word. He refuses to burn incense.— In *re tam justa*, 'regular, ordinary': so *justum iter*, *j. anni, statura, altitudo muri*—[I do not know the word *cærimoniari* elsewhere].

[3] Any grave decision had to be pronounced *de consilii sententia*. The proconsul was bound to consult them but not bound even by a majority of their opinions.

[4] *Acta Proc.* 4. 'Sanguine tuo *sancietur* disciplina.' So Pontius, *Vit.* 17, ...quod sanguine ejus inciperet disciplina sanciri.—'Prior in provincia martyrii primitias dedicavit,' which in 19

XI.   THE BIRTHDAY.   503

He said, 'Your life has long been led in a sacrilegious 'mode of thought—you have associated yourself with a very 'large number of persons in criminal complicity: you have 'constituted yourself an antagonist to the gods of Rome and 'to their sacred observances. Nor have our pious and most 'hallowed princes, Valerian and Gallien the Augusti, and 'Valerian the most noble Cæsar[1], been able to recal you to 'the obedience of their own ceremonial. And therefore, 'whereas you have been clearly detected[2] as the instigator 'and standard-bearer in very bad offences, you shall in your 'own person be a lesson to those'—they were present—'whom 'you have by guilt of your own associated with you. Disci-'pline shall be ratified with your blood.' He then took the prepared tablet and read, 'Our pleasure is that Thascius Cyprianus be executed with the sword.'

'Thanks be to God,' said Cyprian.

To the bosom friends who had realized that this was the revealed 'morrow' and this the sentence suspended in the dream a year ago, every word of the judge seemed beyond himself and spiritual and prophetic in the manner of Caiaphas. It was all true—'standard-bearer' he was—'foe of the gods' he was,—and a fresh 'discipline' of martyrdom was inaugurated, consecrated.

But the Christian multitude broke out in a more human

---

he expands 'sacerdotales coronas in Africa primus imbueret,' &c.

[1] This passage answers Eckhel, who says (vol. VII. p. 427) that the young Valerian never became either Augustus or Cæsar. But in the British Museum there is a beautiful medallion of these three heads with Salonina, inscribed 'Pietas Augustorum, Concordia Augustorum.' Grueber, *Roman Medallions, Br. Mus.* pl. xlvii. 4. Several laws of dates 255—260 are under their names in Codex Justinianus. Gallienus gave him the title of Augustus, and on his tomb at Milan he was called Imperator. Treb. Poll. *Valeriani Duo*, c. 8. The young Valerian was 'forma conspicuus, verecundia probabilis, eruditione pro ætate clarus, moribus perjucundus,' a contrast to his half-brother Gallien.

[2] 'Deprehensus,' *Acta Proc.* 4 : *Cod. Theodos.* 9, 16, 11, quicumque...audierit, deprehenderit, occupaverit. Paul. *Sentt.* 2, 26, 2, deprehenderit. Gaius, 3, 198, in ipso delicto deprehendere.

cry, 'And let us be beheaded too—along with him.' There was something like the beginning of a disturbance[1]. And the great company, whose presence had been invited, moved onwards with him as he left the doors, guarded by a detachment of the famous Third Legion, with its centurions and tribunes on either side of him.

Their short march, still within the grounds of Sextus, was to a level space surrounded with steep high slopes thick with trees. It was an amphitheatre[2], but on a scale too large for distinct seeing, while below the multitude was one mass. Many who were in sympathy (and there were many besides the Christians[3]) with the great old citizen and friend of the city had climbed into the trees to see the end.

They saw the halt. They saw the legionaries enclose a space in the midst of which stood Cyprian with his Deacons, Pontius and others, the Presbyter Julian and Julian the Subdeacon. He undid his shoulder-clasp and took off his white woollen cape; then at once knelt on the ground, and prostrated himself in prayer. When he rose this seemed the moment in which the looked-for prophecy would be uttered.

He had longed, and he had himself expected that his last words on earth would be given to him from above. But now he spoke not. He quietly took off his dalmatic, and gave it to his deacons, and stood upright and silent in his long white and girdled tunic of linen. We should know him very imperfectly if we did not think how his yearning went out to the yearning of his people. No man was more capable of simple moving speech rich with the truth he had loved, and fraught with the full significance of that hour; and it would have been no wonder if, in that exalted frame of mind, the thoughts that gathered

---

[1] *Acta Proc.* 5, '*tumultus* fratrum exortus est.'

[2] Pont. *Vit.* 18, 'Ut...sublime spectaculum præbeat.' For *spectaculum* in this sense of 'a seeing-place,' cf. Orosius, *Hist.* iv. 1, '...Tarentini Romanam classem forte prætereuntem, *spectaculo* theatri prospectam, hostiliter invaserunt.' So *spectacula* is constantly the blocks of seats.

[3] 'Personæ faventes,' Pont. *Vit.* 18.

thick upon him had presented themselves to him as the expected message of God. Nothing could so perpetuate the Unity which he had lived for in the Church as that he should place the seal upon it now[1]. But nothing came to him which he could distinguish from the working of his own mind, nothing which he could recognize as 'given him' in that moment. He knew that his every word would be accepted as an inspiration. And he was silent. He might disappoint them but he would not delude them for their good.

There was a delay in the arrival of the executioner[2]. When he appeared Cyprian with his usual largeness of ideas about money desired his friends to give him twenty-five gold pieces[3]. The grass before his feet was now strewn by the Christian bystanders who stood nearest with linen cloths and handkerchiefs[4].

He took a handkerchief, perhaps one of these; folded it and covered his eyes with it, and began to tie the ends, but

---

[1] So the Martyr Montanus re-enunciated Cyprian's principles, Ruinart, *Passio Montani*.

[2] *Speculator*. The form *spiculator* in *Act. Proc.* 5, is due to a wrong derivation and is not found in the Inscriptions. Livy xxxi. 24, using the word to represent '*hemerodromos* in gens uno die emetientes spatium' incidentally gives the true derivation, *a specula*—a look-out officer. There were to each legion ten such officers of the rank '*principales*,' next below centurions, who carried the dispatches very rapidly, and as alert athletic men were also the usual executioners. They carried Caius' dispatches in state to the Senate on his absurd conquest of Britain, Suet. *Calig.* 44, and brought to Vitellius the news of the submission of the East from Syria and Judæa, Tac. *Hist.* ii. 73. For the other capacity, see Mark vi. 27, 28... σπεκουλάτορα ἐπέταξεν ἐνεχθῆναι τὴν κεφαλὴν αὐτοῦ, καὶ ἀπελθὼν ἀπεκεφάλισεν αὐτὸν ἐν τῇ φυλακῇ.—In Senec. *de Ira*, i. 16 the speculator is the executioner (infr. p. 506, r. 2 on *centurion* and *speculator*). At Lambæse are three inscriptions on *speculateres* of the Third Legion, *Corp. Inscrr. Latt.* VIII. i. 2603, 2890, 2989; another, 4381, at Seriana calls one of the same legion *rarissimus filius*.

[3] The *aureus*, equivalent under Augustus to the forty-sixth part of a *libra* or 126 English grains of gold, had sunk by Gallienus' time to about 70 grains Troy, which in English money would be about 11s. 8d., so that the fee which Cyprian gave was nearly £15. Maximilian gave the *speculator* his new military suit, Ruinart, *Acta Sti. Maximiliani M.* iii.

[4] *Acta Proc.* 5, linteamina et manualia. Manualis, not a classical word. See infr. *The dress of Cyprian*, 4, *laciniæ manuales*, p. 516.

this was not easy, and the two Julians tied them, while he held it to his eyes[1]. He said something to quicken the movements of the soldier. Then occurred a singular circumstance, missed in every rendering of the event which I have seen[2]. Astonished at the good-will expressed to him by so generous a gift for such an office, or touched with the sight of so venerable and unusual a figure awaiting his stroke, or moved by the surrounding sympathy, or it may be by a secret leaning towards the faith, the headsman dropped his hand and could scarcely close his trembling fingers on the hilt of his broadsword.

Seeing him utterly unnerved the centurion in command of the party stepped forward, and, to those who waited for the very ripeness of the hour of this, the promised 'Morrow,' a preternatural strength seemed to be in his one stroke[3].

'And so suffered the blessed Cyprian[4].'

The demeanour of the populace was remarkable. Augustine[5] indeed speaks in a conventional way of the 'savage

---

[1] This is what Pontius means by his slight note of correction to the *Acta*. Up to this point Pontius has left out all detail from the moment that Cyprian entered the 'convallis,' because, as he says in c. 11, *sunt Acta quæ referant*. But here the *Acts*, 5, say, 'beatus Cyprianus manu sua oculos sibi texit, qui cum lacinias manuales ligare sibi non potuisset, Julianus presbyter et Julianus subdiaconus ei ligaverunt.' Pontius, who was close to him, does not wish this to be understood, as it might be, that Cyprian merely placed his hand over his eyes, while his friends put on the handkerchief, and so says (18) 'ligatis *per manus suas* oculis' with the help of his own hands—he held it from slipping down while they tied it, which he could not do. All these little touches put together mark the genuineness of the account.

[2] Marshall, Tillemont, Rettberg, C. Thornton, Wallis and all imagine the *speculator* to be the centurion. Pontius, who was close to them and saw exactly what happened, here again completes the Acts, which say only 'ita beatus Cyprianus passus est.' He relates clearly enough; if only it is known that the *speculator*, or 'carnifex,' 'cujus munus est ferrum,' and the centurion were officers of utterly different grade and position. The headsman failing, his superior officer acted so as to close the painful scene (*Vit.* 18). See note, p. 505, n. 2, and compare Seneca, *de Ira*, i. 16, 'Tunc centurio, supplicio præpositus, condere gladium speculatorem jubet.'

[3] 'Clarificationis hora matura'...'concesso desuper vigore,' Pont. *Vit.* 18.

[4] *Acta Proc.* 5.

[5] S. Aug. *Serm.* 310, 2. '*Calcabatur*' however is metaphorical, as it is in his next sermon.

XI. THE BIRTHDAY.

multitude' as contrasted with the communions of after years held on that same ground. But at the time there was no triumph, no molestation. There was evident surprise. And they wished to gaze more closely on the man who had been an acknowledged benefactor to the city, and yet (so they were assured) was a deadly enemy of the State, head in all Africa of an unfathomable society whose unity was coextensive with the unity of the Empire; a man who would sooner die than consider whether he could honour the gods.

They came and went while daylight lasted. Through the night the Christians, still unhindered[1], bore him with wax lights and torches, with 'prayer and a great triumph,' to the cemetery of Macrobius Candidianus. Bearing the name of a former Procurator as its owner or founder, this resting-place can scarcely have been appropriated yet by Christians. It lay within the beautiful region of the Mapalia, yet close to the busy street and gate of the city proper[2], and near to the cisterns of Maálka into which the enormous aqueduct poured its ceaseless river.

The effect upon the Christian multitude assembled by Galerius was the reverse of what he contemplated. Their Martyr had fallen as he resolved, among them. And he was the first Martyr Bishop of the Church of Carthage, or, as they believed, of Proconsular Africa[3], since its foundation in the Apostolic age. There grew on them also touches of immediate likeness to Christ's Passion—his being carried to judgment between the two apparitors[4], the Zacchæuses who

---

[1] The Proconsul could not at this time have refused, if he would, to give up the body. Ulpianus, libro ix. *de officio proconsulis,* 'Corpora eorum qui capite damnantur cognatis ipsorum neganda non sunt'; but Paulus says, 'Corpora animadversorum quibuslibet petentibus ad sepulturam danda sunt.' Ulpian adds, 'Nonnunquam non permittitur maxime majestatis causa damnatorum,' *Digesta,* 48, 24, 1, 3. (See De Rossi, *Bollettino,* ann. II. p. 27.)

[2] I venture here to assert what I think can be shewn; see p. 509.

[3] We have Pontius' clear statement of this, *Vit.* 17, 19, but it is singular if there was no instance in the province during the Decian persecution.

[4] This is significantly touched in the *Acta,* 2, 'levaverunt in medioque

had climbed the trees to see him approach, the prophecy of the Gentile ruler like that of the High-priest. But even such glorying in him was outdone by a sense of consecration in themselves. For years he had taught them that martyrdom was not a mere opportunity of suffering: that it consisted in clear realization and self-devotion[1]. Never had he expressed this more forcibly than since it was evident that the opportunity would be his. The last words of his last manual were to this effect—'If persecution finds God's soldier in this 'mind...and he is called away without attaining "martyrdom" 'the faith which was ready to welcome it will not lose its 'reward. The wages of God are paid in full without any 'deductions for lack of opportunity. The crown is given for 'field-service in time of persecution; in time of peace it is 'given to him who is certain of His will[2].'

The eyewitness who confesses like a child that, in his own heart, sorrow was stronger than joy, treats the ejaculations of the people—'let us be beheaded too'—as no mere outburst, but as a solemn record made before Christ's eyes in the ears of His blindfold martyr; a message to Himself committed to that faithful ambassador on the part of many that they themselves were very martyrs in will[3]. Cynicism is cheap. But if we recollect in how short a time a frenzy of martyrdom possessed those regions, we may see little reason to doubt that the enthusiasm of the faith made a forward bound that hour; little reason to question the reality of the joy in which after their long vigil, the Christians left Cyprian in the pagan sepulchre, and went home in a consciousness that they too were 'Crowned[4]' in him.

posuerunt,' and somewhat rudely forced by Augustine, *Serm.* 309, 3.

[1] *De mortalitate*, 17. Pontius, *Vit.* 18, says that the people (whose will was truly to suffer with him) 'compassus est; et *sicut ipso tractante semper audierat*, Deo judice coronatus est.' There is here a verbal reference to the quoted close of his *Ad Fortunatum*.

[2] '*Conscientia.*' *Ad Fortunat.* fin.

[3] Pont. *Vit.* 18, 'publicata voce.' Pontius refers again to the *Acta Proc.* 5 init. These concluding lines of Pontius, c. 18, are worth marking.

[4] 'Gaudium passionis,' Pont. *Vit.* 19; 'compassus...coronatus,' Pont. *Vit.* 18.

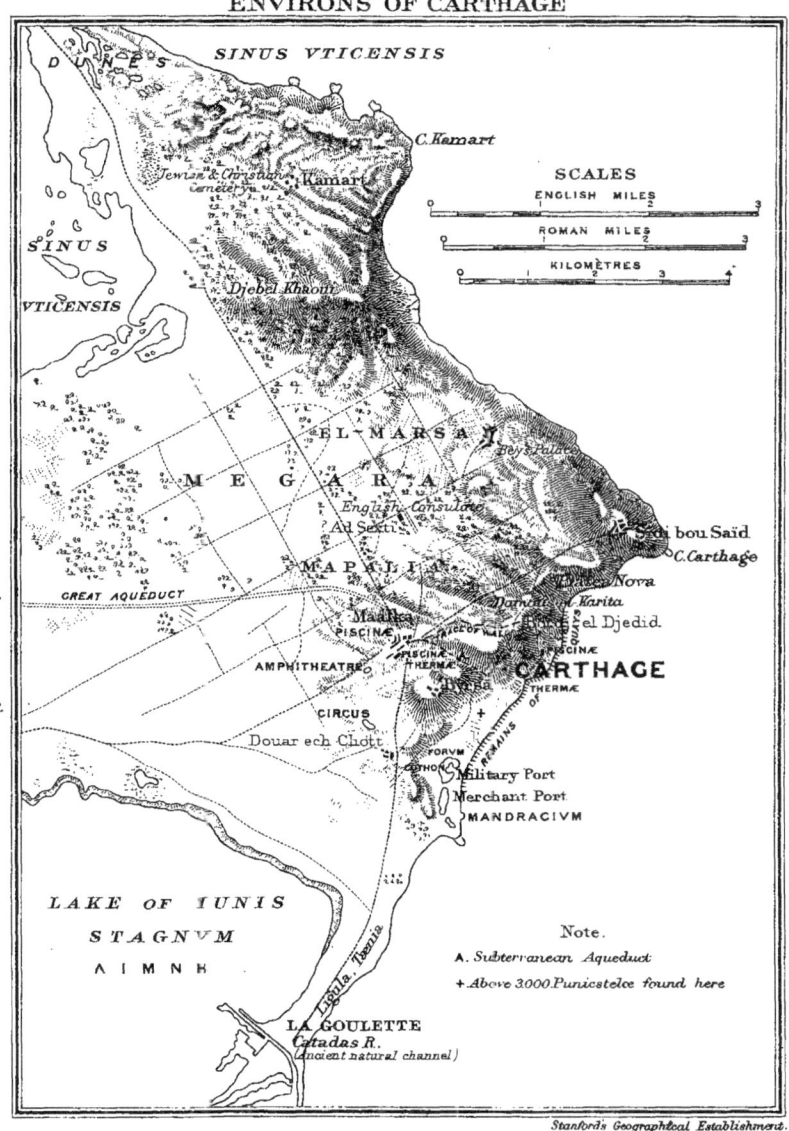

Where was Cyprian Martyr buried[1]?

He was brought with torchlight procession[2] 'ad areas Macrobii Candidiani procuratoris quæ sunt in via Mappaliensi juxta Piscinas.' Here are three points. Tissot has translated the first point to mean 'la maison 'du procurateur Macrobe dans la cour extérieure de laquelle fut enterré 'le corps du martyr[3].' But *Areas* as usual means 'the burial place[4].' And Macrobius could not well be the procurator at that time, because to welcome Cyprian's remains would have implied relations with Christianity at least kindly, and for a great official dangerous, whereas during the vacancy after Galerius' death, which immediately followed Cyprian's, the then procurator governed the province with almost furious rigour against the Christians[5]. [In a proconsular or senatorial province the Procurator was over the branch of the Fiscus, and in matters of inheritance, legacies and various Imperial dues, had concurrent jurisdiction with the Proconsul himself. We have inscriptions relating to three 'Procuratores Africæ Tractus Karthaginiensis[6],' as well as to other 'Tracts,' Hippo, Hadrumetum, Theveste.] These *Areæ* then in which Cyprian was buried were no doubt a cemetery provided or founded by a former procurator, and bearing his name, as those at Rome bore the names of their founders.

Where were these Areæ? They were 'in via Mappaliensi,' a second point. Provided in Roman times, they would probably be outside the city proper. Old Carthage (wrote Cornelius Nepos) 'had the aspect of a double city,' the 'outer town' of the *Magalia* 'embracing' the inner Byrsa and precinct[7]. But the limited space, the wall along the bay, and

---

[1] Since the text and following notes have been in print the third *Livraison* has appeared of the magnificent *Atlas Archéologique de la Tunisie, Édition Spéciale*, published by the *Ministère de la Guerre*, with explanatory text by E. Babelon, R. Cagnat and S. Reinach. Feuille xiv. is *La Marsa*, with a supplementary chart and text. This has not necessitated any alteration in this work, but the plan in this volume is mainly drawn from these maps.

[2] *Acta Proc.* 5.

[3] Tissot, vol. i. p. 660.

[4] Tertull. *ad Scap.* 3, '...sub Hilariano præside cum de areis sepulturarum nostrarum adclamassent Areæ non sint'; also at Carthage Montanus desires '...in medio eorum in area solum servari jussit ut nec sepulturæ consortio privaretur,' *Passio SS. Montani* &c. c. xv. (Ruinart); at Cirta people were shut up 'in area martyrum...in casa majore,' *Gesta apud Zenophilum*, ap. Dupin's *Optatus* (Paris, 1702), p. 170. De Rossi explains, *Bollettino*, ann. 11. p. 27, that *casa* means a sepulchral cell.

[5] Ruinart, *Passio SS. Montani et Lucii*, A.D. 259, ii. vi. &c.

[6] *Corp. Inscrr. Latt.* VIII. i. 1269, 1578, ii. 10570.

[7] Fragm. Cornelii Nep. ap. Servium ad Æn. i. 368 (see Thilo and Hagen's Servius, Leips. 1878), 'Carthago antea

the harbours must have early squeezed out the *Magalia* on those sides and left it lying mainly on the north, but still giving the 'aspect of a double city.' North of the double city, called *Byrsa* from the citadel round which it hung, *Megara*, or 'The New Town,' spread to the sea, and north to the sandy dunes between Kamart and Sidi bou Saïd. It was a vast suburb full of gardens and villas, as it still is, the present El-Marsa, and was not merely coextensive with the region of the *Mapalia*[1], which bore to the latest times the native name of the Hut-farms whose circles once covered it[2]. The *Via Mappaliensis* was no doubt the road or street which ran out by the west of the Byrsa through the *Mapalia*. Such a road there is traversing its whole length; an antient road, with its many cross roads at exact right angles. It was on this street in the Mapalia itself that the *Areæ* lay.

Genseric occupied a number of churches *outside the wall*, and particularly '*two* noble and ample basilicas of the holy martyr Cyprian, one 'where he shed his blood, the other where his body was buried, the place 'which is called Mappalia,' so writes Victor Vitensis[3]. The 'wall outside of which' the Basilica stood was probably either the outer wall of Megara

speciem habuit duplicis oppidi, quasi aliud alterum complecteretur, cujus interior pars Byrsa dicebatur, exterior Magalia.' Quoted by Tissot, v. I. p. 586, as the language of Servius.

[1] Tissot, 1. pp. 569, 579 ff.

[2] *Magalia* is the great suburb of Carthage, one half of Cornelius's 'double city,' in the fragment of Sallust ap. Serv. on Æn. i. 421, 'Magalia sunt circumjecta civitati suburbana ædificia'; in Plaut. *Pœn. Prolog.* 86 (Magaribus); and correctly in Virg. *Æn.* i. 421, iv. 259, as having preceded Punic Carthage.—Kritz on Sall. *Jug.* 18 says after Servius that *măpalia* only differs from *măgalia* in quantity (as above in the *Æneid* compared with *Georg.* iii. 340, Lucan, iv. 684), but *mappalia* with two *p*'s is common at any rate later.—The word meant native African tents, Liv. xxix. 31, which were like inverted boats, Sall. *Jug.* 18, of herdsmen and shepherds, *Geor. l.c.*, then the whole kraal, 'mappalia quasi cohortes rotundæ sunt....' Cato *ap. Fest.* and *Serv.* (*cohors* means 'quod in villa ex pluribus tectis conjungitur et quiddam fit unum'); the Garamantes' villages between Œa and Leptis were so called, Tac. *Hist.* iv. 50; and so were the war-camps of Tacfarinas and the Numidians, *Ann.* iv. 25, iii. 74. — Festus says they were 'casæ Punicæ,' but this is inaccurate and can only be derived from the name of the quarter at Carthage through which the *Via Mappaliensis* ran, as it lay both inside and outside the wall of Megara.—It is interesting to notice that the farm labourers on estates near Hippo were still called Mappalienses in Augustine's time, *Ep.* 66 (3) *ad Crispinum Calamensem.*

[3] Victor Vitensis, i. 5. Augustine, *Serm.* 62, 17, speaks to the people as having heard a Scripture lesson read *in Mappalibus*, which refers no doubt to this Basilica. In Sermons 311, 312 and 313, which he preached in it, he speaks of its 'amplitude,' and of the 'sublimity of its Divine altar,' and says that the site of it had been within living memory a scene of pagan revelries with singing and dancing all night (*Serm.* 311, 5). The present Bishop (*frater noster*) had instituted the 'holy vigils' which displaced them.

itself or the great wall which, though Carthage was dismantled, could not be destroyed (and is not destroyed yet), which went east from Maâlka to the sea, shutting the city proper off from Megara[1]. But it may have been the wall on the west of Megara.

The third point is that the *Areæ* were 'juxta piscinas,' that is no doubt the immense cisterns at Maâlka which are just outside that great wall. The smaller cisterns by the sea do not fit the other points as these exactly do. I cannot doubt then that within a few yards we can mark the site of that Basilica of Cyprian's resting-place—namely by the Piscinæ, outside the antient north wall of the Byrsa, within the Mapalia, and on the long street which traverses it.

There is however a passage which at first sight seems irreconcileable with this locality. Maximilian of Theveste, beheaded in A.D. 295 for refusing as a Christian to serve in the army, was buried *sub monticulo juxta Cyprianum martyrem secus platum*[2], or in the other MS. of this passio, *palatium*. Tissot thence concludes that Cyprian was buried not far from the Proconsular Palace[3], which he elsewhere shews to have been on the eastern slope of the Byrsa-Citadel, which was crowded with buildings. Intramural and Christian interment in such a spot at either date seems impossible, and that spot could not be called *juxta piscinas*.

This being so I think it possible that *palatium* in the 13th cent. MS. was a correction, and that *platum* may represent *plateam*. Near to the *Platea Nova*, and near the shore, there was a *third* church of S. Cyprian, the *Memoria Sancti Cypriani*, in which Monica by Augustine's persuasion spent the night in which he eluded her affection and sailed for

---

[1] Cf. *Atlas Archéol. de la Tunisie*, note on *La Marsa*, lxxx. Cf. *C. I. Semiticarum*, I. p. 243.

[2] The Passion of Maximilian was first printed at the end of the Oxford Edition of Lactantius, *de Mortibus Persecutorum*, 12mo. 1680, from 'membranæ Sarisburienses.' Mabillon, *Vet. Analecta*, tom. IV. 1635, reprints it pp. 565 ff. 'ex codice Sarensi nuper Oxonii Vulgata post Lactantii librum de morte persecutorum, a V. C. Stephano Baluzio primum editum: quam Passionem hic recudere visum est ad superiora [*scil. in tomo iv.*] Martyrum acta illustranda.' Ruinart, *Acta Martyrum sincera*, prints it 'ex codice MS. Montis S. Michaelis cum editis collato.'

The Sarum MS. has disappeared, and we do not know its date. That of Mt. S. Michel is now no. 167 in the Town Library of Avranches. It is only of the 13th century.

In the passage above discussed, the Sarum MS. had *secus platum*, for which the Oxford Editors conjecture *platanum* because Pontius says that the place was *arboribus consitum*, or else *palatium*, because the Cotton MS. of the *Acta Proc.* says Cyprian was beheaded *in agro Sexti post prætorium* (Lactantii *de Mortibus Persecut.* Oxon. 1680, p. 46 n.). But both those expressions refer to the place of execution, not of burial, and there is no indication that the Villa where Galerius was, though properly called a *Prætorium*, was called *Palatium*. The late MS. Mt. S. Mich. had *palatium*, also Ruinart, *Acta MM*.

[3] Tissot, I. 660.

Rome[1]. This locality further answers the description of the place in which Maximilian was buried, for it would be *sub monticulo*, namely under the low hill on which was formed the Platea whose 'giant-steps' descended to the quays[2].

[Is it moreover certain that *platum* itself could not be used, though traces of it are later? '*Platos* est *latum sive planum idem platea*, gloss. MSS. S. Andreæ Avenion.' ap. Ducange[3], who also gives (A.D. 1519) 'super quodem *Platto* dicto *le petit plat* sito Lugduni...']

Where was Cyprian tried and executed?

The Acta Proconsularia are explicit. On the ides of September Cyprian was fetched from his gardens and conveyed in a chariot *in Sexti*, where Galerius was for his health. That day he was too ill to take the case. Cyprian went to the house of the *princeps* for the night. Next morning a great crowd assembled *ad Sexti*. Cyprian was brought up and heard by the proconsul in a certain *atrium*, and was taken *in agrum Sexti* to be executed[4].

Ad Sexti, like many other place-names in Africa, as *ad Atticillæ, ad Cazalis, ad Germani, ad Lali*, represents a villa of importance, or the vicus which had grown up about it—a 'village' proper. Corresponding to these in meaning would be such names as *Vicus Aureli, Vicus Juliani, Villa Marci*. Sextus (or Sextius?) then had been the founder or was the well-known owner of a villa fit to nurse a sick proconsul, and containing at least one hall not unfit for a proconsul's hall of judgment in the trial of a great citizen. It had an *ager* or farm, in some part of which executions could be held in the sight of a great multitude, and on which there were many trees.

Pontius had these Acts in his hands. In the trial before Paternus he says he purposely omits details because the Acts gave them fully. He says that on the first day Cyprian was remanded *from the prætorium*, went on the second day to the *prætorium* to be tried, and left the *prætorium* doors condemned to death[5].

This has led even such authorities as Tissot to look for the scene of

---

[1] Aug. *Conf.* v. 8. Cf. Procop. *B. Vand.* i. 21, ed. Dindorf, vol. I. p. 397.

[2] See Tissot, I. 569, and Falbe's map and note on *La Marsa*, cx. in *Atlas Archéol. de la Tunisie*.

[3] More fully described in his list of authorities.

[4] Bede, *Martyrol.* 18 Kal. Oct., through a misunderstanding about *ad Sexti* and of reports as to Cyprian's third church, has 'martyrium consummavit sexto milliario a Carthagine juxta mare.'

[5] Pontii *Vit.* 15 bis, 18.

the trial near the *Prætorium* or *Palatium Proconsulare* which, as he shews, stood on the steep slope of the citadel and looked towards the ports[1]. But it is next to impossible that a place called *ad Sexti* with an *ager Sexti* and a very large wood could be so situated, even if no reasons carried it elsewhere. But the error arises from imagining the word *prætorium* to be so limited in use. At this time *prætorium*, 'head-quarters,' had passed into a common name for the residence-house and buildings, the *urbana*, of any great estate[2]. Pontius' word 'prætorium' would perfectly suit a villa '*ad Sexti*,' even if the Proconsul did not occupy it. There is no contradiction between Pontius and the Acts.

From the house of the Princeps to *ad Sexti* is called *iter longum*[3], which scarcely could be applied to the distance from near the Palatium to the Cisterns of Maálka; so that *ad Sexti* was probably a good way beyond that—say twice as far. Again, the body was brought back *per noctem*. This was along the Mappalian Way, which probably was also his way out. Its being brought there favours the idea that 'Sextus's' was in that wide, healthy, beautiful region, which has from immemorial time been all gardens and villas, the present El-Marsa in which the English Consulate lies among its gardens and trees. It seems probable that the trial and execution were not far from that. The sites marked out under the auspices of the Cathedral do not claim to be and have no interest in being authentic. They are for the convenience of functions and functionaries. On the spot where he fell was erected the Holy Table of one of those Basilicas which Victor speaks of[4], and it was called '*Mensa Cypriani*.' Augustine[5], while he says that everyone knew it who knew Carthage, finds it well to explain that it had never been used by Cyprian, but only was marked by his offering to be a place for offerings.

The dress of Cyprian.

In preparation for the death-blow he took off first the *lacerna byrrus*, then the *dalmatic*; then he stood in his *linea*. He was unable to fasten the *laciniæ manuales*.

---

[1] Vol. I. p. 660, p. 649. *Atlas Archéol. de la Tunisie* does not hold with any special identification of the ruins, note on *La Marsa*, xlii.

[2] *Digesta*, 50, 16, 198, Ulpian, 'prætoria voluptati tantum deservientia' come under the definition of *urbana prædia*, *i.e.* estates in the country with buildings of town-fashion. Juv. i. 75, 'criminibus debent hortos, *prætoria*, mensas, Argentum vetus.' Suet. *Tib.* 39 'in *prætorio* cui Speluncæ nomen est,' of which Tacitus, *Ann.* iv. 59, speaks as ' in *villa* cui vocabulum Speluncæ'—Suet. *Calig.* 37 'in exstructionibus *prætoriorum* et villarum.'

[3] Pontii *Vit.* 16.

[4] *Ut sup.* Victor Vitensis, i. 5.

[5] Aug. *Serm.* 310, c. 2.

1. *Lacerna byrrus*.

I do not know whether *lacerna byrrus*[1] occur elsewhere in conjunction; but there is copious illustration of each in Ducange, and in the older antiquarians. See also *Dict. Gk. and Rom. Antiquities, s.vv.* The *lacerna* was a man's woollen cape or short cloak, fastened on the shoulder, open down the side, worn over the toga in chilly times or places, and by soldiers. Too common originally for town wear; but had largely come in, when Augustus sarcastically quoted *Romanos rerum dominos gentemque togatam*. As it grew fashionable it might only be white in the theatre; if the Emperor (Claudius) entered the Equites put it off. Finally worn of all colours, and costly. *Birrhus* appears as synonymous with more than one kind of cloak. In the Edictum Diocletiani *de Pretiis Rerum* A.D. 301, the birrhus has a large range of price from the Laodicene, which was very expensive, to the African, which was cheap. The name has nothing to do with πυρρός, and is probably barbaric. Augustine wore a cheap birrhus and sold more expensive ones given to him for his community. *Serm.* 356, 13. Sulp. Sev. *Dial.* i. 21 speaks of it as *rigens*, while the *lacerna* was *fluens*. The *lacerna* was also thinner (Aug. *Serm.* 161, 10). Ascetics disdained it in comparison with the monastic *pallium* to such an extent that the Council of Gangra anathematized their folly (Can. xii.[2]) in the fourth century. In the seventh it was made too costly for monks to wear (Isidor. Hispal. *Reg. Mon.* xii. 2, cf. Jo. Cassian. *de Cœnob. Instit.* i. 7). In Gregory the Great's time men put it on after baptism white, and dedicated it. The hood often attached to the *birrhus* became a 'head-dress,' and thence *birretta*.

We see then that Cyprian wore the unpretentious citizen's dress and rather plain, just as Pontius c. 6 describes him, 'cultus...temperatus et 'ipse de medio...non superbia sæcularis...nec tamen prorsus adfectata 'penuria.'

2. *Dalmatica*.

Dr R. Sinker speaks like other learned authorities of the wearing of the dalmatic by Cyprian as an 'ecclesiastical use,' and this has perhaps something to do with a doubt[3] which he hints as to the authenticity of the *Acta Proconsularia*. The Dalmatian tunic (*chiridota Dalmatarum*)

---

[1] ...*pænulasque, lacernas et chirodotas Dalmatarum...* ap. Jul. Capitol. *Pertinax* 8, with very similar meaning, and we shall note below that *laciniæ manuales* is probably a similar combination in the matter of dress.

[2] Gangra, A.D. 358 (v. Ffoulkes, *Dict. Christ. Antiq. s.v.*), Can. xii. εἴ τις ἀνδρῶν διὰ νομιζομένην ἄσκησιν περιβολαίῳ (Isidor. Mercat. *pallio;* Dion. Exig. *amictu pallii*) χρῆται, καὶ ὡς ἂν ἐκ τούτου τὴν δικαιοσύνην ἔχων καταψηφίσοιτο τῶν μετ' εὐλαβείας τοὺς βήρους φορούντων, καὶ τῇ ἄλλῃ κοινῇ καὶ ἐν συνηθείᾳ οὔσῃ ἐσθῆτι κεχρημένων, ἀνάθεμα ἔστω. Labbe (Mansi), II. col. 1101, Florent. 1759.

[3] See p. 518.

is never heard of among Romans till the end of the second century. The learning about it is too extensive and accessible to repeat. It was squarely constructed, of good material, and being made originally of one width, had a fringe or selvage down the joining of the edges on one side only. The *colobion*, otherwise like it, had no sleeves. The dalmatic had large stiff sleeves as far as the elbow, which were not always sewn up under the arm.

When we consider that as late as A.D. 222 under Elagabalus, a man who wore a dalmatic in public did something *outré*[1], and that in A.D. 301 the Edict of Diocletian[2] fixed the prices of all sorts of dalmatics for men and women, according to their manufacture (the African were cheap) as regular articles of wear, it is impossible to conceive that about halfway between these two dates they had been adopted as solemn ecclesiastical vestments. Further, not till under Silvester I. (314—335), who in his last Council of 335 (according to Roman tradition) certainly magnified their office, was the dalmatic adopted for Deacons instead of the sleeveless *colobion*[3], but this was for the Seven Deacons *of Rome*. Two centuries later, A.D. 513, the Deacons of Arles receive licence to use it, *perinde ac Romanæ ecclesiæ diaconi*[4]. In A.D. 599 Gregory (*Epp*. l. ix. Ind. ii. Ep. 107) grants the use of it 'after much consideration' 'as a new thing' to the *Bishop* of Gap (Vapincum) and his *Archdeacon*, so that the common idea that it was the proper episcopal dress before Silvester cannot be true, and the use was still connected with *Rome*. But when Gregory conceded this, it must be remembered that persons like himself and his father at any rate, who were of senatorial rank, wore it laically (Joann.Diac. *Vit. S. Greg*. iv. 83, 84). Gregory's Sacramentary (ed. Bened. vol. III. col. 65, Paris, 1705) is quoted in proof of the early liturgical use of it, the Pope and the Seven Deacons being directed all to wear dalmatics for the consecration of oil 'on the Thursday in Holy Week.' But whatever the use may have been, these Rubrics are not part of the original[5].

In Spain the dalmatic had not become a clerical vestment in A.D. 633[6]. Considering then the lay use of the dalmatic in the third century and the Roman aspect of its ecclesiastical use later, it is out of the question that it should have been an ecclesiastical vesture in Africa in

---

[1] Lamprid. *Anton. Helagabalus*, 26.

[2] Edictum Diocletiani *de pretiis rerum*, *Corp. Inscrr. Latt*. III. ii. p. 836. W. H. Waddington, *Édit de Dioclétien*, p. 30.

[3] See *Vita Silvestri P*., Labbe (Mansi) vol. I. col. 444, Florent. 1759.

[4] Jaffé, *Regesta Pontificum s. ann.* 513, vol. I. p. 99. *Vita Cæsarii*, 4.

[5] They are not in Muratori's Vatican MS. or in Cod. Ottoboni, both of the early ninth century. They cannot be traced earlier than the *Ordo Romanus I.* of which Muratori has two recensions (*Lit. Rom. Vet.*) vol. II. 992 and 1006, and these Rubrics represent a third. The *Ordo* seems to have been compiled about A.D. 730 and describes the Roman rite of perhaps the seventh century. H.A.W. C.W.

[6] See *Dict. Chris. Antt. s.v. Dalmatica*.

A.D. 258, and worn with a very long cape over it. We see again that Cyprian in fact wore the dress of a quiet Roman gentleman.

Such questions are wholly unimportant except so far as incorrect assertions give for any age a perverse view of how the world looked and what the world felt.

3. *Linea.*

We may take it that no particular change between Cyprian's and Augustine's time took place in this. Augustine speaks of the antient idea of effeminacy attached to long and long-sleeved tunics. So in Virgil, *et tunicæ manicas et habent redimicula mitræ.* 'It was once a 'crime,' says Augustine, 'to have tunics to the ancles and sleeved. But 'now when people of respectable birth wear tunics it is a crime not to 'have them so[1].' Soldiers were very particular that they should fit the body close. The girdle was essential to neatness out of doors, and the tunic was shortened by being drawn up through it.

4. *Laciniæ manuales.*

Words not elsewhere conjoined, and certainly not meaning 'the sleeve of his robe at the wrist' (Thornton). The lexicons abundantly illustrate that successive meanings of *laciniæ* are fringed or cut edges hemmed on to a garment, the hem of the garment itself, the lappet of a dress used among other things to wipe the face. Then of separate strips of cloth, of skin, of land. The notion of 'strips,' and hence of 'folds,' runs through a set of words, *laciniare, -atim, -osus, -ose,* which I should observe are particularly affected by African writers. It is not at all clear to me that Apuleius ever uses the word simply as equivalent to *vestis,* as Hildebrand and others say. *Manualis,* or *-e,* is used by itself as 'a handkerchief.' When Montanus was blindfolded he tore the *manualis* in two and said half should be kept for Flavian *qua oculi post crastinum ligarentur.* Halves of it served the purpose as well as the whole. (Compare *manipulus,* which came to mean a long shaped towel or a towel folded long and narrow.) *Manuales* then may be adjectival, but I should rather think *laciniæ manuales* is constructed like *lacerna birrhus,* and it meant large handkerchiefs, originally of substantial stuff, narrow, or folded narrow, and perhaps two of them used, one over the other.

The Soldiers and Officers named in the Trial.

The more we press every detail in these Cyprianic documents the more their truthfulness stands out. It is very interesting that we can tell exactly who these soldiers of the Proconsul were. A single line in a

[1] *De Doctr. Christiana,* iii. 11, (20).

striking inscription reveals it (*Corp. Inscrr. Latt.* VIII. i. 2532). On the pedestal of a column which formed part of the west gate of the camp at Lambæse the Third Legion inscribed a speech which Hadrian addressed to them on a memorable visit. He says 'the Legate has 'explained to him that he may notice certain deficiencies, and has given 'the reasons for them.' Among these is

OMNIA MIHI PRO VOBIS IPSE DI[*xit quod*] COHORS ABEST QUOD OMNIBUS ANNIS PER VICES IN OFFICIUM PR[*ocon*]SULIS MITTITUR.

That is one cohort of the Third Legion from the camp at Lambæse was always in attendance in annual turns on the Proconsul. If we ask why the whole Third Legion was not under the command of the Proconsul, the answer is in Tacitus, *Hist.* iv. 48. Caligula, insanely jealous of the then Proconsul, took away the control of it and established a Legate to command the Legion and (as we know from elsewhere) the fortresses.

The soldiers then who appear in the narrative with their tribunes, centurions, and the other officers so freely named belonged to that cohort of the Third Legion which for that year was appointed to the officium of the Proconsul.

Of the Massa Candida.

We have seen how Cyprian was summoned to Utica by the Proconsul, undoubtedly with a view to his execution there. From the different mentions of the group known by this curiosity-wakening name of *Massa Candida* it has been inferred by Tillemont as well as others that in 258 A.D., on the 18th or 24th August[1], a great number of Christians were summoned thither, and martyred. But the accounts cannot be put together, or rather there are none which can be put together. The facts are these. (1) Augustine's Enarration of Ps. 144 (or part of it) is a sermon preached at Utica in the 'Basilica of the Massa Candida[2].' He preached Sermon 306 on the solemnity of their 'Natalis'; in Sermon 311, preached at Carthage, in the Memoria of Cyprian on his 'Birthday' (c. 10), he mentions them as '*Uticensis* Massa Candida,' and apparently as having been rich and poor together, but not as being specially connected with Cyprian. That he mentions them along with Cyprian is merely because both illustrate his point. In his Enarration on Ps. 49, c. 9, he speaks of '...sola *in proximo* quæ dicitur Massa Candida'

---

[1] Aug. 24th, IX. Kal. Sept. Uticæ SS. MM. CCC. *Massæ Candidæ*. *Kalendar. Ant. Eccl. Carth.*; Aug. 18th Hieron. *Martyrolog.*; 24th Ado; 24th Usuard.

[2] Heading in Cod. Floriac. 'habitus Uticæ in basilica Massæ Candidæ.' No reason to doubt this, which agrees with the allusions.

(*i.e.* perhaps in the neighbouring Utica), and says they were more numerous than 'the 153 fishes' which he is expounding. He says (*Serm.* 306, c. 2) they were called *massa* because of their number[1], and *candida* for *their martyr-brightness*, which demands a *candida conscientia* in us. It is apparent that no details were known which he could dwell on.

(2) A sermon upon them tastelessly attributed to Augustine, but possibly of his time, speaks of *cruentus percussor, ferrum..., cervicem* as if they were then supposed to have died by the sword[2].

(3) Of what Augustine on the spot did not know Prudentius (*Peristeph.* 13) about the same time in Spain has full particulars. By him our Cyprian is first confounded with Cyprian the magician, Bishop of Antioch. After being brought before the Proconsul he is imprisoned in chains in the dark. His prayer so nerves the Carthaginians that 300 of them being offered their choice between sacrificing or being burnt in a lime-kiln, open at the place where Cyprian was to be executed, all flung themselves into the kiln, and are called *candida* from the whiteness of their bodies in the lime as well as that of their souls. Then Cyprian is brought before the Proconsul and beheaded, 'rejoicing in their martyrdom.'

Thus literally there exists nothing like history. Nothing to shew at what period or in what way the Group suffered. The argument from non-mention is of positive value here. For, if there had been such a large self-martyrdom so early, the advocates of the Circumcellions must have alleged it. And such is the copiousness of Augustine that we must have known both their use of the argument and his answer.

Prudentius' tale as it stands is absurd, and where it is attempted to give it more probability by separating it from Cyprian's execution and putting it nearer to his exile, the attempt, the supposition that a mass of people could have been put to death by the Proconsul of Africa immediately after Valerian's Edict (or Rescript), is a misconception of the whole idea of the legislation up to this point.

It was entirely in the hope of averting such large executions that Valerian's penalties were conceived and directed upon the leaders of the new Society.

Acta Proconsularia.

The *Acta* were certainly older than the Life of Cyprian by Pontius, who was his constant companion and was with him at his death. Pontius quotes from them, and silently but evidently corrects two details in that brief document, so that added to its own accuracy of detail it is scarcely possible for a document to be better accredited.

---

[1] 'De numeri multitudine.' Cf. Optat. ii. 26 ad fin. 'massam pœnitentium facere.' Rarely used of people.

[2] Aug. *Serm. Supposit.* 317.

Pontius, c. 12, says 'quid sacerdos Dei proconsule interrogante responderit, sunt Acta quæ referant.'

Pontius's expression '*publicata voce*,' c. 18, is not intelligible without the exclamation of the people as given in *Acta Procons.* 5 init.

The tying of the handkerchief is a detail in which Pontius corrects the account of the Acts (see Text, p. 505).

So is also his explanation that it was the centurion in command and not the executioner who actually gave the death stroke. (Pont. 18 compared with *Acta* 5. Text, p. 506.)

The short Passion of Cyprian which Fell gives p. 14 'ex MS. S. Victoris nec non Bodleiano I.' and which Rigault (and apparently Fell) thinks the more antient form is nothing but a piece (c. 2—4) of the longer one with abbreviations and interpolations meant to give a more formal appearance, so that it is best presented, as by Hartel, merely in the shape of various readings on the genuine *Acta*. Pontius and Augustine, *Sermm.* 309, 310, and *c. Gaudentium* i. 31, (40) quote only from the longer one phrases and words which have been modified in the shorter and later.

CHAPTER XII.

AFTERMATH.

THERE is not only interest, there is spiritual reassurance in marking how, like a cloud from Atlas floated into the bright air, Cyprian's error disappears in the warmth of the Church's atmosphere.

At Arles, where, in A.D. 314, seven or eight out of thirty-three bishops who signed were Africans, the African custom was quietly overruled.

At Nicæa in A.D. 325 the mere enactment that Paulianists were to be baptized shews how peaceably the enactments of Iconium and Synnada had died, just as that of Agrippinus had died before Cyprian revived it. The Church has never been ruled by its canons except for brief instants. Men collect themselves from time to time and formulate for eternity the standard of the hour, and as soon as it is fixed the stream sets away from it again.

At Carthage in A.D. 349[1] the successors of Cyprian's bishops dispersed by acclamation the 87 reasoned fallacies of their fathers. And afterwards Augustine refuted one by one the suffrages given to the man whose wisdom, power and love he literally adored.

That there was a seed in his teaching which fanatics

[1] *Conc. Carth.* I. *sub Grato.*

could foster to a wild growth, cannot be denied, although Augustine has shewn with what exaggerations the mistake was urged, and what corrections he had himself supplied. But it fell unhappily on a widespread temper, mad for laxities in one direction, mad for exclusion in another, mad for a ceremonial materialism in a third, and a temper charged moreover with political revengefulness.

This was Cyprian's unforeseen contribution to Donatism —the invalidation of an ecclesiastical act on account of subjective imperfection in the minister. For the modern doctrine of Intention he has no responsibility.

The last of that string of canons which, beginning with those of Nicæa, was affirmed in the second canon of the Quini-Sext Council in A.D. 692, was 'the canon put forth by 'Cyprian, that was Archbishop of the land of the Africans and 'Martyr, and the Synod of his time, which canon prevailed in 'the places of the aforesaid prelates, and only according to the 'custom delivered to them.' The Greek acceptance of this Council might seem to commit their Church to Cyprian's practice, unless the canon be interpreted as supposing the practice still extant and still limited to Africa. Some interpretation must be found for it as it stands, for it is in flat contradiction to part of the ninety-fifth of the same Council, and the usage did not prevail among the Greeks.

The canon was however turned into Syriac, accepted by Syrian Churches, and became the ground on which Jacobites rejected the baptism of the orthodox[1].

A strange irony that the unanimous rulings of the African episcopate should be swept away by the resounding *Absit, Absit* of their own successors, too impatient of it to speak or vote, and that the vital necessity of baptism by the orthodox should find its final lodgment with the heterodox.

Not that human hunger for exclusiveness was appeased even in the greater Churches. The exclusions that had been

---

[1] Renaudot, *Liturg. Orient.* vol. II. p. 292.

set aside as untenable Doctrine were revived on special pleas of Form. The Greeks long denied the validity of all other baptism and accepted only 'trine immersion.' The Romans rebaptize all 'conditionally'; that is, upon a theory dating only from Alexander III.[1], and rarely put in practice until the sixteenth century.

As Hero and Saint Cyprian's personality went through scarcely less strange experiences. Gibbon is charmed to call him 'almost a local deity.' It was not long before every Mediterranean sailor called the September gales *Cypriana* from his 'Birthday.' It was kept at Rome in the Cemetery of Callistus long before Cornelius himself was honoured by a joint commemoration with him. He was and is the one non-Roman commemorated in the Roman Canon, the one Latin father really recognised by the world-contemning Greeks. But this recognition was more fantastic than their ignorance. Gregory of Nazianzus looses floods of eloquence upon him. Some of his works he knew; he knew particulars which he could scarcely have derived from anything but memoirs as personal as those of Pontius. Yet he thought that he suffered under Decius, that his chief merit was the restoration of accurate definitions of the Holy Trinity; and he identified him with that Cyprian of Antioch, whose legend, a compound of riotous fancy, pagan theurgy, and new demonology, exercised a depraving influence on the popular religion far down into the middle ages. Near three centuries later he had appeared unto many and quieted the indignation of African Catholics at his sea-side church being in the hands of the Arians—'he would care for himself in his own time.' On his own eve in A.D. 533 Belisarius overthrew the Vandals ten miles from Carthage, and was received in the city with a triumphal welcome. The 'Christians,' Procopius relates, came in, lighted the already prepared lamps, and celebrated the

---

[1] Thomas Aquinas, *Summa Theol.* P. III. Q. lxvi. art. 9.

day in the sanctuary which the Arian priests had splendidly arrayed for the festival[1].

To his own contemporaries he seemed for a time scarcely to have quitted them. The faces of confessors and martyrs beamed with the remembrance that they had been Cyprian's disciples[2]. Almost his very words rose to their lips as at the last moment they spoke of the sufferings of the Church or commended her discipline to their survivors[3]. One questions Cyprian in his dream 'whether it is pain to die[4]?' Another after torture saw him sitting by the Judge, helping him mount the steps to his side, and then giving him water from a fountain[5]. That he spoke as the oracles of God, that he was essentially a Ruler, essentially a Comforter—nothing could better express the intense reverence for Cyprian than these three martyr-thoughts.

Nor is anything lost if we bring that high-wrought emotional view into comparison with the practical analytic measure of the man.

Cyprian was possessed by two overmastering ideas. He burned to make them live and breathe for Christian men as for himself. He did more than any man to house them in the life and polity of the world. The ideas were to each other as soul and body. To him they were one fact, one truth. One was the vital principle, the other was the organism of Christendom.

I. He was certain that human nature (in which Thucydides himself perhaps thought that wickedness was not a permanent, necessary ingredient) could be changed, could be perfectly remoulded. He was convinced that it had in Roman civilization taken the wrong bent; that not only the 'superb falsities[6]' of religion but many contemporary institutions which

---

[1] Procop. *de Bello Vand.* i. 20, 21. See *Appendix on S. Cyprian's Day.*
[2] *Passio SS. Montani et Lucii*, xiii.
[3] *Id.* xiv.
[4] *Id.* xxi.
[5] *Passio SS. Jacobi et Mariani et aliorum*, vi.
[6] Aug. *Serm.* 312, 5.

were the life of society were working powerfully for degradation and destruction. He was assured to demonstration that God had marked another line, provided other institutions, offered powers sufficient to conduct nature along another road to another end. It had been revealed that the individual could be enabled to assume and justify his true place in creation, his true dignity, which was that of the 'Sons of God.' This fact realized was enough to dethrone self, to transform thought, to renovate society. In this view all suffering became probation, death often a duty, always a triumph. Every virtue of the world must be born again and live a resurrection-life. His *Custodi puellas* was felt, strange as that now seems, to be the utterance of a new protective influence, a new kind of 'shepherding.' A plague city need be no more the hell that it had ever been. Perfect altruism would perfect the world.

These were no dreams. They were established experimental facts. He had in his own person tested the power of the 'illumination,' the 'inundation' of grace. In his own consciousness he had ascertained what it was to be born of water and the Spirit. Multitudes drank from the Chalice of the Lord a strength without which no man could be expected to stand.

II. It was no cloud-land, this lofty spiritual future. It was begun. The New City had 'descended.' There had taken place 'the settlement of a Visible Church, of a society dis-
'tinguished from common ones and from the rest of the world
'by peculiar religious institutions; by an instituted method of
'instruction and an instituted form of external religion...'
'The very notion of it implied positive institutions, for the
'visibility of the Church consisted in them.'

'It was mere idle wantonness to insist upon knowing
'why such particular (institutions) were fixed upon rather than
'others[1],' and among those which offered no justification for

[1] Butler's *Analogy*, Part II. i. 1.

themselves, but simply lay there in evidence, in a universal sort of way, with the uniformity and with the variety of the phenomena of nature, was the institute of the Overseership, the episcopacy, of the Church. When Cyprian became a Christian and placed himself under it, its authority was no new object, either when vesting in the individual or in the union of conciliar action. The individual, elected by the communicant 'commons' of Christ's Church, was their representative as truly as the Tribune was the representative of the commons of Rome. But he was no Bishop until he had received the office through bishops by transmission from regions and times in which (as Bp. Lightfoot clearly shewed in his extremely cautious and discriminating essay) 'its prevalence 'in its maturer forms cannot be dissociated from their (the 'Apostles') influence or their sanction[1].' He was Baptizer, Offerer, Teacher, Judge. No one fulfilled any of these functions but as his delegate with no further right of transmission, no power to confer even the humblest Orders.

The Office carried the thoughts of men (whether consciously or not) back to the *Origines* of the three ruling principles of constitutional governments; to Democracy, to the power of the *Aristoi*, to Hierarchy—Levitic or earlier.

Up to this point we are dealing only with what Cyprian received. And Cyprian made no fresh invention, introduced no novel action, modified no method. Yet he did more than any man. Far more than Hildebrand with his inventions of investiture and celibacy. It was not that he summoned Councils and set them to solve Church-problems. Councils had met before and determined questions. But so to speak they had worked in the dark.

Cyprian formulated the 'Theory,' as Brahe, Copernicus or Newton gave the 'Theory' of the Solar System. He 'constructed the Hypothesis'; he 'superinduced the conception upon the facts.' The conception was that the one

[1] 'The Christian Ministry,' Lightfoot's *Ep. to the Philippians*, p. 226.

undivided episcopate constituted not the authority only, but the unity of the Church. Then that followed which follows always in science. The conception 'is a secret, which, once 'uttered, cannot be recalled, even though it be despised by 'those to whom it is imparted. As soon as the leading term 'of a new theory has been pronounced and understood, all the 'phenomena change their aspect. There is a standard to 'which we cannot help referring them[1].'

Why Cyprian never formulated his seemingly serious and palpable purpose of consulting the laity more sedulously, and what would have been the effect of so doing is hard to say, but what he did leave, his leading term, his standard, remains.

And now, whatever exceptions may be taken to his illustrations, his analogies, his interpretings, whatever qualifications may assert themselves in practice, whatever safeguards or subsidiaries may be required to preserve equilibrium, whatever encroachments may have limited, whatever corruptions endangered the institution, still *that* is the 'Theory' which underlies Christendom to-day.

In much of Europe it was overridden by a usurpation which secular events favoured and no scruples impeded,—the usurpation by the principal see of a monarchical, autocratic attitude toward the episcopate, obliterating it except in name, only multiplying phantom names when votes are required.

In North-west Europe intense reaction threw up in some of its countries a counter system which, for the first time, deliberately dispensed with the Episcopate; a hardy venture, a risky asseveration that Episcopacy is not necessary even to itself, that it amply resides in Presbytery. But, once persuaded that there was no Apostolic survival in the Church, successive varieties of management have successfully dotted the globe with truncate communities, generating Ministries for themselves spontaneously, energetic, expansive, sincere. Some of them have sought a Unity in their common repulsion.

[1] See Whewell's *Philosophy of the Inductive Sciences*, vol. II. pp. 59, 50, 53.

We are not now to enquire whether in either case instability of doctrine has had any connexion with the subversion of the primitive preservative organization. In the later instance there are not wanting voices of anxiety, either from within or from those without who love them unloved, lest even that *Didache*, that *Doctrina*, that 'Instruction' in the mysteries of the faith, which it was the first object of Primitive Institutions to secure, should tremble unsafely or slide upon the down-grade.

But in either case where should either that Usurpation or this Revolution look for historic justification? Where but to the age in which the conception of a united Christendom was formulated?

Yet on the one hand the mind of Cyprian, dwelling on all the phenomena which were to be co-ordinated, was found to have been such a blank on that one central point of Roman supremacy that a determined and sustained attempt had to be made to remodel his language. The authorities had their will, and yet Cyprian remains a hopeless difficulty. Even the glozed extract is inadequate without glozing comments. Or let the supposed teaching be tested by the conduct which it formed. If Cyprian meant Roman Unity in principle, then at least the next succeeding stage of the history of the Church of Carthage, which was devoted to him, must have exhibited some approximation to that form of unity,— especially as one of its first acts was the removal of a barrier by the dropping of his obstinate opinion. But what was the fact? The great scholar and critic whose erudition and accuracy adorn the Roman Communion of to-day shall tell us in his own words, ' By the end of the fourth century the 'Africans were already organized, and formed around the 'Bishop of Carthage a close serried phalanx (*faisceau très serré*). 'Carthage was scarcely less autonomous than Alexandria[1].' On the other hand, whither should the extreme reactionaries

---

[1] M. l'Abbé Duchesne, *Fastes Épiscopaux*, I. p. 91.

turn but to the same times of Cyprian in order to find earliest expression given to their views, if Cyprian was really innovating? If Cyprian's theory was a creation of his mind, violently fitted upon phenomena which did not correspond to it, where should we find the protest and the contradictory phenomena but as the readiest armature of the strong parties which so long opposed him? The ecclesiastical circumstances, the action of his contemporaries, must have yielded some refutation of his postulates. Step by step we have explored the rock. And we find no ledge whereon may lie the very egg of a presbyteral fancy.

Cyprian and his times were as innocent of presbyterian and of congregational, as they were of papal catholicity.

We saw that in the first order of the Christian Ministry, as it then subsisted, the strongest threads of primitive constitutions were singularly woven together. The Empire felt how strong that leadership was, though it knew not why, and believed that if only this were eradicated the Christian commons might safely be left their *cultus*. As time went on it was perceived that the Imperial magistracy was powerless against a jurisdiction which rested on moral and spiritual convictions in conflict with which its own material sanctions were utterly despised.

If that perception had not been taken up and acted on, the Christian Ministry would have remained a magistracy to this day, always either dominant or persecuted. The prospect was impossible. Alliance with the Imperial rule, with all its justice and all its lawfulness, became an impending necessity. Then, all history would predict that alliance with the State could not become an accomplished fact without a practical outburst and shock of worldliness probably of a terrific sort. So it was. But the worldliness was a violence to the principle and motive of the alliance, whose strength was its purity, and Reform would henceforth be the salt of every age.

But the maintenance of a position unallied with the State and outside it, independent, indifferent, unaggressive, would have involved a faithless worldliness inaccessible to reform. 'The external bonds may be severed for a time,' says Bp. Lightfoot, 'but the State cannot liberate itself from the 'influence of the Church, nor the Church from the influence of 'the State.... Where there is not an alliance there must be a 'collision. Indifference is impossible, and without indifference 'there can be no strict neutrality[1].'

The Donatist cry, '*Quid christianis cum regibus*[2],' was the earliest and earthliest real sectarianism. It gives up Christianity and it gives up the world. It is content to leave one of the world's 'three measures of meal' unleavened. It is content that States should have no profession of the Truth of Christ. The kingdoms of this world must perish without ever becoming the kingdom of God and of His Christ.

It gives up Christianity. For it confesses that there are powers in the world which Christianity cannot and dare not deal with, gates of hell which must be left to prevail.

For the development of the two overmastering ideas in which he dwelt Cyprian possessed marvellous qualifications of character, of trained literary power, of position.

The character which endeared him to the laity, and which excited warmer and more affectionate feeling than that of any leader in the antient Church, has been noted again and again in these pages.

Exact habits of business suiting a lively innate courtesy kept every authority informed of facts. He was ready to discuss doubts and differences with every earnest and capable enquirer. The generosity possible only to a wealthy man was not curbed by the limits of his wealth until he had denuded himself of his estates. His passion was to work like God in nature 'for good and for bad' alike. In political

---

[1] *Historical Essays*, p. 38.   [2] *Optat.* i. 22.

and party life within the Church he had a singular power of self-recal. In dealing with the pretentious 'martyrs,' the puritans and the lapsed, he was in each instance on the edge of going too far. In each he recovered himself with dignity and carried the Church along with him by his charity. At last the calm settling for himself when and where he would not be martyred, and where he would, and his silence in the last hour when he and all expected a Divine utterance through him, help us to realize that grave and sweet serenity which his contemporaries thought that his manners, his face, his very dress betokened.

His trained literary power appeared not only in his sympathetic approaches, his marshalling of arguments weak or strong, his antithetic point, his rising periods, but in the variety of topics in ethics, doctrine, policy which are grasped and handled by him so lightly, yet so definitely.

We said we might not find in him one of the well-springs of scientific theology. Yet Jerome, that profound and exact critic, considers that he was not a great commentator, only because he was in incessant conflict with the practicalities of so many different situations. The inexhaustible memory of Scripture, the prolific illustrations and adaptations of its language, were to his contemporaries admirable, and to us would be incredible if they were not actual. Of course he contributed to the misleading pile of verbal and mechanical discoveries of symbol. It was almost as true of him as of the Donatists that, as Optatus says, they saw Baptism in every mention of water. But were all those fancies cut away, his argument would seldom disappear. And it was impossible that this error of judgment should not be committed largely when it first began to dawn on men that the world of things and words was all a temporary expression of the eternal. As to theology itself, it must not be forgotten that the simple yet learned straightforwardness of his interpretations made for Augustine a very mine of testimonies against later Separatists as they arose.

The equable grace of his eloquence, 'the calm fountain-like flow,' which the same great judge marks as his characteristic style, almost impedes the recognition of his genius.

He was so thoroughly what we call a scholar that he edited for Christians a phraseological lexicon of Cicero[1].

His diction is not unworthy to be read beside the classical writers of antiquity; stronger than any who had come between him and them, purer and clearer than any contemporary; and that not because his ideas were simpler and easier to render, but because no sort of affectation had lodging in his soul. He left what he had not found, a language which Divinity could use as a facile, finely tempered, unbreakable instrument.

When Tertullian began to write Theological Latin had to be formed. His free, unhesitating, creative genius rough-hewed a new language out of classical literature and African renderings of Hellenistic Greek. It stands like the masses of a fresh-opened quarry. Out of it Cyprian wrought shapely columns, cornices, capitals in perfect finish. It was like the Eocene record opening into the Pleiocene with more articulate forms and forecasts of more to come. Again he had that gift of gifts, the breathing of life into dead or languid phrase. A fiery tongue sat on his brow as on Tertullian's, but of a purer, tenderer radiance. Every Christian Church has learnt of him. The lamp which all runners in the sacred race have received is that which Tertullian lit and Cyprian trimmed.

These gifts of character and of genius met in a man who came to Christ from a Pagan position not very analogous to anything in modern life—a foremost man among the great and wealthy rhetoricians.

They had the most refined and varied culture of their times, experiences of life in every condition. Their reputations were won before the generals as well as the lawyers

---

[1] v. Hartel's *Præfatio*, pp. lxviii, lxix.

of the Empire, and before the whole populace. Their leaders were at home with Proconsuls and Emperors.

For the devotion of his gifts, acquirements and position to the work and life of the New People as they grew in Christ, Carthage offered a fairer, larger field than Rome, because it was at once less officialized and less hopelessly split into classes; and so it continued, until at last the mismanagement of subject races and the degradation of a capital daily reflooded with fresh tides of vice, threw open every door to the barbarian.

Of his great gifts the greatest was his Charity. His Charity was no purple patching. In the letters which are sent for the business-like purpose of keeping authorities informed there is always visible the affectionate desire that they should be in the heart of affairs. That on the other hand it was no mere good nature, appears by the vigour with which he can chastise. A quiet amusement lies suppressed below the encouragement which he gives to Cornelius in his nervousness about Felicissimus. The dignity with which he returns the presuming letter of the Roman presbyters, declining to think it can be genuine, and the immortality which his sarcasm and indignation have conferred on Florentius Puppianus, make it plain that, if he was charitable, his was charity with a will. He was regarded as a special manifestation of that Grace. So Augustine[1], 'Praise be to 'Him! Glory to Him! who made this man what he was, to 'set forth before His Church the greatness of the evils with 'which Charity was to do battle, and the greatness of the 'goodnesses over which Charity was to have precedence, 'and the worthlessness of the Charity of any Christian, 'who would not keep the Unity of Christ. To him that 'Unity was so dear as to make him for very charity not 'spare the bad, and yet for peace' sake endure the bad. 'A man as free in expressing what he felt himself, as

---

[1] Aug. *Serm.* 312, 6 *et passim.*

'he was patient in listening to what he knew his brethren 'felt.'

But when we try to estimate the working of that Charity of his on the great scale the incongruous puzzle seems at first to be that the same man who so evolved and so used the Theory of Unity should have been the man who afterwards went so near to breaking up, by an opinion, the unity that then was.

But indeed in the way of providence that doctrine of his was an actual test of the stability and durableness of his 'Unity.' For certain it is that, however uncatholic that one opinion was, however uncatholic the Roman Bishop in his tone concerning it, Cyprian was never parted from the very heart of the Communion of Saints in Christendom. This was the fullest example possible of that great truth which in word and conduct he enunciated: 'That Christian men must 'be able to differ in opinions without forfeiting or withholding 'from each other the rights of intercommunion[1].'

Wearied and weakened by separations of which the guilt, the loss, and even the suffering can never be truly apportioned as between those who triumph and those who are defeated, the spirit of Christendom has feebly begun to yearn for Reunion in some form, to recognize that a fractured force cannot complete the conquest of Heathendom. Yet each Church is rightly aghast at the thought of purchasing Unity at the cost of Truth.

Cyprian does not recommend such barter to his 'most loved colleagues.'

What Cyprian meant is summed by Augustine and rounded into one exact and perfect phrase. *Salvo jure communionis diversa sentire.* He means that Schools of Thought are not Communions. He means that the Apostleship

---

[1] Aug. *de Bapt. c. Donat.* VI. vii. 10. Salvo jure communionis diversa sentire. The actual words are gathered from Cyprian: *Ep.* 72. 3; *Sentt. Epp. prœm, Ep* 68, fin. The spirit breathes through all Cyprian.

and the Apostolic Creed are enough. He means that the harmony of mankind, in a world which is a world of Beginnings, never will be a harmony intellectual or metaphysical, but that it may even now be a harmony spiritual and sacramental.

Such Unity as the Lord prayed for is a mysterious thing. It is no fantasy, but it answers in no way to the idea that 'one Lord, one Faith, one Baptism' can be condensed into one Rite, one Code, one Chair. A mysterious thing. Nothing formal. mechanical, or limitable by words. That is evident in His very comparison and apposition of that Unity to the relations which subsist within the Holiest Trinity. No intellectual expression can embrace these relations; so neither can intellectual Articles of Faith express that Unity which He defines only by likening it to those Divine relations. Nothing can reach it but some mystery, compact of visible and spiritual; nothing but a Sacrament.

A true Unity has to take account equally of Christ's Prayer and of Christ's Laws: of the Prayer which He offered over the sacrifice of Himself, and of the Laws which Himself, our Creator, impressed on the intellectual existence of our race. One centre we have, but the approaches to it from without, the radii of thought, are infinite.

In that saying lies enfolded the germ of Christ's Prayer—'*jus communionis*'—and the germ of Christ's natural Law '*diversa sentire.*'

The Church which masters that saying, which roots it as the principle of the thought which itself cherishes and encourages, which fructifies it in the action that itself enterprises, that Church was and is the Church of the Future.

APPENDICES.

APPENDIX A.

PRINCIPALIS ECCLESIA. Note on the meaning of *Principalis* (p. 192).

IT is matter of grief when one finds a scholar like Duchesne led by the logic of his position to translate *principalis ecclesia* 'l'église souveraine' (*Origines Chrétiennes*, vol. II. c. xxiv., sect. 6, pp 427, 436).

Postponing the question whether the *principalitas* originated in the *Urbs* (*Civitas*) or the *Ecclesia*, with other questions not belonging to the plan of this book, we should do well to learn accurately first what the word *principalis* meant to Romans under the Empire.

The word is from *princeps*, the ordinary title of the Emperor in daily use, and mediæval or later students may be excused for vaguely concluding that it held in it all that was imperial and dominating, the highest idea of authority on earth. But why was it the title of the Emperor? and what notion did it convey to the Roman world? Constitutional and philological research leave no doubt on these questions.

The theory of the Roman Emperor was that all his powers were conferred upon him by virtue of the separate republican offices with which after his nomination he was invested, at first each by itself, but afterwards by one statute (*Journal of Philology*, XVII. p. 45). This mass of powers was conferred on a person who bore the most unpretending constitutional title, 'a title of courtesy pure and simple' (*Dict. Gk. and R. Antt.* v. II. p. 483[1]).

The Republic itself had been familiar with the idea of a *princeps civitatis* or 'pre-eminent single citizen,' 'the foremost man of the state,' 'and of placing at the head of the Republican system a constitutional

---

[1] In these two paragraphs I have preferred to make no statement of my own but to define the *princeps* solely from Professor H. Pelham's learned and comprehensive papers, written without any ecclesiastical reference, viz., '*Princeps* or *Princeps Senatus* (proving that the former was an independent title not abbreviated from, or in any way representing the latter). *Journal of Philology*, VIII. pp. 323 ff.; 'On some disputed points connected with the "imperium" of Augustus and his successors,' *ibid.* XVII. pp. 27 ff.; 'Princeps,' *Dictionary of Gk. and Rom. Antt.* 3rd ed. vol. II. pp. 483 ff.

'primate—a first citizen—as the best means of securing administrative 'stability and Republican freedom' (*J. of Phil.* VIII. p. 329).—'The sig-'nificance of the term as accorded by popular consent to Augustus and 'his successors was the same.' And still in the time of Ulpian, 'The 'princeps was only a citizen invested by senate and people with certain 'powers.' 'The title did not connote the tenure of any special office or 'prerogative.' 'It implied not only a general pre-eminence as distinct 'from a specific official function, but a constitutional pre-eminence among 'free citizens as opposed to despotic rule (Tac. *Hist.* iv. 3, ...Ceterum ut 'princeps loquebatur, civilia de se, de republica egregia. Plin. *Paneg.* '55, sedem obtinet principis ne sit domino locus).' 'It involved an ex-'plicit recognition of the continued existence of a free commonwealth.' 'The position was created only for each princeps for his life.' 'The 'principate died with the princeps' (*Dict. Gk. and R. Antt.* v. II. pp. 484, 485).

The term *principalis ecclesia*, ἡγεμονική, was the best and most exact possible to make plain to the constitutional subjects of the Roman Empire what was the position claimed by the Roman Church among Churches. First and highest in a great Republic of Churches, securing administrative unity and freedom, possessing a general pre-eminence as distinct from a special function, a constitutional pre-eminence as opposed to despotic rule.

That was the meaning of *principalitas*, *principatus* to any Roman lawyer or citizen. 'Sovereignty,' 'Ruling power' is exactly what was *not* included, implied or allowed in the term. All *imperium* or *potestas* had to be separately and solemnly conferred. So long as the public felt that they had the conferring of each high authority as so many offices, while they called the one who held the many offices nothing but *princeps*, the first citizen, this name enabled them to believe that they were a republic, not a monarchy.

In the case of the See its *principatus* was undoubted. The pre-rogatives of which the sum was autocracy were never conferred on it, and at first not only not claimed, but repudiated by it. The assumption of them came later, but with that assumption came wide and deep disregard for the *principatus* itself.

Let us add some illustrations of the true sense. *Princeps Senatus* was a well-known position in Rome. At no time did it imply power or authority: simply 'the privilege of delivering his *sententia* before the rest of the assembled Fathers.' The *Princeps Juventutis*, first of the *Equites*, had not a tinge of authority.

In Africa itself the *Principales* were a rank to which Sovereignty by no means appertained. They are mentioned after *Decuriones* and before *Cives* (probably because they had no special jurisdiction) in an inscription from Sitifis (*C.I.L.* VIII. i. nn. 14, 4224; ii. n. 8480). Augustine

Ep. 139, 4, commends to Marcellinus 'our son' Ruffinus as *Cirtensis Principalis*[1].

Augustine in his Epistle 43 to Glorius, Eleusius...lays much stress on the principate of the Church of Rome, '...Romanæ ecclesiæ in qua semper apostolicæ cathedræ viguit principatus' (*s.* 7), and urges the Donatists to submit to the judgment of Pope Melchiades and his colleague Bishops given on appeal at Rome (*s.* 14). Then he points out that, supposing that Roman judgment to be wrong, there was still an appeal to a General Council, which might reconsider and reverse the judgment of the Pope and Bishops. 'Ecce putemus illos episcopos, qui Romæ 'judicarunt, non bonos judices fuisse: restabat adhuc plenarium universæ 'Ecclesiæ concilium, ubi etiam cum ipsis judicibus causa posset agitari, 'ut si male judicasse convicti essent, eorum sententiæ solverentur' (*s.* 19). That distinctly expresses the nature of the *principatus*. It was exactly not 'sovereign' in its decisions, great as was the respect to be paid to them.

Tertullian, *de Anima*, cc. 13—15, has to determine the purely abstract metaphysical question of whether the *anima* or the *animus* in man has τὸ ἡγεμονικόν, *principalitas ubi sit? quid cui præest?* 'where resides the *principalitas?* which is over which?' He renders τὸ ἡγεμονικόν by *principale*, the only possible term, ἡγεμών being the equivalent for *princeps*.

He decides of course that the *principale* is in the *anima*, of which the *animus* with its senses and operations is in one view a function 'officium,' in another its furniture or apparatus 'instrumentum.' Next he proceeds to enquire in what 'recess of the body' the *principale* has its shrine, 'esse consecratum.'

There is no analogy drawn or resemblance existent between the metaphysical relations in this most abstract discussion and the practical relations of political or civil ranks, and no one would pretend that the Church is in any sense 'a function,' or 'the furniture,' or 'the apparatus' of a See. No definition of *principalis* is sought or given by Tertullian. The meaning of the word is assumed to be known by any Roman reader. What is here supposed to be ascertained is the pre-eminent place of the *anima*. It is simply shewn that the *principale*, the foremost, chiefest, pre-eminent rank, belongs to the *anima*.

This however is the passage of which the Rev. L. Rivington writes (*Primitive Church and See of Peter*, 1894, p. 58), 'Since Irenæus wrote 'those words about Rome, Tertullian (*de Anim.* 13) had defined the word 'as meaning "that which is over anything" as the soul presides over and

---

[1] [Cf. *C. I. L.* vol. v. ii. n. 7786, viro innocenti principali civitatis.—vol. IX. nn. 259, 1540, 1633. In *Cod. Justin.* 7, 16, 41; 10, 32 (31), 33, 40, 42, and in some inscriptions, it seems like a rank belonging often to a decurion. In Apuleius, in Africa, in this century, it is similarly used of men and of the god Serapis, *Metamorph.* xi. (261), viii. (175); *Florid.* iv. 21. In no case is there a trace of rule or sovereignty.]

rules the body.' There is (as I have said) no attempt to define[1]; the translation and application of *quid cui præest* is too shocking; there is not a trace of the illustration of soul ruling body.

As to 'those words of Irenæus' *c. Hæres.* iii. 3, 2, Mr Rivington observes that 'this expression "principal Church" and its Greek equiva-'lent occurring in S. Irenæus...means the ruling Church.' There is a little slip here, as the passage of Irenæus does not exist in Greek, but the *potentior principalitas* which he assigns to the Church, not the Bishop, of Rome, means of course what it means everywhere. It means what Strabo xvii. 3 calls ἡ προστασία τῆς ἡγεμονίας, the precedence, the presidency, the pre-eminence belonging to the position of princeps. What this was we have seen.

Principatus, principalitas embodied the tradition and the hope of Rome. They expected to maintain the idea of undisputed pre-eminence and to exclude inherent autocracy, making all authority and jurisdiction to be only the exercise of various offices specially conferred. They expected. So did the Christians.

---

[1] When Tertullian *de Præscriptionibus Hæretic.* 31 claims *principalitas* for Truth as against Heresy, he might equally well be said to have 'defined' the word as meaning 'priority in time,'—'sed ab excessu revertar ad *principalitatem* veritatis et *posteritatem* mendacitatis.'

APPENDIX B.

Additional note on Libelli (pp. 81—84).

THE account of the Libelli, pp. 81—84, was constructed many years ago from the various extant references to them. We little thought then to find such actual documents extant after sixteen centuries and a half. But in 1893 and 1894 there appeared two, one in the Brugsch Collection of the Berlin Museum, the other in that of the Archduke Rainer, brought from the province of Faioum, S.W. of Cairo. The former is a papyrus leaf, about 8 inches by 3, much damaged but most skilfully deciphered by Dr Krebs, who acknowledges Dr Harnack's learned assistance in illustrating it ; the fragments of the other have been skilfully pieced together by Prof. K. Wessely[1].

These documents give us a sharpened sense of the suppression planned by Decius—a policy of 'Thorough,' an application of the great Roman administrative forces to any and every individual in the Empire. The scheme extends formally to little villages (Euseb. *H. E.* vi. 42, 1), and takes in country folks outside them, and their wives. The form in Africa is not likely to have differed from that in Egypt. The date, we shall see, is of the year we are describing.

I had concluded formerly[2] that besides the process of Registration there were two kinds of *libelli* or certificates of sacrifice, one an allowed protest or declaration of innocence put in (*traditus*) by the person accused of Christianity, the other a certificate received by him (*acceptus*) from the magistrate that he was satisfied of his paganism. Our second papyrus might have seemed one of the former sort, if it had stood alone, and our first a similar one, attested by the magistrate. But their being in duplicate, except for the personal particulars filled in, and their both praying for attestation, shews that what I thought might be different documents were combined in each *libellus*, the two parts being what was conjectured.

---

[1] The former is described and illustrated with a facsimile by Dr Fritz Krebs in the *Sitzungsberichte d. Königl. Preuss. Akademie d. Wissenschaften zu Berlin*, 1893, 30 Nov., xlviii. p. 1007; and there is an article on it in the *Theolog. Literaturzeitung*, Leipzig, 20 Jan. 1894, by Dr A. Harnack, and one by the Bishop of Salisbury in the *Guardian*, Jan. 31, 1894, p. 167. The second is described by Dr A. Harnack in the *Theolog. Literaturzeitung*, Leipzig, 17 March, 1894 [from *Sitzungsb.d. Kaiserl.Akad.d.Wissensch.* Phil.-Hist. Classe 131 B. Wien, 1894] and by [Dr] A. J. M[ason] in the *Guardian*, March 21, 1894, p. 431.

[2] *Dict. of Christian Antiquities, s.v.* vol. II. p. 981.

APPENDIX B.

I admit also that if there was Registration (which seems essential) it would be the registering of these documents and not a different process.

I (Brugsch).

τοις επι των θυσιων ηρη-
μενοις κω(μης) αλεξ(ανδρου) νησου
παρα αυρηλ(ιου) διογενου(ς) σατα-
βουτος απο κω(μης) αλεξανδ(ρου)
5 νησου ως Lοβ ουλ(η)
οφρυι δεξ(ια) και αει
θυων τοις θεοις διετε-
λεσα και νυν επι πα-
ρουσιν υμειν κατα
        sic
10 τα προστετατα[γμε]
να εθυσα [κα]ι επ[...]
[.]. ι των ι[ε]ρειων [...]
σαμην και αξιω υ[μας]
υποσημιωσασθαι
15   διευτυχειται
αυρηλ[ιος] [δι]ογενης επιδ[ε(δωκα)]
   αυρη(λιος) σ..ρ...[...]
    θυοντα μυσ[...]
     ...νωνος σεσ(ημειωμαι)
20 [Lα] αυτοκρατορο[ς] και[σαρος]
[γα]ιου μεσσιου κ[ο]ιν[του]
[τρ]αι[ανου δε]κιου ευσ[εβους]
[ε]υτ[υχους] σε[β]α[σ]του
επ[ειφ] β

II (Rainer).

τοις επι των θυσιων ηρημενοις
   κωμης φιλαδελφιας
παρα αυρηλιων συρου και πασβειου του
αδελφου και δημητριας και σαραπιαδος
γυναικων [η]μων εξωπυλειτων
αει θυον[τες] τοις θεοις διετελε
σαμεν και νυν επι παροντων υμων
κατα τα προσταχθεντα και εσπισαμεν
και [τω]ν ι[ερειων] ε[γευσαμεθα και]
[αξιουμεν υμας υποσημειω]
σασθαι ημιν   διευτ[υχειτε]
αυρηλ συρος και πασβης επιδεδωκ
ισιδωρος εγρ | υ αυτ αγρ |

I. To the commissioners of the sacrifices of the village of Alexander's island from Aurelius Diogenes [son of] Satabûs of the village of Alexander's island. About 72. Scar on right eyebrow. I was both constant in ever sacrificing to the gods and now in your presence according to the precepts I sacrificed and drank and tasted of the victims and I beseech you to attach your signature.

May you ever prosper.

I Aurelius Diogenes have delivered this.

I Aurelius.........[?saw] him sacrificing I Mys[thes son of]....non have signed.

[first year] of the Emperor Cæsar
                      Gaius Messius Quintus
                      Trajanus Decius Pius
                      Felix Augustus

2ᵈ day of Epiphi.

LIBELLI. 543

II. To the commissioners of the sacrifices of the village of Philadelphia from the Aurelii Syrus and Pasbeius his brother and Demetria and Serapias our wives, Dwellers outside the gates, We were constant in ever sacrificing to the gods and now in your presence according to the precepts we both poured libations and tasted of the victims and we beseech you to attach your signature for us. May you ever prosper.

We Aurelius Syrus and Pasbes have delivered this.
I Isidorus wrote for them *as* unlettered.

The date (ll. 20—24) is not so well written as the declaration, but the signatures of the magistrates (17—19) are hurriedly scribbled with a thick reed pen. Round brackets ( ) indicate abbreviations in the original, square [ ] indicate holes in the papyrus.

I. 1. οἱ ᾑρημένοι are the local commissioners added to the local magistrates, the *quinque primores illi qui edicto nuper magistratibus fuerant copulati* of *Ep.* 43. 3, sup. p. 76, probably selected by higher courts. Cf. turba eorum quos ad investigandos Christianos Polemoni judicia majora sociaverant. Ruinart, *Passio SS. Pionii et socc.* iii.

2. 'Alexander's Island' in one of the former lakes of the Faioum, so called from the veterans settled there by Ptolemy I.

3. *Aurelius* from Caracalla, who gave the *Civitas* to the *Orbis Romanus*, Dion. Cass. 77, 9 and cp. 60, 17. *Dig.* 1, 5, 17. Cf. ὀνομαστί τε καλούμενοι ταῖς...θυσίαις προσῄεσαν, Dionys. *ap. Eus.* vi. 41. Note that the magistrate is an Aurelius too.

7. Nothing indicates whether these Aurelii were genuine pagans or lapsing Christians, cf. ἰσχυριζόμενοι τῇ θρασύτητι τὸ μηδὲ πρότερον Χριστιανοὶ γεγονέναι, Dionys. *ap. Eus.* vi. 41.

10. τὰ προστεταγμένα &c. *i.e.* the provisions of the πρόσταγμα, Eus. vi. 40, 41 ; the Edict, *Ep.* 43. 3, or the *Præceptum* (see pp. 465, n. 4; 492, n. 2).

11. Decipherers hesitated between ἔπ[ιον] and ἔσπεισα καὶ, but the latter is verified by the second libellus.

12. There can be little doubt that the right reading is ἐγευσάμην, which constructs with ἱερείων. Cf. *Passio Pionii*, ii., 'sicut ceteros qui degustabant sacrificia.' *Acta S. Theodori Amas.* (Surius, Nov. 9), 'si execrandos cibos gustassent.' 'Ora maculare, polluere,' is the constant expression about the sacrificati as an essential part of the test, *e.g. Ep.* 20. 2 ; 31. 7 ; 55. 14 ; 59. 12, 13 ; *Ep.* 30. 3 ; *de Lapsis*, 10. 15, 22, 24, 25.

17, 18. The reading of 18 is not certain. These are thought to be the names of the Magistrate Aurelius......and of his Secretary Mys[thes] (not an uncommon name), with the name of his father. Are they not likely to be the signatures of one Magistrate and one Commissioner? However for ΜΥϹ Harnack would read ΓΕΓ(ομενου).

24. 2 Epiphi in Egyptian kalendar is 26 June. By that time in A.D.

251 the persecution was over. Hence the date of the libellus must be 26 June 250, Decius' first year.

II. 2. Philadelphia. Unknown.
12, 13 written in another hand.
13. ἔγραψα ὑπὲρ αὐτῶν ἀγραμμάτων is Harnack's ingenious reading.

APPENDIX C.

The Intrigue about Manutius' Text—Visconti's Letter.
(Note on p. 212, nn. 1 and 2.)

The language of these intriguers at Trent and Rome is so clever and so self-conscious that it is worth while to look at the originals.

Visconti's letters are printed in Mansi's Appendix to *Baluzii Miscellanea* (4 vols. fo. Lucæ, 1761—4), 'from a MS. in the public library at Siena'; not in the first edition 1678—83. Also in 'Lettres, anecdotes et 'mémoires historiques du Nonce Visconti...dont plusieurs intrigues inouïes 'se trouvent dans ces relations, mises au jour, en Italien et François, par 'Mr. Aymon.' 2 vols. 12°. Amsterdam, 1719. Mansi indicates his sources, Vol. III. Index, p. xviii. Aymon does not name his MS.

(1) Mansi (*Baluz. Misc.* III. p. 472), l. xlv (from Trent, Visconti to Borromeo).

Di xxii. Giugno, 1563[1].

Fù scritto, questi di, da Roma che le Opere di San Cipriano, ristampate nuovamente da M. Paolo Manutio[2] non erano state date fuori con quelle corretioni che i correttori havevano notate; ma nel trattare *de authoritate Ecclesiæ*, dove si parla *de Primatu Papæ*[3] erano state mutate alcune parole le quali non si truovano[4] citate nelli Decreti, nè da gli authori, che ne fanno mentione, in quel modo che sono date fuori, & essendomi stato detto, che Monsignor Agostino haveva havuto sovra di ciò littere da Roma, parendomi, che fosse di molta importanza il non lasciare a questo tempo, che si tratta dell' auttorità del Papa, spargere cotali voci, procurai con buona occasione d' intendere dal sodetto Monsignore l' avviso, ch' egli ne haveva, il qual mi disse che molti giorni sono M. Latino un de correttori scrisse a Monsignor Siglicello[5] sopra di questo

---

[1] Aymon, vol. II. p. 84, reads at end of letter di Trento a' 21 di Giugno 1563.

[2] Aymon (p. 78) l' opere...da Monsignore Paulo Manucio.

[3] Aymon, dell' *Autorità Ecclesiastica* dove si tratta *de Primatu Pontificis Romani* (pp. 78—80).

[4] Aym. trovavano.

[5] Aym. Sighuello; Io. Baptista Singhicello, Latino, *Ep. ad Andr. Masium*, II. p. 101 (Hartel, *Præf.* p. ix).

affine, che ne havesse a parlar col Sig. Cardinal Varmiense [Hosius, Bp. of Varmie, Poland] avvertendolo, che 'l Manutio non haveva in quel luogo detto di sopra seguita la correttione fatta dal Faerno & da lui, & che il Faerno, il quale haveva sopra di ciò rincontrato molti essemplari e particolarmente uno, che fu della santa memoria di Marcello [II] haveva notate le sodette parole diversamente da quel che l' haveva poste il Manutio, soggiungendomi il predetto Monsignore, che sendole stata mandata una di queste opere, gli fu scritto anco a lui il medesimo. Di che ne ho avvertito il Sig. Cardinal Simoneta, & crederei che non fosse se non bene, prima che tale opinione si andasse confirmando, trovar modo di levarla, il che si potria fare, se così piacesse a V.S. Illustriss., con dare auttorità a quelle parole che sono date fuori, autenticandole col Testimonio & approbatione di persone che havessero visto e confrontato i codici antichi.

(2) The following is the Note at the end of Manutius' *Cyprian*, Romæ, M.D. LXIII.

The few notes follow the Index and this is on the last page but one signed TTiii. It is on the words 'loquitur...ecclesia' in *Ep*. ix. (Manutius) to Florentius Puppianus, Hartel, *Ep*. 66. 8, p. 732, 25.

'Pag. 106, v. 34 *Loquitur Petrus super quem fundata* [text ædificata] *fuerat ecclesia*. Quantum Petro & illius Cathedræ tribuendum censuerit B. Cyprianus, hic, & multis aliis eximiis probat testimoniis. Nec quidquam illi deperit si extant diversæ doctorum ad verba Christi expositiones. Omnium tandem Catholicorum scopus & finis eò tendit ut recognoscant unum Christi loco in ecclesia esse relictū pro quo & illius sede & successoribus rogavit ne deficeret fides illius, & universum gregem dominicum pasceret. *Nec quemquam movere debet quod alicubi dicat hoc fuisse ceteros apostolos quod fuit & Petrus, pari consortio præditos honoris & potestatis,* [de unit. 4. Manut. p. 139, 32, Hartel, p. 213, 2] quod de æqualitate apostolatus est omnino intelligendum, qui cum apostolis morientibus cessavit nec ad episcopos trāsiit qui succedunt apostolis in ministerio episcopalis dignitatis pro sua quisque portione. In solo Petro remansit omnis plenitudo potestatis ad universalem ecclesiæ totius gubernationem, ut catholici doctores acutissime viderunt et comprobarunt. *Nec est alienum si priscorum patrum scriptis piæ & catholicæ adhibeantur interpretationes, & veri sensus, ad conservandam semper Ecclesiæ unitatem, qua B. Cypriano nil fuit in scribendo optabilius. alioqui hæreseum & schismatum nullus finis.*'

Thus in 1563, instantly after and notwithstanding the interpolations, the papal warning against the teaching of the *De Unitate* has still to be raised.

As there could be no more thorough exposition and example of Roman practice, so there can be no keener comment on its futility.

APPENDIX D.

The Intrigue about the Benedictine Text—*Additional note on* du Mabaret (p. 213).

The Abbé du Mabaret was from 1720 to 1733 Professor of Philosophy and then of Theology at Angers. In 1725, at the age of 28, in a work called *Veritatis triumphus* he refuted Spinoza, 'Protestantism' and Jansenism, and proved Papal Infallibility. To the age of 86 he was a pious patient student of 'vast erudition' without a touch of critical method or power. He disallowed the genuineness of Lactantius 'on the deaths of persecutors'; was the compiler of enormous works which never found editor, publisher or patron, and complains that his contributions to Moreri's *Dictionnaire Historique* are inadequately acknowledged. His one literary success was, as we have seen, the spoiling of Baluze's Cyprian. His feeble 'arguments' on the Interpolation survive among Freppel's. They chiefly rest on the 'Citations.' M. l'Abbé Arbellot published at Limoges 1867 a pamphlet, now rare, which collects the particulars of his writings, and as far as possible admires him.

The following interesting illustrations of the state of feeling at the time were pointed out to me by M. le Vicomte de Cormenin.

The 'Sçavant d'A...' of Oct. 1726 (*Mém. de Trévoux* for that year, p. 1902) says, 'Personne n'ignore avec combien d'éclat et de force M. 'l'Abbé du Plessis d'Argentré, aujourd'hui Evêque de Tulles, a soutenu 'l'authenticité de ce passage.' In Feb. 1743 du Mabaret published in the same memoirs his éloge on du Plessis d'Argentré.

When du Plessis was a young doctor of the Sorbonne he had published in quarto at Paris in 1702, '*Elementa Theologiæ* in quibus de 'autoritate et pondere cujuslibet argumenti theologici diligenter et 'accurate disputatur...autore Carolo du Plessis d'Argentré, socio Sor- 'bonico, e Sacra Facultate Parisiensi Doctore Theologo et Abbate a ' S. Cruce juxta Quinquainpum in Armorica.' The author's estimate of his work was not generally accepted. And in the copy at the *Bibliothèque Nationale* (Inv. D 3616, D 384) is preserved a printed letter of 8 pp. dated 27 Dec. 1707 which describes the Archbishop of Reims (Charles Maurice Le Tellier, 1668—1710) administering to Dr du Plessis what he called a '*Correction*' before a great company at his nephew's, the Abbé de Louvois. 'He did it for him,' he said, 'in his quality of fellowship with him in the Doctorate.' The Controller of his Household revealed that, if he had not thus met him, the Archbishop's intention had been to dine on Christmas Day at the Sorbonne and there correct him before the Doctors. 'His book was full of ignorance and false principles. Never 'had he read a worse. He had written it only from motives of policy 'to pay court to the Jesuits, and, having attained his object of getting 'himself an Abbey, to get a Bishopric. He himself had been much 'scandalized by the book. The Cardinal de Noailles still more. He ought 'to suppress it.'—He did not. And in 1725 he obtained his bishopric.

APPENDIX E.

TEXT OF THE INTERPOLATION OF CYPRIAN DE UNITATE C. IV.

'Bod 1,' (Fell) Bodleian Library Oxford, Laud. Misc. 451   10th century
> fo. ff 199, double columns, well written. 'Of same class as T (Hartel xlv, xlvi) if not a copy of it.' F. M.

'Bod 2,' Bodleian cod. 210   12th cent.
> fo. ff 208, double columns, 'a better MS in some respects than 451 (Bod 1) though written by a careless scribe and afterwards much corrected.' J. W. 'The order of contents resembles μ (H. p. xlvi) and β (lvii).' F. M. It is older than either.

'Bod 3,' Bodleian Laud. Misc. 217   15th cent.
> small 4to. ff 129 rather closely written, full page. '2nd Family. Follows M Q as against T, and Q as against M.' F. M.

'Bod 4,' Bodleian Laud. Misc. 105   10th or 11th cent.
> 4to. ff 163 'seems to be a selection from T M and to agree with the first corrector of T. Considering its resemblance to M Q, with purer readings like T, it may seem a better though more recent representation of the archetype of M Q, coordinate with Hartel $<X>$ and $<Y>$.'

'Bod 5' (so I venture to call it). Bodleian MS add. C. 15   early 10th cent.
> 'acquired at the Libri sale 1859 : a beautiful MS: has *ep. ad Thibaritanos* twice over with different texts.' F. M.

'Ebor,' not in Library.

'Lam,' Archbishop's Library at Lambeth, Codd. Lamb. 106   13th cent.
> 'Epistolæ et tractatus lxxxv...Codex perpulcher' H. Wharton (MS catal. 1688) rubricated, several fine illuminated initials. 'Liber Lanthoniensis Ecclīe. Qui detinuerit: anatema sit.'

'Lin,' Lincoln College Library Oxford n. 47   15th cent.
> fo. ff 231. Order same as B (v. Hartel p. lvi) In fronte '*Vespasianus librarius florentinus hunc librum florentie transcribendum curavit*' '?copied from one at Florence described by Bandini 1. 268, viz. MS laurent. plut 16 cod 22. Has some good ll. but by a careless scribe as these beautiful MSS often are.' J. W.

'NC 1,' New College Oxford 130   12th cent.
> fo. ff 245, 2 col., well writ. 'very interesting MS; seems coordinate with those of the 3rd family, though perhaps independent enough to be regarded as alone of its kind.' F. M.

'NC 2,' New College Oxford 131, 2   15th cent.
> 131, sm. fo. ff 155. 132, sm. fo. ff 137. These two thought to be really one MS; but some treatises occur in both parts; the order of treatises in 132 is mainly that of Q; the epp. in 131 do not answer in order to any of Hartel's. F. M.

'Pem,' Pembroke College Library Cambridge C 20 (1935)   early 13th cent.
> small fo. ff 89, 2 columns, 36 lines, pale. Italian MS. The initials remarkable. Given by Abp Rotheram, Master in A.D. 1480 to Pembroke Hall. Has a note '*istum librum emi in Messana ⚹ 8d^c Venetiis.*'

'Pem 2,' Pem. Coll. Lib. Camb., no press mark, 'Petri Blesensis'   12th cent.
pencil in marg. catal.
> not known to Fell; ff 189, of which 143 contain 'Passio Cypriani et Epistolæ lxxiiii,' of which *De Unitate* is one among other treatises. Large beautiful folio, double columns, finely writ, 40 lines to page.

'Sar,' Cathedral Library Salisbury n. 9.   12th cent.
> 'oblong, well written, injured on outer margin by damp.'

For convenience in following the description in Chapter IV, III I have placed the readings of M Q Bod 3 Bod 4 and Pelagius together. New collations are given of the English manuscripts (on which see Hartel p. lxxxvi) because Fell's are not accurate. For the collations of *Bod* 1, *Bod* 2, *NC* 2, I have to thank the Rev. John Wordsworth (now Bishop of Salisbury): F. Madan, Esq. of the Bodleian for those of *Bod* 1, *Bod* 2 also, as well as of *Bod* 3, *Bod* 4, *NC* 1 and *Linc.* and for the notes on classification: for transcript of *Pem* E. H. C. Smith, Esq., for transcripts also of *Pem* and *Pem* 2, the Rev. E. J. Heriz Smith, Fellow of the College; of *Sarum*, the Rev. H. G. White, Chaplain to the Lord Bishop of Salisbury.

549

Text of the Interpolated Passage in Cyp. *de Unitate* iv. as given in the edition of Paulus Manutius, A.D. 1563 (p. 139). The clause in [ ] is from Pamèle ed. 1568 (p. 254), Rigault 1648, and Baluze (Maran) 1726.

Loquitur Dominus ad Petrum: Ego tibi dico, inquit, quia tu es Petrus, & super istam petram aedificabo Ecclesiam meam, et portae inferorum non vincent eam. Tibi dabo claves regni caelorum, & quae ligaveris super terram, erunt ligata & in caelis: & quaecunque solveris super terram, 5 erunt soluta & in caelis. *Et eidem post resurrectionem suam dicit: Pasce oves meas.* Super *illum* unum aedificat Ecclesiam *suam, & illi pascendas mandat oves suas.* Et quamvis apostolis omnibus post resurrectionem suam parem potestatem tribuat & dicat: Sicut misit me pater, et ego mitto vos, accipite 10

Readings of M (Monacensis) from Hartel with which Q (Trecensis) agrees precisely even in corrections; of Fel.'s *Bod* 3, *Bod* 4 (=Laud Misc. 217 & 105) and of *Ep.* Pelagii Papae ii

1. Et ego B 3. dico tibi M. inquit petre B 4   **2.** hanc petram edificabo B 3   **3.** porte (*et sic semper* e *pro* ae *vel* oe)   **4.** ligaberis B 4, legaveris M   **5.** legata M. celis B 3   **6.** Et idem...meas M B 3 (*om.* suam B 3), et eidem...meas B 4   **7.** illum M 2 B 3. dicit] illi (illi *perlineatum*) B 4. *om.* unum B 3 B 4. edificavit B 3   **8.** *om.* suam M B 3 B 4. et illi pascendas oves mandat suas M B 3 B 4 (*om.* suas B 3 B 4)   **9.** *om.* post resurrectionem suam M B 3 B 4. tribuat potestatem M B 4, tribuit potestatem B 3   **10.** *om.* et dicat...manifestaret, *inserting*

Readings of *Bod* 1, *Bed* 2, *Bod* 5, *Lambeth, Lincoln Coll., New Coll.* 1, 2, *Pembroke Coll. Cam.* 1, 2, and *Sarum*

1. dico tibi Linc. in quid petre Pem   **2.** hanc B 5 Linc Sar. edificabo La Pem Pem 2, hedificabo Linc   **3.** porte Sar. inferiorum Linc. tibi dabo B 1 Linc, et tibi B 2 Pem Pem 2 NC 1, dabo tibi NC 2 *ut H*   **4.** celurum Sar La Pem Pem 2. quecunque Pem, que Sar   **5.** celis Sar Pem, caelo B 5. quecunque Sar Pem   **6.** celis et idem...meas B 2 La Pem Pem 2 NC 1, celis Sar, caelo B 5, celis et eidem...meas Pem Linc, *om.* et Pem, *om.* et eidem...meas B 1 Sar   **7.** *om.* illum B 1 B 2 B 5 NC 1 Linc Sar La Pem 2. *om.* unum Pem. edificat Linc Sar La, edificat (*ma* 1 -avit) ille *delet.* Pem, aedificavit B 2, edificavit NC 1 Pem 2   **8.** *om.* suam B 2 B 5 La NC 1 Pem Pem 2. *om.* suam...suas B 1 Sar, et illi pascendas (tuendasque B 5) oves mandat. Et B 2 NC 1

550   APPENDIX E.

Spiritum sanctum: Si cui remiseritis peccata, remittentur
illi: si cui tenueritis, tenebuntur: tamen ut unitatem manifestaret, *unam cathedram constituit, et* unitatis ejusdem
originem ab uno incipientem sua auctoritate disposuit. Hoc
15 erant utiq, et cæteri apostoli, quod fuit & Petrus, pari
consortio præditi & honoris & potestatis, sed *exordium ab
unitate proficiscitur, & *primatus Petro datur, ut una Ecclesia
Christi et cathedra una monstretur: & pastores sunt omnes, et
grex unus ostenditur, qui & apostolis omnibus unanimi con-
20 sensione pascatur**;* ut Ecclesia Christi una monstretur, quam
unam Ecclesiam etiam in cantico cāticorum Spiritus Sanctus
ex persona Domini designat et dicit: Una est columba mea,
perfecta mea, una est matri suæ, electa genitrici suæ. *Hanc
Ecclesiæ unitatem qui non tenet, tenere se fidem credit?
25 Qui Ecclesiæ renititur et resistit, [*qui cathedram Petri super
quam fundata est Ecclesia deserit,*] in Ecclesia se esse confidit?

Readings of M, Q, *Bod* 3, *Bod* 4 and *Ep.* Pelagii Papæ ii

the tamen *between* unam *and* cathedram M B 3 B 4   **13**. *om.* et B 3. *om.* ejusdem M B 3 B 4   **14**. originem) atque orationis suæ (atque *erased by a second hand*) M, atque rationem sua B 3 B 4. *om.* ab uno incipientem M B 3 B 4   **15**. utique M B 3 B 4. *om.* et B 4. *om.* apostoli M B 3 B 4. *om.* fuit et M, *om.* et B 4, *om.* fuit B 3. *om.* pari...proficiscitur M B 3 B 4.   **16**. * *1st citation in Pelag. begins.*   **17**. sed primatus M B 3 B 4. et *pro* ut B 4   **18**. *om.* Christi M B 3 B 4. Xti eccl. Pel. ut M B 3, et M 2 B 4. *om.* una Pel. monstretur M B 3, monstratur B 4. sed grex M B 3 B 4 Pel.   **19**. ab *for* et M B 3 B 4 Pel. *om.* omnibus Pel.   **20**. ** *in* B 4 *genuine form begins here, v. inf. om.* ut Ecclesia... genitrici suæ M B 3. *om.* ut Ecclesia...confidit B 4   **23**. * *2nd cit. in Pelagius commences.* **24**. et Pauli *for* Ecclesiæ M B 3   **25**. Qui Ecclesiæ renititur et resistit, *om.* Pel. M B 3. Qui Cathedram Petri...deserit *ins.* M B 3; Qui Cath. P. super quam Ecclesia fundata est deserit et resistit Pel. *Here follows in* M B 3 *the repetition from line 2 of words* super unum ædificavit ecclesiam, *and then the whole passage once more in its genuine form without the interpolations.*

Gretser's collation of his Bavarian Codex (supra p. 206) gives ego dico tibi; et idem...meas; *om.* illum; *om.* [Eccl] suam; suas; *om.* post resurrectionem suam; parem tribuat potestatem; *om.* dicat...manifestaret; tamen *between* unam *and* cathedram; *om.* ejusdem; orationis suæ; *om.* ab uno incipientem; *om.* apostoli; et *for* ut; sed (grex); ab *for* et; *om.* ut Ecclesia... genitrici suæ—*all in perfect correspondence with* M (Munich).

Pem La Pem 2. apostolus Sar   **9**. *om.* post resurrectionem Pem. *om.* suam Linc. tribuat potestatem B 2 La NC 1 Pem 2   **11**. cujus remiseritis B 1. si cujus B 2 B 5 La Pem 2. et si cui Pem. remittuntur B 5, NC 2 Pem   **12**. *om.* illi Sar. illis, cujus B 1. si cujus Pem. ei; si cujus La B 2 B 5 Sar. ei si cui Pem 2. retinueritis retenta erunt B 2 La Pem 2, retinueritis retenta sunt NC 1. tenebuntur *in ras* Linc. *om.* ut Pem. manifestarent NC 1   **13**. *om.* unam cath...et B 1 B 2 B 5 La Linc NC 1 NC 2 Pem 2 Sar. unitatis ejus B 1. ejus idem (idem *in rasura* dem *ut udtur scriptum*) Sar   **14**. originem atque rationem B 2 Pem. incipiente B 5 Linc. incipientes Sar. *om.* ab uno incipientem Pem   **15**. *erasure of a letter betw.* cæteri *and* apostoli B 2. fuit Petrus B 5 La Pem 2   **16**. ab uno prof. B 1 NC 2   **17**. *om.* et prim...pascatur B 1 B 2 B 5 La Linc NC 1 NC 2 Pem 2 Sar. *MS of Card. Hosius ap Pamel* hic *for* et. Christi ecclesia, Linc   **18**. monstratur Pem, monstraretur Linc, monstretur *bis* Sar. sed grex Pem   **19**. qui ab Pem   **20**. *om.* ut Ecc...genitrici suæ Pem. dei NC 2. *om.* unitatis suæ NC 2   **21**. in cantica B 1   **22**. de ecclesia *pro* designat et Sar   **23**. matris...genitricis B 1 B 2 B 5 La Linc NC 1 Pem. electa est ex Linc, electa est B 2* La NC 1 Pem 2   **24**. Petri *for* Ecclesiæ Pem. si Pem. *om.* fidem B 2 La Pem 2   **25**. *om.* qui cathedram...deserit B 1 B 2 La Linc NC 1 NC 2 Pem 2 Sar   **26**. quem fundata Ecclesia est Pem. aecclesia B 1 [*Note* Pem *om. from* confidit *to* corrumpat c. 5 *as does also a* MS *at Bologna not otherwise much like* Pem *in this passage, see p.* 352].

INTERPOLATION OF DE UNITATE, C. IV. 551

So ends the interpolated passage in Manutius, and here in the manuscripts M Q B 3 the whole passage is repeated in its genuine form, following the word *confidit*. In B 4 the repetition follows *pascatur* but this Codex leaves out the genuine 'qui Ecclesiae renititur et resistit' and replaces it by the interpolated sentence. Thus (Hartel's text)

super unum aedificat ecclesiam et quamvis apostolis omnibus post resurrectionem suam parem potestatem tribuat et dicat: sicut misit me pater et ego mitto uos. accipite Spiritum sanctum: si cuius remiseritis peccata, remittentur illi: si cuius tenueritis, tenebuntur, tamen ut unitatem mani- 5 festaret, unitatis eiusdem originem ab uno incipientem sua auctoritate disposuit. hoc erant utique et ceteri apostoli quod fuit Petrus, pari consortio praediti et honoris et potestatis, sed exordium ab unitate proficiscitur, ut ecclesia Christi una monstretur. quam unam ecclesiam etiam in cantico canti- 10 corum Spiritus Sanctus ex persona Domini designat et dicit: una est columba mea, perfecta mea, una est matri suae, electa genitrici suae. hanc ecclesiae unitatem qui non tenet tenere se fidem credit? qui ecclesiae renititur et resistit in ecclesia se esse confidit? 15

Readings of M, Q, *Bod* 3, *Bod* 4 and *Ep*. Pelagii Papae ii

1. aedificavit M, edificavit B 3. ecclesiam et quamvis *super litura* B 4. *om*. et B 3   2. resurreccionem B 3   4. quorum B 3. sicut B 4. remittuntur B 4, dimittentur B 3   5. illis M B 3, eis B 4. quorum E 3. unitatem ut B 4. monstraret B 3   6. em *in rasura* B 4. incipiente B 3 B 4   7. erunt Et ceteri B 4. *om*. et B 3. erat B 3   8. prediti B 3 B 4   9. exoritur B 4   10. ecclesiam in cantica B 4   12. perfecta una B 4.   matris B 4. sue B 3. electa est M, electa e genitrice sua *contraction mark over e erased* B 3   13 genetricis B 4   14. ecclesie B 3.   *pro* 'qui ecclesiae...resistit,' qui cathedram petri super quem fundata ecclesia deserit B 4.

Hartel's collations.

1. dico tibi M R. inquit *om*. G   3. dabo tibi S, tibi dabo WGMVR   5. et (*ant* in) *om*. S. super] in S   6. *om*. Hart et eidem...meas *cum* SWGVR   7. *om*. Hart. illum *cum* SWGM'RV   8. *om*. Hart. suam...oves suas *cum* SWGVR   10. sicut *bis* R', si cui *bis* R². rem. accipe S   11. remittuntur R   12. illis M, *om*. G. manifestet R   13. *Hart. om*. unam cathedram constituit et *cum* SWGRV. ejus R   14. ab uno incipientem] atque originem V *teste Rigaltio*   15 et *om*. R. fuit et G   17. *Hart. om*. et primatus...pascatur *cum* SWGVR. ut *s. l. m.* 2 R   18. *om*. Christi V   20 mostretur S   21 etiam *om*. S   22. designat et} de ecclesia G. dicat S   23 electa est M, *om*. S   24 tenet *om*. R   25 *Hart. om*. qui cathedram...deserit.

It will be seen that Bod 1 NC 2 Sar (and Ebor. by Fell's collation), have entirely escaped interpolation: Bod 2 La Linc NC 1 Pem 2 have only the insertion about the post-resurrection charge to Peter.

The curious corruption in B 3 B 4 as to *rationem* and *orationis* seems to me to have their rise in *Ep*. lxx. c. 3, super Petrum origine unitatis et ratione fundata.

Pelagii Papae II Ep. VI Labbe (ed. 1729) vol. VI p. 631

...Sed et beatus Cyprianus egregius martyr in libro quem de unitatis nomine titulavit inter alia sic dicit: Exordium ab unitate proficiscitur: *et primatus Petro datur, ut una Christi ecclesia et cathedra monstretur: et pastores sunt omnes, sed grex unus ostenditur, qui ab apostolis unanimi consensione pascatur.* Et post pauca: Hanc ecclesiae unitatem qui non tenet, tenere se fidem credit? *Qui cathedram Petri, super quam ecclesia fundata est, deserit & resistit*, in ecclesia se esse confidit.

552   APPENDIX F.

A transcript by J. W. from a MS in University Library Bologna (no. 2572, sm. 4°, *saec. xiv or first half xv* in Italian hand), which belonged formerly to S. Salvadore di Canonici Lateranensi, shews the same curious omission from *confidit* to *corrumpat* as *Pem*, which it does not otherwise resemble.

e.g. it has: petram istam—post resurrectionem—tribuat potestatem—et cui remiseritis—et si cui tenueritis—tamen ut unitatem—et ceteri quod fuit et—monstraretur—animi—pascantur—super quam—fundata est ecclesia—[*It has:* et tibi—et idem—originem atque rationem—sed exordium].

APPENDIX F.

On points in the CHRONOLOGY of VALERIAN'S reign (pp. 456 sqq.).

THE confusions of events in Valerian's reign were such that Tillemont felt obliged to take them geographically, not chronologically. The following observations may serve the cause of clearness :—

1. *The end of Valerian's reign.*

Niebuhr (*Lectt. Rom. Hist.* III. p. 279, London, 1850) is unable to decide whether the catastrophe which ended Valerian's reign was in A.D. 256 or 260. There can be no doubt, looking at the varied indications, that it was in 260. (1) The persecution lasted 42 months (Dionys. *ap. Euseb.* vii. 10) until Gallienus repealed the edict after Valerian's disappearance. Supposing Cyprian, on Aug. 30, A.D. 257, to have been the first confessor as is probable[1] in Africa, the edict can scarcely have appeared earlier than July, when Valerian made his arrangements for the empire, departed for the East, and left Macrian to administer. This brings the end of Valerian's power to the end of A.D. 260. (2) Valerian was proclaimed Augustus in Rhætia before the end of 253, since his second year of Tribunitian power dates from Jan. 1, 254. This makes his reign, ending in his 8th year, to end in 260 (cf. Clinton, *F. R.* I. p. 284). (3) There are coins of Valerian struck in his eighth Tribuneship, *i.e.* in 260, at Alexandria in August, and in Cilicia after October, and enactments bearing his name issued through that year up till September 24th[2] (see Clinton, *l.c.*).

How long he lived in captivity is not known. His son Gallienus made no effort to recover him. He was reported dead at Rome, and deified while still alive in captivity. (Treb. Poll. *Gallieni duo*, c. 10.) Whether the headings of two laws which bear his name in 262 and 265 are genuine, and if so whether they prove that he was still living is doubtful (*Cod. Just.* 3, 8, 3 ; 5, 62, 17).

[1] ...Quid nos...dicere deberemus prior apud Acta Proconsulis pronuntiasti et tuba canens &c. in acie prima...primos impetus, *Ep.* 77. 2.

[2] *Codex Justinianus*. They may be found by the Index to the *Corpus Juris Civilis* (Berlin, 1880), v. II. p. 494.

2. *The date of the capture of Antioch.*

The main cause of confusion is difference as to the date of the capture of Antioch by Sapor. Gibbon (c. x. p. 284, ed. Milman, 1846) and Niebuhr (*l. c.* p. 295) place this event after Valerian's capture, in 260, following (they believe) Ammianus Marcellinus (xxiii. 5, 3), who adds a special note to his particular tale, 'These events were in the times of Gallienus,' *i.e.* 260 onward.

Zosimus (i. 32) relates how Valerian engaged himself with Successianus in resettling Antioch after its ruin[1]. The fall of Pityus in 258 was attributed to his withdrawing for that purpose Successianus, who had saved Pityus the year before. Antioch had therefore fallen before 258.

Tillemont tries a hopeless compromise by placing its fall late in 258.

There is, however, no real contradiction between these late but not careless authorities[2]. The fact is that Antioch was *twice* captured by Sapor, once in A.D. 252–3, and again in 260 (v. inf.), having been in the interval restored by Valerian. To this restoration we may refer his coins with the legend RESTITUT. ORIENTIS, RESTITUTOR ORBIS[3].

Zosimus himself (in i. 27, a passage which almost seems to have been overlooked) relates the capture of Antioch by Sapor in the time of Gallus, A.D. 252 or before May 253 when Æmilian was proclaimed. Antioch was unprepared and offered no resistance, and on this occasion, after a great massacre and the destruction of 'every building private or public,' the Persians, 'while the conquest of all Asia lay in their power,' returned immediately home to deposit their masses of captives and spoil. Their method often was destruction and abandonment.

The same author writes (i. 36) that, at the later time when he captured Valerian, Sapor 'was ranging over the East and subduing all before him'

---

[1] τὰ περὶ τὴν Ἀντιόχειαν καὶ τὸν ταύτης οἰκισμὸν οἰκονομοῦντος.

[2] Considering the lateness of their dates, the evident paucity and fragmentary character of their materials and the brevity with which generally they write, the old historians scarcely merit the lavish abuse they receive. It can scarcely be said that the moderns have been more successful as critics in digesting even their materials. Consider that Dionysius Magnus is the only contemporary writer.

Trebellius Pollio wrote his later work under Constantine.

Vopiscus began to write in 291 or 292 and refers to Trebellius (*Divus Aurelianus*, ii.).

Eusebii Chronicon is dated A.D. 325, Jerome's edition, 378.

Aurelius Victor wrote after 350.

Ammianus Marcellinus wrote before 380.

Zosimus *floruit* after 420.

Georgius Syncellus wrote between 780 and 800.

Zonaras *floruit* 1118.

[3] [*Restit. orientis;* a 'turreted female' (*i.e.* a city) presents the Emperor with a crown. *Restitutor Orbis;* the Emperor raises a turreted female. No ground for the statement that these were struck '*in anticipation* of success,' as Stevenson, *Dict. Rom. Coins*, p. 687.] They commemorate the actual restoration.

($\dot{\epsilon}\pi\iota\grave{\omega}\nu$ $\tau\grave{\eta}\nu$ $\dot{\epsilon}\dot{\omega}a\nu$ $\ddot{a}\pi a\nu\tau a$ $\kappa a\tau\epsilon\sigma\tau\rho\dot{\epsilon}\phi\epsilon\tau o$) and (iii. 32) that after his (second) capture of Antioch, which this time he had to take by storm ($\kappa a\tau\grave{a}$ $\kappa\rho\acute{a}\tau os$), he had 'marched across as far as to the Cilician Gates,' when Valerian advancing against him fell into his power (v. infr. sect. 4).

The earlier chronicle of Eusebius places the capture of Valerian in 260, and the ravaging (*depopulatur*) of Syria, Cilicia *i.e.* within 'the Gates,' and Cappadocia in 261 (*s. anno*). This is not inconsistent with Zosimus. Sapor entered Syria not from the south, but from Mesopotamia, made direct for Antioch, and having taken it the second time, ravaged the Syria adjacent to the other two countries and north of Antioch.

Thus the earlier authorities agree in the fourth and fifth century. But when we come to the ninth century we find that Georgius Syncellus (ed. Dind. p. 716) thought this 'ravaging of Syria' in 261 must include the taking of Antioch. So he makes the capture of Valerian precede the taking of Antioch, as well as of Tarsus in Cilicia and Cæsarea of Cappadocia. This is against the earlier testimonies so far as Antioch is concerned. And it is improbable in itself that Valerian, considering what we know of his dilatory tactics, should anticipate the approach of Sapor and throw himself in his way outside Antioch. But Syncellus himself indicates that there was something wrong in his story, for a few lines earlier he says (*l. c.* p. 715) 'Sapor overran Syria, *came to Antioch*, and ravaged all Cappadocia' before the capture of Valerian. He could not have 'come to Antioch' and marched on, leaving such a place in his rear.

In the twelfth century we find that Zonaras gives first an account, which agrees with Zosimus and Eusebius;—the overrunning of Syria followed by the ravage of Cappadocia and then by the siege of Edesa, in attempting to relieve which city Valerian is taken (xii. 23)[1]. He then gives another version, which is nothing but a paraphrase[2] of Syncellus, and puts together the capture of Antioch, Tarsus and Cæsarea as all after Valerian's seizure.

The only discrepancy then which remains on close comparison arises from Syncellus's late misinterpretation. It is clear that the two campaigns of Sapor, in each of which Antioch was taken, at an interval of eight years, were quite differently conceived. The object of the first was the sack of Antioch itself. But in the second the annihilation of the recolonized and restored city was the basis of a vast invasion of the countries north of it.

---

[1] So Aurel. Vict. *Epit.* 32 'in Mesopotamia bellum gerens.'—Cf. *de Cæsaribus*, 32.

[2] In one or two places not even a paraphrase but the very words. Syncell. Dind. ed. p. 715 ἑαυτὸν προὔδωκε...συνθέμενος καὶ τὴν τοῦ πλήθους προδοσίαν, ἣν αἰσθόμενοι Ῥωμαῖοι μόλις διέφυγον ὀλίγων ἀναιρεθέντων. Compare Zonar. xii. 23, προδεδωκὼς ἑαυτόν...ἀλλὰ γνόντες τὴν προδοσίαν διέφυγον, ὀλίγων ἀναιρεθέντων.

To the second assault belongs (it is said) the picturesque story in Ammianus (xxiii. 5, 3) of the actress suddenly exclaiming from the stage 'Is it a dream, or do I see the Persians,' and of the instant overwhelming of the gathered population by the archery[1].

3. *Fall of Cæsarea of Cappadocia.*

Dr Peters[2] says 'Valerian hurried to Cappadocia against Sapor in A.D. 258.'

No antient authority gives an idea that Valerian 'hurried' (inertia was his characteristic) either in that year or any other, or that Sapor was at that time anywhere near Cappadocia.

Valerian set out, as Zosimus says (i. 36), with the view of meeting the 'Scythians,' then ravaging Bithynia; only he got no further than Cappadocia, and returned 'having done nothing but just damage the cities by his transit[3].'

The fall of Cæsarea belongs to that wide sustained campaigning of Sapor (Zosim. i. 36), spoken of under the last head, when, after Antioch was taken for the second time, Valerian, as the Eusebian Chronicle rightly gives it, was captured in A.D. 260, and Syria, Cilicia and Cappadocia were overrun in 261.

4. *The Treachery in the capture of Valerian.*

The capture of Valerian was a tragic but not a politically significant event. It was accompanied by no loss to the Roman armies or administration. It is agreed by historians that it was effected by treachery, but not so agreed where or what the treachery. It is variously attributed to Sapor, to an unknown general, to Macrian, and to Valerian himself. There is, however, no real difficulty in determining the fact.

In the fragment of a contemporary dispatch from some potentate to Sapor with which Trebellius' memoir on 'The Two Valerians' begins the capture is treated as simply Sapor's craft, 'Look to it lest ill befall you for

---

[1] '*Et hæc quidem Gallieni temporibus evenerunt*' unless *Gallieni* is a *mistake* for *Galli*. The features of the story,—the time of peace, the burnt city, the retiring with vast booty,—exactly fit the former fall. But the second does not absolutely refuse them.

Clinton places this sack of Antioch in 262 (*s. anno*) from the notice of that year in Hieronymus' Chron. *Parthi Mesopotamiam tenentes Syriam incursaverunt.* But it is impossible to suppose that the raids of years had been carried on in Syria with the restored Antioch intact in the midst of it. The mere *incursaverunt* is not adequate to such events, and the text shews sufficient reasons for placing this earlier.

[2] Peters, p. 573.

[3] ...καὶ τῇ παρόδῳ μόνον ἐπιτρίψας τὰς πόλεις ὑπέστρεψεν εἰς τοὐπίσω.

Moses Chorenensis (cent. iv.—v.), *Hist. Armen.* l. ii. c. 72, 73 (ed. Whiston, 1736, pp. 1967, 8) states on the authority of Firmilian that Valerian was informed of the danger in which Armenia stood, but did not help, 'ad regionem nostram tutendam Valerianus non pervenit, nec diu vitam traxit.'

having seized the aged emperor and that too by fraud[1].' So Aurelius Victor, 'circumvented by the treachery of the king of the Persians, whose name was Sapor[2].' Zosimus developes the nature of the treachery. In iii. 32 he mentions that Valerian advanced with his troops against Sapor, but in i. 36 relates that he was not inclined to fight, but proposed by ambassadors to buy off the enemy[3]. Sapor requested to see the emperor for personal conference on some essential points. Valerian unreflectingly and uncircumspectly set out with a few attendants, thinking to discuss a truce with Sapor, and was suddenly seized[4].

Thus there is no question among the earlier batch of writers as to whose was the treachery.

Still the 'fraus' in Trebellius was misunderstood, and in an interpolation in his text, quoted as genuine by Gibbon (c. x. IV. p. 283) and Clinton (I. p. 284) we read 'victus est enim a Sapore, rege Persarum, dum ductu 'cujusdam sui ducis, cui summam omnium bellicarum rerum agendarum 'commiserat, seu fraude seu adversa fortuna in ea esset loca deductus, ubi 'nec vigor nec disciplina militaris quin caperetur quicquam valere potuit[5].' Here the fraud has been transferred to one of the Roman officers. Then Tillemont (*Emp*. III. p. 313) and Pearson (*s. anno* 260), taking the προέμενος of Dionysius (Euseb. vii. 23)[6] to mean 'betrayal,' regard Macrian himself, who was far enough away, as the betrayer. Tillemont observing that, though the passage of Trebellius may not be genuine, it fits the history and Macrian's character!

Yet again the later historians formed another misconception of the treachery. They attach it to the unfortunate Valerian himself. According to Georgius Syncellus (p. 715), it is he who, terrified at the mutinous spirit of his hungry troops in Edessa, pretends a battle, and gives himself up to Sapor, having arranged also the betrayal of all his men, but they understood the case in time to escape. Zonaras (xii. 23) gives both stories, paraphrasing the second from Georgius.

Thus the two latest authors, who placed the siege of Antioch wrongly, also make the treachery, which was purely Sapor's, to be a plot of Valerian's to betray the Roman army.

---

[1] Vide ne quod senem imperatorem cepisti et id quidem fraude male tibi cedat. Treb. Poll. *Val. duo*, 4.

[2] Cum...bellum per Mesopotamiam anceps diuturnumque instruit, Persarum regis, cui nomen Sapor erat, dolo circumventus.... Aur. Vict. *de Cæs*. 32.

[3] [So also Petrus Patric. (6th cent., *Fragm*. 9 ap. C. Müller, *Fragmm. Historicorum Græc*. Paris 1851, vol. IV. p. 186) χρυσίον ἄφατον συναγαγὼν...ἐπὶ μεγάλαις δόσεσι τὸν πόλεμον καταλῦσαι βουλόμενος.]

[4] I. 36: ὁ δὲ σὺν οὐδεμίᾳ φρονήσει κατανεύσας τοῖς αἰτουμένοις, ἀπερισκέπτως μετ' ὀλίγων ὁρμήσας ἐπὶ Σαπώρην ὡς δὴ περὶ σπονδῶν αὐτῷ διαλεξόμενος, ἄφνω συλλαμβάνεται παρὰ τῶν πολεμίων.

[5] *Sic ap.* Cæsarum vitæ post Suetonium Tranquillum conscriptæ, Lugd. 1551; Historiæ Rom. Scriptores Latini, de la Rovière 1609; Hist. Augustæ Scriptt. Latt., Sylburg 1589.

[6] Sup. p. 458, n. 1.

APPENDIX G.

On the nameless Epistle Ad Novatianum *and the attribution of it to Xystus* (p. 476).

SINCE the chapters on Xystus were in print, Dr Adolf Harnack has published an essay on 'A hitherto unrecognised Writing of Pope Sixtus II. of the years 257—8[1].' Whether his view is accepted or not, the treatment and the by-learning of the essay are full of interest and suggestiveness. If true his view is so important, that I select those main points which touch our history, and must add the lights in which they appear to me.

His Excursus (pp. 54—64), comparing the Versions of Scripture used in Cyprian and in this author, will not come within our scope, but it is of capital interest and value.

The 'writing' is the well-known *Ad Novatianum*, taken hitherto to be (as described by Hartel) 'The work of a bishop who was on 'Cyprian's side as against Stephen (see H. *Appendix*, p. 55, 4), and 'against the schism of Felicissimus (54, 12), shortly after the Decian 'persecution (57, 25)[2].'

Stephen is not mentioned in it, but the comparison of the Church to the one saving Ark (as Hartel) and the 'domus una id est Christi ecclesia' (*ad Novat.* c. 13, H. 63, 8), are no doubt references to this controversy, and the whole tenor of the tractate is clear. But the reference to Felicissimus is in the supposed pun 'quid ad ista respondeant...in-Felicissimi pauci,' and is in my judgment impossible[3].

---

[1] V. Gebhardt and Harnack, *Texte und Untersuchungen*, XIII. Band, Heft 1, Leipzig, 1895. 'Eine bisher nicht erkannte Schrift des Papstes Sixtus II. vom Jahre 257—8...von Adolf Harnack.'

[2] Hartel's *Cyprian*, vol. III., Pars iii. Appendix, *Opera Spuria*, &c., p. 52. The *Ad Novatianum* first appeared not in Erasmus' ed. 1519, as Hartel's note there, but, as he corrects it (*Præfatio*, pp. lx, lxi), in the *Editio Daventriensis*, 1477. Hartel had corrected previous texts by MS. K, and at the latter page adds the readings of *Ed. Dav.* It was first marked as not Cyprian's in Erasmus' ed. 1520. Cf. Pamel. Cyp. 1568, Antv. pp. 434—5.

[3] There is no other reference to the action or tenets of Felicissimites, *Ap.* 54, 12. *Ed. Dav.* has 'infelicissime,' which certainly cannot be (as Harnack, p. 23 n.) a vocative case.

558   APPENDIX G.

Harnack.
I. The author of 'ad Novatianum'?

I. I shall try to represent accurately, but of course shortly, Harnack's argument.

The Treatise opens thus :

(H. p. 52, 9) 'Cogitanti mihi et intolerabiliter animo æstuanti quid-
'nam agere deberem de miserandis fratribus qui vulnerati non propria
'voluntate sed diaboli sævientis inruptione adhuc usque, hoc est per
'longam temporum seriem, agentes pœnas darent, ecce ex adverso
'obortus est alius hostis et ipsius paternæ pietatis adversarius hæreticus
'Novatianus.' *Ad Novat.* 1.

This language is appropriate from a highly responsible Bishop who was anxious to restore such Lapsed persons as had remained Penitents a very long time, but who found himself confronted by sudden action on Novatian's part. The words *vulnerati* ff. shew that he took a more compassionate view of their temptation than was possible earlier.

That he took Cyprian's view of the Church itself as the one Ark of Salvation appears in the words

(H. p. 55, 3) 'Quæ arca sola cum his quæ secum fuerant liberata est in aqua, at cæteri qui in ea inventi non sunt diluvio perierunt.' *Ad Novat.* 2,

and as the only valid authorized baptizer in

(H. p. 55, 23) '...sacramentum baptismatis, quod in salutem generis humani provisum et soli ecclesiæ cælesti ratione celebrare *permissum*' (permissum add. *H.*). *Ad Novat.* 3.

The limits of date are fixed from the following :

(H. p. 56, 18) 'Cataclysmus...ille qui sub Noe factus est figuram persecutionis quæ per totum orbem nunc nuper supereffusa ostendit.' *Ad Novat.* 5.

(H. p. 57, 24) 'Duplex ergo illa emissio [columbæ ex arca] duplicem
'nobis persecutionis temptationem ostendit : prima in qua qui lapsi sunt
'victi ceciderunt, secunda in qua hi ipsi qui ceciderunt victores extiterunt.
'Nulli enim nostrum dubium vel incertum est, fratres dilectissimi, illos
'qui prima acie id est Deciana persecutione vulnerati fuerunt, hos postea
'id est secundo prœlio ita fortiter perseverasse, ut contemnentes edicta
'sæcularium principum hoc invictum haberent, quod et non metuerunt
'exemplo *boni pastoris animam suam tradere*, sanguinem fundere nec
'ullam insanientis tyranni sævitiam recusare.' *Ad Novat.* 6.

secundo prœlio must mean the persecution of Gallus, which was not over before Aug. 253, but was over when this treatise was written. It can be described by 'nunc nuper,' yet the Penitent Lapsed have been Penitents 'per longam temporum seriem[1],' which would be adequately met by allowing three years or even two since the persecution of Gallus. Even so, some would have been in that condition five years since the

---

[1] Cyprian thought a *triennium* sufficient. *Ep.* 56. 2.

beginning of the persecution of Decius. The persecution of Valerian is plainly not begun. It began Aug. 257, but not in earnest, and for Rome not at all till Aug. 258. We have then the limits fixed between Aug. 255 and Aug. (257 or) 258.

The locality is interestingly fixed by considering who these Lapsi must have been. They fell in the persecution of Decius; many retrieved their honour in that of Gallus, but none have been restored. Now the Carthaginian penitents were restored by the Council of May 252, to arm them for the threatened persecution of Gallus. But there is no indication of any such restoration at Rome. Cyprian was pressed by a lax party who would have absorbed the penitents if these were kept out of the Church much longer. But Stephanus was pressed by the Puritan party of Novatianists, who would have absorbed many Catholics if his action had been indulgent. Stephanus had in the case of Marcian of Arles shewn himself unwilling to be hard on Novatianists, and was ready even to admit their Baptism. The Roman policy had been to keep penitents long waiting.

There are strong touches of Roman colour also in the Christology which writes that Judas '*Deum* prodidit' (H. 64, 22. *Ad Novat.* 14); and in the assumption implied in quoting the baptismal charge as given by Christ '*Petro sed et* ceteris discipulis[1].' (H. 56, 1. *Ad Novat.* 3.)

Our author then is a Bishop at Rome between Aug. 253 and Aug. 257 or 8, anxious to restore meritorious penitents of long standing, his efforts frustrated by Novatian's action.

It being shewn that neither Stephanus nor Lucius could have written the treatise[2], it remains by process of exhaustion that the Bishop in question is Sixtus II., and he had opportunity to write, for it is almost certain that during his eleven months and six days' reign the Christians and he were unmolested at Rome: he and Roman presbyters were in fact peacefully corresponding all the time with Dionysius.

Such is the outline of Harnack's argument, and we certainly are grateful to him for taking us on so interesting a quest.

II. The historic results which he deduces are still more remarkable. Thus: (1) There must have been in the time of Sixtus a new and forceful outbreak of Novatianism, led by Novatian himself.—'ecce ex adverso obortus est alius hostis...Novatianus.' *Ad Novat.* 1. It was sufficient to stem the charitable policy of the Church, or at least to compel it to parley on the question in argument with the 'hæreticus.'

Historical consequences of Sixtus II. being the author.

---

[1] The words of the charge itself are here compounded of Matth. xxviii. 19 and Mark xvi. 15

[2] Argument against the authorship of Stephanus was superfluous, and though the arguments adduced against the authorship of Lucius are not very strong, yet they are satisfactory in the absence of any probability on the other side.

(2) It becomes clear how the Baptismal Controversy ended at Rome —which, as Harnack says (p. 39), was not known to Augustine himself,— namely by Sixtus' adopting the policy and even the formula[1] of Cyprian. This further explains the remark of Dionysius[2] to Sixtus that the Roman presbyters, Dionysius and Philemon, had *formerly* sided with Stephen (συμψήφοις πρότερον Στεφάνῳ γενομένοις).

(3) Sixtus II. becomes much more than the 'bonus et pacificus sacerdos' of Pontius (*Vit.* 14) (an expression, we may remark, to which in his mouth it is possible to attach too much significance).

(4) A comparison of passages (Harn. pp. 35 ff.) shews the closest dependence of the *ad Novatianum* on the *de Unitate*. Twenty places at least are distinct quotations. Besides this there is (pp. 50 ff.) a constant near resemblance to Cyprian's style and use of words. Sixtus II. was in fact a 'Scholar of the great African Bishop,' a 'slavish copyist' of his treatises 'on Unity' and 'on Work and Almsdeeds' and of some of his Epistles, and he adopted his policy in every particular.

In fact in A.D. 257—8 Cyprian 'by his writings spiritually lorded it over the Roman See' (pp. 67 f.).

The above are Harnack's principal historical inferences.

Difficulties in accepting Xystus as the author.

III. This is beyond question a strikingly new aspect of Rome exhibited to the eyes of the historical student, and it requires reflexion. Meantime certain difficulties present themselves.

1. If the Baptismal controversy ended in so round and simple a manner as by Xystus adopting entirely Cyprian's views and language, it is strange that Augustine did not know it, and that others should have given such wild accounts of the reversal.

2. It is strange that no trace of intercourse between Cyprian and Xystus, no mention of either by the other, should have survived or, so far as we know, have ever been known to exist. Cyprian had agents in Rome, and Xystus was corresponding with Dionysius in exile.

3. It is yet more strange, if Xystus thus adopted Cyprian's treatment of heretical baptism, that the treatment which prevailed and continued in the Western Church should have been not that of Cyprian and Xystus but that of Stephen.

4. The Roman inclination to appropriate to Peter language of our Lord which is addressed to others is traced by Harnack in the 'mandat *Petro sed et* ceteris discipulis' noticed above. But there is a much more extraordinary instance of that proclivity which for some reason he does not notice. In c. 11 the *ad Novatianum* quotes at length the conversation between our Lord and Simon the Pharisee over the penitent woman. Three times over our author in his quotation of S. Luke vii. *vv.* 40, 43, 47 substitutes the name of Peter for that of Simon, in the last verse

---

[1] Harn. p. 66.   [2] Euseb. vii. 5.

inserts it. Can this be really Xystus the typical Doctor, he of the Chair, who either confuses Simon Peter with Simon the Pharisee, or thinks to honour the See of Rome by the change?

IV. But there are also other passages which, if this is a genuine letter of those times, might seem to fall in with an earlier year and person. *Indications of earlier date.*

1. The language about Novatian seems more appropriate to his first rise than to a recrudescence. While our author was considering how the Lapsed should be reconciled, '*ecce ex adverso obortus* est alius hostis et ipsius paternæ pietatis adversarius hæreticus Novatianus,' c. 1, H. 52, 12. This is not the phraseology which would be used about one who had now for over six years been pursuing the same policy.

2. In c. 14 Novatian is scarcely addressed as if his sound teaching in the Church belonged to years ago; and the writer proceeds 'hodie retractas an debeant lapsorum curari vulnera,' H. 64, 10, as if his discussion of the question were new, not of such old standing as by Xystus' time it would have become.

3. In c. 1, H. 53, 12 his adherents are called 'suos quos colligit,' not as if they were a long-standing formidable congregation. In c. 2, H. 54, 12 they are 'vel nunc infelicissimi pauci,' just as Cornelius (Euseb. *H. E.* vi. 43) says that Novatian γεγυμνῶσθαι καὶ ἔρημον γεγονέναι, καταλιμπανόντων αὐτὸν καθ' ἡμέραν ἑκάστην τῶν ἀδελφῶν.

4. Compare the already quoted 'ecce ex adverso obortus est alius hostis &c.' and the exclamation of surprise at the attitude of Novatian, 'mirum quot acerba, quot aspera, quot perversa sunt,' c. 1, H. 52, 13 with what Cornelius writes of him (Euseb. *l.c.*), αἰφνίδιον ἐπίσκοπος ὥσπερ ἐκ μαγγάνου τινὸς εἰς τὸ μέσον ῥιφθεὶς ἀναφαίνεται and ἀμήχανον ὅσην....τροπὴν καὶ μεταβολὴν ἐν βραχεῖ καιρῷ ἐθεασάμεθα ἐπ' αὐτοῦ γεγενημένην.

5. Compare c. 1, H. 53, 9 'luporum more tenebrosam caliginem optare...ferina sua crudelitate oves...laniare' with Cornelius' τὴν ἀκοινωνησίαν αὐτοῦ καὶ λυκοφιλίαν.

6. Compare what is said c. 14 of his former position as a teacher, sound on this very subject of penitence, with Cornelius' sneer at him as ὁ δογματιστής, ὁ τῆς ἐκκλησιαστικῆς ἐπιστήμης ὑπερασπιστής.

7. Compare c. 8, H. 59, 1, on their intentional superseding of the name *Christiani* by *Novatiani* with what Cornelius relates of the personal pledges taken to Novatian in the Eucharist itself by his followers[1].

In all these passages the point of view is identical. The personal angles may be different, for c. 13 treats him as having been a tender pastor, which Cornelius does not. But the point of view is the same. It cannot be said that one describes the rise of an enemy, the other the revival of a heretic of several years' standing.

8. The passage 'Duplex ergo &c.' from c. 6, H. p. 57, 24 does not require (as Harnack thinks) that the persecution of Gallus should be *No proof of date*

[1] Euseb. vi. 43.

562   APPENDIX G.

later than over when it was written. It at least admits of an earlier application.
the begin- It only says, in that *secundum prœlium*[1] some who had before lapsed,
ning of 'victores extiterunt,' that they 'fortiter perseverasse...nec ullam in-
the per-
secution of sævientis tyranni sævitiam recusare.' But these noble recoveries
Gallus. were of frequent occurrence. One of the strongest arguments of Cyprian
and the Council 'de pace maturius danda,' A.D. 252, even before the
persecution of Gallus, was the cases of the Lapsed who in a second
trial 'fortiter steterint et adversarium nobiscum in congressione pro-
straverint' (*Ep.* 57. 3) and Epistle 56 is occupied with the case of three
such persons whose endurance was marvellous.

The passage contains no indication that the *secundum prœlium* was
more than begun, and we know that it was not considered to be ended.

No second   9. Harnack thinks (p. 41) that the new outbreak of Novatianism in the
outbreak time of Sixtus II., which he infers from *ad Novat.*, is indicated by Dionysius
of Nova-
tianism de- who, in writing to his namesake the Roman presbyter (Euseb. *H. E.* vii. 8),
scribed by gives these reasons for hostility to Novatian, namely as διακόψαντι τὴν ἐκκλη-
Dionysius σίαν, καί τινας τῶν ἀδελφῶν εἰς ἀσεβείας καὶ βλασφημίας ἑλκύσαντι, καὶ περὶ τοῦ
Alex.
Θεοῦ διδασκαλίαν ἀνοσιωτάτην ἐπεισκυκλήσαντι· καὶ τὸν χρηστότατον Κύριον
ἡμῶν Ἰησοῦν Χριστὸν ὡς ἀνηλεῆ συκοφαντοῦντι, ἐπὶ πᾶσιν δὲ τούτοις τὸ λουτρὸν
ἀθετοῦντι τὸ ἅγιον, καὶ τήν τε πρὸ αὐτοῦ πίστιν καὶ ὁμολογίαν ἀνατρέποντι τό τε
πνεῦμα τὸ ἅγιον ἐξ αὐτῶν, εἰ καί τις ἦν ἐλπὶς τοῦ παραμεῖναι ἢ ἐπανελθεῖν πρὸς
αὐτούς, παντελῶς φυγαδεύοντι.

I am obliged to quote the whole passage in Greek because all turns
upon the participial tenses, which are surely most carefully kept apart,
and lead, as it seems to me, to a conclusion contrary to Harnack's.—The
continuous result is distinguished from the outbreak of the schism. The
violent cleavage of the Church, the perversion of a body of believers to
irreverent and even blasphemous acts (such as the Eucharistic pledges by
which Novatian compacted a following[2]), the introduction of a doctrine
dishonouring to God,—these are told in aorists; they were one group of
actions past, the formation of the heretical schism. But the misrepre-
sentation of Christ's compassionate character, the contempt of the font,
and perversion of the baptismal confession, the keeping of the Holy
Ghost at a distance from those who would repent but are not allowed:

---

[1] We do not doubt the application of these words. Cyprian shews that there was a short interval before it after the Decian persecution, which he calls 'quies et tranquillitas,' but they were even then under the fear 'impendentis prœlii,' 'urguente certamine,' *Ep.* 57. 2, 3, 5.

[2] Harnack, p. 42, thinks this account of Novatian's Eucharist incredible, but holds that it may be a version of his altering the Baptismal Creed. But let us observe that the account is the original of Cornelius, describing the very gestures and words of Novatian. Cornelius had such particulars of his τεχνάσματα καὶ πονηρεύματα from Maximus, Urbanus, Sidonius and Celerinus (Eus. *l.c.*).

these are the continuous operation, not new strokes, of Novatianism, and so are related in the present tense. The passage distinctly differences from each other the first energetic movement and the continuous result. The former it places in past time, but gives no sign of new development or even revival in the time of Xystus.

V. There remains one external argument for the book being by Sixtus. The *Prædestinatus*, which belongs to the middle of the fifth century (so Harnack, pp. 44—49)[1], has in its Part I., The Catalogue of Heresies, this notice. *The testimony of the Præ-destinatus.*

'XXXVIII. hæresis est Catharorum qui se ipsos isto nomine quasi propter munditiam superbissime appellarunt, secundas nuptias non admittunt, pænitentiam denegant, Novatum sectantes hæreticum, unde etiam Novatiani appellantur. contra hunc beatus Xystus martyr et episcopus et venerabilis Cyprianus martyr Christi tunc Carthaginiensis pontifex scripsit contra Novatum librum de lapsis quod possint per pænitentiam recuperare gratiam quam labendo perdiderant, quod Novatus adserebat fieri omnino non posse.'

This description of the book '*contra Novatum*' is an account exactly to the point of this fragment *ad Novatianum*, but has no relation to Cyprian's *de Lapsis*. I suggest that it was the occurrence of these two words *de lapsis* which caused some erudite scribe to *insert* all the words '*et venerabilis...pontifex.*' Fortunately the word *scripsit* remains, which by its construction makes the insertion certain. The rest of the statement I must leave for what it is worth. The Catalogue of Heresies is of course admitted by Harnack himself to be much of it quite valueless. But his historic *Erkenntniss* assures him that its assignment of the authorship of this obscure fragment is correct.

VI. Upon the whole, I believe that if this fragment (which does not present many points to lay hold of) is not an historic and theological study but a book genuinely addressed to Novatian, it is the work of a responsible Bishop in or about Rome. But to identify the writer with Xystus is to create a view of that doctor himself, of Rome as under the influence of Cyprian, and of the end of the Baptismal controversy, which is not warranted, but discredited by our other knowledge of the times.

---

[1] [First published by Jacques Sirmond, Paris 1643. Printed in Sirmondi *Opera varia*, vol. I. pp. 465 ff. (Paris 1696); La Bigne, *Max. Bibl. vett. Patr.*, vol. XXVII. p. 543 (Lyon 1677); Galland. *Bibl. vett. Patr.*, vol. x. p. 359 (Ven. 1774). Book I edited by Oehler, *Corpus hæreseologicum*, Berlin, 1856, *Part I.*, The Catalogue of Heresies, is full of blunders. *Part II.* absurdly professes to be Augustine's. *Part III.* professes to condemn the Pelagians, but is full of Pelagianism.] In the passage given in the text 'qui se ipsos ... appellarunt' is copied from Augustine, *De hæres.* 30.

But there is nothing which would not fall in with the conditions of five or six years earlier, the anxious days in which Cornelius and Cyprian were with great unanimity dealing with the rise of Novatianism and the proper treatment of the Lapsed; when Cyprian was sending Cornelius his new book *de Unitate*; and the kinder view of the Lapsed, as 'vulnerati a diabolo,' and not as wilful sinners, had already come in, see Cyprian's *Ep.* 55. 19 (H. p. 637, 22), *Ep.* 58. 13 (H. 680, 16) *et passim*. It might be carried (if so desired) almost to the end of Cornelius's life.

It is not inconceivable that the author might be Cornelius[1]. Yet its general, abstract style contrasts too much with the detailed, definite, personal style in which he handles Novatian in the letter to Fabius (Euseb. *H. E.* vi. 43), even allowing for the different situations. I am also loth to impute to him either the confusion between Simon the Pharisee and Simon Peter, or the lengthy, feeble and inextricably confused applications of the flights of Noah's dove to the fall and recovery of the Lapsed.

There were other Bishops near to Rome who were quite capable of inditing the book and who (like Hippolytus before this time) may have felt their responsibility for all that went on as even superior to that of the Pope.

These observations I make with diffidence, with a lively appreciation of the interest of Dr Harnack's paper, and with gratitude for the incidental lights which in brief space he has thrown on the subject and its literature.

---

[1] Erasmus thought so, but only through misapprehension of Jerome, *de Viris Illustribus*, lxvi., 'Cornelius ...scripsit epistolam ad Fabium...et aliam de Novatiano et de his qui lapsi sunt,' as if this could describe the *ad Novatianum*. Erasmus's *adnotatiuncula* (in Fo. 500) prefixed to his Cyprian, 1520; repeated in ed. 1530.

APPENDIX H.

Examination of the Lists of Bishops attending the Councils.
(Genuineness, Seniority.)

THERE are four lists of Bishops, varying in number from 36 to 86, who were assembled in Councils, or were formally addressed by Councils, from the year 252 to 256 A.D. (*Epp.* 57, 67, 70, and *Sentt. Episc.*).

The African bishops sat by seniority according to Codex Canonum Eccles. Africanæ Can. 86, which comes from Concil. Milevit. A.D. 416, Labbe, II. c. 1316, III. cc. 383, 4. This, as all the bishops there affirmed, represented the tradition. Augustine complains of breaches of the rule, *Ep.* 59. 1. They sate under their primates, and it is evident in the list of the Council of 256 A.D. that they did not sit by provinces from the mixture of Proconsular and Numidian sees.

If the Cyprianic lists were genuine, then

(1) From an episcopate so large and so widespread, we should expect that in lists so far short of the whole number some names would recur in more than one list, but many would appear only once.

Also we should find certain relations among the recurrent names.

(2) Names which appeared in more than one list would, when intervening non-recurrent names were struck out, stand in nearly the same order in different lists, allowance being made for incidents such as disputable precedence which might arise, for instance, from date of consecration being uncertain or other causes, such as appear in Augustine and the Canon as cited above.

(3) The percentage of recurrent names would dwindle in later lists on account of deaths.

(4) In a longer list the recurrent names would be more spread out, dotted along its whole length. The later names in a list of 36 *might* be the later in a list of 86, but if the largest list be the latest it would probably have at the end a number of junior names not occurring in earlier ones.

If those conditions were met the genuineness of the lists would be established. In forged lists such conditions would find no place, unless they had been clearly foreseen, and the names arranged upon a skeleton drawn before to ensure the appearances. But the multiplicity and complication of the relations between the names on these lists and in other parts of the Cyprianic correspondence is far too great to have been invented and constructed by any romancer. Disturbances we do find, but small in proportion. Some of them are singular and explicable, while the very presence of other disturbances to which we find no clue, in a case where most is coherent and our knowledge so limited, indicates that at least they are not shaped on a plan.

APPENDIX H.

TABLE I.

THE FOUR LISTS.

IInd Council, A.D. 252, *Ep.* 57.	IVth Council, A.D. 254, *Ep.* 67.	Vth Council, A.D. 255, *Ep.* 70.
1 Liberalis	1 Cæcilius	1 Liberalis
2 Caldonius	2 Primus	2 Caldonius
3 Nicomedes	3 Polycarpus	3 Junius
4 Cæcilius	4 Nicomedes	4 Primus
5 Junius	5 Lucianus	5 Cæcilius
6 Marrutius	6 Successus	6 Polycarpus
7 Felix	7 Sedatus	7 Nicomedes
8 Successus	8 Fortunatus	8 Felix
9 Faustinus	9 Januarius I.	9 Marrutius
10 Fortunatus I.	10 Secundus	10 Successus
11 Victor	11 Pomponius	11 Lucianus
12 Saturninus I.	12 Honoratus	12 Honoratus
13 Saturninus II.	13 Victor	13 Fortunatus
14 Rogatianus	14 Aurelius I.	14 Victor I.
15 Tertullus	15 Sattius	15 Donatus I.
16 Lucianus	16 Petrus	16 Lucius
17 Sattius	17 Januarius II.	17 Herculanus
18 Secundinus	18 Saturninus I.	18 Pomponius
19 Saturninus III.	19 Aurelius II.	19 Demetrius
20 Eutyches	20 Venantius	20 Quintus
21 Ampius	21 Quietus	21 Saturninus I.
22 Saturninus IV.	22 Rogatianus	[22 Januarius I.]
23 Aurelius	23 Tenax	23 Marcus
24 Priscus	24 Felix	24 Saturninus II.
25 Herculaneus	25 Faustus	25 Donatus II.
26 Victoricus	26 Quintus	26 Rogatianus
27 Quintus	27 Saturninus II.	27 Sedatus
28 Honoratus	28 Lucius	28 Tertullus
29 Manthaneus	29 Vincentius	29 Hortensianus
30 Hortensianus	30 Libosus	30 Saturninus III.
31 Verianus	31 Geminius	31 Sattius
32 Iambus	32 Marcellus	32 Januario II. (*Numidian*)
33 Donatus I.	33 Iambus	33 Saturnino IV. ,,
34 Pomponius	34 Adelphius	34 Maximo ,,
35 Polycarpus	35 Victoricus	35 Victori II. ,,
36 Demetrius	36 Paulus	36 Victori III. ,,
37 Donatus II.		37 Cassio ,,
38 Privatianus		38 Proculo ,,
39 Fortunatus II.		39 Modiano ,,
40 Rogatus		40 Cittino ,,
41 Monnulus		41 Gargilio I. ,,
		42 Eutichiano ,,
		43 Gargilio II. ,,
		44 Saturnino V. ,,
		45 Nemesiano ,,
		46 Nampulo ,,
		47 Antoniano ,,
		48 Rogatiano ,,
		49 Honorato ,,

22 Saturninus IV. *om. Oxon.*
25 Herculanus M.

22 Januarius *om.* Hartel, though in C L M R.

TABLE I. (*continued*).

THE FOUR LISTS.

VIIth COUNCIL,
A.D. 256, *Sentt. Epp.*

1 Cæcilius
2 Primus
3 Polycarpus
4 Novatus
5 Nemesianus
6 Januarius I.
7 Lucius I.
8 Crescens
9 Nicomedes
10 Monnulus
11 Secundinus I.
12 Felix I.
13 Polianus
14 Theogenes
15 Dativus
16 Successus
17 Fortunatus
18 Sedatus
19 Privatianus
20 Privatus
21 Hortensianus
22 Cassius
23 Januarius II.
24 Secundinus II.
25 Victoricus
26 Felix II.
27 Quietus
28 Castus
29 Eucratius
30 Libosus
31 Leucius
32 Eugenius
33 Felix III.
34 Januarius III.
35 Adelphius
36 Demetrius
37 Vincentius
38 Marcus
39 Sattius
40 Victor I.
41 Aurelius I.
42 Iambus
43 Lucianus
44 Pelagianus
45 Iader
46 Felix IV.
47 Paulus
48 Pomponius
49 Venantius
50 Ahymnus
51 Saturninus I.
52 Saturninus II.
53 Marcellus
54 Irenæus
55 Donatus
56 Zosimus
57 Julianus I.
58 Faustus
59 Geminius
60 Rogatianus
61 Therapius
62 Lucius II.
63 Felix V.
64 Saturninus III.
65 Quintus
66 Julianus II.
67 Tenax
68 Victor II.
69 Donatulus
70 Verulus
71 Pudentianus
72 Petrus
73 Lucius III.
74 Felix VI.
75 Pusillus
76 Salvianus
77 Honoratus
78 Victor III.
79 Clarus
80 Secundianus
81 Aurelius II.
82 Litteus
83 Natalis
84 Pompeius
85 Dioga
86 Junius

568   APPENDIX H.

1. If we turn now to the actual lists given in Table I. side by side, complete as they are found in the MSS. of Cyprian, and again as opposite in Table II., with the omission of names which occur only in one list, and of very common names like Felix, where nothing points to identification, we shall find upon an inspection of the numbers which give their position in each list, that the identified names do follow in the same sequence in each to such an extent as to shew at once the genuineness of the documents and the existence in Cyprian's time of the rule of seniority.

An inspection of Table II. will at once shew the force of this argument. The number of names which have their sequence exact is remarkable.

LISTS OF BISHOPS. 569

TABLE II.

IDENTICAL NAMES IN THE LISTS OF THE COUNCILS.

IInd, A.D. 252, Ep. 57.		IVth, A.D. 254, Ep. 67.		Vth, A.D. 255, Ep. 70.		VIIth, A.D. 256, Sentt. Epp.	
1	Liberalis			1	Liberalis		
2	Caldonius			2	Caldonius		
3	Nicomedes			3	Junius		
4	Cæcilius	1	Cæcilius	4	Primus	1	Cæcilius
		2	Primus	5	Cæcilius	2	Primus
		3	Polycarpus	6	Polycarpus	3	Polycarpus
5	Junius	4	Nicomedes	7	Nicomedes	9	Nicomedes
6	Marrutius			8	Felix	12	Felix I.
7	Felix			9	Marrutius		
8	Successus	6	Successus	10	Successus	16	Successus
10	Fortunatus	7	Sedatus	13	Fortunatus	17	Fortunatus
		8	Fortunatus	27	Sedatus]	18	Sedatus
		12	Pomponius				
11	Victor	13	Victor	14	Victor I.	40	Victor I.
		17	Januarius I.	18	Pomponius	23	Januarius II.
						48	Pomponius
				19	Demetrius	36	Demetrius
		18	Saturninus I.	21	Saturninus I.	51	Saturninus I.
				22	Januarius		
				23	Marcus	38	Marcus
13	Saturninus II.	22	Rogatianus	24	Saturninus II.	52	Saturninus II.
14	Rogatianus	27	Saturninus II.	26	Rogatianus	60	Rogatianus
		29	Vincentius			37	Vincentius]
16	Lucianus			11	Lucianus	43	Lucianus
17	Sattius	15	Sattius]	31	Sattius	39	Sattius
18	Secundinus					24	Secundinus II.]
19	Saturninus III.			30	Saturninus III.	54	Saturninus III.
23	Aurelius	19	Aurelius			41	Aurelius
		20	Venantius			49	Venantius
		21	Quietus			27	Quietus]
		23	Tenax			57	Tenax
		28	Lucius	16	Lucius	62	Lucius
25	Herculaneus			17	Herculanus]		
26	Victoricus	35	Victoricus]			25	Victoricus]
27	Quintus	26	Quintus	20	Quintus]	65	Quintus
30	Hortensianus			29	Hortensianus	21	Hortensianus]
		30	Libosus			30	Libosus]
		31	Geminius			59	Geminius
		32	Marcellus				
32	Iambus	33	Iambus			42	Iambus
		34	Adelphius			35	Adelphius]
		36	Paulus			47	Paulus
						53	Marcellus
33	Donatus I.			25	Donatus II.]	55	Donatus
				49	Honoratus	77	Honoratus
34	Pomponius						
35	Polycarpus	3	. . .	6	. . .	3	
36	Demetrius		. . .	19	. . .	36	
37	Donatus II.		. . .	15	Donatus or 25]		
38	Privatianus		. . .		. . .	19	Privatianus]
39	Fortunatus II.						
41	Monnulus		. . .		. . .	10	Monnulus]

570   APPENDIX H.

2. We next ascertain that of the names which can be identified throughout the lists,

>30 occur in the first list of 41 (A.D. 252), or 73·2 per cent.
>28 ,, ,, second ,, 36 (A.D. 254), ,, 77·8 ,, ,,
>30 ,, ,, third ,, 49 (A.D. 255), ,, 61·2 ,, ,,
>39 ,, ,, fourth ,, 86 (A.D. 256), ,, 45·3 ,, ,,

So that the second test as to the diminution is fulfilled, except in the second list, where the percentage rises[1].

3. The third test is seen upon inspection to be fulfilled. After the 77th bishop, Honoratus, or the 78th (which is more doubtful, since the name Victor is so common) no names in the last longest list of 86 correspond to names in the other lists.

The instances of disturbance are curious, and worth consideration :—

(1) In list of Council V. the reversal of the order of Primus and Cæcilius, the variation of Junius and Nicomedes on either side of them, and the stability of Polycarp, while as a group these five hold their place.

(2) The similar disturbance of Felix and Marrutius in same list.

(3) The disturbance of Sedatus and Fortunatus, and in V. the depression of Sedatus.

(4) The disturbance of Rogatianus and Saturninus II.

(5) The alternation visible in the above instances as to pairs of names is extended to groups of four in Councils IV., V., VII., where (IV. 11 sqq.) Pomponius, Januarius, Demetrius, Saturninus, are intermixed, Victor keeping his place among them; and again (IV. 32 sqq.) Marcellus, Iambus, Adelphius, Paulus, of whom Adelphius is in VII. much higher.

(6) Other isolated variations are pointed out by a *square bracket*] *after the names*.

(7) At the close of list of Council II. occurs a very evident depression of seven names *en masse*. While they are last in this list they (all save one, not again mentioned) occupy very high places in the other lists. These appear without omission below the line at the end of Table II., and are nos. 34 to 41 in the list of Council II.

Now 35 Polycarpus was bishop of Hadrumetum. He and his clergy had already addressed Cornelius as duly elected Pope of Rome, before the Council met which was to decide for or against his recognition. When the Council had determined to await the arrival of more authentic information as to the character of the election, Cyprian the Metropolitan and Liberalis the senior bishop visited Hadrumetum together during

---

[1] In this list it will be found that there is twice as large a proportion of attendances from the immediate vicinity of Carthage, from places within the 45 miles radius (v. *Appendix on Cities*, p. 578).

the pause (pp. 152, 133). The result of that visit was (and Cornelius complained of it accordingly) that the clergy of Hadrumetum in addressing a second ecclesiastical letter to Rome, directed it this time not to Cornelius but to the presbyter and deacons of the city.

What was the object of this visit of Cyprian and Liberalis if it was not to induce the bishop and clergy of a city which had been precipitate in its recognition to suspend their judgment? And would the visit have been necessary if Polycarp had been with them at Carthage?

The presumption is not weak that Polycarp was absent from the first and present at the later sittings, and when we consider the names and numbers which follow, especially such an instance as that of Monnulus, we must assume (it would appear) some formal cause for the anomalous depression of these members below their usual place; and deferred attendance seems to be at least one rational way of accounting for the fact.

(8) In the long list of the 86 bishops of Council VII. there are two lines of disturbance clearly not accidental, yet without more knowledge inexplicable.

a. It will be seen that the bishops numbered 40, 48, 51, 52, 60, 64, 67, 62? 65? are all placed in this list much lower than in the others, but that *their seniority among themselves* is very slightly deranged.

b. In same list 24, 27, 21, 25, 30, 36, are all much higher than in other lists, but again *their seniority among themselves* is respected.

Notes. (1) The bishop VII. 71, Pudentianus, speaks of his own juniority.

(2) It appears that Junius VII. 86 unless he came late can scarcely be the same as v. 3 Junius.

(3) In treating VII. 52 as Numidian Tucca, and VII. 77 as Proconsular Tucca, Morcelli has transposed them. For VII. 77 Honoratus is the Numidian by *Epp.* 62, 70, and answers to 49 in Council V.

VII. 52 Saturninus of Tucca (Terebinthina) is the proconsular bishop, and comes in his proper place according to the other lists.

(4) I have forborne to collate some of the name of Felix, or to identify VII. 58 Faustus with IV. 25.

(5) On VII. 27 see note on Quietus of Buruc, p. 363. If that view is right then VII. 27 will not be identified with IV. 21 Quietus, but would *as Quintus* take the place now given to VII. 65 Quintus. This would be more in order, which would again still further confirm the view taken in that note.

Lists of Numidian Bishops.

Taking out the Numidian bishops by themselves for a similar comparison we have a similar result. There are about 25 (some uncertain) in the longest list, that of Council VII.; there are 18 in the superscription of their Epistle 70, and 8 in that of their Epistle 62. All of these earliest eight recur in one of the other two, and all in the same order (with others intervening), except that in the first two lists Proculus and one Victor change places, and that Nemesian is low in both of these and highest but one in the third. He is also the first named in the two letters 76, 77 to and from the Numidian Confessor-Bishops. These two however are not formal documents as the others are, and their agreement is more general.

Inspection of the following Numidian names found in more than one list will detect the facts.

TABLE III.

ORDER OF NUMIDIAN BISHOPS IN THE HEADINGS OF *Epp.* 62 *and* 70, AND IN THE *Seventh Council*, AND IN THE HEADINGS OF *Epp.* 76, 77.

Epistle 62 (8 Bishops)		*Epistle* 70 (18 Bishops)		VIIth *Council* (? 25 Bishops)		*Epistles* 76	77
				5	Nemesianus	1	1
1	Januarius	1	Januarius	6	Januarius		
				7	Lucius	3	
				12	Felix	2	3 ?
				13	Polianus	6	
				15	Dativus	9	2
2	Maximus	3	Maximus				
4	Victor	4	Victor				
		5	Victor				
		6	Cassius	22	Cassius		
3	Proculus	7	Proculus				
5	Modianus	8	Modianus				
				33	Felix ? III.	4	3 ?
6	Nemesianus	14	Nemesianus				
7	Nampulus	15	Nampulus				
8	Honoratus	18	Honoratus	77	Honoratus		
				78	Victor III.	7	4
				82	Litteus	5	

To conclude. In documents of which the coincidences are so subtle yet so substantial as in these Council-Lists, the difficulties so insoluble and yet so evidently capable of being unlocked in whole groups by a little more knowledge, we are sure that we have genuine documents, belonging to the times and scenes which they lay claim to. They are evidently documents, so to speak, which made themselves and took no pains to clear themselves.

APPENDICES I, K.

The Cities.

APPENDIX I.

INDEX TO CITIES.

City	PAGE	City	PAGE
Abbamaccora ?	608	(Meninx)	598
Abbir Germaniciana	603, 608	Midili	608
Aggya	609	Mileou	584
Ammedera	595	Misgirpa	608
Assuras	602	Musula	595
Ausafa	604	Neapolis	579
Ausuaga	608	Nova	607
Avitinæ	581, 609	Obba	595
Bagai	591	Octavu	609
Bamacora	608	Oea	596
Biltha	608	Rucuma	608
Bulla Regia	581	Rusicade	584
Buruc	607	Sabrata	597
a Buslacenis	609	Segermes	579
Capsa	599	Sicca Veneria	582
Carpos	579	Sicilibba	581
a Castra Galbæ	609	Sufes	601
Cedias	590	Sufetula	601
Chullabi	584	Thabraca	581
Cibaliana	609	(Thagaste)	582
Cirta	583	a Thambis	609
Cuicul	584	Thamugadi	589
Dionysiana	608	Tharassa	608
Furni	580	Thasualthe	608
Gazaufala	585	Thelepte	600
Gemellæ	592, 599	Thenæ	603
Germaniciana	603	Theveste	588, 593
Girba	598	(Theveste Road)	594
Giru Marcelli ?	608	Thibaris	583
Gor	580	Thimida Regia	580
a Gurgitibus	609	Thinisa	579
Hadrumetum	606	Thubunæ	592
Hippo Diarrhytus	578	Thuburbo Majus	579
Hippo Regius	582	Thuccaboris	580
Horrea Cælia	606	(Tripolis)	597
Lamasba	591	Tucca (Num. & Maur.)	585
Lambæsis	586	Tucca Terebinthina	602
Laribus	594	Ululæ	608
Leptiminus	605	Uthina	580
Leptis Magna	596	Utica	578
Luperciana	609	(Uzappa)	604
Macomades	585	Vada	608
Mactharis	604	Vaga	581
Marazana	604	Victoriana	609
Marcelliana ?	608	Vicus Cæsaris	581, 608
Mascula	591	Zama Regia	605
Membresa	581		

APPENDIX K.

Note on the Cities *from which the* Bishops *came to the* Seventh Council *of Cyprian and Third on Baptism on the first of September,* A.D. 256[1] (pp. 366 sqq.).

A short sketch has been given in the text of the interests which invested most of these cities under the Empire. But the cities and their

---

[1] *Principal Authorities:*

Inscriptiones Africæ Latinæ, Gust. Wilmanns (*Corp. Inscriptt. Latt.*, vol. VIII. i., ii.), fo., Berl., 1881 and *Supplementum* (Afr. Proc.), R. Cagnat et Johan. Schmidt, fo., Berl , 1891.

Inscriptions Romaines d'Algérie, L. Rénier, Paris, 1858 ff.

Société Archéologique de la Province de Constantine. Annuaire 1853 ff.

Revue Africaine, Alger, Paris, Constantine, 1856 ff.

Fouilles à Carthage, M. Beulé, 4to., Paris, 1861.

Explorations Épigraphiques et Archéologiques en Tunisie, M. R. Cagnat, 3 fascicules, Paris 1883—1886.

Géographie comparée de la Province Romaine d'Afrique, C. Tissot (*Exploration Scientifique de la Tunisie*), Paris, 1884—1888. 2 vols. 4to. and Atlas.

Remains of the Roman occupation of N. Africa with special reference to Algeria, Al. Graham (*Transactions of R. Inst. of British Architects,* vol. I. N.S., Lond., 1885).

Travels in the Footsteps of Bruce, Col. Sir R. L. Playfair, 4to., Lond., 1887.

Various Monographs on Discoveries at Carthage, by le R. P. Delattre, 8vo., Lille (Desclée), 1888—1890.

Trésor de Chronologie, d'Histoire et de Géographie, Cte de Mas Latrie, fo., Paris, 1889.

Untersuchungen über die äussere Entwicklung der Afrikanischen Kirche, Dr A. Schwarze, Göttingen, 1892.

Excursions in the Mediterranean, Algeria and Tunis, Sir Grenville T. Temple, Lond., 1835.

Four Months in Algeria, J. W. Blakesley, 8vo., Cambridge, 1859.

occupation of the country are indeed so remarkable that I have cast into the form of a long Note fuller particulars. This Note cannot pretend to originality, although I felt it a duty and found it an intense enjoyment to visit some of these remarkable sites. I have to rely on published investigations and, where possible, I have verified the authorities, although mistakes are, I fear, inevitable in summarizing so large a number of statements.

Some explorations have been so assiduous and their records so monumental that increasing research will rather increase than lessen their value[1]. The gratitude of learning will never be withdrawn from Charles Tissot or Gustavus Wilmanns.

To recapitulate a few necessary points.

The Council of Carthage of the year 256 (September 1) is described in contemporaneous minutes as 'The meeting of very many Bishops of the province of Africa, Numidia, Mauritania.' It must not be understood as if the 87 were an approximately even representation of the sees of the continent[2]. At the most two Mauritanian Bishops, and one whose see

Great Sahara, H. B. Tristram, 8vo., London, 1860.
Carthage and her Remains, Dr N. Davis, 8vo., London, 1861.
Ruined Cities within Numidian and Carthaginian Territory, N. Davis, 8vo., London, 1862.
Travels in Tunisia, A. Graham and H. S. Ashbee, imp. 8vo., London, 1887.
Maps: Carthage, Caillat, 1877.   Perthes (Afrika), West Sahara (1), Central Sahara (2).   Spruner-Menke, Atlas antiq. no. xxxi.   Afrique Reg. Septentrionale (Service géographique de l'Armée—R. de Lannoy de Bissy), 1, 2, 6. Carte de Reconnaissance (Serv. géogr. de l'Armée) Tunisie iii.   Environs de la Tunisie et de Carthage, Paris, Dépôt de la Guerre.   Algérie et Tunisie, Pelet, 1891.   Above all, the grand Atlas archéologique de la Tunisie (Ministère de l'Instruction Publique), Paris, 3 livraisons, 1893-5.

[1] *Note* that the margin gives the antient names of the towns from the *Corpus Inscriptionum Latinarum*; and the modern names of the towns generally as in Tissot; the figures are the dates at which their Bishops appear, mostly in Councils. The date of Cyprian's Council, 256 A.D., is not entered because the Bishops of all the towns treated of were there. Nearly all the other dates belong to the following Councils:

A.D.
256. Synodus Carthaginensis sub Cypriano VII. de Baptismo III.
305. Synodus Cirtæ Celebrata.
314. Synodus Arelatensis I.

A.D.
349. Synodus Carthagin. sub Grato.
393. Synodus Maximianistarum [Concilium apud Cabursussi].
397. Synodus Carthaginensis.
411. Collatio Carthagine habita inter Catholicos et Donatistas.
419. Synodus Carthaginensis.
484. Collatio Carthagine habita inter Catholicos et Arianos.
525. Concilium Carthaginense.
641. Concilium Byzacenum.
646. IV. Concilia Africana.

[2] Poole, *Life and Times of Cyprian*, p. 366, 'the far greater part of the Bishops of Africa, Numidia and Mauritania.'

was half in Numidia, appear for this vast Province. There were twice as many from the Proconsular Province as from the larger Numidia, and of the 55 who represented the Province 12 came from within five and forty miles of Carthage.

The bare roll of the eighty-seven names would be a wonderful witness to the commanding influence of Cyprian, but to review their cities is to realize the material which was being shaped into Christendom.

If we could revive but a faint picture of those cities, their number, their beauty, their wealth, resources and administration, we should stand amazed at the power and the policy, the magnificence and the elaboration with which Rome organized so resourceful a continent so wickedly won.

But a separate interest still lies in the fact that the Christians had so immediately and so vigorously laid hold on the centres of life and activity, and faced on new principles the problems which defied that Roman genius of rule and grew more intricate both in spite of and in consequence of its efforts.

Buildings may be mentioned in this Note which belong to a later century than Cyprian's, but already in his time many of the cities were full grown and magnificent, and it is strange to remember how actively heathen growth was going on side by side with Christian growth.

In most of these towns which lay so thick in that resourceful region there was a bishop, a stipendiary[1] staff of presbyters, organized on a collegiate or quasi-canonical plan of life and work, and a set of deacons administering the more secular affairs and providing for the monetary needs of the Church. Many of these places have ruins of more than one Christian basilica, which no doubt succeeded to private halls, secular rooms, and 'fabricæ' like Fabian's, which were used in Cyprian's time.

The bishop was everywhere elected by and represented an enlightened and steadily increasing portion of the community. What his powers were, sole or joint, we have seen. He had been brought up like every educated Roman within constant sight of the administration of firm justice, of revenue, of military force, within sound, and possibly in the practice, of eloquence and argumentation, amid the publicity of the wildest pleasures, and with his precise place assigned him in the body politic, under the name but without the least substance of liberty. The only liberty known was that which was being re-formed under the new constitution which he himself represented.

The *Episcopus Christianorum* was called *sacerdos*. There were many *sacerdotes* in every town: flamens, pontiffs, ministers of the beautiful temples, and countless altars. The higher of these were great civilians and generals who officiated from time to time for an hour of their secular day. Some were hereditary keepers of the gods' homes and of the gods themselves; some were nominated and lived partly by endowments, partly

---

[1] *Epp.* 1. 1; 34. 4; 39. 5; see note 3 on p. 305 sup.

on offerings. But the new *sacerdotes* had begun to live among them, each at once the elect of men and the successor to powers which 'loved not the world, neither the things which were in the world.' He was the ambassador of One God who had had and was having real dealings with men, touching things inexpressible by the voices of heathen prayer; things which had nothing to do with prosperity, or material, or disease, which triplet was the hope or fear of the heathen.

It was some such person, who with his personal equation as various as tides of life could make it, came glowing with the faith of Christ from each of eighty-six cities to the central chair of the Province.

The list runs off merely, as it would seem, according to the seniority of the prelates, with perhaps a queue of late comers. But with a little effort we can cast those cities into groups, we can even now attach somewhat of a living idea to their names. We shall thus appreciate the significance of the list and the force of the thoughts which rise out of it.

I will group them as follows, merely for convenience and easy recognition on the map, as they lay in the eye of neighbours or travellers.

 1. The circle of cities about Carthage.
 2. The circle of Cirta.
 3. The circle of Mount Aures.
 4. The Theveste Road.
 5. Three Routes to Carthage from the cities on the Syrtes and upwards.
 6. Mauretania.
 7. The cities unidentified.

1. *The Circle of Carthage.*

First; from the group of sees close round the Metropolis, within a radius of 45 miles, twelve bishops came to the Council.

Municipium Julium Utika: Colonia Julia Ælia Hadriana Augusta Utika. *Bou-Châter.* Bishops in A.D. 303; at Arles 314, 339, 411, 419, 484, 525, 556, 646, 684.

UTICA, with memories of primæval rivalry with Carthage, still ranked as the second city of Africa, but was now fast ceding that place to Hadrumetum, for the Bagradas was silting up its grand military and merchant harbours, and banking the sea out further every year from immense structures reared for the health, pleasure, and defence of its many generations. In its miles of fragments we trace Phœnician works almost as extensive and more solid than the finest Roman. From Cape Carthage Utica lies full in view across the curve of the bay, pale against the hills which hide Bizerte on the northern trend of the coast.

Colonia Julia Hippo Diarrhytus. Ἱππῶν διάρρυτος, Ptol. Hippone Zarito, Itin. *Benzert, Bizerte.*—Bps. 401—404, 411, 484, 525, 646.

Bizerte, even in its strangely altered name, is HIPPO DIARRHYTUS. It occupied picturesquely both banks and the mid-island of the tidal adit of its north lake with its garden shores. The fame of neither city seemed ever clear from the unpatriotic memory of having deserted Carthage in its extremity, and Hippo was now a poor-spirited, self-contained provincial town[1], living by its marvellous fisheries.

---

[1] See the pretty sarcastic story of Pliny, *Ep.* ix. 33.

THE CITIES.

From THINISA, which lay on the coast between the two, came the Bishop Venantius; from Hippo Petrus, and from Utica Aurelius[1]. *Θίνισσα*, Ptol. Thinissa, Tuneiza, Tuniza, It. Ant. *Ras el Djebel.* Bps. 411, 484.

From Carthage, looking due east across the glorious gulf, a good way beyond the eastern spur of the Horns of Ben Gournin, Secundinus would discern his own CARPOS[2], with its fashionable hot-springs—scene later on of Donatist savagery. Colonia Julia Karpis. *Κάρπις*, Pt. *Mraïsa.* Bps. 411, 419, 484, 525, 646.

Out of sight on the far side of the same eastern promontory lay NEAPOLIS, the north horn of the gulf then called after it, now Gulf of Hammamet—an African Bay of Naples. It was a Carthaginian factory, the nearest African harbour to Sicily[3], captured by Agathocles and by Piso, and an early 'Colonia.' Edrisi saw great ruins of it, but they have all passed into the mean carcase of the Arab town. Col. Julia Neapolis. *Nebel.* Bps. 411, 419, 484, 525, 646.

Its Bishop Junius was the last who spoke in the Council. He speaks of the earlier conciliar decisions as 'what we once for all sanctioned[4],' and in each of the former Council-lists his name appears—and as a senior. Some element of either distance or lateness enters into the list of A.D. 257, as the Tripolitan Bishops are all together at the end.

Southward a few miles, between Mount Zaghouan and the sea, was SEGERMES, only ruins still to us, not identified until 1884[5]. Nicomedes was one of the seniors. Municipium Aurelianum Augustum Segermes. *Harat.*

The tiny Oued Meliana, with its deep torrent channel, drains into the Lake of Tunis a fertile waste once thick with cities. In its upper dale it skirts on the south-east the site of GREAT THUBURBO[6], one of Pliny's 'eight Colonies,' founded by Julius, improved by Commodus. One of Bps. 411, 484, 641. Colonia Julia Aurelia Commoda Thuburbo Majus. *Kasbat.* Bps. 314 (Arles), 411, 484.

---

[1] *Sentt. Epp.* 49, 72, 41.

[2] *Sentt. Epp.* 24. On form of name see p. 421, n. 2.

[3] Thucydides vii. 50. He calls Neapolis a Καρχηδονιακὸν ἐμπόριον; that is, not one of the Emporia proper which were the towns on the little Syrtis from Thenæ, though those between the two Syrtes are sometimes understood in the word. Morcelli thought Neapolis of Tripoli was here meant, since it follows the other Tripolitan sees and Leptis Magna. Tissot holds this Neapolis to be only a new quarter of Leptis Magna. Still the order is remarkable; although geographical arrangement does not appear (except as above) in the list, and the non-representation of the greater Neapolis might seem unlikely too.

[4] Quod semel censuimus, *Sentt. Epp.* 86.

[5] *Sentt. Epp.* 9—*C. I. L.* VIII. i. n. 910, and *Suppl.* I., p. 1164, nn. 11170 and 11172. Cf. *Bullet. archéol. du Com. des Trav. Hist.* 1885, p. 162, 1886, p. 71.

[6] *Sentt. Epp.* 18. No reason to doubt that the see is Thuburbo *majus*. Now and in 314 at Arles there is no appearance of two synonymous cities. But in 411, bishops from 'Thuburbo majus' and 'minus' attend the Collation of Carthage.

Tuburbis, *Plin.* Θουβουρβώ, *Ptol.* Tuburbo Majus, *Peut.* Tuburb, Thubur, *Inscrr.* But the great inscription, by finding which in 1857 M. Tissot first identified the place, has Thuburbo, like the text of Cyprian.

37—2

the noble Roman Cities of Peace, now 'lying among the pots'—fragments of three temples, great Phœnician stones in the fort-walls, and four more 'grand edifices.' Under Genseric and Huneric its martyrs were many.

Sedatus, its bishop, thought that 'as water was hallowed by the 'bishop's prayer in the church, so it was tainted into a cancer by the 'speech of heresy.'

<small>Civitas, s. Respublica Goritana. *Drâa el Gamra.*</small>

Over the Meliana opposite was GOR[1]—pure Punic for 'Hospice'—its lands bestridden by the great aqueduct of Carthage.

<small>'Respublica Thimidensium Regiorum.' *Sidi Ali-es-Sedjini.* Bps. 484, 525, 646. Uthina 'Colonia,' Pl. Οὔθινα, Pt. *Oudena.* Bps. 314 (Arles), 411, 525.</small>

In its lower valley was the 'most splendid commonwealth' of THIMIDA ROYAL—that is, an ancient seat of Numidian kings, and higher up the mountain slopes is another of the earlier Colonies, UTHINA.

It is difficult to speak of the majesty of its ruins, never rebuilt by Byzantine general nor quarried by Arab. They are all of the best time of Roman art. This apparent indication of its abandonment after the Vandal sack is strengthened by the fact that in A.D. 525 it had no bishop of its own[2]. In Tertullian's time the character of its bishop had been a weapon of his against Catholics. When Felix came to Cyprian, its square miles of undulating plateau covered with buildings, as now with relics, required those enormous sets of cisterns, that massy and complicated citadel for its defence, and that perfectly appointed amphitheatre for its ferocious pleasure. It presented one and all of those social problems which Cyprian saw spread out before Christianity.

<small>Tuccabor. *Toukkâbeur.* Bps. 411, 646.</small>

The Lower Bagradas Valley, of untold agricultural wealth, spreads to the north past Carthage. The river is alternately a brooklet and a wide sudden stream, laden with alluvium. On a buttress of hills overlooking its plain from the north, hung THUCCABORIS, 40 miles in a direct line west of Carthage. It still is inhabited meanly in its old insulæ on their own foundations, below the great rock cisterns which it bears in its name[3], within fortifications of enormous blocks; for it had its Roman and its Punic quarters, and the native cultus of Cælestis and of Baal as Hercules Conservator, was served with Imperial temples. The bishop's name was Fortunatus.

<small>Furni. *El-Mssaâdin.* Bps. a Donat. 411, 525.</small>

On the other side of the valley, eight and twenty miles from Carthage, lying on the chord of a long sweep in Hadrian's road to Theveste, and giving its name to the gate by which that road started from Carthage, stood FURNI[4]. This was the place in which Cyprian applied his first act

---

[1] Gorduba, Hartel; two of the best MSS. and Aug. have Gor. Two inscriptions identify with Henchir Drâa el Gamra, and mention its annual magistrates, perpetual flamen, ordo and decuriones.

[2] Felicissimus episcopus plebis Sedelensis qui et Utinensis. *Syn. Carth. Bonifacii Episcopi*, A.D. 525. Labbe, V. 771.

[3] 'Bor' seems to be identical in Hebrew and Punic. Tissot, II. 292 n.

[4] I adopt as probable Tissot's identification of the see with the Furni which

THE CITIES.

of clergy discipline in the Geminian family. One of that same family was now its bishop.

In this same Lower Medjerda Valley, threaded by the great Road, were SICILIBBA[1], in whose extended ruins are relics of good architecture; and MEMBRESA, of Punic origin, a difficult unfortified hill-town[2], overhanging an elbow of the river,—the key both to its upper valley and to the rich agricultural vale of Vaga. Here it was that, aided by the invincible north-west gale of the region, Belisarius dispersed the rebel forces of Stotzas. Near Membresa was the yet unfound AVITINÆ[3]. The three bishops were Sattius, Lucius, Saturninus.

At VAGA, seated on the high western end of the tract which it commands, there were no doubt traces of the large Italian population of which Sallust speaks, connected with its great trade in other commodities besides corn. It had been specially made over to Masinissa, and became the principal centre of Numidian commerce.

Through the Upper Medjerda Valley, above Membresa, road and river run together until near the Numidian frontier, passing Vicus Augusti, which some would identify with that otherwise unknown VICUS CÆSARIS, which sent Januarius to the Council. It lies some twenty-six miles onward, and after yet another twenty-nine is BULLA REGIA, which sent Therapius.

'King's Bulla,' with its massy Punic Byrsa (lately pulled down to metal the railway), with crag-defended plateau and a vast water-storage[4], with marshes below prolific of eel and barbel, with hot sulphur baths, sweet fountains reverently enshrined, theatre and amphitheatre, covers many acres with its ruins. It was, like Samaria, 'The Head of the Fat Valley.'

North of Bulla the mountains rise to a height of 3,326 feet at Aïn Draham. Thence the 'smiling hills of the Tell' fall in terrace and slope to the sea level. And due north, where the bewilderingly fertile and feverous valley of Oued-el-Kebir, the antient partition of Numidia and the Province, enters the sea, lies THABRACA[5], on mainland and

Sidenotes: Sicilibba, It. Ant. *El Alouenim.* Bps. bef. 337 a Donat.; 4 II, a Donat. 419, ?484. Membressa, It. Ant. *Medjez-el-Bab.* Bps. a Donat. 393, 411, 484, 525; 646. [Avitinæ] Bps. bef. 404?, 411, 440, 525, 646. Colonia Septimia Vaga. *Badja.* Bps. 411, 484, 495. ? Vicus Cæsaris. Bps. a Donat. 393, 411. Bulla Regia. Oppidum liberum, Pl. *Hammam Darradji.* Bps. 390, 411. Thabraca, colonia, Pt. *Tabarka.* Bps. 398, 411; Tabrac. Monast. Vict. Vit. Pers. Vand. i. 32.

---

he here discovered, and not with the Henchir Aïn Fournou 130 miles away, near Zama Regia. But it is not demonstrated.

[1] *Al.* Sicilibra, Sicilbra, Sicilippa, Sciliba also Itin. Ant. Cf. Itin. Anc. Fortia d' Urban (1845). p. 12.

[2] Ἐν χωρίῳ ὑψηλῷ τε καὶ δυσκόλῳ, Procop. *B. V.* ii. 15, ap. Tissot, II. 327, with plan.

[3] Neighbourhood is implied in the horrid story of the religious ill-usage of the Membresitan Bishop Salvius by the people of Avitinæ. Augustin. *c. Ep. Parmen.* iii. 29, with *c. Crescon.* iv. 49 (t. ix. c. 77, and note).

[4] Dr Carton, *Bullet. archéol. du Comité des Trav. Hist.* 1891, p. 212, describes this feature; not only its public cisterns, but, p. 247, 'pas d'habitation, si modeste fût elle, qui ne possédât de ces réservoirs.' On its Punic necropolis see *Id.* 1892, p. 69.

[5] *Sentt. Epp.* 25.

582   APPENDIX K.

island. The mainland is still dense with 'glorious forest-lands,' the 'shadowed glades[1]' of Juvenal, among whose immense oaks were hunted lions and leopards as well as deer. The island is a towering fortified rock, four hundred feet high, forming and sheltering a slight roadstead. The sea is rich in coral, whose fishers have carried their craft and their native name in colonies to Sardinia and Spain[2].

From either Hippo and from Bulla roads converged on Thabraca, bringing material from east, west and south for embarkation along with its own rich local exports. It is difficult to explore, but the basilica and some mosaics of the Christians have emerged[3]. Their bishop was at Cyprian's Council, Victoricus.

Hippo Regius Colonia, It. Ant. Annaba; Bône. Bps. ?304, ?350, bef. 388, Don. ?396, Don. 409, S. Augustine (395—430).

Fifty-one miles west along the coast-road is another Royal Numidian town, HIPPO REGIUS[4], on high ground between the marshy mouths of the Seyboux and a lesser stream. The Seyboux draws waters from Augustine's home, Thagaste, on the high Medjerda valley, and delivers them at this home of his labour and his rest. Of the six or seven known basilicas and churches of his time no trace yet appears. Relics of the cisterns, aqueduct, quay and bridge remain of what up to the sixth century, long after its fall, was a strong city still. Five important roads converged here, for, though an insecure harbour until the French dominion, it was one of the best along the iron-bound seaboard. King's Hippo then was an active place. Its bishop now was Theogenes, one of the Seniors, a martyr in whose Memoria at Hippo Augustine sometimes celebrated[5].

Colonia Julia Veneria Cirta Nova Sicca. Colonia Julia Cirta Nova. El Kef. Bps. 349, 411, 418, 483?, 646.

Above the valley of the Mellag, a great branch of the Upper Medjerda system, towers the strongest, most commanding place in Tunisia, El Kef, 'The Rock.' This is SICCA VENERIA[6], known also by either name severally. It is on the road to Cirta from Carthage, more than 21 miles beyond Thacia, where it forks off from the Theveste road. A Royal City of Masinissa, and first to join the Romans after the Battle of Muthul, thence honoured as a 'Julian' Colony. Seat of infamous, originally Punic, rites. A fine inscription honours the Restorer of a Venus stolen by thieves 'interrupta templi munitione.' Arnobius born here, who is very strong on the Heathen vice which such a place fostered. Another inscription describes a charitable foundation for 300 boys and 300 girls. Its bishop was Castus and his text the duty of preferring truth to custom.

And in another southern side-valley of the Upper Medjerda, the Oued

---

[1] Quales umbriferos ubi pandit Thabraca saltus. Juv. *Sat.* x. 194.

[2] Tabarcini in Sardinia and also near Alicanti.

[3] Toutain, *Bull. Trav. Hist.* 1892, p. 195, speaks of a 'nécropole Chrétienne.'

[4] *Sentt. Epp.* 14. Antiquis dilectus regibus, Sil. Ital. iii. 259. The changes of its name are curious, Ubbo, Phœn.? 'marsh'—Ἱππώνη, Bona, Bône. Its Arab name *Annaba* is from its jujube trees.

[5] *Serm. ad Populum*, 273, 7.

[6] *Sentt. Epp.* 28; Tissot, II. 375; C. *I. L.* VIII. i. nn. 1632, 1648.

Tibar[1], is THIBARIS, to whose 'plebs consistens' Cyprian wrote his 58th epistle, to nerve them for the expected persecution of Gallus. The basilica of their descendants is traceable. The bishop of Thibaris was Vincentius.

Resp.
Thibaris.
Amänet.
Bp. 411.

2. *The Circle of Cirta.*

We pass to the heart of Numidia. The Circle of Cirta, as we may call it, was a unique group of towns. Each sent its Christian bishop to the Council. 'Lordly CIRTA,' the tragic capital of the Numidian kings, has well been thought 'the noblest site in the whole world.' A gigantic foursquare pedestal of rock, a cubic mountain (like that of the Apocalypse) touches the surrounding country at one point, islanded otherwise by streams. Its precipices grow to a thousand feet in height as the plateau of the city tilts slowly up, while the ravine bed of the Rummel, spanned here and there by giant arches of rock, slopes to its beautiful cascades.

Colonia Julia Juvenalis Honoris et Virtutis Cirta. *Constantine.*
Bps. 303, 305, 330, bef. 407, bef. 410, 411, 416, 484.

Antient epithets for it vied with one another—'the most fenced city,' 'the most opulent.' Palaces and temples rimmed the highest edge where the hideous barrack is now, and left marvellous remains even till the French came. The most prosaic of races is still clearing away everything that is picturesque. Inscriptions record how many were its priests, pontiffs, augurs and flamens.

Very antiently it had some close bond with surrounding *pagi*, and the Roman wisdom of colonization is eminent in that it not only allowed the exemption of so proud a place for a time from proconsular jurisdiction and even from that of the quæstor, but gave to the four greater pagi the title of *Colonies*. At the same time there was appointed to each a præfect of its own, apparently under a 'præfect of the colonies[2].' The union certainly existed under Trajan; is not recorded after Alexander Severus[3], and perhaps at the time of the Council was becoming needless

---

[1] *Sentt. Epp.* 37. This name together with an inscription. *C. I. L.* VIII. *Suppl.* i. p. 1486, n. 15435, fix the place but not its name, GENIO THIBARIS AUGUSTO SACRUM R P THIB. Dd. Tissot calls it Thibar. It is within Byzacena.

[2] *C. I. L.* I. 6944, 6711, 7978. See Mommsen's article *C. I. L.* VIII. i. p. 618. The title conferred shews that they were not reduced to the rank of *præfecturæ*; and so, I think, the appointment of a *præfectus* no longer conveyed the idea of chastisement for revolt as antiently in the case of Capua, &c., yet was still desirable as a security.

[3] M. Tissot, vol. II. p. 401, says: 'Une inscription de Milev prouve que [la confédération] fut *dissoute*, probablement dans le cours ou vers la fin du IIIᵉ siècle.' I understand the inscription to shew that the Confederation was still active at the date of the inscription, and that sometimes as a mark of respect the towns paid the fees or subscriptions expected from members of the magistracy on their appointment.

D. M. Commodi. . aedilis auguris. . III viri præfectura jure dicundo in colonia Rusicadensi et *in colonia* Chullitana *et* bis in colonia Milevitana functi

as a matter of policy. Yet as a matter of sentiment it remained still and long after[1].

The 'Four Cirtensian Colonies' were Cirta, Rusicade, Chullu and Mileou, and with them was sometimes associated 'the Fifth Colony of Cuicul[2].'

Colonia Sarnensis Milevitana.
Bps. bef. 375, ? 399, 408—25, 484, 553.

The MILEOU of to-day was Mileou in its bishop's signature in A.D. 553. It can almost be seen from Constantine, 18 miles away, with the snowy Djirdjura for a background. When Cæsar recompensed his strange ally, the Catilinarian P. Sittius Nucerinus, by the grant of West Numidia to his Italian and Spanish volunteers, the exile touchingly disfigured the unchangeable name of the city into a reminiscence of his own native stream, the Sarnus. It perhaps never was a very large place, yet its Church life was memorable. Two Councils were held here in 402 to try reconciliation with the Donatists, and in 416 against the Pelagians. Here S. Optatus ruled, and wrote his vigorous and accurate[3] history. Of one Bishop Honorius there was a dark story. Another was Severus, in whom was the 'large and holy deep of heart.' To another Optatus Augustine wrote on the 'Origin of Souls,' and one was banished with the other bishops by Huneric.

Colonia Veneria Rusicade. Philippeville.
Bps. 305, 411.

RUSICADE[4] was in reality the port of Cirta, thirty-seven miles distant due north. The same reason for which France has re-created it into the fine harbour of Philippeville led Rome to place it under the Legate of Numidia, namely, to insure the most direct communication with themselves. The area and variety of its ruins seemed to make it not so much a centre as a group of centres. The contractor and the archæologist have nowhere captured so much prey.

Colonia Minervia Chullu. Kollo.
Bp. 411.

Twenty miles west of Philippeville, on the same wide open bay, is Collo, once Chullu or Chulli, which the Greek form Κόλλοψ connects with the CHULLABI of the Council—the second city of Numidia. Its purple manufacturers competed with those of Tyre. On till the 17th century A.D. it was the great mart for Kabyle wax and hides and wheat. But merchantmen and warships had to make the best of its harbour.

CUICUL was sometimes counted a Fifth Colony with those of

---

quinquennalis, item *soluta* contributione a Cirtensib*us* iterum in colo*nia* Mile*vitana* patria sua primi III viri flam*inis* p*er*p*etui* quod ei ad legitimam qua*n*t*it*atem pro adfectionum in ord*i*ne adq*ue* in populo meritis suff*r*agio oblatum est.... *C. I. L.* VIII. i. n. 8210.

[1] Under Constantine and Constans the *Ordo* of the Colonia of Milev, one of the Four, erect a statue in the Forum at Cirta '...*ubi honorificentius erigendam credidit*...' *C. I. L.* VIII. i. n. 7013.

[2] On the two basilicas of Cirta and the Christian inscriptions see Schwarze, pp. 80, 81.

[3] [See the important discovery of materials described by the Abbé Duchesne in *Acad. d. Inscrr.* Nov. 1890.]

[4] The name is thought to be from the Phœnician pharos *Rus ikda*, 'Headland of fire,' its cases appear as Rusicadis, -i, -em; it survives in Cape Skikda.

THE CITIES.

Cirta[1], seventy-five Roman miles from it (*It. Ant.*), on the road to Sitifis, and close on the frontier of Mauretania. Remains of its Christian basilica lie among temples, theatre, and triumphal arch (to Severus, Julia Domna and Caracalla). Its bishop at the Council was one of the juniors who voted acquiescently—Pudentianus.

MACOMADES was 43 miles from Cirta, about 25 beyond Sigus, the Confessors' mine, along the road to Theveste. Traces of fine irrigation, 100 acres of ruins, baths, an aisled basilica 100 feet long: so Tissot. Cassius its bishop rather copious and rhetorical in a short space[2].

GAZAUFALA (depraved from Gadiaufala, like Zaritus from Diarrhytus). It was 'two days' journey from Cirta,' as Procopius says, being about 45 miles from it on the road to Carthage. A curious inscription on a native veteran, who had campaigned in Britain, fixes the place and the spelling[3]. The Bishop Salvian based his easy inference on the self-evident proposition 'Haereticos nihil habere constat[4].'

TUCCA. Unfound. It was 46 miles from Ilgilgilis, 60 from Cuicul[5]. It was 'near the sea.' It 'commanded both river and sea[6].' It was 'divided between the provinces of Numidia and Mauretania.' Ptolemy counts it Numidian and Pliny Mauretanian. At the collation of 411 its bishop was Numidian; in relations with Mileou. Before Huneric, in 484, its bishop was Mauretanian. Hence scholars have thought of two cities and two sees, synonymous. But the conditions are fulfilled if we think of it as a double city, like Buda-Pesth or Mayence, seated on both banks of the Ampsaga, where that stream, pouring down from Cirta, becomes, at its confluence with Oued Endja, the boundary of the two provinces. Their bishop now was Honoratus, who appears as a

Respublica Cuicuiitano-rum, Colonia Cuicuiitano-rum.
Djemila.
Bps. 349, 411, 484, 553.
Macomades, Pl.
Μακόμαδα, Pt.
Merekeb-Talha.
Bps. bef.
406, 411, 484.
Gadiaufala, Gasaufula, It. Ant.
Γαζόφυλα, Procop.
Ksar Sbai,
Bp. 484.

Oppidum Tuccae, Pl.
Zaouiat-el-Barka?
Bps. 411, 484, 646.

---

[1] Cuiculi (It. Ant.) is ablative. Cf. inscr. of A.D. 256 RESP CVICVL DEVOT, Cagnat, *Bull. Arch. Com. Trav. hist.* 1892, p. 303. Cuiculum is not really proved by *C. I. L.* VIII. i. 8318, 8319....FL · P · P · IIII · COL · CIRT · ET · CVIC · PONT · OMNIBVS · Q · HONORIBVS · IN · V · COL · FVNCTVS... ('Flamen perpetuus IIII coloniarum Cirtensium et Cuiculi'......), but Cagnat, *Bull. des Ant. de France*, 1889, p. 179, gives 'Miles morans *Coiclo* ann v et menses VIIII.'

[2] *Sentt. Epp.* 22. Tissot, II. p. 477.

[3] *C. I. L.* VIII. n. 4800.

[4] *Sentt. Epp.* 76. Procop. *de B. Vand.* ii. 15.

[5] Tab. Peut., cf. Tissot, II. pp. 411, 412.

[6] Tissot (II. 27) is warrant for the finding of the distances (I cannot quite verify them) of the Peutinger Table, which make it at least out of the question that Tucca should have been where Wilmanns places it, on the mouth of the Ampsaga. He speaks of the city as on the left bank (p. 413), and thinks therefore the boundary shifted. But the difficulty removes itself at the explicit statement: *Ravennat. Anonymi Cosmograph*: 'Civitas Tuca quae juxta mare magnum dividitur inter...provinciam Numidiam et ipsam Mauritaniam Sitifensem' [III. vii.] This *juxta mare magnum* and Pliny's 'impositam mari et flumini' (*H. N.* v. 1, 2) are fulfilled by the strategic position.

Numidian in Epistles 62 and 70. He allows Tradition no standing against Truth[1].

3. *The Circle of Aures.*

Betwixt South Numidia and the Great Desert lies that grand mass of the Southern Atlas which ranks by itself as Aurasius—the range of Aures. Its outer and inner plateaux, most fertile of corn and fruit, commanded by village-clustered crests, its central heights of between seven and eight thousand feet, its almost inaccessible rock castles and camps of refuge[2], its copious springs, its endless valleys and ravines, with their perennial waters and cedar forests, made Aures the nursing-ground, the impenetrable warren and impregnable citadel of the Berber tribes and chieftains.

The Phœnicians had skirted but not pierced it. To the Romans it was the borderland of danger. Yet it was to Aures that in this continent they devoted their chief attention. They circled it with roads and strong towns, and in its circuit founded model cities on lands higher than Helvellyn, 'most splendid[3]' even to Roman conceptions. Aures waited and finally reconquered all.

Civitas Lambæsis, Municipium Lambæsitanum, Colonia Lambæsitana, Respublica Lambæsis. Lambèse. Bps. 240 (Cypr. Ep. 36), 411.

From Augustus to Diocletian the Third Legion Augusta held the tribes in check from LAMBÆSIS[4], a camp and city of its own creation. This three centuries was the longest time that any Roman Legion was fixed in one head-quarters. Its history gives us an idea of what a Roman Legion had to do—and further, what massive elements Christianity had to grapple with. Its camp and extant prætorium are a magnificent, a grammatical specimen of a military centre. Outside the camp, detached from it by a considerable space, the town grew up. Hadrian ran a great road 191 Roman miles direct from Carthage to Theveste, engineered by his legate P. Metilius Secundus the Proprætor, constructed by the labour of the legion[5], and finished A.D. 123.

---

[1] *Sentt. Epp.* 77 and 52. Tissot, II. p. 619. (See note on Tucca Terebinthina in 'Three Routes,' Route 1, p. 602.)

[2] Masqueray, *de M. Aurasio*, pp. 13, 53.

[3] '...in splendi·issimis civita·ib duabus col·· amug et mu· icipi Lambæsitani....' *C. I. L.* VIII. i. 2407. And Theveste was in fact more 'splendid' than either Thamugadi or Lambæsis.

[4] *Inscrr.* rarely Lambesis, Lambesitan. The modern French *Lambessa* in imitation of Tebessa is too barbarous.

[5] A milliarium found at Carthage (*C. I. L.* VIII. ii. 10048) is inscribed:

Imp·Cæs·| Divi·Nervae·Nepos | Divi·Traiani·Parthici·F·| Traianus· Hadrianus | Aug·Pont·Max·Trib·| Pot·VII·Cos·III|viam·a·Karthagine| Thevestem·stravit | Per leg·III·Aug | P·Metilio·Secundo | Leg·Aug·Pr· Pr·| LXXXV |

An inscription at Tebessa gives the distance which modern measurements accurately verify:

Imp Cæs | divi Traiani | Parthici F Divi | Nervæ Nepos | Traianus | Had-

THE CITIES.

They had nearly if not quite finished their permanent stone camp at Lambæsis, having occupied two temporary ones before, when Hadrian visited them in July A.D. 128. He delivered to them a great allocution which stands recorded on a special monument[1]. He speaks of the number of their works as having in no degree impaired the excellence of their manœuvring.

The town long remained a Vicus only. It was made a Municipium probably when in A.D. 207 Numidia was made a Province. Its citizens were enrolled in Trajan's own tribe Papiria.

Severus claimed to be a great reformer, and soldiers held him to be a great corruptor of military life. Legionaries could not contract valid marriage before, but from him they received the *jus conubii* with *cives Romanæ* and leave to reside with their wives[2]. At Lambæsis are many traces of the working of the plan, in monuments to the sons and daughters of soldiers, in the curious elsewhere unknown fact that their children by Roman citizen-women were enrolled in a special tribe *Pollia* of their own, and not in *Collina*, the tribe of the spurious, and particularly in the gradual covering of the great spaces of the camp itself by large buildings,—among them numerous *scholæ* for the *collegia* and military clubs. It is palpable that the legionaries were allowed to live in the town.

Around us now spread miles of fragments with immense remains of public buildings, a 'Prætorium' constructed for military pomps beyond our conceiving, arches, temples of singular but somewhat irregular beauty. The triple shrine of Æsculapius, Serapis and Silvanus is on a fantastic yet most elegant ground plan. We know the very years of most of these buildings[3]. They were all erected, whether in the camp or city (except perhaps the Capitol) by the Legion itself, and the temples themselves were retained under military guardianship. In the camp was no temple. It will not be thought surprising that these and many more particulars of the life of the great head-quarters are known to us when it

---

rianus Aug | Pontif Max Trib | Pot VII Cos III viam | a Carthagine The|vestem Mil P CXCI | DCCXXX stravit | P. Metilio | Secundo leg | Aug Pro Pr | Cos Desig | Per | leg III Aug | | (*C. I. L.* VIII. ii. 10114.)

leg III *Aug* has been erased and restored, a fact which will be explained presently.

[1] *C. I. L.* VIII. i. n. 2532.

[2] Herodianus, iii. 8. Papinian and Ulpian, in and just after Severus' time, speak of their *matrimonium* as if it were in all respects *justum*. *Digesta* 23, 2, 35; 23, 2, 45; 3; 49, 17, 16. But to assert that their children by foreign wives were citizens seems difficult.

See Wilmanns' essay, giving Mommsen's views, *C. I. L.* VIII. i. p. 283. The monumental work is Cagnat, *Armée de l'Afrique*, Paris, 1892.

[3] *E.g.*—The great temple of Neptune 148, dedicated 158, enlarged 174. Isis and Serapis 158, Æsculapius and Salus 162, finished 211 with the addition of Jupiter and Silvanus. Silvanus restored 198—203.

is realized that this one place yields to the *Corpus* over 1600 inscriptions. Probably as many more are built into the French prison walls.

The Christians after awhile had at least four basilicas of dates unknown at present. We have already heard of the early Council here of ninety bishops, and of the 'old heretic' Privatus[1]. Wilmanns and Tissot mention that no Christian inscription has been found. I copied there two large sculptures of the labarum with A and ω within a wreath, and on one of them the Dove[2]. It is interesting that the time of Cyprian was a marked period in the history of Lambæsis. He is the only author who tells us that it ever was a Colony[3]. From A.D. 238 to 253 the Third Legion was disbanded, and this is thought to be the time when the town rose to that dignity, when the Capitol was founded and the noble temple of Jupiter Optimus Maximus built on it.

The Legion was restored and replaced by Gallienus and Valerian[4] in A.D 253, but only for about 40 years, up till the time of Diocletian[5]. Its bishop appears in our Council, but apparently not in that of 411[6], and as no bishop appears in 484 or ever again, it is likely that after its abandonment as the seat of the Legate Proprætor under Constantine it fell into decline. The ceasing of inscriptions tells the same tale.

It has seemed worth while to dwell upon Lambæsis on account of the vividness with which its life and its necessary problems for Christianity suggest themselves. But what would be the interest of Thamugadi, what of Theveste, if their story were as clear?

Colonia Theveste. *Tebessa.* Bps. 349, 411, 484.

THEVESTE[7], at the north-east corner of the Aures system, is no doubt the place which the Greeks regarded as the capital of Libya, and as a 'Hundred-gated' city not quite distinguishable from Thebes. Yet in the best Roman age and until Vespasian none but geographers name it. Then, while Lambæsis was the military centre, Theveste was the centre of communication. Eight great roads linked it to Cirta, Sitifis, Lambæsis,

---

[1] Cypr. *Ep.* 36. 4; *Ep.* 59. 10, 11.

[2] Another, Dr Schwarze, p. 75.

[3] *Ep.* 59. 10 Lambesitana Colonia, agreeing thus with the inscriptions *C. I. L.* VIII. i. 2661, 2720, 2721, ii. 10228, 10229, 10256, 10259.

[4] This inscription on a statue base, which I copied in the Prætorium, relates to their return. It is *C. I. L.* VIII. i. 2634.

DEO | MARTI MĹITIÆ | POTEŃI STATVᴡ | IN HONOREM LEG | III AVG VALERIᴀ/Æ | GALLIENÆ VALERIᴀ/Æ | SATTONIVS IV|CVNDVS ⚜ PP QVI|PRIMVS LEG RENo|VATA ⚜ APVT AQVI|LAM VITEM POSV|IT VOTVM DEDIT | DEDICANTE|VETVRIO VETV|RIANO ⚜ VC ⚜ LEG | AVGGG PR PR |

[5] The arguments of Wilmanns for this will be generally thought stronger than those of Mommsen against him. *C. I. L.* VIII. i. tit. *Lambæsis*, and Momms. *C. I. L.* vol. VIII. i., pp. xxii, xxiii.

[6] In spite of Masqueray I must agree with Wilmanns that *Lambiensis* is not a likely appellative from Lambæsis.

[7] *Sentt. Epp.* 31, Thebeste MSS. Lauresh, Veron. H.

THE CITIES.

Tacape, Sufetula and Thysdrus; Hadrian (we have seen) developed the most important, that to Carthage.

A favourable station for Christian pioneering, it has been said, and the remark seems to be borne out by the number and apparently early date of Christian inscriptions[1] from that region.

Procurators managed imperial estates in the neighbourhood. Settlers on military tenure of knight-service held wide lands, and were protected with elaborate care. They planted out groups of towers throughout the domains, with an eye to the raids from Aures.

The scale and splendour of the place are marvellous: its water-works, its baths, its drainage. The careful arrangement of its forum and market with its marble pavement, marble screens, and cloisters, and with stabling for troops of horses. African architecture like African Latin has marked peculiarities, and the fine temple of Jupiter is an excellent instance of them, as is also the quadruple Janus, finer than that of Rome, and again the simple grand basilica with its stately steps and mosaic floor, exactly contemporary with Cyprian, and stopped, three or four centuries later, in actual process of conversion into an immense church and establishment. Rude Christian capitals lie ready to be hoisted, and an immense array of monks' cells in solid masonry has been already added, together with a bishop's house and chapel and a baptistry, the whole defended vainly by the Byzantine ramparts[2]. The Vandals were driven back, but the spirit of the dry places returned to his garnished house, and the Arabs sit marketing by thousands in the dust among their camels, and the débris of the city are spread out for miles.

The third of these glorious cities, which we must notice, that was so grandly placed to do the work which Rome conceived to be hers in the wild world, was THAMUGADI, Timgâd—'the African Pompeii.' *(Colonia Ulpia Thamugadis, Col. Marcia Trajana Thamugad. Timgâd.)*

Verecunda was a fourth not so much known to us nor represented at Carthage (a see? Morcelli).

Thamugadi was founded in A.D. 100 with a true soldier's eye by L. Munatius Gallus, Trajan's legate and proprætor, to control the adits to the very heart of Aures by the veterans of the Thirtieth Legion, Ulpia *(Bps. 320, Optatus † 398, 411, 484.)*

---

[1] See Schwarze, pp. 63 ff.

[2] I gratefully acknowledge the courtesy of the Abbé Délapart, the accomplished antiquarian and self-devoted parish priest of Tebessa, of the Commandant des Armes, and the Commandant des Indigènes, Captains Martineau and Empiroget. One of M. Délapart's most singular discoveries is the mosaic plaque of a cross placed within an apse between A and G, which he found some feet beneath the altar of the basilica, where he expected to find some token of consecration. For fine illustrations of Lambæsis, Theveste and Thamugadis see Mr Graham's Paper on the 'Remains of the Roman Occupation of N. Africa,' *Transactions of R. Inst. of Brit. Architects*, vol. I. N.S. part 3; Sir L. Playfair's *Travels;* Duthoit, Soc. Arch. de Constantine, 1884, and especially Boeswillwald and Cagnat's *Timgad*.

Victrix, as colonists. They were enrolled in the Emperor's own tribe, Papiria, and held a richer, wider territory than any African colony. It is unmentioned except by geographers, until with Bagai it is very much mentioned for its Donatist terrors, and for 'the ten years long groaning of all Africa' under its Bishop Optatus, the 'Dux Circumcellionum.' But who shall say what the long groaning of real Africa had been under Roman Africa, or what the misery of the dispossessed and destitute natives who listened to him? The scene of his harangues in the curia and the forum needs little imagination to complete it. After the disappearance of the baffled Vandals it was the Maurusii who poured in, depopulated Timgad, and made it uninhabitable, so that no civilized being might find in it a pretext for even approaching Aures[1]. It was reoccupied by Solomon about A.D. 538; not restored, but quarried for his fortifications.

The long white streak beneath the mountain brow, which you watch for hours as you approach it, develops at last into an almost perfect city which looks as if roofs and capitals had been taken away a year ago, leaving walls and floors and bases perfect. The whole aspect is that of a city built on a perfectly considered and beautiful plan. Its fine triumphal arch takes you into the long street with its smooth wheel-grooved pavements and shady colonnades towards the north breeze. These lead on to the macellum, to the forum with its cloisters and statuary, and then to the basilica and public offices. A short stroll brings you to the beautiful theatre in the hillside. Ever in your ears is the rush of waters which once poured through these dry troughs, channels and fountains, and charged the vast baths.

It is notable that the fine temple of Jupiter Capitolinus was built under a severe Christian Emperor Valentinian I., and that when the Arabs came a new basilica was in building[2].

Respublica Cediensium. Oum Kif. Bp. a Donat. 411.

From Theveste the road which encircles the ridges and defiles of Aures and commands the plateaux and skirts the salt-basins that lie northwards, goes west through CEDIAS, whose ruins as yet serve only to identify it. It was like Mascula a seat of Donatism. Two Christians at some time built a church near, and dedicated it as 'men of Cedias, sinners,' perhaps on their restoration to the Church[3]. The road passes

---

[1] Procop. *de Bell. Vand.* ii. 13, 'civibus sublatis,' perhaps; but 'æquaverant solo,' no; for that is not its state even now.

[2] Thimgad is essentially a *civil* city as Lambæsis is a military one, but laid out with its main streets crossing at right angles, *Cardo* N. and S. towards Constantine, *Decumanus* E. and W. towards Lambæsis. Cagnat *ap. Acad. d. Inscr.* May 1891.

[3] This noteworthy record is in *C. I. L.* VIII. i. n. 2309 ' IN · ATRI · DOMINI | DÈF QUI ÈST SÈRMONI | DONATUS ÈT NAVIS | IUS FÈCÈRUNT CÈDI | ÈNSÈS PÈCKATORÈS,' corrected and (?) explained by De Rossi as In nomine Patris domini *dei qui est sermoni.*

THE CITIES. 591

on through the wide strewn ruins of MASCULA, on the north-east spur of Aures, a critical strategic post, then and now commanding one of the main passes of Aures, and covering the direct route from the Tell to Sahara; to begin with, a great corn and cattle station[1].

Colonia Mascula. *Khenchela.* Bps. 305, 411, 484, 525.

It communicated with BAGAI near the salt lake. Bagai and Timgad the Donatists claimed as all their own. Augustine sarcastically makes one of them argue 'And ours too is a "Great Congregation." What do you think of Thamugade and Bagai[2]?' Here was held their Council of 310 Bishops in A.D. 394[3]. Donatus the Circumcellion leader was a native of Bagai, and here were perpetrated many of the horrors of the faction[4].

Bagai. *Ksar Baghaï.* Bps. Donatus † 348, 394, 402, ? 403, 404, a Donat. 411, 484.

These places were all revived into Byzantine fortresses by Solomon, but were never likely to hold a country, whose cities had failed, by mere force of arms. Yet they seem all to have retained their Christianity long after the Arabs had exterminated it elsewhere.

The bishops of Cedias, Mascula and Bagai were now Secundinus, Clarus and Felix[5].

Facing from Lambæsis towards Sitifis, capital of Mauretania, 21 mountainous miles would bring you to LAMASBA, the last station but one on the Numidian side of the border, a great depot for the products of the fertile plains beyond. A great inscription on the distribution of water, probably for the use of the numberless oil-mills, is an instance of the perfection with which the Roman farmers were attended to[6]. Pusillus, a rare name, was their bishop.

Resp. Lamasbensis Antoniniana. Municipium Lamasba. Lamasua, *Notit.* Lamasbua, *Peut.* *Merouana.* Bps. 411, 484.

Westward and then southward, about 62 kilometres more, the road from Lambæsis sweeps round down the stern deep defile which the Romans called 'Hercules' Shoe' and the Arabs, in amazement at the

---

Donatus et Navigius fecerunt Cedienses peccatores. Mommsen's suggestion *in patre domini* (i.e. *in deo*) *defunctus qui est* seems unnatural. Schwarze, p. 69, quotes for *Dominus Deus* (of Christ) *C. I. L.* VIII. i. n. 2079: *In nomine Domini dei nostri atque salbatoris* IHU XPI; *C. I. L.* VIII. ii. n. 8429 *In nomine ℟ Domini Dei*; and on *Sermo* for Λóγος Tert. *adv. Prax.* v.

I would therefore emend simply *In Patre Domini Dei qui est sermo Dei,* 'In the Father of the Lord God Who is the Word of God.'

[1] Masqueray has a treatise *Ruines anciennes de Kherchela.* Paris, 1879. Cf. Schwarze, p. 73.

[2] Aug. *Enarr. i. on Psalm* xxi. 26.

[3] Aug. *Contr. Crescon. Donat.* iv. 10.

[4] Neander, vol. III. p. 271 (Bohn), on the question whether Donatus a Casis Nigris and Donatus Magnus were one and the same, says 'Optatus seems to have knowledge of only one Donatus.' Optatus expressly distinguishes them, lib. iii. init. and says, 'Donatus Bagaiensis collected the "insana multitudo."'

[5] *Sentt. Epp.* 11, 79 12. It is interesting that from the neighbourhoods of Cedias, Bagai, Mascula, Theveste come the inscriptions with 'Deo laudes,' the Donatist greeting adopted instead of the Catholic 'Deo gratias.' See Schwarze, pp. 69 f.

[6] *Sentt. Epp.* 75. *C. I. L.* VIII. i. n. 4440.

592   APPENDIX K.

Roman bridge 'El Kantara'; then it suddenly bursts into that vision of a hundred thousand palm trees which startle every traveller into the sense that he has touched a new zone, and a world in which the sons of Japhet will never be at home.

<small>Tubunæ munic. Θούβουν, Pt. Tubonæ and Tobonæ, *Peut.* Aug. Bps. 411, 484.</small> From El Kantara, a Roman road, quarried through wonderful defiles and set all along with towers and ruins, turns up to THUBUNÆ, the westernmost frontier town and castle of Numidia, though Wilmanns almost assigns it to Mauretania[1]. Its Nemesian was a very senior bishop and the lengthiest speaker—twice as long as Cyprian.

Then from Biskra, about 112 kilom. from Lambæsis[2], the inexorable road sets itself back eastward to enchain the precipice walls of Mount Aures on the south, with nothing but the sandy rock of Sahara in front and far beyond the horizons of many days.

Out into the desert of Mokrân five-and-thirty kilometres south-west of Biskra, the Roman planted his last outpost, the immense and manifoldly fortified camp of GEMELLÆ. We shall come to it by another route[3].

Great stations, Ad Badias and others, watched the valleys which poured out their torrents of waters and of Berbers through the mountain posterns.

By such a tremendous chain of fortresses, cities and colonies, by 'wardens of the marches' and tenants inheriting and holding lands by military service, by actual 'moss-troopers' in the marshlands, the whole vast frontier was continuously guarded.

From Leptis Magna the *limites* ran westward in this order, Thamellensis, Badiensis (then came Aurasius itself, which need not and could not be a *limes*[4]), Gemellensis, Tubunensis. A similar line of *limites* then ran northward to the sea, and behind was Mauretania Cæsariensis itself (apparently) all held by this tenure. Alexander Severus had, just before Cyprian's time, taken important measures for the security of the '*limitanei duces et milites* and their *heredes*' in their '*sola*,' and for keeping up their stock of cattle and slaves '*ne desererentur rura vicina barbariæ.*'

On the colonies and principal towns every delight which could make a Rome in miniature was lavished. Officers of family, augurs, legates,

---

[1] A Thubunas. *Sentt. Epp.* 5, Tissot, II. pp. 512 and 518.

[2] *C. I. L.* VIII. i. p. 275.

[3] See infr. 'Three Routes'—Rte. (1).

[4] Masqueray seems much impressed and puzzled by the fact. But Aures was absolutely ringed round with forts and camps and legions, and certainly very little of it could be farmed. See his interesting sketch (*de Aurasio M.*, pp. 70 ff.) of the *limites* and their conditions, as also the laws against extortion by these armed farmers. The marshlands are particularly noticed ('agros limitaneos universos, cum paludibus,') in *Cod. lib.* XI. tit. LIX. (LX.).

propraetors devoted themselves to the enrichment of the new homes. Thus at Theveste, before A.D. 212, C. Cornelius Egrilianus, an old præfect of the 14th Legion, who belonged to a family which has left many monuments at Lambæsis, bequeaths £5,000, half to found the extant Triumphal Arch, half for gymnastic games in the Thermæ on fixed days through the year, as well as sets of large silver and gold vessels for the Capitol.

But not amusement only was provided, whether fierce or luxurious. The courts indicate elaborate administrations complete upon the spot. There were curiæ and rostra and the appointments of an apparent republic. The marriage privileges, the tribal arrangements all were for the purpose of founding not only garrison cities for the marches but communities perfect in themselves yet identified in every interest with the Empire. The country probably could not at this time have been held at all, or cultivated to profit if it had not been distributed in vast *latifundia* to capitalists (often members of the imperial families and even ladies) and by them partly furnished for themselves with fortified country houses (such as we see in the African mosaics) surrounded by large villes, and partly sublet to Roman farmers and contractors[1].

It is evident that this civilization cannot have been carried on without the co-operation of vast numbers of native tenants as labourers, as well as poor colonists. To them we must ascribe the abundant traces of small farmsteads in some of the larger and safer valleys. Spots which still are called 'Roman Gardens' of olives and fruit trees seem as likely to be Berber copies as to be original Roman plantations, which would probably have borne Roman names.

When Rome grew Christian the mountaineers too were so soaked with Christian usages that to this day they keep Christmas[2]. They call the months by Latin names and measure the year, like Christians, by the sun and not by moons.

Yet these cities were not at last captured by Vandals, but deliberately desolated by their neighbours the first hour that the invasion called the garrison away.

Yes. Civilization and Christianity were unable to overcome animosity of race and wildness of temper. That is how we put it. Rather—Civilization and Christianity sate helpless, not knowing or thinking how to deal with the prodigious, multiplying masses of dispossessed, impoverished, harried natives, whom mile by mile soldiers and settlers drove out before them.

The Circumcellions had weakened everything long before the Vandals came. They liberated slaves, destroyed account books, broke up villas, drove the gentry round and round in the mills. Their weapons were sticks. They were accompanied by troops of women. Their numbers were everywhere immense—'such herds,' 'such crowds,' 'so many thousands.'

[1] See ap. Masqueray, *De Auras. Monte*, pp. 50, 57.   [2] Moolid, 'The Nativity.'

594 APPENDIX K.

What they hated was proprietorship. The controversy was nothing to such people. They attached themselves to the Donatists because these were the disaffected party in Church and State. They had no hold on life except life. When life was too miserable they quitted it by the thousand[1]. It seems plain who and what they were.

Material wonders are being worked in other parts of the world before our own eyes.

4. *The Theveste Road.*

There were 20 stations on 197 Roman miles of direct road between Carthage and Theveste; on the average $9\frac{1}{3}$ Roman miles apart[2]. From eleven of these station-towns bishops attended the Collation of Carthage in the year A.D. 411. Between Thurris and Thignica the road was double, and on the second line the town of Valli sent a bishop to the same conference. Besides there is no reason to doubt that three other stationtowns which had bishops before (two of them also afterwards) had bishops in A.D. 411—Ad Pertusa, Thurris, Thacia.

<small>Pertusa, It. Ant. Ad Pertusa. *El Haraïria.* Bp. 393.</small>

This makes 15 sees, or as nearly as possible a see every 13 miles.

<small>Thurris, It. Ant. *El Djemel.* Bps. 396, a Donat. 411.</small>

Whether these all were sees in Cyprian's time there is no knowing. Bishops from five of them, distributed all along the line, attended the Council, viz. from Sicilibba (33 miles), Membresa (54), Laribus (117), Ad Medĕra (172), Theveste (197).

<small>Thacia, Tab. Peut. Θασία, Pt. *Bordj Messaoudi.* Bps. 348, a Donat. 393, 525, 646.</small>

With the exception of one or two older Liby-Punic towns, the others were probably little more than travelling stations founded with the road, and gathering settlements about them. Not much is known of them but their distances in the Itineraries and their Christianity.

SICILIBBA and MEMBRESA, in the Lower Medjerda valley, have been described. A hundred and seventeen miles from Carthage we come upon *Lorbeus*, which represents LARIBUS, which again, from being an incessantly used case, had become (first on barbarian lips) as in other instances a substitute for the true *Lares*[3]. Widespread ruins in an uninhabited land once rich with forest; built out of them, Justinian's walls; a Christian basilica which saw the massacre of 30,000 Christians and became a mosque. Its bishop, Hortensianus[4], had attended the Councils of 252 and 255 A.D.

<small>Colonia Ælia Augusta. Lares. Laribus. *Lorbeus.* Bps. 411, 483, 525.</small>

---

[1] Augustine supplies such particulars *passim*.

[2] The stations are: *Ad Pertusa* (14), Ad Mercurium (18), *Inuca* (20), SICILIBBA (33), *Thurris* (38), *Chisiduo* (44), [2nd route *Valli* (44),] *MEMBRESA* (54), Tichilla (64), *Thignica* (78), Agbia (84), *Musti* (91), *Thacia* (98), *Drusiliana* (105), LARIBUS (117), *Obba* (124), *Altuburos* (140), Mutia (156), *AD MEDERA* (172), Ad Mercurium (186), *THEVESTE* (197). (Tissot, II. 443.) The italicized were sees early in the fifth century, or earlier. The capitals mark the sees from which bishops came to Cyprian. The figures shew the distances from Carthage.

[3] Εἰς Λάριβον, Λαρίβους, Procop. *de Bell. Vand.* ii. 23, 28.

[4] *Sentt. Epp.* 21. Coripp. Joh. vi.

Seven miles further Ebba, Orba in the Peutinger Table, miswritten it seems for OBBA, where the bishop was Paulus[1]. He thought the error of 'aliquis' a fall from the faith.

Then Mutia, and then AMMEDERA[2], rather more than 19 miles from Theveste. Great ruins on both sides of the river, quays, great theatre, five Christian churches, two triumphal arches, one very fine, A.D. 195. Hyginus relates how it was gated and streeted as a camp, and we can recognize it.

Eugenius' speech consists of the four least offensive words of his fanatical neighbour whom he followed immediately.

Obba.
Ebba.
Bps. 411,
484, 553.

Colonia Flavia Augusta emerita Ammaedara. *Haïdra.* Bp. 411.

5. *Three Routes.*

Three main routes linked the Theveste road to that grand coast line which, south from Cape Bon, sweeps out the great gulf of Hammamet and that of Gabes (Tacape), which forms the crescent of the lesser Syrtis[3], and then trends south-east to the great Syrtis. (1) The coast road from Leptis Magna throws off at Tacape, the last of the Emporia, a great road passing the end of the salt lakes, and working northward through the highlands, until it meets at Asturas (2) a second road from Thenae, where the Emporia began; then from Assuras a loop-line ran to two stations on the Theveste road, Althiburos and Thacia. (3) At Coreva, higher up on this same road, a third route falls in from Hadrumetum.

There was a MUSULA on the great Syrtis, 150 miles beyond Leptis Magna, between Dissio and ad Ficum, which Tissot makes no attempt to identify with the see of Januarius Muzulensis. But why not? Nothing but its distance seems against it[4].

143 (ap. Tiss.), Urbs Laribus surgit mediis tutissima silvis Et muris munita novis quam condidit ipse Justinianus apex.

[1] *Sentt. Epp.* 47.

[2] Sic *Sentt. Epp.* 32.—'Αμμαίδαρα, *Pt.*—Ammaedara, Ammædera, *Corp. Inscrr.* (It has yielded 282 inscriptions, 34 of them Christian. See Schwarze, p. 50, on two Christians of the family *Astius* bearing the title *flamen perpetuus*, sc. of Roma and Augustus, in 6th century.)—Ad Medera, *Peut.*—Ad Medera, Admedera Ad Medra, *It. Ant.* —Admedera, *Hygin.*—Αύμετέρα, *Proc.* —Metridera, *Oros.*

[3] Procopius dwells on the crescent, *de Ædif.* vi. 3: ἐς κόλπον μηνοειδῆ. 4: ἡ θάλασσα ἐν στενῷ θλιβομένη ἀπεργάζεται μηνοειδῆ κόλπον...

[4] *Sentt. Epp.* 34, Tissot, II. pp. 228, 231.

There is no ground for Morcelli's (adopted by De Mas Latrie) identification of 'Januarius Muzulensis' with Muzuca. There are two Muzucas near Lama (Tissot, II. 603 f. Pl. xix.). Morcelli says readings vary, as Mucuza, Muzuca, Muzucha, Muzulensis, Mosulensis, Mutucensis. Hartel gives no variant in Cyp. save Mozulensis *Cod. Seg.*, though Rigault alleges 'a Muzucha *Cod. Corb.*' and Holsten 'Muzuca.' On the other hand the only reading in list

596   APPENDIX K.

Other roads too connected the towns[1], but these three lines striking the coast road, and traversing the inland, would bring up representatives of at least three-and-twenty sees to Carthage.

Hadrumetum was about 108 Roman miles from Carthage[2], and Great Leptis about 650[3] by the coast from Hadrumetum. The last hundred miles of this were the sand-deluged coast of the Tripolis, a name which then meant the three early Phœnician Marts of Sabratoun, Oïat, and Lebki[4], but which, as its two neighbours decayed, settled upon Oïat or Oea and so remains. The conditions of life in the Tripolis differed much from all that we have been considering.

Colonia Ulpia Trajana Leptis. Leptis Magna, Pl. *Lebda*. Bps. a Donat. 393, a Donat. 411, 484.

To Livy[5] LEPTIS seemed 'the only city' there worth mention. Its constitution must have been strong, since in our first century it was still ruled by the old Canaanite 'Judges' or Sufetes[6]. As Gibeon from Joshua, so Leptis from Bestia sought and obtained instant conditions of peace when the Romans appeared on the soil in the outset of the Jugurthan war.

Its enormous imports and exports may be estimated from its antient tribute of an Euboic talent daily to Carthage[7], and from the permanent impost with which C. Julius Cæsar visited its reception of the shattered Pompeians.

Oëa, Ocea, Colonia, It. Ant. Civitas Ocensis, Oensis, Pl. *Tripoli*. Bps. a Donat. 411, 484.

The splendour of OEA[8] is witnessed still by the grandest Four-fronted Janus extant[9]. It had been built by a chief magistrate, and dedicated by a proconsul about a century before our date, and was probably surpassed by the edifices with which Septimius Severus adorned this his birthplace.

of 484 A.D. (Labbe, V. 266) and list of 411 (Labbe, III. 199) which refers to the province is Muzucensis.

The use of the adjectival form in *Cyprian's time* has a bearing on the geography, see p. 597, n. 6.

[1] From Thenæ the first route might be struck at Sufetula.

[2] *It. Ant.*; but *It. Peut.* 114.

[3] *It. Ant.*; but *It. Peut.* 632.

[4] Hence the Latin appellative Lepcitanus side by side with Leptitanus.

[5] Livy xxxiv. 62.

[6] Their notable monument in the British Museum had strange English adventures under our Fourth George and William. Wilmanns, *C. I. L.* VIII. i. p. 3.

[7] Liv. xxxiv. 62. Hirtii *de B. Afric.* c. 97, tricies centena millia pondo olei annually.

[8] *Sentt. Epp.* 83. Coins, Ouïath, Oeath; Oeath bilath Makar, 'town of Makar,' the Tyrian 'Hercules'; the final *t* is the Punic feminine. Literary forms Osa, Oza, Oca, &c.

[9] It praises itself as 'ex marmore solido' and far surpasses the great Roman specimen in material, construction and decoration. It is Bruce's 'most exquisite and elaborate' sketch, Sir Lambert Playfair's *Travels*, p. 280. Calpurnius was 'curator muneris publici munerarius, duumvir quinquennalis et flamen perfectus.' Ser. Cornelius Scipio Orfitus was proconsul about 163 A.D.

I may remark that if Quintilian, viii. 3, is right (and the reading right) in ascribing the first use of *Munerarius* to Augustus, it is interesting that in African inscriptions, in Tertullian and Cyprian, Munerarius occurs several times and Munerator never.

THE CITIES.

The position of SABRATA appears perhaps in the fact that the cause in which Apuleius had triumphantly pleaded for himself on the charge of magic employed in winning his wealthy lady was tried there though all the parties belonged to Oea. Travellers have seen its amphitheatre, the marble floor of its temple or basilica, and its pier amid the sand. A vast space, apparently never built on, is included in its walls. This may be what the Punic name of Sabratoun[1] is thought to describe—a 'Corn-Market' of nations.

Sabrata Colonia, It. Ant. Σάβραθα, Pt. Sabratha } Pl. Sabathra } Sabra. Bps. a Donat. 393?, 411, 450, 484.

The Tripolis was at our date somewhat more than trilingual, and the fusion of its population was never accomplished, any more than that of its three tongues, Libycized Punic[2], Siceliot Greek and Latin.

The Tripolis was held together at least[3] by an annual council, but so unsubstantially that Oea about A.D. 70 brought in the Garamantes to help her quarrel with Leptis.

It is a mirror for colonists who think it policy to be liberally indifferent to the religion of nations with whom they dwell, or to the barbarism which looks across their pale.

Thenceforth the drift of the Sahara sand, successfully resisted for so many ages, was seconded by the drift of Sahara tribes no less multitudinous[4]. Protectors like Count Romanus made resistance to them hopeless. Leptis was destroyed once more by the Ausuritani in A.D. 370, yet bishops of all three towns appeared in 411. None however after their banishment by Huneric in 484. So that the towns sank probably soon after that to the condition in which Justinian found them, mounded deep in sand[5]. His splendid revivals were soon buried again, and of Great Leptis nothing now emerges but white sea-walls and a ghostly likeness to Carthage.

The self-governing organization which, adverse to war and unifying as it expanded, had arisen in that antient scene of industrious wealth and anxious splendour was the salt of their old world. It could not here become the seed of the new. That element in Tripolis was represented at the Council by Natalis of Oea, who with his own suffrage brought the proxies of Pompey of Sabrata and Dioga of Great Leptis six or seven hundred miles, and—as Augustine says—begged the question[6].

---

[1] Which is also its other Greek name Ἀβρότονον, *Scyl. Peripl.* 110. *Procop. d. Ædif.* vi. 4 Ἀλλὰ καὶ Σαβαραθὰν ἐτείχισατο πόλιν, οὗ δὴ καὶ λόγου ἀξίαν πολλοῦ ἐκκλησίαν ἐδείματο.

[2] Sall. *Jug.* 78. Silius, *Pun.* iii. 256, writes of their pre-Roman age not without discrimination. Sabratha tum Tyrium vulgus, Sarranaque Leptis, Oeaque Trinacrios Afris permixta colonos.

[3] The diffident particle is due to Wilmanns' protest against any idea of confederation. *C. I. L.* VIII. i. p. 2.

[4] 'Globi supervenere barbarici.' Ammianus at the end of lib. xxviii. relates the 'terrific tragedy' with feeling and justice.

[5] Ψάμμου πλήθει τὰ πολλὰ τῷ ἀπημελῆσθαι καταχωσθεῖσα. Procop. *de Ædif.* vi. 4.

[6] *Sentt. Epp.* 83—85. The two absentee bishops are quoted in the forms

APPENDIX K.

Route (1). *Oea to Assuras by the Salt Lakes and Capsa.*

Now if we may make so bold with this said Natalis of Oea as to watch his journey to Carthage by one or other of these routes, he would, for any of them, take first the coast-road as far as Tacape, now Gabes. Thence he might turn inland to Capsa, thence by Thelepte, Sufetula, Sufes, Tucca Terebinthina to Assuras. These all, save Tacape, were sees which sent their bishops to Council with Cyprian.

From between the gulf and the dunes, below the curved escarpments of the Nefousa hills, which do their best to break the endless drifts of sand and catch them in their valley parallels, his road emerged on a level of vast lagoons beyond which, but as if among them, lay the low island of Meninx, which in these very years was beginning to be called GIRBA[1] as it is now. It was the Lotus Eaters' Isle. The Canaanites had brought to it date palms and the arts of the purple dye. But the superior brilliance of the colour made here, and the marvellous fruitage of the isle, are due still to the unbroken industry of the Berbers, who received and survived the Tyrians, resisted the Mahommedans, though they accepted their creed, and speak their original tongue among themselves to this day.

(margin: Girba, Aur. Vict. Djerba. Bps. a Donat. 393, 411, 450, 484, 525.)

Like the Kabyles they accepted and dropped Christianity. They had a bishop already in Cyprian's day, and he went to the Council, a senior bishop, Monnulus by name. Besides his singular bad grammar, it is interesting to find him expressing 'a stain' by using a technical term of dyeing, and that in a form nowhere else existing[2].

Then on Natalis' left opened out the extraordinary chain of the three salt water Chotts, 215 miles of lake-basins[3], full of quicksands, crusted thick with salt which has conveyed and betrayed armies and caravans in single file for thousands of years—a crust spread like 'floors of camphor,'

Sabratensis and *Leptimagnensis*; all the others as *e.g.* Natalis *ab Oea*. The use of this form at this time *in this district only* itself inclines one to believe that *Muzulensis* in *Sentt. Epp.* 34 relates to Musula on the Great Syrtis.

Later, when local designations became territorial titles, the temporal lords used the *a* or the *de*, the bishops kept (to this day) the adjective.

[1] Between A.D. 252 and 260; v. Tissot, I. p. 195 n. There is no ground for inventing another Girba (as Morcelli does) in the Proconsular Province.

[2] *Sentt. Epp.* 10. Monnulus 'Debent... baptizari, ut cancer quod habebant et damnationis iram et erroris offecturam per sanctum et caeleste lavacrum sanc-

tificetur.' Hartel, *ind.* p. 440, explains offectura as = 'tenebrae.' But it means a *dye* specially for the conversion of one colour into another. 'Infectores qui alienum colorem in lanam conjiciunt: offectores qui proprio colori novum officiunt.' Festus, lib. ix.

[3] *Lacus Salinarum* = Sebkha.

It was only in 1853 that the first real exploration of this strange country was made, by M. Tissot.

The lacustrine valley is 348 kilomètres long in the Carte de Reconnaissance, 1881—1887. Sir L. Playfair's map gives 370 and Tissot's apparently 273, vol. I. p. 100. 'The size of the Chotts varies every month.'

THE CITIES.

an 'arctic landscape under a sky of fire,' and set with fathomless lakes that shine among the mirage like molten metal. The first and greatest is the mystical Lake Tritonis. The traveller crossed only 'the Mouth' and passed behind 'the Lips'—these are the Arab names for the gap where Sahara comes upon the sea, and for the low north ranges which fringe it. Sheltered from the August heat of the weird valleys he would use Roman roads and stations until, a hundred miles beyond Gabes, he reached Capsa.

CAPSA[1] is but an oasis set in a great breach of the same perpendicular north cliff which continuing beyond Biskra walls in the salt desert. There three vast valleys meet from north, north-west and east, and pour streams and roads and merchandise out through the Mountain-gate. For from the days of 'the Libyan Hercules'—the first Phœnicians—the city is warder of the mountain plateaux of the Tell, and keeps the gate of Sahara and Soudan[2]. Mediæval travellers could still admire its fortress, defences and masonry; we have only its vast reservoirs and bathing tanks. The Roman historians were amazed at its lonely greatness, 'amid immeasurable solitudes,' as Sallust writes, and at its security 'in mid Afric fenced with sands and serpents' says Florus. No figure of speech; the French columns of to-day keep fires burning through their quarters, not to scare the cerastes, but for instant cautery[3]. *(margin: Capsa municipium. Respublica Capsensium. Justiniana. Capsa Civitas. Kafsa. Bps. 349, 393 a Donat. 411, 484.)*

Marius is still a legendary hero there on account of his preternatural capture of the fortress in mere lust of battle. The Christians of the district (Pliny observes that it is more of a clan (*natio*) than a city[4]) had no bloody contest with Islam, but held their faith longer than others with a quietude which is described as still characteristic of them.

Donatulus, who went to the Council, was[5] a junior bishop consecrated as we have seen in A.D. 252, and it is rather amusing to notice that he begins his brief speech with 'Et ego semper sensi.'

Far away, quite at the western end of the same vast valley of the salt lakes, the Roman military road swept down south through another grand defile, the famous El Kantara, and onward for some 50 miles to reach the fine oasis of Mlili; thence it returned up to Biskra, and ran east under Aures and the long vertical cliffs which rim Sahara. It reached the Chott-el-Djerid, embraced it and went on to Gabes.

This military road was the south boundary of the Roman Province, here called Limes Gemellensis, for the oasis which made its corner was *(margin: Gemellæ. Mlili. Bp. a Donat. 411.)*

---

[1] Morcelli dreams of two Capsas also.

[2] *Sentt. Epp.* 69; Capse, H. I omit the frequent statement that Capsa was the treasure city of Jugurtha, because Wilmanns, *C. I. L.* VIII. i. p. 22, reasonably questions the accuracy of the text of Strabo.

[3] Bruce did not find this necessary. Playfair, p. 286.

[4] ...ex reliquo numero non civitates tantum sed pleræque etiam nationes jure dici possunt ut Natabudes, *Capsitani*... *H. N.* v. 4.

[5] *Sentt. Epp.* 69. Cf. *Ep.* 56.

GEMELLÆ. It was nothing but one magnificent fortified camp and precinct with every known form of defence, with outlying forts and outposts. It was the bastion of Rome against wild Africa. There is still on the spot a monument erected in the year 253, while Carthage was most angry with Cyprian; a monument of the gratitude of a squadron (vexillatio) a thousand strong of the Third Legion, 'Augusta,' disbanded by Gordian and lately reconstituted and recalled from Rhætia[1], which on Oct. 23rd in that year marched back into its old quarters, '*Gemell(as) Regressi*[2].'

The present desert of Mokrân became a garden, for Sahara soil wants nothing but water, and the troops completely intersected the whole tract as far as the first salt lake, Chott Melghigh, with channels from their river and cross channels and ditches. The great camp had its bishop Litteus who went to Carthage, and there drew the metaphor by which he proved his position, from the 'blind leading the blind into the ditch[3].'

No other Catholic bishop of the place is ever mentioned, and Burcaton, the Donatist bishop of the year 411, states that he had never known one[4].

Colonia Thelepte.
? *Medinat el Kdima.*
? *Haouch el Khima.*
Eps. a Donat. 411, 484.

The north road from Capsa 'climbs by immense stairs' to the high plateau on which THELEPTE stands; a city of the usual inland type— theatre, baths, an old citadel and a Byzantine one as at Tebessa, a circuit of $3\frac{1}{2}$ miles, and its *insulæ* traceable. That is, if Medinat el Kdima be Thelepte. If Thelepte is Haouch el Khima[5] it is on a still higher plateau to the eastward, and still a city of similar type. But our two great authorities differ as to the distance[6], and no inscription has yet decided between them. Its bishop, Julian[7], was at the Council.

[1] Cp. sup. Lambæsis, p. 586.

[2] *C. I. L.* VIII. i. no. 2482 and Mommsen's *Preface* xxii.

[3] *Sentt. Epp.* 82.

[4] His delicate dissenting style is 'Traditorem non habeo neque unquam habui.' It is intelligible that a fortress should cease to be the seat of a bishop. (At Durham or Carlisle the bishop was in command.) But it would be hard to explain if this had been, as Morcelli thinks, Gemellæ of Numidia (*Kherbet Frain*), or the Gemellæ one stage north of Capsa.

The inscription and the fragment 'Mlili' prove that the Peutinger Table (see Spruner) erred in placing Gemellæ east of Biskra. A glance at the map (Tissot, pl. xxii.) explains the mistake. I do not understand why the last named accurate author omits Gemellæ altogether from his *Notices Episcopales*, vol. II. pp. 770 ff.

[5] Cagnat, III. p. 5, does not mention either Haouch el Khima or Henchir Mzira, two localities shewn near together in Tissot, pl. xix., but he describes considerable ruins at Henschir-el-Khima-ruta-Zarouia, a name in which both seem to appear. The difficulties of exploration are great here. See Wilmanns' tale of miseries and misgivings, VIII. i. p. 31.

[6] The Peutinger Table gives 44 (Roman) miles as the distance of Thelepte from Capsa, and the Itinerary of Antoninus gives 71; these numbers fairly correspond to the distances of the two towns named above.

[7] *Sentt. Epp.* 57. The Gentile name Julius was common here; C. Julius Saturninus of Thelepte and C. Julius

THE CITIES. 601

From either Thelepte to Sufetula[1] is about 37 miles. The bishop of Sufetula, SUFETULA, Privatianus[2], came from a town unlike any type we have described. It was the very seat of wealth and of security. It was not even walled, and its spoil astounded its captors. It stood where the great road from Theveste to the sea crossed the great road from Carthage to Sahara. Its regular streets are full of beautiful relics of architecture without a single Arab structure ever having been raised among them, and its range of three tall temples[3], side by side, in golden limestone, with their great gate and cloisters, was of unsurpassed beauty. These are of the Aurelius and Verus age, while a great triumphal arch is fifty years later than the Council, dedicated to Maximian and Constantine. There are many temples traceable, and many churches.

Sufetula, It. Ant. (? Colonia). Sbeitla. Bps. 411— 418, 484.

The destruction of the Christian 'Tyrant' Gregorius by Ibn Saad was a crucial event, which closed the Christianity of this region twelve centuries and a half ago.

The country below and all west of Sbeïtla to the sea is one monumental test of what Islam has done for civilization. The crystal river of the city, 'copious as Zaghouan,' and many streams besides lose themselves in the sand. The now trackless, treeless, scorching plains were once alive with 'villages[4] that touched each other,' says the Arab historian, along infinite woods. The soil is all strewn with hewn stones. Dry fountains and broken stations dot the wayside. Roman oil mills stand with no olives in sight, save some glorious giant which the Arab is burning piecemeal. The very soil, no longer bound together by roots, is washed from the hills.

For all this denudation, physical and moral, Islam is to be thanked, yet some earlier thanks are due to Christian sects which, unlearning all that Cyprian and Augustine had taught, sank for lack of charity into a controversial and political religion, and armed opinion with material forces.

Sufetula may, to judge from its sound, be a daughter of SUFES, and Jovinus of Thelepte are the names of two officers at Lambæsis. *C. I. L.* VIII. i. 2568, 2569.

[1] 'Probabiliter Colonia' *C. I. L.* VIII. i. p. 40. But how established? Not so in *Itin. Ant.* nor in any inscription. *C. I. L.* VIII. i. p. 40, Suppl. i. p. 1180. Its people called themselves Sufetulentes as well as Suffetulenses, *C. I. L.* VIII. i. 233.

[2] *Sentt. Epp.* 15.

[3] The two side temples of the Corinthian order, flanking a middle which is Composite, are said to be one large design. Yet this division of styles, taken with the fact that the great entrance is not centric to the façade, seem to me to indicate extension at some period. Two beautiful drawings of Bruce's have been reproduced by Sir Lambert Playfair, p. 155, while Mr Alex. Graham (*Travels in Tunisia*) has two interesting sketches and a restoration of the Triple Temple.

[4] This word of Ibn Khaldoun, their own historian, seems to me to account for Wilmanns' surprise at finding so few inscriptions among so many remains.

602   APPENDIX K.

<small>Sufes.
Colonia
Sufetana.
...Aurelia
Sufetana.
Castellum
Sufetanum.
Shiba.
Bps. 411, 484,
Playf. 191.</small>

Sufes seems a primæval Berber name from its '*Souf*' or river. The straight north road thither runs about nineteen miles along one of the wondrous valleys of the Tell. About A.D. 399 the blood of sixty Christians was shed here for a broken Hercules whom Augustine scornfully offered to replace, and who in a fine inscription is yet honoured there as 'Genius of the Fatherland.' That means an early settlement of Phœnicians; and one of the oldest Roman inscriptions in the country records the new settlings under or before Augustus[1]. The present bishop was Privatus[2].

<small>Tucca Terebinthina,
It. Ant.
Dougga.</small>

The next stage was the next see, TUCCA TEREBINTHINA. The bishop was Saturninus, for Honoratus belongs to Tucca of Numidia[3]. Saturninus is familiar with the teaching of Marcion.

Twelve Roman miles bring us to ASSURAS[4], again a noble regularly

---

[1] *C. I. L.* VIII. i. nos. 262, 258. Wilmanns points out that the address of Augustine's indignant note (*Ep.* 50) should have Sufetanæ for Suffectanæ. The same correction appears to have been made in Victor Vitensis, *Persec. Afric.* I. 7.

[2] There are at Sufetula two graceful little epitaphs which set forth those prevalent views of Life and Death which Privatus was set to dispel. *C. I. L.* VIII. i. no. 241. Marcéllus hic quiéscit | Medicá nobilis árte | Annís qui fere víxit | Trigínta et duóbus. Sed cúm cuncta parásset | Edendo, placíturus | Tertiúm muneris ánte | Validá febre cremátus | Diem defunctus obiit. [Edendo *muneri* Tertium *diem.*]

No. 251, *acrostich.* Génitor Junonem dédicat | Alteque Pompeiaé locat | Levámen hoc dolóribus | Lacrimisque pausam crédidit | At núnc videndo júgiter | Et flétum et gemitus integrat.

[3] *Sentt. Epp.* 52. Alius Saturninus a Tucca, *Hartel*; a tucga, *Cod. Seg.*; attu*ca, *Cod. Regin.*; a Thucca, *edd.* ἀπὸ Συκῆς, *Gk. vers.* Morcelli transposes them.

Sentt. Epp. 77 Honoratus a Thucca, *no v.l.*; ἀπὸ Λούγκης, *Gk. vers.* (? Δούγκης).

Where Tucca Terebinthina should be by the stages in the Itinerary of Antoninus we find *Henschir Dougga.*

Another *Dougga* near Tibursicum has remains 'the most exquisite in Africa' (Playfair) of a temple and mausoleum from which the British Museum has the bilingual Libyan-Phœnician inscription which gives us the key to the Libyan alphabet. It is now being fully explored by Dr Carton. I do not venture to identify, as Wilmanns does, either Tucca (Thucca) with this *Dougga* because its spelling Thugga, Thugge, Tugga, does not vary in a dozen inscriptions which name it. In 411 a Catholic bishop (Sabinus) is called Tuccensis and a Donatist bishop (Paschasius) is called Tuggensis. In 649, Victor is called Episcopus Municipii Togiæ.

Neither do the MSS. of Cyprian encourage us to follow Wilmanns in choosing either see as Terebinthina or in writing either of them Thugga to correspond with the Proconsular city. Procopius however calls Thugge Τοῦκκα (*de Ædif.* vi. 5), and Ptolemy Τούκκα. Wilmanns declines to decide what Tucca is meant by Dio Cassius, 48. 21, ἐν τῇ πόλει Τούκκῃ; but one may modestly point out that the person and the scene are concerned with Numidia. On Numidian Tucca see Circle of Cirta, p. 583.

[4] Hatsor, Punic 'precinct.' Ἄσσουρος, Ptol.; Assuræ and indecl. ab Assuras *It. Ant.*; Assures, *Tab. Peut.*; and Ædil-

THE CITIES.   603

laid out city; one of its traceable great gates very perfect, with wall   Colonia Julia
and inscription adoring Caracalla; theatre with remarkably long stage;   Assuras.
fine Corinthian portions of its temple. Like Sufes, its two names shew it   Zanfour.
to be of earliest Punic settling and earliest Roman resettling.   Bps. a Donat. 393, 397, 401, 484.

Route (2). *Oea to Assuras by Thenæ.*

And now at Assuras swept in another road which Natalis of Oea might have travelled, if (not turning inland at Gabes) he kept the coast beyond Thenæ and turned inland to Thysdrus. He would by this route pass by sees as many as between Capsa and Assuras.

The little acropolis of THENÆ rises sternly over the sea, the northern-   Colonia
most of the Emporia. Its port silted up. Its solid city wall two miles in   Ælia Augusta
circuit; nothing within but small stones and potsherds. The great   Mercurialis
necropolis marks its antiquity of settlement, and in the reign of Augustus   Thænitanorum.
it still coined money bearing its old name Tainat in Punic lettering. Yet   Tina. Bps. 411,
the name is thought to be the Berber of 'date palms[1].'   484, 525, 641.

Its bishop was now Eucratius—a man of precision and violence. 'Blasphemy of the Trinity' is his phrase for heretic baptism.

The great foss which in A.D. 146 the Romans made to bound their first province ran over the continent from the river Tusca over against Tabraca, and it just took in Thenæ.

From Thysdrus (it sent no bishop to Carthage), at its star of roads, with amphitheatre almost rivalling in size, and studied as if to excel the grandest known, a straight thirty-four Roman miles in two stages would bring our Natalis to GERMANICIANA. So stands the Itinerary of An-   Germani-
tonine[2]. Many ruins about; no verifying inscription. It is this place   ciana
which is commonly assumed to have sent Bishop Iambus to the Council[3].   It. Ant.

It was of course a different place from ABBIR GERMANICIANA[4], whose

col. Assuribus, *C. I. L.* VIII. i. 631; ab Assuras, *Sentt. Epp.* 68; plebi Assuras consistenti, Cypr. *Ep.* 65. Graham and Ashbee, p. 164, name the plain Bled-es-Sers. (? a trace of Assuras.)

[1] Then(æ), *C. I. L.* VIII. i. n. 2991; Plin., Itin. Ant. Θένα, Θαῖνα, Strab. Θέαιναι, Ptol. ἀπὸ Θένων, *Sentt. Epp. Græce.* Tenitanus, coll. 411, notit. 484. Civitatis Thenisiis, *Syn. Ep.* 649 (ap. Wilmanns). Es beam Thænat, 'of the people of Thenæ,' Punic Inscr. *Acad. d. Inscrr.* Jan. 1890.

[2] Tissot, II. p. 588.

[3] *Sentt. Epp.* 42.

[4] The perplexity of Abbirs and Germanicianas is thus resolved by Wilmanns, *C. I. L.* VIII. i. p. 102. Abbir Majus (coll. 411) and Abbir Cellense (Municipium Julianum Philippianum Abbir Cellense) or Cella (*Not. Epp.*) are one city; Abbir 411, 484, Abbir Minus, and Abbir Germaniciana, or Germanicianorum, are one city. This may be, but I have failed to find any trace of the name Abbir Minus. Wilmanns also does not note Augustine's Germanicianenses.

604   APPENDIX K.

Abbir Germaniciana. Bps. 411, 419.

bishop now was Successus[1], and which had its bishop also in 411 and in 419 A.D., but has not its site made clear by either itinerary or inscription.

The Roman see had under Gregory the Great a patrimony at Germaniciana, of which he made the notary and record-keeper, Hilarus, 'Rector.'

Marazanæ, Marazanis, It. Ant. Bps. 411, 484, 641.

Beyond Germaniciana, twenty-two miles by the Itinerary, lay another great centre of roads, Aquæ Regiæ, and on a cross road between this and Sufes was MARAZANA, not visited yet, but its ruins heard of in Arab rumour. In this highland was a Council held, of unknown date, but four of its canons survive[2], and its bishops appear in three other crises; as in this Council of ours Felix[3] did—with eleven weighty words.

Civitas Mactaritanorum. Colonia Ælia Aurelia Mactaris. Col. Ælia Aurelia Augusta Mactaris s. Mactarina. Makter. Bps. a Donat. 411, 484.

From either Aquæ Regiæ or Sufes we rise fast among the high plateaux. MACTHARIS[4] is 944 feet above the sea[5]. The name has lived orally, though not entered in itineraries nor, until the other day, found in inscription. Yet in the Ælian century Mactharis must have been one of the stateliest of African cities. The ruins cover miles of ground —buildings finished in the noble if not strictly grammatical style of the country. Aqueduct and amphitheatre, arches of triumph, bath and palace, mausolea with stone doors on their pivots, and columbaria[6]. Bruce's beautiful drawings[7] prove how fast they disappear,—like the surrounding Aleppo pines which the Turk taxes for pitch and neglects to preserve.

Marcus the bishop gave not only his suffrage but a severe side stroke at Stephen.

Civitas Uzappa— Uzappensis.

Mactharis lay high on the left of our road from Aquæ Regiæ, which leads to AUSAFA or Uzappa[8]. Great ruins, lately discovered, partly of the

---

[1] *Sentt. Epp.* 16.
Greg. M. *Epp.* I. 75, 77; *Vita* (Joan. Diac.) II. 53. Tissot does not mention that Augustine (*Ep.* iv. 251) speaks of Germanicianenses within his own jurisdiction of Hippo. It might be doubtful whether the Roman estates and the bishop at Carthage belonged to the distant or to the nearer place, but that in the Collation of 411 and before Huneric in 484 (Labbe, V. 265 A, III. 184 A, the latter in the Numidian list) there appear bishops called Germanienses—so that the town may have been Germania, and Germanicianensis only the long drawn out adjective which the Africans affected.

[2] Ferrandus, Breviatio Canon. 44, 76, 127, 220.—Harduin, Conc. I. col. 1251.

[3] *Sentt. Epp.* 46.

[4] *Sentt. Epp.* 38, a Macthari (Hartel), ἀπὸ Μαθάρων (Gk. vers.), the slip Machari in Cod. Regin., and the modern Mukthert (Playfair) suppose an aspirate in the middle letters. But Cod. Seguier, Mactari; the Episcopal Lists, Mactaritanus; *C. I. L.* Supplem. i. nn. 11801, 11809 Mactaris, 11813 RP. Col. Mactaritanæ.

[5] Pelet, *Nouv. Atl. des Col. Franç.* carte 1 (1891).

[6] Nécropoles de Mactaris, Cagnat, *Bull. arch. du Com. des Trav. hist.* 1891, p. 509 sq. 'entièrement entourée de nécropoles.'

[7] Six, reproduced by Sir L. Playfair, pp. 194 ff.; Plan of 'Macteur,' Tissot, II. p. 621. *C. I. L.* VIII. Suppl. i. n. 11804.

[8] Ausafa, *Sentt. Epp.* 73; Αὐσάφη,

THE CITIES. 605

best age; undisturbed sepulchres, beside a stream still called Ousapha; identified by inscriptions and answering to the itinerary. Lucius, bishop, speaks with a quiet piety.   Municipium Uzappa— Uzappense. Ksour Abd-el-Melek.

Twenty-three Roman miles to Seggo, and the road sweeps west twenty more to ZAMA REGIA, for from Aquæ Regiæ to Assuras it circles by the high valleys round some very lofty plateaux and mountain heads.   Bp. a Don. 393. Zama Regia.

There was not an African or Roman in Africa who did not hold the field of Zama to have determined, as Polybius clearly saw[1] it must do, the dominion not of Libya or Europe, but of the world. The warring powers, the fortresses and genius of the commanders, and the prize contended for had 'trifled former knowings.' But Zama has little to shew—very broken ground, an eminence among eminences; its old work very solid[2], and abundant evidence that at our epoch the place was populous, rich and artistic.   Colonia Ælia Hadriana Augusta Zama Regia. Ζάμα μείζων, Pt. Djiâma. Bp. 411.

Marcellus[3] was the bishop. He put the controversy in a nutshell.

Another ten miles completed this cross-country route, if we may call it so, from Thenæ to Assuras. Thence the Theveste road to Carthage.

Route (3). Oea by Thenæ and Hadrumetum to Carthage.

Another perhaps easier way to Carthage was open to the traveller from Oea when he had reached Thenæ. He might go on from Thysdrus to Hadrumetum, either direct or by Leptiminus.

LEPTIS, LEPTIMINUS[4] was built to the waterside, with a fine roadstead but difficult to make[5]. A small city, but splendidly fortified from the days of the first solid fort which sufficed the Phœnicians until it was fixed upon as one of the two residences of the Governor of the Byzacene. It had sided at once like its larger namesake with Rome when she appeared on the ground and reaped its advantage, in being a free and exempt town for ever.   Leptiminus, It. Ant. Λέπτις μικρά, Pt. Lemta. Bps. 411, 484, 641.

Demetrius the bishop[6] merely turns the whole question under discussion into an assertion.

Zonar. (ap. Tissot), II. p. 575. Found only in 1884. Baal Usappân, 'citizen of Usappa.' Punic Inscr. *Acad. des Inscriptions*, Jan. 1890.

[1] Polyb. xv. 9, 3.

[2] This agrees with Sallust, *Jug.* 56, who says it was 'magis opere quam natura munita.'

[3] *Sentt. Epp.* 53.

[4] Coins until Tiberius Λέπτι (Phœnician), then Λέπτις. Leptis (Λέπτη, Procop.) until μικρά added in the second century. Then Leptiminus (indecl.); Lepteminus; *Anonym. Ravennat. Cosmograph.* Leptis minus (Leptis Parva in Tissot's Index, not antient).

[5] Wilmanns misreads what is said of this in Stadiasmus, as if the port had been destroyed in the third century.

The Christian (Phœnician?) burials at Leptiminus are curious; Schwarze, pp. 54, 55, and 59 and Tafel i.

[6] *Sentt. Epp.* 36.

APPENDIX K.

Colonia Concordia Ulpia Trajana Augusta Frugifera Hadrunetina. Colonia Concordia Ulpia Hadrumetum. Justinianopolis. Susa, Sousse. Bps. 348, a Donat. 393, 397, 411, 451, 453, 551.

HADRUMETUM[1] rose picturesquely, a white pyramid, over its elaborately created harbour[2] with mighty breakwater and secluded cothon like Carthage. As at Carthage, a massive yellow-coated temple topped the citadel, and a noble suburb overspread the walls. For it came direct from Tyre,—an older settlement than Carthage,—and now was second city of the province. It never had a history, for it was strong, 'frugiferous,' commercial, opulent, and unpatriotic. Cæsar had stalked round its triple walls, and knew he could not afford to take them. When the war was over, he would make them pay for their regard to Pompey. It was chief of the seven cities which, at the first scent of danger, had gone over to Rome. Henceforth it is styled a Free City. Trajan made it a colony. Its forts, cisterns, circus, grandly porticoed theatre, and huge edifices of undivined intention date through all its ages. The two events which the critic records of it, its long litigation with Thysdrus over a temple, and its rough reception of Vespasian as Proconsul, are less significant to real history than Cyprian's visit to its clergy and instructions about the Roman see. Its bishop, Polycarp, had perhaps not been in attendance at Carthage before this. He missed no Council of which the list remains[3], and at this of A.D. 255 he assisted with six sufficient words[4].

Horrea Cælia, It. Ant. Hergla. Bps. a Donat. 411, 419.

The traveller, leaving Hadrumetum for the north, whether he kept close to the sea or pursued the parallel road a few miles inland, soon saw before him, clear against water and sky, a castle-crowned promontory. This was one of the great grain depots. It gave its name to the small town of quays and magazines which surrounded it, HORREA CÆLIA[5]. This too had a bishop, Tenax, who begins *scriptum est*, inserts *ecclesia una* in Eph. iv. 5, and so proves his point easily. Tenax might be taken up by the way, or might join the travellers from Oea further on. The bishop of SEGERMES[6] might also join them at Bibæ (Djeradorl or Bir-el-Foouâra), and thence the way was short through beautiful Zaghouan

---

[1] 'Αδρύμης, -μητος, -μητός, 'Αδρούμητος, 'Αδραμύτης, -μυτος, -μητος, -μεντος. In Greek never aspirate. In Latin medals and inscriptions always, Hadrumetum, -imetum, -ymetum. Elsewhere Adrimetum, -umetum, -ymetum. In Mysia was also an 'Αδραμύττιον, -υτεῖον; in Lycia an 'Αδραμύττις, and an Arab tribe is called 'Αδραμιταί. (W. and P.)

[2] Is it presumptuous to think that ἀλίμενος (Stadiasm. c. 116) means with no natural harbour, and not (as Wilmanns) that in the third century its port had disappeared? For the breakwater must have been serviceable when Justinian repaired it, and in the twelfth century El-Bekri speaks of its fine harbour.

[3] See p. 569 sup., A.D. 252, *Ep.* 57; 254, *Ep.* 67; 255, *Ep.* 70; 256, *Sentt. Epp.* 3.

[4] *Sentt. Epp.* 3, a senior place. On his low place in Council II. see *Appendix*, p. 566.

[5] *Sentt. Epp.* 67. The text of Cyprian has (without v. l.) 'ab Horreis Cæliæ,' the Greek ἀπὸ 'Ορι ῶν Κελλίων; *It. Ant.*, 'Horrea Cælia vicus.' The variants of the bishops' titles are several, at last 'Oρρεοκίλης; and its now contracted name is Hergla.—From Hadrumetum, 18 miles (*It. Ant.*).

[6] Above, p. 579.

THE CITIES.   607

and Gor and Thuburbo Majus into Carthage[1], striking the Theveste road usually at Coreva.

6. *Mauretania.*

The proëm of the Council says that there were assembled at it 'Bishops very many, out of the Province Africa, Numidia, Mauretania.' Mauretania seems to have been represented, except as claiming to itself a half share in the bishop of Tucca, only by the bishops of BURUC and NOVA. Wilmanns thinks Thubunæ[2] might be claimed for Mauretania, but does not claim it. Whatever the reasons in favour, they are not the same as for Tucca. ?Βούρκα, Ft. ?Bp. a Donat. 411.

BURUC. There are independent reasons for believing *Quietus*[3] to be wrongly read for Quintus, and Quintus to be the correspondent of Cyprian's seventy-first epistle. Quintus was a Mauretanian, 'our colleague established in Mauretania,' and if so BURUC was a Mauretanian see, which from other considerations also is more likely than not[4].

As for NOVA, two bishops, each styled Nobensis, both of Mauretania, from different cities, presented themselves before Huneric in A.D. 484, and were banished. One of them, Mingin, barbarous name, died in exile[5]. Also a bishop from one of them assisted in A.D. 411 at the Collation of Carthage. Bps. 411, 484.

There is no African Nova except in South Egypt, but two cities called OPPIDUM NOVUM are in Mauretania. One of these is too far, only 62 Roman miles from Tangiers, 1613 from Carthage. It. Ant.

The other is near Manliana and only about 210 miles beyond the Numidian frontier. This may be the NOVA of our very explicit bishop Rogatianus. Ptol. and It. Ant.

7. *The Cities Unidentified.*

[This list seems complete as far as was known up to 1893; it is possible that fresh identifications have been conjectured or proved since. E. F. BENSON.]

It only remains to add the names of the sees which yet await discovery and identification. The disinterment of inscriptions alone could

---

[1] Route, Tissot, II. p. 539. Tab. Peut. Bibæ to Onellana (Zaghouan) 16 miles, Onellana to Thuburbo Majus 15.

[2] *C. I. L.* VIII. i. p. 453.

[3] Note on Quintus appears p. 363 before the Third Council.

[4] *Epp.* 71, 72, 1. In *Sentt. Epp.* 27 MSS. have and editions attest 'Buruc' and 'Burug.' It is no way impossible that these should be latinised as Buruca, Burugia, and that Ptolemy's Βούρκα, Mauretanian Burca, and the Burugiatensis Episcopus of A.D. 411 (Labbe, III. 233 B) may belong to it. Leontius Burcensis, A.D. 484 (Labbe, V. 263) is of Numidia. Rigault has Buruch, Baluze Baruch.

[5] *Sentt. Epp.* 60, 'a Nova.' In Labbe, V. 268 B, per stands for peregre; see also 269 B, III. 326 D. Nobensis; so Nobabarbarensis, Nobagermaniensis, Nobasparsensis, &c.

set at rest the questions which arise, so that further criticism would be mostly misspent. There is a list of late authorities in Tissot, II. p. 771, note 1. The MS. readings are from Hartel.

In Numidia.

	Sententia			
[?Οὐατα, Str.] Bp. 484.		15	Vada.	[Dativus]
		23	Vicus Cæsaris=V. Augusti?	
Bps. 411, 484.		33	Bamaccora *H*. Ab amacora *Lauresh*. Abbamaccora T. (*Regin.*) ab amaccura Aug. *de Bapt. c. Donatt.* VI. xl. [Felix]	

(Vamaccorensis. The reading *Coll. Carth.* with Pliny v. 4 Bamacures, a Numidian tribe, shews that B belongs to name. Tissot II. p. 777 gives it among known see-sites, but no more.)

Bps. a Donat. 411, 484.		45	Midili *H. cod. Seg. Regin.* Madili *Lauresh*. Midila August. *de Baptism. contr. Donatt.* VII. ix.	[Iader]

(Numidia by list of 484, and therefore not as Morcelli, 'Pagus Mercurialis Veteranorum Medilitanorum,' which was found in Prov. Proc. Tiss. II. 591.)

(The Bishop's name IADER has a Barbarian look. It occurs elsewhere only in a Christian inscription at Tebessa, *Acad. des Inscrr. Mai* 1890, 'Iulio Iaderi patri dulcissimo in pace a ω.')

Bp. 484.		54	? Ululæ ('ab Ululis'). Morc. would identify with ? Ullæ (Ullitanus, A.D. 484, Labbe V. 265).	[Irenæus]
Bp. 484.		56	Tharassa *H*. Tharasa.	[Zosimas]
Bps. 411, 484.		66	Marcelliana, ? Giru Marcelli.	[Julianus]

In Provincia.

Bps. a Donat. 411, 525, 646.		1	Biltha *H*. Bilta. Vilta August. *de Baptism. contr. Donatt.* VI. viii.	[Cæcilius]
Bps. 397, 411, 484.		2	Misgirpa *H*. miscirpa *Lauresh*. Migirpa August. *de Baptism. contr. Donatt.* VI. ix.	[Primus]
Bps. ? 411, 419.		16	Abbir germaniciana *H*. Abbis *Lauresh*. germanicipiana *Regin*.	[Successus]
Bps. a Donat. 393, 397, 411, 484.		35	Thasualthe *H*. Thasuate *Regin*. Thasualte, Thasbalte August. *de Baptism. contr. Donatt.* VI. xlii. ? Tabalta *It. Ant.* [? omitted by Tissot] (Byzac.).	[Adelphius]
Bp. 646.		43	Rucuma *H*. rucuna *Seg*. rucima *Lauresh*.	[Lucianus]
Bps. a Donat. 393, a Donat. 411; 484 (vacant). Bp. a Donat. 411.		48	Dionysiana (Byzac.).	[Pomponius]
		50	Ausuaga *H*. ausuago *Seg*. Ausuagga *Lauresh*. adausuagga *Regin*. Auzagga *Coll. Carth.*	[Ahymnus]

(Two sees of that name, as Primianus, Donatist bishop at Carthage, explains in the Collation of Carthage A.D. 411, Prima Cognitio 179, Labbe III. p. 218.)

THE CITIES.

Sententia 51 Victoriana *H.* Victorina *Seg.* (Byzac.).   [Saturninus] Bps. 393, 484, 553.
  (Οὐικταρία, Pt. in Mauretania Cæsariensis...'Victoriana dicitur villa,
  ab Hippone Regio minus xxx milibus abest,' August. *de Civ. Dei*
  22, 3, 7.)

  64 Avitirae, Abitinae.   [*al.* Saturninus] Bps. before 304, 411, 440, 525, 649.
  Tissot II. 771 infers neighbourhood of Membresa from Aug. *c.*
  Epist. Parmen. iii. 6. (In 411 Bp. of Avitta also present.) 'In
  civitate Abitinensi,' *ap. Acta SS. Saturnini, Dativi et aliorum
  in Africa* (A.D. 304), Ruinart *Act. Martyr.*

  65 Aggya *H.* so August. *de Baptism. contr. Donatt.* VII. xxix. Bp. 646.
  acbia *Mon. Regin.* acdia *Lauresh.*   [Quintus]
  (? Agensis *Ep. Syn. ad Paul. Constant.* ? A.D. 646.)

  80 a Thambis *H.* Thanbis *Seg.* Thambeis August. *de Baptism.* Bps. a Donat. 393, 411, 484.
  contr. Donatt. VII. xliv. (Tambaiensis 411, Tambeitanus 484)
  (Byzac.).   [Secundianus]

Province Uncertain.

  7 A Castra Galbæ *H.* Castro Aug. *de Bapt. c. Donatt.* VI. xiv.
         [Lucius]
  44 Luperciana.   [Pelagianus]
  55 Cibaliana, ? Djebeliana Tissot II. 781 [near Usilla on Lesser Bp. a Donat. 411.
  Syrtis].   [Donatus]
  63 a Busiacenis *H.* abustiacgenis *Lauresh.* abustlaccens *Reg.*
  abusti lacceni *Monac.*   [*al.* Felix]
  (Morc. conjectures contraction of Bisica Lucana, west of Thuburbo
  Majus; Tissot II. p. 333.   ? Visicensis in *Coll. Carth.*
  411, and in *Ep. Syn. ad Paulum Constant.* ? A.D. 646. Labbe III.
  1880.

  74 a Gurgitibus ? Gurgaitensis (Byzac.) *Morc.*   [*al.* Felix] Bp. 484.
  (The regular form *a gurgitibus* can scarcely be traced to any proba-
  ble corruption from *Gergis* in Byzac. 'Stadiasm. 102; Procop.
  Ædif. vi. 4; C. L. Müller *Numismatique de l'ancienne Afrique*
  II. p. 35. B. V. Head *Historia Numorum* p. 735 read GERG. for
  Gergis on a medal in Brit. Mus.—but ? CERC (Cercine).')

  78 Octavu   [Victor] Bp. 484.
  (Octabensis in Numidia 484; massacre by Circumcellions, Optat.
  iii. 4. Octabensis, Octabiensis in Byzacene 484.)

Readings of Cities in Crawford MS.

The following are the readings of the cities in the Crawford MS. which differ from Hartel's. Hartel's MSS. which they resemble are noted. When no MS. is noted none agrees. *A* or *ab* noted only when necessary.

3 adrimeto   4 thamoga   7 galha   10 girpa   11 accedias T
12 bacai S 15 badis L (*Aug*)   17 ad huc·cabori, dhuccabori LT
27 buruch *editiones aliquot*   31 theveste LV 33 abamaccora, ab amacora L
35 thevalthe   40 gor LT (*Aug*)   42 ger maniciana   45 medeli
47 a bobba T (*Aug*)   48 dionisiana   50 a bausuagga, ausuagga L ad ausuagga T
51 victoria (Οὐικτορία *Ptol.*)   54 Ubulis   62 Membressa L 63 a bustlacgenis, a bustiacgenis L abustlaccens T 65 achia   67 orreis cæliæ   68 asurag
70 rusicca   71 cuiguli   72 hip pomine harit to   76 gazauphala, gazauphalia LT
77 tucca   78 octaviu   81 chulabi.

APPENDIX L.

S. Cyprian's Day in Kalendars

And how it comes to be in England on the 26th instead of the 14th September.

THIS enquiry is not so trivial as it may seem. It is not only archæologically curious as a good instance of the gradual formation of kalendars, but it has a spiritual side, too, of which we will say a word when we have finished[1].

S. Cyprian suffered on the 14th of September. Accordingly in the Martyrology of the African Church and in the earlier Roman kalendars this was the day of his commemoration by himself alone. The '*depositio martirum*' of Rome in the middle of the fourth century records the memorable fact that, (though his relics were of course not there,) his Day was celebrated in the Cemetery of Callistus. The Missal of the Mozarabic rite and the Sanctorale of its Breviary also give complete evidence how he was at first commemorated alone in the Services, although there have been uncritical and unhistorical guesses hazarded about Cornelius' absence from the *Depositio*. (*Note* A.)

The first change made was by uniting in the commemoration with

---

[1] In the collation and verification of some of the kalendars I am greatly indebted to M. Larpent.

Cyprian his friend Cornelius, who had died in June 253. The change was made at Rome, and it is notable that the Pope was placed on Cyprian's Day, not Cyprian transferred to his; but the name of Cornelius is placed first.

This is what we find in the Leonian Sacramentary and in a kalendar of the fourth or fifth century from MSS. once at Grasse and Avignon. (*Note* B.)

The Feast of the Exaltation of the Holy Cross, commemorated in the West the recovery of that precious relic from the Persians by Heraclius in A.D. 628. The date of the introduction of the Festival is unknown, but it was kept on the 14th September, as if traditionally the day on which the cross was re-erected. The addition of that commemoration, usually in the first place, is the next change in the observance of the day. This we see in the Gelasian and Gregorian Sacramentaries as they stand. (*Note* C.)

For a long time after these, which have the appearance of having been neatly re-edited, kalendars shew themselves to be copied carefully from older ones by the perpetuation of the word *Romæ* after the observance had become universal, and of *Karthagine* after Carthage had ceased to be. This continues, though diminishingly, until quite the end of the tenth century. (*Note* D.)

From this period the local origins of the commemorations disappear. They are at home everywhere. But at the very same time singular instances occur of the saints themselves too disappearing from the kalendars. This does not, however, mean that they disappeared from the Offices, although it shews the increased appreciation of the Exaltation. (*Note* E.)

But all the time the Celebration of Holy Cross Day was growing in popularity and observance, and was also of civil importance as the unreformed Quarter Day. The commemoration of Cornelius and Cyprian on the same day became inconvenient, and began to be moved to various days. The first to move it was Cardinal Quignon in the Reformed Breviary of 1535, which was allowed to be used by secular clergy who desired it. (*Licence of Paul PP. III.*, Feb. 5, 1535.) He moved it on to the next day, the 15th. (*Note* F.)

England throughout had the same usage, but with a curious groundwork for future confusions. In the Sarum Breviary Calendar, 1531 (as in the Roman Missal of 1477), Cornelius and Cyprian are omitted, though their commemoration is provided for in the Office itself. Perhaps this was for typographical reasons, but even so it shews that Holy Cross Day had quite overshadowed theirs. And this had occurred in earlier kalendars, English and foreign. Nevertheless the Ambrosian Missal still exhibited the old order—the Saints first. (*Note* G.)

The ordinary entry then has now become XVIII *Kal. Oct. Exaltatio Stæ Crucis SS. Cornelii et Cypriani*, and so remains until the Council of Trent, after which, in 1570, the new Roman books appear and remove the true and antient commemoration of S. Cyprian as Quignon had done, but to one day later still. (*Note* H.)

The Bull A.D. 1568, 'Quod a nobis postulat ratio,' abolishes Quignon's and substitutes the New Breviary. In the first post-tridentine Roman Missal and Breviary Cornelius and Cyprian are transferred to the 16th September. (*Note* I.) In the Gelasian Sacramentary stood the error XVI *Kal. Oct.* (Sept. 16). (*Note* C.) It is impossible to say whether this error had anything to do with the new selection, but there it was.

It is interesting to mark in the early *Drafts* (*Note* K) for our own Common Prayer (to which Dom Gasquet called attention) that Cranmer did not follow Quignon, but restored Cyprian to his own day without the Exaltation, and also in his own handwriting replaced Cornelius, who was at first left out. Sept. 26, with Cyprian and Justina, is dropped in both drafts. But in the *Festivale*, a collection of Third Lessons for Holydays, in this book, there is a long lesson for this day, composed of extracts from Gregory Nazianzen (*Orat.* xxiv.), and from the Acta Proconsularia, simplified and with some interpolations, beginning as in Sarum with the examination before Paternus. Cyprian is here identified fully with the magician-bishop of the Justina legend. It must have seemed then that the two Cyprians were one, and that there ought not to be a second day.

Archbishop Parker and his Commission for framing our own 'New Calendar' in 1561 had no difficulty as to concurrence of services and increasing of commemorations as there were no collects or lessons for these black letter days, but they returned to the principle of the earliest kalendars to have but one name or event on one day.

It was desirable to retain Holy Cross Day, not merely for its historic interest, but on account of the civil functions which depended on it.

Where to place Cyprian?

We do not know whether they had before them Cranmer's drafts, dropping the other Cyprian and Justina on the 26th, restoring Cyprian to his 14th, and adding Cornelius[1]. But if they had, the drafts were misleading because the 'Third Lesson' identified the two Cyprians with each other, and thus gave a colour for choosing the 26th.

They had old kalendars before them which omitted the Cyprian from the 16th and named a Cyprian alone on the 26th.

Further and separately, Dr Wickham Legg has pointed to the mediæval accumulations of namesakes on the same day. Thus in the *Acta Sanctorum*, taking days at random, *e.g.* from Feb. 7—17 there is not a day which has not two or more saints of the same name. Feb. 14 has two Valentines (Bolland, *Acta Sanctt.* Febr. vol. II. Antv. 1658). And there are instances in almost every week.

---

[1] They were asked for by the Convocation of 1547. Whether produced is not recorded. F. A. Gasquet and E. Bishop, *Edward VI and the Bk. of Common Prayer*, p. 2.

Each of these three conditions supplied a fair argument, and probably each had its effect:—'We must have the 14th for Holy Cross Day, and 'there are abundance of old kalendars which have no mention of S. 'Cyprian on that day. Even if it is his feast we are bound to move him. 'We had better move him, according to precedent, and not arbitrarily, to 'the next S. Cyprian on the 25th. And in all probability those two 'Cyprians are but one.'

This was what the Commissioners under Parker did. They left Holy Cross Day paramount on Cyprian's true festival, and translated Cyprian by himself to the 26th. At any rate they substituted a true saint for an intolerable legendary wizard.

We said that this enquiry was not trivial, not merely an illustration of the nature of entries in kalendars, but had somewhat of the spiritual to exhibit.

We have seen the reverence with which such entries had been made by Cyprian himself (*Ep.* 12. 2; *Ep.* 38. 3); we have seen the way in which his own commemoration was welcomed in other countries. After that, we have seen the passing away of the original local setting in favour of new interests. But the instance in question shews also the original moral force of commemoration infringed first by the jealous dignity of another Church, then gradually pushed off by an imperial association of little or no moral power but of much superstition, and finally subsiding into a mere application for patronal help.

Parallel to and typical of many ideals lowered and lost. Spiritual powers allowed to depart while we cherish material symbols. That persistence of nature against which the Church needs all her energy.

NOTE A.

* *Martyrologium Ecclesiæ Africanæ* (Morcelli, *Africa Christiana*, vol. II. p. 372).

XVIII *Kal. Oct. Carthagine S. M. Cypriani Episc.*

* *Depositio martirum* (ap. Th. Mommsen, *Chronogr. v. J.* 354, p. 633). (*Bucher. Kalendar.*)

XVIII *Kl. Octob. Cypriani Africæ Romæ celebratur in Calisti.*

Muratori, *Lit. Rom. Vet.* I. c. 39 n. (*c*), makes the unhappy conjecture 'in postremis verbis fortasse excidit nomen Cornelii Papæ' in which, alas, De Rossi and Mommsen have followed, the latter dreaming (*op. cit.* p. 633 n.) that *celebratur* may be a corruption of Cornelii.

* *Missale mixtum secundum regulam beati Isidori dictum Mozarabes* (ed. Card. Ximenes A.D. 1500) has fo. ccclxxix (verso) the missa *In Festo Sancti Cipriani* without Cornelius and fo. ccclxxv (verso) *Exaltatio sancte Crucis*. (So also ed. A. Lesley, 1755, pp. 379, 375; Migne, *Lit. Moz.* I. c. 856, 848.)

The kalendar has a mass of late entries.

* *Breviarium secundum regulas beati Iysidori*, ed. Card. Ximenes A.D. 1502.
Kalendar. XVIII *Kls Octobris Exaltatio Sce* ✠ VI *capparū Cipriani* IX *lc*.
(without Cornelius).

* Sanctorale : in *Festa Septembris*, fo. cccc *Exaltatio Sancte Crucis*....*In festo sancti Cipriani epi. Ad Vesperū....Hymn*. Urbis magister tuscie : fo. ccccii... *In festo sancti cornelii epi mris*...

(Ed. Ant. Lorenzana, Matriti, 1775) *Kalendar*. XVIII *Kalendas Octobris Cypriani novem lectionum.*

Sanctorale p. ccxcii *Festa Septembris die* XIV *in Festo Sancti Cypriani episcopi* (without Cornelius). [The kalendar has been corrected by Lorenzana and *Exaltatio* and *Cornelius* rejected. *Appendix*, p. 17; Migne, II. c. 1341. The obvious slip in printing the September days reappears in Migne, II. c. 41.] ['Tasciæ' for 'Tusciæ' *Hymn. ad Vesp.* correctly, though embodying a peculiar theory of Cyprian's name.]

NOTE B.

* The *Leonian Sacramentary* (Muratori, *Liturg. Rom. Vetus*, I. c. 404, cod. bef. cent. x.).

XVIII *Kal. Octobris Natale sanctorum Cornelii et Cypriani.*

* *Missale (Gallo-)Gothicum* (Muratori, II. c. 629, cod. bef. cent. ix.).
in *Natale Sanctorum Martyrum Cornili et Cypriani.*

* *Ant. Kalendarium* S. R. E. ex MSS. codd. *Grassensis* monasterii et S. Andreæ *Avenionensis* (cent. iv or v. acc. to Martène and Durand, *Thesaur. nov. Anecdd.* vol. v. c. 76, Paris, 1717).

die XIV *mensis Septembris natal. SS. Cornelii et Cypriani, secundum Lucam cap.* CXL (sic) *Dicebat...*usque*...generatione.*

Very curious kalendar ; has no saint later than Sylvester, cent. iv. init. ; no feast or commemoration in Lent ; (the 10th Council of Toledo, A.D. 656, decrees this 'sicut ex antiquitate regulari cautum est,' ap. Bruns, *Cann. Apostt. et Concill.* I. p. 298 ; as Council of Laodicea had done, A.D. 352, canon 51, Bruns, I. p. 78 ;) no mention of *Exaltatio S. Crucis* ; no feast of B. V. M. *except Assumption*, which must be interpolated if (as appears) it is as a whole genuine—for this feast was later than the Annuntiation and the Nativity and was not called at first *Assumptio* but *Transitus, Dormitio, Pausatio.*

NOTE C.

* The *Gelasian Sacramentary* (our recension—Muratori, I. c. 667, 8) has
LVI *In Exaltat. Sanctæ Crucis* XVIII *Kal. Octob.*
LVII *In Natal. Sanctorum Corneli et Cypriani* XVI *Kal. Octob.*

This XVI is no doubt an antient error corrected without remark in Muratori's *Index*, I. c. 771.

In Exaltatione Sanctæ Crucis XVIII *Kal. Oct.*
In natal. Sanctorum Cornelii et Cypriani. Item XVIII *Kal. Octob.*
And in his *Kalendar. Gelasianum* (Murat. I. c. 49).

XVIII *Kal. Octob. exaltatio Sanctæ Crucis. Item Sanctorum Cornelii et Cypriani.*

But it is a question whether the error had not a remarkable permanent result in the Roman post-tridentine books, see above and *Note* I infra.

* The *Gregoriæn Sacramentary*, Muratori, II. c. 119.

> XVIII *Kalendas Octobris id est* XIV *die Mensis Septemb.*
> *Natale Sanctorum Cornelii et Cypriani*
> *Item eodem die* XIV *dicti mensis Septembris*
> *Exaltatio Sanctæ Crucis.*

[How long the association with Cornelius was in spreading from Rome is possibly exemplified in the *Vetus Marmoreum S. Eccl. Neapolitanæ Kalendarium*, which is given in Lesley's note on *Liturg. Mozarab.* Migne, I. c. 855.

XIII (?) *P.S. Cipr. et exalt. See Crucis.*]

* *Vetustius Occidentalis Ecclesiæ Martyrologium* D. Hieronymo a Cassiodoro, Beda, Walfrido, Notkero, aliisque scriptoribus tributum, Quod nuncupandum esse Romanum a Magno Gregorio descriptum, ab Adone laudatum, Proximioribus sæculis præteritum et expetitum non leviora argumenta suadent. Franciscus Maria Florentinius nob. Lucensis ex suo præsertim, ac Patriæ Majoris Ecclesiæ, &c. integre vulgav.t. Lucæ, MDCLXVIII.

> XVIII *Kal. Octobris. Exaltatio Sanctæ Crucis. Romæ in Cimiterio Via Appia natalis Corneli Episcopi…in Africa civitate Certagine natalis S. Cypriani Episcopi* [? cent. vii, viii, E.C.].

* *Martyrologium vetustissimum* S. Hieronymi presb. nomine insignitum, ed. D'Achery, Migne, *P. L.* t. XXX. c. 475: cent. ? vii, viii (acc. to Bede vi or vii *Retract. in Act. App.* c. 1).

> XVIII *Kal. Oct. Exaltatio Sanctæ Crucis. Romæ via Appia in cœmeterio Calesti natalis Sanctorum Cornelii episcopi et confessoris. In Africa civitate Carthagine natalis sancti Cypriani episcopi et*…….

NOTE D.

* '*Romanum Parvum*,' so called by Sollier as the source of Ado; 'Vetus Romanum,' Rosweyd; 'venerabile et perantiquum martyrologium' Ado, who first edited it, having found it at Ravenna; given by the Roman pontiff 'cuidam sto episcopo' at Aquileia. (Cent. viii or end of vii.)

> XVIII *K. Octob. Romæ Cornelii episcopi et martyris Carthagine Cypriani episcopi et Martyris. Exaltatio Stæ Crucis ab Heraclio imperatore a Persis Hierosylmam reportatæ quando et Romæ lignus salutiferum Crucis a Sergio Papa inventum ab omni populo veneratur.* (Had Rome a rival Cross?)

* *Martyrologium Vetus* ab annis circiter mille sub nomine *Hieronymi* compactum ex MS. *S. Germani Antissiodorensis* (cent. viii—ix) (Martène and Durand, *Thes. Nov. Anecdott.* III. c. 1560).

> XVIII *Calendas Octobris Romæ Cornelii, Cypriani martyris, et Salutatio S. Crucis.*

(If this implies knowledge that Cornelius was not a martyr it represents some much earlier source.)

616   APPENDIX L.

* *Kalendarium Frontonis.* 'Kal. Romanum nongentis annis antiquius ex MS. Monast. S. Genovefæ Parisiensis in monte, aureis characteribus &c. ed....F. Joannes Fronto [Fronteau] Can. Reg. S. T. Prof. in Mon. S. Genovefæ, & in Acad. Paris. Cancellarius' (Paris, 1552) (A.D. 714—741 F.).

It seems distinctly Roman.

> *Die* XIV *mens. Sept. Natal. SS. Corneli Pontif. et Cypriani. Secund. Luc. cap.* CXL (sic) *Dicebat...usque...accusarent eum.*
> *Die sups. exaltatio S. Crucis secund. Joann. cap.* XXIII *Erat homo... Nicodemus...usque...æternam.*

This very curious kalendar numbers and calls the *Weeks* between S. Cyprian's Day and the 4th week before the Nativity '*Hebd.* I. II. III. IV. V. VI. *post S. Cypriani Hebd.* VII.' (meaning also post S. Cypriani)[1].

It has close affinity with the above-named *Grassense*, but Cornelius is not mentioned; *exaltatio S. Crucis* has been added, but *after* S. Cyprian. And it has four Feasts of the Virgin. 1. In Octabas Domini [i.e. ? Jan. 11] die supras. Natal. S. Mariæ[2]. 2. (Mar. 25) adnuntiatio *Domini.* 3. Die XV mens. Aug. Sollemnia de *Pausatione* S. Mariæ. 4. Die IX (? unice) mens. Sep. Nativitas S. Mariæ. It has often two *missæ* for the same day with the same Epistles and Gospels as Grassense for that which is common to both—only longer.

Grassense counts the six Sundays '*Dominica* I &c. a Festo Sancti Angeli' [Michaelis].

* *Bedæ Martyrologium* (as edited by Florus, A.D. 830).

> XVIII *Kalend. Oct. Romæ natale S. Cornelii episcopi...Item Sancti Cypriani episcopi...martyrium consummavit sexto milliario a Carthagine, juxta mare. Eodem die exaltatio Sanctæ Crucis...*

* His *Martyrologium Poeticum* agrees.

* *Martyrologium Gellonense* sive Monasterii S. Guillelmi de Deserto O. B. Diœcesis Lutevensis pervetustum, ineunte scilicet sæculo nono anno circiter 804 [ap. D'Achery, *Spicilegium*, II. p. 25 (Paris, 1723)].

(Printed at end of old editions of Gelasian and Gregorian Sacramentaries.)

> XVIII *Kal. Octobris Roma* (sic). *Cornelii et Cypriani Mart.......Et salutatio Sanctæ Crucis.*

* *Rabanus Maurus*, A.D. cir. 845, has dropped *Romæ* &c.

> XVIII *Kal. Oct. Sancti Cornelii episcopi....Eodem die natale Sancti Episcopi...eodem die exaltatio est Sanctæ Crucis.*

But 'Rome' and 'Africa' were still perpetuated to a much later date, at least to the end of the 10th century.

* *Wandalbert*, Deacon and Monk in the diocese of Treves, fl. 854. His *Martyrologium* in verse gives the Exaltation, Cornelius at Rome and Cyprian at Carthage on this day. (One line versified from Jerome—'totum Ecclesiæ scribunt cujus sacra dicta per orbem,' ap. D'Achery, *Spicilegium*, II. p. 38.)

---

[1] So the Mozarabic Breviary dates the September fast by his feast, 'Incipit Officium Jejuniorum Kalendarum [Nov]embrium, quod observatur tribus diebus ante festum Sancti Cypriani....' Lorenzana, *Brev. Goth.* p. 431. Migne, II. c. 708.

[2] Cf. 'de S. Maria in Octava Domini' *Antiphonar.*, *Greg. M.* ap. Pamelium: *Liturgic.* (1571) II. p. 71.

S. CYPRIAN'S DAY IN KALENDARS.

* *Ado.* Not so much a kalendar as brief memoirs, which accounts sufficiently for Holy Cross being postponed here. *Obiit* A.D. 875.

> XVIII *Kal. Oct. Romæ via Appia in cœmeterio Callisti natale Sancti Cornelii episcopi: qui sub persecutione Decii &c.*
> *Item apud Africam natale beati Cypriani episcopi Valeriano et Gallieno impp. Galerio maximo proconsule &c.* (from Pontius mainly)... *Referuntur autem cum beato Cypriano passi Crescentius &c.* (scil. the four commemorated same day in *Kal. Eccl. Afric.*).
> *Eodem die Exaltatio Stæ Crucis.*

* *Usuard,* A.D. 875 *circ.*

> XVIII *Kal. Oct. Exaltatio Stæ Crucis...Romæ via Appia beati Cornelii papæ...In Africa sancti Cypriani episcopi...martyrium consummavit sexto milliario a Carthagine juxta mare* (from Beda sup.) *Referuntur cum eo passi Cresc. &c.* (from Ado).

* *Ant. Kal. Corbeiense,* written for Abbot Rathold, who died 986.

> XVIII *Cal. Oct. Exaltatio Sanctæ Crucis. Romæ Cornelii papæ Kartagine sancti Cypriani episcopi et martyris* (*Papæ*; cf. sup. Usuard).
>
> (Martène and Durand, *Th. Nov.* III. cc. 1548, 1601.)

* *Ant. Martyrol. Morbacense,* xth cent.

> XVIII *Cal.* [Oct.] *Romæ Cornelii Cypriani et exaltatio S. Crucis.*
>
> (Mart. and Dur. *Th. Nov.* III. c. 1569.)

NOTE E.

* *Missale Vet. Hibernicum* ap. C.C.C. Oxford (cent. xii) p. 39 (ed. F. E. Warren, 1879).

> XVIII *Kal. Oct. Exaltatio Sancte Crucis.*

* *Antiquum Corbeiensis monasterii Martyrologium* (cent. x).

> XVIII *Cal. Oct. Exaltatio S. Crucis.*
>
> (Mart. and Dur. *Th. Nov.* III. c. 1583.)

NOTE F.

* *Brev. Romanum a Fr. Card. Quignonio edit.* A.D. 1535 (ed. J. W. Legg, p. xli).

> XVIII *Cal.'* (Sept.) 14 *Exaltatio sanctæ Crucis duplex majus*
> XVII *Cal.'* 15 *Cornelius et Cyprianus. Fuerunt heri.*

* *Sanctorum historiæ* [i.e. *Proprium Sanctorum* abbreviated]. The Third Lesson is of Cornelius and Cyprian [said rightly in Index to be from Platina et cæteri, but the Cyprian part of it seems paraphrased from Jerome, *Vv. Ill.* lxvii. and the Cornelius part from the *Liber Pontificalis* (ed. Duchesne, I. pp. 150, 151)].

The note *fuerunt heri* and that on Sept. 8, the Nativity of the Virgin, *habet octavam,* shew that Quignon made the change to the 15th deliberately. But afterwards Cyprian and Cornelius were not ordinarily moved to that day, probably because it was the octave of the Nativity of the Virgin, a feast much observed, though dating only from A.D. 1245.

Note G.

* *Missale Romanum*, Venet. 1477.
>Kalendar. XVIII *Kl. Octobris Exaltatio Sancte Crucis* Propr. Temporis. *in exaltatione Sacte Crucis et fit commemoratio de Sactis* [Oratio Secreta P. Comm. Corn. et Cyp.].

* *Missale Ambrosianum*, Mediol. 1475.
>XVIII *Kl. Oct. S̄tor Cornelii et Cipriani m̄. eodē die exaltatio Sce Crucis* Propr. temp. (no octave of Nativity B.V.M.) fo. clxvi (verso) *in sc̄or martyr cornelii et cypriani*, fo. clxvii *eodem die exaltatio Scte Crucis.* [Cornelius and Cyprian still first.]

* *Calendarium Anglicanum* (cod. anno circ. M. exaratum), Martène and Durand, *Vett. Scriptorum et Monum. amplissima Coll.* VI. cc. 635, 651 (Paris, 1729).
>XVIII *Kal. Octembres. Exaltatio Ste Crucis et SS. Cornelii et Cypriani.*

* *Leofric Missal*, Exeter, 1050—1072 (ed. F. E. Warren, Oxford, 1883) Kalendar. p. 31.
>XVIII *Kl. Oct. Exaltatio Sce Crucis, Cornelii, et Cipriani.*

* *Sarum Missal*, Rothom. 1492 [ed. F. H. Dickenson, p. 25** &c. 902].
>XVIII *Kl. Octobris. Exaltatio Sce Crucis mi. dup. nov. lect. med. lc. de SS. Cornelio et Cypriano.*

(The note about the lessons, assigning the middle three of the nine lessons to Cornelius and Cyprian, applies to the Breviary.)

The *Proprium Sanctorum* provides a Memoria, Secreta and Post-Communion for their commemoration on Holy Cross Day.

* *Sarum Breviary Kalendar*, Chevallon, 1531 (ed. F. Procter and C. Wordsworth, fasc. 1).
>XVIII *Kalen. Octobris. Exaltatio S. Crucis festum minus duplex* IX *lectiones.*

Cornelius and Cyprian omitted in the kalendar, but provided for in the Offices with Collect and Lessons.

Proprium Sanctorum (Fasc. 3, pp. 810, 815):—
>*Memoria fiat de martyribus Cornelio et Cypriano cum Ant. &c.*
>*Mediæ lectiones fiant de martyribus Cornelio et Cypriano.*

(In the middle of the middle lesson Cyprian begins. It is a shortened and edificatory version of Pontius, beginning with the examination before Paternus.)

* W. Maskell, *Monumenta Ritualia Eccl. Anglic.* (1846) vol. II. pp. 179 ff., *Appendix to the Prymer*, gives three early and 'valuable' English Kalendars, viz.
>1. *In Bodleian* (Bodl. MS. 85) XVIII (Kl. Oct.) *Exultacion*[1] *of the crois...*VI *Seint Ciprian.*—2. (Douce 275) XVIII *Kl. Reisyng of the cros.* VI *Kl. S. Ciprian bischop.*—3. *Enchiridion ad usum Sarum* (Maskell Collection), Paris, 1530. XVIII *Kl. Exaltatio S. crucis.* VI *Kl. Cypriani et Justinæ.*

There must have been many such. Here we have three, chosen only for their value, omitting Cyprian on the right day and two of them giving Cyprian alone on the 26th. For foreign examples see *Note* C above.

---
[1] So *exultatio* sometimes in foreign Kalendars.

S. CYPRIAN'S DAY IN KALENDARS.

* *York Missal Kalendar* (v. I. p. xxxviii, ed, Surtees Soc. 1874).
  XVIII *Kal. Octobris Exaltatio Sanctæ Crucis. S. Cornelii et Cypriani, mediæ lectiones.* IX *lect.* (see Comparative Calendar, v. II. p. 267).
(v. II. p. 101) *Proprium Missarum de Sanctis*
  in Festo Exaltationis Sanctæ Crucis. (XVIII Kal. Oct.)
p. 102, *eodem die Sanctorum martyrum Cornelii et Cypriani oratio.*
p. 104, *secreta...postcomm.*

* *Hereford Missal Kalendar* (W. G. Henderson, 1874, p. xxix).
  XVIII *Kal. Octobris. Exaltatio Sanctæ Crucis festum duplex, SS. Cornelii et Cypriani commemoratio* IX *lect.*
Proprium Sanctorum (*id.* p. 323). *In exaltatione Sanctæ Crucis.* The second collect is 'memoria de martyribus Cornelio et Cypriano, Oratio...alia Secreta...alia Post-Communio.'

* *Hereford Missal*, 1502.
  XVIII *Kl. Octobr.* Exaltatio S. ✠ Corneliī et Cipriāi m̄t.

* It is to this stage that the *Calendarium Mozarabicum* '*sæpius auctum*' has been brought down (*Lit. Moz.* Migne, I. c. 101)
  XVIII *Kal. Octobris Exaltatio sancte crucis* VI *capp.*
    Cornelii et Cipriani IX *lect.*

Note H.

So for example *Calendaria Verdunense, Stabulense, Antissiodorense* (all cent. x—xi), the last adding Pantaleon (as many do) and the four African martyrs of the day.
  (*Mart.* and Dur. *Vett. Scrr. et Mon.* VI. c. 720.)

* *Kalend. Sitonianum* (called from its owner in 18th cent. Carnillo Sitonio of Milan) (cent. xi).
  XVIII *Kal. Oct. SS. Cornelii et Cypriani eodem die S.* Nicomedis et *exaltatio S. Crucis ad* Dionysium.
    Muratori, *Rer. Ital. Scrr.* t. II. pt. 2, p. 1040 (Mediol. 1726).)

* *Antiq. Calendarium ex* MS. *Lyrensis monasterii* (cent. xi—xii)
  XVIII *Kal. Oct. Exaltatio S. Crucis SS. Cornelii et Cypriani.*
    (Mart. and Dur. *Thes. Nov.* III. c. 1614.)

And thus *Missale Romanum*, 1533.
  XVIII *Kal. Octobris Exalta. S. Cru. d. mi. mis.* 211 *Cornelii et Cipriani m. oro* 211.

* *Breviarium Romanum*, 1534 (Venet.).
  XVIII *Kal. Octobris Exaltatio Ste Crucis d. mi. omnia* 320 *Et Cornelii et Cypriani martyrū oro lec.* IX 322.

1564, Venet. (the last known edition of the Old Breviary, superseded 1568).
  XVIII *Cal.* 14 *Octobris. Exaltatio see Crucis du. mi.* 340.
  Cornelii & Cypriani martyrum, 342.

NOTE I.

* *Breviarium Romanum* ex decr. sacrosanct. Conc. Tridentini restitutum, Pii V. Pont. Max. jussu, ed. Rome, 1570 (Manutius).
  XVIII 14 Exaltatio S. Crucis du. cū cōm Oct. Nat. S. Ma. 821.
  XVI 16 Cornelii et Cipriani pont. et Mart. semid.

It appoints the 4th and 5th Lessons for Cornelius, and the 6th for Cyprian. This latter is taken from Jerome, *de Viris Illustribus*, lxvi.

* *Missale Romanum* ex decr. Conc. Pii V. jussu, ed. A.D. 1572, Venet.
  XVIII *Sept.* Cal. 14 *Exaltatio San. Crucis* dup. cum commemo. Octavæ Nativitatis Sanctæ Mariæ, 189.
  XVII Cal. 15 Octava Nativitatis beatæ Mariæ dup. cum commemora. San. Nicomedis mar. 190.
  XVI Cal. 16 *Cornelii et Cypriani pont. & mar.* Sanc. dup. &c.

* In the modern *Roman* books, A.D. 1631 &c.
  Missal, XVI *Kal. Sep.* 16 *Cornelii et Cypriani Pont. et M. semi-d.*
  Breviary, XVI *Kal. Sep.* 16 *SS. Cornelii et Cypriani Pont. et Mart. semi-d.*

* *Lyons*, A.D. 1737, has Cornelius on 16th and Cyprian on 17th.

The following references were sent to the Archbishop by his friend the Rev. Christopher Wordsworth:

Breviarium Sanctæ Lugdunensis Ecclesiæ primæ Galliarum sedis, Lugduni, M.DCC.XXXVII.
  XVIII 14 *Exaltatio Sanctæ Crucis. Duplex minus. an.* 326.
  XVII 15 *Octava Nativit. B. Mariæ Virginis. Semiduplex minus....*
  XVI 16 *Cornelii Papæ et Martyris (è die* 14). *Simplex. an.* 252....
  XV 17 *Cypriani Carthaginensis Episcopi et Martyris. Simplex (è die* 14). [*In ecclesia Primatiali. Semiduplex majus*] *an.* 258.

These curious entries witness to the transfer and to the reasons for it.

* *Brev. Ambrosian.* (Mediol. 1582 and 1841). 12 *Prid. Id. SS. Cornelii papæ et Cypriani ep. mm.*

* *Brev. Paris.* A.D. 1778 commemorates Cornelius (Pap. & Mart.) on Holy Cross Day, but also keeps the semi-double feast of Cyprian (Episc. Eccl. Doct. & Mart.) on 16th.

NOTE K.

* *British Museum*, Royal MS. 7, B. IV.
  First Kalendar *September* 14 *Cyprianus.*
  Second Kalendar *Cyprianus et Cornelius.*
Et Cornelius added in Archbishop Cranmer's own handwriting.
  F. A. Gasquet and E. Bishop, *Edward VI. and the Book of Common Prayer*, 1890, p. 16.

LIST OF BOOKS QUOTED.

Many authorities are quoted in this book and some important works (*e.g.* Mommsen, *On the Chronography of* A.D. 354; Lipsius, *On the Chronology of the Roman Bishops;* Morcelli's *Africa Christiana*, Tissot's great work *On the Roman Province of Africa*, &c.) have been of necessity referred to in an abbreviated form. It has been thought that the reader would find it convenient to consult a more complete description of some of these authorities.

ALEXANDRE, Charles. Oracula Sibyllina.... Paris, 1841. 1 vol. 8vo. Editio altera 1869.

AUBESPINE, Gabriel de l'. S. Optati...Opera cum observationibus et notis G. Albaspinæi.... 1631. Fol.—De Veteribus Ecclesiæ ritibus.... Lutetiæ Parisiorum, 1623. 3 vols. 4to.

BALLERINI, Pietro. De vi ac ratione primatus Romanorum Pontificum et de ipsorum infallibilitate in definiendis controversiis fidei. Veronæ, 1766. New edition by E. W. Westhoff. Monasterii Westphalorum, 1865. 8vo.

BALUZE, Étienne. Sancti Cæcilii Cypriani...opera...studio et labore Stephani Baluzii Tutelensis. Absolvit post Baluzium ac Præfationem et Vitam Sancti Cypriani adornavit unus ex monachis Congregationis S. Mauri (Dom Prudent MARAN). Parisiis, ex Typographia regia, 1726. Fol. Editio secunda, Veneta, 1758. Fol.

BALUZE, Étienne. Capitularia regum Francorum......Accessere vita Baluzii partim ab ipso scripta, catalogus et index. Curante *P. de Chiniac*. Parisiis, 1780. 2 vols. Fol.

Stephani BALUZII miscellanea. Parisiis, 1678—83. 4 vols. 8vo. ...novo ordine digesta et non paucis ineditis monumentis opportunisque animadversionibus aucta opera ac studio *J. D. Mansi*. Lucæ, 1761—64. 4 vols. Fol.

BARONIUS, Cæsar. Annales Ecclesiastici [A.D. 1—1198]......continuatione O. RAYNALDI......(edited by G. D. Mansi and D. Georgius). Lucæ, 1738—59. Fol. 38 vols.

BINGHAM, Joseph. Works, quoted from the Oxford edition. 1855. 10 vols.

BOECKHIUS, Augustus. Corpus Inscriptionum Græcarum. Berolini, 1828—1867. 4 vols. Fol.

BRIGHT, William. Select Anti-Pelagian Treatises of S. Augustine. London, 1880. 8vo.

BRUNS, Herman Theodor. Canones Apostolorum et Conciliorum veterum selecti. Berolini, 1839. 2 vols. 8vo.

BUNSEN, Christian Carl Josias. Hippolytus and his Age. London, 1852. 4 vols. 8vo.—Christianity and Mankind... 7 vols. Hippolytus and his Age. (1, 2.) Analecta Ante-Nicæna. (5, 6, 7.) London, 1854.

LIST OF BOOKS QUOTED.

BURN, Robert. Rome and the Campagna. London, 1871—6. 4to.

BURNET, Gilbert. Some letters ; containing accounts of what seemed most remarkable in Switzerland, Italy, &c. Amsterdam, 1686. 2 vols. 12mo.

CECCONI, Eugenio. Studi storici sul concilio di Firenze con documenti inediti o nuovamente datti alla luce sui manoscritti di Firenze e di Roma. Firenze, 1868. 8vo.

CHINIAC, P. de. See Baluze : Capitularia Regum Francorum. Histoire des Capitulaires des Rois François de la première et seconde race ou traduction de la preface mise par É. B. à la tête de son édition des Capitulaires. Avec la vie de Baluze...... Paris, 1779. 8vo.

CLINTON, H. F. Fasti Romani. Oxford, 1845. 2 vols. 4to.

CORPUS INSCRIPTIONUM LATINARUM. Berolini, 1873—1891. Chiefly vol. VIII., parts i, ii. Inscriptiones Africæ Latinæ, collegit Gustavus Wilmanns. 1881. Supplementum ediderunt Renatus Cagnat et Johannes Schmidt. 1891.

CORPUS JURIS CIVILIS (edited by Theodor Mommsen and Paul Krueger). Berolini, 1888. 2 vols. 8vo.

COUNCILS. When no special mention of editions occurs, Councils are quoted from :
    LABBE, Philippe, and COSSART, G., Sacrosancta concilia ad regiam editionem exacta... 25 vols. (Apparatus 2 vols.)... Supplementum...collegit J. D. Mansi. Venetiis, 1728—52. 29 vols. Fol.
    When references are made to Mansi, the reader will consult the following edition :
    MANSI, J. D. Sacrorum conciliorum nova et amplissima collectio ...... Florentiæ, Venetiis, 1759—98. 31 vols. Fol.

CYPRIAN. The works of Cyprian are quoted from the following edition :
    S. THASCI CÆCILI CYPRIANI opera omnia, recensuit et commentario critico instruxit *Guilelmus Hartel*. Vindobonæ, apud C. Geroldi Filium Bibliopolam Academiæ, 1868—1871. 3 vols. 8vo.

DIRKSEN, Heinrich Eduard. Manuale Latinitatis fontium juris civilis Romanorum. Berolini, 1837. 4to.

DODWELL, Henry. Dissertationes Cyprianicæ. Ap. J. Fell's edition of Cyprian. Oxonii, 1682.

DŒLLINGER, Johann Joseph Ignaz von. Hippolytus und Kallistus. Regensburg, 1853. 8vo.

DU CANGE, Charles Du Fresne. Glossarium mediæ et infimæ Latinitatis. Niort, 1883—1887. 10 vols.

DUCHESNE, Louis. Le Liber Pontificalis. Paris, 1884. 2 vols. 4to.—Le Dossier du Donatisme. 1890.—Fastes Épiscopaux de l'Ancienne Gaule. 1894.—Les Origines Chrétiennes. ? 1891. 2 vols. 4to. (Lithographed throughout.)—Origines du Culte Chrétien. Étude sur la liturgie latine avant Charlemagne. 1889.

EWALD, Georg Heinrich August von. Die Propheten des Alten Bundes... 1840. 8vo.

FECHTRUP, Bernhard. Der hl. Cyprian. Sein Leben und seine Lehre. Münster, 1878. 8vo.

FELL. Sancti Cæcilii Cypriani opera. Accedunt Annales Cyprianici...per Joannem Cestriensem. (PEARSON.) Oxonii, 1682.

FORTIA D'URBAN. Recueil des Itinéraires anciens.... Paris, 1844. 4to.

FREPPEL, Charles Émile. Les Pères Apostoliques et leur Époque.... Paris, 1859. 8vo.—Saint Cyprien et l'Église d'Afrique au IIIme siècle. Paris, 1864—5. 8vo.

FRIEDLAENDER, Ludwig. Darstellungen aus der Sittengeschichte Roms in der Zeit von August bis zum Ausgang der Antonine. Leipzig, 1862—71. 8vo. 3 Thle.—Sechste...vermehrte Auflage. Leipzig, 1888—90. 3 Thle.

FRONTEAU, Jean. Kalendarium Romanum nongentis annis antiquius.... 1652. 8vo.—Epistolæ et dissertationes ecclesiasticæ.... Veronæ, 1733. 8vo.

GALLANDIUS, Andreas. Bibliotheca Veterum Patrum Antiquorumque Scriptorum Ecclesiasticorum. Venetiis, 1765—81. Fol. 14 vols.

GAMS, Bonifacius. Series Episcoporum. Ratisbon, 1873. 4to.

GOAR, Jacobus. Euchologion sive Rituale Græcorum. Paris, 1647. Fol.

GRETSER, J. De jure et more prohibendi, expurgandi et abolendi libros hereticos et noxios.... Ingoldstadii, 1603. 8vo.

GRISAR, H. (S. J.) Le Tombe Apostoliche di Roma. Roma, 1892. 4to.

GRYNÆUS, Johan Jacob. Monumenta S. Patrum Orthodoxographa.... Basileæ, 1569. Fol. 3 vols.

HARNACK, Adolf. Geschichte der altchristlichen Litteratur bis Eusebius. Leipzig, 1893. 2 vols. 8vo.—Sources of the Apostolic Canons, with a treatise on the origin of the Readership and other lower orders.... Translated by L. A. Wheatley. London, 1895. 8vo.—Die Briefe des römischen Klerus aus der Zeit der Sedisvacanz im Jahre 250. Ap. Theologische Abhandlungen.—Carl von Weizsäcker, zu seinem siebzigsten Geburtstage... Freiburg i. B. 1892. 8vo.—Articles ap. Texte und Untersuchungen zur Geschichte der altchristlichen Literatur von Oscar von Gebhardt und Adolf Harnack.

HEFELE, Carl Joseph von. Conciliengeschichte. Histoire des Conciles... traduite de l'Allemand par M. l'abbé Delarc. 12 vols. 8vo. Paris, 1869—70.

HODGKIN, Thomas. Italy and her Invaders. 2nd edition. 6 vols. Oxford, 1892.

HURTER, Heinrich von. Sanctorum Patrum opuscula selecta. Œniponti, 1868—1874—1885.

JAFFÉ, Philippus. Regesta Pontificum Romanorum. Lipsiæ, 1885. 2 vols. 4to.

JUSTEL, Christophe. Codex Canonum Ecclesiæ Africanæ. Paris, 1614. 8vo.

KLEIN, Josephus. Fasti Consulares. Lipsiæ, 1881.

LA BIGNE, Margarinus de. Maxima Bibliotheca Veterum Patrum et Antiquorum Scriptorum Ecclesiasticorum.... Coloniæ Agrippinæ, 1618—22. 15 vols. Fol.

LANCIANI, Rodolfo Amadeo. Pagan and Christian Rome. London, 1892. 8vo.

LATINIUS, Latinus. Bibliotheca sacra et profana. Romæ, 1677. 2 tom. Fol.—Epistolæ.... Romæ, 1659. 2 tom. 4to.

LE NAIN DE TILLEMONT, Louis Sébastien. Histoire des Empereurs.... Paris, 1700—36. 6 vols. 4to.—Mémoires pour servir à l'histoire ecclésiastique des six premiers siècles.... Paris, 1701—12. 16 vols. 4to.

LEYDEKKER, Melchior. Historia Ecclesiæ Africanæ. Ultrajecti, 1690. 4to.
LIGHTFOOT, Bishop Joseph Barber. Epistles of S. Paul [Galatians, Philippians, Colossians, Philemon]. London, 1865. 8vo.—The Apostolic Fathers. Part I. S. Clement of Rome. London, 1890. 2 vols. 8vo. Part II. S. Ignatius, S. Polycarp. London, 1889. 3 vols. 8vo.—Historical Essays. London, 1895. 8vo.—On a fresh revision of the English New Testament. London, 1871. 2nd edition, 1872. 8vo.
LIPSIUS, Richard Adelbert. Chronologie der Römischen Bischöfe. Kiel, 1869.
MABILLON, Jean. Vetera Analecta. Parisiis, 1675. 4 vols. 8vo.
MABILLON, Jean, and GERMAIN, Michel. Museum Italicum. Lutetiæ Parisiorum, 1687—89. 2 vols. 4to.
MANSEL, Henry Longueville. The Gnostic Heresies of the First and Second Centuries....Edited by J. B. Lightfoot. London, 1875. 8vo.
MARAN, Prudent. Vita Sancti Cypriani, ap. Étienne Baluze's edition of Cyprian. Paris, 1726.
MARTÈNE, Edmond. De antiquis Ecclesiæ Ritibus. Antwerpiæ, 1736—37. 3 vols. Fol.
MARTÈNE, Edmond, and DURAND, Ursin. Thesaurus novus Anecdotorum. Parisiis, 1717. 5 vols. Fol.—Veterum Scriptorum Monumentorum... amplissima Collectio. Parisiis, 1724—33. Fol.
MASKELL, William. Monumenta Ritualia Ecclesiæ Anglicanæ. London, 1846—47. 3 vols. 8vo.—Second Edition. Oxford, 1882. 3 vols. 8vo.
MIGNE, J. P. Patrologiæ Cursus Completus. Series Latina. Paris, 1844 —1864. 221 vols. 4to. Series Græca. Paris, 1857—1866. 162 vols. 4to.
MOMMSEN, Theodor. De Collegiis et Sodaliciis Romanorum. Kiliæ, 1843. Ueber den Chronographen vom J. 354: ap. Abhandlungen der Philologisch-Historischen Classe der Königlich Sächsischen Gesellschaft der Wissenschaften (erster Band). Leipzig, 1850.
    M. is quoted constantly in connection with the *Corpus Inscriptionum Latinarum.*
MORCELLI, Stefano Antonio. Africa Christiana. Brixiæ, 1816—17. 3 vols. 4to.
MÜNTER, Frederic Christian Carl Henrik. Primordia Ecclesiæ Africanæ. Hafniæ. 1829. 4to.
MURATORI, Lodovico Antonio. Liturgia Romana Vetus. Venetiis, 1748. 2 vols. Fol.—Rerum Italarum Scriptores. Mediolani, 1723—1751. 25 vols. Fol.
NEANDER, J. A. W. History of the Christian Religion and Church. Bohn's Standard Library. London, 1850—58. 9 vols. 8vo.
ŒHLER, Franciscus. Corpus Hæreologicum. Vol. I. Berolini, 1856. 8vo.
OTTO, Johann Carl Theodor von. Corpus Apologetarum Christianorum Sæculi Secundi. Jenæ, 1851—76—81. 9 vols. 8vo.
PAMELIUS, Jacobus. Liturgia Latinorum... Coloniæ Agrippinæ, 1571. 2 vols. 4to.
PANVINIO, Onofrio. De Primatu Petri et Apostolicæ sedis potestate... Veronæ, 1589. 4to.
PARKER, John Henry. The Archæology of Rome (chiefly on the Catacombs). London, 1878. 8vo.

LIST OF BOOKS QUOTED.

PEARSON, John. Annales Cyprianici, ap. J. Fell's edition of Cyprian. Oxonii, 1682.—Minor Theological Works. Oxford, 1844. 2 vols. 8vo.—Vindiciæ Epistolarum S. Ignatii. Cantabrigiæ, 1672. 4to.—Editio nova. Oxonii, 1852. 2 vols. 8vo.

PETERS, Johannes. Der heilige Cyprian von Karthago...in seinen Leben und Wirken dargestellt. Regensburg, 1877. 8vo.

PITRA, Jean Baptiste. Spicilegium Solesmense....Paris, 1852—58. 4 vols. 8vo.

PUSEY, Edward Bouverie. The Councils of the Church from the Council of Jerusalem, A.D. 51, to the Council of Constantinople, A.D. 381. Oxford, 1857. 8vo.

RENAUDOT, Eusèbe. Liturgiarum Orientalium Collectio.... Parisiis, 1716. 4to. 2 vols.

RETTBERG, Friedrich Wilhelm. Thascius Cäcilius Cyprianus, Bischof von Carthage, dargestellt nach seinen Leben und Wirken. Göttingen, 1831. 8vo.

RITSCHL, Otto. Cyprian von Karthago und die Verfassung der Kirche. Göttingen, 1885. 8vo.

ROBERT, Ulysse. Bullaire du Pape Calixte II. Paris, 1891. 8vo. 2 vols.

RŒNSCH, Hermann. Itala und Vulgata.... Leipzig, 1869. 8vo.—Das neue Testament Tertullian's...mit...Anmerkungen.... Leipzig, 1871. 8vo.

ROSSI, Giovanni Battista de. Inscriptiones Christianæ Urbis Romæ septimo sæculo antiquiores. Romæ, 1861.... 2 vols. Fol.—La Roma Sotterranea Cristiana descritta ed illustrata. Roma, 1864.... 3 vols. Fol.

ROUTH, Martin Joseph. Reliquiæ Sacræ. Oxonii, 1846—48. 5 vols. 8vo.

RUINART, Thierry. Acta Martyrum. Ratisbonæ, 1859.

SABATIER, P. Bibliorum sacrorum Latinæ versiones antiquæ, seu *Vetus Italica*.... Rheims, 1743—49. 3 vols. Fol.

SCHELSTRATE, Emanuel. Ecclesia Africana sub Primate Carthaginiensi. Paris, 1679. 4to.

SHEPHERD, Edward John. A First (—fifth) Letter to the Rev. S. R. Maitland on the genuineness of the writings ascribed to Cyprian, Bishop of Carthage. London, 1852—53. 8vo.

SIRMOND, Jacques. Opera varia. Paris, 1696. 5 vols. Fol.

STEVENSON, Seth William. A Dictionary of Roman Coins. London, 1889. 8vo.

TISSOT, Charles. Exploration scientifique de la Tunisie.—Géographie comparée de la Province Romaine d'Afrique. Paris, 1884—1888. 2 vols. 4to. and Atlas.

WETSTEIN, Johann Jacob. Novum Testamentum Græcum, 1751.—Epistola ad...H. Venema: de duabus Clementis Romani ad Virgines epistolis ex Codice Syriaco nuper editis. Amstelædami, 1751. 8vo.

WORDSWORTH, Christopher, Bishop of Lincoln. S. Hippolytus and the Church of Rome.... (Second edition.) London, 1880. 8vo.

WORDSWORTH, John, Bishop of Salisbury, and H. J. WHITE. Novum Testamentum Domini Nostri Jesu Christi, Latine secundum editionem Sancti Hieronymi. Oxonii, 1891. 4 vols.—Old Latin Biblical Texts. Oxford, 1883.... 8vo.

INDEX.

NOTE. The Reader will kindly bear in mind that a special Geographical Table —the work of the University Press—is given at page 574; that table relates to the Appendix on the Cities, but the towns mentioned in the body of the Book have been entered in the Index.

Abstinere, sense of the word in Cyprian, 143, n.
Acta Proconsularia, 518
Actors, 46
Adam (date for), 266, n.
Adsertor, use of the word, 6, n.
Adunatio—adunatus, use of the words, 386 and nn.; 407
Æmilius, the Martyr, 78
Æmulus princeps, Valens, opportunity afforded for the election of Cornelius, 126, n.
Agrippinus. See Baptismal Question. Tradition of Africa, 337; date of Council, 337, 348
Alexander Severus, the Emperor, his organization of the city of Rome (curatores), 67 and n.
Alexander III., Pope (Conditional Baptism), 522
Amantius, acolyte, carries with others Cyprian's letters to the Numidian Bishop-Confessors, 473
Ambrose, S., 11, n.; 55, n.; 272, n.; 286, 384, n.; 491, n.
Antioch (Council of), 167, 168, 347; Councils on Paul of Samosata, 376 and n.
Antioch (first and second capture of). See special note on Points in the Chronology of Valerian's reign, 552
Antonianus (Letter of Cyprian to), 156, n.; 157 and n.; 167, n.
Apollo Salutaris, allusion to the Plague on Coins and Medals, 243, n.

Apostolic Canons and Constitutions, 27, n.; 46, n.; 54, n.; 294, n.; 341, n.; 404, n.; 420, n.
Apostolic Succession, 34, 389, 525
Arles (Church of). See Gaulish Appeal. Foundation of this Church, Trophimus and the tradition handed down by Stephen V. and Gregory of Tours, 314, 315, 316. Council of Arles : see Councils
Assuras, a town, 232 and n.; 369, 602
Atrium Sanciolum, 501 and n.
Auctor Schismatis, sense of the words, 136, n.
Augendus, a deacon, joins Felicissimus (see name), 113, 136, 137, n.
Augustine, S., 23, n.; 42; 43, nn.; 55, n.; 59, n.; 81, n.; 112, n.; 147, n.; 174, n.; 249, n.; 259, n.; 271, n.; 272, n.; 273 and n.; 283; 285, n.; 291, n.; 296 and n.; 331; 334, n.; 338, n.; 343, n.; 369, n.; 402, n.; 403, n.; 405, n.; 409, n.; 412, n.; 413, n.; 415, n.; 417, n.; reaffirms the teaching of Stephen on Baptism, 418, sqq.; 424, n.; 433, n.; 434, n.; 437 and n.; 443, n.; 445, n.; 448, n.; 451, n.; 453, n.; 471, n.; 493; 499, n.; 506, n.; 510, n.; 512, n.; 513, n.; 517; 519; 523, n.; 533 and n.; 538
Aurelius, a young Confessor (Persecution of Decius), 71; his name used by Lucianus, 93
Aureus, value of the aureus in Gallienus' time, 505, n.

INDEX.   627

Baluze, Étienne, his edition of Cyprian published after his death by Dom Maran; the interpolations introduced, 212, 213, 214, 215, 216, n.; 231, n.

Baptism and Baptismal Question (the), 231, 295, 331, sqq.; Tradition of Africa, 335; Tradition of Asia Minor, East, 339; Councils of Iconium and Synnada (dates), 340, 348; Cyprian's First and Second Council on Baptism, 349, 351; Attitude of Stephanus, 351; Dionysius of Alexandria, 354; Third Council on Baptism, 364; Towns which sent their Bishops, 366, sqq. See also Appendix on Cities and Index of same Appendix.—*Sententiæ Episcoporum*, authenticity of the document, 371, 372; Cyprian's Arguments on Rebaptism, 401; Baptism performed by a demoniac woman, 410; The Councils failed,— why, 424.

Baptism by one that is dead, sense of the words, 411

Baptism in the Name of Christ alone, 398 and n.; 406, 407

Basil, S., 54, n.; 166, n.; on Dionysius the Great, 356 and n.; on Firmilian, 375 and n.

Basilicæ, 41, n.; 68 and n.; 296, n.

Basilides, a lapsed Bishop, 37, n.; 233. See also Spanish Appeal, 311, sqq.

BENSON, EDWARD WHITE (died October 11, 1896). His 'juvenile lucubration' on the Martyrdom and Commemoration of S. Hippolytus, and Bishop Lightfoot's Comments on it, 169, n.; his article on Agrippinus, 337, n.

Berber Raid (the), 236, sqq.

Biennium, use of the word, 128, n.

Birrhus, 514 and nn. See Lacerna

Bishops. See Apostolic Succession, Episcopate; see also Examination of the Lists of Bishops attending the Councils, Appendix, 564; also Cities from which the Bishops came to the Seventh Council, Appendix, 573, sqq.

Bona (Persecution of Decius), her history, 78

Budinarius, 117

Bulla Regia, a town, 231, n.; 581

Bunsen, 27, nn.; 28 n.; 45, n.; 46, n.; 54, n.; 72, n.; 337, n.; 341, n.; 404, n.

Butler, Bp., on Resentment, 250; see also 524

Byzantium to Rome. Distance, journey from, 479, n.

Cæcilianus the presbyter, 7, 9, 18, 19, 48

Cæcilius, Bishop, on junior Clerics and professed virgins, 47 the same as Cæcilius of Biltha

Cæcilius, Bishop of Biltha, 291

Cæsarea, 373; date of its fall, 373, n.; 555

Cæsariani, sense of the word, 480, n.

Caius (Hippolytus himself), 482

Caldonius, a bishop, 84; one of Cyprian's five representatives during his retirement, 107; excommunicates Felicissimus, 113, 114, n.; sent to Rome (see 'the Title of Cornelius'), 131, 133, 145. See also Herculanus, Numidicus, Rogatianus, Victor

Callistus, the Pope, 31, 308, 336 and n., 348

Callixtus II., Pope, his citation of *de Unitate*, 218 and n.

Canonize (to), origin of the word, 90, n.

Capsa, a town, 223, 368, 599

Captives (redemption of), 238

Carpos, a town, 421, n.; 579

Carthage. See Introduction. *Carthage and her Society; where was Cyprian Martyr buried?* 509; where was Cyprian tried and executed? 512; also 45, n.; 79, n.; 112, 113, 359, n.; 497, 498, 500 and n.

Castus, the Martyr, 78

Catacombs, 61, 481, sqq.

Celerina, the Martyr, 69, 70

Celerinus (Persecution of Decius), his family; his history, 69, sqq.; 93. See Confessors at Rome

Cemeteries, 233, 481, sqq. See also Catacombs and Collegia

Chromatius of Aquileia, 280, sqq.

Chrysostom, S. John, 52, n.; 284, 294, n.

Church of the Future (the), 534

Cirta, a town, 368, 583

Clement of Rome (Epistles to Virgins attributed to), 56, n.

Clement of Alexandria, 37, 355 and n.; 412, n.

Clementianus, one of the Lapsed; triennium of penance, 223

Clinical baptism, 121, n.; 404, n.

Clypea, a town, 467

Collegia, 61, n.; 233. See also Cemeteries and Catacombs

Commentarii (Commentarienses), sense of the word, 495, n.

Commission of five representatives appointed by Cyprian during his retirement, 107. See also Caldonius, Rogatianus, Herculanus, Victor, Numidicus

Conditional Baptism, 522 and n.

Confessors at Rome (Persecution of Decius), 69, sqq. (See also Moyses, Maximus, Rufinus, Nicostratus, Urbanus, Sidonius, Macarius, Celerinus.) After the death of Moyses (119, 120) they place themselves on the side of Novatian, 140, sqq.; the 'brief letter' of Cyprian, 146; Letter of Dionysius of Alexandria, 147; Restoration of Roman Confessors, 159, sqq.; on Nicostratus, delegate of Novatian to Carthage, permanently alienated from the Church, 159, 160

Confirmation, 394, n.; 404, n.; 420, 421
Consessus, 20, 21, 324, 325 and n.
Contestatio, use of the word, 372, n.
Coprianus, 5, n.
Cornelius, the Pope, 70; his character, his family, 124, sqq.; his election (date discussed), 127 and n.; First Council of Cyprian, the title of Cornelius, 129, sqq.; letters of recognition sent to him—Novatian, the schism, 134, sqq.; Restoration of Roman Confessors, 159, sqq.; Roman Council, 163; his letters, 168 and n.; Felicissimus goes to Rome as legate of Fortunatus, attitude of Cornelius, 228; Cornelius banished to Centumcellæ, 298; his death, 299; date of his death, 299, n.; place of his repose, 301; Commemoration of Cornelius, 303
Cornelius and *Cyprian* Companion Saints in Kalendar and Collect, 310 and n. See also S. Cyprian's Day in Kalendars, 610, sqq.
Councils of Cyprian. First, 129; Second, 224; Third, 231; Fourth, 233; Fifth (I. on Baptism), 349; Sixth (II. on Baptism), 351; Seventh (III. on Baptism), 364; the Baptismal Councils failed doctrinally and why? 424, sqq.
Councils. African, but not Cyprianic, 36, n.; 43, n.; 49, nn.; 53, n.; 55, n; 114, n.; 129, n.; 163, n.; 237, n.; 520
Councils (not African), quoted. Antioch, 167, 168, 347, 376, nn.; Arles, 173, n.; 312, n.; 520; Basle, 429, n.; Constance, 415, n.; Elvira, 43, n.; 46, n.; 79, n.; 166, n.; 173, n.; 312, n.; 499, n.; Florence, 292, n.; London, 415, n.; Mâcon, 501; Neo-Cæsarea, 166, n.; 244, n.; Nicæa, 55, n.; 163, 166, n.; 333, n.; 520; Nid, 432, n.; Orange, 429, n.; Quini-Sext, 294, n.; 521; Trent, 293, n.; Tribur, 292, n.
Crementius, a sub-deacon sent to Rome (retirement of Cyprian), 100, n.
Crescens, Bishop of Cirta, 371, n.; 420, n.
Crimen Majestatis, 61 and n.
Curubis (Cyprian deported to), 467 and n.
Custodia, use of the word, 499, n.

CYPRIAN, his name, 1, n.; his wealth, 4; at the African bar, 2—5; his person and place, 5; Cyprian Catechumen, 7; Influence of Tertullian and Minucius Felix, 9; his first exercise, 9; *Quod Idola dii non sint; the Grace of God*, 13; Cyprian Deacon, 17; his charity, 18; Cyprian Presbyter, 19, sqq.; Scripture studies, *Testimonies*, 22, sqq.; Cyprian Bishop of Carthage, 25, sqq.; his title of Papa, 29; his view of the Authority and the Design of the Episcopate, 31, sqq.; his work as a Bishop, 41, sqq.; Virginal life in Carthage, 51; *The Dress of Virgins*, 55; his retirement (Persecution of Decius), 84, sqq.; his scheme for restorative discipline, 95, sqq.; the thirteen Epistles of which Cyprian sent copies to the Romans, 102, sqq.; his Diocesan disquietudes, and his confidence in the Plebes, 106; his five representatives, 107; Ecclesiastical parties at Carthage, the Five Presbyters, 108, sqq.; return of Cyprian to Carthage, 128; First Council; Cyprian at Hadrumetum, 129, 132, 133, n.; Novatian's delegacies to Carthage, 143, 159; Cyprian on the return of the Confessors to the Church, 163, 174; Analysis of the *de Lapsis*, 174; of the *de Unitate Ecclesiæ*, 180, sqq.; Catena of Cyprianic passages on the Unity signified in the Charge to Peter, 197, sqq.; Persecution of Gallus, 222; Second Council, 224; softening of the Penance, 224; Maximus and Fortunatus made anti-popes at Carthage, 226, sqq.; Third Council, 231; characteristic mistake of Cyprian, 232; Fourth Council; Intercourse of Churches and Dioceses, 233, 234; Cyprian's Charity during the Berber Raid, 236, sqq.; the Plague; the work of Cyprian, 240, sqq.; *on Work and Alms deeds*, 246; *ad Demetrianum*, 249, sqq.; *de Mortalitate*, 256, sqq.; Cyprian's Epistle to the people of Thibaris, 258; *ad Fortunatum*, 264, sqq. (also 474, 475); *on the Lord's Prayer*, 267, sqq.; Cyprian on the mixed cup, 289, sqq.; his views on the dignity of the Roman See, 307; the Spanish Appeal to Carthage, 311, sqq.; the Gaulish Appeal, 314, sqq.; the Baptismal Question, 331, sqq.; Tradition of Africa, 335; First and Second Council on Baptism, 349, 351; Attitude of Cyprian towards Stephanus, 351, 352; Cyprian's letter to Pompey, 358, sqq.; Third Council on Baptism, 364, sqq.; speech of Cyprian,

INDEX.

369; Arguments of Cyprian on Rebaptism, 401, sqq.; the Catholic and Ultramontane estimate of Cyprian, 432, sqq.; *of the Good of Patience*, 437; *of Jealousy and Envy*, 448, sqq.; Cyprian sent to exile, 466; Cyprian at Curubis, 467; Cyprian's dream, 469; the Numidian Bishop Confessors, 471, sqq.; Cyprian returns to Carthage, 494; his *horti*; Cyprian condemned to death, 503; martyrdom, 505, 506; where was Cyprian buried? 509; where was Cyprian tried and executed? 512; Dress of Cyprian, 513—516; Ideal of Cyprian, see Chapter XII. Aftermath, 620, sqq.; S. Cyprian's Day in Kalendars, 610, sqq.; Mai's supposed fragment of Cyprian, 179

Cyprian and *Cornelius*, Companion Saints in Kalendar and Collect, 310 and n. See also S. Cyprian's Day in Kalendars, 610, sqq.

Dalmatica, 514
Damasus, the Pope, 30; on Hippolytus, 165, n.; his inscriptions, 95, n.; 301 and n.; 483, n.; 484, n.; 488, 489, 490, n.
Dativus, Bishop of Vada, 471, n.
Deacons, Hic (Fabianus) regiones divisit Diaconibus, 67 and n.; 68 and n.; (the third priesthood), 114; case of a contumelious Deacon, 234; as administrators of churches, 312, n.
Decius, the Emperor, 64; the persecution, 64, sqq.; 75, sqq; his death, 127 and n.
Demetrianus (ad D.), 249, sqq.; D. perhaps one of the Five *Primores*, 250, n.; Tertullian's *ad Scapulam* compared, 251; Style of the 'Demetrian,' 256
Deprehendere, in its legal sense, 503, n.
Didache, Teaching of the XII. Apostles, 44, n.; 294, n.; 410, n.
Dionysius the Great, of Alexandria, 29; 79, n.; 65, 158; on Novatian and Novatianism, 121, 142, 147, 164; his 'diaconal letter' 'through Hippolytus,' 164, 167, 169, 171; Baptismal question, 341, 353, 354, sqq.; on Stephen's liberality, 311; on Firmilian, 375; letters to Xystus, 355, 358; his exile to Kephron, 456, 463
Doctor Audientium, 44, n.
Döllinger, 337, n.; 340, n.; 342, n.
Donatulus, Bishop of Capsa, date of his ordination, 224, n.
Donatus, fellow neophyte of Cyprian, 4, 13; Ad Donatum, 13, sqq.; 445, n.

Donatus, Bishop of Carthage, predecessor of Cyprian, 7, 25, 227
Donatus, one of the Five Presbyters, original opponents of Cyprian, 111, n. See also Novatus
Dress, of Virgins (of the), 51, sqq.; 57, sqq.
Duchesne, Abbé L., 68, n.; on Deacons as administrators of churches, 312, n.; on the Vicariate of Arles, 315, n.; on the autonomy of Carthage, 4th century, 527; on Principalis Ecclesia, 537; also 483, n.; 484, n.; 485, n.; 490, n.; 491, n.; 492, n.

Edicta feralia, 222, n.
Egnatius, the Martyr, 70
End (nearness of the), 266 and n.
Ennodius, 30, n. 3
Epictetus, Bishop of Assuras, elected after the lapse of Fortunatianus, 232
Episcopate. Election and Consecration of Bishops, 27, 35, sqq.; 327; the Order is of Divine creation; Character derived from the Apostles, 34; Authority of the Episcopate, 31, sqq.; 106, 193, 195, 196; Unity of the Episcopate, 181, 182; Restoration of Lapsed Bishops, 166 (and n.), 230; Bishops and the rights of the Laity, 313, 327; Government of churches when the See is vacant or the Bishop absent, 329
Episcopus Episcoporum, 30, 31, 197
Etecusa (Persecution of Decius), 71; note on her name, 74
Eucharist (the Holy), 45, 86 and n.; 90, 92, 108, 225, 248, 259, 268, 284, 285, 289—295, 410 and n.
Eucratius, Bp. of Thenæ (the training of actors), 45, 46
Eusebius (questions of dates), 14, n.; 128, n.; 347, 463, 487, n.
Evangelium, character of, strictness attached to this word (Novatianism), 147 and n.
Evaristus, a Bishop, the promoter of Novatianism, 136, 160
Evil (Deliver us from), on the clause, 272
Exomologesis, 98, 99
Exorcism, 10 and n.; 253, 258, 409, n.
Extorres, use of the word, 102, 103, 107, n.; 114, n.

Fabian, the Pope, his death, 65; F. 'divided the Regions to the Deacons,' 67, 88, 90, 120, 227
Fabius of Antioch, his leaning towards the schism; letter of Cornelius to him, 167, 168. (See also Council of Antioch.)

630 INDEX.

Fechtrup, B., 19, n.; 65, n.; 83, n.; 88, n.; 94, n.; 111, n.; 115, n.; 116, n.; 130, n.; 158, n.; 163, n.; 166, n.; 336, n.; 342, n.; 396, n.; 416, n.

Felicissimus, a layman, one of the earliest Confessors at Carthage in the Persecution of Decius, 77

Felicissimus, a Deacon who joined Novatus...non communicaturos in Monte secum...the Five Presbyters 'his satellites,' 113 and nn.; was already a Deacon when he joined Novatus, 116. First Council of Carthage: Decision on Felicissimus, 131, 133...180; his journey to Rome as a legate of Fortunatus, 228

Felix, Bishop of Bagai, 471, n.

Felix, Bishop of (?) Bamaccora, 413, n.; 471, n.

Felix, pseudo bishop of Privatus (of Lambæsis, see name), appointment, 227

Felix III., Pope...Penitential discipline, 167, n.

Fidus, a Bishop: his views on penitential discipline and infant Baptism, 231, 295, 296, 297

Firmare concilium, 363, n.

Firmilianus, Bishop of Cæsarea, his letter to Cyprian, 372, sqq.; Genuineness of this Letter, 377; Greek locutions, 381; Quotations of Scripture in his letter, 386; Origen and Firmilian, 374; Dionysius of Alexandria on Firmilian, 375; Basil on Firmilian, 375, 388; Firmilian's influence in assembling Councils, 376 and n.; Latino Latini on the Letter of Firmilian, 378

Florentini (his Martyrology quoted), 483, n.; 615

Florida (confessio), floridiores...use of the words, 78, n.

Florus, one of the Lapsed; triennium of penance, 223

Fortunatianus, Proconsul at Carthage, Persecution of Decius, 76, n.

Fortunatianus, the lapsed Bishop of Assuras, 232

Fortunatus (ad F., Exhortation to Confessorship), 264, sqq.; 474, 475

Fortunatus, Bishop of Thuccabor, 402, n.

Fortunatus, a Bishop, sent to Rome with Caldonius (see name), 131, 133, 145

Fortunatus, a sub-deacon, sent by Cyprian to the clergy of Rome, 110 and n.

Fortunatus, one of the original opponents of Cyprian, 111, n.; anti-pope at Carthage, 227, sqq.; the Five Bishops who created him anti-pope, 227, n.

Fortunatus, Venantius, 280, sqq.

Freppel, Mgr., 26, n.; 55, n.; 66, n.; 87, n.; 91, n.; 94, 97, n.; 98, 201, 202, 218, 227, n.; 267, n.; 307, n.; 321, 370, n.; 475, n.

Furni, a town, 45, n.; 580

Gaius of Dida and his deacon, 107, 113, n.; 328

Galerius, the Proconsul, 502

Gallienus, the Emperor, 300; concessions made long ago to the Christians, 304 and n.; 458, 460, 477 and n.

Gallus (Persecution of), 222

Gaulish Appeal to Carthage (the), 314, sqq.

Gemellæ, a town, 369, 592, 599

Geminius, Bishop of Furni, 50

Geminius Victor, of Furni, nominates a presbyter as tutor, 45—47

Geminius Faustinus, the presbyter, appointed as tutor, 45, 47

Girba (the isle of Meninx), 367, 598

Gordius, one of the Five Presbyters, original opponents of Cyprian, 111, n. See also Novatus

Græcising-Latin Inscriptions, 306 and n.

Gratia Dei (de), 13. See Donatus

Gratian (Decretum of), Quotations of *De Unitate*, 219

Gregory of Nyssa, 27, n.; 54, n.; 65, n.; 90, n.; 242, n.; 284

Gregory Nazianzen, 3, n.; 5, n.; 6, n.; 8, n.; 11, n.; 240, n.; 432, 433, n.

Gregory Thaumaturgus, 27, n.; 29, n.; 65, n.; 242, n.

Gregory the Great, 315, 515

Gregory of Tours, on Trophimus of Arles, 316 and n.

Gretser, his Bavarian manuscript, 206, 207 and n.; 209 and n.

Harnack, Dr A., 67, n.; 389; see note 'Cyprian before the Roman Presbyters,' 150. See Appendix, Additional note on Libelli, 541, sqq. and Appendix, On the Nameless Epistle *ad Novatianum* and the attribution of it to Xystus, 557, sqq.

Hartel (readings of his edition of Cyprian), 8, n.; 22, n.; 23, n.; 34, n.; 44, n.; 70, n.; 80, n.; 85, n.; 87, n.; 88, n.; 107, n.; 112, n.; 116, n.; 130, n.; 144, n.; 145, n.; 146, n.; 185, n.; 204, n.; 205, n.; 206, n.; 207, n.; 208, n.; 209, n.; 210, n.; 211, n.; 288, n.; 313, n.; 363, 371, n.; 393, n.; 394, n.; 469, n.; 473, n.; 481, n.; 531, n.

Hefele, on 'votum decisivum' and

'votum consultativum' in Councils, 431, n.
Heraclas, his title of Pope, 29
Herculanus, a Bishop, one of Cyprian's five representatives during his retirement, 107. See also Caldonius, Rogatianus, Victor, Numidicus
Herennianus, a sub-deacon, carries with others Cyprian's letter to the Numidian Bishop Confessors, 473
Hilary, S., 280 and n.; 286
Hippo Diarrhytus, 367, 578
Hippolytus of Portus, 31, n.; Difficulties in identifying Hippolytus through whom Dionysius wrote to the Romans with Hippolytus of Portus, 169; on Callistus, 336, n.
Hooker, 325, n.; 334—335
Hort, Dr, 8, n.; 42, n.; 427, n.
Horti (Cyprian's), 28, 494, 496
Hosius, Cardinal, his Codex of *de Unitate*, 211, 216

Iader, Bishop of Midili, 471, n.
Iconium and Synnada (Councils of), 340—342, 347, 348
'Idols are not Gods' (That), 10, sqq.
Indulgence granted by Lucianus to 'all Lapsed' in the name of 'all Confessors,' 93, 109
Infant Baptism, 231, 295, 296
Intercourse of Churches or Dioceses, 232, 233. See Aftermath, end
Interpolations (*de Unitate*), 200, sqq.; 547
Irenæus, on the Episcopate, 38, n.; 427, 540

Januarius, Bishop of Lambæsis, 227, n.
Jerome, S., 1, n.; 3; 6, n.; 10, n.; 12, n.; 21, n.; 53, n.; 54, n.; 72. n.; 112, n.; 141, n.; 164, n.; 255 and n.; 351, n.; 356, n.; 359, 374, n.; 391, 404, n.; 448, n.; 474, n.
Jewish priesthood. 33
Jovinus, a lapsed Bishop, 227
Jubaianus, a Bishop of Mauretania, his Letter to Cyprian, 352; Cyprian's Letter to J., 352, 372, 373, n.; 398, 399
Justin Martyr, 37, 38, n.

Kephron and the Lands of Kolluthion, 463, 464

Lacerna birrhus, 514
Laciniæ manuales, 516
Lactantius, 5, n.; 255, 266, n.; 462, n.
Laity. See Plebes
Lambæsis, a town, 226, n.; 586
Lapsi, 79, sqq.; the Lapsed and the Martyrs, 89, sqq.; 106, sqq.; 156, sqq.; 164, sqq.; the treatise *De Lapsis*, 174, sqq.; 230, 259, 298, 305. See also Spanish Appeal, 311, sqq.
Latino Latini, withdraws his annotations from Manutius' edition of Cyprian, 209, 210; on the Letter of Firmilian, 378
Laurentinus, the Martyr, 70
Laurentius, S., Martyr, his dialogue with Xystus, 491 and n.
Laying on of hands, 400. Cyprian's and Stephen's explanation. Three intentions with which it was used besides that of ordination, 420 and n.
Leo I., Pope, 166, n.; 315, nn.
Levitica tribus, 36, n.
Lex Regia, 62, n.
Libelli, 31, 82, 265; additional note, 541. See also Martyrs (Letters from)
Liberalis, a Bishop, accompanies Cyprian to Hadrumetum, 132
Lightfoot, Bp., on Hippolytus of Portus, 169 and nn.; on Dionysius' Epistle called diaconic, 171; 11, n.; 20, n.; 37, n.; 38, n.; 39, n.; 40, n.; 57, n.; 68, n.; 116, n.; 164, n.; 165, nn.; 284, n.; 445, n.; 452, n.; 476, n.; 484, n.; 485, n.; 525, 529
Linea, 516
Lipsius, 65, n.; 67, n.; 120, n.; 126, n. (on the date of the election of Cornelius, 127, n.); 133, n.; 138, n.; 145, n.; 299, n.; 304, n.; 316, n.; 373, n.; 485, n.; 488, n.
Litteus, Bishop of Gemellæ, 369 and n.; 471, n.
Liturgies (mixed cup symbolism), 293, n.
Longinus, a member of the first Novatianist delegacy to Carthage, 136
Lucanus, acolyte, carries with others the letter of Cyprian to the Numidian Bishop-Confessors, 473
Lucianus, a Carthaginian friend of Celerinus (see name), Persecution of Decius, 70, 93. See letters from Martyrs. Grant of a general indulgence to 'all Lapsed' in the name of 'all Confessors,' 93, 109
Lucius, the Pope, successor of Cornelius, his exile and recall, 304, 305; a 'precept' attributed to him; his treatment of the Lapsed, 305; his death, 306

Mabaret, Abbé du, his letter ap. 'Mémoires de Trévoux'...the interpolations (*de Unitate*) are restored in Baluze's edition, 213, sqq.; Appendix, 546
Macarius, Roman Confessor (Persecution of Decius), 69. See Confessors at Rome

Machæus, a member of the first Novatianist delegacy to Carthage, 136
Macrianus, his influence on Valerian, 457, sqq.
Mactharis, a town, 369, 604
Magalia, Mapalia, Mappalia, 510, n.
Magister Sacrorum, 61
Magnus (Letter of Cyprian to), 349
Majestas. See Crimen Majestatis
Manualis, -e, 516. See Laciniæ
Manutius' edition of Cyprian's works, 209—212. Special note, Appendix, 544
Mappalicus, the Martyr, 77, 92
Maran, Dom Prudent, see Baluze; 213, 214, n.; 215, n.
Marcianus, Novatianist Bishop of Arles, 317, sqq. See Gaulish Appeal
Marcion, Marcionites, 347, 398
Martialis, a lapsed Bishop, 37, n.; 233. See also Spanish Appeal, 311, sqq.
Martyrs (Acts of the). See Notarii and Eucharist
Martyrs (Letters from), see the Lapsed and the Martyrs; 89, 92, sqq.; 172, 173, n.
Massa Candida, 517
Maximus, Roman Presbyter and Confessor (Persecution of Decius), 69; joins the schism of Novatian, 140, 141; is reconciled to Cornelius and becomes his supporter, 160—162; Loculus, 69, 162
Maximus, Novatianist Roman Presbyter sent by Novatian to Carthage to announce the election of Novatian as Antipope, 136; made Antipope at Carthage, 226
Maximus, acolyte, carries with others Cyprian's Letter to the Numidian Bishop-Confessors, 473
Metator (of Antichrist), sense of the word, 70
Mettius, a sub-deacon sent to Rome with Nicephorus the acolyte, 145
Minucius Felix, 9, sqq.
Mixed Cup (the), 289, sqq.
Mommsen, 61, n.; 67, n.; 162, n.; 231, n.; 237, n.; 300, n.; 303, n.; 472, n.; 485, n.; 488, n.; 491, n.
Monnulus, Bishop of Girba, 367 and n.
Mons, in Monte, *i.e.* Bozra, 112 and n.; 113, n.
Moses of Chorene on Firmilian, 375 and n.; 555, n.
Moyses, Roman Presbyter and Confessor (Persecution of Decius), 69, 70; refuses to act with Novatian, 120, sqq.; his death, 119, 120
Munerarii, use of the word, 248 and n.

Natalis, Bishop of Oea, 360
Neapolis, a town, 467
Nemesianus, Bishop of Thubunæ, 371, n.; 387; 412; 421, n.; 471, n.
Nicephorus, an acolyte, sent to Rome with Mettius the sub-deacon, 145
Nicostratus, Deacon, Roman Confessor (Persecution of Decius), 69. See Confessors at Rome. N. delegate of Novatian to Carthage; his character; permanently alienated from the Church, 159, 160
Ninus, one of the Lapsed, triennium of penance, 223
Notarii, 67, n.; 90, n. See also Acts of the Martyrs
Novatianus, 88; his character and talents, 120, sqq.; his works, 123; the schism, 134, sqq.; Novatian's delegacies to Carthage, 136, 143, 159; the Roman Confessors join Novatianus, 140; Maximus the head of the first legation made Antipope at Carthage, 226
Novatianus, on the Nameless Epistle *ad Novatianum*, and the attribution of it to Xystus. Special note, Appendix, 557
Novatus, Bishop of Thamugadi, 337
Novatus, the presbyter, his life and intrigues, 110, 111, sqq.; *in Monte* or *in morte*, 112, n.; Novatus leader of the Five Presbyters, 112 and n.; did N. confer orders upon Felicissimus, 115; his connection with Novatianism, 136, sqq.; his journey to Rome, 137, 138, n.
Numeria, see Etecusa
Numidian Bishop-Confessors. Persecution of Valerian, 471, sqq.; their names, 471, n.
Numidicus, a Carthaginian Presbyter (Persecution of Decius), 77; one of Cyprian's five representatives during his retirement, 107. See also Caldonius, Herculanus, Rogatianus, Victor

Offering sacrifice pro dormitione, 45, 323, n.
Offerre nomen, use of the word, 92 and n.
Optatus, the reader, made Teacher of Catechumens, 44
Optatus of Milev, 18, n.; 42, n.; 68, n.; 147, n.; 157 and n.; 231, n.; 313, n.; 394, n.; 409, n.; 413, n.; 416, n.; 427, n.; 459, n.; 471, n.; 529, n.
Ordo, the clergy, 19
Origen, 36, n.; 41, n.; 65; O. and Firmilian, 374; O. on Baptism into Christ,

INDEX. 633

407; on consultation of the laity by Bishops, 428 and n.
Orosius, 504, n.
Ostensiones, 222, n. See also Visions of Cyprian

Pallium, the philosopher's pall, 5 and n.
Pamèle, Jacques de, his edition of Cyprian's works, 205, 216, n. 3
Papa, Title of, 29
Paternus, the Proconsul. See Treatment of Cyprian, 464, sqq.
Paul of Samosata, 376 and n.
Paula Sarcinatrix, 117
Paulinianists, 333, n.; 520
Paulus, the Confessor, at his request Lucianus begins the system of Indulgence to the Lapsed, 93, 109
Pearson, 4, n.; 18, n.; 29 and n.; 71, n.; 77, n.; 85, n.; 90, n.; 105; 163, n.; 224, n.; 235, n.; 250, n.; 258, n.; 259, n.; 289, n.; 291, n.; 299, nn.; 341, n.; 373, n.; 479, n.
Pelagius II., Pope, 217; his letters to the Bishops of Istria, 220, 221. See Appendix, 549—551. See also Interpolations (*de Unitate*)
Penitential discipline, 166 and n.; 176, 229, 230, sqq.
Perferre coronam sense of the words, 223, n.
Persecutions, Roman theory, 60. See Decius, Gallus, Valerian
Peter (the Charge to the Apostle), catena of Cyprianic passages on the unity signified in the Charge to Peter, 197
Peter and Paul (the Apostles), removed to the Catacombs, 484, 485, 486
Peter of Alexandria, S., 81, nn.; 82, 95, n.
Peters, Dr, 5, n.; 24, n.; 146, n.; 319, n.; 321, n.; 343, n.; 348; 350, n.; 351, n.; 353, n.; 370, n.; 373, n.; 398, n.; 409, n.; 416, n.; 434, n.; 435, nn.; 436; 440, n.; 459, n.; 475, n.; 476, n.
Philip, the Emperor, his toleration of the Christians, 64 and n.
Plague (the), 240, sqq.
Platonia (see also Damasus), 483 and n.
Plebes, the Commons (the Laity), 19, 32, n.; 36, 105, 173, n.; 188, 430, 431; Right of the Laity of withdrawing from the Communion of sacrilegious or sinful Bishops, 194, n.; 313, 314, 327; the Laity silent in the Baptismal Councils 426, sqq.
Polianus, Bishop of Milev, 471, n.
Polycarpus, Bishop of Hadrumetum, 371, n.

Pompeius, an African Bishop, present at the Consecration of Cornelius, 135 (also 133, n.)
Pompeius, Bishop of Sabrata (Letter of Cyprian to), 358; special note on this Letter, 361
Pomponius, Bishop of Dionysiana, 371, n.
Pontianus, the Pope, 169, 170
Pontiff (the title of), 33, 197
Præceptum, 465, n.; 492, n.
Prærogativa (martyrum), sense of the word, 91, n.
Præscriptio, use of the word, 313
Præsens, Præsentes, use of the words, 32, n; 88, 96, n.; 328, 329, 430, n.
Præses (of Numidia), 472, n.
Prayers, thrice daily, 269
Presbyterian theories with regard to Novatus, 115 and n.; Presbyterianism, 528
Presbyters, 36, 193, n.; Presbyters as members of the Administration, 323, sqq.; 381
Presbyters (the Five), a faction hostile to Cyprian's election and authority, 25, 26, 109 and n.; Novatus their leader; their identification, 110, n.
Priesthood, of the Laity, 20, 37, 38, 404, n.
Primitivus, a presbyter, sent to Cornelius, 145
Primores quinque, Commissioners at Carthage, Persecution of Decius, 76 and n.; 113
Princeps, sense of the word, 537, 538, 404, n.
Principalis, Principales, sense and use of the words, 495, 538, 539
Principalis Ecclesia, 192, 234; special note, 537
Principalitas, sense and use of the word, 539, 540 and n.
Principes, use of the word, 497
Privatus, Bp. of Lambæsis, condemned of heresy, 226, 227
Probation (idea of), 254, 258, sqq.
Prophets, 410, n. (the Cappadocian case of a professed prophetess)
Prudentius, 2, n.; 7, n.; 165, n.; 169, n.; 404, n.; 491, n.
Puppianus (Letter of Cyprian to), 28, n.; 37

Quadriennium, use of the word, 41, n.
Quintus, Mauretanian Bishop, 350; Letter of Cyprian to Q., 350. Special note: that Quietus of Buruch (*Sentt. Epp.* 27) is Quintus, Recipient of *Ep.* 71, 363
Quirinus, a lay friend of Cyprian; the *Testimonia* compiled and classified for

him, 22, sqq.; 473; his liberality to the Numidian Bishop-Confessors, 473

Rebaptism. See Baptismal Question
Rebaptismate (de), the Nameless Author, 390; antiquity of the Treatise, genuine reading of S. John vii. 39, 392 and n.; arguments, 393, sqq.; did the Author know Cyprian's later writings on Baptism? 396; had Cyprian read the Author? 397; possibly the Treatise which Jubaianus submitted to Cyprian, 399
Receptum eum...continuit..., use of the words, 498, n.
Repostus of Tuburnuc, apostate Bishop, 80
Repræsentare, 324, n.
Resentment (on), 249
Respondere Natalibus, 245
Restoration of Clerics, 166 and nn.; 230
Rettberg, F.W., 15, n.; 23, n.; 54, n.; 65, n.; 111, n.; 161, n.; 225, n.; 255, n.; 289, n.; 349, n.; 351, n.; 357, n.; 373, n.
Ritschl, O., 18, n.; 40, n.; 85, n.; 94, n.; 125, n.; 130, n.; 135, n.; 143, n.; 144, n. See notes: 'Cyprian before his own presbyters,' 148; 'Felicissimus as a more faithful representative of the Church,' 153; 'Evanescence of Novatus under Ritschl's analysis,' 154—161, n.; 166, n.; 189, n.; 191, n.; 196, n.; 235, n.; 289, n.; 311, n.; 330; 373, n.; on *Ep.* 74 to Pompeius, 361; on *Ep.* 72 to Stephanus, 362; on *Ep.* 75 (Firmilian's), 382, sqq.
Ritual. See Mixed Cup, Water, Wine, Unction
Rivington, Rev. L., 220, 539, 540
Rogatianus, Bishop of Nova, case of a contumelious deacon (Cypr. *Ep.* 3), 234, 235
Rogatianus, presbyter at Carthage, trustee of Cyprian's charities during his absence, 77, 85; one of Cyprian's representatives during his retirement, 107. See also Caldonius, Herculanus, Numidicus, Victor
Rogatianus, a deacon, who carried the Letter of Firmilian, 372
Rome (the Church of), under Fabian, 67; interference of the C. of R. (Persecution of Decius), 87; Cornelius elected, 127; Novatianism, 134, sqq.; the C. of R. under Lucius, 304, 305; under Stephanus, 307, sqq.; the Spanish Appeal to Carthage, 311, sqq.; the Gaulish Appeal to Carthage, 314, sqq.; tradition on rebaptism of Schismatics, 336; the C. of R. under Xystus, 475, sqq.
Rome (claims of the Modern Church of R.), 208, sqq. See 'Principalis Ecclesia,' Freppel, Peters, Rivington
Rossi, G. B. de, 5, n.; 30, n.; 69, n.; 72, n.; 95, n.; 125, n.; 162, n.; 183, n.; 300, n.; 301, n.; 303, n.; 483, nn.; 484, n.; 487, nn.; 488, n.; 489, n.; 490, nn.; 491, n.
Rufinus, Deacon, Roman Confessor (Persecution of Decius), 69. See Confessors at Rome

Sabrata, a town, 358, 597
Sacerdos, Sacerdotium, use of the words, 33, n.; 36, 166, n.
Sacrificati (Persecution of Decius), 80, 166, n. See also 223
Sacrilegium, 502, n.
Salonina, Cornelia, wife of Gallienus, probably a Christian, 300, 458, n.
Salzburg Itinerary, 482, 490, n.
Sanctificare, use of the word, 404, n.
Sarcinatrix, 117
Saturus, appointed to read the lesson at Easter, 41, n.; 44, n.; 45
Scruples (a case recorded by Dionysius of Alexandria), 355
Secretarium, 464
Secundinus, Bishop of Carpos, 421, n.
Sedatus, Bishop of Thuburbo, 404, n.
Seniores Plebis, in later African Councils, 427, n.
Sententiæ Episcoporum, authenticity of the document, 371, 372
Sexti (ad), 500, 512, 513
Shepherd, Rev. E. J., 47—51, 224, 280, 297, 364, 371, 379
Sicily. First mention of a Christian Church in that island, 95 and n.
Sidgwick, H., on Christian Humility, 441, n.
Sidonius, Roman Confessor (Persecution of Decius), 69. See Confessors at Rome
Sigus (the mines of), 473 and n.
Sin (original), 273, 297 and n.
Slavery, slaves, 14, 81, 252, n.; 260
Soldiers and officers named in Cyprian's trial, 516
Soliassus, budinarius, 117
Sorrows (Interpretation of), 256, &c.
Spanish Appeal to Carthage, 311, sqq. See also Basilides and Martialis
Spectaculum, use of the word, 504, n.
Speculator, 505, n.; 506, n.
Spisina (Espesina), 74 and n.
Sportula, '...sportulantium fratrum...,' 325, n.

INDEX.   635

Stantes (The), at Carthage (Persecution of Decius), 75, sqq.
Stephen V., the Pope, on Trophimus of Arles, 315 and n.
Stephanus, the Pope, 307. His character and policy, 309, sqq.; Spanish Appeal to Carthage, 311; Gaulish Appeal, 314; the Baptismal Question, 331, sqq.; Tradition of the Roman Church on Rebaptism of Schismatics, 336; First and Second Council of Cyprian on Baptism, 349, 351; some African Bishops in sympathy with Stephanus, 351; a deputation of Bishops from Cyprian waits on Stephanus, his attitude, 352; he threatens to withdraw from the Communion of the Bishops of Asia Minor, 353; note on ὡς οὐ κοινωνήσων, 354; are Letters missing from the correspondence with Stephanus? 360; special note on the Epistle to Pompey, 362; Cyprian's Third Council on Baptism, 364, sqq.; 370, n.; arguments of Stephanus on Baptism, 413, sqq.; note on Stephen's 'Nihil innovetur nisi,' 421
Stephanus, an African Bishop, present at the Consecration of Cornelius, his return to Carthage, 135 (also 133, n.)
Strator, use of the word, 497, n.
Subintroductæ, 47, 54, n.
Successus, Bishop of Abbir Germaniciana (Letter of Cyprian to), 493
Suffragium, use of the word, 25, n.; 28, n.
Superius, a Bishop (See unknown), 224
Superstitions, 265
Synnada (site of), 340, n.

Taylor, Jeremy, on Stephen the Pope, 310; on Stephen and Cyprian, 335
Te Deum (clauses of), 264
Tertium genus, 6... See also Introduction
Tertullian, 'the master,' 9; on the priesthood of the laity, 20, 38; on '*Episcopus Episcoporum*,' 30, 31, 197; on Virginal life, 52, sqq.; *de Fuga in Persecutione*, 85; on the Prayer, 269; Table shewing the verbal debts to Tertullian in Cyprian's Treatise *de Dominica Oratione*, 276, 277, 278; date of the *de Baptismo*, 338, 348. Tertullian's *de Patientia*, 443, sqq.; References: 5, n.; 13, n.; 20 nn.; 21, n.; 33, n.; 38, n.; 39, n.; 41, n.; 43, n.; 45, n.; 51, n.; 52, nn.; 53, nn.; 54, n.; 56, n.; 57, n.; 58, nn.; 59, nn.; 61, n.; 64, n.; 85, n.; 89, 91; 197, n.; 250, n.; 251 and n.; 254, nn.; 265, n.; 266, n.; 267, n.; 269, nn.; 270, nn.; 271, nn.; 272, nn.; 283,

nn.; 293, n.; 339, n.; 343, n.; 364, n.; 392, n.; 402, nn.; 403, n.; 404, n.; 408, n.; 409, n.; 414, n.; 439, nn.; 441, n.; 443, nn.; 444, nn.; 445, n.; 446, nn.; 447, nn.; 474, n.; 501, n.; 509, n.
Tertullus, a presbyter of Carthage, advocate of the concealment of Cyprian, 86
Thabraca (the island rock of), 367, 581
Thamugadi, a town, 337, 368, 589
Thelepte, a town, 369, 600
Thenæ, a town, 45 and n.; 603
Theophilus of Antioch (Introduction of the word 'Trinity'), 269, n.
Therapius, Bishop of Bulla, 232 and n.
Theveste (road to), 368, 588, 593
Thibaris (the Epistle to the people of), 258
Thibaris, a town, 258, 583
Thirteen Epistles (the), of which Cyprian sent copies to the Romans, special note, 102, 103, 104, 105
Thomas Aquinas, Conditional Baptism, 522, n.
Thuburbo, a town, 369, 579
Thurificati (Persecution of Decius), 80, 166, n.
Timesitheus, on the name, 3, n.
Tinguere, *i.e.* Baptizare, 387
Tractatus, Tractare, sense of the words, 32, n.; 165, n.; 508, n.
Traditor, Traditores (disqualification of, by the Donatists), 415 and n.
Traversaria, sense of the word, 472, n.
Tria Fata (temple of the), 71, n.
Triennium, use of the word, 223, n.
Trinity, Τριάς (earliest use of the word), 269, n.
Trinity, '...sacrament of the Trinity...,' 269 and n.
Tripolis, a town, 367, 596, 597
Trofimus, a lapsed Bishop, restored to the Church as a layman, 166. See also Penitential Discipline
Trophimus of Arles, 314, sqq.
Tuburnuc, a town, 80 and n.
Tutores (clerics), 45, 46, 47

Unam Sanctam (Bull), 322, n.
Unction (baptism, confirmation), 403, n.
Unity of the Catholic Church, Treatise of, 180, sqq.; Codices of *de Unitate*, 204, sqq. See also Appendix, 547, sqq.
Urbanus, Roman Confessor (Persecution of Decius), 69. See Confessors at Rome
Ursinus, supposed author of *de Rebaptismate*, 391

INDEX.

Valens, Æmulus, princeps, opportunity afforded for the election of Cornelius, 126, n.
Valerian, the Persecution of; the Edict and its occasion, 456, sqq., 459; his departure to the East, 460; the levée of Byzantium, 477, sqq.; the Rescript (its date), 479, and n.; 480; special note on Points in the Chronology of Valerian's reign, Appendix, 552
Vatican decrees, 322, n.
Veil (to take the), original meaning of the words, 53 and n.
Victor, a Bishop, one of Cyprian's five representatives during his retirement, 107. See also Caldonius, Herculanus, Numidicus, Rogatianus
Victor, Bishop of Gorduba, 402, n.
Victor, Bishop of Octavu, 471, n.
Victor, a presbyter readmitted to Communion by Therapius, Bishop of Bulla, 224, n.; 231
Viduatus, the Order of Widows; their seat of honour in the church, their functions, 53 and n.
Vigil of the Martyr, 499
Vincent of Lerins, 311, n.; 335, 422
Vincentius, Bishop of Thibaris, 371, n.; 414, n.
Virginal life in Carthage, 51, sqq.
Virgines (custodi virgines), a word of Cyprian before his death, 499 and n.
Visconti, Carlo; his letter concerning the edition of Cyprian (1563), 211, 212. See also Appendix, 544

Visions of Cyprian, 60, 85, n. See also Ostensiones

Water (instead of Wine) in the Eucharist, 290 and nn.; water alone cannot be offered and reason why, 292; water in Baptism, 403, 404 and n.; profaned and polluted water, 351 and n.; 404, n.; 412 and n. Water used instead of oil for consignation of the baptized, 404 n.
Westcott, Bishop, 9 n.; 57, n.; 427, n.
William of Malmesbury, 483, n.
Wine alone cannot be offered, the reason why, 292
Wordsworth, Bp. Christopher, on the Diaconal Epistle of Hippolytus of Portus, 171
Wordsworth, Bp. John, on Latin MSS. of the Gospel, 272, n.; 392, n.
Work and Alms Deeds (treatise on), 246
Wyclif, 415; Wyclifite proposition condemned, 415, n.

Xystus, the Pope, his Election, 475; his immunity, 477; Memorials of Xystus and his Martyrdom, 487, sqq.; on the Nameless Epistle *ad Novatianum* and the attribution of it to Xystus, 557

Zephyrinus, Bishop of Rome (date), 348
Zosimus, Pope, on the Rights of the Metropolitan of Arles, 315 and n.

www.ingramcontent.com/pod-product-compliance
Lightning Source LLC
Chambersburg PA
CBHW071214290426
44108CB00013B/1180